GLOBAL RULES

GLOBAL RULES

AMERICA, BRITAIN AND A DISORDERED WORLD

JAMES E. CRONIN

YALE UNIVERSITY PRESS

NEW HAVEN AND LONDON

For information about this and other Yale University Press publications, please contact:

U.S. Office: sales.press@yale.edu   www.yalebooks.com
Europe Office: sales@yaleup.co.uk   www.yalebooks.co.uk

Typeset in Minion Pro by IDSUK (DataConnection) Ltd
Printed in Great Britain by TJ International Ltd, Padstow, Cornwall

Library of Congress Cataloging-in-Publication Data

Cronin, James E.
  Global rules: America, Britain and a disordered world/James E. Cronin.
    pages cm
  Includes bibliographical references and index.
  ISBN 978-0-300-15148-0 (cl: alk. paper)
1. World politics—1945–1989. 2. World politics—1989– 3. United States—Foreign relations—1945–1989. 4. Great Britain—Foreign relations—1945– 5. United States—Foreign relations—1989– 6. Cold War. 7. Security, International. I. Title.
D840.C76 2014
909.82—dc23

2014014229

A catalogue record for this book is available from the British Library.

10 9 8 7 6 5 4 3 2 1

Contents

Prologue

The United States does not rule the world, either alone or in league with Great Britain. Nor do the two countries seek to do so. They have, however, largely made the rules that order the world and fashioned the institutions and alliances that govern the relations between states and economies and that define the character of states, confer legitimacy upon them, and specify the rights of their citizens. The United States and Britain played a critical role in structuring the world order that came into being after World War II; and it was a vision worked out in the U.S. and Britain during the 1980s that set the terms on which the Cold War ended and guided the making of the post–Cold War order. Together, these two efforts have shaped the world order that exists today. The goal of this study is to understand and explain this recent, and mostly successful, effort to establish the rules and norms of global order and to create, or recreate, the framework of institutions through which it functions.

The ending of the Cold War brought to a close an entire era and effectively resolved existential issues about democracy and dictatorship and about capitalism and socialism. It also opened enormous new possibilities for the design of political and economic systems, for the relations between states and for the international economy. It mattered greatly that as the Cold War loosened its grip on people and their fates those who prevailed in the struggle had at hand a model, if not quite a blueprint, for what the world after the Cold War should look like. At its core were commitments to free markets, to market-based democracies and to human rights. Backing up these principles was a newly assertive and rearmed United States that in the 1980s was determined to confront the Soviet Union and reduce its influence beyond its borders.

These ideas, and American military power, were not new, but they were all redefined, strengthened and more closely linked during the 1980s. This reconfiguration of policies was prompted by a pervasive sense of crisis and lack of control that grew over the course of the 1970s. The economy faltered, and prices soared with the oil shocks of 1973–4 and 1978–9. The United States experienced defeat in Vietnam and confronted a Soviet Union that had achieved a rough parity in nuclear weapons and was determined to push its interests in the Third World. Britain, America's closest ally in war and postwar, was forced by its straitened circumstances to reduce its global reach, granting independence to most of its empire and pulling back from positions staked out when its influence spanned the world. For a quarter-century its economy had grown more slowly than those of its European allies and competitors, and efforts to spur growth led to controversial policies that shattered the social compact and political consensus that had prevailed since the 1940s. By the 1970s, government seemed unable to steer the economy or to project power on even a modest scale. These parallel difficulties diminished the importance of the alliance between the two countries, for there was little that either could or would do for the other on the issues that mattered most. At the same time, the Western alliance became strained as the Soviet threat in Europe appeared to recede and divergent interests reemerged.

It required a crisis of this breadth and intensity to bring about a break from the pattern of governance and economic policy-making of postwar and the alliances and security policies in which they were anchored. The elections of Margaret Thatcher and Ronald Reagan were the most visible markers of the break. The two conservative leaders oversaw the sharp turn toward markets and against the state, as well as the ratcheting up of the rhetoric of the Cold War and of military spending. The attempt to reassert American and, to a lesser extent, British power in the world met resistance at home and abroad. The fact that it was now a postimperial, postcolonial and, in America, a post-Vietnam and post-Watergate world meant that policy needed to be reworked to take account of demands for peace, for human rights and for democracy. By the late 1980s, U.S. and U.K. strategy had therefore come to include not only the prefer-ence for open markets and hostility to communism but also the promotion of human rights and democracy.

This new formula was in place, in fact dominant, when the Cold War ended and opened up the possibility of applying it on a vast new scale. It was the vision that informed transitions in Eastern Europe and even, to some extent, in the former Soviet Union; and these prescriptions were to be enshrined in law and international agreements and in the norms they typically proclaimed. They were also embedded in international institutions such as the United Nations and the World Trade Organization, as well as the European Union, which were in theory committed to these principles and ready to enforce them. Alliances such as NATO – and other security arrangements bargained out between the United States and local allies – would provide the muscle that these other groupings often lacked. This post–Cold War order represented the extension of what can be labeled "Atlantic Rules" to the rest of the world. It was a major undertaking – it could also be considered heroic, or arrogant, or utopian. The effort met with much success, frequent resistance, and numerous if not fatal setbacks in the 1990s and after.

This post–Cold War order was still in place a quarter-century after the collapse of socialism in 1989, though it was rather battered and compromised. The progress of democracy had visibly slowed after 2000, and after the debacle in Iraq the idea of humanitarian intervention or regime change to guarantee human rights lost whatever appeal it might have had. The economic model, based on free markets and the increasingly free flow of goods, services, money and even people, suffered a major blow with the "great recession" of 2008. Almost inevitably, the states and leaders who had not been in a position to establish the rules of the new order insisted that, as it evolved, they should have a major role in shaping its future. That insistence coincided with a new wariness on the part of voters and elites in the United States and Britain over their position in the world. The promise of openness had slowly morphed into a threat; and the prospect of leading the world came to be seen as an unwelcome and unaffordable burden.

Would the post–Cold War order endure? It proved surprisingly resilient during the troubled first decade of the new century, but support had clearly eroded by its end. The looming question was whether rising powers, which joined up to the new order without serious input into its creation, would join with the United States, Britain and the other advanced democracies that bargained out the system's principles and institutional framework, in making it work. Were they sufficiently invested in its functioning? If not, had they a common interest in altering the system, and did they have an alternative vision to offer? The great attraction of a system of rules and institutions is that it can be, and typically is designed to be, open – to new entrants and interests and arrangements. Whether that is enough to ensure the successful adaptation and hence the future of the post–Cold War order is not yet clear, but much is at stake. Telling the story of how the global rules and institutions now in place came to be, and charting their effects throughout the world, will, it is hoped, generate a proper appreciation of just how much.

CHAPTER 1

Remaking the World, Again

The end of the Cold War resolved the two great questions of the twentieth century – about capitalism versus socialism, about dictatorship or democracy – and the superpower rivalry through which they were expressed. History did not end, for legacies and memories and institutions persisted and the resolution of the questions posed to the twentieth century allowed new and unforeseen problems to emerge. Still, the post–Cold War world was a new beginning and effectively the start of the new century.[1] The terms on which the Cold War ended, and the institutions and assumptions put in place in its aftermath, define the framework within which states and peoples will work out their fates in the new century. Understanding these terms and the lineaments of the new post–Cold War order is the essential precondition for understanding what comes next.

Three times in the twentieth century the United States and Great Britain came together in an effort to put in place a world order that would provide a framework which would enhance the prospects of peace, democracy and prosperity. The ending of the Great War was the occasion for perhaps the grandest vision, though its implementation would largely fail. World War II offered another chance, and the postwar order that emerged from that conflict was far more successful, though its reach and effects were limited by the Cold War and the superpower rivalry. The collapse of the socialist states in Eastern Europe in 1989 and the disappearance of the Soviet Union just two years later created an opportunity to fashion a world order that would operate on a still wider scale.[2]

Why this repeated quest for a structure with which to order the world? The simple answer is that, without a set of institutions and principles to govern international relations and the international economy, it is not unreasonable to assume that disorder will prevail, and with disorder will come instability, war and economic crisis.[3] Empirically, however, it was not this abstract consideration that motivated these ambitious efforts, but the actual horror of world war.[4] It is hard at this distance to recall fully the trauma of World War I and its revolutionary consequences, a trauma that affected soldiers and citizens high and low. The war's destructiveness exceeded the expectations and experiences of all who lived through it and transformed the understanding of what modern war meant. Its ending, with four great European empires disappeared and new regimes claiming to be their rightful successors, made clear that the world after the war desperately needed guidance and organization. The Bolshevik Revolution in Russia demonstrated to established elites just what needed to be organized against and in what direction new states and their restive populations had to be guided.

If a new postwar order was to be stable, it would also have to be economically viable. The Great War had produced massive losses, extensive disruption and dislocation across the industrial nations. It also caused a near cessation of trade, the end of currency convertibility and rates of inflation that would make the restoration of old parities and trading relationships extremely difficult. Constructing a better world would therefore require a new set of states based on new principles of membership and legitimacy, new mechanisms to regulate the relations between them, and the reconstruction of the international economy. The vision of world order associated with Woodrow Wilson – and influenced strongly by British traditions – was meant to meet these varied requirements, but it was a very tall order that the Versailles settlement failed to meet.[5]

World War II brought even greater losses and created a new standard for evil in the world. And because it followed the deepest and most prolonged crisis in the history of capitalism, the determination to reorder both international relations *and* the world economy was that much greater. The character of the enemy also dictated that the order had to be "antifascist." Germany and Japan promised new orders in Europe and East Asia, but their political visions were racist and undemocratic and their economic plans closed and autarkic.[6] In response, the British and the Americans felt the need to craft a world order premised on democracy, racial equality and economic openness, even if these lofty goals sat uneasily alongside the practice of racial inequality in the U.S. and the U.K.'s commitment to maintaining its empire.[7] The Soviets were determined in their antifascism, but guided in practice by a realist calculation of geopolitics and untroubled by the contradiction between a rhetorically democratic foreign policy and a brutal authoritarianism at home.[8]

The effort to build a new postwar order was overseen by leaders who were more pragmatic than idealistic, and it had the support of the United States, by now the world's dominant power, and of Britain, once the world's dominant power and still possessed of a global reach.[9] It therefore "took," and the postwar order proved remarkably durable and allowed the major powers to avoid war with one another and, especially in the West, to experience rapid and sustained economic growth. It was of necessity a Cold War order, which meant that the peace was highly armed and that nations on the periphery – in Asia, Africa and Latin America – and unlucky enough to be the object of superpower rivalry, experienced repeated and deadly conflicts.[10] It meant, too, that the prosperity of the postwar era was limited to peoples and countries in Western Europe, North America and Japan, while the socialist states limped along and the developing countries developed at a very slow pace. The political freedom enjoyed in "the West" was also not afforded to those trapped within the socialist bloc and was only intermittently on offer for people in the Third World as well.

The revolutions of 1989, and the Soviet collapse that followed, provided the third opportunity to create a new order, one that would reconstruct economies, societies and political systems in the formerly socialist world and reconfigure international institutions and the global economy. The end of the Cold War and the eclipse of the socialist idea, and economic model, also altered the options available to what had been the "Third World." The outcome of this latest effort is still unclear: much has changed, but some things remain the same; not every change has been positive; and the dreams that attended the end of the Cold War have been tempered by awkward realities and unforeseen problems. Still, the contrast between the worlds before and after 1989 is stark, and demands detailed study and at least a provisional assessment.[11]

It was also the very opportunity to remake the world – in 1918, 1945 and 1989 – that elicited the effort. With destruction all around and old institutions in ruins, there was literally no alternative but to begin anew with a different vision. Just what vision would prevail and how effectively it would be embodied in institutions and rules was what the politics of the immediate postwar (or post–Cold War) eras would be about. What is striking about all three moments, however, is the extent to which the ideas on offer were Anglo-American in origin and inspiration and, less surprising perhaps, that it was largely Britain and the United States that would dominate the process of turning them into reality. Clearly, it mattered that they had been allies in the two world wars, and in the Cold War, and that they had prevailed in those contests. But what was it that produced such a measure of agreement between the two countries, and what facilitated their cooperation? Was it the shared culture, the similar polit-ical institutions and the common commitment to a liberal capitalism that brought, and kept, the two countries together? Or was it a common stance toward the world? Both countries were protected from rivals by geographic distance, by being "offshore" in relation to Europe and its continental powers; and both saw their connections to the rest of the world in terms of commerce, the flow of goods and people and money across borders and great distances, rather than in armaments, alliances or territorial aggrandizement.[12] Britain had a formal empire, of course, but the goal was to run it like a business, to devolve power to locals and native elites and to govern lightly even if British rule did not always feel so light to those who endured it. American expansion across the continent was often brutal, but once it was accomplished the United States had little appetite for things imperial, although there had been a brief flirtation with empire around the turn of the century.[13]

The Anglo-American connection, or "special relationship" as Churchill dubbed it, has fascinated observers for a long time and produced a large and perceptive literature. It is a history filled with ambivalence, with resentment and condescension as well as pride and affection. Overall, the literature depicts an intimacy that is unusual and surely produced a predisposition to be allies rather than rivals or enemies, even if it did not prevent recurring episodes of estrangement.[14] The fact that Britain and the United States have also staked out a similar relationship with the rest of the world has been less remarked, but not entirely unnoticed. It also served to predispose the two countries to take the same side in the great conflicts of the twentieth century and, especially after 1940, to work out their fates collectively. So, too, did the extensive economic ties between the two dominant states within what was still until 1914 a "British world system."[15]

Explaining why the U.S. and the U.K. have been allied is therefore not terribly difficult. The point of this study, however, is not when and why the alliance flourished, but to what effect. What mattered to the world were the consequences of the joint actions, the common projects, that Britain and America undertook. It mattered a great deal, after all, that they joined together against the Germans in two world wars; and it mattered greatly that the U.S. and Britain were at the center of the alliance system through which the Cold War was largely fought out. And it would matter enormously that the Cold War ended at a moment when the two nations were more or less united in an effort to make the world safe for markets and democracy. During the 1980s British and American leaders – Margaret Thatcher and Ronald Reagan in particular – embarked on a controversial effort to shift the boundaries between state and market toward the market, to roll back the state, to expand trade and to remove barriers to the free flow of goods and money, if not people, and to convince others – developed and less developed countries alike – that the path to prosperity ran through more open and competitive markets.

The U.S. and the U.K. also took to preaching the virtues of democracy and of human rights, even if their record was patchy and their enthusiasm of recent vintage. Just as the turn to markets was aimed at restoring the U.S. and its ally to a position of economic leadership, so the policies of the "Second Cold War" –

increased armaments, an escalation in anti-Soviet rhetoric and a plan to cause the Soviets trouble at the further reaches of their sphere of influence – were designed to rebuild American (and Western) influence globally. But the world would exact a price, for in a postimperial and postcolonial era dominance would be bargained rather than simply asserted. Self-determination and democracy were by the 1980s the accepted norms in international relations and the aspiration to lead would require a vision that acknowledged these. Democracy and human rights were thus added to open markets and private property as key components in what the U.S. and the U.K. proposed in their quest to recover and extend their influence.[16]

This reimagined vision, which united the two allies, was shared at least in part by others, though not to the same extent; and it was the vision that would guide the work of constructing the post–Cold War world. The end of the Cold War meant that the principles proclaimed by the Americans and their British allies could be applied in places previously closed off and to societies that had been ruled by opposing principles. The campaign to extend the reach of "markets, rights and democracy" and to make them the standard against which institutions were judged was the central feature of the post–Cold War era. It produced mixed results, and the verdict is still awaited on the overall effect, but it was a vast undertaking with real and enduring consequences. And because it was largely an American project, with Anglo-American roots, it was also resented and resisted as a further extension of U.S. dominance or hegemony.

The purpose of this book is twofold. The first aim is to describe and explain the formula – with its new emphasis on markets, democracy and human rights, its greater antipathy to communism and its insistence on fighting and winning the Cold War – that emerged in the 1980s as a consequence of the relaunch of the "special relationship." Its second goal is to assess its impact on the ending of the Cold War and the construction, and later the functioning, of the post–Cold war world. Understanding the dramatic turn taken in the 1980s will necessitate an examination of the mounting crises of the 1970s that seemed to overwhelm Britain and the United States domestically and internationally. These crises, part of a more systemic challenge to the Cold War order that prevailed during the quarter-century after 1945, led to the political triumph of more conservative parties and politicians who chose to pursue a crusade for markets and market-oriented democracy. The success of this "neoliberal" turn in the U.S. and the U.K., and its capture of international institutions and the ideas that governed them, goes a long way toward explaining just how consequential these policies and the vision informing them were, not in winning the Cold War but in imposing a new framework to govern national and international politics and the world economy after its ending. Understanding these origins should make it possible to analyze, tentatively of course, the effectiveness of the new paradigm and institutional structure in dealing with the often unexpected problems of the new and more thoroughly globalized world that has emerged after the Cold War.

The beginnings of the story therefore lie in the 1970s, when Britain and America both found that the policies that had brought stability and prosperity since the late 1940s no longer worked and that something new was required. The old approach, the set of beliefs and institutions and policies that had been crafted with such care in the 1940s and worked well enough, indeed very well, up until the 1970s, had three distinct features. The relations between states were formally governed by the United Nations, founded in 1945 on the ruins of the League of Nations and gradually expanded to include most of the world's states. In practice, the world was split into rival camps – one structured around the United States and Great Britain, the other around the Soviet Union – and military alliances, primarily NATO and the Warsaw Pact but also regional compacts cobbled together by the United States. Belonging to one camp or another did not completely dictate the character of domestic policies and politics, but nearly so: the core states in the Soviet orbit had party and state structures, and economies, that mimicked those in the Soviet Union; in the U.S. sphere of influence the norm for the major countries was political democracy and a form of capitalism tempered by more or less generous social provision and a far greater degree of state intervention in the economy than had been the case before 1939. Economic policy was largely, if not completely, Keynesian in inspiration. Democratic politics, firmly established at the center of the "Western" alliance, were less common on the periphery of the system and by definition the European empires were not democracies. Decolonization would proceed rapidly in the postwar era, however, and in theory the process would spread democracy along with self-determination. The reality, of course, often failed to live up to the rhetoric or the theory.

The international economy, like the world of geopolitics, was divided. A socialist bloc of countries existed largely outside the world market, though there were exceptions and over time trade increased across the blocs. The market economies operated within the framework agreed at Bretton Woods in 1944 and formally governed by the International Monetary Fund, the World Bank, and the General Agreement on Tariffs and Trade (GATT). It was putatively an open system, but the actual movement of goods, capital and people was hindered by restrictions left over from the Depression and World War II and kept in place, in theory on a temporary basis, after 1945. Successive rounds of trade negotiations and decisions freeing up the exchange of currencies would gradually produce a more genuinely open global economy, though it would take until the late 1970s and 1980s for it to approach the level of openness that had existed before 1914.

It is not easy to summarize and label this package of ideas, institutions and policies that governed the non-communist part of this Cold War order. It was a kind of reformed capitalism that tolerated a larger or smaller welfare state, a product of a de facto "social-democratic settlement" that was settled upon by parties and leaders of both the center-left and the center-right. The growth model has been termed "Fordist" in recognition not merely of its roots but also of its self-reinforcing mix of mass consumption and mass production. Politically, it was a system that, formally democratic, empowered the well organized and on a daily basis involved "corporatist bargaining" between big unions, the largest employers and the state, with little input from voters. It was also, at least for most of the states in Europe and North America, a military alliance that was poised to confront the Soviet Union and its allies, a coalition that was highly armed, with weapons that could destroy the world.

The Cold War order, east and west, was not an ideal world. If it managed to avoid outright war between the superpowers, it did so at a high price; and the prospect of "mutually assured destruction," the doctrine that came to guide military strategy, was terrifying. And there was no end to violence, which was displaced onto the Third World but no less real. Still, the outcome was a relatively stable arrangement that allowed the process of decolonization to proceed peacefully, at least in most cases. The exceptions were notably brutal, but they were exceptions. This bifurcated world also led to political stability on both sides, again at a cost. Within the Soviet bloc, it required an iron fist, a stifling bureaucracy and an intrusive and extensive security apparatus. In the "West" – a geographical term which, for political and ideological purposes, included Japan – stability was the result of mostly democratic politics. The greatest successes were in Germany and Japan, both of which emerged from allied occupation as democratic polities, and also Italy, whose political system offered no model for effective governance but was no longer fascist. The most important achievement was undoubtedly prosperity, with the surge of growth in the capitalist countries far exceeding what the mobilizations of the command economies could accomplish. Over time, the differences in economic performance would become more stark, with fateful consequences for the regimes in Eastern Europe and for the Soviet Union, but even into the early 1970s it was possible to see growth continuing and stability enduring within both camps.

The postwar order in the "West" was mainly the work of the United States and Britain. Only three states really mattered in 1945 – the U.S., the U.K. and the USSR – and the Soviets had a limited agenda focused primarily on defense. The other states to which a veto was accorded in the United Nations Security

Council – China and France – were in no position to lead. The Chinese government was tottering, and France had to be liberated by its allies during the war and rebuilt by the French themselves after the war. Japan and Germany were enemies, recently defeated, occupied and subject to reeducation. The principles around which the postwar settlement was constructed thus had their origins in the United States and Britain. The two states had staked out their basic commitments in the Atlantic Charter, agreed in August 1941, even before the U.S. had entered the war. It renounced territorial gains, promised serious efforts to promote peace and disarmament, reasserted the right of self-determination and committed the U.S. and U.K. to work for an open economic order. Detailed planning began soon after, though obviously the prosecution of the war was the top priority. The British were not excited by the prospect of opening their empire to America and the world, and they would try to circumscribe the application of self-determination within the empire. Still, they had no choice but to agree, for American aid and military support were essential to the war effort.[17] The Charter was the basis for the United Nations, the name attached to the coalition that fought the war and, not coincidentally, the organization that came to replace the discredited League of Nations at the end of the war.

It would require several years for the postwar order to take on its more or less permanent shape. The Bretton Woods institutions and policies were mostly settled in 1944, but the effort to establish an open trading system and convertible currencies would be delayed and compromised. Most important, by 1947 it was clear that recovery would be harder to achieve than first thought and the U.S. felt compelled to offer what became known as the Marshall Plan to aid in the transition. Geopolitics and military strategy also remained in flux as the U.S. and USSR tested each other's intentions and capabilities. As of 1945 there was no real determination to see a Cold War replace the blazing hostilities that had just ended and neither superpower was quite ready to to call off their collaboration. By 1947, however, they did so: early in the year the "Truman Doctrine" called on the U.S. and its allies to stand up to Soviet advances and in September the Soviets returned to a rhetoric of confrontation. In short order they had crushed dissent and installed compliant regimes across Eastern Europe. Antagonisms only hardened with the Berlin crisis of 1948; and in 1949 the Soviets exploded their first atom bomb, the Chinese Communists came to power and the North Atlantic Treaty Organization (NATO), was formed. The Korean War broke out in June 1950. It led to massive rearmament and convinced President Harry Truman to sign on to the national security strategy outlined in NSC-68, with its emphasis on containment and its call for a massive increase in defense spending.[18] Britain would also agree to a higher level of military spending, though somewhat reluctantly. By the early 1950s, as a result of these choices and events, Cold War alignments and policies were set on both sides, and the contest had become much more highly militarized.

The outcome was decidedly an Anglo-American construction. Experts from the two allied nations worked out the details of Bretton Woods, and the United Nations was largely a product of American and British planning.[19] Of course, all planning was forced to reckon with the reality of the Soviet Union, which was determined to secure its own vital interests. The structure of the new organization was crafted to ensure that the most important powers – and this included the Soviet Union – did not feel threatened; hence the Security Council veto. The bargaining that went into the economic side of the postwar settlement also provided at least a brief opportunity for countries other than Britain and the U.S. to push for their particular interests and understandings; and the construction of NATO (and, later, alliances in Asia, the Middle East and elsewhere) had to acknowledge the different perspectives, traditions and capacities that allies brought to the task of mutual defense. Nevertheless, the initiative and inspiration typically came from the U.S. and the U.K. It was the British request for support in Greece that elicited the Truman Doctrine; and Britain was the first and most enthusiastic supporter of the Marshall Plan and of NATO. The link between Britain and the United States was the assumed starting point for crafting both the economic and security architecture of the postwar order. As Dean Acheson, the U.S. Secretary of State, explained in 1949, "it was in the very nature of things that the United Kingdom was our staunchest and most valuable ally in all quarters of the world. They were not only important to us in a military sense, but political and economic as well."[20] The United States and Great Britain would thus find themselves fighting together in Korea, with only token participation from others, and the two countries made the greatest efforts to rearm in response to that conflict. In sum, the postwar order owed much to the U.S. and the U.K. and to the alliance between them.

Less heroic efforts would be needed to keep the new order running and its routine functioning would provide the framework within which long-term trends would work themselves out. Two of these were closely linked: decolonization and Britain's relative eclipse as a global power. Inevitably, the terms of the Anglo-American alliance were altered. The United States had little interest in shoring up European colonial empires and effectively abetted in their demise. Its support for decolonization was qualified in practice, however, by fears that the disintegration of empire would provide opportunities for the advance of communism or Soviet influence. As a result, the United States acquiesced in the maintenance of imperial control in the early years of the Cold War and was persuaded more than once to shore up regimes threatened by left-wing insurgencies. Vietnam was the most important example.

Overall, however, U.S. policy was to support the granting of independence to former colonies and to seek to woo the emerging states to its side in the Cold War. Neither the British nor the French – nor the Dutch in Indonesia or the Portuguese in Africa – could count on U.S. support in resisting calls for self-determination. The dissolution of empire became inevitable. The turning point was Suez in 1956. Gamal Abdel Nasser, the Egyptian nationalist and pan-Arab leader, had taken control of the Suez Canal and in response Britain and France, in alliance with Israel, concocted a plan to take it back. Israel was to attack, the British and French would come in to mediate and restore order, Nasser would be defeated and discredited. The Eisenhower administration refused to go along with the idea, however, and the invasion was aborted. Anthony Eden, the British Prime Minister, resigned in disgrace; and the Suez debacle was the signal that Britain and France were no longer in a position to defend what remained – and a lot remained even at this late date – of their colonial possessions. The "wind of change," as Harold Macmillan termed it in 1960, soon became irresistible and by the mid-1960s the British and French empires had largely disappeared. Britain's retreat from empire was accompanied by a series of defense cutbacks that sharply reduced its global military presence. In the wake of the 1967 financial crisis that had resulted in the devaluation of the pound, the Labour government decided to pull back British military forces from "east of Suez" by 1971. The Conservative government of Edward Heath, taking office in 1970, reluctantly went along with the decision.

While Britain's global reach shrank, its economy grew, but only modestly. Unemployment remained low into the 1970s, but the rate of growth was far less impressive than what was achieved by its competitors. Germany and Japan rebuilt their economies quickly and, starting from a low base, achieved impressive rates of growth. The French and Italian economies also grew substantially in the three decades after the war. In response Labour and Tory governments alike became fixated on how to create a more dynamic economy and reverse what was seen, mistakenly but understandably, as industrial decline. Labour's solutions tended toward greater state involvement and the Wilson government, elected in 1964, sought to combine economic planning with a focus on unleashing the "white heat of technology." In theory Conservatives preferred market mechanisms, but sought to lure investment by keeping inflation, which they attributed to rising wages, under control; and that meant quite *dirigiste* incomes policies. Neither worked well and by the mid–1970s inflation was much higher and growth more elusive.

The other remedy for slow growth was for Britain to sign up for the Common Market or, as it came to be known, the European Community. Although the U.K. was a major supporter of the Marshall Plan and encouraged the rest of Europe to come together, it held aloof from the Common Market in its early years. It chose instead to pursue a "national strategy" that would make use of its global status – its formal and informal empire and Commonwealth, its historic role in international finance, its extensive trading network and its still considerable military clout – to forge an independent path to growth. Britain would push for faster and wider trade liberalization rather than the protectionist security offered by a European customs union and hoped to enlist U.S. support for the project.[21] The strategy was plausible enough but did not work, and in 1961 Britain began to explore the possibility of becoming a member of the Common Market. The application was vetoed by De Gaulle in January 1963, as was a second effort in December 1967, but the determination to join survived the two rejections. With the departure of De Gaulle in 1968 Britain applied again and was finally admitted, formally joining at the beginning of 1973. The turn to Europe was unable, however, to prevent the economic crisis of the 1970s, when inflation rose dramatically, growth petered out, and unemployment began a sustained and seemingly irreversible rise.

Britain's loss of empire, its military retrenchment and its slow growth complicated its relations with the United States. What had been, not just during the war but in the early Cold War era, an unequal alliance became more of a dependency. The Suez disaster showed the limits of Britain's freedom of maneuver in international relations and cast doubts upon its judgment as well. The United States was deeply displeased: a State Department review of the events leading up to the invasion concluded that Britain and France not only engaged in "collusion and deception" but that "it was directed not only against Egypt but against the U.S. government."[22] Equally damning, this had all occurred in a bad cause. As John Foster Dulles told the British Foreign Minister shortly after, the reason the U.S. did not support Britain was not that it "liked the Egyptians better" but because "we were convinced that there would be little chance of establishing a world order or avoiding World War III if we acquiesced in the British action."[23] Suez was followed in August 1957 by the publication of Duncan Sandys' Defence White Paper, which was interpreted by the U.S. as a further indication of Britain's retreat and decline.[24] The Joint Chiefs believed that "the British were reducing their forces to the point where they could no longer be considered a major reliance in dealing with problems around the world."[25]

Though Britain now brought less to the collaboration, the United States still needed allies and so Eisenhower worked to repair the relationship. Macmillan, of course, was desperate to do so. The outcome was a set of agreements on nuclear cooperation of considerable benefit to the U.K. The first, announced in early 1957, involved the deployment in East Anglia of sixty intermediate-range ballistic missiles; in 1958 the U.S. Congress was persuaded to pass the Mutual Defence Agreement which allowed the administration to resume cooperation with Britain on nuclear weapons development; and in 1960 the United States agreed to supply the U.K. with the Skybolt missile in exchange for allowing the Americans to station nuclear submarines in Scotland.[26]

Relations were more complicated during the Kennedy administration. The President was personally close to the British Ambassador, David Ormsby-Gore (later Lord Harlech), who was part of Kennedy's inner circle during the Cuban missile crisis; and Kennedy chose to surround himself with what his successor referred to as "men with the temperament of Rhodes scholars, dangerously sympathetic to the U.K."[27] Macmillan also sought to charm the American leader, and with some success. Issues and events got in the way, however, none more important than the matter of nuclear weapons. The Skybolt program, on whose successful development Britain's future as a nuclear power now depended, was beset by high costs and technical failures, and in late November 1962 the Americans decided to scrap it altogether. What might replace it would be discussed at a meeting in the Bahamas a month later. Shortly before the meeting convened, the former Secretary of State, Dean Acheson, spoke at West Point and asserted that "Great Britain has lost an empire and has not yet found a role." Still worse, "its attempt to play a separate power role – that is, a role apart from Europe, a role based on a 'special relationship' with the United States, a role based on being the head of a 'Commonwealth' ... – this role is about to be played out."[28] The British were incensed, proof perhaps of the accuracy of the remarks, and the subsequent meeting was fraught. The outcome, however, was that Kennedy agreed – indeed he had already decided on this – to let Britain have Polaris missiles. Britain would remain a nuclear power and the alliance would be reaffirmed.[29] De Gaulle was not pleased and vetoed the U.K.'s application to join the European Economic Community (EEC) the very next month.

Britain's reliance on the United States for atomic weapons reinforced the message about the U.K.'s declining capabilities; and its inability throughout the 1960s to develop a distinctly British model of economic growth raised serious doubts about what Britain, on its own, could and would contribute to the alliance. A variety of factors held the British economy back, but nothing was as debilitating as its insecure financial position. Efforts to stimulate the economy would regularly produce problems with the balance of payments and these would threaten the value of the pound. The result was a frustrating "stop-go" pattern of growth. Devaluation was the logical remedy, but successive governments were reluctant; instead, they relied on American assistance to get them through what they hoped were temporary difficulties. The United States became increasingly impatient and urged more drastic measures of retrenchment that the Labour government was reluctant to undertake. Embattled over Vietnam, Lyndon Johnson was desperate to get support from other countries, and especially from Britain. "A platoon of bagpipers would be sufficient; it was the British flag that was wanted," Johnson reportedly said; and his advisor McGeorge Bundy put it even more bluntly when he stated that "a battalion would be worth a billion."[30] George Ball, Under Secretary of State, told Wilson that "it would be a great mistake if the United Kingdom failed to understand that the American effort to relieve Sterling was inextricably related to the commitment of the United Kingdom to maintain its commitments around the world."[31] The Prime Minister, Harold Wilson, nevertheless resisted the linkage and persisted in his refusal to send forces to Vietnam. His subsequent and rather unhelpful diplomacy over Vietnam offered yet further evidence that the special relationship was no longer delivering special benefits.[32]

Not only did financial difficulties confronting Britain fail to convince the government to send troops to Vietnam, but instead they led it to decide that the country could no longer afford to maintain a military presence "east of Suez," in places such as Malaysia, Singapore, Hong Kong, the Persian Gulf and Aden.[33] American leaders were appalled and Johnson wrote to Wilson on January 11, 1968 saying:

> If these steps are taken, they will be tantamount to British withdrawal from world affairs, with all that means for the future safety and health of the free world. The structure of peace-keeping will be shaken to its foundations. Our own capability and political will could be gravely weakened if we have to man the ramparts all alone.

Four days later, the President even threatened retribution: if the U.K. cancelled orders for F–111 jets, the decision would threaten the system of joint procurement, and could lead to the cancellation of contracts to U.K. firms. The next day the British reaffirmed their decision. The effect was to lower still further American expectations of what Britain could and would contribute to the relationship. A State Department paper the following June spoke of a "historical transformation of British foreign policy" and proceeded to describe "the Britain of the future as, at best, a middle-sized, European power, albeit one with a nuclear capability, a residual sense of extra-European responsibility, and a continuing, if diminished, status as a favored partner of the United States."[34]

Even before the decisions to devalue and retrench were taken, U.S. policymakers had begun to rethink Britain's role in the world. George Ball, for example, wrote at length to Johnson in 1966 and explained that the U.S. had adopted various ad hoc policies to assist the United Kingdom since the war, but it was now time to get serious. As he put it:

Britain must recognize that she is no longer the center of a world system but that she can nevertheless play a role by applying her talents and resources to the leadership of Western Europe. We, on our part, should face the fact that it is basically unhealthy to encourage the U.K. to continue as America's poor relation, living beyond her means by periodic American bailouts.

Since Britain was no longer much help beyond Europe, its most useful role would be within, where "Britain should seek to turn Europe outward both in its commercial policy and its political interests."[35] The United States had long advocated greater European cohesion and with Britain part of Europe it could encourage a united Europe in what it regarded as the right direction.[36] The move would also benefit Britain, whose sclerotic economy would experience "the cold douche of a big market," as Macmillan had once said, and it would also relieve the U.S. from repeated demands to assist it.

As the rationale for the Anglo-American alliance weakened, British officials cast about for reasons to keep it going. A long paper by the British Embassy in Washington and the Planning Staff of the Foreign Office was prepared in January 1969 to guide policy during the Nixon administration. Its starting point was the frank acceptance that "the maintenance of close relations and mutual confidence between the United States and Britain is a matter of strong practical concern," if only because the U.S. "can do us the most damage if we do not handle our relations in a way which ensures that our interests are properly taken into account." On a more positive note, "U.S. objectives with regard to world order and the evolution of open societies generally correspond more closely than those of other countries to our own ideals and requirements (even if we might differ on methods)." Britain was also specially capable of serving as America's closest ally because of shared strategic objectives, a unique ability to speak to and understand one another, the U.K.'s experience in world affairs, and all the cultural and sentimental ties that bound the two countries. The report nevertheless conceded that "most of these are declining assets."

> The inescapable conclusion is that our direct leverage on U.S. policies is bound to decline unless we can acquire a new power base from which to operate. (This indeed is the main political rationale for our European policy.) A further conclusion is that in order to retain the privileged position which we now enjoy in American counsels we may have to accept increasing servitude.

In short, "we may have to pay more for the right to influence the conduct of the United States."[37] By the beginning of 1969, therefore, policy-makers at the

Foreign Office had come to much the same position as George Ball and his allies in the State Department: Britain's new role, and the price of its continued role in the Anglo-American alliance, was entry into Europe and a willingness to work within Europe for the sorts of policies that the U.S. and the U.K. had long advocated.

This emerging consensus, to which not all as yet adhered, was presumably what Henry Kissinger ran into when he took office and found himself surrounded by people who doubted the value of the "special relationship." With his old world attachments, the new National Security Advisor looked more favorably on the connection and in 1969 explained that "we do not suffer in the world from such an excess of friends that we should discourage those who feel that they have a special friendship for us."[38] His benign views would be tested by the awkwardness of Heath's term as prime minister and his lack of enthusiasm for the "special relationship," and by the fact that, after 1972 and Watergate, nobody – except for Mao Zedong – wanted a special relationship with a government led by Richard Nixon. Kissinger also understood the realities of power that limited Britain's influence, however, and was full of respect for its ability to finesse the issue: as he later explained, "Only a morally strong and cohesive society could have undertaken this tour de force of preserving its identity through an act of ostensible subordination . . . Britain based its claim to special consideration on performance and a persistent, subtle, and pervasive discipline unobtrusively conveyed through growing habits of familiarity."[39]

The connection between the U.K. and the U.S. would survive, and even be revived, but the fraying of the relationship was an example as well as a symbol of America's increasing difficulties in keeping Cold War alliances together. America faced a genuine dilemma: its "preponderance of power" and its determination to confront the Soviet Union across the globe meant that allies were less invested in the structure of security and regularly tempted, if not actually to defect, to minimize their contributions and to demand more independence and to criticize.[40] The management of alliances was an ongoing necessity, for allies conferred legitimacy internationally and were also required if the foreign policies of successive governments were to maintain domestic support. As the Cold War became less pressing to the American public and as its foci shifted from Europe to the developing world, where the Soviets had considerable advantages, the task of keeping allies loyal, and citizens and rival politicians on side, became still more urgent.

The United States therefore confronted its own set of challenges that grew more intractable during the 1960s and early 1970s. Especially troubling was the steady increase in the military clout of the Soviet Union. As early as 1949, when the Soviets exploded their own atomic bomb, it became clear that the USSR would seek to match and even exceed U.S. military might. The dilemma for the United States, and its allies in NATO, was that the Soviet Union began the arms race with a massive advantage in conventional forces in Europe, which seemed to demand a response in terms of both conventional and nuclear armaments. The launch of Sputnik in October 1957 opened yet another front in the competition by projecting the rivalry into space and by demonstrating that the Soviets would soon develop the capacity to launch missiles aimed directly at the United States. The effect was a race in which one side would leapfrog over the other, its opponent would match that advance and initiate yet another new technology or deployment, which would in turn meet its match. The cost was staggering enough, but the worrying thing was that by the late 1960s the Soviets and their allies seem to have achieved parity in nuclear weapons while maintaining their advantage in conventional forces.

Military strength was accompanied by an expansion in the geographic reach of the Soviet Union. The outbreak of war in Korea had signaled that the Cold War would be fought out not in Europe where it had begun, but in Asia, Africa and Latin America. It would be determined in places where the Western powers, by dint of prior and ongoing imperial involvement, were not well liked or admired. After 1945 all the European empires were on the defensive and both the U.S. and the USSR claimed to be in favor of independence for colonial peoples. The Soviet claim was more credible, for the Americans were formally allied with the European colonial powers and the Soviet Union had long styled itself as the product of the first anticolonial revolution. The Soviet Union also offered a model of development outside the capitalist world economy, which was so closely bound up with empire, and it was a model that accorded a dominating role to the states that revolutionary leaders were intent on creating and controlling. Newly independent and developing states typically declared themselves "non-aligned" in the battle between East and West, but more often than not were to be found arrayed against the U.S., the U.K. and their allies in the United Nations and other international organizations.

The Vietnam War emerged from this shifting "correlation of forces," as the Soviets were wont to say, for the U.S. chose to regard the conflict as proof of its resolve and capacity to hold firm against these adverse trends. Instead, it demonstrated the limits of American power and influence and served further to weaken it. It also highlighted an obvious distinction between the American and Soviet spheres. The United States led an alliance of mostly democratic countries; the Soviet Union presided over an empire of undemocratic regimes. U.S. leaders made choices that could be questioned and ultimately reversed by its citizens, as the successful protests against the Vietnam War demonstrated. So, too, did British political leaders. Domestic considerations have always played a part in the framing of foreign policy, even in undemocratic countries, but the unrest and opposition that arose in the 1960s and early 1970s made international affairs, normally the preserve of elites, the stuff of daily political conflict. In the United States the civil rights and antiwar movements, which saw the Vietnam conflict in similar terms, made life very difficult for two successive Presidents, Johnson and Nixon, and materially affected the prosecution of the war.[41] Opposition to the war was also vocal, and sporadically violent, in Britain, despite the government's refusal to send troops.[42] Popular protest occurred elsewhere in the West, most notably in France in May 1968, and it induced a sense of crisis and malaise that led some to wonder whether the democracies were becoming "ungovernable."[43] A more compelling case could be made that the upheavals of the 1960s tested and expanded democracy, though it surely looked like an excess of democracy to those in charge.

Because America's allies needed to be persuaded, European leaders were forced at least to acknowledge dissent and perhaps even to defer to it. Unruly publics demanded attention in democratic systems; and wayward allies required negotiation, compromise and the occasional exchange of favors. America's overwhelming military dominance at the beginning of the Cold War and its towering strength at its end has tended to obscure the fact that the Cold War was mainly organized and prosecuted multilaterally, through alliances, and that unilateral moves were rare.[44] Managing foreign policy was thus an altogether different and more difficult matter for the U.S. and its allies than it was for the Soviet Union, which could command obedience if not enthusiasm from its de facto empire. Both sides faced material constraints, of course, but the political constraints were completely different. It could be argued that, over the long term, democratic polities could make more credible commitments and, when citizens gave their assent, mobilize greater resources, and that those resources were multiplied through joint action with allies, but the Cold War typically presented itself as a set of short-term engagements rather than as the sustained confrontation that it in fact was.

America's difficulties were mainly political, and geopolitical, through the 1960s and its economy, unlike Britain's, remained strong. Still, the United States and Britain entered the 1970s with a list of problems that would only grow and would require major readjustments by both countries. The growth model they largely shared, though with varying results, was beginning to falter and would fail to cope with the oil shocks of the next decade; neither wielded the global influence that was theirs in 1945; their relations with allies and with one another were not what they had been; and large numbers of their citizens were unhappy and resentful. Things were destined to get worse: the economic crises and the geopolitical setbacks that marked the 1970s threw troubled political systems into further disrepute and dysfunction and rendered shaky economies even more difficult to manage. By 1979, leaders in both countries were thoroughly on the defensive and appeared powerless to control events. Our detailed story begins with an effort to understand this crisis and its lasting effects.[45]

CHAPTER 2

Vietnam to Helsinki:
A Seventies Trip

History comes to us with labels and meanings attached. Before historians get to define an era, it has defined itself with an array of images, memories and understandings that scholars must start with before they begin their work of revising, elaborating and complicating. For the United States and for Britain, few decades have produced such a rich stock of symbolic moments and impressions as the 1970s. Most were negative. America began the decade with the incursion into Cambodia, which elicited massive protests and resulted, at Kent State and Jackson State, in soldiers firing on and killing students. The image bank flashes forward to Nixon and Watergate, with the nation mesmerized during the summer of 1973 by the Congressional hearings that caused the unraveling of the entire "imperial presidency," as it was termed, and then completely stunned when in August 1974 the President himself resigned rather than face impeachment hearings. As that drama was unfolding, Americans confronted the unprecedented need to wait in long lines for gasoline as the effects of the Yom Kippur War and the subsequent Arab oil boycott worked their way through to consumers. Rationing was something that happened in war, and mostly to other people, not in America in peacetime. More traumatic images were to come. At the end of April 1975 President Ford, on the advice of Secretary of State Henry Kissinger, ordered the evacuation of all Americans from Saigon. The plan was dubbed "Operation Frequent Wind" and it was not pretty: the last American soldiers lifted off from the embassy, with Vietnamese supporters and allies – who, having worked with and for the U.S., faced terrible retribution if they were unable to leave – trying vainly to board the departing helicopters while many more waited below.[1] The fall of Saigon was about as inglorious an end as possible for the decades-long engagement, but it was rivaled by what transpired in Iran in 1979. Islamist revolutionaries not only removed from office a regime put in power by the U.S. a quarter-century before, and long sustained by American arms and diplomatic support, but also proceeded to take over the U.S. Embassy and to seize those trapped inside.[2] The hostages would be held for the duration of the Carter administration by supporters of the Ayatollah Khomeini, and they were not released until the morning of Ronald Reagan's inauguration in January 1981.

It would be hard for Britain to match the drama and poignancy of these images, but the more prosaic images that marked the same era in the U.K. were just as negative. The decade had begun with a change in government that implied a deep dissatisfaction with existing policies and ways of doing business, but the initiatives of the Heath government faltered and it was soon forced to reverse itself. It would be brought down by the election of February 1974, which concluded a dismal stretch. The coal miners had gone on strike in December 1973 and, making use of "flying pickets" that not only shut down the mines but also prevented deliveries of coal to power stations, crippled the economy. The government imposed a three-day week to conserve power and called an election framed around the question of whether the miners or the government should rule. However noble the miners' cause, the fact that the government felt compelled to ask voters for permission to govern was a sign that, in truth, those who were supposed to be in charge no longer were. The fact that the answer from voters was a turn away from both major parties said further that, unless and until something dramatically changed, authority would not be easily restored.

The truly big shift for Britain in the early 1970s, of course, involved the decision to join the European Communities (EC). A wise move economically, at least in the long run, but the moment was not ideal and the terms poor; together, these things augured a troubled future for Britain in Europe. The choice to proceed was a clear indication, moreover, that Britain's lingering global role could not mask or compensate for economic weakness. On the contrary, retreat from empire was made necessary by Britain's lagging economy. The decision to join the EC, within which Britain would work out its postimperial future, actually reinforced the perception of decline; and it also, for a time, seemed to threaten Britain's relationship with its oldest and strongest ally. Heath saw the turn to Europe as requiring a turning away from America. While it was reasonable enough to put some distance between his government and the developing failures of the Nixon administration, doing so left Britain largely without allies, without resources and without influence abroad at precisely the moment when domestic politics and policy-making began to come undone.[3]

Heath's departure brought to power a Labour Party whose leaders had not expected to win and whose goal was to "manage the crisis." Their strategic innovation was the "social contract" with the trade unions.[4] The unions would voluntarily keep wages down and discourage strikes if the government delivered on a series of promises to increase benefits and to restore and extend trade union rights. The bargain held for over four years and brought a semblance of industrial peace, but the price was high: the government had ceded to unions a veto over policy that further reduced its authority and room for maneuver. The symbol for the arrangement was the regular consultation between ministers and union representatives – "beer and sandwiches at No. 10" – and it represented a high point for the "corporatist" policies that prevailed during the long postwar era of social compromise. It left government ultimately passive, however, pushed back and forth between the preferences of its friends, the demands of its critics and the realities of the world outside. A striking example came in the fall of 1976, when Labour was forced to seek a loan from the International Monetary Fund (IMF). IMF negotiators arrived in London on November 1 and spent the next several weeks bargaining over how much the government would have to cut expenditure as the condition for the loan. In the end the Cabinet accepted £3 billion in cuts over two years, not a terrible deal for a country with little bargaining power. But that was precisely the issue: Britain had very little clout. James Callaghan, who had succeeded Harold Wilson as Labour Prime Minister earlier that year, was barely in control of his government; the government was not in control of the economy; and allies such as the U.S. and Germany chose not to use their clout on Britain's behalf. The message was clear enough; and if it was not yet understood by the public, the unions took care of that two years later when they refused to agree to another period of pay restraint and in effect gave the signal for the "winter of discontent." Trains, buses and ambulances ceased to operate, garbage piled up in London and graves were not dug in Liverpool. These were images not soon forgotten, and they produced the election of Margaret Thatcher in 1979.

In both Britain and the United States, then, the 1970s were a time of decline, of what would come to be termed "malaise," of an apparent inability to control either the economy or the world outside. Most important, it was a time when the techniques and strategies at the disposal of governments visibly failed to work. There were new and difficult challenges to confront: the "Fordist" model of growth began to exhaust its potential at the very moment when geopolitical shifts enabled oil producers to ratchet up prices, which overwhelmed local measures to control inflation; and the coming of superpower parity meant that the global "correlation of forces" was no longer so favorable to the United States, Britain and their allies. What was most painful and frustrating to leaders and members of the public however, was the failure of what had worked for the past quarter-century to work again. Beneath the arresting images and the depressed atmosphere were, therefore, two separate but related stories: a dimly perceived and poorly understood story of the unexpected and unprecedented economic and political realities that emerged to confound the U.S. and the U.K.; and the deceptively simple story of the incapacity that ruined careers and reputations and overwhelmed the efforts of both governments to respond.

Kissinger's Year of Europe, and Heath's

It was only by experiencing repeated failures of policy that rulers and ruled alike came gradually to grasp the structural shifts that rendered efforts at control or resolution unsuccessful. There were many examples, too many to recount in detail, but a brief review will make it possible to recreate the learning process that led to the dramatic shifts in policy and political philosophy with which the decade ended. As a first step, it is perhaps useful to focus on one failure that has largely been forgotten but that was nonetheless unusually revealing: the so-called Year of Europe.[5] The "Year of Europe" was Kissinger's proposal, a plan to reinvigorate the Atlantic alliance in 1973, but it was in 1973 that Britain joined the European Community and Edward Heath was determined to make a success of it. The two goals clashed, ensuring that 1973 would be a year of tension and discord within the alliance.

The U.K.'s position was understandable. For much of the postwar era, Britain could not make up its mind whether to join what began as a Common Market or to seek its fate outside it.[6] That stance had become untenable by the early 1960s, but not until 1973 did the U.K. formally become a member of the EC. For Britain, and for Heath, the turn to Europe would provide the stimulus for economic revival, opening new markets and compelling British firms to become more competitive. Equally important, becoming a part of a growing and more assertive geopolitical bloc would also offer Britain a new means for exercising global influence. Heath had reluctantly accepted the decision to withdraw from "east of Suez," but the move reinforced the sense that Britain had somehow to redefine its role in the world, and Europe was clearly how to do it.[7] There were two schools of thought about what a turn to Europe would mean.[8] For some, the Prime Minister included, it would require that Britain move away from the United States and develop a genuinely new and European identity. Others believed it was possible to become closer to Europe and still maintain the Atlantic alliance. This was more or less the official view. As the Foreign Office saw it, "While the United Kingdom is becoming less indispensable to American interests, the United States is as important to the United Kingdom as ever." Europe was the key, for "If we fail to become part of a more united Europe, we shall become increasingly peripheral to U.S. concerns." For that to happen, of course, Britain needed to convince Europe that it "is in no sense a Trojan horse for the United States."[9] Europe beckoned, therefore, but a fuller engagement would complicate relations with the United States.

Whichever of these views one held to, it was imperative that when Britain formally joined in January 1973 it should make every effort to dispel the skepticism of its new partners. This posture also sat well with heads of state in the European Economic Community. At the Hague Summit in December 1969, European leaders had already committed themselves to closer economic integration and to the need to develop "European Political Coordination" on issues of foreign policy.[10] At the Paris Summit in October 1972, the first to include representatives of all "the Nine," there was still more talk of this sort and there were even higher hopes for closer cooperation on defense and foreign policy and a formal pledge to attain monetary union by 1980. As the final communiqué put it, "the Member States of the Community, the driving wheels of European construction, declare their intention of converting their entire relationship into a European Union before the end of this decade."[11] Heath was especially taken with the vision and wrote to Nixon informing him of this great "success," which he hoped would "provide the impulse for the next stage in the Community's development ..."[12] When the two met at Camp David the following February, it was clear that Heath envisioned a genuinely new balance between the U.S. and Europe: as Kissinger noted, "He wanted Europe as a unit to formulate answers to our queries; he was determined to avoid any whiff of Anglo-American collusion."[13]

The possibility of Europe, with Britain now on the inside, developing an independent identity and adopting policies of its own choosing separate from the U.S., was made still more urgent and consequential by the recent disarray in the governance of the international economy. Mounting inflation in the United States in the late 1960s and early 1970s made the continued use of the dollar as the key international currency impossible. On August 15, 1971 Nixon stunned the world by announcing his New Economic Program. It had both domestic and international components: tax cuts and credits to stimulate employment, spending cuts, a ninety-day freeze on wages and prices, a 10 percent surcharge, and the suspension of dollar convertibility. This was the beginning of the dismantling of the Bretton Woods system. The process would not be completed until March 1973, precisely the moment that Kissinger was beginning to talk with European leaders about his plan for the Year of Europe.

The United States had a different set of reasons for launching the "Year of Europe." The key was Vietnam and its aftermath: the United States and North Vietnam concluded the Paris Peace Accords in late January 1973 and immediately Nixon and Kissinger turned to urgent matters elsewhere.[14] The debacle in Vietnam had left America weak, internally divided and isolated internationally.[15] Its response to its isolation was a flurry of diplomatic activity that began even before the deal was struck over Vietnam. The U.S. had been pursuing détente with the Soviet Union since the early days of the Nixon administration and it would continue to do so, but from 1970 it also moved to open up relations with China: Kissinger would visit Beijing in July 1971 and Nixon famously followed at the end of February 1972.[16] "Triangular diplomacy," as Kissinger labeled it, could give the United States leverage both with the Soviet Union and with Vietnam, which relied on the USSR and China for support.[17] It was coupled with a series of initiatives labeled "the Nixon Doctrine" that involved an effort to identify the conditions under which America would get involved abroad, especially in Asia. The idea was to rule out future Vietnams by insisting that nations should take primary responsibility for their security both internally and externally, though the U.S. could and would provide support. In practice, the policy devolved into one of deciding which medium-size powers could, with American military aid and "goodwill," provide stability in regions where the U.S. preferred not to become more directly involved. The classic case was Iran under the Shah. It was reasonably strong, loyal to the U.S. and very anti-Soviet; as such, it received massive support.[18] The Nixon Doctrine was meant to accompany détente; together, they would provide stability at the center – East/West relations – and on the periphery; and the "linkage" between the two arenas would reinforce progress in both. The outcome would be a recalibration of global power: the U.S., having lost its overall preponderance with the emergence of superpower parity, would try to engineer an "imperial multipolarity" instead.[19] Nixon and Kissinger, obsessed with the relative decline of U.S. influence, would follow a set of policies inspired by "metaphors of control: *balance of power, equilibrium, structure of peace*" and meant to achieve precisely these objectives.[20]

But what of America's traditional allies in Europe, where East/West relations were matters of more immediate and intimate concern? Despite strong ties of sympathy and self-interest and the institutional connections surrounding NATO, the Europeans had by and large not supported the U.S. in Vietnam and worked to distance themselves from American policy. U.S. leaders recognized this and decided it was time to repair the connection. Nixon and Heath met in January 1973 and began to discuss the prospects, and then again in February at Camp David. Heath was distinctly unhelpful and Kissinger concluded that the Prime Minister's "nearly impenetrable opacity . . . had to be deliberate . . ."[21] Kissinger was nonetheless expected to move forward and he further sounded out the Heath government as well as Pompidou, the French president, and also conferred with Jean Monnet, the great founding figure of the European

Community. The Germans were kept informed as well. Finally, on April 23 Kissinger gave a major speech in New York proclaiming 1973 as the "Year of Europe" and calling for a new Atlantic Charter to be worked out between the U.S. and its allies and, presumably, signed during a Nixon visit to Europe later in the year.

Nixon's visit never happened; the declaration, when it came more than a year later, was anodyne and largely ignored.[22] The project was seen to be failing just a few months after it was launched, and by the end of the year relations between the United States and Europe, and between the U.S. and its closest ally, the U.K., were at their lowest point since before World War II. The U.S. and its allies were by then unable to agree on how to respond to the Arab-Israel War, the Arab oil boycott and the faltering world economy. Why such utter failure? The most obvious and proximate reason was Watergate, which in discrediting Nixon stripped away the incentives for European leaders to risk their own credibility by associating with him or by indulging in any public gestures of support. Watergate was also a huge distraction for American policy-makers and it fueled domestic efforts to curtail what the administration could do abroad. But there were more important and long-term reasons as well: the idea of reasserting what had been bold and innovative in the 1940s so many years later was quite simply a mistake. As Kissinger put it in an unusual display of self-criticism, we in the U.S. were not only eager to "shift our atten-tion back to the West and away from Southeast Asia" but, "seduced by our own nostalgia for historic initiatives, we ran afoul of conditions that had changed drastically since 1947."[23] The frustrations that attended the venture revealed how much the world had changed since the days of the Atlantic Charter and the Marshall Plan.

The frustrations came quickly.[24] The day after Kissinger's speech the Foreign Office labeled it "important," but proposed to discuss it "with our European allies"; two days later, the French Cabinet took note and promised to respond "in the spirit which had always been ours, that of faithfulness to the Alliance in the context of respect for our independence." These formal expressions of support were weak and meant little and difficulties soon became apparent. When Willy Brandt visited Washington on May 1, for example, he raised two issues that appeared merely procedural but were in fact substantive and that would dog all subsequent negotiations: the first was the need to separate discussions on different issues rather than to "globalize" them, as the U.S. supposedly wanted and the Europeans did not; the second was the question of who spoke for Europe. The U.S. opposed separate negotiations on economic and political matters, for it did not want to allow the Europeans to feel that they could count on America for security but oppose the U.S. on economic policy.

The question of who spoke for whom was really about whether the Europeans would gradually develop a distinct European position and act as a "third force" across the globe, particularly in terms of the Cold War. The Americans were not reassured by the pronouncements of their allies: "None of us," Brandt proclaimed in a toast to his hosts, "meets you any longer as the representative of his own country but at the same time already, to a certain degree, as a representative of the European Community as well." The communiqué issued at the end of the Brandt/Nixon meeting pointedly omitted any reference to the proposed new "Atlantic Charter." These early responses prefigured a process that would not go well, that would demonstrate "institutional tangle" deliberately made more complex, that would be marked by "farcical maneuvering" and produce the opposite of what was intended. As a thoughtful observer argued, "Commitments are best defined in crisis. Kissinger's pressure produced a crisis that exacerbated differences."[25]

Kissinger tried to elicit more support when he stopped in London on May 10, but before he arrived, a senior Foreign Office official circulated a dismissive memo to colleagues explaining that talk of a new Atlantic Charter was based on a misunderstanding of the first.[26] Once again, Kissinger encountered a diffident audience and found himself again debating procedures and institutions, and he came away convinced that the British would defer to the French. Paris was thus the obvious next stop, where on May 17 Kissinger met with the new French Foreign Minister, Michel Jobert, who expressed a willingness to cooperate and even asked if the U.S. could draft the beginnings of a declaration. Jobert objected to talks with the European Community, however, and recommended bilateral discussions with Britain, Germany and France. The effect was to render the process more complicated and to multiply the possibilities for misunderstandings. It also allowed the French to portray the effort as an American venture rather than a shared project and it afforded them repeated opportunities to criticize the plan, which they did both privately and in public. Nixon and French President Pompidou, who was ailing and so not the force he might have been, met in Iceland at the end of May. In honor of the hosts, the meeting was prefaced by a wrangle over codfish; later, Jobert rattled off a series of criticisms of the U.S. initiative. His fundamental point was that it was all about U.S. pressuring and dominating Europe and diminishing not only Europe but particularly France. The next day, in his meeting with Nixon, Pompidou raised again the procedural difficulties, though in a more elevated and profound manner: who could make a commitment to a refashioned Atlantic Charter, he asked, if the membership of NATO and the European Community did not completely overlap and if the latter was still just a common market that was only beginning to develop a more robust identity? The outcome was a decision to keep talking, but the forum and the level of talks were left unclear. It was agreed that the U.S. would prepare a more extensive draft to present to Jobert at the end of June in San Clemente; prior to that, nothing of substance could happen; after that, what happened was a confrontation that worsened the relations between erstwhile friends and allies.

Stasis did not sit well with Kissinger and he voiced his irritation to Burke Trend, the Cabinet Secretary, the Ambassador Lord Cromer, and other British officials during a June meeting at the embassy in Washington. Kissinger recounted the French charge that "the Americans were trying to create a new Atlantic organization to force France back into NATO, that they were trying to 'abridge French autonomy'; were seeking to force decisions which would split the European Community; and were trying to organize a Soviet/U.S. condominium." He insisted that his, and Nixon's, primary concern had been to shore up U.S. support for the continued commitment to Europe in the face of Congressional pressures for disengagement. The French seemed to think that because it was in America's interest to keep the Soviets out of Europe, they would keep troops there anywhere. Kissinger disagreed, but in the end confessed that "He could not understand what game they (the French) were playing."[27] He did not say, but he was also coming to believe that the British, at Heath's direction, were also playing on the French team and merely humoring their U.S. allies. They were more willing, if necessary, to "give the Americans the symbolic satisfaction they seek" by offering them "a new form of words" on the Atlantic relationship, but nothing of substance. Indeed, the official British position was "to trade form for substance"[28]

The U.S. continued to go back and forth with France and Britain to no avail. Eventually drafts were exchanged, but not agreed, and egos were bruised over the question of who got to see which document first and who was, or might have been, left out. Eventually, the Europeans met in Copenhagen on July 23 and decided that officials would prepare a draft for ministers by mid-September and only after that would an agreed draft be delivered to Washington by a Community representative who would have no authority to negotiate. In the interim the U.S. was not to get involved: in fact, Edward Heath cabled Nixon to the effect that the content of any discussions between U.S. and U.K. was henceforth to be shared. They would therefore largely cease to happen. Instead, the Europeans would work together to define their "identity . . . vis-à-vis the United States." What had begun as an effort to proclaim the shared values and interests which supposedly underpinned the alliance had evolved into an exercise in deciding how they differed and where their interests did not align. Europeans would agree that their "shared culture and a common attachment to parliamentary democracy, to freedom of opinion, to equality of rights and to social justice" had by the 1970s "been diffused throughout the rest of the world and shared by the United States." To this extent the objectives of the U.S. and Europe were "at one." "Where they sometimes differ is in their choice of methods, particularly in the legitimate emphasis accorded by the Nine to the priority objective of progressively developing their own unity and creating a strong and independent entity in the international arena." The Nine, or some of them, also had "historical associations linking Europe with the Middle East, Africa and other overseas territories down the centuries. Europe's lack of raw materials will require her to seek special relations with the countries concerned in the future as it has in the past."

Such was the understanding of European identity evolved by the Foreign Office as of August 1973.[29] The text was not apparently shared with U.S. leaders or officials, who might well have noted how recently some of the Nine had become committed to democracy and freedom and queried the phrase "historical associations" to describe Europe's connection to its former colonies.[30] Nevertheless, it was obviously the intellectual framework through which many European leaders viewed the transatlantic relationship, and it inevitably came to inform the content of the Declaration proposed by the Europeans. Equally inevitably, "the form of words" – which eschewed terms such as "partnership" and "interdependence" – would not, and did not, satisfy the United States. The wrangling would drag on well into the next year, but by the end of September 1973 the rift between the U.S. and its allies had widened and the Year of Europe was largely dead.

Well before burial, however, Kissinger met with Douglas-Home in late September for an early post-mortem.[31] The Foreign Secretary acknowledged "misunderstandings" but sought to attribute them to inadequate "machinery at the lower levels" and to minimize their significance. Kissinger was not appeased.[32] "Britain had never been treated as a foreign country," he insisted, but now it was unclear what sort of exchanges the U.S. and the U.K. could have. Nor was it clear what kinds of communications were possible with Europe. The Europeans had decided in Copenhagen that their deliberations should be their own and that only when they were done would the spokesman for the Community convey the results to the U.S. At the time this "European personality" was embodied in the Danish Foreign Minister Knut Andersen, who chaired the meeting of foreign ministers and who was to present the European draft declaration. "What," Kissinger asked in exasperation, "was the position of Mr. Andersen? Who did he really represent? He was little more than an emissary. America was in danger of losing her traditional contacts in return for not the most qualified of interlocutors . . . This was an unsatisfactory relationship with America's closest allies. It was worse than dealing with the Soviets . . ." The British representatives continued to insist that the big problem was that Europe as an entity was still in formation and it would take time to get things right; meanwhile, Britain would continue to consult with the Americans. For his part Kissinger kept arguing that the aim behind the "Year of Europe" was not to achieve "a propaganda success" but actually to strengthen the relationship at a moment when the "Administration was facing a coalition of liberals and conservatives in Congress who could wreck America's foreign policy." For this they needed a positive European response and what they got was "confrontation." The meeting resolved little, and Heath was unrepentant: as late as November he reportedly told a group of American correspondents that "Apparently, Dr. Kissinger did not like having a Dane speaking for Europe. Well, he would have to get used to it."[33]

The September encounter might have served to release tensions just a bit, but the antipathy would be revived soon enough. The meeting ended with desultory discussions of Iceland and the "cod wars," and, more important, of the Middle East. On the latter Kissinger agreed with the British desire to move toward a settlement but acknowledged that "the Americans were not engaged in serious talks at the moment . . ." There seemed no sense of urgency on that score, however, either for the British or the U.S, and when the British Ambassador cabled London on October 3, he described a "reasonably satisfactory picture" in the Middle East.[34] Heath, for his part, was later reported to have said that "The only warlike Egyptians I have ever heard of were in Aida."[35] Such complacency would be short-lived, for on October 6 war broke out between Israel and its Arab neighbors. The Arab-Israel War would have deadly consequences for its victims and participants, and serious effects far beyond. It would bring the superpowers close to confrontation, it would quadruple the cost of oil and make its availability a matter of politics, and it would plunge the world into a recession which crippled growth into the 1980s. It created huge difficulties for the United States and its allies, whose responses were uncoordinated and often at odds. Their disarray would have precluded effective action even if the problems had been properly understood and the solutions had been clear, which of course they were not.

Alliances and Their Discontents

The failure of the Year of Europe makes it clear that the troubles with allies had begun earlier and were based on real differences in interest and outlook. When Europeans criticized the U.S., they spoke in familiar accents: the French reverted to long-standing criticisms of American domination; the Germans stressed the need for complexity and flexibility; and the British explained as they typically did that it was a matter of misunderstanding and unskilled diplomacy, implying that the British would have done better. Nevertheless, the arguments about the Year of Europe also contained three interesting and somewhat novel elements: real worries over détente and a possible U.S./Soviet condominium, a genuine wariness over trade and monetary issues, and a keener sense of the implications of European integration for foreign policy in general and the Atlantic Alliance in particular. These interacted with still deeper economic problems and an altered world balance to make cooperation and resolution extremely difficult.

The major European states were officially supportive of détente and of the arms limitations which accompanied it. It was difficult to be otherwise. But there was also ambivalence and a potential divergence of interests. Most Europeans recognized that their defense rested ultimately on American arms, both nuclear and conventional, and were comfortable dealing with the East on that basis. The Germans, for example, could count on ultimate U.S. support against the Soviets while they themselves undertook overtures to the East designed to lessen tensions and improve the lot of Germans caught on the wrong side of the East–West divide. This was the essence of *Ostpolitik* and its pursuit was the centerpiece of German policy under Willy Brandt.[36] French policy was similar, even if the rationale was different. The Gaullist aspiration for independence from the U.S. and preeminence within Europe encouraged French leaders to argue that reliance on the American defense umbrella did not, and should not, limit or define France's own relationship with the East or, for that matter, with the rest of the world. They maintained that since it was in the interests of the U.S. to keep the Soviets out of Western Europe, France should be free to approach Moscow in its own way. France could do this, moreover, from a position of relative strength, for as of 1964 it had its own nuclear weapons.

Britain also had its own weapons and its own history of dealing with the rest of the world, though it had long since decided that its influence could best be maintained alongside rather than in opposition to the U.S. But it, too, found itself ambivalent about the policy of détente: Labour, when it was in power until 1970, continued to believe that left could speak to left and so believed that it could communicate better and more effectively with Soviet leaders. The Conservatives, in power from 1970 into early 1974, simultaneously worried about being left out of U.S./Soviet negotiations and worked to keep the U.S. out of European deliberations. They fretted, too, about the implications of any arms agreements for the British nuclear deterrent. U.K. officials were also concerned about ongoing negotiations on conventional forces in Europe (MBFR, mutual and balanced force reductions, was the acronym), fearing that the Soviets' aim was "to bring about reductions in the level of American forces in Europe, and to reduce the credibility of the American guarantee to Western Europe."[37]

The U.S. decision to push forward with détente was by definition a recalibration of the American defense posture vis-à-vis the Soviet Union and had to involve the region where East and West most directly confronted one another. That was in Europe. The choice for America was premised on the Soviet achievement of nuclear parity. By the late 1960s, as a report to the National Security Council put it, the "Soviets have evinced greater confidence in the existence of a state of mutual deterrence . . ." in large part because it was "their assessment that the United States shares this view of the balance."[38] With "the consolidation of strategic nuclear parity," it became "generally understood . . . that neither the United States nor the Soviet Union would initiate the use of nuclear weapons against the other . . ."[39] It was not out of the question that the USSR might "look for opportunities to project Soviet influence under the shadow of nuclear equality"; what was not in question was that strategic parity had "reduced the credibility of America's nuclear protection" for its European allies. For the United States, the new configuration of forces could be best managed by détente, which meant not only arms limitation but the elaboration of a network of agreements designed to limit tensions across a range of issues and regions. For the Europeans détente meant two different things: it meant settling outstanding issues and threats to peace in Eastern Europe, Germany especially; but it also meant that the U.S. role in the provision of security would inevitably be different and, in all probability, would amount to something less. With less of a guarantee, Europe could choose to increase its own contributions to defense, something most countries were reluctant to do; or to reassess its relations with the Soviets and their allies. Europeans therefore had reasons to fear the consequences of détente even if they approved the lessening of tensions between the rival blocs.

The disagreements over détente, implicit at first, became more visible during the Year of Europe. The rapprochement between the U.S. and the Soviet Union and the Strategic Arms Limitation Talks (SALT) had by then resulted in the Interim Agreement on strategic arms and the Anti-Ballistic Missile (ABM) Treaty, both agreed at the Moscow Summit of May 1972, combined with a formal statement on the "Basic Principles of Relations" between the super-powers committing them to creating "the conditions which promote the reduction of tensions in the world and the strengthening of universal security and international cooperation." These efforts were supplemented and extended geographically by the Nuclear Non-Proliferation Treaty that came into force in 1970 and the Biological Weapons Convention, approved in April 1972 and effective in 1975. Within Europe the process of negotiation had produced a series of three treaties involving the Federal Republic of Germany and its neighbors to the east – the first with the Soviets in August 1970, the second with Poland, and the third with East Germany. To these was added the Four-Power Agreement on Berlin. These were all in place by 1971. Soon after, it was agreed to begin discussions on a broader settlement in Europe. The Conference on Security and Cooperation in Europe (CSCE) was set up in 1972, began meeting in 1973, and would ultimately result in the Helsinki Accords of August 1, 1975.[40]

These clear achievements did not, however, eliminate the uncertainty among Europeans about the long-term consequences of détente. A telling example was the response by the U.S., and Britain, to a July 1972 proposal from the Soviets for a formal treaty on the "Prevention of Nuclear War." Again, it was difficult formally to oppose such a move, but Britain – and, it would turn out, other European powers – had serious reservations about the effects on Europe and on the British nuclear deterrent. Thus in February 1973 Heath told Nixon that in proposing such a treaty the Soviets "aimed at depriving NATO of the protection of the United States nuclear deterrent." "Europe," he insisted, "could not afford to rely on a wholly conventional defence." Nixon and Kissinger saw the declaration differently, as a tactical move. As Kissinger later admitted, "We had next to no interest in the project" itself.[41] Nixon explained that the Soviets "had not really done very well out of their advocacy of a policy of détente" and so needed something to show for it. The U.S. wanted to give them a symbol, provided it could be done "without really meaning anything much at all" by it. The U.S. also hoped to gain time: "United States domestic opinion now needed a year or so in which to recover from the psychological trauma of the Vietnam war," the President believed, and the "whole point of the operation would be to hold the prospect of some further deal with the Soviet Union continuously dangling just ahead in order to keep the Soviet Government in play and at the same time to fend off, month by month, Congressional pressure for United States troop reductions in Europe."[42]

To assuage British fears, the U.S. arranged for Thomas Brimelow, a top Foreign Office official, to take a hand in drafting the declaration. Cromer, the British Ambassador, could hardly believe the arrangement – code-named "Operation Hullaboo" – noting "the astonishing anomaly of the most powerful nation in the world invoking the aid of a foreign government to do its drafting of it, while totally excluding its own Ministry of Foreign Affairs."[43] The U.S. would continue to consult closely with Britain as it finalized the agreement, which was duly signed at the Washington Summit in late June 1973. Despite the British role in drafting the agreement and prior consultations with other

European countries, it would nevertheless be interpreted by Europeans as threatening a "U.S./Soviet condominium" under which Europe's interests might be damaged. Heath had worried over a situation in which Europe would be forced to rely on conventional forces; Pompidou worried over that as well and also over Soviet advances "camouflaged ... as a 'progressive tide.'" [44] It would thus serve as yet a further obstacle to the negotiations over the proposal for a new Atlantic Charter.

The Europeans were also deeply concerned about America's economic policies. Developments on both sides of the Atlantic were at work. The enlargement of the Common Market in 1973 and its transformation into the European Community meant that tariff barriers were now in place around most of the European continent. The reach of the Common Agricultural Policy was also extended. Europe was to this extent opting out of the broader effort to reduce tariffs, and Europeans not unreasonably feared that the United States would demand compensation or a shift in policy. The United States was focused largely on the question of trade: America had run a trade surplus for the entire twentieth century, but preliminary figures for 1971 pointed to a deficit which administration experts attributed to an overvalued dollar. That led in turn to pressure against the dollar which built throughout the spring and summer. On June 2, Paul McCracken, Chair of the Council of Economic Advisors (CEA), wrote to Nixon saying that "We have just muddled through another international monetary crisis." Something needed to be done, for "A system that combines rigidly fixed exchange rates with free trade and capital movements appears to be unworkable."[45]

On August 13, in the middle of yet another dollar crisis, Nixon retreated to Camp David with his key economic advisors, the most important of whom was Treasury Secretary John Connally. Both the Secretary of State, William Rogers, and Kissinger, the National Security Advisor, were left out of the discussion which led to the most important moment in international economic policy since 1944.[46] The decision was apparently not to be dominated by the concerns of diplomats and foreign policy experts. The result was not long in coming: in the middle of August Nixon announced his New Economic Program that suspended the dollar's convertibility into gold, froze wages and prices and imposed a 10 percent important surcharge. In a desire to boost the economy so as to shore up his electoral prospects, Nixon had broken with the Bretton Woods system of fixed exchange rates, based on the dollar, upon which the postwar economy had been based and under which it had flourished for over a quarter of a century.[47] U.S. allies and trading partners were left utterly unsure of what was to come and feared that Nixon, under domestic pressures to which he was unusually sensitive, would move further in the direction of protection, devaluation, or both.[48] The postwar economic order seemed, in consequence, under immediate and potentially dire threat.

The system did not fall apart right away. The U.S. used the leverage of the import surcharge, as well as the suspension of gold payments, to effect a major realignment. After hard bargaining and considerable resistance, the Smithsonian Agreement of December 1971 set new exchange rates that added up to an upward revaluation vis-à-vis the dollar of roughly 8 percent among its trading partners. In fact, the German mark was pegged at a level more than 13.5 percent higher and the yen at a point nearly 17 percent higher than before the "Nixon shock." The adjustment did serve to stimulate the U.S. economy and helped to produce the boom that Nixon rode to victory on in November 1972. U.S. allies hoped that the new rates would hold steady and allow a return to fixed rates and the resumption of gold payments. This did not happen, partly because the U.S. chose not to agree, but also because a period of fluctuation and adjustment was clearly in order so as to allow currencies to find the appropriate levels. Over the next year or so the price of gold rose dramatically, the British decided to float the pound in a de facto devaluation in June 1972 and the U.S. trade balance again worsened. The dollar was further devalued in February 1973, by just over 11 percent against the mark and the franc, but came under more pressure a month later. In mid-March both the U.S. and the Europeans decided not to try to maintain the dollar's value. It was at that moment that the Bretton Woods system definitively ended, a victim of a U.S. choice not to "bear any burden" or "pay any price" to make the system as a whole work. The outcome may have been inevitable, given the shifting balance of economic power, but the decision had been taken more or less unilaterally by the U.S. and sent a signal about American priorities in coping with this new balance.

Uncertainties over the effects of détente on America's relations with Europe combined with those over U.S. economic policy led European leaders to consider their options. Hence the focus on the European project and European identity that manifested itself during the Year of Europe. Though Nixon and Kissinger insisted on the importance of relations with Britain, American policy on issues of security and the international economy actually reinforced Heath's predisposition to put Europe first and, as a corollary, to downgrade the Anglo-American connection. Heath had little or no sympathetic attachment to the U.S. and, unlike most previous and subsequent British leaders, he was unusual in his skepticism about the "special relationship." In the early 1960s Macmillan had placed Heath in charge of negotiations for British entry into Europe, and Heath was stung by De Gaulle's veto and largely accepted his rationale for it: that the U.K. was too close to the United States and could well become a "Trojan horse" within the Community. Convinced that Britain's future lay with Europe, he was determined not to allow such a charge to derail his government's application for membership in the EEC. His attitude was enduring, and shortly after taking office in 1970 Heath was faced with U.S. requests for the use of "our remaining island dependencies" for defense purposes; in response he asked Douglas-Home just "what we get in return for all this from the Americans." "I may be wrong," he admitted, "but so far this seems to me to be very much a one-way movement." The Foreign Secretary tried to explain to the Prime Minister that Britain's possession of these "island dependencies" allowed it to make "a considerable contribution to an alliance which is important to both of us but in which otherwise our respective contributions might be very ill-balanced." In other words, the U.K. received substantial benefits with a modest contribution. Douglas-Home proceeded to append a long list of specific exchanges and agreements. Apparently this intervention satisfied Heath, at least for the moment, but his views did not change fundamentally.[49] He never warmed to Nixon or to Kissinger and was at pains in the run-up to British membership in the European Community to do nothing that would imply a prior, or greater, loyalty to the American alliance.

Heath was not alone in his views, however, for they found echoes among old-fashioned conservatives who felt betrayed by America over empire and by more forward-looking diplomats and officials such as Con O'Neill and Michael Palliser, who were strongly committed to a European future.[50] Typically, the highly educated and well-connected men who staffed the Foreign Office were strong supporters of the Anglo-American alliance, but they were also worldly and cosmopolitan and felt themselves superior to the cruder sorts who ran American foreign policy. Their predispositions could therefore cut both ways and often produced an ambivalence that allowed them to pursue seemingly conflicting policies at the same time. There was also a genuine dilemma confronting Britain in its postimperial era: how would the U.K. combine a novel attachment to Europe with its established link with the U.S.? In the context it was almost inevitable that the effort to sign up as good Europeans would entail at least a momentary shift on Britain's part away from the U.S. That the moment should come when Heath was in power and when the U.S. was eager for a reaffirmation of the links with its traditional allies turned the move into a confrontation.

It became, too, an occasion to rehearse old grievances and to revisit old prejudices. While the Europeans were deciding how to respond to Kissinger, Walt Rostow dined with Edward Heath and had what must have been a decidedly unpleasant evening. Rostow insisted that Nixon and Kissinger "needed help in dealing with isolationist and protectionist influences at home." Heath would have no part of this and claimed that "For the last 25 years Britain had been divesting itself, largely to please the Americans, of Imperial responsibilities and creating a Commonwealth of independent countries. The result was of little benefit and of some liability to the United Kingdom." "Now," he said, the U.S. was "going through a similar process. She was now no longer 'No. 1', either militarily or in economic or trade affairs":

> The United States had allowed her nuclear superiority to be eroded. The fashionable talk was of parity; but Soviet strength was constantly growing. Americans must not be surprised if the Europeans were apprehensive about this development. In the meantime Europe – in the shape of an enlarged European community – now existed. This meant that the United States could no longer deal with European countries on the old basis.

The Prime Minister admitted that Europe had as yet "no defence personality" but even in that sphere "Europe could do with less preaching" from the U.S.[51] Heath's curious views on decolonization and America's impending decline were perhaps not widely shared, but his sense of frustration at Britain's own loss of influence and of its need to reinvent itself presumably was. And there can be little question that the government as a whole believed that Britain's accession to the EC was both essential and extremely complicated.[52] So, too, did other Europeans who believed enlargement would lead on to a new European identity, to enhanced influence in foreign affairs and security, and to closer economic and financial integration. None of these objectives would prove easy to attain, and the failures which greeted the first efforts probably served only to make things harder.

There was more than a little irony in the fact that the European attempt to assert an independent identity should have run afoul of an initiative designed by Henry Kissinger, for Kissinger had always placed transatlantic relations at the center of his schemes for ordering the world. During the 1960s, for example, he had proposed the creation of an "Atlantic Confederacy" which would have given the Europeans greater clout within the alliance. He favored a "directorate" of the big powers – the U.S., Britain, France, Germany and maybe Italy – and envisioned a situation in which Britain and France would have more control of their own defense and the deployment and potential use of their own nuclear weapons.[53] Kissinger assumed that nuclear weapons in the hands of U.S. allies would complicate Soviet defense policy and so, rather than discourage proliferation, the U.S. should try to manage it.[54] The preoccupation with Vietnam forced Kissinger to put such schemes aside during the first Nixon administration, although the thinking behind them informed U.S. foreign policy more broadly, and they were never abandoned. On the contrary, they would lead logically to the proposal for a new Atlantic Charter. It was not to be, of course, but the difficulties attending the Year of Europe did not stem from misunderstandings or poor procedure or lack of consultation, although these did not help, but from genuine divergences that in turn arose from the changed circumstances of the 1970s. The settled facts and established relationships, indeed the entire postwar order of things economic and political and strategic, were no longer settled, and the outlines of any future order or reordering were as yet completely unclear. Nor would they become clear in the near term, for the differences that wrecked the Year of Europe would only get worse.

Oil, the Middle East and "the West"

The outbreak of the Arab-Israeli War in October 1973 ought not to have come as a surprise, but it did. More genuinely surprising was the initial success of the Arab forces, which in the first few days succeeded in driving the Israelis out of the Sinai and pushing them back on the Golan Heights as well. It would have been an even bigger surprise, however, if the Israelis had failed to regroup, counterattack and ultimately regain what they had lost and drive further into Arab lands. All this they did, so that by late October the outcome was yet another Arab defeat and another vindication of Israeli military superiority. But the costs had been considerable, and the consequences would be more serious than anyone had imagined. Indeed, much the most remarkable feature of the war was how quickly it engaged states and leaders and peoples far away from the conflict itself. This was partly due to the fact that neither the Israelis nor the Arab states could make war without weapons and support from one or the other of the superpowers, who were thus inevitably drawn in; and partly due to oil.

Egypt, Syria and Iraq were all armed by the Soviets. Their military forces had been decimated by the Israelis in the Six-Day War of 1967 and they had turned to the Soviet Union to rebuild their forces. There were occasional disputes, especially between Egypt and the USSR, but whatever success those states had in 1973 was due to weapons supplied by the Soviet Union or its allies. The Israelis were equally dependent after 1967 on U.S. support, although they bought weapons from others as well. After the first few days of fighting, therefore, both sides needed to be resupplied. The Soviets responded quickly, but the U.S. waited a bit. It would seem that neither of the superpowers wished for a decisive victory, for they preferred a balance that would encourage negotiation and a broader settlement. Modest gains by Egypt and Syria would not seriously jeopardize Israel's security and might also assuage revanchist sentiments and allow the normal give and take of diplomacy to take hold in the region. As Kissinger later argued, the U.S. had been determined to defend Israel, but "it was not in our interest that the war end with Egypt's humiliation. We had wanted to prevent a victory of Soviet arms. We did not want to see Sadat overthrown or Egypt radicalized by total defeat."[55] Events on the ground conspired against U.S. and Soviet efforts to manage the conflict, however: setbacks for the Israelis led to insistent demands for U.S. logistical support; Israel's subsequent successes deprived the Arab states of what they seemed for a brief moment to have gained on the battlefield; and the Israelis were in no mood to compromise after being invaded on Yom Kippur. The rapid ebb and flow of battle also complicated its ending and brought the superpowers close to confrontation. The U.S. and the Soviets wanted a ceasefire, as did others, but there was no agreement on borders. Would it be the borders in place before or after the 1967 war, or along some new line of demarcation? The ceasefire agreed on October 21 was ambiguous and the Israelis sought to use the ambiguity to continue their advance. The Egyptians, and the Soviets, were alarmed and the Soviets proposed that U.S. and Soviet forces be deployed to police the ceasefire. The U.S. refused, fearing a Soviet military presence in yet another region of the world, but the Soviets insisted. In response, the U.S. put its forces, both conventional and nuclear, on alert (DefCon III, as it was called) on October 24. The crisis quickly passed and the ceasefire held as of October 28, but the incident highlighted both the fragility of détente and the explosive potential of conflict in the Middle East.

The full consequences of the war were in any event still unfolding. During the second week of the war, the Organization of the Petroleum Exporting Countries (OPEC) announced a near doubling of oil prices. The Arab oil producers then announced a decision to cut oil production by 5 percent and to keep cutting if Israel did not withdraw from Arab lands. On October 19 the U.S. administration proposed a $2.2 billion program of assistance to Israel, a decision that prompted the Arab members of OPEC to declare a boycott on sales to the U.S. (as well as the Netherlands, South Africa and Portugal). In December, long after the ceasefire that ended hostilities on the ground, OPEC announced another price increase. The immediate effect was to bring about a the price rise of nearly five times in less than a year. This jump in the cost of energy caused a sharp spike in inflation as it worked its way across the world and through all the industries that made use of oil. Inflation had been creeping upward in all the industrial counties during the late 1960s: in the United States it was just under 6 percent in 1970; in Europe it had averaged just 3.1 percent for the period 1961–9, then more than doubled for the years 1969–73, when it ran at 6.4 percent, and nearly doubled again to just under 12 percent for

1973–9. In the United States inflation ran at over 11 percent in 1974; in Britain it would hit 24 percent in 1975.[56] What had been a modest concern during the 1960s became a mounting crisis in the 1970s. It had an obviously depressing effect on the global economy, which was already beginning to slow down. The combination of growing unemployment and inflation was labeled "stagflation," a phenomenon that was in theory not supposed to occur and that, in consequence, economists and policy-makers had difficulty explaining.

Coping with the emerging economic crisis would become the dominant issue of the 1970s. What complicated matters was that economic problems were all wrapped up in politics. The decisions to raise oil prices and to impose the boycott represented a political choice, and it would elicit a series of essentially political responses. Wages and prices and unemployment were economic phenomena, but they instantly became political issues requiring government action for their resolution and discrediting successive administrations and strategies in more than one country. In fact, the short-term political responses both to the energy crisis and to the problems of the domestic economy would prove largely ineffective, for the difficulties were not so easily diagnosed or treated; and it would take several years of repeated failure before governments, in the U.S. and the U.K. at least, developed an alternative approach. Before that could happen, leaders would be driven to distraction, and to defeat, by the intractability of the problems they faced.

The oil crisis caused distress everywhere, but it created a near panic among America's allies. Europe was much more dependent on imported oil than the U.S., and Japan imported almost all its oil. The result was an embarrassingly rapid shift toward more public support for the Arab cause. The new stance took concrete form in the refusal of European countries to allow U.S. bases to be used to resupply Israel. Even Britain, whose military forces were so deeply interconnected with those of the U.S., hesitated over whether to allow U.S. ships to refuel its ships in Singapore and Hong Kong. The British acquiesced, but did so only "in confidence and stressing that it is in our two governments' common interest that we should not be seen to be circumventing the Arab embargo."[57] Other allies were even less cooperative, and demonstrably so. This would be followed by efforts to strike individual deals with particular exporting nations. France, for example, was actively involved in arranging bilateral deals that involved arms for oil; and Edward Heath sent an emissary to Saudi Arabia to work out an agreement by which the Saudis would guarantee British oil supplies for twenty years "in return for a major program of industrial cooperation."[58]

Tensions between the U.S. and Europe flared anew. Europeans largely blamed the U.S. for Israel's behavior, which they saw as the root cause of the war. As Heath explained in another not quite "off-the-record" encounter on November 28, "There has never been a joint understanding between the U.S. and Europe on the Mideast . . . During the past six years – since the 1967 war – the U.S. had ample opportunity to bring pressure on Israel to negotiate and has done nothing." America's allies were even more outraged at the U.S. "alert" of October 24–25, over which they had not been consulted. A week before, on October 17, Jobert spoke to the National Assembly and blamed the U.S. and USSR equally for the war: "We see Mr. Brezhnev, the apostle of détente, and Dr. Kissinger, now a Nobel Peace Prize winner, shaking hands while sending thousands of tons of arms by air." To the French, to Heath and to other Europeans, the war and the oil crisis were taken as further proof that Europe required a distinct and independent position in the world.[59] Although the U.S. had by the autumn of 1973 largely given up on the crafting of a new Atlantic Charter, Europeans were still at work on a draft and, as Lord Cromer observed on November 3, "We Europeans have been taking credit for ourselves in the ability of the Nine . . . to agree" on a declaration, while the U.S. had been taking offense.[60] As the now largely once-sided process continued, the Europeans continued to define their global role as distinct from that of the U.S.: though "at the present moment there is no alternative to the security provided by the nuclear weapons of the United States and by the presence of their forces in Europe," one version of the "identity paper" grudgingly conceded, there was a "determination" to "take up common positions in the field of foreign policy" and to do so "acting as a distinct identity."[61] When speaking to the Americans, the British blamed the French for the hostile tone, but the U.S. understood that Britain was at the time eager to work closely with France and reluctant to oppose it. Defense Secretary James Schlesinger went so far as to label British policies "decayed Gaullism."[62]

The U.S. was also appalled at what seemed to be the "appeasement of the Arab oil producing countries in a state of panic by the consumers."[63] Arab states had initiated the recent war with Israel and it was fellow Arabs who were largely responsible for the oil crisis. Equally important, the U.S. was convinced that efforts to solve the crisis country by country would be futile. Kissinger was particularly incensed that, as he flew from place to place in the Middle East, and to and from Moscow, the Europeans met in Brussels on November 6 and issued their own declaration on how the conflict should be settled. They insisted on an Israeli withdrawal to the 1967 borders and on recognition of the "legitimate rights of Palestinians."[64] Even more objectionable was the proposal for a Euro-Arab Dialogue adopted at the European Summit in Copenhagen in mid-December.[65] As Kissinger explained to Douglas-Home, "any getting together of all the Arab states – moderates and radicals – would have most unfortunate consequences. It is bound to lead the radicals to make extreme statements which will be very difficult for the moderates to resist. This will immediately lead to pressures on the European leaders to endorse every point on the Arab radicals' program."[66] It was also a mistake, the Americans argued, to begin bargaining with the oil producers without first having brought together consuming nations to coordinate their policies.

The U.S. response was largely crafted by Kissinger, whose authority was enhanced by Nixon's deepening troubles over Watergate. He sought to turn the crisis into an opportunity for the exercise of U.S. leadership and took it upon himself both to conceive and execute the necessary moves. The top priority was to prevent the Soviets from extracting any advantage. This was achieved in part by the "alert," which helped to block plans for direct involvement by the USSR in policing the ceasefire, and in part by the successful Israeli counteroffensive. These events left the Arab states aware that if they wanted any kind of settlement with Israel, they needed to rely on the U.S. Progress toward a settlement, the U.S. decided, would come in small steps, with country-by-country agreements on plans for disengagement; and Kissinger would take an active part in each of these bilateral deals in what became known as "shuttle diplomacy." Eventually, a formal peace conference would be convened in Geneva with the U.S. and USSR presiding. This was largely a formality, for the real bargaining would be done elsewhere, and beforehand, and it would not involve the Soviets. The confrontation between Arabs and Jews would in this way be dissipated, with U.S. leadership confirmed.[67]

The U.S. also sought a dominant role in resolving the oil crisis, though the rhetoric was all about multilateral cooperation. The fact that the U.S. was only minimally dependent on Middle East oil gave it a degree of leverage and flexibility that its allies could not afford. America was not only better able to cope with high prices and shortages, although it would not acquit itself well on this score, but it was also capable of offering meaningful support to allies in a crisis. Strategy was in this case not worked out solely by Kissinger. He was not an economist, and there were other players involved – among them George Shultz, William Simon, Arthur Burns at the Federal Reserve, and Peter Peterson – but since the problems were international in origin and scope, he would play a major role in their execution. The basic U.S. approach was simultaneously political and economic and it made sense, for a degree of consumer solidarity would enhance the developed nations' bargaining position with the oil producers, and U.S.-led efforts to negotiate with individual countries could and did weaken the power of the oil cartel. In December 1973 the U.S. proposed the creation of an Energy Action Group made up of experts from the major industrial countries; on January 10, it proposed the convening of a major energy conference in Washington the following month. Both proposals were in competition with the proposed Euro-Arab Dialogue, favored especially by the French, and by efforts on the part of individual countries to strike bilateral deals with producers. The success or failure of the Washington Energy Conference would determine which approach prevailed.

The negotiations, and the posturing, preceding the meeting were a replay of earlier arguments over the Year of Europe and the appropriate response to the Yom Kippur War. Would Europe adopt a separate role, a distinct identity and strategy in dealing with the oil producers? The French insisted that they should and offered a scheme in which the industrial countries would cooperate on high-tech projects and conservation measures but bargain separately with oil producers. The aim was to prevent the formation of a consumers' front that might provoke a confrontation with the oil cartel. Other European countries were not so sure, for it seemed that the confrontation had already occurred and that on matters of energy the prospects were better working with the U.S. than alongside or in opposition to it. If the Europeans opted for bilateral deals, moreover, the U.S. would do likewise and in all likelihood secure much better terms. The balance of advantage lay with the U.S. and the balance of the arguments therefore led to a choice for "multilateral" efforts to achieve consumer solidarity. The rhetoric of European identity aside, when the conference met in Washington on February 11–13 the French found themselves isolated and the meeting agreed to create what would become the International Energy Agency. The precise details of the compromise were worked out largely by Douglas-Home, whose actions signaled that the U.K. had chosen to cast its fate with the U.S. and that its role in Europe would not be what Edward Heath had envisioned.

The Washington Energy Conference was an important turning point in the relations between the U.S. and Europe, in Anglo-American relations, and in the linked issues of the Arab-Israeli conflict and the energy crisis. Shortly after it broke up, the U.S. managed to convince the Arab states to lift the oil embargo; and Kissinger's "shuttle diplomacy" began to make headway in getting Israel and its adversaries to disengage. Even before that, Heath and the Conservative Party would be defeated in a general election and replaced by a Labour government deeply split over the issue of Europe and so ready to realign itself more closely with the United States. On April 2, President Pompidou died and soon after Jobert was replaced as Foreign Minister. Pompidou's successor, Valéry Giscard d'Estaing, was less skeptical of U.S. intentions and moved French foreign policy closer to Washington's. At virtually the same moment Willy Brandt's government was rocked by a spying scandal and Brandt himself resigned on May 7, 1974. The new configuration of leaders at the top allowed for the adoption in June 1974 of the Ottawa Declaration that, in reaffirming NATO's mission and the transatlantic commitment of all parties, produced something like the new Atlantic Charter that had been the objective of the Year of Europe.

The outcome was a real, if modest, achievement for U.S. policy and for Kissinger personally, although its benefits were short-lived. What was more lasting was the failure of the effort to establish a clear and independent European identity and a distinct "personality" on matters of foreign policy and security. Europe was tested by the crises in the Middle East and in energy, and it proved incapable of affecting either without assistance from the U.S. All the European powers realized this and, for good or ill, all came around to a greater willingness to work in tandem with the U.S. Nowhere was the shift more dramatic than in Britain. As late as mid-October 1973, even as fighting continued in the Middle East, opinion among British officials was that the policy of working through and with the Nine, and in opposition to or at least separate from the U.S., was working. Douglas-Home, for example, traditionally a supporter of the alliance, wrote to British representatives abroad that the "new diplomacy," centered on Europe, offered Britain new options and flexibility. Although U.S. leaders "were not altogether happy" with its procedures, Britain would persist and try to "make sure that the advantages are substantial and the difficulties minimal." The U.S., he felt, would come around and understand not only that European unity was a good thing in general but also that "the U.K. has had a beneficial influence on the positions of the community (e.g. multilateral trade negotiation and preferential trading blocs) and in the political cooperation work since we joined the Community."[68] This confidence evaporated as the Arab-Israeli War dragged on and as the effects of the oil price increase and boycott spread.

The U.K. began seriously to reconsider its position in November 1973, when Kissinger and Nixon publicly criticized their allies for lack of support. Cromer reported to London in late November, for example, that Kissinger believed that "the special relationship was collapsing." "Our entry into the European Community should have raised Europe to the level of Britain," Kissinger was reported to have said, but "instead it had reduced Britain to the level of Europe." Britain had also been an enabler of the French: "Objectively," Kissinger insisted, "the U.K. made it possible for France to pursue its policies."[69] Douglas-Home and, it seems, even Heath clearly got the message, which was reinforced by the realization that only in alliance with the U.S. was it possible to make progress on energy or on a solution for the Middle East. British leaders also came to feel that, with North Sea oil gradually coming on line, a collective European oil strategy might not be so attractive.[70] Reassuring words were spoken on both sides on the occasion of Kissinger's December 12 speech to the Pilgrims Society in London.[71] In addition, the U.K. government seems to have been genuinely embarrassed by the EC summit meeting of December 14–15, where the leaders of key Arab countries somehow showed up and were welcomed and the Euro-Arab Dialogue agreed.[72] It provided confirmation that a turn was necessary.

The reconciliation continued in the new year. On January 10 Cromer warned his superiors about the likely negative effects of a possible "Euro-Arab conference" and argued the importance of cooperation with the U.S.; and he followed that up with a long memo to the Foreign Secretary about "The Middle East War and U.S./U.K. Relations" which was more sympathetic to U.S. complaints, and even to Kissinger himself, than many earlier communications. British officials in London and in Washington debated to what extent it was possible to work with the U.S., and Kissinger in particular, but there was no real debate about the fact that the European option was much less attractive than it had appeared just a short while before.[73] The decision to support the U.S. position at the Washington Energy Conference was therefore not taken lightly, or with any illusions, but it did put the U.S. and the U.K. back on more or less the same side on what was at that moment the most pressing global issue.

The Curious Path to Helsinki

The Watergate saga climaxed with the resignation of Richard Nixon on August 8, 1974. Over a six-month period the top leaders of Britain, France, Germany and now the U.S. had been replaced. Would diplomacy shift as well? Would new leaders depart from previous policies, chart new courses, undertake more fundamental reassessments of the maladies simultaneously affecting international relations and the world economy? Gerard Ford's decision to keep Kissinger foretold a basic continuity, though a continuation of policies that did not work would, and eventually did, lead to their abandonment. But first, more muddling through, more failed initiatives and unexpected and often unwanted outcomes.

Those who came to power in 1974 confronted the same set of issues that had bedeviled their predecessors, with less drama but no less seriousness. The oil embargo had been called off in March, and "shuttle diplomacy" had lessened tensions on both the Egyptian and Syrian fronts by May 1974. The sense of immediate crisis diminished, but further progress on all fronts would be elusive. The energy crisis, for example, would continue to unfold: minor political or diplomatic victories combined with short-term price stability to mask a steady worsening of the underlying economic reality. The strategy of uniting the consumers and dividing OPEC began to work and paid dividends for a while, but the confrontation soon broadened. Inspired by the success of OPEC, other less developed countries began to argue for a "new international economic order" based on "commodity power" and grounded specifically on an agreement to boost the prices of a wide range of raw materials produced by the developing countries. The program grew out of efforts centered around the UN Conference on Trade and Development (UNCTAD), pushed forcefully by the Non-Aligned Conference at Algiers in 1973, and formally approved by the UN in 1974.

The effort to achieve a new bargain between North and South would be blunted, at least temporarily, as OPEC began to fragment and the world economy adjusted, albeit with difficulty, to the oil price shock.[74] Policy also contributed, for after initial disunity the leading industrial nations learned to cooperate. As the UN met in New York in late September 1974, ministers from Britain, France, Germany, Japan and the U.S. met in Washington. Just prior to that, the U.S. initiated a plan to counter oil with food, agreeing to work toward ameliorating the spike in food prices that inevitably followed the jump in oil prices by lifting restrictions on the production and export of food and setting up a mechanism to help pay for it. At roughly the same moment Ford proclaimed that "Sovereign nations cannot allow their policies to be dictated or their fate decided by artificial rigging and distortion of world commodity markets."[75] The International Energy Agency was also established in November 1974. Meanwhile, the U.S. pursued oil deals with Saudi Arabia, with Iran and, later, with the Soviet Union. The industrial countries, especially the U.S. and U.K., also undertook to create facilities to handle, and recirculate, the enormous funds now in the hands of OPEC nations in a way that would blunt their independence and discourage solidarity between the oil-rich nations and the rest of the developing world. They would also be encouraged to spend, for it was only the industrial nations that could provide the goods and services they wanted; and this, too, would reinforce their links to the West. A British official put it nicely when he explained the value of exports to OPEC countries: "The West will need these outlets. Moreover, the faster the oil producers can spend, the smaller their accumulation of financial surpluses; and, further into the future, the more they can be hooked on a high propensity to consume, the more difficult they will find it to cut oil output."[76]

The diplomacy of the oil crisis revealed that OPEC had for the moment lost the advantage it recently had. The new French President was much more willing to work with the U.S., Britain and Germany and helped prepare the way for more formal and institutionalized collaboration, though he did not necessarily follow a straight path. In October 1974 Giscard proposed a joint meeting of producing and consuming nations. The U.S. resisted such a meeting until the achievement of a greater measure of "consumer solidarity" and convinced other allies on this point. The French acquiesced and agreed on a joint strategy with the U.S. in December. The consumers would create a system of oil reserves and undertake a variety of conservation measures; after that, they would meet the producers. It was also agreed to create a group of top experts representing the industrial countries, the so-called G5, who would work together on a shared strategy.[77] The meeting with producers was put off, and when officials met in Paris in April 1975 to plan it, there was no agreement on an agenda: OPEC and the developing countries insisted on their proposal for increasing the prices of a wide range of commodities; the industrial countries resisted. The conference was finally held in December, but by that time the industrial countries presented a united front that resulted in frustration for the advocates of a new international order.

The front had come together officially a month before, with the first economic summit at Rambouillet in mid-November. That gathering was held largely on the initiative of Giscard, who outlined his intentions in June: The capitalist countries seemed absolutely unable to manage their economic and monetary situations, yet "we never have a serious conversation among the great capitalist leaders to say what do we do now . . ."[78] His partners were by now eager to sign up to the conversation, for they understood, as Harold Wilson put it, that "We have won ourselves a breathing space. The initiative on these issues has, at least partially, been transferred to the sort of people sitting around this table." It was a moment when it made sense to fall in with the effort, as Kissinger explained it,

> to break what the Chancellor [Schmidt] called the unholy alliance between the LDCs [less developed countries] and OPEC. This can happen, and we can achieve our results, if they know that their disruptive actions could stop discussions on commodities or that they will pay a price in terms of cooperation, or military exports. In this way we can combat our dependence with a coherent strategy.[79]

For their part, European leaders hoped to get U.S. support on trade and on reflationary measures to combat the worsening recession. The strictly economic results would disappoint, but a measure of unity had been recreated among the major industrial powers – for good or ill.

Capitalist solidarity, or transatlantic cooperation, was evident on matters of security as well. While Europe and the U.S. had found themselves at odds over a new Atlantic Charter, they worked together much more effectively at the

Conference on Security and Cooperation in Europe (CSCE) which culminated in the signing of the Helsinki Final Act on August 1, 1975. The result was ironic: in struggling to reach agreement with the U.S. during the "Year of Europe," Europeans irritated the Americans and they ultimately fell out with one another over energy; in negotiating with the Soviets, by contrast, the Europeans would demonstrate their attachment to the Western alliance and to one another. The Helsinki Accord was to be the climax, and by some accounts truly the last act, of détente. It grew from a Soviet proposal of April 1969 for a meeting, and presumably an agreement, that the USSR believed would ratify its hegemonic role in Eastern Europe by recognizing the "inviolability" of borders and declaring that each nation had the right to run its own affairs and craft its own social system without international interference. The Soviets had long sought to declare the postwar settlement, through which they dominated the nations on their periphery, permanently settled and legitimate. Their determination was increased after the invasion of Czechoslovakia in August 1968 and the proclamation in November of the so-called Brezhnev Doctrine. "When forces that are hostile to socialism try to turn the development of some socialist country towards capitalism," the Soviet leader insisted, "it becomes not only a problem of the country concerned, but a common problem and concern of all socialist countries." A problem that, moreover, might well require foreign intervention.

Neither the U.S. nor the U.K. governments wished to ratify the Brezhnev Doctrine, and they were not terribly eager for the conference. Nor were the French. There was, however, strong support from the Germans, who saw it as part and parcel of *Ostpolitik*, from at least some other European countries, and from Western publics eager to opt out of the Cold War and to reduce defense expenditure.[80] In the United States, revulsion against the war in Vietnam had produced a broader reluctance to intervene abroad and to sustain a defense establishment on the scale that previous policies had required. The Senate Majority Leader, Mike Mansfield, shared these sentiments and threatened repeatedly to introduce legislation to cut back U.S. troop levels in Europe. Though his amendment to that effect was defeated in May 1971, the Nixon administration was apoplectic and became constantly worried about its ability to maintain domestic support for its global stance.[81] It therefore felt compelled to participate in the CSCE and in a set of parallel negotiations designed to achieve "Mutual and Balanced Force Reductions" in Europe. It did so with little enthusiasm, however: Kissinger reminded his colleagues at the NATO meeting in Ottawa in June 1974 that "The United States never wanted the European Security Conference." "They had," nevertheless, "gone along ... at the prompting of the Europeans and in order not to be isolated."[82]

The negotiations proved trying and seemed endless, to this extent justifying initial skepticism. The issues were divided into three categories: Basket I was all about security, borders and frontiers; Basket II focused on commerce and technical exchanges; and Basket III involved "human contacts" and what would occasionally be called "human rights." The Soviets were most interested in Basket I, which they believed would recognize and guarantee their rights and perquisites as a superpower. All sides were keen on Basket II, for the Soviets and the East Europeans wanted and needed trade and access to Western goods and technologies, while the U.S., Europe and Japan were eager to expand markets for both economic and political reasons. The Germans wanted trade to further *Ostpolitik*, while the U.S. regarded trade as a key component of détente. It was the Western nations, especially the Europeans, who were most interested in Basket III. The U.S. supported the effort to increase access and openness in the East, but had little faith it would succeed. Kissinger, for example, was unimpressed: "The Soviet system," he argued, "had survived for 50 years and would not be changed if Western newspapers were put on sale in a few kiosks in Moscow."[83] The USSR was largely opposed.

The debate was not uninteresting. The Soviets, for example, insisted that "the inviolability" of frontiers was more or less absolute, while the West (and the Germans in particular) held out for the possibility of the peaceful adjustment of borders; likewise, to the Soviets the same principle precluded "hostile propaganda" and required "respect for the cultural foundations of states," which, of course, meant no challenge to the socialist character of the system. For its part, the West insisted on a freer press and the rights of journalists, and on the right of citizens to travel and even to emigrate. There was surprisingly little rhetoric about human rights as a broad set of principles. The Helsinki Accords would in the end play a huge role in advancing the politics of human rights, but it would be hard to predict that based on the discussions that ultimately produced the agreement.[84]

In fact, it was not at all obvious to participants in the negotiations that anything at all would result. They succeeded in the end because all sides came to believe they had something to gain. The United States, for example, wanted an agreement to shore up and further détente and, in the aftermath of Watergate and the fall of Saigon, desperately desired an achievement of some sort. The Europeans saw Helsinki as an opportunity to put their stamp on détente and ensure that it was not simply a matter for the superpowers. The Soviets were most eager for an accord and proved willing, as negotiations dragged on, to pay a real price for it by accepting Basket III. Had they understood how much the modest commitments to human rights in Basket III would undermine their authority in Eastern Europe, they might well not have agreed, but at the time nobody – not the Europeans, not the United States, and not the leaders of the Soviet Union – grasped the potential of human rights politics.

The successful conclusion of the Security Conference was also a product of a desire for unity among the Western allies. The antipathy that attended the Year of Europe and which was magnified by the Arab-Israeli War and ensuing oil crisis was not truly welcome on either side of the Atlantic, and it was not at all helpful in developing a sustained policy for dealing with the Middle East, the oil crisis or the economic problems that were becoming ever more severe and less tractable. The new leaders who took office in 1974 were thus eager to repair relations. In the CSCE negotiations, therefore, the U.S. and its allies worked more closely and effectively. A part of the reason was that the U.S. played a less prominent role, which in turn gave the French less reason to assume an oppositional stance. The Germans, in the aftermath of Brandt's difficulties and having already secured the agreements they cared about, now decided to be more aggressive in their dealings with the East. These shifts made it easier in turn for the U.K. to play a greater role in coordinating the European and the NATO positions. As Britain's chief negotiator put it with a measure of self-satisfaction, "In the politics of the Conference, we are as it were at the centre of the Western group, and enjoy the weight that goes with it."[85]

Britain's role as mediator but also as the key U.S. ally during 1974–5, on matters of oil and in the CSCE, represented a decisive shift from the role it had played during Edward Heath's time in office. The effect was to reassert the Anglo-American connection that had been so strained in Britain's first year in the EC. In his memoirs Kissinger attributed the new warmth in the relationship to personalities – to Gerald Ford and Harold Wilson and especially James Callaghan. "Trust does not come to me spontaneously," Kissinger wrote in a classic understatement, "But Callaghan managed to gain my confidence by the solidity of his judgment, his calm in crisis, and his practicality. He never specifically invoked the special relationship; rather he brought it to life by his conduct. I came to rely heavily on Callaghan's judgment . . ."[86] There were also hard-headed calculations behind the British choice to realign itself. The Labour Party had won the election of February 1974 with a promise to renegotiate its relationship with the Europe. The party was in fact deeply split over Europe, with the left of the party very much opposed and the center and the right largely, though not uniformly, in favor. Wilson had over the years straddled the left and the center, but oversaw the previous Labour government's decision to make a second (and also unsuccessful) application to join the EEC. Callaghan was skeptical, but ambivalent. Neither really wanted to take Britain out of Europe, but both were under pressure from the left. The result was that for over a year the two leaders sought ways to soften the terms of British membership before submitting them to a referendum in June 1975.[87] Voters chose to stay in Europe by a margin of 2 to 1. Before the referendum, however, the British government could not allow itself to be seen to be too pro-European, as Heath increasingly had been; and the alternative was a more traditional reliance on the U.S.

The choice for the U.S. was not hard, of course, for the events of 1973–4 had effectively demonstrated the weakness of Europe and the still formidable clout of the United States.[88] But the choice was not made enthusiastically or naively. Official papers prepared during the election that ousted Heath, for example, suggest a deep ambivalence. What prompted the papers was the sense that the ongoing election raised unprecedented questions and created the possibility of a major departure. Heath had decided to confront the miners and turned the election into a referendum on whether the government or the unions should rule. The outcome, key officials felt, could be dire. Equally important, the Labour Party in opposition had adopted a quite radical program. Although the top leaders, such as Wilson and Callaghan, seemed unlikely to implement it, it was not impossible that policy would veer sharply to the left. In response, the Permanent Secretaries got together to consider what an alternative foreign policy might look like.[89] It was broadly agreed that present difficulties demonstrated "the degree to which Britain's internal and foreign policies had become over-extended in relation to the resources available for their support." For the next few years, in consequence, "aspirations of an altruistic or intangible kind . . . will be luxuries" and unaffordable; the main task of the 1970s instead "will be to insure national survival." In this context it made little sense to turn to Europe; on the contrary, "the U.S. would henceforward be a stronger, and more rewarding, source of potential support than the EEC."[90] The immediate question was financial and dealing with it required that the U.K. stay on good terms with the U.S., Europe and the Arab oil producers, but if it came to a choice, the U.S. option would prevail. The Arabs might well think that Britain was "too close to the United States . . . Yet if we are not on close terms with the United Sates, the financial difficulties . . . are likely to be enhanced." Great Britain would eventually solve its energy problem with its own resources from the North Sea, officials believed or at least pretended to believe, but could anticipate a difficult transition during which "the U.S. will be important to us." So long as the oil crisis persisted in its current form, it was essential to work closely with America, and Britain, it was agreed, "cannot afford to allow the French to block or water down cooperation with the Americans."[91] Surveying the options on offer in early 1974, "tilting towards America" was clearly the best alternative.

The reaffirmation of the U.S./U.K. alliance was a choice consciously made by all the key players. On the British side, it was a decision taken by Tories who realized the unhappy consequences of Heath's preferential option for Europe; by Labour leaders who, wary of Europe and not entirely enamored of the U.S., nevertheless chose continuity over any more fundamental reorientation; and by officials tasked with minding the nation's interests at home and abroad. On the American side, it was an option that appealed because the alternative was isolation, and even undependable and weak allies were better than none. It was clearly not a matter of sentiment but necessity, the result of the careful calculation of advantage, a move therefore lacking conviction and an accompanying strategic agenda.[92] In a world that seemed very much out of control, for both the U.S. and the U.K. and their beleaguered political leaders, the logic was to stick with what worked or what seemed to have worked over the past quarter-century. It was this preference for the traditional, for patching up the system and making minor modifications, that characterized much of foreign policy during the period from the conclusion of the Paris Peace Accords to the signing of the Helsinki Accords and including the economic summit meeting at Rambouillet. The summit was an institutional innovation; so, too, was the creation of the International Energy Agency and so was Helsinki, for it left in place an agreement, a set of principles, a permanent organization, and the machinery for follow-up. What is striking, however, is that these new institutions were created to carry out existing policies conceived in an earlier era and modified only marginally, and reluctantly, to cope with the emerging crises of the 1970s. It was the response to be expected from a thinker like Kissinger and from politicians nurtured in the stable environment of the postwar economic boom, what the French labeled *les trente glorieuses*. It should come as no surprise that it proved insufficient and that, without a more fundamental reassessment and a more decisive shift in outlook and policy, the problems of the 1970s would only get worse.

CHAPTER 3

Détente, Human Rights and Economic Crisis

Détente reached a formal climax with the signing of the Helsinki Accords in the summer of 1975. It then unraveled; a "second Cold War" and a renewed arms race would follow, though not immediately.[1] The allies who had been so disunited in responding to the oil crisis of 1973–4 were by 1975 cooperating again, their relationships at least partly repaired as they came to realize they had more interests in common with each other than they did with oil producers, the "global South," or the Soviet Union. The Soviets, newly secure in their borders and with their hegemony in eastern and central Europe granted de facto legitimacy by Helsinki, at least for a time, now had less reason to compromise with the West. They chose instead to use their increased clout to extend their influence further; and they ignored the implications of the Helsinki Accords for the expression of human rights, seeming, for a time, to suffer no ill consequences. The United States, chastened in Vietnam, sought desperately to rebuild its reputation and restore its influence, though it could not decide how to do it. Kissinger preferred the conventional route; Jimmy Carter and his advisors opted for a departure that proved impossible to sustain. The course of global politics continued to baffle those whose job it was to predict and direct it and nothing quite seemed to work. Meanwhile, the world economy slowed while prices kept rising.

Trouble at Home

Nothing that happened in the sphere of international relations had quite the effect of the worsening economic crisis, at least in Britain and the United States. Of course, economics and foreign affairs were closely linked, for the most visible economic problem – the price of oil and its escalating consequences – came from abroad. So, too, did the increased competition faced by American and British industries as Germany and Japan, and eventually the rest of Europe, came to challenge British and American firms in domestic and export markets. For Britain, moreover, the most obvious sign of the nation's industrial difficulties came in the form of recurring balance of payments crises and budget deficits that threatened, but also stemmed from, its role in the international economy. It was surely appropriate that at the time and in retrospect the critical moment in the economic history of the decade was understood to be the decision in 1976 to request a loan from the IMF and the need, as a precondition, to agree to spending cuts that put an end to the government's strategy for getting through the economic crisis.

Believing that the source of economic problems was external was not completely wrong, but it had the unfortunate consequence of leading policy-makers astray. It delayed a full and proper reckoning with the failures, or deficiencies, of the domestic economy and of economic policy in Britain and America, and in the advanced economies more broadly. In retrospect, it seems that the Fordist model of growth, so effective for a quarter-century, was falling victim to diminishing returns. The technologies that drove the postwar boom had been widely adopted across the developed countries and the industries in which they had the greatest impact experienced increased competition and declining profits. Renewed growth would require new markets, new technologies and new products, but the precise shape of the post-Fordist economy was as yet unclear. In the best of circumstances, the transition would be rough. The difficult circumstances of the 1970s ensured that it would be very rough and would entail a radical break in policy that would cause much pain and strife.[2]

The immediate effect of the delayed reckoning was to prolong existing but increasingly ineffective patterns of policy-making, with governments tinkering or adapting or at times just waiting for things to improve. It meant, more precisely, a continuation of Keynesian policies in a setting far different from that in which they had first been worked out. In the United States, Keynesianism had evolved into a policy centered on growth, on the understanding that growth could be effectively engineered and that it would help solve all variety of social problems, resolve or adjourn conflicts over who got what, and provide more or less full employment. In Britain, Keynes came to mean primarily full employment and stability, though Keynesianism had gradually come to involve a commitment to growth and greater affluence as well. Other advanced countries developed their own varieties of policy, some more and some less Keynesian, but they shared a fundamental belief that government could effectively control the ups and downs of economic life and chart a path toward sustained growth.[3]

These beliefs were not to survive the decade, with its confounding combination of unwelcome phenomena. Particularly difficult to understand was the coexistence of increasing inflation and rising unemployment: stagnation increased unemployment, which was was in theory supposed to reduce prices; and rising prices were a sign of increasing demand that should produce more jobs. The economy had somehow ceased to behave this way, and instead offered up the phenomenon of "stagflation," a combination of both evils. How did governments respond to this confusing picture?

Initially, they chose to give priority to continued growth while seeking to control inflation through a series of ad hoc adjustments. The pattern began with Nixon and Edward Heath. The Heath administration began by promising to abandon established policies and move away from corporatism and government intervention and toward free or freer markets. It hoped, too, that joining the Common Market would thrust Britain into a bracing new environment that would encourage growth and innovation. Soon, however, it was compelled to execute a famous U-turn which left it propping up failing industries, giving in to the demands of the more aggressive trade unions – the miners in particular – and shifting back toward wage and price controls. Incomes policy would be the solution, the device that would get Britain through a difficult period and allow growth to resume. Nixon also imposed wage and price controls in 1971, but this was coupled with more aggressive moves internationally. The U.S. abandoned the Bretton Woods system and in the process devalued its currency. Throughout the 1970s the industrialized nations would jostle with each other over currencies and domestic economic policies in a desperate effort to maintain an open trading system while seeking maximum advantage within it. With oil-induced inflation spreading throughout the system and vast sums circulating through the emerging new world of international finance, stability was hard to achieve, but a major net effect was to depreciate the dollar and allow U.S. exporters a decisive short-term edge.

American policy also focused on the Middle East. The crises produced by the Arab-Israeli War of 1973 and the oil embargo and accompanying price increases had the curious effect of strengthening U.S. leverage in the region. The Soviets were effectively blocked from acting as a major player in the conflict and the possibility of a separate European initiative quickly receded. All sides realized that the U.S. would be key to any settlement, for only the U.S. was thought capable of exerting pressure on Israel. The United States also had two major allies in the region, Iran and Saudi Arabia, and for a time they could be counted on to keep oil price increases within reason and to keep OPEC from using its near-monopoly over supply. Oil price increases did ease in the late 1970s, and there was at least a brief economic recovery during 1977–8. It was short-lived, however, and even before the second oil shock produced by the Iranian Revolution inflation was taking off again.

The failure to cope with the economic slowdown and with inflation would ultimately undermine the Keynesian assumptions on which policy had been based since World War II, but it did not happen quickly and easily. Unhappily, but perhaps appropriately, it fell to James Callaghan and Jimmy Carter to preside over the discrediting of Keynes in their respective countries. It was a tortuous process. Carter's personal instincts were cautious, and he was not a profligate governor in Georgia, but he ran for President on a campaign that promised expansion. Inflation ran at over 9 percent for 1975 and unemployment hit 9 percent in May of that year. The economy revived in the latter half of 1975, but not enough, and it dipped again during the election year. Carter's advisors, in a classically Keynesian formulation, argued that the economy was running at 10 percent below its potential; and Carter would implement policies designed to realize that potential. Indeed, the U.S. took to arguing that the expansion of the American economy would act as a "locomotive" to restart growth across the developed world, if only other economies would do likewise.[4] The new administration thus began with an expansionary budget. Over the next several years, however, it would vacillate between expansionary budgets and recurring second thoughts that brought fiscal tightening and monetary restraint. The effect was a period of growth – GDP increased by close to 10 percent over the Carter era and unemployment was no worse in 1979 than in 1971 – but one in which the rewards were undermined by repeated bouts of inflation. In the period 1967–73, for example, real hourly wages had risen nearly 3 percent per year; during 1973–9 they stagnated. Over the course of the Carter presidency (1977–81) retail prices increased by fully half.[5]

Policy clearly favored employment over price stability, but the political effect was to convince policy-makers and the public that this was a mistake. Carter himself wavered and in August 1979 finally came down in favor of controlling inflation as his administration's top priority: he replaced Michael Blumenthal as Treasury Secretary and at the same time appointed Paul Volcker to be head of the Federal Reserve.[6] Volcker proceeded to raise interest rates dramatically, and kept them high into the 1980s, in order to wring inflation out of the economy. It was a move that signaled a decisive shift in priorities – inflation was now the chief enemy and full employment no longer feasible as a goal of government economic policy – and the abandonment of the Keynesian assumptions that had guided policy-makers since the 1940s. Keynesian ideas had already begun to lose their sway among economists, large numbers of whom became convinced that, as Milton Friedman famously argued in 1967, there was a "natural rate of unemployment" that could not be lowered by

inflationary policies and that "there is no permanent trade-off" between inflation and unemployment. The argument against Keynes advanced still further
in the 1970s, when yet another group of economists claimed that government
intervention to create growth was ineffective, for the "rational expectations" of
economic actors cancelled out the effects of public policy.[7] Discussions of this
sort had little resonance among the broader American public, but failure did,
and the failure to combat inflation even as unemployment reached new levels
produced a conviction that existing policies needed to be abandoned and a
new framework developed and adopted.

The turn away from the Keynesian paradigm was even more drastic in
Britain.[8] Again, repeated failure played the key role. The purely academic criticism of Keynes was more muted in Britain, and the critics more marginal and
clearly partisan. But economic difficulties were worse and the inability of
government to deal with them more prolonged and pronounced. Since at least
the 1960s governments had been fixated on increasing the rate of growth, but
they had not succeeded. They kept bumping into balance of payments
constraints that required, or seemed to require, fiscal and monetary policies
that cut off growth before it could become sustaining. The resulting "stop-go"
pattern became endemic. Labour had sought to escape through planning
during the 1960s, but it did not break the cycle. In response, both parties turned
to incomes policies that brought government into regular consultation, and
into repeated conflict, with the trade unions. The Heath government tried to
break with this "corporatist" style of governance and economic policy-making
and put in its place greater recourse to market mechanisms alongside legislation to control trade unions and make it harder to strike. It, too, failed to bring
this off and the government fell when in February 1974 voters refused to give
their backing during an extended contest with the miners.

Labour returned to office with a very confused set of plans. The party had
recently committed itself to a new and quite radical program of extensive
state intervention and direction of the economy, with promises to expand
public ownership. At the same time Labour's key leaders had negotiated a
"social contract" with the unions that called for increases in social spending,
the "social wage," in exchange for an informal system of wage controls
policed by the unions themselves.[9] The inevitable tension between these
visions undermined the government and guaranteed recurring criticism from
the left of the party. For their part the unions kept to the bargain they had made
for as long as the rank-and-file would put up with it. It fell apart in late 1978
when the Callaghan government sought to impose yet another year of modest
wage increases and union membership resisted. The big test would come
at Ford Motor Company, where the unions demanded a major increase and

the government went back and forth between trying to firm up management by offering to protect its market share and threatening sanctions if the company agreed to an excessive settlement.[10] It was all very unseemly, and when the government ultimately proposed sanctions on Ford in December, they were voted down in Parliament. Ford workers had thus secured, against the insistence of government, a 16 percent rise. Other workers, especially in the public sector, were keen to follow their example: the result was the "winter of discontent."

Labour's policies during 1974–9 were basically Keynesian and the government sought desperately to make them work in trying circumstances. Fiscal policy remained moderately expansionist for most of the period, but the problem of inflation and government borrowing continually undermined that stance. Equally important, the unions had grown much stronger during the 1960s and early 1970s and had made wage gains that they fought to keep and even extend. Trade union leaders were sympathetic with government efforts to hold down wages and prices, but they had increasing difficulty convincing their members to go along with this. The result was steady upward pressure on wages, inflation and public spending. That led in turn to a crisis of confidence and the run on the pound that forced the government to seek a loan from the International Monetary Fund in September 1976. The terms of the loan required serious cuts in public spending that many in the government, and in the Labour Party, were reluctant to accept. The lengthy argument about precisely what those terms should be, and whether to accept them, was a defining moment in the history of the Wilson-Callaghan government, of the Labour Party, and of an entire era of economic policy-making in Britain.[11]

Callaghan and the Chancellor, Denis Healey, considered the loan a necessity and felt that, however unfair the judgments of the financial community, confidence needed to be maintained if the economy was not to grind to a halt. They were nevertheless keen to keep the cuts to a minimum. More committed Keynesians, such as Tony Crosland, were reluctant to accept any serious package of cuts and believed that they could essentially call the bluff of the IMF and international finance. Britain was simply too important to fail. The left within the Cabinet, led by Tony Benn, regarded the crisis as a moment to move Britain toward socialism and greater social justice even if that required a major increase in spending and state intervention. Benn's position was based largely on the quite radical proposals contained in *Labour's Programme 1973*, which had been adopted while in opposition and while the party's top leaders, like Wilson and Callaghan and Crosland, were focused elsewhere. It would become known as the "alternative economic strategy." A critical feature, or at least an essential corollary, was import controls which, it was widely understood, would create a more autarkic "siege" economy for a lengthy period of transition. The consequence would be a dramatic break – with the essential orientation of the economy, with Britain's identity as a nation dependent on trade and as a center for global finance and with its historic attachment to openness. It would also likely violate GATT rules and the rules of the Common Market. Just the year before voters had opted, by a two-to-one margin, to remain in Europe. The "alternative economic strategy" would reverse that.

Callaghan and Healey brought far greater resources to the battle, for they could call on the Treasury as well at the Prime Minister's advisors for data and for argument. Still, the debate dragged on for roughly two months and the outcome was a least partly a product of fatigue. Callaghan waited out his opponents, persisted, and got the Cabinet to endorse the loan and its terms. The consequences were economically quite beneficial: the balance of payments and borrowing (the phrase at the time was the "public sector borrowing requirement" or PSBR) improved quickly and the government did not even use up the entire proceeds of the loan; inflation was curbed, if temporarily; spending cuts were kept within reason and were distributed fairly; and the economy began marginally to improve.

Politically, the effects were rather more damaging: the crisis made it clear to just about everyone, inside government and out, that the old Keynesian formulas were not working and that, as Callaghan told the Labour Party conference, "the cosy world we were told would go on forever, where full employment would be guaranteed by the stroke of the Chancellor's pen, cutting taxes, deficit spending, that world is gone."[12] The rejection of the party's favored mantras – which were not an accurate summary of what Keynesian policy should mean or what the party did in practice – was accompanied by a reassertion of Britain's commitment to participation in the world market. The country would not seal itself off from international trade and investment and would continue its integration into the large market that was Europe. The decision came at a highly significant juncture, for the consequences of increased competition and floating currencies had made protectionist policies more attractive. In fact, the competitive devaluations that began with the U.S. decision to abandon Bretton Woods in 1971 and the hard bargaining over trade that followed were to some extent the equivalent of protection even if their effect, and purpose, was to avoid a still greater turn to protection. By opting for the market, even at the cost of higher unemployment, the Labour government effectively foreclosed both Keynesian and more collectivist solutions to the economic crisis.

Not that everyone accepted the result. In fact, the full implications remained unclear for a couple of years because of the surprising, if temporary, recovery of 1977–8 and because the coming on line of North Sea oil offered a lifeline to those who still clung to hopes of growth through planning and state initiatives. The government began to reap substantial revenues from oil in the late 1970s and it was confidently, and accurately, predicted that Britain would become a net exporter of oil by 1980. The prospect opened up two specific possibilities: first, there would be real money available for expenditure designed to stimulate the economy or support particular industries; and second, the balance of payments constraint on steady growth would be removed. With growth should come increases in productivity and competitiveness – the goals that had eluded successive governments of the left and of the right for a quarter of a century. The government spelled out these hopes in the White Paper on *The Challenge of North Sea Oil*, published in March 1978. As Callaghan argued at the time, North Sea oil would make it possible to "regenerate those traditional industries" that had long been languishing. Moreover, he claimed, the government's earlier tough decisions, which had supposedly put industries such as gas and electricity on a sound footing, now meant that "if you have cases coming along like British steel because of the recession and Leylands and the rest of it, we are in a much better position to finance them . . ." When asked what the government's priorities were for the use of oil revenues, he gave an answer that could just as easily have come from Tony Benn: "industrial strategy is given the first priority together with Government incentives for investment and selective assistance of various sorts . . ." The Prime Minister even went on to mention the National Enterprise Board, the agency in which the left of the party had put such great faith, and he concluded in a remarkable rhetorical flourish in response to a question about socialism: "the whole White Paper," he asserted, "would match my definition of Socialism."[13]

This optimism, and sense of confidence, would be dissipated over the next year, as the deal with the unions foundered and as the "winter of discontent" destroyed the centerpiece of the government's economic strategy. The second oil shock would ruin all calculations by causing a massive boost in inflation and a huge drop in global demand. Together, these events made it obvious to British voters that a radical departure was in order. It happened in May 1979 with the election of a Conservative government with Margaret Thatcher as Prime Minister, a politician determined to break with the policies of the previous era and willing to break eggs, bust heads and put up with, even thrive upon, the intense antipathy that her policies would arouse. Tutored by ideologues thoroughly committed to the market, Thatcher would preside over a thorough reversal of political philosophy and a transformation in the relationship between the market and the state.

Even before the oil price increases of 1978–9 the underpinnings of economic strategy in both Britain and the U.S. had been seriously weakened. The impact of the second oil shock was in this sense to demonstrate what was already well underway, for policy-makers were unwilling or unable to grasp what was happening until they were in fact overwhelmed by the consequences. At the Bonn summit of July 1978, for example, the U.S. and the U.K. collaborated to push the Germans and the Japanese to adopt more expansionist policies. Carter and Callaghan still believed in a kind of locomotive strategy, though by this time they realized that the thrust would have to come from others.[14] The Germans and Japanese suffered much less from inflation and so had more room for expansion, but they in turn demanded greater fiscal responsibility from both the U.S. and U.K. and insisted that the U.S. decontrol oil prices. A deal was done, but soon its very foundations were swept away by another round of oil price increases.[15] By 1979–80, governments in both America and Britain found themselves struggling unsuccessfully with what seemed an unprecedented set of problems. A sense of cumulative failure grew up around their efforts, eroded confidence in the ruling parties and the reigning orthodoxies and produced, in the end, a repudiation by voters that ushered in new governments, new policies and new ideas. The elections first of Margaret Thatcher and then of Ronald Reagan brought an effective end to the policies and public philosophies that had governed the postwar era. Just what new policies and underlying visions would be adopted were not immediately clear; and it would take still longer to judge their efficacy and durability. But the world was about to change.

And Trouble Abroad

The fact that the final stages of the unraveling involved, yet again, foreign actors and what was not unreasonably regarded as U.S. and U.K. weakness in the world helped to ensure that the developing crisis, and the ensuing shifts, would involve both foreign and domestic policy, security and the governance of the economy. As with economic policy, international relations during the late 1970s defied quite serious efforts to manage them. The big problem was the shifting balance in the Cold War; second to that, but not by much, was the intractability of the Middle East.

Since the United States and Britain confronted many of the same issues in foreign policy, they often did so together. Indeed, the tensions between the two countries so evident in the early 1970s lessened considerably after the defeat of Edward Heath in February 1974. As Kissinger explained, "When Harold Wilson succeeded Heath, he wasted no time in restoring the special relationship." Kissinger would get on especially well with Callaghan, Wilson's Foreign Secretary and then successor as Prime Minister.[16] Kissinger would also get on surprisingly well with Tony Crosland, who became Foreign Secretary in 1976 and who was happy to report that during his tenure "A high degree of confidence has been established with Dr. Kissinger ..."[17] Though Kissinger was initially put off by Crosland's "articulate petulance" and "supercilious behavior," they quickly developed a rapport on the major issues.[18]

This personal rapprochement did little, however, to alter the fundamental fact that Britain was in a far weaker position, both absolutely and relatively, during the 1970s than it had been for the previous thirty years. The big issues in foreign policy would therefore be confronted primarily by the United States, which was itself weaker than before but which alone seemed to have the global reach and capacity to intervene decisively throughout the world. That did not mean it would succeed, but it did mean that it felt compelled to act, and sometimes alone. Still, if there was an ally that most often moved in concert with the U.S., it was the U.K. The United States and Britain were also pushed closer together because they inhabited a similar place in the world of states: they were allied over most East-West issues; they found themselves working together on a range of imperial or postimperial issues and conflicts; and they shared political cultures that allowed them to act together in an international relations arena that gave new prominence to the question of human rights.

Indeed, while the shifting balances, terms and venues of the Cold War constituted the most critical foreign policy issue of the late 1970s and the Middle East the second, it was the unprecedented emphasis on human rights that was truly novel in the international politics of the late 1970s. Human rights, and human rights talk, reshaped the contest between East and West and the relationship between North and South. Even Henry Kissinger, the archetypal realist who ridiculed the influence of sympathy on matters of security and diplomacy, found himself forced at least to gesture in the direction of human rights. For others such as Jimmy Carter it was far more than a gesture; and foreign policy professionals all had to learn a new language, whatever their meaning or intention.

The politics of human rights was, of course, not invented *de novo* in the 1970s. Its origins went back at least to the French Revolution and an abstract commitment to the "rights of man" had been a part of democratic political discourse ever since. Questions of human rights were nevertheless seldom at the top of the agenda of international relations. They began to become important during the "Wilsonian moment" that emerged at the end of the Great War. Even then there was a tension between the principle of self-determination, which accorded more or less absolute sovereignty in internal affairs to nation states, and the rights of individuals and of minorities who might not fare so well at the hands of national majorities. The League of Nations sought to resolve, or mitigate, this tension by providing specific protection for minorities, although selectively. The horrors of the Nazi regime and the catastrophes associated with racial and ethnic politics during World War II brought a shift toward a broader and more compelling insistence on human rights. The new emphasis was articulated in the early postwar era in the UN's Universal Declaration of Human Rights, adopted in 1948, and in the European Convention on Human Rights.[19]

This more expanded definition of human rights was not accompanied, however, by any mechanism for its enforcement, so its practical effects were for many years exceedingly modest. The United States, for example, had a long history of expressing support for such principles but exempting itself from their detailed application, and the promotion of human rights was often sacrificed to the perceived exigencies of the Cold War.[20] Its superpower rival was much worse, in practice if not in theory. Progress would resume in the 1960s, as decolonization proceeded and the denial of human rights in places such as South Africa and Rhodesia became less and less defensible. The association between decolonization and human rights was very fraught, however, for postcolonial states and their rulers often tended toward authoritarianism, or worse, and were unwilling to grant to their own citizens the individual rights that a more universal politics of human rights would imply. Instead, they argued for a version of "cultural relativism" in which it was regularly asserted that the same principles could not be applied equally to developed and less developed countries. In its extreme form, the argument led to the assertion that human rights was a new form of colonialism. A perhaps fitting illustration of the difficulties came in April 1968, when the first "World Congress on Human Rights" – called to mark the twentieth anniversary of the Universal Declaration – was held in Tehran and hosted by the Shah.[21]

The politics of human rights would be transformed in the next decade as these contradictory visions clashed and as Western countries and publics saw the possibilities inherent in this emerging discourse. A key step was the Helsinki Process. A formal commitment to a very basic package of human rights was part of the Helsinki Final Act in 1975 and served to redefine Cold War politics in the language and politics of human rights.[22] The effects of the Helsinki Accords would be considerable, if indirect and very much unanticipated, particularly in Eastern Europe and the Soviet Union. Until the mid-1970s, however, the concern for human rights was typically focused elsewhere, particularly in Latin America. The most egregious case was Chile, where General Pinochet began a brutal repression after the coup against Allende in September 1973. The precise role of the U.S. in carrying out the coup remains in dispute, but what is not in dispute is that the United States welcomed it and

gave strong support to the Pinochet dictatorship even after reports of government brutality became widespread.[23] The effects of what happened in Chile
were spread further and faster because 200,000 people, many of them artists
and writers, fled the regime's terror and were welcomed across the Spanish-
speaking world and in the United States and Europe. There was also the
connection between events in Chile and a broader effort known as "Operation
Condor" launched in 1975. This was a campaign of assassination and intimidation carried out by dictatorships in Chile, Argentina, Bolivia, Brazil, Paraguay
and Uruguay and aimed at the left. It received at least tacit support from the
United States, and probably more.[24] The debate over political repression in
Latin America was largely conducted in the language of human rights. Kissinger
would privately tell Chile's foreign minister in June 1976 that "We wish the new
government well. We wish it will succeed. We will do what we can to help it
succeed."[25] Nevertheless, just two days before he had felt forced publicly to
proclaim at a meeting of the Organization of American States (OAS) that
"human rights must be preserved, cherished and defended if peace and prosperity are to be more than hollow technical achievements." And he went on to
admit that "violations continue to occur" and that "the condition of human
rights as assessed by the OAS Human Rights Commission has impaired our
relationship with Chile."[26] Kissinger's statements were in fact largely directed to
the Senate and Congress, where the Kennedy Amendment (1974) and the
Harkin Amendment (1975) had restricted aid first to Chile and then to kindred
regimes guilty of human rights violations.

The debate over human rights violations in specific countries thus had the
unintended consequence of broadening and advancing the global case for
human rights. This process was also furthered by the tactic, adopted by the
U.S. and by Britain, of trying to deflect concern over human rights violations
in Chile by pointing to all the other violations of human rights across the
world. The U.K. was the first major country to develop a list of countries
that abused human rights when it did so in 1976. British interest in human
rights was prompted by three distinct concerns: the first and most enduring
was the legacy of empire which had still not been extinguished; the second
was the ongoing debate about whether the U.K. should adopt the European
Convention on Human Rights, an issue that became more pressing when the
U.K. joined the European Communities in 1973; and the third was Northern
Ireland. Civil rights agitation begun in the late 1960s had moved on quickly
to a revived nationalist insurgency. British leaders soon realized that any
solution would most likely require a bill of rights for Catholics in that troubled
province, but could a bill of rights be created just for Northern Ireland? Clearly
not, and this meant that British governments and officials were forced to

reckon with the broader question of human rights as both domestic and foreign policy.

In the United States, support for human rights had still more curious origins. As part of détente Kissinger and Nixon had offered trading concessions to the Soviet Union, presumably in exchange for help in Vietnam. The proposal in 1972 to grant the USSR "most favored nation" status nevertheless created an opportunity for critics of détente and of Nixon and Kissinger. The chief instigator was Senator Henry "Scoop" Jackson of Washington, who proposed an amendment to the legislation aimed at withholding this benefit to states that denied citizens the right to emigrate. The Jackson-Vanik Amendment was specifically aimed at recent Soviet moves to restrict emigration by forcing emigrants to pay an "education tax," a provision that fell most heavily on Jews.[27] Nixon and Kissinger were apoplectic about the implications for détente and for their control of negotiations with the Soviets, though Kissinger later conceded that the move was "a tactically brilliant stroke."[28] Jackson was quite politically adept and managed to gain support from a wide coalition of supporters that stretched from union leader Lane Kirkland, head of the AFL-CIO, to the Soviet nuclear physicist and dissident Andrei Sakharov.[29] When he reintroduced the amendment in March 1973, he claimed to be "upholding our traditional commitment to liberty – a commitment enshrined in the Universal Declaration of Human Rights unanimously adopted by the United Nations more than 25 years ago."[30] The amendment passed but the administration resisted and spent a year working on a compromise that never came off. It became law in January 1975. Later that year the Helsinki Accords added another explicit requirement that states recognize certain critical human rights. The Soviets had no more intention of fulfilling it than they had of agreeing to Jackson-Vanik, but their resistance to both measures would prove counterproductive to the regime and would serve to undermine détente.

These diverse actions and debates helped to put human rights at the top of the agenda of international relations. So, too, did activism on the ground. The most prominent organization was Amnesty International, which had been founded in 1961 to bring to light the fate of "prisoners of conscience" and put pressure on governments. Local groups would focus on specific prisoners whose cases they would publicize. The strategy relied on naming and shaming and lobbying, and it was consciously directed at abuses in the West as well as the East and in both developed and less developed states. The roots of Amnesty were in the activism of the 1960s, but its tactics allowed it to survive into the more quiescent 1970s. In the new context it thrived: by 1979 it had 200,000 members; it had by then earned a place in the counsels of international organizations and had access to government officials who could more effectively press individual cases; and it had been instrumental in the push to ratify the two UN Covenants on Human Rights, which came into force in 1976.[31]

Well before the election of Jimmy Carter in November 1976, then, considerations of human rights were becoming much more central at least to the rhetoric of foreign policy. Still, it was during Carter's presidency that human rights began to have direct and unambiguous effects on the conduct of U.S. policy. The advocacy of human rights served two immediate ends. The first was Carter's evident desire to adopt a righteous stance in world affairs. Carter really was different from previous presidents, and from most politicians, in the extent of his religiosity and moral commitment. It was a question of principle, but also a means of distinguishing himself from his rivals. The second was the desperate need for a new departure in American foreign policy. The legacy of Vietnam was powerful, both domestically and internationally, and it was almost entirely negative: the U.S. was viewed as arrogant, imperialist and hostile to the aspirations of people seeking freedom from colonial or postcolonial domination. To recover its reputation and, in the process, to regain leverage, the United States needed to craft a foreign policy for what Nicholas Henderson, Thatcher's first Ambassador to the United States, called a "post-imperial, post-Vietnam, post-Watergate climate."[32] What was required was a stance and set of policies that would put it on the side of democracy, peace and self-determination, and, geopolitically, on the side of the increasingly important and independent developing nations whose support both the U.S. and the Soviet Union regarded as critical in their global rivalry. The promotion of human rights was that policy.

The conversion to a policy of promoting human rights, and its tensions and contradictions, are illustrated quite clearly in discussions between the U.K. and the U.S. Britain's involvement in Northern Ireland and its membership among "the Nine" had put the issue on the agenda of the Foreign Office and the Cabinet even before Helsinki, but there had been little action.[33] In January 1976 the Home Office reported that the arguments for and against a more explicit set of commitments were finely balanced: adherence to the European Convention might be part of the solution to the crisis in Ireland but it might also get in the way of necessary "measures against terrorism."[34] It might also cause difficulties in industrial relations and education: the "closed shop" might become illegal; and Labour's plans to abolish private schools might be blocked on the grounds that they interfered with freedom of religion. Worries of this sort meant that many on the left of the Labour Party who might otherwise have been expected to support a stronger human rights regime – such as Tony Benn and Michael Foot – in practice did not.[35]

What is notable about this moment is how insular the British debate was, despite the implications for foreign policy. This began to change in 1976. As Evan Luard, David Owen's Parliamentary Under-Secretary, explained to colleagues in Washington, pressure to take action over South Africa and Chile led the government to propose the "observance of human rights on a more systematic basis."[36] That led to an exercise in which British diplomats across the world were asked to provide information that would provide the basis for a "comparative assessment" in which countries would be grouped into five "bands" depending on their support for, or suppression of, human rights. Officials complied, but not without a certain cynicism: in his report from Buenos Aires, the British diplomat J. W. R. Shakespeare confessed:

> I cannot help reflecting wryly that many of those people we are now busy trying to help on the instructions of the Department have earmarked officials like myself and others in the Embassy as targets for kidnapping, maiming, torture and even murder – and would do so again, no doubt, if they had the opportunity.[37]

The assessment was nevertheless produced by the Planning Staff of the Foreign Office in November 1976 and used subsequently to shape diplomacy toward countries ranked in the bottom bands.

In the U.S. the Carter administration had come into office determined to break with the amoral realism that seemed to characterize foreign policy in the era of Nixon, Ford and Kissinger.[38] Zbigniew Brzezinski, soon to be Carter's National Security Advisor, claimed in 1976 that the previous Republican administrations had "elevated amorality to the level of principle."[39] "For too many years," Carter himself insisted in May 1977, "we have been willing to adopt the flawed and erroneous principles of our adversaries, sometimes abandoning our own values for theirs ... This approach failed," he went on, "with Vietnam the best example of its intellectual and moral poverty." Failure was in truth even more widespread, for America's "inordinate fear of communism ... led us to embrace any dictator who joined us in that fear" and that unholy embrace repelled people across the globe. In response, it was essential to reaffirm "America's commitment to human rights as a fundamental tenet of our foreign policy."[40] Under Carter, at least in the early years of his administration, human rights would dominate the rhetoric of foreign policy and inform, if not quite govern, its actual conduct. As Carter put it in February 1978, "It shall be a major objective of U.S. foreign policy to promote the observance of human rights throughout the world."[41] Carter had already created a new section of the State Department devoted to monitoring and enforcing human rights, led by

Patricia Derian; and considerations of human rights would lead to critical shifts in U.S. policy toward the Soviet Union and toward allies with dubious human rights records such as Iran and Nicaragua.

The new thrust inevitably affected relationships with America's European allies, Britain in particular. The U.K.'s prior effort to assess human rights across countries served as a model. In addition, the deep British and American involvement in southern Africa elicited close coordination on what was ultimately a matter of human rights. The British government, on the other hand, was rather more committed to détente than was the Carter administration and so was eager to work out with the U.S. a joint position on the implementation of the Helsinki Accords, one that would advance human rights without jeopardizing relations with the Soviets.[42] The U.S. and the U.K. were also the most important backers of an effort to upgrade the human rights machinery of the United Nations through the appointment of a High Commissioner for Human Rights.[43] Nevertheless, British leaders and officials were more than a bit puzzled by the Carter phenomenon: "President Carter has a strong, almost evangelical, sense of international morality," explained the head of the North American Department in the Foreign Office; and David Owen was certainly not alone in finding his sense of "moral certainty . . . unattractive."[44] Owen also argued that an excessive focus on human rights would harm the policy of détente with the Soviet Union.[45] The issue was more vexing to British policy-makers because it coincided with the realization that Britain's economic and political weakness had "weakened the U.S. confidence in our [Britain's] standing as an ally," a view that was shared by Carter and many in his administration.[46]

Whatever the precise balance between the U.S. and U.K., during the late 1970s the foreign policies of both countries would be sharply influenced by the turn to human rights. It was in certain respects an appropriate turn for the era after Vietnam, when both nations understood their situation as basically "post-imperial" and desperately sought a new role and rationale for their conduct abroad. Whether it was appropriate for the particular problems they faced at the time is a more complicated question. The world after Vietnam, after Helsinki and after the first oil shock was not after all a very welcoming place; nor was it likely to respond to a softer tone and loftier rhetoric on the part of the world's dominant superpower and its ally, which had until just recently been the world largest colonial power. It was a world predisposed to be hostile toward the United States and, to the extent that it mattered, toward Britain. Both countries were seen as reluctant to accept the full logic of decolonization or to support the efforts of Third World countries to develop independently of the West and to achieve what they regarded as their due. Whatever the intentions of American and British leaders, U.S. intervention in Vietnam defined the United States in global public opinion, and Britain still could not escape the association with empire and with its nasty legacies in southern Africa.

Global Challenges

The fact that the U.S. and the U.K. were, and were understood to be, weaker than before did nothing to reverse these antipathies. On the contrary, they encouraged further criticism and aroused irritation at the continuing efforts of both countries to exercise influence on a broad front. Weakness also tempted opponents to extend their own geopolitical reach. The Soviet Union was particularly eager to take advantage of what it saw as a new geographical balance that favored the Soviet Union over the United States and an expanded range of opportunities in the Third World.[47] The Soviet stance was quite complex and not always consistent. The Soviet leadership was genuinely committed to détente and saw big advantages in continuing the policy, but it also sought to restrict the application of détente to Europe. Beyond Europe, it asserted the right to promote its interests just as the United States had done and continued to do. When James Callaghan visited Moscow in August 1973, for example, he reported back that the Soviets "did not . . . see anything unnatural or disturbing about the Soviet Union wishing to expand its influence, nor would they accept that such an expansion of influence or interest should be of concern to the countries of Western Europe . . ."[48] The U.S. saw things differently and chose to regard détente as a global bargain with all sorts of "linkages." As such, the Americans interpreted Soviet efforts and advances outside Europe as evidence of bad faith and of the failure of détente to elicit good behavior from the Soviets. The consequence was that from the mid–1970s a series of engagements or crises on the periphery of the two camps – in Portugal and its former African colonies, in southern Africa and also the Horn of Africa, in Nicaragua and later in Afghanistan – seriously began to erode support for détente. Even those generally supportive of détente came to recognize that the Soviet Union's "arms buildup did not stop when it reached parity" and that its "self-restraint in the Third World . . . ended quite spectacularly in the mid–1970s."[49] The Iranian Revolution of 1978–9 was obviously not an engagement between the superpowers and the Ayatollah Khomeini was nobody's man but his own, or perhaps God's. To many in the U.S., however, the Islamic Revolution in Iran felt like another setback in the struggle between East and West. Out of these varied conflicts and trouble spots would emerge a sense that the world had entered a "second Cold War."[50]

The difficulty that the U.S. and the U.K. had in controlling these events was illustrated early on even closer to home. Two set of developments converged and complicated the Cold War balance on Europe's "southern flank": the first was the decay and fall of authoritarian regimes in Greece, Portugal and Spain, and the consequent dissolution of the Portuguese empire in Africa; the second was the emergence of Eurocommunism, especially in Italy and Spain.[51] The "challenge of Eurocommunism" was particularly worrying to Henry Kissinger, who feared that the possible entry of Communist parties into government would undermine NATO. The issue was posed most sharply in Italy, where the fragmentation of parties rendered normal politics largely unworkable. Throughout the postwar era the Christian Democrats (DC) dominated a succession of coalition governments while the Italian Communist Party (PCI), to whom most workers gave their votes, was largely frozen out of office at national level. The PCI nevertheless held power locally and performed quite credibly in that role. The Italian Communist Party was also more moderate and flexible than its counterparts elsewhere in Europe, and although heavily dependent on Moscow for funding, it had visibly departed from the Soviet position on more than one occasion. All this led to talk of a "historic compromise" between the two big parties – the Christian Democrats and the Communists – and of a possible coalition government. The U.S. exerted what leverage it could to prevent this. There were rumors, and some evidence, of a role for the CIA; Kissinger told all who would listen that including the Communists in the government was unacceptable; and Gerald Ford warned at Helsinki that "We do not see how it is possible to tolerate a Marxist government in NATO."[52] The Italians did not seem inclined to listen and the Communists won over 34 percent of the vote in June 1976. This would prove to be the limit of the PCI's success, however, and the fortunes of Eurocommunism subsequently declined, but more because of its inherent implausibility than because the Americans disapproved.[53]

The other major Eurocommunist party was in Spain, where forty years of repression was coming to an end and the Communists realized that they would fare better in the new era if they struck a pose of moderation. They did, but the performance of the Spanish Communists was soon eclipsed by that of its rivals, especially the Socialists, who went on to dominate Spanish politics throughout the 1980s. Communists in Portugal were less Eurocommunist and more rigid than those in Italy and Spain, and it was therefore in Portugal that the possibility of a decisive shift to the left was greatest. The regime of Marcello Caetano had been overthrown in late April 1974 by the Junta of National Salvation (JNS) supported by the Armed Forces Movement (MFA). The Portuguese military had been involved in nasty colonial wars that occupied over 150,000 troops by 1974, provoking serious discontent, particularly among younger officers who would become the backbone of the revolution. The transition to a stable democratic regime was to prove complicated and protracted. As the British Ambassador condescendingly observed a few weeks after the collapse of the old regime, "The Portuguese are, by and large, a docile people, not unduly addicted to intellectual activity, and a paternalistic regime is not by its nature unwelcome to many of them. But the increasing rigidity of the regime," he explained, had led to its fall and "the sudden removal of all restraints had a highly unsettling effect." The "impression one gets," he concluded, "is of an ant-heap which has been broken open. Frenzied activity is in progress and ants are scurrying in all directions . . ."[54]

The direction became clear soon enough as successive governments moved steadily to the left. A coalition regime including Communists, Socialists and moderates took office in mid-May, but the Junta and MFA remained dominant; by August 1974 a more openly left-wing administration, led by General Gonçalves, was in place; and in September there was a move to oust the more moderate elements in the regime. Moderates and conservatives pushed back and organized an unsuccessful coup in March 1975, which in turn prompted a further move to the left, with the radicals in the military setting up a Supreme Council of the Revolution and Communists holding key ministries. A Constituent Assembly was elected on April 25, but prior to the vote the Supreme Council forced the contending parties to sign a "Constitution Pact" leaving the MFA and the Council with extensive supervisory powers. The actual vote proved a setback for the left, however. The moderate Socialist Party emerged with roughly 38 percent of the vote, the Popular Democrats with a quarter and the Communists with only about 13 percent. Tensions came to a head over the summer: the MFA pushed for a series of more radical measures despite the outcome of the vote; the moderate parties withdrew from the governing coalition in July; and there were growing fears of a left-wing coup. The appointment in August of a government sharply tilted to the left led to widespread protests, which eventually led to the ousting of General Gonçalves. In September, a new coalition government, in which offices were distributed in accord with the recent election results, took office. In late November a mutiny of left-wing officers was suppressed and a centrist stability achieved.

The crisis in Portugal was a test for the U.S. and the USSR as well as for the U.K. and the rest of Europe. The long repression exercised by the Salazar regime meant the atrophy of democratic parties and institutions. When the system collapsed, authority devolved on to the only institution left standing: the military; and the Communists – historically better suited to operating clandestinely and thus surviving under right-wing dictators – emerged as the party with the most extensive influence across the country, with particular strength in the expanding trade unions, the media and the military. A gradual return to normalcy would in all likelihood serve to diminish the clout of the Communists, but would the situation permit such an evolution? The United States believed it would not and feared that Moscow would take advantage of the unrest to establish a communist outpost. Kissinger's pessimism led him to tell Mario Soares, leader of the Socialist Party, "You are a Kerensky."[55]

The Wilson/Callaghan government was rather more sanguine, but not naively so. The Labour government's main advantages were its ability, as a trade union-based and theoretically socialist party, to get access to Portuguese trade unionists and social democrats such as Soares, and the intuition, derived again from its own identity, that, left to their own devices, workers would not ordinarily turn to the far left. When Callaghan visited Lisbon in February 1975 and met with Soares, he therefore counseled patience while agreeing to send a representative of the Labour Party to advise the Socialists in the upcoming elections.[56] While the internal crisis unfolded, of course, the economy deteriorated, and the Europeans were soon asked for substantial aid. Portugal's need for economic assistance gave Europe, and the U.S., additional leverage to use with the regime. Just how hard to push, and how generous or restrictive to be in granting aid, became the subjects of intense, but not acrimonious, consultations among the Europeans and between them and the U.S. The varied responses revealed the different approaches of the British, the French, the Germans and the Americans. Kissinger, chastened by recent rifts, chose to regard the differences as the occasion for the Western allies to adopt a division of labor: "it was decided," he explained later, "that each ally should play its own hand while keeping the others closely informed. Ford and Giscard took on the role of the 'bad cops,' Schmidt the good one, and Callaghan the mediating father figure trying to meld both policies."[57] Callaghan saw his role in much the same way. At a meeting of European Socialist leaders the day after the signing of the Helsinki Accords, he took a middle position between those, like Joop den Uyl of the Netherlands, who advocated a general strike against the regime, and those, like the Danish Prime Minister, who "warned against continued demonstrations" by those opposed to the regime. "Time for words is still with us," Callaghan insisted, "but it was also time for action, which should be discussed in a smaller group."[58]

The role of the Soviets was harder to gauge. To some, it was obvious that they were behind the actions of the Portuguese Communists. Others were less clear: the British Embassy in Moscow told Callaghan that while we "can take for granted that Moscow is paying the PCP and must assume that it can directly influence not only the PCP but also elements within the AFM [MFA], I know of no evidence that could be used to prove this incontrovertibly."[59] Whether the Soviets were calling the shots or not, it was obvious that they would have a say in the resolution. Their top consideration was détente and, in particular, the proposed signing of the Helsinki Accords in the summer of 1975. The United States and Britain repeatedly used the negotiations over Helsinki to pressure the Soviets not to cause trouble in Portugal and instead to push the Portuguese leftists to reverse course. Harold Wilson delivered a stern lecture to Portuguese President Costa Gomes in Helsinki on the very day the Accords were signed, for example, and it must be assumed he did so with the blessing of the U.S.[60] The pressure seems to have been effective. The Soviets watched events carefully and defended the actions of the Portuguese Communists and their allies, attacked Soares and other moderates for not being "proper socialists," and even criticized communists who allied with social democrats, but ultimately they chose détente over confrontation, at least in Europe.[61]

Beyond Europe détente was less secure, for the Soviets perceived opportunities in America's retreats and vulnerabilities. The former Portuguese colony of Angola would be the site for a confrontation by proxy, in which the Soviets gave aid and the Cubans sent troops to assist the Popular Movement for the Liberation of Angola (MPLA) while the United States gave inconsistent, and largely ineffective, backing to its rivals: the National Front for the Liberation of Angola (FNLA) and the National Union for the Total Independence of Angola (UNITA). It was a messy situation in which the United States found itself at one moment backing the same group as the Chinese, the FNLA, and at another the same group as the South Africans, UNITA. Events on the ground were especially confusing and local loyalties were significantly more important than ideologies or outside allies. In the U.S. neither the State Department nor the military were especially eager to get involved, and even the CIA was hesitant about an extensive covert program, but Kissinger pressed forward, convinced that Soviet and Cuban involvement represented a bold move in an area far away from traditional Soviet interests and that it had to be resisted. In the summer of 1975 the U.S. instituted a substantial secret program to give funds, supplies and advice to UNITA and the FNLA and in the fall Kissinger sought to expand it. The effort failed to generate political support at home and Congress cut off funds for U.S. involvement in January 1976. Americans were simply unwilling to get involved in anything that looked or felt like Vietnam. The MPLA prevailed, and the world did not fall apart, though the Soviet Union did regard the outcome as a sign that "the world is turning in our direction."[62] Kissinger drew much the same lesson and lectured Congress on its folly: "If the U.S. is seen to emasculate itself in the face of massive, unprecedented Soviet and Cuban intervention, what will be the perception of leaders around the world as they make decisions regarding their future security?"[63] Of course, this new Soviet assertiveness in Africa constituted yet another argument against the policy of détente and the Ford administration actually ceased using the term in 1976.[64]

The reassessment of Soviet intentions and of the value of détente was also influenced by events on the Horn of Africa. In Ethiopia the aging Emperor Haile Selassie was overthrown in 1974 by a movement centered on the military. Again, the revolution was a confused and complex affair, but it soon moved left under the direction of Colonel Mengistu and its leaders began to reassess the country's dependence on the United States for its military needs. While still taking delivery of American supplies, which Kissinger was eager to provide as a way to keep contact with the new regime, they approached the Soviets with a set of requests early in 1975. The Soviets were wary, not so much because of worries about the U.S. response but because they were at that moment supporting the government of Siad Barre in Somalia, where they had a naval base, and the insurgency in Eritrea. The Ethiopian government was in conflict with both, and it would be difficult for the Soviets to develop relations with all sides. The Soviets eventually overcame their hesitations and concluded a major deal in late 1976. They understood that an alliance with Ethiopia would enhance their influence in a region of growing strategic importance. They had also become less enthusiastic about their Somali allies, who were increasingly coming under the influence of conservative Arab states. In addition, they were attracted by Mengistu's style and decisiveness as he moved to consolidate his rule by murdering foes and former allies in a "Red Terror."[65] By 1977, U.S. intelligence estimated that 400 tanks and 50 MiG jet fighters had been sent to Ethiopia from the Soviet Union, along with advisors to train in their use, and there were 10,000–11,000 Cuban troops in the country as well.[66] This Soviet and Cuban support would prove critical in the 1977–8 war with Somalia, now a U.S. ally but a source of embarrassment, over the Ogaden region of Ethiopia. Soviet success there, in a rocky desert utterly lacking in resources or geopolitical significance, caused a further deterioration in superpower relations: as Brzezinski put it in an obvious overstatement, "SALT (the Strategic Arms Limitation Talks) [and by implication détente] lies buried in the sands of the Ogaden."[67]

While policy-makers found ominous portents in events in the former Portuguese colonies and the Horn of Africa, their remoteness meant that these developments did not much exercise the imaginations or engage the sympathies of wider publics in the U.S., Britain or the rest of Europe. The festering crisis in southern Africa did, however, and the projection of Cold War rivalries into Africa vastly complicated the last stages of decolonization in Rhodesia (Zimbabwe), South West Africa (Namibia) and South Africa. The fate of southern Africa was especially critical for Britain, for it was there that the legacy of empire was most evident and toxic. Since neither Britain nor other countries had recognized Rhodesia's "Unilateral Declaration of Independence" in 1965, the U.K. remained officially sovereign. The region was equally critical for the United States, which came to understand that its relationships with the Third World hinged on its perceived response to continued racial oppression. The legacy of colonialism in southern Africa prevented Britain from becoming a genuinely postimperial power and playing a distinctively different role in the world and in Europe; and the United States, in its quest for a post-Vietnam and hence effectively postimperial stance, also felt compelled to prove itself in that most difficult part of the Third World. Shared need once again pushed the U.S. and U.K. together and led them to coordinate policy on southern Africa.

Doing so required a shift for both countries. British ties to the white settler regimes were extensive and successive British governments had combined public calls for decolonization and majority rule with covert support or at least inaction. The American position varied: the Johnson administration was extremely critical and had told the South Africans that they must end apartheid. Nixon and Kissinger saw the issue differently: not only was southern Africa a decisive front in the Cold War, but support for the government in South Africa fit well within the "Nixon Doctrine" which sought to recruit local surrogates to exercise power on behalf of U.S., or Western, interests. The Nixon administration was well aware of the dilemmas facing the U.S. As a National Security Council study explained in December 1969:

> Racial repression by white minority regimes in Africa has international political ramifications . . . Politically conscious blacks elsewhere in Africa and the world deeply resent the continuation of discrimination, identify with the repressed majorities in southern Africa and tend in varying degrees to see the relationship of outside powers to the white regimes as at least tacit acceptance of racism . . . The communist states have been quick to seize on this issue and to support black aspirations. Thus our policy toward the white regimes in southern Africa affects, though it might not necessarily govern, our standing with African and other states on issues in the United Nations and bilaterally.

Nevertheless, for Nixon and Kissinger the most useful policy was a turn to "at least tacit acceptance": "We would maintain public opposition to racial repression but relax political isolation and economic restrictions on the white states."[68]

The Soviet/Cuban breakthrough in Angola provoked a reorientation. Though Kissinger continued to see African conflicts through the lens of the Cold War and would have preferred to stick with South Africa, he felt compelled to tell the white South Africans that their time was running out. He also undertook a tour of Africa in April 1976 during which he announced a fundamentally new U.S. policy: "Of all the purposes we have in common," he said in Lusaka, "racial justice is one of the most basic . . . Our support for this principle in southern Africa is not simply a matter of foreign policy, but an imperative of our moral heritage." Kissinger went on to promise U.S. support for majority rule throughout the region and, in the short term, to treat the white regime in Rhodesia with "unrelenting opposition until a negotiated settlement is achieved"; and he outlined a ten-point program toward that end. In September he returned to Africa and worked out a proposal for a two-year transition to majority rule in that country. The plan was formally accepted, but detailed agreement was elusive and the subsequent Geneva conference broke down and left the issue unresolved. Nevertheless, a major reversal in U.S. policy had occurred and a path to majority rule in Rhodesia was at least charted on paper.[69] It would not happen until the Lancaster House Agreement of December 1979, but there was no longer any real doubt about the direction of change or the ultimate outcome.[70]

British policy had already moved in a similar direction under the Labour government which took office in 1974, but rhetoric and reality were at variance here as well. Though Britain never came to terms with Rhodesia and consistently opposed the continuation of white rule, its attitude toward sanctions was inconsistent, at times even illegal. As early as 1967 George Brown, then Foreign Secretary, explained the choice facing the U.K.: "To apply sanctions to South Africa or to turn a blind eye to Rhodesian sanctions being evaded with the help of South Africa."[71] Labour and Conservative governments, backed up by higher civil servants, chose the latter; consequently, British firms connived at the supply and resupply of both regimes. Britain's efforts to seek a resolution in southern Africa were thus compromised not only by its imperial legacy, but by its recent complicity in dealing with the regimes. In addition, there were economic and political ties with the settler governments, and these were especially strong among Tories. Even within the Labour government, the Foreign Secretary David Owen found that key economic ministers – Denis Healey, Edmund Dell and Harold Lever – were opposed to sanctions. At the same time, the left within the party was eager to press for majority black rule. There was also, on the left and on the right, resistance to an active U.S. role. British political leaders recognized that American support was essential to a breakthrough, but they did not much like it. Kissinger's initiatives were inherently suspect, and he and Crosland had a difficult collaboration on the matter during 1976. The American Secretary of State attempted to work closely with Callaghan and Crosland, but the British were wary of failure and of Cabinet resistance. In the end, cooperation prevailed, though not without some lingering resentment.

David Owen and Cyrus Vance would do better. They agreed on a basic strategy, appointed a "consultative group" of officials and diplomats to develop detailed plans, and jointly crafted the proposals that would revive the failed negotiations and become the basis for the final settlement. The Carter administration's broader commitment to human rights – symbolized by, among other things, Andrew Young's appointment as UN Ambassador – clearly helped to create a favorable climate as well for, as Vance argued, "If the United States did not support social and political justice in Rhodesia, Namibia and South Africa itself, Africans would correctly dismiss our human rights policy as mere cold war propaganda, employed at the expense of the people of Africa."[72] Success remained elusive, however, for the "front-line" African states set tough conditions and the white regimes resisted. In South Africa the highly suspect death in prison of Steve Biko in September 1977 signaled the beginning of a period of harsh repression, while in Rhodesia the government launched a plan for an "internal settlement" with moderate black leaders that would exclude the more radical liberation groups. The Carter administration found itself under increasing right-wing pressure to lift sanctions as a sign of support for such a deal, however inadequate it might be, and during 1979 the U.S. began to play a less public role.[73] The British inevitably found it "quite difficult dealing with the Carter administration" and its problems juggling domestic constituencies and competing principles.[74] The U.S. did maintain sanctions, however, and in the end sanctions and the refusal – by the liberation forces, by the "front-line states," by the U.K. and by the Commonwealth countries – to accept the gambit of an "internal settlement" that failed to deliver majority rule produced the desired effect.[75] After much wrangling, the Lancaster House meeting would bring an end to the Rhodesian government and in 1980 Zimbabwe elected its first majority black government. It was ironic that Thatcher should have presided over the outcome. Not only was it far from her preferred resolution, but she understood her success as a largely British achievement rather than as the result of an Anglo-American collaboration. That understanding, and that definition of Britain's role in the world, would come later for her, and only after Carter had left office. The reality was that the U.S./U.K. connection had been essential and that the process had served to recast both Britain and the United Sates as powers prepared to oppose what remained of colonialism.

The beginning of the end of the racist regimes in southern Africa could in this sense be regarded as a triumph for the new politics of human rights. The signing and, in the spring of 1978, ratification of the Panama Canal Treaty could be seen in a similar light.[76] In other cases the concern for human rights – and the rights of small nations – was less marked and in still other places the issue of human rights was more or less irrelevant. The Carter administration's greatest diplomatic success, after all, was the Camp David Accords of September 1978, which may have marginally advanced the cause of peace in the Middle East but did little to extend the remit of human rights in that troubled region. Carter did commit the U.S. to the notion that the Palestinians had legitimate rights that could not be ignored, but the diplomacy he initiated did precisely that. Thus the Camp David agreements acknowledged "the legitimate rights of the Palestinian people," but what was practically agreed was a peace treaty between Egypt and Israel which was signed in March 1979 but left the fate of the Palestinians unchanged. It was a major achievement for Carter, for the Egyptian President Anwar Sadat, and for Menachim Begin – and Callaghan played an important role as interlocutor – but this very partial success merely stored up problems for the long term and did little to further the principles that the U.S. sought more generally to articulate.[77] Soon enough, Carter was out of office and unable to back up his rhetoric; Sadat would be assassinated in October 1981 for his efforts; the Arab world generally denounced the treaty; and the Israelis would use the easing of tensions with Egypt to turn their attention to driving the Palestinian Liberation Organization (PLO) out of Lebanon, which they invaded in June 1982, and to a sustained effort to implant Jewish settlements in the occupied territories.

The other major preoccupation of American foreign policy during the late 1970s was the quest for a second installment in the process of strategic arms limitation. Again, human rights was not much of a consideration, though at times the rhetoric of human rights seemed an impediment. Three problems hung over the negotiations and impeded an agreement. The first was the decay of détente, as more and more Americans came to see it as one-sided and not in the interests of the United States. Détente also came to be criticized as fundamentally immoral, for it implied a willingness to compromise with a regime whose very existence was an affront to the principles of human rights. A second was largely technical: arms control was complicated, and while it was possible to agree on the broad outlines, the details were less easy to control and compliance was hard to verify. Inevitably, they invited dissembling and dispute. Third, the first set of agreements – SALT, agreed in 1972, as well as the interim agreement reached at Vladivostok in 1974 – dealt in broad aggregates and covered a limited range of weapons and uses, and outside these limits the two sides continued to make improvements and to deploy new and updated armaments where not strictly prohibited. The Soviets, for example, decided in 1976 to deploy SS–20s in its European territory. The U.S. and its NATO allies interpreted the decision as a serious threat, while the Soviets argued that they were merely replacing older and outdated weapons and, in the process, providing a counter to NATO's "Forward Base Systems" and the separate U.K. and French nuclear deterrents. The perceived need for both sides to match the technical progress of the other tossed up a series of issues that would become the subjects of intense debate, within and between the blocs, and tough bargaining. Despite the agreement not to develop anti-ballistic missile defenses, for example, the U.S. and the USSR worked steadily to "harden" systems to protect them from attack. The effort led to plans for new missile systems that would be less vulnerable because they would be mobile or because they would be deployed on submarines.

It therefore proved difficult to get and then to sell a second arms control agreement. In the U.S., for example, prominent conservatives formed a Committee on the Present Danger to argue for a tougher stance toward the Soviet Union and opposed what it regarded as further concessions. Its spokesman Paul Nitze argued in 1976 that SALT had not stabilized the arms race to the mutual benefit of the U.S. and the USSR, but rather "that under the terms of the SALT agreements the Soviet Union will continue to pursue a nuclear superiority that is not merely quantitative but designed to produce a war-winning capability."[78] Worries over Soviet intentions were clearly intensified by what was going on in Africa and by lingering uncertainty about developments on Europe's "southern flank." The Carter administration also had to deal with Soviet discomfiture and resentment over its human rights policies. Brezhnev and his advisors, like the Foreign Minister Andrei Gromyko, were irritated by efforts to promote human rights in the USSR and Eastern Europe, and America's European allies were worried that an aggressive human rights agenda would set back détente between the superpowers. The Foreign Office, for example, urged that the debate over the implementation of Helsinki be conducted gently and not allowed "to degenerate into polemics": "we have to be careful not to press Soviet tolerance too far."[79] The Germans felt much the same way, for the entire project of *Ostpolitik* involved such compromises.[80] Eventually, the Carter government got the Soviets back to the bargaining table, but as they worked out the terms of SALT II, they were forced to appease domestic critics as well.

This was done by abandoning the hopes for major arms reductions with which the new administration had first taken office and the adoption of a tougher stance in negotiations. Shortly after taking office, the Carter administration had proposed a series of quite massive reductions in nuclear arms. The USSR was suspicious – a "cheap and shady maneuver" was how Gromyko described it – and rejected the idea out of hand.[81] Negotiations would resume later that year, but the path to an agreement was difficult. It was made tougher still by relations with allies, particularly in Europe. European leaders were extremely worried over the deployment of SS–20s, for it raised anew the question of the U.S. nuclear guarantee. Soviet weapons that could be used against Europe quickly and easily might, it was feared, make the U.S. reluctant to risk its own cities in defense of Europe. Helmut Schmidt gave an important speech to the International Institute for Strategic Studies in London in 1977 and argued that because "SALT codifies the nuclear strategic balance between the Soviet Union and the United States" it also effectively "neutralizes their strategic capabilities. In Europe this magnifies the significance of the disparities between East and West in nuclear and conventional weapons." He warned that "strategic arms limitations confined to the United States and the Soviet Union will inevitably impair the security of the West European members of the alliance vis-à-vis Soviet military superiority in Europe if we do not succeed in removing the disparities in Europe parallel to the SALT negotiations."[82]

Schmidt's worries were military but also political, and would set in motion responses at both levels.[83] Militarily, NATO would move to modernize and increase its weapons in Europe. The first proposal was to develop and deploy the "neutron bomb" or, as it was officially known, the Enhanced Radiation Weapon (ERW). Europeans early on agreed with the plan, but began to back off as criticism of the ultimate "capitalist weapon," which would kill people but spare property, began to increase. The U.S. put considerable pressure on its NATO allies to accept the weapon and they mostly stood firm. When Carter himself decided in March 1978 against that option, they were seriously miffed. Relations became very strained and Carter was increasingly seen as weak and unreliable. The focus then shifted to an alternative proposal for the deployment of a new package of intermediate range nuclear weapons, Cruise and Pershing II missiles. That choice was informally agreed at a meeting in Guadalupe in January 1979 involving Carter, Schmidt, Giscard and Callaghan. On the side of that gathering, Callaghan also got Carter's agreement to provide Trident missiles to the U.K. to replace its aging Polaris missiles. Resolving the military issue, at least temporarily, allowed for closer collaboration between the U.S. and the Europeans on the SALT negotiations and removed at least one obstacle to reaching an agreement, but it also angered the Soviets and to that extent retarded progress on arms limitation.

The Soviets were also disturbed by the administration's decision to "play the China card." The opening to China pursued by Nixon and Kissinger had been a spectacular coup, but progress on normalizing relations was slow and essentially put on hold until the death of Mao and Zhou Enlai and the defeat of the so-called "gang of four" in 1976. The continued tension with the Soviets made the Chinese eager for a better relationship with the West, however, and with

U.S./Soviet rivalries intensifying, the U.S. looked ever more favorably upon the China connection. Closer ties between the U.S. and China would be rightly understood by Soviet leaders as a threat, but that was what made the prospect so attractive. Within the Carter administration Cyrus Vance was hesitant about such a move, but Brzezinski was excited by it; and Carter sided with his National Security advisor, who was sent to China in May 1978. It was agreed that full "normalization" would take place on January 1, 1979, and Deng Xiaoping visited Washington before the end of that month.[84] The public position on both sides was that the connection was not an alliance and not directed at anyone, but again, everybody understood its meaning. In fact, normalization was accompanied by military and intelligence cooperation. As early as April 1978 the British Air Marshal and Chief of the Defence Staff, Sir Neil Cameron, had told the Chinese "that he looked forward to closer cooperation with the Chinese armed forces against their common enemy, Moscow."[85] Apparently Tony Benn objected in a Cabinet meeting, but his was a solitary voice, and the meaning of these initiatives was transparent. They undoubtedly produced anger in Moscow, but they might well have put pressure on the Soviets in the negotiations over arms control.

A deal on nuclear weapons nevertheless proved elusive, and tensions between the U.S. and the USSR continued to mount. Carter was forced, by external events and by domestic politics, to proceed on two fronts simultaneously: he would continue to negotiate with the Soviets, but the U.S. would also undertake a military buildup of its own. Détente had given way to renewed arms competition.[86] At the beginning of 1978 Carter proposed that NATO defense budgets should be increased by 3 percent annually and he pledged to boost U.S. defense spending by 6 percent in 1979.[87] The administration also undertook what Brzezinski labeled a "strategic renewal" that involved plans for a Rapid Reaction Force and for more advanced weaponry and a drastic rethinking of deterrence strategy. These decisions were part of a broader shift in which the rather dovish and conciliatory foreign policy articulated in the first year of the Carter administration was replaced by a more hawkish and anti-Soviet stance that would be largely in place when the U.S. and the USSR signed the SALT II agreement in June 1979. The agreement itself was unremarkable, for it mainly fleshed out the terms of the interim Vladivostok agreement with its numerical limits on long-range missiles.[88] It was never ratified, but honored by both sides into the 1980s.

The failure to ratify SALT II, or even to propose its approval, was not the biggest setback for the Carter administration during 1979. That year, which would see the fall of the Labour government in Britain and the election of Margaret Thatcher, was in fact disastrous for both the U.S. and the U.K. It witnessed huge reversals on the economy and in foreign policy, and the two countries were strongly linked in practice and in the public mind, which did not forgive the party in power in either country. The link between economics and international relations was most clearly demonstrated in the Middle East. The Islamist revolution in Iran was understood by all parties as "a geopolitical disaster" and a major defeat for the West, and for the U.S. in particular.[89] It would trigger yet another round of oil price increases. This second oil price shock set off a further bout of inflation just when the effects of the first oil shock seemed to have been absorbed. The result was an increase in prices that decreased demand and lowered output and that led to anti-inflationary policies which further depressed the global economy. The immediate political consequence was to create an impression of impotence and vulnerability that overwhelmed the governments of both the U.K. and the U.S. Callaghan bargained and cajoled but failed to end the "winter of discontent" before it shattered Labour's claim to competence. Carter was seen to fail on virtually every front: abroad in dealings with the Soviets, in Iran, in Nicaragua where the Sandinistas ousted the dictator and former U.S. ally Somoza; and at home in an inability to respond effectively to a devastating combination of inflation and rising unemployment.

No issue came to symbolize mounting and cumulative failure more than the Iranian Revolution and the subsequent hostage crisis.[90] The roots of hostility between Iran, the United States and the U.K. went back to the coup of 1953 that overthrew Mossadegh and put the Shah back on the throne. During the 1970s, with the Shah still in power and now bolstered by inflated oil prices, "Iran was very much part of the whole American system . . . for maintaining stability in the whole area."[91] Carter followed a particularly confused policy, at one moment criticizing the Shah's regime over human rights violations and limiting U.S. support, at another praising Iran as "an island of stability in one of the most troubled areas of the world." In a speech at a New Year's Eve party in Tehran at the end of 1977 Carter went still further in his praise of the Shah: "This is a great tribute to you, Your Majesty, and to your leadership and to the respect and admiration and love which your people give to you . . ."[92] Within weeks the Shah's forces unleashed a political attack on the Ayatollah Khomeini and suppressed the resulting uproar at Qom with lethal violence. The British government's attitude was no more enlightened: its policy remained "support for the Shah, warts and all, while occasionally offering treatment for the warts."[93] The lack of understanding of what was happening inside Iran was widely shared in the West, and it produced a mistaken conception not only of the regime but also of the opposition. In his report on the internal situation in Iran at the end of January 1978, Sir Anthony Parsons, the British Ambassador, listed the various forces – students, middle-class professionals, workers, and religious leaders – opposed to the Shah but concluded that "there is no question of the Shah or his Government being confronted with a united opposition posing a significant threat . . ."[94] There was some dissent within the embassy, with one analyst arguing in early March that "The most important and complicated development of recent months has been the reappearance of the religious community as a major force," a new political phenomenon linked to "the widespread Islamic revival that has been noticeable throughout Iranian society over the last year or so . . ."[95] More characteristic was the rather frivolous reaction of the head of the Foreign Office department to whom the embassy reported. Responding to the reports of unrest, he asked "[W]hatever happened to Hajji Baba? Having been accustomed to regard your average Persian as the epitome of idleness, deceitfulness, corruption, charm and conceit, are we now in fact witnessing a change in the national character?" On a more sanguine note, he concluded in his note to Parsons that, "as you say the troubles you describe do not add up to a plausible threat to the regime in face of the continued loyalty of the Armed Forces and the effectiveness of Savak."[96]

By late October 1978 it had become clear to the U.S. and U.K. that the Shah's regime might not be so stable. They began contingency planning and started to speculate about the nature of Iran after the Shah, but they still fretted as much over nationalist, liberal and communist opponents of the Shah as over the prospects of the Islamist insurgency that was visibly gaining strength.[97] They were thus very much taken aback by the emergence of the Ayatollah Khomeini, whom they greatly underestimated, and utterly confounded by his outlook and his intransigence. The U.S. stood by the Shah and hoped that some mix of repression and liberalizing reforms would stabilize the situation. It is highly unlikely that the formula would have worked, but in any event the Shah did not follow it. Instead, he bluffed, compromised and ultimately yielded to his foes, departing the country on January 16, 1979.

The interim government the Shah left in place did not last: on February 1 the Ayatollah returned to Tehran from his Paris exile and within days a new regime took over; the Islamic Republic was proclaimed on April 1 and an Islamist constitution, granting ultimate power to religious authorities, approved in December. The U.S. response continued to be confused and inconsistent. American policy-makers had wavered over whether to push the Shah toward a more confrontational and repressive stance; with the Shah gone, it sought to deal with the moderates whose power was destined to dissolve as the revolution took its violent and yet predictable course. Under pressure from the Shah's U.S. friends, Kissinger and Nelson Rockefeller prominent among them, Carter allowed the ailing Shah to enter the U.S. for medical treatment in October; less than three weeks later militants had seized the U.S. Embassy in Iran and taken sixty-six hostages. The hostage crisis would not end while Carter was President and it would overshadow his last year in the job. Diplomatic efforts were tried, and failed, and on April 24, 1980 a military operation failed as well.[98] The hostages were finally released minutes after the swearing in of Ronald Reagan, 444 days after their seizure.[99] Carter would visit them the next day at a military base in Germany, but he was then no longer President.[100]

The Iranian Revolution was not only a sign of the limits of U.S., and Western, power, but a catalyst for a new definition of global strategy on the part of the United States. What seemed an adverse turn in the Cold War was now reinforced by a turn to radical Islam that was seen further to weaken the U.S. position. The deterioration was then worsened, or so it seemed, by the Soviet invasion of Afghanistan in late December 1979. The hostages languished in Tehran while Soviet troops entered Kabul, oil prices continued to rise and the lights on the White House Christmas tree remained turned off. Whatever the connections between these disparate events, they seemed connected by geography, for the locus of chaos was in an "arc of crisis" stretching from the Horn of Africa to the Indian Ocean, with the Persian Gulf at its center. Within the Carter administration hardliners such as Brzezinski identified this enormous and diverse part of the world as "America's New Strategic Area" and began pushing for a "regional security framework" to encompass that region and to protect it, not so much from Islamist militancy as from Soviet pressure.[101] Protecting it would also make its resources accessible to the United States and to the global economy.

Carter himself came around to this view and in his State of the Union address in January 1980 announced what would become known as the "Carter Doctrine." "Let our position be absolutely clear," he warned. "An attempt by any outside force to gain control of the Persian Gulf region will be regarded as an assault on the vital interests of the United States of America and such an assault will be repelled by any means necessary, including military force." The new framework explicitly linked the Iranian Revolution and the Soviet incursion into Afghanistan, but it was the apparent Soviet advance that was of primary concern:

> The region which is now threatened by Soviet troops in Afghanistan is of great strategic importance: It contains more than two-thirds of the world's exportable oil. The Soviet effort to dominate Afghanistan has brought Soviet military forces to within 300 miles of the Indian Ocean and close to the Straits of Hormuz, a waterway through which most of the world's oil must flow. The Soviet Union is now attempting to consolidate a strategic position, therefore, that poses a grave threat to the free movement of Middle East oil.[102]

The challenge would be met by a series of actions aimed at the Soviets: an embargo on grain and on the transfer of advanced technology, a boycott of the Moscow Olympics, and limits on cultural ties and exchanges. Most important, the Carter administration would undertake a "strategic renewal" that began with a call for a 5 percent increase in defense spending and the establishment of a "Rapid Deployment Force." Still more ominously, in July 1980 Carter signed Presidential Directive 59, which replaced the by now traditional theory of deterrence with a policy that envisioned "limited" nuclear war focused not on cities and populations but on more precise political, military and economic targets.[103]

This reorientation of U.S. strategy was extremely significant. Prior to the Carter Doctrine, the U.S. was an important player in the Middle East, but the area had been of secondary importance; now the U.S. had declared an interest in whatever went on there and would in future be implicated, for good or ill, in whatever transpired. Détente had been in retreat throughout the late 1970s, but from 1980 it was effectively dead and a revived Cold War was proclaimed and planned for. In the new era, moreover, the old inhibitions on the use of nuclear weapons would be relaxed, at least in the minds of military planners, and a much more dangerous escalation would become possible. For all intents and purposes, the Reagan/Thatcher era in foreign and defense policy had begun.

Still, Carter got no credit from either the left or the right and he was rebuked by allies and opponents and, in the end, by the voters. Whether Carter's rejection by the electorate was due primarily to perceived failures in foreign policy, which came fast and furiously and relentlessly, or to the nation's economic difficulties is impossible to say, for problems at home and abroad were linked in reality and in public perception. It was the deteriorating economy, however, that would be the centerpiece of the Republican campaign against Carter. Carter had himself attacked Gerald Ford for presiding over an economy with a "misery index" (a simple adding up of the inflation rate and the unemployment rate) of over 13 percent; four years later it was nearly 22 percent; and Ronald Reagan used his only debate with Carter to ask Americans "Are you better off than you were four years ago?"[104] The answer was clearly no, though if it had been asked just a year earlier, it would have been different.[105] What had intervened was the second oil shock, whose intensity and suddenness destroyed any and all progress made in Carter's first two years in office.

The Economy, Again

American economic policy in the mid–1970s was not completely ineffectual: growth was substantial in 1977–8 and, with oil prices roughly stable from 1974

through 1978, inflation moderated as well. Unemployment had fallen to
5.8 percent by the end of 1978. But the respite was not used to good effect. With
varying degrees of intensity, Nixon, Ford and Carter had all pushed for conservation and alternative fuels, but Congress repeatedly failed to act. Part of the
reason was that Americans were unwilling to endure the pain of increased gas
prices. Instead, subsidies were maintained, consumption remained high, and
the share of imports coming from Arab oil exporters actually increased.
Another part of the reason was that the United States was able to use inflation
as a mechanism to cope with the earlier price increase. Oil was denominated in
dollars and producers mostly paid with dollars; in consequence, a huge share of
the increased profits of oil-producing countries flowed back into the U.S. and,
to a lesser but important extent, to the U.K. Money from oil was in fact a fundamental cause of the broader expansion of U.S. and global finance during the
1970s. The United States was also able to benefit from the flexible exchange
rates brought about by its abandonment of Bretton Woods. Floating rates
meant, in effect, regular depreciations in the value of the dollar; the effect was
to stimulate U.S. exports, which grew substantially during the 1970s.

For a variety of reasons, then, the U.S. for a time coped reasonably well with
the economic problems of the 1970s. Successful adaptation, with increased
trade and increasingly mobile capital and a more globally oriented financial
sector, combined as well to keep the U.S. committed to a more or less open
world economy. The Japanese and the Europeans had good reason in the 1970s
to worry that the U.S. would turn in a more protectionist direction in response
to the gathering economic crisis, but it did not happen. The U.S. did bargain
hard with the Japanese over market opening and insisted on "orderly marketing
agreements" that limited Japanese imports, but the system overall remained
open. A series of economic summit meetings produced reaffirmations from
the major countries of the virtues and value of trade, a development that
reflected a sense that, despite periodic tensions and intensified competition,
economic problems were largely shared.[106] It also reflected a decision
to counter demands for a new international economic order to redress the
North–South balance with short-term plans to finance the oil purchases of
developing countries and a more long-term promise to facilitate access to the
markets of the developed countries.[107] The international system would actually
become more open with the conclusion of the Tokyo Round of GATT negotiations in 1979, which saw the first steps toward extending the process of trade
opening from tariff reductions to the elimination of non-tariff barriers.[108]

These were more than mere ad hoc arrangements, but much less than the
more fundamental reorientation that the depths of the decline required. Still, it
required yet another crisis to drive home that truth. It began when oil production

virtually stopped in Iran as the revolution gathered pace in late 1978. Oil prices started to rise again, though as much from panic as from real shortages of supply, and with predictable consequences.[109] Between 1978 and 1981 crude oil prices grew by one and a half times; and over the same period consumer prices in the U.S. rose by 40 percent. American prices overall were rising at a rate of over 13 percent throughout 1980, as Carter fought for reelection, first against Ted Kennedy running to his left and then against Ronald Reagan running to his right. Unemployment grew simultaneously as well, averaging over 7 percent in 1980–1 and rising to 9.7 percent in the depths of recession in 1982.

Again, however, it was not simply the return of "stagflation" but rather the growing perception that government was incapable of coping that would prove disastrous for Carter and his administration and for the policy-making para-digm within which he worked. The ideas and tools with which Carter worked were fundamentally Keynesian, though oddly distorted. Keynesian approaches to running the economy had been in place for the entire postwar era, but their meaning and significance had evolved. By the 1960s Keynes meant not just stability but steady growth. During the 1970s, growth had slowed and by the time Carter became President faith in sustained economic expansion had begun to dim. Carter's policies were thus a mix of what had become the conven-tional wisdom of the Keynesian era and a new emphasis on stability and secu-rity in a time defined by a new set of apparent "limits to growth."[110] Ambivalence about growth, its possibility and its usefulness, was not the reason for the vacil-lations in U.S. economic policy under Carter – these were prompted by more immediate shifts in economic variables – but it could have been.

The sense that the era of growth was coming to an end certainly came across in Carter's energy proposals. The President had promised to make the issue a top priority and in April 1977 he addressed the American people on the problem: "Tonight," he said, "I want to have an unpleasant talk with you." Carter proceeded to enumerate a set of proposals that "will cause you to put up with inconveniences and to make sacrifices." "Ours is the most wasteful nation on Earth," he explained; and "If we fail to act soon, we will face an economic, social and political crisis that will threaten our free institutions."[111] The substance of Carter's proposals – for conservation, energy security, decontrol of prices and the development of alternative fuels – were all sensible and worth debating, but the lecturing and the self-righteousness of the argument were distinctly unhelpful. The public simply did not want to hear about changes in lifestyle and had no desire to "rediscover small-scale, more creative ways of satisfying our needs," as Carter urged.[112] Nor did Congress, whose members were more politically attuned to their constituents and often more closely tied to interests that might be disadvantaged by Carter's initiatives.

The effect was that Carter's proposals were defeated or severely watered down. When the second oil shock hit in 1978–9, the administration would try again but with even less success politically. Deciding how to respond to the latest round of price increases was the dominant issue at the Tokyo Economic Summit in late June 1979. It was a difficult meeting, with Carter confiding to his diary, "This is the first day of the economic summit, and one of the worst days of my diplomatic life."[113] OPEC was meeting at the very same time and chose the moment to announce further price increases while blaming the Western consuming nations for the economic distress the move would create. The effect was to spread gloom and uncertainty and a sense of impotence. The United States wanted restrictions and quotas to cut consumption; the Japanese and the Europeans were reluctant to agree to specifics. They were not eager to do what the Americans had so far been unable or unwilling to do themselves and feared being locked into decisions that would not be reciprocated and that would therefore not produce the desired results. At the same time, the OPEC decisions convinced summit leaders of the need for consumer solidarity against seemingly unreasonable producers and to that extent undercut those, like the French, who still favored dialogue with the oil producers. The leaders of the major industrial countries became more convinced of the need to cope on their own and hence agreed on specific targets for consumption and imports; they also choose to give top priority to the fight against inflation even if that meant fiscal tightening, slower growth and higher unemployment. This stance would be combined with a sharp rebuke to OPEC and what looked at the time to be serious plans to limit oil imports, encourage conservation and move toward alternative supplies of energy.[114]

Success would depend, however, on the ability of the developed countries to reduce domestic consumption. To that end Carter planned a major speech in July 1979 aimed at generating support for a revamped set of initiatives. By now, however, Carter and his aides understood that the moralizing approach deployed over the previous two years had produced increased cynicism and that one more speech in the same vein would likely be ignored. The realization led Carter to postpone the speech and to spend eleven days sequestered at Camp David where he discussed the state of the nation with all sorts of people. He talked with critics such as Jesse Jackson, with the labor leader Lane Kirkland, with clergymen and academic pundits like Christopher Lasch, and with policy-makers; he also relied heavily on polling done by his advisor Patrick Caddell and on the ideas of his speechwriters. Like so much else that Carter did, the exercise was intrinsically worthy but the politics deeply misguided. On July 15 he emerged and went on television to explain why he had departed from his earlier plan to talk just about the energy crisis: "For the fifth time," he explained,

"I would have described the urgency of the problem and laid out a series of legislative recommendations to Congress." He had come to realize, however, that the problems were "much deeper . . . deeper even than inflation or recession." He detected "a crisis of confidence . . . that strikes at the heart and soul and spirit of our national will" and "is threatening to destroy the social and the political fabric of America." The crisis was manifest in a loss of faith "not only in government itself but in the ability as citizens to serve as the ultimate rulers and shapers of our democracy," in growing disrespect for "for churches and for schools," and in a troubling tendency "to worship self-indulgence and consumption." The President was particularly glum about the inability of the political system to produce effective action; instead, he lamented, the public was compelled to witness "a balanced and fair approach that demands sacrifice, a little sacrifice from everyone, abandoned like an orphan without support and without friends."[115]

Once again, Carter proposed a plan and Congress responded with far less than he asked.[116] More important than the legislative outcome was the political message. When Carter complained of good policies "abandoned like an orphan," he was transparently speaking of his own plans and his own fate. This confession of failure came, moreover, before the seizure of hostages in Iran and before the economic effects of the second oil shock were fully evident. In 1979 the United States did appear impotent, unable to respond effectively to a worsening economy. The U.S. was equally incapable of controlling the international environment and getting its way with a world that seemed out of control. There was in fact a loss of confidence and a loss of control, and the effect was to discredit those in power and their ideas and policy frameworks. When things do not work, democratic publics demand new leaders, ideas and strategies. The process is grossly unfair, for it punishes leaders who just happen to be in office when things stop working. It is nevertheless the mechanism by which democracies register choice and, perhaps, make progress. By the end of the 1970s, a succession of failures had elicited a revulsion against those in power and against the shared assumptions by which they governed; and it would usher in a huge shift in politics. The beneficiaries would be Ronald Reagan in the United States and Margaret Thatcher in the U.K. The election of two tough conservatives determined to transform politics as it had recently been practiced was in many ways coincidental, but in a deeper sense no accident at all.

CHAPTER 4

Thatcher, Reagan and the Market

A New Vision, a Recharged Relationship

Neither Margaret Thatcher nor Ronald Reagan looked inevitable before they were elected. Thatcher's popularity lagged behind that of her party, and her opponent, James Callaghan, might well have beaten her if he had called the election in the autumn of 1978, as he had planned and many had expected. He delayed, the "winter of discontent" wrecked his administration, and Thatcher won a solid but not spectacular victory in May 1979. Reagan ran against a government for which nothing went right, at home or abroad, and against a decidedly uncharismatic incumbent. Even so, the polls remained close until a week before the actual vote. His victory was decisive, but neither his triumph nor Thatcher's seemed to be the outcome of an unstoppable process.

Nor was it obvious that their elections would prove decisive in matters of policy or political philosophy. Callaghan did say that there are moments when politics undergoes a "sea-change" and that the election of 1979 was one of them, but his view was not widely shared. Respectable opinion regarded Thatcher and Reagan as to some extent aberrations, produced by unusually unhappy times, and the difficulties they confronted and the resistance they at first aroused suggested that they would not rule long enough to implement any radical new vision. Callaghan was proved right, and Reagan and Thatcher would genuinely transform politics in the countries they governed. The transformation would be first and foremost a matter of domestic policy, where the two regimes preached and practiced a return to markets and a sharp turn away from the state and from the assumption that the state not only had a responsibility for ensuring full employment and economic well-being but that it also had the ability to do so. It was also, and more or less simultaneously, a matter of the role of the U.S. and the U.K. in the world: if markets and democracy worked at home, the same combination should work everywhere and there was

no need to compromise with communism and its advocates. Fierce anticommunism, a commitment to creating the military strength required to back up
this policy, and an intense belief in markets were to be the defining features of
the foreign and domestic policies of the Thatcher and Reagan governments.
That the world's most powerful nation and its closest ally shared equally in this
vision greatly magnified its effect.

Especially important for the fate of that vision was the fact that Thatcher
and Reagan were determined from the beginning to use the crises they inherited to bring about a major shift in policy. When Thatcher took office in May
1979, virtually her first act was to insist that all departments immediately assess
the commitments they had inherited from the Labour government with an eye
to reversing course. Just two days into the job, Keith Joseph could report back
from the Department of Trade that he had found a new eagerness there "to
create a more encouraging framework for enterprise and effort," but that
"substantial savings will have to be made in what I regard as the unrealistic and
irresponsible pledges made by our predecessors . . ." Not all ministers were so
eager to cut back on what their new departments could or would do, but the
tone was set and would be maintained.[1] Within a month the Chancellor,
Geoffrey Howe, would introduce the government's first budget and begin in
earnest the process of lowering taxes and paring down expenditure.

In the United States the Reagan administration came into office in January
1981 with a similar resolve. Richard Allen, Reagan's National Security Advisor,
remembered more than a quarter-century later the "teams of Reaganauts
dispatched to each department or agency" armed with blueprints from right-
wing think tanks. "The plan from the outset was to put in place the Reagan
economic program as the major priority and foundation for every major initiative, domestic and foreign."[2] The country's new leaders understood the need to
act quickly and decisively.[3] An "Initial Actions Project" was put in place even
before Reagan assumed office. It operated on the assumption that the American
people, "Hoping for change . . . had elected Ronald Reagan to preside over a
restructuring and redirecting of public policy for the country." "The public
sense of urgency requires that the new President immediately undertake to
steer a new course, to advance policies designed to support that new direction,
and to follow those policies with firmness and consistency." More specifically,
the project's report argued, "The initial days of the new Reagan Administration
will be the time when his presidency will be under its closest scrutiny. What is
done or not done may well cast the die for what is recorded about the entire
four-year performance of the first Reagan Administration."[4]

Thatcher's and Reagan's shared enthusiasm for markets allowed for, indeed
encouraged, an ever closer connection between the two governments; and they

appeared to inspire one another. The "special relationship" between Britain and the United States did not appear all that special in 1979–80. Carter and Callaghan had got on reasonably well, and the United States and Britain continued to take the same side on most matters of foreign policy, but the link did not constitute a major force in international affairs. Peter Jay, U.K. Ambassador to Washington, reported to his superiors in February 1979 that "No one is now so foolish as to think that we are as important to the Americans as the United States is to us" and "Britain is not anywhere near central to the American world vision." The British were still "consulted for a second opinion on a wider range of problems overall than any other government"; and cooperation on matters of defense remained critical. And, of course, "our similarity of view and purpose over a wide area of world problems constitutes the most important feature of our relationship."[5]

Thatcher's election later that spring did little to bring the two countries and their leaders closer. Carter was an embattled president and nothing about him or his politics encouraged Thatcher to expect much from him. Their first serious encounter came at the Tokyo Economic Summit near the end of June 1979.[6] The American President was desperately seeking commitments from other countries to limit oil imports and to encourage conservation and alternative fuels. Thatcher believed that the market would take care of the oil crisis; besides, with North Sea oil flowing, Britain was better positioned to withstand shortages. Her main objective was to control inflation, which she believed had largely domestic sources in Britain. The U.S. wanted the U.K. on board, but Thatcher's approach differed fundamentally from Carter's. After the meeting, Carter wrote in his diary that Thatcher was "A tough lady . . . highly opinionated, strong willed, cannot admit she doesn't know anything."[7] Thatcher would claim later that "It was impossible not to like Jimmy Carter." It was obvious, however, that she did not respect him. He had stumbled into office because of Watergate: as a top official put it, "he was chosen because he was not a racist, not a war-monger, and not a crook."[8] He had not been elected, Thatcher argued, "because he had persuaded Americans of the rightness of his analysis" which, she believed "was badly flawed. He had an unsure handle on economics," was naive in foreign affairs and "in general he had no large vision of America's future." "In addition to these political flaws, he was in some ways ill-suited to the presidency, agonizing over big decisions and too concerned with detail."[9] And, maybe most important, he was unlucky.

There was not much personal warmth in these assessments, but it was also the case that the two leaders confronted enormous problems and had no reason to believe that closer ties would be of much use. Both countries were largely on the defensive in international affairs and neither seemed able to control its economic fate; and these fundamental weaknesses undermined both stable policy-making and historic alliances. During the 1970s the U.S. had seen reversals and challenges from the Middle East to Latin America, not to mention Vietnam; and it was forced to acknowledge and confront the strength and aggressiveness of the Soviet Union. Foreign policy for the U.K. had been a question of managing a strategic retreat while waiting and hoping for better times. When the mandarins of the Foreign Office worried about "surviving the 70s," that fearful perception defined the limits of their ambitions. The alliance with America would help, but not much, just as British support was mildly helpful to Kissinger and his schemes and later on to the Carter administration, but the alliance was never enough in a world that seemed so hostile and out of control to both countries and their beleaguered governments. The regular intercourse between diplomats, soldiers and spies sustained an infrastructure of mutual support, but its practical value was hard to see in the prevailing sense of crisis and in the absence of a strategy to reverse it.

The coming to power of Thatcher and Reagan did not make either country stronger or more useful to the other, at least not right away. Nor did it remove the resentments that were as much a part of the connection as the shared interests, values and heritage that held it together. What it did, however, was to unite the two countries, or their leaders, behind a common agenda. The promotion of markets and market-based democracy and increased resistance to Soviet communism, at least at the level of rhetoric, pushed Reagan and Thatcher into a uniquely close embrace. Reagan, and the United States, had other allies and some were more powerful economically than Britain; Thatcher had few soulmates, even within her own party at first, but Britain was a member of the European Community and European connections were becoming more pervasive. But with no other leaders, in Europe or elsewhere, did Reagan or Thatcher share a common view of the world, a common belief in the superiority of the market, a common antipathy to the state and what went with it – public ownership, public responsibility for the health of the economy, and extensive state provision of services – and an uncommonly intense hatred of communism.

Within days of Reagan's inauguration, the new closeness was publicly proclaimed. On January 29, 1981 Thatcher spoke to the Pilgrims Society in London about the supposed bases of the relationship between Britain and the U.S.: "representative democracy . . . economic liberty, and . . . the rule of law." More pointedly, she endorsed the new President's belief "that in the present crisis government is not the solution, it is part of the problem" and proceeded to note that "the economic policies of the new administration and of Her Majesty's Government are also strikingly similar." Both sought, she explained, to remove regulations and "set free the natural energies of our people."

"The President intends to increase incentives by reducing tax rates," while "We have already reduced rates of income tax and this Government believes that we must get government out of the pockets of our people." Thatcher ended with a promise to side with the U.S. on foreign policy and to join together to meet the Soviet challenge. Reagan responded to the Prime Minister just three days later and with enthusiasm, assuring Thatcher that "we share a very special concern for democracy and for liberty. That is the essence of the special relationship ..."[10] The similarity of views, and the conviction that they were both right and their opponents wrong, meant that a common agenda would become a joint crusade, a heroic effort to reshape domestic politics and the international system and to create, in effect, a new world order.

The common vision would be reinforced by what became a close personal relationship. The initial expression of mutual support was quickly followed by Thatcher's visit to the U.S. in late February. In her subsequent letter of thanks to Reagan, Thatcher was effusive: "We shall never have a happier visit," she concluded. Before he could respond, Reagan was shot by a would-be assassin on March 30. Thatcher immediately expressed her shock and concern and Reagan replied as soon as he was able. Already, his aides understood "the special relationship" between them and took care to convey an appropriate degree of intimacy.[11] It became more of a working relationship when Reagan attended his first economic summit in Ottawa in late June. The two met privately and Thatcher was keen to show support and deflect criticism of the U.S. Reagan in turn said that in dealing with other, and more experienced, leaders, he much appreciated "having Maggie on his side" and months later, he would recall how brilliantly she performed at the meeting and conclude a letter to "Margaret" by saying that "I look forward to the closest possible relations between our two countries. You know, of course, the esteem in which I hold our personal friendship."[12] In a very short time the alliance between the two states had not only become personal, but the personal attachments and beliefs of its leaders had begun largely to define the meaning of the alliance. The relationship was not always happy, for the short-term interests of the two countries were not always aligned. But the two leaders were also close enough and perceptive enough to be aware of one another's faults, and such intimate knowledge would serve to smooth over the rough patches.[13]

Reagan and Thatcher also seemed to understand that to support one another was to further their shared agenda. On occasion, each was encouraged to put some distance between himself, or herself, and the other, but they chose not to. In April 1981, for example, John Louis was appointed U.S. Ambassador to London and was reminded by his superiors of "the exceptionally good personal chemistry between the two leaders, the keen interest which the President has in Thatcher's leadership, and our desire to build on that essential rapport." Nevertheless, in July 1981 Louis sent back a "sobering picture" of a "troubling political, social and economic drift ... in London" and even suggested that "Thatcher has lost her grip on the political rudder."[14] The doubts apparently had no effect on the President's judgment then or later. Three years later, another Ambassador, Charles Price, forwarded to Reagan a piece from the *Economist* critical of Thatcher's style of running foreign policy. Reagan again refused to criticize, even in private, and told Price that the article "reminded me of U.S. media criticism of my policies. Margaret's perseverance and persuasiveness ..." he added, "have always been among her greatest strengths."[15] Reagan and Thatcher were also mindful of each other's domestic political needs, even when dealing with the wider world. The economic summit at Williamsburg in 1983 was held while Thatcher was fighting a general election campaign and the London Summit of 1984 took place while Reagan sought a second term. A British official noted the impact:

> Williamsburg had occurred in the middle of the British election campaign, and that fact had to a great extent dominated the proceedings, for nobody had wanted to complicate her job of fighting the election. There was the same feeling this year [1984] all through the preparations and at the summit itself. Everyone understood that President Reagan was in the middle of a campaign and no one wanted to rock the boat for him.[16]

Predictably enough, Reagan was "overjoyed" at Thatcher's 1983 victory and Thatcher could barely contain her excitement at Reagan's triumph in 1984: "What a victory! I cannot tell you how delighted I am."[17]

Not merely the personal relationship, then, but the broader effort by Thatcher and Reagan to make the world safe for markets and inhospitable for the enemies of capitalism would be sustained throughout the 1980s. Inevitably, the campaign was not always successful, but it had many successes; and the effect was to create a new paradigm informing domestic and foreign policy. It was a vision, moreover, that would not only appear to be justified by the return of economic growth and the taming of inflation by the mid–1980s but would appear to be vindicated in more dramatic fashion at the end of the 1980s, with the collapse of "actually existing socialism," first in Eastern Europe and then in the Soviet Union itself.[18] This unexpected result had the effect of ratifying the new framework and making it the starting point for policy after the end of the Cold War. If this outcome involved a great deal of luck, then it was fortune favoring those with a plan.

The paradigm has been called neoliberal in that it sought a return to the ideas of classical liberal political economy and the commitment to free trade and laissez-faire that characterized British economic policy after the repeal of the Corn Laws in 1846 and that had largely informed U.K. thinking and policy-making through the Great War.[19] The term does not resonate with Americans, however, who may be the most committed neoliberals but for whom liberalism has come to mean something rather different. It would seem better simply to speak about an era in which open markets are given special prominence. The outlook has also been termed "market fundamentalism," mainly by critics, and there has surely been something fanatical in the faith with which advocates of the market have pushed their belief.[20] What the usage misses, however, is the extent to which the turn to markets was based not merely on faith and ideology but on a reasoned critique of policies that were visibly failing. The world economy had slowed down in the 1970s and the policies adopted by governments, mostly Keynesian in inspiration, had failed to deal effectively with slow growth and rampant inflation. Policy failure did not mean that Keynes was wrong, merely that the problems confronting the major economies at the end of the "golden age" were not those toward which Keynesian thinking had been directed or for which Keynesian solutions had been devised. Nevertheless, the intractability of the economic challenges of the 1970s rendered a major rethinking of economic assumptions almost inevitable, and the desperation displayed by governments like those of Jimmy Carter and James Callaghan led understandably to the conclusion that the political philosophies and policy-making assumptions which guided their actions had seen their day. Indeed, the political discourse of the late 1970s was filled with confessions of failure and proclamations of the end of an era, however the era had been defined.

The emerging conventional wisdom was not merely a function of the collapse of the previously dominant Keynesian vision. It was also a product of a protracted effort at thinking, planning and debating the role of markets. Success was further aided by the simultaneous crisis in international relations. Although the economic woes of the 1970s were only indirectly related to the setbacks that the United States and Britain experienced in foreign policy, they were easily and plausibly linked at the level of perception and rhetoric: U.S. economic dominance seemed to evaporate at roughly the same time as its capacity effectively to confront opponents; and the government's failure to control rising prices seemed a product of America's inability to compel the Arab states to supply oil at reasonable prices; decline in Britain was a multifaceted affair in which imperial retreat and economic decline came to be understood as manifestations of a broader phenomenon. All this combined to make the late 1970s and early 1980s a time when new, or not so new, ideas were given a hearing.

Even so, the thinkers and politicians who fought to move politics away from reliance on the state and toward markets deserve considerable credit. As a group they had been largely ignored in the 1950s and 1960s, their belief in markets regarded as quaintly irrelevant and their antipathy toward the state considered not merely wrong but dangerously reactionary, yet they persisted. The key thinker, with influence in both the U.S. and the U.K., was Friedrich Hayek. Hayek was an Austrian émigré economist who taught at the London School of Economics (LSE) and at the University of Chicago before concluding his career at Freiburg. In the 1920s he was greatly influenced by a fellow Austrian, Ludwig von Mises, who insisted that the "economic calculation problem" rendered socialism impossible. Hayek worked for and collaborated with von Mises, who would also leave Austria to teach first in Geneva and then in the United States.

Both men were deeply moved by their first-hand experience of fascism and perhaps the key feature of their outlook was the conflation of communism and fascism. In 1944 Hayek put his arguments and fears into words in his famous book *The Road to Serfdom*.[21] The book's emotional intensity owed a great deal to Hayek's antipathy to, and understanding of, fascism. In fact, one might reasonably argue that "the real subject of the book is Germany."[22] The volume was nevertheless dedicated to "the socialists of all parties" and its argument condemned all attempts at planning as leading ineluctably to centralized control and some form of dictatorship. Leaders of the British Conservative Party were much impressed and the attack on socialism as inimical to freedom became the central theme of the Tory election campaign in 1945. Churchill's famous suggestion that Labour in power would need "some form of Gestapo" to do its business reflected, at least indirectly, Hayek's influence; and the Conservatives sought desperately to get an abridged version of the book published in time for the election. In the U.S., *Reader's Digest* succeeded in the task in April 1945, but it was not available in Britain. It is unlikely that wide-spread distribution would have altered the outcome of the election, but its prominence in the debate ensured that the essay would be read again and again and become the leading antisocialist tract of the postwar era.

Hayek was also a surprisingly effective organizer, and in the late 1940s he joined with other free-market advocates to create an international association that took its name from the Swiss resort where it first met in 1947: the Mont Pelerin Society.[23] The avowed aim was to emulate the Fabians earlier in the century, who sought to win over elites to their vision of the future. There was little expectation of immediate success; rather, the plan was a prolonged effort to undermine what economic liberals regarded as the reigning consensus – a mix of Keynes, state ownership, and collective social provision underpinned by over-mighty trade unions. Hayek was himself inspired by Keynes's comments about the lasting power of ideas, about how politicians – even "Madmen … who hear voices in the air" – "are distilling their frenzy from some academic scribbler of a few years back" and his insistence that "it is ideas, not vested interests, which are dangerous for good or evil." As he told the first meeting of the Mont Pelerin Society, "It is … from this long run point of view that we must look at our task."[24] The strategy was to fight the battle of ideas over a protracted period so as to keep them alive and fresh when an opportunity arose to implement them. On this, Milton Friedman, a close ally of Hayek's, was even clearer:

> There is enormous inertia – a tyranny of the status quo – in private and especially governmental arrangements. Only a crisis – actual or perceived – produces real change. When that crisis occurs, the actions that are taken depend on the ideas that are lying around. That, I believe, is our basic function: to develop alternatives to existing policies, to keep them alive and available until the politically impossible becomes politically inevitable.[25]

Hayek estimated that although "in each country those who think actively on these questions [and who presumably agreed with him] are comparatively few, combined they represent a considerable force …"[26] It was with this understanding that Hayek and friends put together a widespread network of economic liberals across Europe, and especially in the U.K. and the U.S. Their efforts were assisted by friendly businessmen and conservative business organizations who provided the funds; and the movement achieved a real measure of respectability from the fact that its intellectual leaders were employed by the LSE and the University of Chicago. Hayek himself taught at both places; Lionel Robbins, a very effective organizer, was at the LSE; and Friedman was at Chicago. Politically, support came mainly from the right, though Hayek himself had some hopes for a revival of the Liberal Party on the basis of free-market principles and was quite suspicious of British Conservatives, with their paternalistic traditions and apparent comfort with an expanded state, and who in the 1950s and 1960s seemed to have acquiesced in the dominance of Keynesian economics and come to terms with the welfare state.

These market enthusiasts were ambivalent about all political parties, because parties aimed to win elections and to govern. That typically led parties to appeal to the political center and to adopt policies that did not depart substantially from the current consensus. Ideologues, in contrast, are free to propagate their ideas without worrying about voters' reactions; and that was what the odd collection of economic liberals in the U.S. and the U.K. did in the postwar era. They wrote, they conferred, and they founded think tanks. The earliest and most important of the latter were the American Enterprise Institute, which dated back to 1938, and, in the U.K., the Institute of Economic Affairs, founded in 1955. Their critiques had little impact during the 1950s, at least in part because centrist conservatives were in power in both countries for most of the decade, but their message began to get more of a hearing in the 1960s. In the United States, the backlash against the extension of civil rights, the counterculture and the movement against the Vietnam War created an atmosphere in which criticism of the state managed take root. In Britain, the policy failures of the Wilson government gave new force to arguments against the state. The economic difficulties of the 1970s and the desperation of governments unable to cope with them provoked a still more decisive turn away from what had been the orthodoxies of postwar and toward the message on offer from free-market conservatives. The context would inspire the formation of a host of new think tanks – such as the Heritage Foundation and the Cato Institute in the U.S., and the Adam Smith Institute in the U.K. – and it would also lead to their growing influence within the major parties of the right. In Britain, Keith Joseph founded the Centre for Policy Studies in 1974 in order "to convert the Tory Party" to the merits of the market.[27] The Heritage Foundation played much the same role in America and it is reported that Ronald Reagan gave every member of his Cabinet a copy of the Foundation's report, *Mandate for Leadership*, at its very first meeting.[28]

A Touch of Class War

Advocates of the market thus worked hard to change minds, but without the multiple crises of the 1970s neither voters nor politicians would have been convinced. Public opinion was unsettled and angry in both countries and politicians felt compelled to respond. American politics became increasingly polarized from the late 1960s, as the Republican Party sought consciously to put together a new majority based on resentment toward students, blacks and antiwar protesters.[29] Richard Nixon was the perfect embodiment of the sentiment and an early beneficiary of the strategy.[30] Watergate served to deepen the sense of rage within the body politic. So, too, did the ongoing debate about race. Liberal attempts to use government to redress the wrongs visited upon generations of African Americans might have worked in an era of sustained prosperity, but at a time of economic dislocation they produced deep resentment among whites, and not only those who lived in the South. Talk of "welfare queens," fear of rising crime in the cities and proposals for affirmative action and "community control" of schools all neatly mixed criticisms of specific public policies with the question of race. It was out of this highly charged discourse that the first identifiable neoconservatives emerged: they were essentially New Deal liberals who "had been mugged by reality," in this case the realities of race in contemporary America.[31] Tough times also led to widespread and almost spontaneous tax revolts.[32] The most successful was the movement that passed Proposition 13 in California, which in 1978 placed restrictions on property taxes that have remained in place ever since, and it had many successful imitators elsewhere.

This agitation on the political right meant that the election of Ronald Reagan in November 1980 was the triumph of a movement, though it was rather less an intellectual phenomenon than a genuine reaction. The election of Thatcher was equally a triumph of reaction, though the movement in the U.K. was rather less populist in character and focused not so much on government policy or issues of race but on and against the trade unions. The Labour government of 1974 had been uniquely dependent on the goodwill of the unions and when that goodwill was withdrawn it provoked a sense of outrage that the fate of the nation and the economy should be so vulnerable. It mattered little that trade union leaders had worked hard for several years to hold back their members and assist the government in managing the economy; nor did it matter much that trade unionists, particularly in the public sector, had fallen behind economically. What did matter was that unelected officials in the unions could derail the plans of the elected government and that the government, in turn, had been unable to get control of the situation.

This imbalance was evident even before the "winter of discontent," and it had been demonstrated with devastating effect in the confrontations between the Heath government and the miners in 1972 and in 1973–4. The latter conflict led to the imposition of a three-day week and cuts in power, and prompted Heath to call an election on the question of who should rule – the government or the unions. The electorate gave a confusing answer in February 1974, when it refused to provide a mandate for either party. Clearly, however, Heath had lost and memories of the defeat inflicted on the party by the miners came to haunt Conservatives throughout the 1970s. The coming to office of the Labour Party in 1974 gave unions even more clout, for they were now genuine partners in government, but public opinion had already begun to turn. In the run-up to 1979 the Conservatives were cautious in what they promised about the unions, but privately they seethed over the extent of union power and what it meant for the sovereignty of Parliament. Thatcher had already made the case at the party conference of 1975: "If we are told that a Conservative government could not govern because extreme leaders would not let it, then general elections are a mockery, we have arrived at the one-party state and parliamentary democracy in this country will have perished."[33] Although Thatcher insisted that the good sense of union members would guarantee that it never came to that, her dissatisfaction with the present state of affairs was palpable and she encouraged people in her entourage to think bold thoughts about how to handle the unions. Her iconoclastic advisors, John Hoskyns and Norman Strauss, responded in late 1977 with "Stepping Stones," a paper which insisted that for a Tory government to achieve success, it would have to take on the trade unions and defeat them. "The task of the next Tory government – national recovery – will be of a different order from that facing any other post-war government," proclaimed the authors. For that reason "The Tory Party's pre-election strategy must ensure that the preparation of policy includes plans for the removal of political obstacles to its implementation . . . There is one major obstacle – the negative role of the trades unions."[34] The paper was too forceful and explicit for some of Thatcher's Shadow Cabinet colleagues and so did not become party policy before the election; and once in office Thatcher would move with caution. However, as the miners above all would discover in 1984–5, when she moved, she moved decisively; and they would be crushed.

So the victories of Thatcher and Reagan were simultaneously more and less than intellectual triumphs and not merely the occasions for paradigm shifts on matters of public policy. They were that, but they were something else as well: they were elections that transferred power from the cluster of interests and actors who had overseen the politics of postwar and had become invested in it to interests and movements that had felt disadvantaged and increasingly resentful. It was a transfer with winners and losers and with great consequences; and it would not take long for the new balance of power to become evident. The clearest examples were in tax policy and industrial relations. In Britain, the Thatcher government inherited an unprecedented rate of inflation and sought desperately to rein in prices, but it refused to countenance the kind of incomes policy that would have given the trade unions a voice in economic management. Nor, despite rising unemployment and a generally sluggish economy, would Thatcher consider any measures to stimulate the economy. The Prime Minister, according to one of her aides, "believes there can be no scope for a stimulus to demand until we see real improvements on the supply side of the economy."[35] Instead, the focus would be on reducing government borrowing and thus reducing the burden and limiting the extent of government involvement in the economy. When the Chancellor and the Treasury produced a plan that did rather less than she wanted, Thatcher called them all together and told them pointedly that "The Treasury approach . . . was not nearly tough enough," and that "In her view, the Chancellor should be aiming to reduce the PSBR [Public Sector Borrowing Requirement] to £7.5 billion in

1979/80 – rather than the £8 billion he was apparently thinking of."[36] Among the Thatcher government's very first acts, therefore, was "a dogmatically inegalitarian budget" that drastically cut the standard rate of income tax as well as the top rates of tax. This was made possible only by a near doubling of the Value Added Tax (VAT) on goods and services, the pain of which was in theory spread across all income levels but which in fact hurt the lower and middle classes much more than the wealthy. These were accompanied by sharp reductions in spending, particularly on subsidies to nationalized industries, and the beginnings of sales of government assets – including £500 million worth of BP shares.[37]

In the United States, Reagan likewise announced a "program for economic recovery". Within weeks of taking office he called for 10 percent reductions in income tax rates in each of the next three years, a cut of roughly $47 billion from Carter's last budget, and various kinds of direct support to business through new depreciation rules and regulatory relief.[38] Congressional passage was more or less guaranteed by the new President's popularity, by the fact that previous policies were seen to have failed, and by the fact that the economy was in crisis. As Murray Weidenbaum, Reagan's economic advisor, explained, "The American economy is in many ways in its worst shape since the Great Depression."[39] This was not quite how the program was presented. Rhetorically, the package was framed around the fashion for "supply-side economics," which at the time incorporated the slightly fantastic "Laffer curve" with its claim that lowering taxes would more or less automatically increase revenue by unleashing entrepreneurial spirits.[40] Behind the fantasy, however, was a cold logic of redistribution from the bottom to the top. And once again there would be very definite winners and losers.[41]

It is not always easy to see who wins and loses in battles over the budget. A shift from direct to indirect taxes, for example, can be more or less regressive depending on what is taxed and what is exempt. The VAT increase by the Thatcher government exempted very little and thus redistributed income in a regressive fashion, but because it was embedded in prices, it was not particularly visible. It boosted inflation in the short term, but after that the increased rate was the new norm and compensated for reduced income tax rates. The reduction in income tax rates in both countries was more clearly regressive, though the unpopularity of income tax probably muted the opposition to the shifts. The distributional effects of raising or lowering the rates of income tax are in any event less straightforward than is often assumed, for the actual impact will depend on allowances, deductions and loopholes. The Reagan budget not only lowered the rates for people with higher incomes, but gave businessmen and the wealthy new opportunities to deduct expenses. The claim was that this would lead to more investment, but it also shifted the tax burden from the well-to-do to ordinary taxpayers. The first budgets of both Thatcher and Reagan were in this sense clear examples of class legislation, even if they were couched in a populist rhetoric.

The winners and losers were still clearer in the battles between the two governments and the trade unions. The unions were the key interest supporting both the Labour Party in Britain and the Democrats in the U.S.; and they had also been major beneficiaries of the economic and social policies of the postwar era. Weakening them was a top objective for conservatives in both countries. The process would be aided, perhaps even begun, by the recession of the early 1980s, and furthered after that by industrial shifts that reduced employment in the industries where unions were strong and increased it where they had yet to gain a foothold. But it was reinforced, and decisively so, by legal offensives and industrial confrontations.

The matter was of greatest import in Britain, where unions were far stronger than in the United States and where they were deeply integrated into the corporatist style of governance. Thatcher's first moves involved downgrading and then abolishing the key institution through which such policy-making occurred: the National Economic Development Council (NEDC). The routine consultations that had almost defined politics during the previous Labour government simply ended. The government's subsequent moves were carefully chosen. The previous Conservative government had been brought down in a confrontation with the miners and the Callaghan government was done in by the "winter of discontent." Thatcher learned the lesson and took great care to have the government prepare for its battles with the unions and to fight only when confident of winning.

Instead of a direct attack, the Thatcher government began with legislation that constrained the activities of the unions, particularly during strikes. For leaders in the Trades Union Congress (TUC), a major reason for acquiescing in the "social contract" and working to sustain the Labour government in office after 1974 had been the fear that the Tories would impose legislation regulating the activities of the trade unions. The government proceeded incrementally: the 1980 legislation restricted picketing and made secondary action unlawful; it granted compensation to workers who ran afoul of the closed shop and made it harder to establish closed shop arrangements; and it allocated government money to unions to hold ballots. The 1982 Act went a bit further: it imposed further restrictions on the closed shop; made unions liable for damages resulting from illegal strikes and industrial action; and it narrowed the range of acceptable industrial disputes to disagreements with employers on pay and conditions and thus ruled out strike action on other issues or designed to affect third parties – such as government or other employers.

The Tories' legislation brought predictable cries of outrage and repeated calls for "days of action," but it was implemented. The unions were hampered by the fact that, after the "winter of discontent," they enjoyed diminished public support. They were crippled as well by the way in which rising unemployment undermined their industrial strength; and they were further thwarted by the care with which the government waged its campaign to curb union power. Despite her reputation as a combative foe, Thatcher avoided provocation and proceeded one step at a time, all the while allowing unemployment to do indirectly what Edward Heath had been unable to accomplish directly. With a solid electoral victory in 1983, it became possible for the government to move more decisively against its opponents.

The critical event was the defeat of the miners' strike in 1984–5.[42] It was the miners who had pioneered a new level and style of industrial militancy in 1972 – with "flying pickets" and secondary boycotts – and it was they who had effectively brought down the government in 1974. The Thatcher government was determined to exact revenge, but moved with caution. During her first term, Thatcher faced down strikes by steelworkers in 1980, civil servants in 1981, health workers in 1982 and water workers the next year. In January 1984 the staff at the spy agency GCHQ Cheltenham were informed that they were not allowed to belong to a union because of national security considerations. The decision was handled clumsily by Geoffrey Howe, who had moved from being Chancellor of the Exchequer to Foreign Secretary in 1983: he was repeatedly forced to deny that he was acting at the behest of the U.S. but managed to convince everyone that he was.[43] It was nevertheless clear that public sector unions, so central to the "winter of discontent," no longer had privileged access to, or sympathy from, the state they served.

The Thatcher government backed away from a confrontation over pit closures in 1981 and would avoid taking on the miners until Thatcher's second term. It did so only after key pieces of legislation were in place, coal supplies were abundant, and contingency plans had been made to protect the movement of coal throughout the country. The thoroughness with which the government prepared for battle was not matched by a comparable tactical intelligence on the part of the miners. Arthur Scargill, who succeeded to the presidency of the National Union of Mineworkers (NUM) in 1982, had first become known as a militant local leader during the conflicts of the 1970s, and he was very much on the left of the labor movement. Immersed in the world of the miners, he failed to grasp that the conditions which had facilitated the union's earlier victories had altered fundamentally, and that in Margaret Thatcher he faced a far more determined opponent than Edward Heath. Upon taking office as NUM president, Scargill moved its headquarters from London to Sheffield – a suitably democratic gesture that nonetheless signaled what would become a pattern of ignoring unpleasant political realities at the national level and focusing instead on the local, the familiar and the reassuring. This was reinforced by the fact that the national context was far less hospitable: the government was proceeding with plans to build up coal stocks for a future dispute; closures were continuing; and in September 1983 Ian MacGregor, the scourge of the steel industry's workers, was appointed to head the National Coal Board. Discontent in the coalfields simmered, but in ballots held in October 1982 and again in March 1983 over 60 percent of miners voted not to strike. The government presumably took note of the pessimism among the miners; Scargill did not.

The strike broke out in March 1984 when pickets were called out in Yorkshire in response to a decision to close a local pit and to a plan for more extensive closures. The stoppage soon spread to Scotland, South Wales and Kent and quickly became a de facto national strike. The NUM argued correctly that the government planned to close a large number of pits and so felt justified in utilizing pickets to spread the dispute into a national confrontation. But Scargill never chanced a vote, and his refusal to ballot the members gave the government an effective propaganda weapon. Neil Kinnock, the new leader of the Labour Party, was appalled at the tactics of the miners' leaders and their determination to press ahead with a prolonged stoppage in the face of the sure knowledge that the Coal Board could hold out for a long time. He also grasped immediately that Scargill was making a tactical mistake by not holding a ballot and told him explicitly that what the Tories wanted most was "no ballot" for they foresaw "enormous political profit for them if they can use the taunt of no ballot." Indeed, not just the Tories but the "people in the street" felt that the consultations undertaken by the miners' executive did not have "the validity of the national ballot that was being called for." Scargill resisted and confided to Kinnock that he might only get the support of 54 to 57 percent of the members, possibly less, and fretted over the impact of such a narrow margin.[44] Even after Kinnock went public with his support for a ballot, the NUM refused. The choice undermined the legitimacy of the miners' case and raised profound doubts about Scargill's leadership. The sense that he, and the strikers, might not be speaking for the entire workforce was further reinforced by the fact that coal continued to be mined and transported from the more profitable pits in Nottinghamshire. The dispute would drag on for a year and the consequences lingered long after. Its conduct was marked by violence on the picket line, partly provoked by the police but made almost inevitable by the miners' tactics. Various compromise solutions were floated, but none were agreed. In

December 1984 Scargill and the left urged a general strike, but received little response. By January, the drift back to work was increasing; and the strike formally ended on March 5, 1985.

A particularly tense moment in the confrontation came during the summer of 1984, when dockworkers joined the miners on strike. At precisely that moment, Thatcher received a letter from Washington. On July 18, President Reagan wrote:

> In recent weeks I have thought often of you with considerable empathy as I follow the activities of the miners' and dockworkers' unions. I know they present a difficult set of issues for your government . . . I just wanted you to know that my thoughts are with you as you address these important issues; I'm confident as ever that you and your government will come out of this well.

Thatcher responded a week later saying that she "was touched by your message." She had waited to reply until she had learned that the dockers' dispute was settled and the ports were open again. "The miners' dispute," she explained, "has not yet been resolved" but she was "confident that in due course firmness and patience will achieve a victory for the forces of moderation and common-sense which are Britain's traditional sources of strength." Thatcher ended by confiding that when dealing with such issues it was "good to know that we have the support of our friends."[45] Presumably, heads of state often sympathize with each other and the problems with which they have to deal, although just as often they must experience a touch of *Schadenfreude* at others' difficulties. What is rather more rare is such a frank admission that they are in close sympathy on matters of a purely domestic character. But Reagan and Thatcher were in fact locked in what was understood as a joint venture in remaking the political and economic landscape of the two countries. As Antony Acland, British Ambassador to Washington from 1986, put it, "Margaret Thatcher believed in the same things as Reagan. That's why they had this good relationship, because they both believed in the same things."[46]

Again, however, the realities they faced differed considerably. Trade unions in the United States were much weaker than in Britain and the Reagan administration had less reason to orchestrate a campaign against them. Republicans were on the whole not terribly sympathetic to the claims and pretensions of unions, but organized labor was not seen as the enemy in quite the way it was in Britain. In fact, there were notable pockets of support for the Republicans among trade unionists, particularly white workers in the building trades. Still, in a critical early contest the Reagan government displayed its fundamental lack of sympathy by inflicting a decisive defeat upon the air traffic controllers.

In the summer of 1981 their union, PATCO, called a strike which had the potential to shut down the nation's airways. PATCO had actually endorsed Reagan for President in 1980 and apparently calculated that its politics and its strategic position gave it an advantage. The union judged wrong, for Reagan responded in resolute fashion: he used military personnel to do the jobs vacated by the strikers and fired 11,000 of them. The union was effectively destroyed and an unmistakable message had been sent: as Reagan himself later wrote, it was "an important juncture for our new administration . . . it convinced people who might have thought otherwise that I meant what I said."[47]

Freeing the Market

The full working out of Reagan and Thatcher's vision would involve a much wider array of policy initiatives.[48] The two free-market crusaders would look to one another for inspiration, but because Britain and the United States were different countries with different economies, inherited structures and political traditions, they faced different challenges and opportunities. Put very simply, Britain had created a universal and comprehensive welfare state after World War II, while the United States had scattered, incoherent and far less generous systems of support that did not merit the phrase "welfare state." The U.S. had welfare, but it was considered anomalous and many of its beneficiaries undeserving. The Labour governments of 1945–51, which did so much to establish the welfare state, had also nationalized large parts of the economy. The mines, the railways, the electrical industry, even for a while steel and sections of road transport, were taken into public ownership, and the economic difficulties of the 1970s led to a further wave of interventions that amounted to nationalization. Equally important, many in the Labour Party and in the governments of 1964–70 and 1974–9 believed that the secret to sustained growth was still more government enterprise. Conservatives tended to disagree, but at the margins. In the United States, by contrast, government was traditionally more favorably predisposed toward business and reluctant to intervene in the economy, and both Democrats and Republicans tended to defer to the market. This stance was combined, however, with a much greater willingness to impose formal legal regulation on business. Consumer protection, antitrust, and bank regulation were the traditional mechanisms through which this was done. The approach was developed further during the 1970s. The crisis of Republicanism brought about by Watergate, which distracted and weakened Nixon before destroying him, allowed for a surge of legislation on the environment, occupational health and safety and the rights of women and minorities that built upon and extended these precedents.[49]

Advocates of free and unregulated markets and opponents of state involvement therefore faced different realities in the two countries. In both countries, there was the issue of inflation and the desire to rein in government expenditure. In Britain, this took the form of controls on the money supply and on government borrowing justified by a variation on free-market economics known as "monetarism," which focused on controlling the money supply. Monetarism per se proved ineffective as government found itself unable to measure or control the amount of money in circulation, but the policy sent the appropriate macroeconomic message and the economy experienced a massive slowdown. Recession pushed some expenditures up, such as unemployment benefits, but the overall impact was to slow at least the rate of growth of public spending. In the United States, the anti-inflationary work was mainly done by the unprecedentedly high interest rates set by the Federal Reserve under Paul Volcker, who had actually been appointed by Reagan's predecessor. The Federal Funds rate reached 20 percent in June 1981, and the prime rate actually hit 21.5 percent a year later. The Reagan administration's strategy was to cut tax rates and it claimed the reductions would be matched with cuts in expenditure. This did not happen, but it did lead to deficits that could be used to argue against increases in spending that the administration did not like. David Stockman, Reagan's budget chief, later admitted that this was the objective. These restrictive policies differed technically, but combined to produce huge job losses in both the U.S. and the U.K. In fact, the recession of 1981–2 was the worst since World War II and inevitably the two governments were placed on the defensive.

Despite growing criticism and dismal poll numbers, however, the two regimes did not reverse course. Instead, they worked even harder to implement their free-market vision. Thatcher gave classic expression to her, and later Reagan's, resolve when she told the House of Commons in July 1980 that "It is no good dreaming of U-turns" and, more famously, when she said to the Conservative Party conference in October: "You turn if you want to, the Lady's not for turning." In practical terms that would mean a reassertion of the primacy of the fight against inflation and further efforts to abandon government ownership and responsibility. The decisive moment came with the massively deflationary budget of March 1981, denounced not just by the government's political opponents but by almost everyone, including many in the business community. No fewer than 364 university economists wrote to *The Times* (March 30, 1981) asserting that "There is no basis in economic theory or supporting evidence for the Government's belief that in deflating demand they will bring inflation permanently under control and thereby introduce an automatic recovery in output and employment." But protests made little impact and the fiscal stance remained austere; at the same time, the government began moving forward with its efforts to shrink the public sector.

Nigel Lawson, the energy secretary and future Chancellor, announced in November 1981, for example, that "No industry should remain under State ownership unless there is a positive and overwhelming case for doing so."[50] Ultimately, huge chunks of industry would be privatized and sold off to investors. In addition, the houses and apartments in which so many working people lived, and which had been built with state support and run by local authorities, would be sold off to their tenants at bargain prices. These parallel tasks would take more than two full terms in office to complete, and in her first term Thatcher mainly prepared the ground by seeking to restructure the nationalized industries so as to reduce the subsidies that government paid out and to make them more attractive to potential investors. As early as 1979 the government had begun the selling off of its stake in British Petroleum and dismantling the National Enterprise Board with its public holdings in a variety of firms; over the next decade it oversaw the privatization of Amersham International (a pharmaceutical company), British Telecom, British Aerospace, the British National Oil Company or Britoil (responsible for much of the development of North Sea oil), British Sugar, British Shipbuilders, Cable and Wireless, Jaguar, British Gas, British Airways, Rolls-Royce PLC, British Airports, British Steel, the water authorities and electricity generation, while British Rail sold off its most profitable assets.[51]

Reagan was a great fan of Thatcher's privatization program, but in the United States there was little to privatize. There were, however, numerous regulations to rescind or undo; and there was always scope for further tax reductions. The politics of deficits and taxation differed considerably in the two countries. London's historic role as the world's great financial center and as the seat of an enormous empire had led the U.K. to adopt a commitment to fiscal responsibility. Paying tax and balancing the state's budget were the price to be paid. The United States was different in that the nation's wealth and productivity made fiscal irresponsibility easier and allowed a popular antipathy to the state and to taxation to thrive without serious consequences and to become embedded in the nation's political culture. The focus of British Conservatives on deficits and debt therefore grew from a long tradition; and the Reagan administration's more casual attitude toward deficits, which tripled over Reagan's two terms, likewise stemmed from America's fiscal history. The result was that the Thatcher government's efforts to control spending were more sustained and effective throughout the 1980s; under Reagan, by contrast, lower taxes did not prompt comparable reductions in spending overall, and lower spending on specific social services was regularly offset by higher spending on defense.

If deficit reduction was hard, it was easier and more rewarding for Republicans to take aim at public policies and government programs to which they were ideologically hostile. They worked tirelessly to remove regulations on the environment and occupational health and safety and did whatever they could to weaken enforcement. Republicans even proposed on more than one occasion to eliminate the Education Department, for its mere existence bespoke a government role in what Republicans considered the preserve of individuals, families, states, localities and, of course, churches. It got a reprieve in 1985 with the appointment as Secretary of William Bennett, who used it as a vehicle to attack allegedly failing schools and teachers' unions, to promote a conservative social agenda, and to launch a career as a right-wing pundit. A particular revealing and appropriate appointment was that of James Watt. The founder of the Mountain States Legal Foundation, which fought legal battles on behalf of property rights, and a fundamentalist Christian, Watt became Reagan's first Secretary of the Interior and as such was charged with protecting and preserving the country's environment and natural resources. His preference for markets and his willingness to deplete the resources available to future generations went together perfectly, for his faith in capitalism was intertwined with his belief that the world would soon end. "I do not know how many future generations we can count on before the Lord returns," he once told Congress. Why worry about a future that might never arrive?

Republicans' dislike of government also led to a rather cavalier attitude toward running its offices and programs. It therefore came as little surprise when an unusually high number of administration officials were charged with, and occasionally convicted of, fraud and mismanagement. If public programs were a waste of taxpayers' money, why not use them for private enrichment while seeking to limit or abolish them? Reagan and his allies betrayed a special animus toward those agencies and policies that had been put in place to further a liberal agenda. A commitment to "affirmative action" was replaced by a concern with the "reverse discrimination" that supposedly resulted from its application; and the administration was eager to back off from laws and judgments that were meant to guarantee rights for women, labor and minorities. In 1981 administration supporters also launched a campaign to "defund the left," which aimed to reduce funding to public programs that provided lawyers to represent the poor or otherwise provided support for efforts to claim from government rights that had been enacted by Congress or mandated by the courts.

The focus on enforcement – on reducing its reach and effectiveness – and on adjudication was smart strategy for Republicans, for it recognized that many of the major achievements of liberal politics had come by way of the courts or through legislation that endowed citizens with the legal status to seek redress for grievances. Whatever rights such laws or rulings established would be rendered meaningless if they were not enforced. Likewise, getting the courts to change their minds and overturning legislation or limiting its effects would have the same result. In consequence, nothing did more to advance the administration's conservative and free-market objectives than the large number of judicial appointments that Reagan was able to make. The President elevated William Rehnquist to Chief Justice of the Supreme Court and appointed three new justices. He failed with the nomination of Robert Bork, but overall managed to move the Court sharply to the right; and he succeeded in appointing over 350 judges in lower courts.[52]

Embedding the Market Revolution

The "Reagan revolution" in domestic policy was meant to be enduring. It not only changed specific policies but rearranged the political landscape by altering the relationship between state and society, the government and the economy, in such a way that subsequent administrations would have great difficulty reversing course. The Thatcher governments aimed at a similar transformation in the U.K. The British state had been able to involve itself in the affairs of industry throughout the postwar era because it had in place many direct and indirect controls and because it actually owned big sections of the economy. Removing controls wherever possible and divesting itself of ownership removed from the state's grasp these critical levers over the economy. In both the U.S. and the U.K. the state continued to have at its disposal powerful tools for managing the economy: government set fiscal and monetary policy and retained responsibility for international economic policy, although membership in the European Community meant that British trade policy was mostly made in Europe. These were blunt instruments that operated at the aggregate or macro level, however, and more precise and refined interventions became harder to carry out and thus harder to contemplate. Equally important, both the Reagan and Thatcher governments insisted that this was as it should be and that the state was not responsible for protecting particular industries or guaranteeing employment. They insisted further that shrinking the state and getting government out of the way would be a more effective means of promoting growth.

Such claims were hard to sustain during the steep recession of 1981–2. Neither government backed off, however, and over time the economy improved. Most important in the short term was the retreat of oil prices and hence inflation, visible in both countries by late 1981. This was in part a by-product of the recession itself. Because it had been the inability of previous governments to stem the rise in prices that did so much to discredit their policies, however, success in the battle against inflation constituted a major achievement for the Reagan and Thatcher governments. It made it possible for them to claim credit for tackling what had been seen, and what they had identified, as the major economic problem they had inherited on taking office.

It would be largely on this claim that they would fight and win the elections of 1983 and 1984. Neither of these campaigns would have been successful had the question of jobs risen to the top of the list of voters' concerns, for although recovery began in late 1982, employment revived more slowly. Indeed, the slowdown in the world economy produced by the second oil shock and its reduction in purchasing power was especially severe in the two countries, for it was reinforced in the U.K. by fiercely deflationary budgets and in the U.S. by extremely high interest rates. One in ten workers in both countries were unemployed in 1982; and as of January 1983, U.S. unemployment averaged 11.4 percent and the U.K. figure was 11 percent.[53] The political effects were unambiguous: in the opinion polls Thatcher lagged far behind her opponents throughout the first half of 1982 and in the U.S. the Republicans would lose twenty-six seats in the House of Representatives in the midterm elections of November 1982.

Thatcher and Reagan nevertheless went on to win reelection by large margins; and securing a second term allowed the two kindred regimes not only to go on and advance their agendas, but to claim a mandate for doing so. Just how they won differed, though both profited greatly from the easing of inflation and from the inadequacy of their opponents. Reagan was also buoyed by what had, by late 1983, become a strong economic recovery. When American voters had gone to the polls for the midterm elections of 1982, unemployment was 10.8 percent and the Republicans lost badly; just two years later, it stood at 7.2 percent, a drop of better than 3 percent. In Britain, in contrast, Thatcher's political fortunes began to recover well before the economy did. In fact, unemployment peaked at almost 12 percent in 1984 and did not dip below 10 percent until late 1987, after yet a third Tory victory.[54] For the Conservatives, improving poll results followed closely on the heels of victory in the Falklands War. The expedition to the South Atlantic was in fact a risky affair and the British stance was not beyond challenge. On the other hand, the foe was a brutal and reckless dictatorship, so when the military operation succeeded, doubts and criticisms dissipated and the government could make a claim to competence and to military prowess that, in echoing a past receding from memory, put the recent sorry record of weakness and retreat in sharp relief.

At least as important in ensuring Thatcher's victory was the division and incoherence of the opposition. Defeat in May 1979 brought no respite to the troubled Labour leadership: Callaghan, beaten and tired, hung on and those who made his time in office so difficult continued to torment him. The left of the party persisted in its pursuit of two main goals: committing the party to a left-wing program; and, more important, making sure that future governments would carry out such policies by somehow binding Members of Parliament and party leaders. The effort led to demands for the routine reselection of candidates for Parliament, and thus the very real possibility of deselection if local activists felt betrayed; for taking away from MPs the power to choose the party's leaders and vesting it instead in some form of "electoral college" that would empower constituency activists and trade unions; and for control by the party as a whole of the election manifesto. These were the key items on the agenda of the Campaign for Labour Party Democracy (CLPD), which for a time could count on support from people such as Tony Benn and certain trade union leaders. The previous government was an easy target and the demand for "Labour Party democracy" made steady headway in 1979–80 and climaxed at a special party conference at Wembley in January 1981. There it was decided that an electoral college, in which constituency parties had 30 percent of the vote, MPs another 30 percent and the trade unions fully 40 percent, would choose the leader of the party.

Centrist members of the party were appalled and a "gang of four" – Roy Jenkins, Shirley Williams, William Rodgers and David Owen – came together to launch what would become the Social Democratic Party in March 1981. Through 1981 and 1982 the new party did spectacularly well in the polls, and once-cautious observers and scholars thought it might well "break the mold" of British politics. In the fall of 1981 the new party formed an alliance with the Liberal Party, with which they would fight the election of 1983. The effect of this venture, aimed at a realignment toward the political center, would be anything but. It weakened Labour, and the opposition to Thatcher in general, while abandoning the effort to move the Labour Party back on to center ground. Without its moderate leaders, there was no force within Labour to offer serious resistance to the shift to the left; and Labour went into the election of 1983 with an ineffective leader of the "soft left," Michael Foot, and a program – dubbed "the longest suicide note in history" – that was largely written by the so-called "hard left." The Conservatives won the election with 42.4 percent of the vote and 397 seats in Parliament; Labour got 27.6 percent and 209 seats; the "Alliance" 25.4 percent but a mere 23 seats, giving Thatcher an unassailable majority.

The Presidential election of 1984 in the U.S. was not complicated by break-away parties and candidates. It involved a straightforward contest between a

Democratic Party that clung to its roots, its past and its constituencies, and a Republican Party that proclaimed rhetorically that "It's morning again in America" and that could plausibly claim to have halted inflation, restarted growth, and stood up to the Soviet Union. The Republican strategy was to "Paint Reagan as the personification of all that is right with or heroized by America. Leave Mondale in a position where an attack on Reagan is an attack on America's idealized image of itself." Reagan would go on to win 59 percent of the popular vote and to sweep the Electoral College; and all that Tip O'Neill, Democratic Speaker of the House, could say on the night was that at least the Democrats would not have to run against Reagan ever again.[55]

They would nevertheless have to deal with Reagan in power for another four years, just as Thatcher's opponents were forced to deal with her until 1990. In these second and, for Thatcher after 1987, third terms the two governments would effectively consolidate the advances made in the early 1980s. They did not prevail on every issue, but they did so often enough, and the very longevity of their dominance allowed their policies to become the norm. The fact that Reagan was succeeded by his Vice-President, George Bush, and that Thatcher, though pushed out of office rather brutally, was replaced by her protégé, John Major, served further to entrench the policies and assumptions of the market-oriented framework that the two conservative governments had introduced.

Thatcher and Reagan also worked hard to secure their legacies. Emboldened by victories in 1983 and again in 1987, Margaret Thatcher continued to press her advantage.[56] In a somewhat rocky moment in March 1986, Thatcher took note of "the odd report that Thatcherism has run its course." Not true, she responded, and explained why: "You might feel that the first seven years of Conservative Government have produced some benefits for Britain. And so they have. But the next seven years are going to produce more – many more. And the next seven after that, more still."[57] A telling example of her determination to prevail over the long term was the decision in 1986 to abolish the Greater London Council (GLC) and other metropolitan governments. Despite crushing defeats in successive general elections, Labour continued to resist the government's policies, especially on matters of local finance and the privatization of council housing. Britain's government is unitary, with power vested in Parliament, but local authorities had sufficient leeway to slow down and frustrate policies emanating from the center. The major metropolitan authorities, all of which were Labour controlled, were fundamentally hostile to Thatcher and what she stood for. Her reaction was to assert the supremacy of Parliament and simply abolish the entire tier of government. The Greater London Council, led by the flamboyant and clever Ken ("Red Ken" to some) Livingstone, was the major adversary and it was done away with at the end of March 1986. A much weaker version of the GLC would be recreated in the late 1990s, and Livingstone became London's mayor, but Thatcher's reshaping of the very structure of local government largely remained.

The Conservative government also pushed ahead with its major effort to restructure political life through further privatization. Selling off state assets not only bolstered the government's finances, but also rendered alternative policies impossible. Whenever the Conservatives lost a general election and were replaced by their opponents in the Labour Party, there would be little a new government could do, for the state would lack the capacity to influence the economy. In addition, Tories believed that by selling off public housing to former tenants they would effectively sever one of the strongest links between the Labour Party and its supporters. It was assumed that so long as council tenants rented flats at cheap rates from Labour-controlled authorities, they would keep voting for Labour; if they became owners of those properties, it was hoped, they would be free to vote for other parties. It did not quite work out that way, but it was a bold and inspired plan. Privatization within industry was also accompanied by painful restructuring. As late as 1979, employment in traditional industries was substantial. Coal mining was the classic example, but there were larger numbers of workers employed in old industries like textiles and shipbuilding and in not quite so old industries like steel and automobile manufacturing. These industries were hardest hit by the recession of the early 1980s and they never really recovered. When unemployment began to drop as a consequence of the so-called "Lawson boom" in the late 1980s, employment growth centered in new industries and new places, notably the service sector and the southeast. For the Tories, a happy side-effect was that the already weakened unions stayed weak.

The radicalism that marked Thatcher's policies, even in her third term, would in the end be her undoing. The key mistake was the "poll tax" or "community charge." It was an effort to do away with local rates, property taxes that fell mostly on the better off and that were massively unpopular among Thatcher's middle-class, property-owning supporters who had long been gripped by a "politics of municipal resentment" that the Prime Minister herself shared.[58] The plan was not hers alone, but a collective product; once she had signed on, however, Thatcher was determined and the poll tax came to be identified with her. The new charge could be defended on the grounds that everyone should pay for local services, but the idea that rich and poor should pay the same, and be assessed as individuals, provoked vocal opposition when the implications became clear. It was first imposed in Scotland in April 1989, with England and Wales to follow a year later. Widespread resistance ensued, with large numbers refusing to pay, and a demonstration in Trafalgar Square in late

March 1990 turned into a riot. Thatcher responded angrily – "I was appalled at such wickedness," she recalled in her memoirs – but the government was forced to backtrack, first coming up with subsidies to ease the pain and eventually abandoning the plan.[59] The issue then faded, but before it did, Mrs. Thatcher herself was gone. She was forced out of office in November 1990, and while there were reasons beyond the poll tax – Europe was obviously critical – it was the poll tax that had first revealed that her political judgment was beginning to fail and that had made her fellow Conservatives fear for their own political futures.

Reagan's second term was likewise not entirely triumphant, though it would end on a better note than Thatcher's. Reagan was older than Thatcher and clearly less dogged and he had never harbored quasi-biblical visions of a battle lasting seven years, then seven more and seven again. In addition, the 1984 election campaign had been marred by a poor debate performance that offered viewers a glimpse of a President who was tired and far less nimble on his feet than in the past.[60] He and his team were thus moved to adopt a shorter time horizon than Thatcher and by 1985 they were looking for ways to lock in the major achievements of the "Reagan revolution." Perhaps inevitably, questions of budget, tax and deficits would loom large.

The combination of tax cuts and increases in defense spending meant that the U.S. was running enormous budget deficits by the mid–1980s. The high interest rates adopted by the Federal Reserve to tame inflation, and kept high by the need to finance mounting deficits, meant in turn that the dollar was overvalued. The administration had no difficulty borrowing funds to cover shortfalls, but it faced considerable international pressure to lower the deficit, interest rates and the value of the dollar. It would eventually move to address all three issues during 1985.[61] The priority, however, was tax reform, for it seemed to promise a long-term fiscal settlement that would make it much harder for subsequent governments to raise taxes and expand spending and the scope of government. As Reagan himself would later claim, "With the tax cuts of 1981 and the Tax Reform Act of 1986, I'd accomplished a lot of what I'd come to Washington to do."[62] The 1986 legislation had its origins in Reagan's State of the Union speech in 1984, when he promised a major revision of the tax code. The task of drafting the legislation was assigned to Donald Regan and officials at the Treasury, but nothing would emerge until well after the election, by which time Regan had been replaced by James Baker. The primary objective of the plan was to lower the rates of taxation. To do this a wide range of loopholes and deductions would have to be eliminated, but the hope was that, once reduced, it would be more or less impossible to raise overall rates of tax on individuals. The Act was formally sponsored by two Democrats, Bill Bradley and Richard

Gephardt, and supported by other leading Democrats, who were attracted by the effort to simplify the system and get rid of the more outrageous ways of avoiding tax. They also managed to exempt many people on low incomes from tax liability. The most important provisions were the simplification of the rate structure with fewer bands of tax; the reduction of the top rate from 50 percent to 28 percent; the lowering of the corporate tax rate from 48 percent to 34 percent; an increase in the lowest rate from 11 percent to 15 percent; and increased exemptions and deductions that allowed 6 million to escape tax completely.[63]

In reforming taxes the administration ensured that they would not be easily increased. What, then, to do about the deficit? One response was Gramm-Rudman, a measure passed in December 1985.[64] It was a resolution that called for government to reduce deficits by specific amounts leading to a balanced budget by 1991. If government failed to meet its targets, funds would be automatically "sequestered" and programs cut. It was a crude measure – a "bad idea whose time has come," as Rudman put it – whose main effect, again according to Rudman, was as an "intimidation factor."[65] It served to put the deficit on the agenda in a way that even Reagan could not ignore.

A policy of studied ignorance was the other response to deficits and it was Reagan's preference. He and his more ideologically committed advisors chose to retain their faith in the original supply-side promise, or fantasy, that lower tax rates would stimulate economic growth and tax revenues and automatically reduce deficits. More pragmatic advisors disagreed: James Baker, for example, was moved to deliver a grim warning to "the boss" in 1987. The administration's past economic successes, he explained, were due in large part to having earned the confidence of financial markets. "However, the persistence of the large trade deficit and concern that the U.S. budget deficit will not decline in the future . . . have begun to erode the financial markets' positive spirit." The Treasury Secretary went on to suggest a combination of "respectable expenditure cuts" and increased taxes or, as he put it, "more of revenues in the nature of miscellaneous 'cats and dogs.'"[66] Reagan did little in response and instead reiterated supply-side claims until the end of his term. Even after leaving office, he chose to blame Congress and "vested interests" when the predicted balanced budget did not materialize. "Presidents," he boldly asserted, "don't create deficits, Congress does. Presidents can't appropriate a dollar of taxpayers' money; only Congress can – and Congress is susceptible to all sorts of pressures that have nothing to do with good government."[67] Reagan's attitude effectively guaranteed that initiatives such as Gramm-Rudman would fail and that the problem would be left to Reagan's successor. Nevertheless, the combination of Reagan's reluctance to tax, his determined unwillingness to restrain spending on programs he favored such as defense, and the pressure to lower deficits created a very inhospitable climate for spending increases. However noble the cause and however real the need, it was almost impossible to pry more money out of Congress and the administration. The effect was what David Stockman had envisioned early on: without money and a readiness to incur debt the beast of big government would be starved. And this downward pressure on spending and the consequent drying up of funds for government programs would continue after Reagan left office, a more or less permanent legacy of the Reagan era.

Perhaps reflecting this fiscal impasse, the Reagan administration launched few new domestic initiatives after the midterm elections of 1986. It contented itself with the contradictory budgetary moves that left what one might call the fiscal settlement of 1986 in place, and with a range of largely symbolic gestures. The administration was also beset by the political crisis created by the Iran-Contra Affair, which broke just after the midterm elections. For the next two years, the administration would deal with the fallout, and the effort would sap its energy and erode its credibility, further limiting what Reagan could do at home. It would not stop the progress of Reagan's foreign policy and his dealings with the Soviet Union, where he would achieve a genuine and world-historical breakthrough, but it constrained the administration on other fronts. Iran-Contra was itself a direct result of the Reagan administration's foreign policy and an obvious instance of its failures and blindnessses. At the same time, the scandal was also a matter of domestic policy, or at least domestic politics. The President's fixation on freeing American hostages held in the Middle East came in part from his memory of what the Iran hostage crisis had done to Carter and his presidency, while his refusal to cease meddling in Central America was a way of satisfying a part of his political base. Reagan also truly believed in both causes, but they had important domestic political resonances as well.

If efforts to reshape the relationship between state and society and increase the role of markets had begun to peter out by the late 1980s, it would nevertheless be a mistake to interpret the slowing down of new initiatives as failure. On the contrary, what the two Conservative allies achieved was a genuine transformation whose success can be measured by the extent to which the new paradigms they articulated became the conventional wisdom of politics and the inheritance that their successors and opponents would seek to modify and transcend, but not to reverse. The continuity in policy that characterized the governments of John Major and George Bush testifies to this; even more telling were the efforts by Bill Clinton and Tony Blair to get their parties to accept the Reagan and Thatcher legacies as the starting point for any new departures.

CHAPTER 5

Market Rules and the International Economy

The most obvious source of the troubles affecting the British and American economies in the late 1970s was the world economy. The oil crisis came from outside, more specifically from the actions of states whose participation in global commerce was limited to selling one very valuable commodity. The resulting inflation masked the more fundamental slowdown in the growth of demand worldwide for the products of the advanced economies and the increasing competition to fill that demand. The "Fordist" model that under-pinned *les trente gloriouses* of postwar was bumping up against its social and geographic limits, as Europe and Japan rebuilt and as domestic markets in the developed countries neared saturation. An external boost was wanting, however. The gradual decline of America's dominance in production and trade also led to financial imbalances, as dollars accumulated elsewhere and tested the U.S. commitment to maintain the dollar's value and its assigned role in the global financial system. Nixon's decision in 1971 to suspend convert-ibility initiated an era of uncertainty characterized by floating rates, competi-tive devaluations and revaluations and tortured efforts to recreate the certainties of the Bretton Woods system. Such efforts would fail, in part because it was in the interest of the U.S. to see them fail, but also because of the surge of prices and the vast and unanticipated expansion of international monetary flows due to the first and second oil shocks. Capital movements across borders had been modest and controlled through the 1960s, but exploded after that. The U.S. abandoned capital controls in 1974 and the U.K. in 1979, and both the United States and Great Britain sought to put themselves at the center of the burgeoning financial networks that were emerging and so resisted efforts to control financial flows or to coordinate the management of various currencies in the post–Bretton Woods era.[1] They succeeded in securing dominant positions in global finance, but the contest prevented the balance and stability that might have facilitated an expansion of effective demand.

It might be thought that the "shock of the global" during the 1970s would elicit a coordinated global response. And it is true that Reagan and Thatcher were eager proselytizers for an open world economic order – for open markets, free trade and the free movement of capital.[2] In practice, however, the steps that the U.S. and the U.K. took to induce economic recovery were basically domestic and unilateral. The Thatcher government's austerity measures, its tax policies and its efforts to disengage government from detailed economic management and to dispose of state assets were of interest abroad, but took effect only at home. The Reagan administration's tax and budget policies affected the domestic economy first and foremost. What did hit other economies hard was American interest rate policy: the extremely high interest rates in the U.S. drew capital from abroad and led to the appreciation of the dollar.[3] While this helped the exports of America's trading partners, it hurt their finances and weakened investment everywhere; it also crippled U.S. exports. The large deficits produced by the Reagan administration's tax cuts and increases in defense spending had similar destabilizing effects. British fiscal policy in the early 1980s also served to reduce worldwide demand, if on a lesser scale. In both cases policy was intended to cure domestic ills, inflation primarily, even at the expense of growth and employment at home and abroad and even in the teeth of criticism from other nations whose economies inevitably suffered in response.

Economic Summits and Market Liberalization

This stance ensured that Britain and the U.S. would often find themselves on the defensive at international gatherings such as the annual economic summits held to develop a measure of cooperation in global economic policy-making. The summits had begun at Rambouillet in 1975, a moment when the Keynesian consensus was fraying but still dominant. In the late 1970s, therefore, the summits were used to generate support for international efforts to keep up the momentum of growth even in the face of mounting inflation: at one point, the U.S. was to act as a "locomotive" for the international economy; later, the Germans and Japanese would be asked to take on that role.[4] By the time the summit met in Tokyo in 1979, however, combating inflation had become the main objective. Carter sought to do so by controlling consumption in response to the second oil crisis; Thatcher supported the goal but disapproved of the necessary controls. Heads of government convened again in Venice in 1980, but there were no major initiatives. Several leaders were locked in election battles whose possible outcomes were unclear or likely to be adverse for those in power, and economic circumstances had altered little since the last meeting. If anything, the imperative to battle inflation was rather greater as the second oil shock began to bite.

Reagan's first summit was in Ottawa in July 1981 and he was still recovering from the attempt on his life at the end of March. He leaned heavily on Thatcher for support and was extremely grateful: "Margaret Thatcher is a tower of strength and a solid friend of the U.S.," he wrote in his diary."[5] The meeting did not accomplish much, but it set a new pattern. Oil prices had begun to stabilize. U.S. interest rates were now at roughly 20 percent, however, and the value of the dollar had increased by approximately 30 percent over the prior year. In response, "summit participants would be unanimous in complaining about U.S. interest rates, the budget deficit and the strength of the dollar." The Americans, with Britain usually but not always in support, resisted at this and later summits. "'Wait a while', was their message in Ottawa; 'Let's study it', the approach at Versailles [in 1982]; 'Our boom will solve it', the line in Williamsburg [in 1983]; and 'After our elections', the promise at London II [in 1984]." Reagan explained his approach more directly to the World Bank and IMF in September 1981: "The most important contribution any country can make to world development is to pursue sound economic policies at home."[6] His sense of priorities was shared by Thatcher and soon echoed by the new German Chancellor, Helmut Kohl, who took office in October 1982. The Japanese also tended to agree. The effect of this emerging consensus was that the twin crises of the early 1980s – first the massive price increase caused by the second oil shock, then the deep recession of 1981–2 – did not produce concerted action of the sort envisioned during the 1970s and throughout the entire Keynesian era. The preferred approach was to focus on domestic policy and market mechanisms to overcome the problems originating in the world economy.

There was as yet no consensus on a new model of how to run the economy, for while states like Germany and Japan may have opted for fiscal restraint over expansion, policy in these two states remained highly interventionist on a variety of measures. They were far from adopting a liberal "Anglo-American" model of political economy. Still, the shift away from efforts to manage global demand was significant, and it was pushed even further by the reversal of French economic policy. François Mitterrand had stormed to victory in May 1981 on a promise to revitalize the French economy through a series of nationalizations and efforts to stimulate growth. Social spending would also increase. The French tried hard to maintain an expansionary policy despite the global recession, but without success. By mid–1982 France was facing high inflation, serious capital flight and, with the prospect of devaluation looming, mounting speculation against the franc. It was widely thought that the U.S. Treasury was encouraging the market in its behavior, but the market needed little encouragement.

Because of its membership in the emerging European Monetary System (EMS), devaluation in France would require austerity measures that would undercut the effort to expand. The more left-wing ministers in the government developed a plan to devalue, to leave the EMS and to impose restrictions on capital movements and imports. Mitterrand's commitment to Europe, and to EMS, precluded that option and he proposed instead that the European Community as a whole should impose capital controls to protect itself from speculation and from the impact of high U.S. interest rates. Britain was opposed, and the Germans skeptical, so the suggestion died. Instead, in June 1982 the French government reluctantly agreed on a devaluation of 10 percent and a series of modest austerity measures. The plan worked for a time, but by the following March the very same problems had returned. Again, debate went back and forth between a plan for a siege economy that might allow for continued expansion, or cuts. Within the government, the Prime Minister Pierre Mauroy and the Finance Minister Jacques Delors argued the case for austerity, with support from Michel Camdessus – head of the Bank of France and destined to become chief of the IMF in 1987 – and finally convinced Mitterrand. In late March 1983 the government announced a further devaluation coupled with tough austerity measures: wages were frozen along with prices, and budgets were slashed. Soon the nationalizations were reversed. As of 1983, French policy had come into much closer alignment with British and U.S. policy: austerity was in vogue nearly everywhere, efforts to stimulate demand had mostly been abandoned, and challenges to participation in international markets largely beaten back.[7]

Key decisions were typically taken by the technocrats who ran France whichever party was in power, but what was distinctive about the 1983 turn was how its leaders understood it as a step in the modernization of the country. One such person was Jean-Claude Trichet, a close ally of Mitterrand's, who felt that "France in the 1980s was a country of vast potential, but it was being held back by its own rules. There was an urgency to make France a 'normal' advanced industrialized economy with market institutions." More telling still was the view of Jean-Claude Naouri, another top official, who understood that this definition of modernity was widely held and pursued by "French technocrats – a technocratic elite from the Treasury. This elite shared a collective culture in favor of modernization. The question was how to lead France into modernity, into the Anglo-Saxon world . . ."[8] It was a moment not unlike that of 1976, when Great Britain had been forced to demonstrate its commitment to international markets and forsake its ambitions to control rather than acquiesce to market outcomes. The French choice may have had even greater significance because of its more central role in Europe.

Again, the faith in markets preached by Thatcher and Reagan was not triumphant everywhere, but there was a widespread recognition that their experiments had been more or less successful and there was less and less faith in alternatives that relied more heavily on the state. Thatcher's and Reagan's impressive reelection victories in 1983 and 1984 reinforced such judgments. Perhaps as important, the two governments had been reasonably successful in their early efforts to impose market solutions and market discipline and survived the severe depression of 1981–2 without abandoning their basic approach; and they emerged from these difficult years ready to argue their case to a broader audience. It helped, too, that foreign affairs in both governments were soon entrusted to people with massive experience and understanding of economic policy. In the U.S. George Shultz, a trained economist and a great believer in markets, replaced Alexander Haig as Secretary of State in July 1982; in the U.K. Geoffrey Howe, the former Chancellor of the Exchequer, went to the Foreign Office in June 1983. The appointment in early 1985 of James Baker as Treasury Secretary, eager as he was to be involved in foreign policy, also helped to focus the attention of both governments on the matter of making the turn to markets a more global affair.[9]

Fortified by solid electoral performances and able to call upon new talents, Thatcher and Reagan found themselves well positioned to make their vision of a world of markets into a new orthodoxy in international economic policy. An important step was the resolution of two issues that put had them at odds with allies. The first was the value of the dollar; the second the fractious argument about Britain's contribution to the budget of the European Community. Even with the recovery gathering strength in the mid–1980s, the U.S. continued to run large budget deficits which kept interest rates high and encouraged an inflow of foreign capital and, in turn, an overvalued dollar. With the dollar so strong, exporters faced a huge disadvantage and the result was a growing trade deficit. In Congress, attentive to the demands of both organized labor and industry, there were calls for protectionist measures that the administration had great difficulty in resisting. The U.S. was also forced to resist pressures from its allies, including Margaret Thatcher, to reduce its deficit and to take steps to lower the value of the dollar. Treasury Secretary Regan rather defensively and unconvincingly told fellow economics ministers in April 1984 that "Quite simply, the U.S. budget deficit is not the cause of all the world's economic problems, nor would reducing our deficit be a panacea." He disputed the notion that there was a "systematic link between the United States budget deficit, the behavior of the United States' interest rate, and secular trends in the value of the U.S. dollar."[10]

James Baker, Regan's successor at the Treasury, accepted that there was a relationship and became convinced not only that the dollar should be devalued but that there needed to be closer cooperation – "a process for macroeconomic policy coordination" – between the people in charge of the major economies.[11] Baker's views were close to Shultz's and he was more capable of controlling the policy agenda. In Reagan's first term, responsibility for economic policy was widely diffused. In the second term, the administration centralized decision-making and put Baker firmly in charge.[12] Immediately upon taking office Baker agreed with his counterparts – the finance ministers in the other G5 countries – "to work towards greater exchange rate stability" and the Treasury began gradually to allow the dollar to move downwards. In September 1985 the G5 finance ministers met at the Plaza Hotel in New York and agreed that an "orderly appreciation of the main non-dollar currencies against the dollar" was desirable and appropriate. Within a short time the dollar's value had declined substantially.[13] The group also agreed to coordinate exchange rates and the U.S. began to work on reining in the deficit. The passage of Gramm-Rudman in December imparted still greater urgency to the effort.[14] The adoption of such self-denying "fiscal rules" in fact became widespread among developed countries, though their effectiveness was limited.[15]

The dispute about how much Britain should pay to Europe was perhaps more difficult to resolve in that it involved fundamental issues about the "European project." The Community had begun as a customs union, but with grander aspirations. In theory it was liberal and in favor of more open trade and exchange, but creating a more open market internally meant protecting it against external competitors. This contradiction would not be quickly or easily resolved. Equally important, the most significant achievement of the common market in its first decade was the Common Agricultural Policy (CAP), which was supposed to modernize agriculture but which in the main protected and subsidized it. In the 1970s and 1980s, CAP payments were the Community's biggest expenditure: French farmers were the biggest winners, but German agriculture also did well out of it.

The original "Six" became "Nine" in 1973 when Britain, Ireland and Denmark joined and during the 1980s Greece, Portugal and Spain would join as well. Enlargement meant a gradual shift of priorities. Ireland and the southern European countries were less developed and in need of what would become regional development funds that would only become available if the CAP were decreased or overall contributions raised. Britain posed a special problem because, in his eagerness to get in, Edward Heath did not bargain a very good deal. The budget was central, for Britain was locked into quite large contributions, due to its size and its level of imports, but received very little in return. Its agricultural sector was very small and what remained of it was highly efficient, unlike that of the French and others, so the U.K. got little from the CAP but paid a lot into it. The United Kingdom was also different in its attitude toward Europe and European integration. Not only had Britain once ruled the world's largest empire, but it still claimed intimate connections to the Commonwealth and other countries it had previously ruled; and it carried into Europe a prior and very consequential relationship with the United States. Almost inevitably, British public opinion toward Europe was ambivalent, even as its elites became more and more sympathetic to membership.

The Labour Party in 1974 promised a referendum on Europe. Wilson as Prime Minister and Callaghan as Foreign Minister traveled around Europe and collected a set of promises that allowed them to claim that they had now negotiated a better deal. In the referendum in June 1975 voters chose to remain in Europe by a two-to-one margin.[16] The issue did not end there, however, for at least two reasons. The first was Britain's continuing economic difficulties, which meant that nothing was settled in terms of the country's economic future, and which led to the financial crisis of 1976. The recourse to the IMF revived interest in an "alternative economic strategy" premised on import controls and a possible withdrawal from Europe. The alternative strategy was rejected, and with it the *dirigiste* and autarkic strategy that it implied, but the idea left a legacy and, for some, a longing.

Britain's position in Europe remained unsettled. The Thatcher government, elected in 1979, was convinced that Britain was still severely disadvantaged in its budgetary relationship to the European Community. Thatcher herself had campaigned in favor of the 1975 referendum and was in 1979 mildly pro-European, but it was estimated that in 1980 Britain paid in to Europe roughly £1,000 million more than it received. The disparity led her to undertake a sustained campaign demanding "our money back" and she caused no end of annoyance to European leaders and officials. At the European Council meeting in Strasbourg on June 21–22, 1979 Thatcher insisted that the matter be brought up early so that in the final communiqué there would be some acknowledgment of the need to address it. The French President began to bring the first day's last session to a close prior to drinks and dinner and asked if that was acceptable to Thatcher. She proudly said "no" and went on to explain the British position. Not everyone was charmed.[17]

At the European Council meeting in Dublin the following November, it was proposed to refund £350 million of the British contribution. Thatcher derisively labeled the sum "a third of a loaf" but, after much angry argument, took it and prepared for a later showdown in April in Luxembourg. Offered almost two-thirds of a loaf, or £700 million, at that meeting, Thatcher still refused to agree. Again, a compromise was brokered in May at the meeting of foreign ministers in Brussels. Britain's representatives, Lord Carrington and Ian Gilmour, got their counterparts to agree on the same amount, but to extend it for three years. Thatcher was tough to convince, but eventually relented.

The deal would run to 1984, when a final arrangement was effected at Fontainebleau under the French presidency of the Council. In the intervening years Thatcher kept making trouble. In 1979 she had instructed officials to develop a "'checklist' . . . of forthcoming Community meetings in the context of possible obstruction of Community business in the event that we do not get an acceptable solution on the budget at Dublin."[18] She repeatedly threatened to hold back money. Though Thatcher did not act on the threat, the British did refuse to agree to various European initiatives, in particular to proposals to raise VAT to fund the Community. Thatcher's relatively crude efforts failed to secure any better deal, however, and at Fontainebleau in June 1984 she chose to accept a permanent refund of 66 percent of Britain's contribution. It was less than she had wanted, but substantial nonetheless, and the deal allowed the issue to go away.[19]

The election victories of Reagan and Thatcher gave them confidence in the wisdom of their choices, while their willingness to settle outstanding differences with other leading economic powers allowed for increased coordination in matters of policy. The effect was that the market-oriented, neoliberal agenda espoused by the U.S. and U.K. became more acceptable internationally and provided the background for further rounds of liberalization both domestically and internationally.[20] In the U.S., the huge deficits created by the tax cuts of the early 1980s constituted a ready argument against government spending and exerted sustained downward pressure on social spending throughout the decade; in the U.K. the Thatcher government not only continued to cut and to sell off state assets, but also legislated to eliminate local governments that might choose otherwise and resist. Elsewhere, the turn to markets also accelerated: in Japan, for example, capital markets were opened up in 1984; France began to deregulate financial markets the same year; and under Helmut Kohl the Germans began to move in a similar direction.

The most important steps toward economic liberalization came at the international level. The effort to create "a single market" in Europe promised not just to transform Europe internally but also to recast its role in the global economy. More or less simultaneously, there was a determined effort to resist domestic pressures for protection and to resume progress toward a more open, global trading system. The U.S. took the initiative in pressing for the Uruguay

Round of GATT negotiations and, with the U.K. also in favor, the European Community would go along as well. Its successful conclusion in 1993 would lead directly to the establishment in 1995 of the World Trade Organization, a key step toward a world order based on rules favorable to trade, markets and the free movement of goods, resources, people and capital. At roughly the same moment the emergence and triumph of the "Washington Consensus" on matters of finance and debt meant the extension of market orthodoxy beyond the developed nations to all countries seeking to gain access to the international economy.[21] Behind all these developments was the vision shared and promulgated by Thatcher and Reagan, and the persuasive (some might say coercive) clout of the hegemonic power and its closest ally.

The European Community may have been distracted by the issue of the British budget contribution, but it was more deeply troubled by lagging economic growth. Recovery from the recession of 1981–2 was slow and uneven and European leaders came gradually to believe in the need to introduce greater dynamism into the economies of member states. Keynesian and more statist remedies had become discredited and were effectively precluded by the international consensus on the primacy of the battle against inflation. Policy eventually converged around a program of market-based reforms leading to the "completion of the single market" as anticipated in the Treaty of Rome. The turn in France was a precondition for reaching agreement on the new approach: when the Mitterrand government reversed its strategy of state-led development and opted instead for fiscal austerity, disengagement and, in the end, actual privatization in certain sectors, it found itself aligned with priorities in Germany and in the United Kingdom. It was also during this particular French presidency that the budget dispute with Britain was resolved. The effect of this realignment was a shared determination by the three major players in the Community to move toward market solutions to Europe's economic stagnation.[22] For Germany and France, the single market was one component in a broader project of European integration and "the progressive construction of European union," a goal toward which Britain at least formally acquiesced in agreeing to the "Solemn Declaration on European Union" at the Council meeting in Stuttgart in June 1983. For Britain, however, the single market was the goal, the commitment to further integration merely a "process" that would take a very long time and might well never reach its conclusion. In any case, as Thatcher argued, "the [Stuttgart] document had no legal force."[23]

As the budget dispute neared resolution the British government submitted a preliminary paper on the single market in September 1983. A more formal document of British provenance, *Europe – The Future*, was delivered to

European leaders at the Fontainebleau meeting in June 1984. It proclaimed the need for further economic integration:

> We must create the genuine common market in goods and services which is envisaged in the Treaty of Rome and will be crucial to our ability to meet the U.S. and Japanese technological challenge. Only by a sustained effort to remove remaining obstacles to intra-Community trade can we enable the citizens of Europe to benefit from the dynamic effects of a fully integrated common market with immense purchasing power.

Uncharacteristically, and rather boldly, the American example was specifically invoked in this European discussion: "The success of the United States in job creation shows what can be achieved when internal barriers to business and trade come down."[24]

Progress toward the creation of the single market was, predictably, contentious. The lingering distrust between Britain and its European partners meant that the recent convergence of aims did not translate smoothly into cooperation on details. The French and the Germans remained committed to working together as the dominant bloc in the Community, and the prospect of enlargement – Spain and Portugal were set to join in 1986 – kept their focus on political rules and institutions as well as on the economy and their support for greater union did not sit well with Thatcher. Nevertheless, the need to move forward with efforts to open up the economy at least within Europe's borders was a matter of mutual interest. In addition, the European Commission became firmly attached to the project under its new president, Jacques Delors. Delors was a moderate socialist with a Catholic background and he had played a major role in turning around French policy in 1982–3. His appointment was secured by a deal between France and Germany, but the U.K. was not opposed; and as a kind of compensation, David Williamson, a British civil servant, was made Secretary General of the Commission in 1987. It was Delors who announced on taking office "a decision to remove all the borders inside Europe between now and 1992" and who superintended the process by which the Single European Act was agreed by heads of government in late 1985 and ratified by 1987.[25] He was assisted in his efforts by several other Frenchmen – his chief of staff, Pascal Lamy, Jean-Paul Mingasson and Jean-Pierre Baché in the Economic and Financial Affairs section of the Commission, and also Joly Dixon, from the U.K.[26]

Actual implementation was very much the handiwork of another British representative, Arthur Cockfield, the former managing director of Boots and a member of the Cabinet before becoming European Commissioner for the Internal Market in January 1985. Lord Cockfield drafted the White Paper,

Completing the Internal Market (June 1985) that set the agenda and timetable, identifying over three hundred decisions required to eliminate barriers to the free movement of goods and services and proposing a detailed plan for how to accomplish all this by 1992. Those decisions were largely taken, and in timely fashion, and the project was successful. Cockfield was aided in his mission by successive Commissioners for Competition: the Irish lawyer, politician and later banker Peter Sutherland, who held the job from 1985 to 1989, and another British Conservative, Leon Brittan, who succeeded Sutherland in 1989. Between 1986 and 1992, as a result, the European Community truly became an open market and goods and money moved more freely within this new economic space than ever before. Anomalies remained, especially in the realm of services and on issues such as credentials and licenses, but the direction of change was set. Equally important, the changes went in only one direction and it was almost impossible that they would be reversed. Indeed, the Sutherland Report of October 1992 proposed a series of measures designed to further the process.[27]

A particularly important feature of these efforts was that they encompassed markets for capital as well as for manufactured goods. Again, the United States and Britain had put the issue on the agenda and the Germans and the Danes were more or less on board from the beginning. Japan fell in line reasonably soon and France after the turn. Getting international institutions in line took a bit longer. The IMF, though generally liberal on most issues, had sufficient experience with capital movements and fiscal crises to be wary and so hesitated. In its absence, the Organisation for Economic Co-operation and Development (OECD) and the European Community would play the critical roles. The "single market" initiative envisioned some liberalization of capital controls, but Delors soon came to believe that "the free movement of capital was essential to the creation of the single market." It was a matter of coherence and consistency, and in June 1988 the Council mandated the abolition of capital controls by July 1, 1990.[28] The OECD operated differently, and was like a club with agreed rules but no legal means of enforcement. Since 1961 it had had in place a Code of Liberalisation of Capital Movements that, in its early years, was not terribly liberal. It was amended several times, however, most significantly in 1989. That revision mandated the "full liberalisation of capital movements."[29] It was carried out under the leadership of another French bureaucrat, Henri Chavranski, and was intended not only to encourage the process of economic globalization but also, and importantly, to be largely irreversible.[30]

Opening up European markets was therefore a central achievement of the liberal project in the 1980s, but none of this meant that the EU was committed wholeheartedly to open competition, freer trade and deregulation. Margaret Thatcher insisted that "The Community was formed to expand trade, not to protect home markets," but the fact that she felt a need to make the claim was proof enough that it had not always acted that way.[31] Delors's decision to push forward with policies to promote "economic and social cohesion," adding a "social dimension" to the single market project, would offer further evidence that Europe was not a thoroughly liberal political entity. It was this commitment by Delors that served as the provocation that lay behind Thatcher's justly famous Bruges speech in September 1988.[32]

On balance, however, it would seem reasonable to argue that Europe has been a force for trade liberalization over the long term and that the U.K. did its best to encourage that. As a close observer of British foreign relations noted in the early 1990s, "Britain has nailed its free trade colors to the mast in the past decade, though not everyone else in the system has done so."[33] Indeed, no other European country had quite the interest in open markets as Britain, although most European countries were keen to export. It would also seem that a defining feature of the Community has predisposed it to support trade liberalization: the Treaty of Rome stipulated that Europe would speak with a single voice on trade and by concentrating the process of trade negotiation at the center local concerns could be at least partly or temporarily overridden. This "pooling of sovereignty," according to Leon Brittan – European Commissioner for Competition, 1989–95 and for Trade and External Affairs, 1995–9 – "has made Europe a powerful force for open markets across the world, giving her the lead in trade liberalization, securing access for European firms abroad and preventing the worst excesses of predatory trading by our partners."[34] The effort to complete the single market after 1985, by getting Europe to open itself to greater access and competition within its borders, tilted the balance still further in the direction of open markets and liberal trade policies beyond those borders.

Trade Politics

The balance between protection and openness was not dissimilar in the United States. U.S. trade policy had been fundamentally liberal, with consistent efforts to lower tariffs and remove trade barriers throughout the first quarter-century after the war. America was committed to expanding markets, largely because its products were highly desirable and attractively priced, and its leaders further believed that open trade made for a more prosperous and peaceful world. The leaders of both major parties had long supported open markets, although this consensus did not preclude partisan bickering and opposition in Congress.

To overcome such resistance, successive administrations sought broad authority to conduct trade negotiations without excessive interference and in 1963 the Office of the Special Trade Representative was established. Its role steadily expanded and the role of the USTR and the President was buttressed by the repeated grant of "fast-track" authority.[35] Neither of these initiatives, however, sufficed to distract interest groups seeking protection or their advocates in Congress.

Still, through the various rounds of negotiations under the auspices of GATT (General Agreement on Tariffs and Trade, established in 1947), tariff barriers were much reduced and the United States, and its allies and trading partners, enjoyed the benefits of expanding world trade. The onset of slower growth in the 1970s coincided, however, with more intense international competition and with a steady growth of imports in U.S. domestic markets. The result was a more intense and contentious era in trade politics during which protectionist pressures increased markedly.[36] Those hurt or threatened by imports – first textiles, apparel and shoes, then steel and automobiles, and always agriculture – mobilized and pressed for special relief or outright protection. The successful conclusion of the Tokyo Round in spring 1979 lessened the pressures by promising export gains, and the subsequent Trade Agreements Act of 1979 passed easily. The issue revived under Ronald Reagan, as the deep recession of the early 1980s and the rise in the value of the dollar put the administration, despite its ideological commitment to open markets, very much on the defensive and Congress became more partisan and active on questions of trade.[37]

Reagan had long supported free trade as part of his broader pro-market philosophy and his administration set to work quickly on a strategy of further liberalizing trade, with a particular emphasis on trade in services.[38] The effort had to contend with an angry political climate in which the difficulties of American industry were regularly attributed to foreign competition. While still campaigning, Reagan was confronted with demands from the auto industry to curb the import of Japanese cars; in May 1981 he announced a voluntary export restraint (VER) agreement with Japan. The administration followed this up by putting pressure on Japan to bargain about "non-tariff barriers" to trade. In July, the administration's Trade Representative, William Brock, presented Congress with a "Statement on U.S. Trade Policy" proclaiming the objective of "free trade, consistent with mutually acceptable trading relations."[39] In response, Democrats began to rally behind a "domestic content" bill that would mandate that cars sold in the United States contain a prescribed share of parts manufactured in the U.S. or Canada. The debate was ongoing and, with the economy reeling, intensified during the midterm election campaign in 1982, with

Democrats promising action and the administration countering by getting Japan to agree to extend voluntary restrictions for a year and by striking a similar deal with European steel producers.

The Reagan administration also formally proposed a new round of trade negotiations at the GATT meeting in Geneva in late November 1982.[40] The move was badly timed, taking place at the depth of a recession affecting virtually all countries. In addition, the Europeans were still angry over the U.S. decision to prohibit the Europeans, and others, from helping and profiting from the construction of a new gas pipeline to the Soviet Union, a clumsy effort to punish the Soviets over Poland.[41] Equally controversial, the Americans wanted to extend negotiations to cover "trade in services."[42] The proposal was resisted both by the Europeans, who did not yet see the advantage of freer trade in services and who were worried about defending the CAP, and also by developing countries like India and Brazil, which were still committed to state-led policies of development and to the protection of local agriculture as well as nascent manufacturing and service industries. The meeting ended with a vague and weak communiqué that accomplished little concrete, but it did register the administration's intentions and begin to shape the agenda for future negotiations.

Democrats in Congress were undeterred: they kept up the pressure and approved the domestic content bill in December 1982. It would die in the Senate, but another version passed the House the following year. It, too, was never enacted, but its revival reflected the continued salience of the issue. The debate on trade continued during 1983–4, as did negotiations between the U.S. and Japan and the European Community. The Reagan administration came up with a succession of ad hoc measures affecting specific industries, but pushed back against plans and proposals for more protectionist legislation. Their strategy of making concessions on detail while holding out for the general principle of free trade allowed the government to get Congress to pass a relatively non-protectionist bill, the Trade and Tariff Act, shortly before the 1984 election. What made this possible was the economic revival that began near the end of 1982 and was by then in full swing.

That very same revival nevertheless kept trade at the center of the political agenda, for by the beginning of Reagan's second term the trade deficit was growing massively. It was close to $125 billion in 1984 and would increase by another $25 billion in 1985. Prosperity was sucking in imports much faster than U.S. exports could revive, and exporters were crippled by the overvalued dollar which, by some calculations, had the effect of a 50 percent tariff. Both Democrats and Republicans argued for a more aggressive U.S. stance on trade. Reagan, however, had just won a decisive election victory and was less inclined to respond to the pressure. He and his advisors also wanted a big and lasting domestic achievement and so decided instead to put their efforts behind tax reform. The choice left the administration vulnerable, however, and its opponents saw an opening. In July 1985 three Democratic politicians – Congressmen Richard Gephardt, Dan Rostenkowski and Senator Lloyd Bentsen – proposed an import surcharge of 25 percent on goods from Japan, Taiwan, South Korea and Brazil. It was one of an estimated 300 bills before Congress dealing with trade and it made clear that something had to be done.

Even if Reagan was focused on taxes, others on his team were more aware of the problem with trade and its potential to derail or at least limit the economic recovery. The administration had presided over a big drop in unemployment between 1982 and 1984, when it fell from nearly 11 percent to 7.2 percent. Unemployment stayed at roughly that level for most of the next two years, however, and there was a growing sense that the administration lacked a model for generating sustained growth.[43] Attention turned to the overvalued dollar, to huge deficits and high interest rates, and to the need to expand trade if growth were to continue. Baker's move to the Treasury gave him a leading role on these questions and he began crafting a strategy that would deal first with the overvalued dollar and then move on to a broader effort to open up global markets. While Baker prepared the ground for the Plaza Accord in September, the administration kept up its selective interventions. In May it unveiled a plan to encourage agricultural exports by promising to distribute $2 billion worth of surpluses to countries that bought U.S. grains; and in June Reagan chose to retaliate against EC preferences for Mediterranean citrus fruits by imposing tariffs on pasta. In September Reagan announced that his administration would launch three Section 301 cases against Japan, South Korea and Brazil, which were alleged to have imposed unfair restrictions on the sale of tobacco, on insurance and on computers, respectively. Section 301 referred to a provision in the 1974 trade bill that allowed the U.S. to retaliate when other countries violated trade rules or discriminated against U.S. interests. In the past, such actions had been initiated by specific industries, but now it was the administration itself beginning the process. The decision to make use of these mechanisms would become part of a more sustained "Trade Policy Action Plan" which Reagan laid out on September 23, the day after the meeting at the Plaza.

The administration followed up with hard and protracted bargaining with Japan over semiconductors and with Europe over Airbus. The U.S. also calculated that the entry of Spain and Portugal into the EC in 1986 would cause an immediate drop in exports of animal feed worth roughly $500 million annually and so demanded compensation. The administration won a reasonably favorable compromise, but none of this stilled the debate over trade. Instead, Congressional opponents developed their own action plan and centered it on a new trade bill. Seeking to avoid that outcome, the administration took action on Japanese machine tools and on wood products from Canada. The bill passed anyway, and the battle continued, with the focus shifting to textiles which, Democrats hoped, would help the party in the South. The administration countered by securing a five-year extension of the "Multi-Fiber Agreement," blunting the effort, and Reagan proceeded to veto the legislation.[44] A Congressional attempt to override the veto in August just failed, but the Democratic leader, Tip O'Neill, promised that "There will be another trade vote on November 4."[45] Protectionist legislation was thus forestalled, and the Democrats would learn from the 1986 midterm elections that a fight over trade would produce only limited political gains. They won seats, and regained control of the Senate, but they gained far less than hoped for. And just before those elections, data were released showing that the trade deficit was finally dropping, suggesting that the trade issue might be dissipating.

The administration did its part in trying to make the issue go away by continuing what was now an accepted strategy of taking specific measures to block or restrict imports that undercut American domestic production in unfair ways or to pry open closed markets abroad. These were obvious deviations from free trade orthodoxy, but they were regarded by the administration as necessary compromises. Simultaneously, the U.S. fought hard for a multilateral agreement through a new round of GATT negotiations. America's first effort had been rebuffed in 1982, but the Reagan administration persisted. In March 1985, at precisely the moment when the single market initiative was being developed, the EC agreed to a new round of negotiations. Preparations took more than a year, but in September 1986 GATT convened at Punta del Este, Uruguay, and began work. Inevitably, there were sharp disagreements, but it was agreed that the new round would include agriculture, textiles, services, investment and intellectual property.[46] Not everyone was happy, but the broad amalgam of issues raised the prospect of potential gains for a wide variety of countries. The Europeans were as usual reluctant to discuss agriculture, but had decided that they could compete well in services. The EC's Commissioner for External Affairs, Willy De Clercq, claimed that the Community was "the biggest world exporter of services" and so not afraid of competition.[47] More open investment policies would presumably benefit most advanced economies with well-developed financial institutions and capital markets; and establishing firmer protection of intellectual property rights helped those who held patents and hurt those, particularly in developing nations, seeking to infringe them and produce cheaper copies; developing countries could imagine an easier time exporting textiles and, more importantly, agricultural products. It was a recipe not for harmony but for tough bargaining, and the ensuing negotiations would be extremely difficult – indeed they would stall repeatedly and come close to a complete collapse in Brussels in 1990 – but the process had begun and it served as a sign that the two major economic powers, the U.S. and the EC, had decided that a further opening of the world economy was in their joint interest; and that developing nations would at least participate.

There were still signs of antagonism over trade. The U.S. and the EC continued to do battle on what was now quite familiar terrain. More important, Japanese imports to the U.S. kept growing, while American firms had little success in penetrating the Japanese market; and Congress remained restive. A more interesting and, for free traders, possibly more promising development was the U.S.–Canada Free Trade Agreement, reached in October 1987. There were, and remain, arguments about whether such regional trading blocs are "stumbling blocks" or "building blocks" in the process of creating an open multilateral system, and it seems clear that for U.S. policy-makers the option of striking a deal in North America was both a means of bargaining for a broader agreement and a "fallback" position. Because of the importance of the trade to both countries, however, freeing it up was a major quantitative contribution to freeing up world trade.

The ambiguity of trade politics, with movements forward and backward often cancelling each other out and with the path toward more open trade littered with deviations and deals on the side, was illustrated as well by the passage of the Omnibus Trade and Competitiveness Act of 1988. Early in 1987 Democratic leaders in Congress began drafting a trade bill whose aim was to get tough on America's trading partners and rivals. It would give the administration "fast-track" authority for the Uruguay Round, but would require stronger action in cases affecting specific industries. The bill also created a new trade weapon, "Super 301," which would force the administration to name countries that maintained unfair trade barriers against the products of U.S. industry and undertake negotiations to remove them. If the effort failed, the U.S. would retaliate. The bill was extremely broad and included much that the administration opposed. It nevertheless passed both the House and the Senate and came close to becoming law, or at least inviting a Presidential veto to prevent that from happening. The penultimate step was a House-Senate Conference scheduled for late October 1987. Just before it was to convene, the stock market took a dive, losing over 22 percent of its value on "Black Monday," October 19, 1987. Quickly Congress backed off for fear that aggressive trade legislation would frighten business at home and abroad and make things worse.

The crisis passed and by January the trade bill was back on the table. It was also now a Presidential election year and Democrats felt that Reagan's departure gave them a real chance to reclaim the White House. They were eager therefore to craft a message that would appeal to voters who had failed to benefit from administration policies and they also believed it was possible to win support from businesses that were facing stiffer competition from abroad. The legislation was redrafted but it was basically similar to the law that did not quite happen the previous year. In places it was milder, but included a controversial provision that placed restrictions on plant closings. It was this that led Reagan to veto the bill in May.[48] The override effort fell just short, so Congress sent the President a new version stripped of the section on plant closings. Somewhat reluctantly, Reagan signed it in August, in large part at the urging of George Bush, who was now running for President. The law was a further demonstration of what had become the basic pattern of U.S. trade policy. It was more aggressive on exports than America's rhetorical and practical commitment to free trade might have allowed in the past, and while it gave more power to the executive – the USTR and the President – it also set deadlines and mandated reports to Congress. It also gave the President the authority to proceed with the Uruguay Round. The making of trade policy was by the late 1980s less consensual than it had been a generation before, but then again trade itself was more important to the economy and more interests were engaged. The mix and mess and the contestation looked rather dysfunctional, but did provide a mechanism for orchestrating a further opening of world trade.[49]

Toward the Washington Consensus

In consequence, by the time Reagan left office in 1989 the United States and Europe, with British prodding, had become far more market-oriented economies and they were joined in an effort to promote trade liberalization. The goal was some way off, and disagreements numerous, but a possible deal was becoming visible. Over the same period the free market orthodoxy had also come to dominate the workings of the international financial system and the organizations that ran it – the International Monetary Fund and the development banks, the most important of which was the World Bank. The advent of this "Washington Consensus" was the result of a series of enormous transformations in global finance that began when the United States abandoned the Bretton Woods system of fixed exchange rates in 1971. Currency volatility was accentuated by the abolition of exchange controls, first in the United States, then in Britain and then elsewhere. Money moved more freely and rapidly and there was more of it, for the two oil shocks put huge sums of money in the hands of countries which lacked the institutions to handle them or the oppor-tunities for domestic investment that could have absorbed them. British and American banks were eager to compete for these petrodollars and largely succeeded, so while inflation ravaged the real economy in both countries, the banks were awash in capital. This success led other countries to compete in banking and finance and to open capital markets that were previously closed or at least restricted. A hugely symbolic event in this competition was the "Big Bang" in October 1986 in which trading in the City of London was liberalized, allowing London firms to compete more effectively with New York and with firms in Paris and Berlin.[50] It was also the moment when decisions to end capital controls throughout Europe were taken.[51]

Finance was thus becoming more open and globalized, partly in conse-quence of policy changes and in part because of technological and organiza-tional developments within the financial sector.[52] The effects were widespread. Rapid shifts in the fortunes of one or another currency meant corresponding shifts in the economic health of one or another country; and this led to repeated efforts to stabilize exchange rates. These efforts were regularly frustrated by the fact that for a long time it was not in the interest of the United States to do so and without American cooperation any new regime was bound to be unstable. The United States had freed itself from Bretton Woods in order to cut a better deal with creditors and competitors. That forced adjustment was still far from complete when the oil crisis of 1979 caused a surge in inflation that was met by a dramatic rise in U.S. interest rates. The key objective of economic policy in the early 1980s, in the U.S. and the U.K., had been to control inflation, and that in turn meant that high interest rates were maintained in the mid–1980s. The Plaza Agreement of 1985 marked not merely the loosening of that policy but the reestablishment of financial coordination between the major economic powers. The Europeans had established a European Monetary System in March 1979, and once French and German fiscal policies became more aligned after 1983, and more in line with Britain's policies of austerity, it provided a reason-able measure of stability. When the U.S. decided in 1985 that it preferred a degree of stability, it became possible to replicate the success of the Europeans on a broader and more consistent basis.

The most direct and tangible effect of the revolution in finance was to expand lending and borrowing. Not only were funds readily available, but the demand was unusually great. The oil crisis was again a major factor: devel-oping countries in particular needed imported oil for their continued growth and, so long as inflation was high, the cost of borrowing to pay for it was minimal. As inflation subsided, however, interest rates did not, and nations with large debts found themselves unable to pay. The result was a series of defaults, or near defaults, by developing countries. The debt crisis was a mark of the integration of the global South into the international economy, and its resolution would decide the terms of that integration. It was an often bitter process, as battles between debtors and creditors often are, and involved clashes of interests, ideas and politics. Rescue packages would typically be negotiated by the debtor countries and the IMF, working alongside the World Bank. The two international institutions were also compelled to work in close concert with the countries that funded them and with the banks holding loans that were not about to be repaid. Since the U.S. provided the largest share of funds and since it was largely U.S. banks at risk, the circumstances afforded the Reagan administration a unique opportunity to set the rules of lending and to begin enforcing them.[53] The U.S. could exert pressure on the institutions routinely, but it could do so more effectively when it came time to increase contributions to them.[54] The World Bank expanded its resources considerably during the 1970s and early 1980s by securing contributions to the International Development Association. IMF borrowing quotas increased by roughly half in 1983 and again in 1990, and on each occasion the U.S. insisted on quite specific conditions and practices.[55]

The U.S., with the U.K. usually alongside and in agreement, brought to these negotiations a set of ideas that were in sharp conflict with those prevailing in the debtor countries and in the developing countries more broadly. During the 1950s and 1960s development was thought to depend largely on the state: the state would promote modern industries, perhaps through direct ownership, or through protection and subsidies; it would also discourage agriculture because it was not very productive and also because of the fear that specialization in agricultural commodities would create dependency on world markets and their erratic fluctuations. It was also believed that the long-term trend in commodity prices was downward, while industrial products would steadily rise in price, at least relatively. The terms of trade would thus also work against developing countries. The overall strategy was referred to as "import substitution industrialization" and it was a vision in which Third World countries would seek to work out their economic futures outside the world market or in a relationship with the market that was highly regulated. These ideas gained wide currency through the meetings of UNCTAD, beginning in 1964.[56]

To this statist approach was added during the 1970s a further focus, not entirely compatible, on keeping commodity prices high. OPEC was obviously the model and although the long-term objective was not to be like the OPEC countries but to industrialize and diversify out of the export of primary products, in the short and medium term it was important to keep prices high. This package formed the basis for the demand for a "New International Economic

Order," supported by the UN General Assembly in May 1974, for the ensuing "North–South dialogue" that gathered so much attention and for the Brandt Commission, which was its ultimate venue and advocate.[57] The Commission published its main report in 1980 and the Ottawa Economic Summit of July 1981 endorsed the idea of "global negotiations" based upon the report. The upshot was a conference held at Cancun in October 1981. Neither the Americans nor the British much liked the report or the prospect of a new global bargain, and U.K. officials fretted that "Cancun is likely to be a difficult meeting for the United Kingdom. Our general line is tougher than any other participant except the United States and perhaps Germany."[58] Thatcher and Reagan nevertheless felt it was politically wise to attend the meeting "both to argue for our positions and to forestall criticism that we were uninterested in the developing world."[59] They were determined in particular to block a proposal that the IMF and World Bank be put under the control of the UN. They largely succeeded: Reagan spoke on the priority of getting the domestic economy right and about how doing so "represents one of the most important contributions the U.S. can make to greater growth and development abroad." "We should not," he added, "seek to create new institutions."[60] Thatcher delivered a similar message, and the meeting would prove to be the end rather than a continuation of the North–South dialogue.

The debt crisis began the next year and would provoke a major confrontation between rival conceptions of how to engineer development. The initiative had by then passed to the advocates of free markets, however, and they would press their advantage in negotiations over debt. The collapse of commodity prices, the deep recession and increasing real interest rates deprived developing countries of what leverage they had possessed, or thought they had possessed, in the previous decade and exposed underlying vulnerabilities. The consequence was that during the 1980s a "silent revolution" occurred in the world of global finance: "From a starting point at which the state was viewed as holding a primary responsibility for controlling economic development, the 'third world' gradually diminished and even rejected that role in favor of privatization and reliance on market incentives."[61] It was indeed a revolution, but by no means was it entirely silent; nor was the shift uncontested.

The Reagan administration had taken office determined to scale back the role of the United States in institutions such as the IMF and World Bank, in part to save money, in part because of hostility to the very notion of lending to developing countries, and in part because it opposed the development policies in place at the banks and in the borrowing countries. The development banks included not just the World Bank, which began life as the International Bank for Reconstruction and Development, and its offshoots – the International

Financial Corporation (IFC), founded in 1956, and the International Development Association (IDA), established in 1960 – but also the Inter-American Development Bank (IDB), which was begun in 1959 and then gave birth to its own Fund for Special Operations (FSO) in 1964, the Asian Development Bank (AsDB), created in 1965, and the African Development Bank (AfDB), established in 1964.[62] Though the donor countries had consider-able influence in these institutions, they were not totally controlled by the West and on occasion showed genuine independence. The Latin American and African banks, for example, gave countries in the region a large say in deciding policy and were often at odds with the U.S. and its preferences. Nor was the World Bank simply a branch of the U.S. Treasury: under Robert McNamara's leadership it adopted relatively generous loan policies toward developing coun-tries and McNamara himself was deeply involved in establishing the Brandt Commission.

The first instinct of the new U.S. administration was to cut the banks down to size. The problem with this strategy was that if the U.S. reduced its contributions, it reduced its influence. In order to avoid that and the inter-national criticism that stance would elicit, the administration instead did a formal evaluation of the banks, their policies and the role of the United States within them. The report was published in February 1982 and explained that the U.S. had "a major role in the MDB [multilateral development banks] decision making process by tradition, law and practice" and it should not be given up. Rather, the U.S. should continue funding the banks, if at a somewhat reduced level, but support "should be designed to encourage adherence to free and open markets, emphasis on the private sector as a vehicle for growth, minimal government involvement, and assistance to the needy who are willing to help themselves."[63]

The principles that would guide American policy toward development and finance were to this extent already in place when the Mexican debt crisis erupted. What happened in Mexico began with a series of quiet phone calls to Washington on August 12, 1982, but the news that the nation would soon have to default on its $80 billion in loan obligations spread quickly and was heard loud and clear in the world's major financial centers.[64] Paul Volcker, Chair of the Federal Reserve, and Gordon Richardson of the Bank of England responded rapidly and offered a temporary loan; and in late August Volker oversaw a meeting between Mexican officials and major creditors. Volcker was also in close and regular contact with Jacques de Larosière, head of the IMF. The bankers agreed on a temporary suspension of payments but insisted that Mexican authorities accept an austerity program. An IMF team traveled to Mexico in mid-August. A deal seemed within reach but fell apart, largely because of the fractured character of Mexican politics and economic policy-making. The President, José López Portillo, was slated to leave office later in the year and would be succeeded by Miguel de la Madrid. López Portillo had come to office in 1976, just as Mexico was concluding an earlier deal with the IMF, and he was eager not to leave office having agreed to another. His instincts in terms of economic development were radical and statist and led him to appoint advocates of planning and state intervention to important posts, most notably Carlos Tell, who became minister of planning and budget and then head of the central bank. His policies were inconsistent, however, for he also appointed more market-oriented policy-makers like Jesus Silva Herzog, who had become Finance Minister in March 1982. He also effectively chose the economically orthodox Miguel de la Madrid as the next president. In short, Mexicans were split on how to deal with the debt crisis and over the role of the IMF and the foreign banks.[65]

The choice to confront international finance was taken at the end of August, when López Portillo signed decrees nationalizing the banks and imposing exchange controls. The next day, September 1, he spoke to Parliament and denounced the prospective agreement with the IMF and the system it represented:

> The financing plague is wreaking greater and greater havoc throughout the world. As in Medieval times, it is scourging country after country. It is trans-mitted by rats and and its consequences are unemployment and poverty, industrial bankruptcy and speculative enrichment. The remedy of the witch doctors is to deprive the patient of food and subject him to compulsory rest. Those who protest must be purged, those who survive bear witness to their virtue before the doctors of obsolete and prepotent dogma and of blind hegemoniacal egoism.

Special animosity was directed at the agents of capital flight, those Mexicans – "sacadolares" – "who have taken more out of the country than the empires that have exploited us since the beginning of time." "They have looted us," the President insisted, and he gave them a month "to meditate and decide where their loyalties lie." They had to bring their money back or face dire consequences.[66]

Three months would pass until López Portillo handed over to his successor. While negotiations continued over the Mexican package, the debt crisis spread to Argentina and Brazil. The government in Argentina had fallen after its defeat in the Falklands War and its successor was incapable of exerting any serious control over the economy; in Brazil, stronger growth had meant even higher debts. By November 1982 an agreement was reached between Mexico and the IMF and similar accords were later struck with Argentina and Brazil. In order to raise the necessary capital, the IMF tapped the private bankers to whom money was owed and insisted that they come up with additional funds. The ultimate aim, as Nigel Lawson explained, was to "buy time . . . for the western banks to rebuild their shattered balance sheets to the point where they could afford to write off their bad sovereign debts . . ." The price of that assistance was that those same banks would be subjected to "forced lending" to those same debtors.[67] The rescue of the banks would proceed apace with the rescue of the countries that owed them money.

The Mexicans ultimately agreed to a "reform program" – the Progama Inmediato de Reordenación Económica – that involved devaluation and tax increases. Conditions improved for a time, but the continued drop in oil prices caused a further crisis in 1985–6. Another bailout was arranged as Mexico agreed to measures to liberalize trade, to join the GATT and to begin a major effort at privatization. Such moves would eventuate in the decision to pursue a free trade agreement with the United States, which would become the North American Free Trade Agreement. Stabilization and "reform" would thus not come quickly or easily, and countries such as Mexico would have to come back more than once to the IMF and international lenders for support, each time exposing themselves to further installments of liberal or neoliberal reform.[68]

The IMF agreement with Mexico in December 1982 nevertheless became the norm for rescue packages for Argentina, Brazil and other debtor countries. Indeed, Mexican officials would play a major role in negotiating deals with other countries, for they now possessed the needed expertise and they had a keen interest in ensuring that no one got a better deal. Argentina was forced to agree to cut public expenditure from 8 percent of GDP in 1983 to 3 percent in 1984, to put up taxes on fuel, to reduce its balance of payments deficit, to stop indexing wages to inflation, and to take modest steps toward the liberalization of trade. The demands were too much and the arrangement soon had to be suspended, with a new deal reached in late 1984. Problems continued throughout the 1980s, and in 1985 Argentina balked at IMF demands and adopted a "heterodox" package aimed at growth over stabilization. Movements of this sort were not unusual, for in countries such as Argentina the requirements for political stability vied with the demands of fiscal stabilization. Still, by 1988 the government was negotiating with the IMF once again. A more secure agreement, involving all the familiar steps toward a more open and market-based economy, was finally put in place by 1991.

Brazil was in a similar position, in that it was also in the process of democratic transition and would for some time remain an unstable democracy that had trouble taking tough decisions, and its path toward fiscal rectitude was likewise marked by detours and resistances. As part of its rescue package in late 1982, Brazil agreed to cut public sector borrowing, to reduce its trade deficit, and to cut various subsidies. The plans did not work and when a new, civilian government took over in 1985 it lurched back to the left with a "developmentalist" agenda and another "heterodox" initiative, the "Cruzado Plan" of 1986. A partial default would follow and a year later the government sought new discussions with the "international financial community." A deal was reached in May 1988 and a package entailing deficit reduction, privatization, and financial reform was accepted. Stability returned. Remarkably, the tough treatment meted out by international finance did not bring about a reversal of the process of democratic transition, though it is unlikely to have helped.

Events in Mexico, Argentina and Brazil were replicated across Latin America and in other developing countries. No fewer than thirty rescue packages had been negotiated by the end of 1984. The extent of the crisis prompted Baker to propose a plan for more systematic relief at the IMF meeting in October 1985. He listed fifteen countries in serious need of relief – Argentina, Bolivia, Brazil, Chile, Colombia, Côte d'Ivoire, Ecuador, Mexico, Morocco, Nigeria, Peru, the Philippines, Uruguay, Venezuela and Yugoslavia – and urged that banks and institutions such as the IMF and World Bank offer new funds while debtors adopted adjustment plans. The Baker Plan was intended at least in part to counter efforts by countries in debt to shift the burden of adjustment onto creditor nations. A meeting in Cartagena in May 1984, for example, produced calls for lower interest rates, more access to markets in the advanced economies, more generous terms for the rescheduling of debt and a different set of indicators to assess economic performance. There were fears that the initiative could lead to a wider action and even to a debtors' version of OPEC, "debtpec." Such worries were probably exaggerated, but not entirely without basis, and they illustrate that the process by which a market-oriented set of solutions to the debt crisis was adopted was by no means consensual. Gestures of resistance to market-oriented solutions also served to concentrate the minds of policy-makers in the developed countries and to push them toward marginally more generous provisions.

Baker's initiative on debt coincided with the agreement to reduce the value of the dollar and to try to reduce the U.S. deficit, and both were aimed at correcting imbalances and rigidities within the world economy that limited the growth of U.S. exports. Economic recovery in the United States had been largely based on deficit spending, much of it on defense, but that path was not viable in the long term. The alternative was exports, which would be increased by lowering the value of the dollar, by forcing Japan to import more and export less, and by striking a global deal on trade – a key part of which would involve getting developing countries to open their markets. The Baker Plan was thus not only broader and more systematic than earlier, ad hoc efforts on debt, but its aims were bolder as well. It sought to pry open the economies of debtor countries by more aggressive use of "structural adjustment lending." The idea of structural adjustment originated at the World Bank in 1979 and a modest program was begun in 1980. The Reagan administration was at first not much interested and focused instead on getting debtors to adopt macroeconomic policies to lower inflation, expenditure and borrowing. The Baker Plan proposed to make greater use of structural adjustment and "conditionality" to get countries to adopt market-friendly policies.[69] The U.S. pushed hard for privatization, for an end to subsidies and for tax reforms favorable to investors.

The Baker Plan was not terribly successful in reducing debt. That goal would have to wait on the Brady Plan of 1989, named for another Treasury Secretary, which called for a more flexible set of options through which debt could be rescheduled and made less burdensome. Nevertheless, the Baker Plan was effective in pushing the development banks and debtor countries to adopt more market-oriented policies. The leaders of the Latin American bank, the IDB, put up sustained resistance. It had already irritated the U.S. by loaning money to Nicaragua, and in negotiations for new funding in 1986 its president refused to agree to U.S. demands. In the end, he was forced to resign and a compromise was reached that brought the IDB's policies in line with U.S. policy. A similar process occurred with the African bank, though its ability to resist was limited by the desperate needs of African countries.[70]

The IMF and the banks would continue to make loans throughout the late 1980s and beyond, for indebtedness was deeply rooted, and they would consistently involve strict "conditionality" and commitments to structural adjustment. The adjustments and conditions added up to what would be labeled the "Washington Consensus."[71] It was a list of ten reforms that Washington – in this case meaning Congress and the administration and also "the technocratic Washington of the international financial institutions, the economic agencies of the U.S. government, the Federal Reserve Board and the think tanks" – had in mind when it told debtors to get "their houses in order" and that had come together in a coherent consensus as of 1989.[72] The ten specific issues could be reduced to three broad preferences: for "macroeconomic discipline, a market economy, and openness to the world (at least in terms of trade and FDI [foreign direct investment]."[73] It was a neoliberal vision that a decade earlier had been shared by a few and that came to be dominant through a sustained debate with serious consequences and with big winners and probably even more losers, at least in the short run. It was a triumph for Thatcher and Reagan and their supporters and a defeat for the more Keynesian and growth-oriented and statist vision of their opponents. By the 1990s, in fact, it was hard for many to imagine a world economy that was not run on these market-oriented principles. Anne Krueger, chief economist at the World Bank during 1982–6, used her presidential address to the American Economic Association in January 1997 to reflect on the huge shift in perspective that had occurred on matters of trade and asked rhetorically "How could it happen that a profession, for which the principle of comparative advantage was one of its key tenets, embraced such protectionist policies?"[74] She wondered similarly about views on "the appropriate role for the state" in development. Her answer focused on the ideas and the research of economists, which were surely relevant. The argument here, by contrast, is that it was more a matter of politics, in which one side prevailed and another lost.

CHAPTER 6

Cold War Ironies: Reagan and Thatcher at Large

Domestic crises brought Thatcher and Reagan to office and presented them with problems requiring immediate attention. They came to office armed with ideologies that told them what to do at home. It was not easy for either to impose her or his vision on societies and polities with established ways of thinking that were not compatible with their pro-market outlook and with deeply rooted interests that would stand to lose from the implementation of pro-market policies. Resistance was stiff, and not unworthy, but it did fail, if only because the experience of the 1970s had done so much to discredit the conventional wisdom and established policies that Reagan and Thatcher were so eager to replace.

Foreign policy proved rather more difficult.[1] Thatcher brought with her a traditional English patriotism mixed with a uniquely intense commitment to markets and their virtues and a passionate anticommunism. Reagan's views on foreign policy were not dissimilar: he held to a view of the United States as a beacon of freedom and democracy that he had worked up into a set-piece speech while lecturing on behalf of General Electric. Both leaders had therefore a long history of opposition to communism and they had not moderated their views in the era of détente. To Reagan it was obvious that the Soviet Union was ultimately to blame for America's difficulties across the globe: while campaigning for President, he insisted that "The Soviet Union underlies all the unrest that is going on."[2] Thatcher was hardly less vocal. She was also very clear about the "Soviet threat" and insisted on the connection between democracy and capitalism. Thatcher attacked all varieties of "Socialism," "both in its more extreme forms in the Communist world, and in its compromise versions" practiced elsewhere, and lectured the Zurich Economic Society in 1977 on both "the material superiority of the free society" and its moral superiority: "The economic results are better," she claimed, "because the moral philosophy is superior." The next year she explained to fellow European conservatives that "Democracy depends on private enterprise as well as the ballot box and countries which have the first are more likely to be able to move towards the second. Free enterprise has historically usually preceded freedom and political freedom has never long survived the end of free enterprise."[3] In the worldview of both Thatcher and Reagan, anticommunism, free enterprise and freedom were inextricably linked. Who better, then, to articulate the rationale for a new effort to confront the challenge of the Soviet Union?

Broad predispositions in favor of capitalism and democracy and opposed to communism did not, however, translate easily into the specific decisions that make up the details of foreign policy. It would take time for Reagan's stance on confronting communism to become crystallized as the "Reagan Doctrine," and even then it was of little practical use in deciding how, for example, to assess and approach Mikhail Gorbachev. Thatcher, leading a country whose influence was not what it had been, was even more handicapped in moving from political philosophy to policy. When the Prime Minister visited Reagan in the White House shortly after his election, he noted that she was "as firm as ever re the Soviets," but that shared antipathy did not determine what stance to adopt with the Soviets or even with each other.[4] It did not, for example, prevent Thatcher and Reagan from clashing less than a year later over the effects on British firms of the U.S.-imposed embargo on trade with the Soviets in the aftermath of the crackdown on Poland. Nor would it prevent tension and awkwardness over the Falklands in 1982 or the U.S. invasion of Grenada a year later.[5] These were nevertheless the stuff of foreign policy and required serious negotiation, even among allies. Broader strategy was even harder to prescribe and before Reagan and Thatcher could try to end the Cold War, they had to decide what positions to take at a succession of summit meetings, what stance to adopt in NATO, what policies to advocate in the counsels of the IMF, the World Bank and ongoing trade negotiations, how to keep unreliable allies in line, and how to deal with publics increasingly wary about the arms race.

However significant the long-term consequences of the Thatcher and Reagan revolutions, at home and broad, the immediate effects on foreign policy were decidedly modest. What happened in international relations was not a transformation but rather a continuation, and intensification, of Cold War tensions and competition. The election of two noted anticommunist leaders would obviously result in a more bellicose posture and an acceleration of the arms race, though the move was not entirely of their choosing. The Soviets had convinced themselves in the early 1970s that the global balance had shifted in their direction and despite détente they were determined to press their advantage, if only on the margins.[6] On the other side, the United States and its allies, not least Britain, believed that they confronted not merely a strong and aggressive Soviet Union but also a developing world over which they had little control.

The Iranian Revolution may have done little or nothing to advance Soviet interests, but it was taken as proof that Western interests were not in control in that volatile and valuable part of the world. The ensuing second oil shock seemed an apt demonstration of U.S./U.K., and more generally Western, vulnerabilities and dependencies and served to enhance the sense that things were slipping beyond their control. Even before Thatcher and Reagan took office, their predecessors in Britain and the United States had responded by committing themselves to substantial increases in defense expenditure and the U.S. and the Europeans had agreed on the need to deploy a new generation of intermediate-range missiles across Europe.

With the election of Thatcher and Reagan, it could be said that this emerging Second Cold War got the leaders it demanded. And yet, these two convinced anticommunists were compelled to deal with a political landscape vastly different from what it had been when they first imbibed their distaste for communism. Not only was the Soviet Union now the military equal, more or less, of its superpower rival, but the "socialist bloc" seemed stable, fenced off by the Brezhnev doctrine and accorded a degree of formal legitimacy by Helsinki. There was also, at least in Western countries, the matter of popular opinion. Large sections of the public in the U.S., in Europe and in Japan had tired of the Cold War and become skeptical of the need to continue spending on defense and deeply fearful of nuclear weapons. The contest for influence in the developing world was much more finely balanced as well. The West had considerable resources to bring to the competition, but the Soviets did as well, as their successes during the 1970s testified. It was also obvious to all sides that the norms that governed, or supposedly governed, international relations had shifted. Empire, so recently the ordering mechanism connecting "the West and the rest," was simply no longer defensible, and decolonization, where it had not already occurred, was irresistible. It was also becoming much harder for the United States to exert its influence in Latin America through supporting local strongmen. Resentment at U.S. meddling was pervasive in the region, and after Vietnam it was matched by a wary reluctance among the U.S. public.

In addition, the United States, Britain, and the Soviets were all constrained by the newly powerful rhetoric of human rights. Even Mrs. Thatcher understood the need to assert that "Respect for human rights is the foundation of our democratic way of life," despite misgivings as to the application of the principle. Reagan likewise felt the need to reassert U.S. commitment to human rights despite a transparent desire to distance himself from what his administration considered Carter's excessive and naive fixation on rights instead of security.[7] Alexander Haig, Reagan's first Secretary of State, sought to switch the focus from human rights to terrorism and, by linking the Soviets to terror, to turn the issue around. Immediately upon his appointment, he proclaimed that "international terrorism will take the place of human rights in our concern because it is the ultimate abuse of human rights . . ." Or, as Elliott Abrams put it later on, "By taking a strong stand against the Soviet Union, we are dealing with the human-rights problem wholesale rather than retail. The Soviet Union is the center of a Communist system that is the worst enemy of human rights." This rhetorical move did not take, and neither did the earlier and comparable effort by Reagan's future UN Ambassador Jeane Kirkpatrick, to explain the difference between "moderate autocrats friendly to American interests" and "less friendly autocrats of extremist persuasion" and to articulate a rearguard defense of the former. Authoritarian regimes of a more moderate type, she insisted, could become democratic, while others could not: as she put it, "Although there is no instance of a revolutionary 'socialist' or Communist society being democratized, right-wing autocracies do sometimes evolve into democracies." The failure of the Carter administration, she insisted, was that it had "little idea of how to go about encouraging the liberalization of an autocracy." Instead, it acquiesced in the coming to power of extremists.[8] Even Kirkpatrick, however, was forced to argue in terms of what would or would not bring about more democratic regimes that would be more favorable to human rights. Equally important, human rights were increasingly linked to the very definition of democracy and securing them meant a commitment to "democracy promotion" and "good governance" and, more concretely, to democratic elections.

The Reagan and Thatcher administrations, in short, were forced to develop policies on a more complicated terrain that precluded the simple reassertion of Western or Anglo-American dominance. They had no doubts about the need to restore American and, if Thatcher had her way, British power and influence, but the path would lead in directions that the conservative leaders in the two nations could not foresee and with effects that were not anticipated. The consequences were deeply ironic. Efforts to assert Western, especially American, influence in the developing world meant that the U.S. (and the U.K. where applicable) shifted from supporting dictators to arranging for their retirement, if not overthrow, and to ensuring transitions to democratic rule.[9] The American and British decisions to rearm – increasing defense spending, proceeding with the deployment of intermediate-range missiles, initiating the Strategic Defense Initiative (SDI) or "Star Wars," and dragging out and effectively stalling arms negotiations – would produce an equally confounding result. Public opinion became deeply alarmed at a new arms race and the talk about fighting and even winning a nuclear war. To counter such sentiment, the Reagan administration began to couple its aggressive stance with a proclaimed commitment to peace and disarmament. Under its aging leaders the Soviet Union became confused and defensive and did not effectively call Reagan on the contradiction between strategy and rhetoric, but the relationship was transformed with the coming to power of Mikhail Gorbachev in 1985. And Reagan responded to the new Soviet leader by agreeing to arms reductions that stunned and upset his more hawkish advisors and that deeply worried Margaret Thatcher; and he and Gorbachev took the critical steps that ended the Cold War.[10] None of this was predicted, or predictable, in 1980 and it was the curious result of the confrontation between the renewed aggressiveness of the U.S. and its major ally and the new realities of international power and the evolution of new norms of legitimacy in the relations between states.

The Strange Course of the Global Cold War

The Cold War had many fronts in terms of geography but two basic issues: the strategic confrontation between the U.S. and the USSR; and the competition between the superpowers for allies and influence in the developing and often "non-aligned" world. The strategic relationship was also a matter of creating alliances and keeping them together. The framework of alliances had been forged in the late 1940s and 1950s.[11] The Soviets created their sphere of influence in Eastern Europe by installing like-minded regimes and the U.S., more subtly, moved to broaden the alliance that won the war by bringing the defeated nations within the fold in Europe and in Asia and in helping to create stable market-based democracies. The Chinese Revolution added massively to the global reach and potential clout of the Soviet sphere, at least for a while. The two systems took on their basic shape in the aftermath of the Korean War and they persisted for nearly forty years. There would be changes over time: the first defection from the Soviet camp was Yugoslavia; far more important was the Sino-Soviet rift, which had deep roots but became manifest only in the 1960s; for the U.S., there were recurring disputes with allies but no major break, although by the 1970s it would seem that the unity of the West had become notably weaker. The French always had trouble reconciling themselves to U.S. predominance, and by the 1970s the German strategy of *Ostpolitik* represented a reorientation of policy by the nation at the very center of earlier Cold War disputes. Détente also seemed to threaten the strength of the alliance by demonstrating the possibility of a rapprochement at the top that would leave the Europeans, west and east, unsure of the superpower commitments that underpinned their defense. These centrifugal tendencies were nevertheless just that, tendencies that were held in check as of the late 1970s and early 1980s, when relations between the U.S. and USSR turned markedly more hostile.

Reagan and Thatcher had long been critical of the policy of détente, but there was little left of it by the time they took office and little to be done of more than symbolic value. Because East–West relations were already at an impasse, there was also little prospect of serious negotiations between the superpowers. Arms control discussions were stalemated, and enhanced economic ties and plans for increased cultural exchanges became victims of the deterioration produced by the Soviet invasion of Afghanistan and, two years later, the suppression of Solidarity, Poland's independent trade union movement.[12] Neither side seemed to have much hope for improved relations and acted accordingly. The Soviet leadership was visibly aging, unable or unwilling to consider alternatives to existing patterns of Cold War rivalry. The problem of succession loomed in the USSR, and whatever underlying weaknesses lurked behind the facade of Soviet power, they were not perceived as threatening the basis of that power; addressing them could thus be postponed. The effect was that Reagan watched the Soviet Union bury three leaders – Brezhnev, Yuri Andropov and Konstantin Chernenko – before he held his first summit meeting.

The United States was also uninterested in negotiations while its leaders believed the Soviets might have the stronger hand. Experts were divided on the balance of advantage in nuclear weapons and the Reagan administration was careful not to claim that the Soviets were ahead: as Haig put it, "We have not lost the strategic balance that exists between the Soviet Union and ourselves." The argument was that the trends were adverse and required a determined effort to reverse them. Reagan was personally impressed by a briefing he received in February 1981 "on Soviet Arms. It was a sobering experience," he confided to his diary, "There can be no argument against our re-arming when one sees the production complex they have established for the mfg. [manufacture] of every kind of weapon and war machine." In his first formal letter to Brezhnev, therefore, Reagan spoke of "the USSR's unremitting and comprehensive military build up over the past fifteen years, a build up which in our view exceeds purely defensive requirements and carries disturbing implications of a search for military superiority." Perhaps carried away by rhetoric or by politics, by March 1982 Reagan had convinced himself "that, on balance, the Soviet Union does have a definite margin of superiority."[13] The perception that the Soviets were either ahead in the arms race or aggressively seeking to get ahead was enhanced by the very real fact that the USSR had begun in the late 1970s to deploy a new type of intermediate-range missile – the SS20 – in positions from which it could easily reach Europe, and had put in service a new Backfire bomber with impressive capabilities. The precise effect of the new weapons on the nuclear balance was as yet unclear, but they were new and visible: as Margaret Thatcher insisted, "The fact is that the Soviet

Union has the latest nuclear missile – the SS20 – and it is facing Europe. We must have a deterrent."[14]

The immediate goal for the Reagan administration, then, was "to rearm America," as Defense Secretary Caspar Weinberger announced in January 1981. A sharp increase in defense spending was proposed and approved shortly after Reagan took office. Spending on defense would increase by over a third (34 percent) in Reagan's first term and a number of new weapons systems were pushed forward – the MX missile, the B–1 bomber, the submarine-based Trident missile and cruise missiles.[15] Rearming the West would not only counter the Soviet Union's alleged gains, but it would also impose costs on them. Reagan explained his reasoning to a group of newspaper editors in October 1981:

> There's one thing sure. They [the Soviets] cannot vastly increase their military productivity because they've already got their people on a starvation diet as far as consumer products are concerned. But they know our potential capacity industrially, and they can't match it. So, we've got the chip this time, that if we show them the will and determination to go forward with a military buildup in our own defense and the defense of our allies, they then have to weigh, do they want to meet us realistically on a program of disarmament or do they want to face a legitimate arms race in which we're racing.[16]

The most important and, to many, the scariest program was the Strategic Defense Initiative, dubbed "Star Wars" by its critics, which Reagan announced in March 1983.[17]

The U.S. also pressed other members of NATO to increase defense spending. Britain did, others demurred; and Britain also arranged in 1982 for an upgrade and new deployment of Trident strategic missiles. At the same time, the U.S. and Britain resolved to proceed with the deployment of Pershing and Cruise missiles in Europe to counter the threat from Soviet SS20s. The plan had its origins in 1979, when Carter agreed to a request from the German Chancellor, Helmut Schmidt, for a NATO response to the Soviet initiative. The Labour government in Britain had also been in favor. The move was immediately controversial; it was denounced by the Soviets as upsetting the nuclear balance and opposition soon took root across Europe. The decision was nevertheless confirmed at a meeting of NATO ministers in December 1979. It was there agreed to pursue a "dual track" – negotiating the removal of such weapons with the Soviets while moving forward toward a planned deployment in 1983. The time lag between the choice for "Euromissiles" and their deployment would provide an opportunity for popular resistance to grow.[18] As it did, it became ever more important for Reagan and Thatcher to prevail over it.

It was not only against Euromissiles that opposition crystallized, but against the entire rearmament policy, and Reagan and Thatcher were forced to take notice. It might even be argued that the progress of the arms buildup and, later, of arms control negotiations was governed less by the back and forth between the U.S. (alongside Britain and the rest of NATO) and the Soviet Union than by the interaction between Western leaders, particularly in the U.S., and the publics they governed. Specifically, the audience to whom proposals for military spending and for arms control or disarmament were directed was mainly in the U.S., the U.K. and Europe. The heightened public involvement in, and skepticism toward, such issues was a distinctly new, or at least newly effective, feature of democratic politics in the era after Watergate and it was impossible even for leaders as determined and forceful as Reagan and Thatcher to ignore it.

The Reagan administration was especially vulnerable since, unable actually to do much to deter the Soviet Union, it choose instead to ratchet up its rhetoric. At his first news conference on January 29, 1981 Reagan spoke of the sustained Soviet commitment to "the promotion of world revolution and a one-world Socialist or Communist state" and explained further that "the only morality they recognize is what will further their cause . . ." U.S. military planners, including the Secretary of Defense, were heard to say things about planning to fight and "prevail" in a nuclear war and Weinberger spoke ominously of "horizontal escalation," a doctrine that would justify military action aimed at vulnerable locations within the broader Soviet sphere of influence. The administration was especially determined to question the legitimacy of Soviet involvement beyond its borders and to deny its status as a co-equal power. Recent actions in Afghanistan were repeatedly denounced, as were supposed aggressive moves in Central America. The crackdown in Poland in December 1981 was further evidence of Soviet perfidy. The climax of this ideological offensive was Reagan's speech to the National Association of Evangelicals in March 1983 in which he charged Soviet leaders with being "the focus of evil in the modern world" and urged Americans not to allow the "soothing tones of brotherhood and peace" emanating from Soviet leaders to disguise the "aggressive impulses of an evil empire."[19] Another round of Soviet-bashing would occur later that same year, when Soviet pilots shot down a civilian Korean Airlines flight, KAL007, on August 31, [20] Whether verbal confrontations of this sort actually worsened relations with the Soviet Union is not clear, but they could and did stimulate fear among Western publics and fueled opposition to the policies pursued by Reagan and Thatcher.[21]

The resistance to the deployment of "theater nuclear weapons" in Europe brought out huge crowds and was particularly intense in Germany, the Netherlands and Britain. Helmut Schmidt faced mounting criticism from within his own party and from the "Greens," and although he won reelection in November 1980, his fall from office in October 1982 was in part due to disillusion over planned Euromissile deployment. Helmut Kohl, his conservative successor, faced less opposition from within his party, but he still had to deal with a hostile public. In Holland the government was split and the Prime Minister told Margaret Thatcher in December 1979 that "half the sermons in Dutch churches were now dealing with nuclear disarmament . . ."[22] In Britain the prospect of Euromissiles led to the revival of the Campaign for Nuclear Disarmament, which had been a major force in the late 1950s and 1960s but had then languished until the late 1970s. Between 1979 and 1984 its membership increased from 4,000 to 100,000. New groups also arose, most notably the Greenham Common Women's Peace Camp. The camp was established in September 1981 and became the focus of efforts to blockade the local air base and prevent delivery of the new missiles: 30,000 women staged the "embrace the base" event in December 1982 and 70,000 people showed up on April 1, 1983 to form a human chain from Greenham to weapons production facilities at Aldermaston and Burghfield. In December, 50,000 protesters showed up as the missiles were being deployed. They did not block deployment, but effectively registered their displeasure.

The antinuclear movement in Britain made particular headway in the Labour Party, which adopted a unilateralist position in 1982 and would fight the election of 1983 under the leadership of Michael Foot, a long-time opponent of nuclear weapons. The link to Labour would prove a mixed blessing, however, because the party was itself in crisis after its defeat in 1979. Its program had moved sharply left, provoking leaders on the right of the party to defect and form the Social Democratic Party. Adding a unilateralist plank confirmed the leftward drift and – whatever the merits of the case against Cruise and Pershing missiles, or against Trident – the party lost contact with the political center. The link between Labour and the antinuclear movement damaged both in the end, for when Thatcher triumphed in the election of 1983, she could claim a mandate for both her domestic policies and for her foreign and security policies.

The American experience was not dissimilar. In April 1980 a coalition of peace groups published a "Call to Halt the Nuclear Arms Race" by means of "a mutual freeze on the testing, production, and deployment of nuclear weapons and of missiles, and new aircraft designed primarily to deliver nuclear weapons." It was a response to the failure to ratify SALT II and the arms buildup begun by Carter. With the election of Reagan, the "nuclear freeze" movement grew massively and came quickly to be regarded as "a dagger pointed at the heart of the administration's defense program."[23] Congress passed a freeze resolution in 1982 and on June 12 of that year close to a million people rallied for the freeze in Central Park on the occasion of the UN Special Session on Disarmament. The Democratic Party met to plan strategy a couple of weeks later in Philadelphia and there embraced the freeze movement.[24] In the elections of November pro-freeze referenda passed across the country. When the Democrats met two years later to nominate Walter Mondale for President, the convention was again strongly in favor of the freeze and the candidate agreed. In the campaign itself, however, Mondale was very much put on the defensive on the issue and he was trounced in November. Reagan, like Thatcher in 1983, could interpret his victory as a popular endorsement of his views on nuclear arms. The nuclear freeze movement would soon fade from view.

The large-scale opposition to the rearmament of the early 1980s was not without effect, however. Thatcher and Reagan were keenly aware and deeply concerned and policy was directly shaped by the desire to counter the proposals and arguments of those opposed to nuclear weapons. The "dual track" strategy owed its origin to the fear of criticism; Reagan's proposal in 1981 for a "zero-zero option" – no SS20s and no Euromissiles – was prompted by growing opposition to the pending deployment of Pershing and Cruise missiles; the administration's proposal to begin talks on a Strategic Arms Reduction Treaty (START) came as support for the nuclear freeze movement was increasing; and even the Strategic Defense Initiative was proclaimed as the path to peace that so many were demanding.[25] Reagan and Thatcher also put great effort into responding to their opponents. Reagan decided it was necessary in 1982 to go to Europe to defend U.S. policy and to try to disprove the widespread image "depicting me as a shoot-from-the-hip cowboy aching to pull out my nuclear six-shooter and bring on doomsday." He formally addressed the British and German parliaments and visited Paris and Rome as well. Reagan also spent serious time fretting over the nuclear freeze movement and even allowed his daughter to convince him to meet with Helen Caldicott, a prominent supporter of the freeze campaign.[26] Combating the campaign seems to have pushed Reagan in opposite directions: at moments he would talk eloquently about ending the arms race and eliminating nuclear weapons, but he was also driven to his most extreme formulations about the Soviet Union in making the case against a nuclear freeze. In his "evil empire" speech, for example, it was because the Soviets were so evil and aggressive that a mere freeze of weapons would not make the world a safer place. It is clear from her memoir that Margaret Thatcher also paid close attention to the antinuclear movement and mobilized to stem its advance. In November 1982, for example, she chaired meetings of ministers and party officials to plan strategy against the disarmers.[27] Within the government Douglas Hurd was assigned responsibility for making the case for missile deployment, but Thatcher herself was regularly involved.[28]

Much of this was posturing, and propaganda. "Dual track," "zero-zero," and START were not expected to produce serious negotiations but to give the appearance of a willingness to bargain. It is nonetheless likely that the very public debate on the arms buildup and the sustained mobilization against it, and the efforts of the Reagan and Thatcher governments to respond, had a real impact, at least indirectly. It is not impossible that it had a particularly strong effect on Reagan who, after all, had been trained to read and respond to an audience and whose behavior has left many puzzled.[29] He presided over a massive increase in defense spending, pressed ahead with the deployment of a new generation of theater nuclear weapons and with the development of entire new classes of weapons – and not just the fanciful "Stars Wars" plan. Yet he also claimed that he differed fundamentally with his generals over the doctrine of "mutually assured destruction" and longed for a world without nuclear weapons. There is no reason to expect Reagan to be any more consistent than other mortals and it is common enough for people in high and low positions to hold contradictory ideas at the same time and to believe deeply in them.[30] It is also possible, however, that the escalating discourse on nuclear weapons in the early 1980s moved Reagan into his almost utopian advocacy of disarmament. Thatcher, made of sterner stuff, never followed Reagan on that path and sought repeatedly to slow him down.

Third World Challenges

New constraints also affected British and American policies toward the Third World, where the competition for influence was becoming more intense. The civil wars and crises that attended the last stages of decolonization in Africa made the new realities evident even before the Reagan administration took power. Neither Britain nor the U.S. was happy with the tendency of postcolonial rulers and states to throw in their lot with the Soviets or the "non-aligned movement" or otherwise to oppose Western interests and policies, and they were particularly opposed to Soviet efforts to gather new allies by providing arms and funds or, through Cuba, troops to anticolonial insurgencies. Nevertheless, the United States and Britain understood that they had no choice but to support local rule and to help put an end to what remained of colonialism if they were to resolve the conflicts whose persistence invited Soviet involvement and encouraged anti-Western sentiment. To regain or increase their influence, therefore, the U.S. and U.K. needed to stand for independence and majority rule.

The experience of what became Zimbabwe was a good example.[31] When Margaret Thatcher asked her Cabinet about inherited problems and commitments, Lord Carrington listed Rhodesia as the top concern of the Foreign Office. As of 1979 it was clear that the civil war between the white regime and its opponents, who were divided into two main rebel groups led by Robert Mugabe and Joshua Nkomo that came together tactically as the "Patriotic Front," was not going to be won by the government side. The regime had been on the defensive since its inception and was further weakened by the collapse of Portuguese rule in Africa in 1975. Sensing which way the political winds and the guerrilla war were heading, Henry Kissinger belatedly began talking of human rights and tried to do a deal in 1976. The scheme failed, but the Vance-Owen Plan of 1977 demonstrated that the U.S. and U.K. continued to feel pressure for an agreement. The regime itself came to understand the need for compromise, but it chose to maintain as much control as possible by arranging an "internal settlement." This would allow elections with the partici-pation of moderate black nationalists inside the country but would exclude rebels with bases in neighboring states. Bishop Muzorewa was duly elected in April 1979 and became Prime Minister in June, but the white minority retained control of the police and military and were given an effective veto over what the government could actually decide; the rebels, reasonably enough, refused to recognize the results or the government. So did the international commu-nity, including the Carter administration.

Before assuming office Thatcher had supported the plan for an "internal settlement" and hoped when in power to get it accepted. But, as she would later explain: "unpleasant realities had to be faced. Peter Carrington's view was that it was essential to secure the widest possible recognition for the Rhodesian regime, for that country held the key to the whole South African region. He turned out to be right."[32] The U.S. Senate was willing to grant legitimacy to the new regime and lift sanctions, but the President was not. In Africa there was stiff opposition from the so-called "front line" states in the region. The new Conservative government in the U.K. decided that its best option was to give up on the regime and press for a new constitution and new elections. Doing so would not only serve to end the conflict, but it also offered an opportunity for Britain to regain some measure of the authority which its recent conduct in Africa had lost it. The pressure and the possibilities would come together at the Commonwealth Conference to be held in Lusaka, Zambia in early August 1979. The British press fretted in anticipation over the safety of the Queen, and Thatcher told Carrington while en route that she expected to have acid thrown in her face upon landing.[33]

African states within the Commonwealth were resolute in their determina-tion to effect the transition to majority rule. What Thatcher and Carrington decided was to assume responsibility and, if possible, take credit for a deal.

They were equally determined not to involve the United Nations, and for that reason the Commonwealth was the preferred vehicle through which to work.[34] Thatcher would tell the Lusaka conference that "The British Government are wholly committed to genuine black majority rule in Rhodesia" and outlined a plan in which Britain would formally reassert its status as colonial ruler and in that capacity negotiate a new constitution, a ceasefire and a transition. The result was a call to meet in September at Lancaster House in London. The conference was tough-going and protracted, but an agreement was reached in December. It would give power to the majority, but the rebels agreed to a ten-year moratorium on land transfers. Britain took over the reins of power earlier that month and supervised elections which brought Robert Mugabe to power. Soon enough Zimbabwe had turned into a one-party state, but Britain had extricated itself successfully.

Whether in the process the U.K. had regained broader influence in the world – or within Africa or the Commonwealth – may well be debated. What is not in doubt is that the confrontation with reality, and the need for strategic adjustments, would be repeated whenever and wherever the U.S. and the U.K. chose to invest energy and resources in hopes of greater influence. This did not necessarily signify a genuine conversion experience for Thatcher, Reagan and their supporters. They remained who they were, with all the prejudices and antipathies they had carried with them into office.[35] But the two leaders and the governments they led were also pragmatic and when necessary altered their stance to win broader acceptance. Reagan and Thatcher repeatedly had to bow to the newly powerful rhetoric of human rights and to pledge their support for democracy and self-determination. They were ideologues, to be sure, or "conviction politicians" as Thatcher styled herself and Reagan, but success was more alluring than ideological purity. Thatcher figured this out quickly, perhaps because Britain was in a weaker position all around. Reagan took longer, but he would learn as well, and the effect would be a dramatic transfor-mation in America's relations with the Soviet Union, in the arms race and in the U.S. stance toward the Third World.

The adaptation by the U.S. and Britain to the imperatives of a postcolonial world where human rights and democracy were becoming the norm, at least in theory, was not simple. It mattered a great deal to the Reagan administration whether the Soviet Union or its "proxies" were closely involved, whether the superpowers had already taken sides and squared off, and whether the regime in question was considered strategically vital to efforts to resist the Soviets. Afghanistan was close to a direct conflict and was fought out with a set of rules that left little room for human rights or for transparency. Because the Soviets had invaded, the contest was by definition righteous; and because the U.S.

response was covert and also by proxy – though by proxies with no interest in democracy or human rights – very little attention was paid to rights or democratic processes. Afghanistan was too good an opportunity to harass the Soviets to fret over details. When he visited Afghanistan in 1984, Gorbachev realized that it was a losing cause; when in 1985 he become General Secretary of the Communist Party, he began discussing how to disengage; and in 1986 labeled the engagement "a bleeding wound." The U.S. showed no interest in compromise, however, and in March 1985 decided to intensify the effort to push the USSR out of Afghanistan and to do so "by all means available." A year later the U.S. chose to provide the insurgents with more sophisticated weapons, including Stinger missiles. And even as the Soviets sought a formula that would allow a graceful exit, the Reagan administration kept up pressure for a complete withdrawal.[36]

Conflicts in Nicaragua and El Salvador were also viewed through a Cold War lens that made it more difficult for the U.S. to adapt to local conditions and to respond with appropriate flexibility and with attention to the new constraints affecting policy. Hence the near obsession with the supposed links between the Soviets, Cuba, the Sandinistas in Nicaragua and the rebels in El Salvador, and the sustained U.S. effort to destabilize Nicaragua by aiding the counterrevolutionaries, or "Contras." Hence, too, the U.S. support for murderous regimes in El Salvador and Guatemala. The Reagan administration's intense fear of Soviet influence in Latin America also led the United States to look very favorably upon the very nasty military leaders in charge in Argentina, people who were not merely anticommunist themselves but who worked closely with the U.S. and the CIA in combating the left throughout the region. They had played a leading role in "Operation Condor" during the 1970s, a secret international effort supervised and financed by the United States to hunt down and eliminate leftist rebels in South America. Estimates of the number of victims run to the tens of thousands.[37] These were apparently the sorts of authoritarian rulers and regimes that Jeane Kirkpatrick had in mind when she criticized the Carter administration's efforts to break with, or pressure, repressive but anticommunist governments on matters of human rights.

It was therefore only logical that Kirkpatrick, U.S. Ambassador to the UN, would be reluctant to side openly and decisively with Britain in its conflict with the Argentine junta over the Falklands in 1982. She and Secretary of State Alexander Haig sought a compromise resolution that would not embarrass the dictatorship or jeopardize its continued cooperation with the United States in anticommunist efforts across Latin America.[38] The British were understandably upset, but mollified when Reagan overruled his two top foreign policy officials and insisted on providing the U.K. with political and logistical support; and in the meantime, Caspar Weinberger had already given orders to the military to offer full cooperation with the British military effort to regain the islands.[39]

Despite the tilt toward Britain, the U.S. administration remained worried about the likely fate of the Argentine junta. Reagan himself was prevailed upon to phone Thatcher on May 31, after the British had landed and taken casualties, and ask her to negotiate so as not to humiliate the regime's leaders. Reagan explained that he was worried "about what happens if the present government, as bad as it's been in this whole affair, if it falls and is replaced as they would be by the leftist Peronists."[40] Thatcher countered by asking the President what he would do if Alaska were invaded and occupied by a hostile power. Reagan's answer kept being interrupted by Thatcher, who was not in a mood to compromise. On balance, and somewhat ironically, the Falklands War probably served to reinforce the Anglo-American connection by revealing how much Britain needed the U.S. and how effective it could be with American help, and also by showing the United States that it had at least one ally willing to deploy military force. This did not happen before testing the alliance just a bit, however, and the United States would continue to fret about its credibility among Latin American dictators accustomed to its coddling and support.[41] The United States would further test the loyalty of its closest ally with the invasion of Grenada in 1983 and again in its use of U.K. bases to launch air attacks on Libya in April 1986.[42] Grenada was particularly trying for Thatcher, for it came just days before the delivery of Euromisssiles in Britain.

The fate of other nations was not so closely related to the Cold War, or to the Soviets and Cubans. In such cases the United States, along with Britain where it mattered, was able to deploy its new post-Vietnam stance in favor of human rights and democracy and play a more positive role. Thus "Haiti was not part of the cold war context," or so Secretary of State George Shultz argued, and so there the United States happily said good-bye to "Baby Doc" Duvalier in early 1986.[43] In places like this a different logic was at work. The broader context in which international relations were conducted had changed, with democracy and non-intervention increasingly the norm, and more political actors – domestic and international – were able to make use of the new transparency of politics to hold the superpowers to a higher standard. Consequently, the United States would find itself in situations where it made sense to abandon dictators, even if they were old friends, and to acquiesce in or even encourage democratic outcomes. Forced to accept the fact that authoritarian rule was no longer a viable option, the Reagan administration had decided by at least the mid–1980s to embrace the promotion of democracy and human rights. The wave of democratic transitions across Latin America and in Asia during the 1980s had many causes, internal and external, but surely the transformation of U.S. policy was of real importance. The U.S. had long been supportive of local elites who claimed that the alternative to their privileged position was chaos and, from chaos, communism. When their patron no longer accepted that rationale, or reinterpreted it to mean that social, economic and political reforms were necessary to avoid such stark choices, the dictators' grip on power quickly loosened.

The turn to democracy was widespread, affecting Brazil, Argentina, Bolivia, Uruguay, Paraguay (a bit later), and eventually even Chile in South America, most of Central America, if incompletely, as well as South Korea, Taiwan and the Philippines in Asia.[44] A particularly telling case was the Philippines. In 1986 Ferdinand Marcos, who had ruled the archipelago with an iron hand, a corrupt family and U.S. support for two decades, was overthrown in the self-proclaimed "People Power Revolution" that brought Corazon Aquino to office. Ronald Reagan was unhappy, and he withdrew his support for the ailing strongman only grudgingly and at the very last minute. The reluctance to abandon Marcos is easy enough to explain. More complicated is to understand why and how Reagan's officials and advisors decided that Marcos had to go and pushed Reagan to acknowledge this reality. The Philippines were not entirely peripheral to the Cold War, for it had a left-wing insurgency, the New People's Army, with modest support, and the U.S. was eager to keep it from spreading. Its strength was estimated at between 16,000 and 20,000 in early 1986, and growing, though it did not seem an imminent threat.[45] More worrying to U.S. officials was that the regime was incompetent and the economy seemed on the verge of collapse. Collapse, disorder and disintegration could lead to instability with unpredictable results. It was this scenario that was more troubling, in large part because it might threaten the future of two U.S. military installations, Clark Air Force Base and Subic Bay Naval Station, leased from the government and regarded as critical for the entire U.S. strategic posture in the Pacific. George Shultz's memoir makes it clear that for him and ultimately for Reagan maintaining this posture was more important than keeping Marcos in power, whatever the President's personal preferences.

The policy question thus came down to whether it was possible to do both. Lurking behind all the short-term calculations, of course, was the memory of Vietnam and the fear of becoming tied down in another futile guerrilla war on behalf of a local leader too corrupt and too inept to survive on his own. The "Vietnam syndrome" was directly invoked in discussions of the Philippines and Marcos. Shultz put it very clearly: "There had to be reform in Philippine politics and within the military if the country was to deal effectively with the ... communist guerillas ..." "Throughout the 1980s," he recalled, "every time the United States tried to deal with a regional conflict anywhere, the cries of 'another Vietnam' were immediately heard; this time, such a fear might be warranted."[46]

There was also the more diffuse but no less urgent sense that democracy and free elections were now the norm and that regimes like the one led by Marcos had to undertake the transition to a government run by these stand-ards.[47] Why these new norms should be applied so readily to the Philippines had much to do with the prior history of the U.S. in the Philippines and their continuing engagement. It would also seem that the longstanding ties between the Philippines, the United States and Europe and the fact that English was one of two official languages guaranteed that what happened there was accessible and more widely reported on than events elsewhere in the developing world.[48] The movement of peoples between the Philippines and the U.S. reinforced this pattern. The effect, as Shultz explained, was decisive, for while the intelligence community predicted that Marcos would win the snap election on February 7,

> The American media were reporting a different view ... Via CNN millions followed the Philippine drama as it was occurring ... The Filipino media, in turn, were simultaneously rebroadcasting the American coverage back to the Philippines. So the Filipino people were watching themselves and hearing themselves analyzed primarily through American eyes. From the U.S. media, the Filipino public was getting the strong impression that Corazon Aquino had won and that Marcos was not going to accept her victory.[49]

No doubt a part of the public fascination stemmed from the crassness of the regime. Imelda Marcos, after all, became the butt of regular jokes on late-night television and even featured in popular song. And long after their fall, treasure hunters kept looking for the Marcos's stolen loot. Even so, the attention had political roots as well, and serious political effects. The U.S. abandoned Marcos and encouraged a peaceful democratic transition.

The focus on elections and democracy had roots in U.S. foreign policy more broadly. Again, it was the confrontation between the Reagan administra-tion's will to reassert American power and the recalcitrant world in which this would be done that produced the new turn in policy. What would become known as the "Reagan Doctrine" was premised on the notion that the main challenge to the U.S. came from the Soviet Union which, "despite increasing pressures on its economy," had nonetheless managed not only "to expand and modernize its military forces" but also to expand its global reach. As the "U.S. National Security Strategy" of April 1982 put it, "Using proxies and a diversified arsenal of arms, military training, logistical assistance, propaganda and economic aid, the USSR, in opportunistic fashion, exploits indigenous unrest in many regions to undermine U.S. influence, to bring Soviet sympathizers to power, and to acquire additional military bases."[50] The United States would respond on a variety of levels in different parts of the world, but a major innovation by the Reagan administration was to cause trouble at the periphery of the Soviet empire by taking on its clients and proxies wherever they were weak and exposed. They would, for example, work to aid resistance in Poland, continue to aid the mujahedeen in Afghanistan and pressure the Cubans in Africa. The key front, however, was in Latin America, where the Reagan administration would provide massive aid to friendly regimes and seek to undermine hostile governments. El Salvador and Nicaragua were of particular concern, and help in dealing with these trouble spots was the major reason for looking fondly upon states such as Argentina.

What was required for this campaign – in addition to local allies, money and acquiescence from Congress – was a rhetoric and a set of objectives. It was simply not possible to support empires, dictators and repressive regimes in the way it might have been in the early years of the Cold War. In a postcolonial world suffused with talk of human rights and democracy, the United States had to frame its goals in the very same terms. The reassertion of American power would have to be achieved on a new basis. Rather than simply shoring up authoritarian regimes, the goal would be to encourage a transition to democracy. In theory, that implied that Soviet or Cuban forces not interfere and that indigenous political forces take the lead. As the Reagan administration saw it, this did not preclude U.S. aid to existing governments and their military and police forces, aimed at combating insurgents and maintaining stability. The prohibition on outside interference was thus radically asymmetrical and to this extent hypocritical. Nevertheless, in this new era aid was to be coupled with efforts to move toward more democracy. There were also now precedents and institutions for monitoring these linkages and conditions, both within the United States and in the international community.

The emphasis on democratic transition was manifest in official U.S. policy toward both El Salvador and Nicaragua, even if it was accompanied by actions that supported a repressive government in the former and a nasty insurgency against a democratically elected government in the latter. Upon coming to office the U.S. administration adopted a hard-line position, stressing military aid over political reform, but even during Reagan's first term he faced stiff opposition from Congress and the public that forced the administration to couple human rights and democratization with support for defeating the rebels or, in the case of Nicaragua, the legitimate government. A turning point of sorts occurred in March 1982, when successful parliamentary elections were held in El Salvador. Reagan made great play with the substantial turnout and held it up as a model. The civil war in that country would drag on for another decade, but the United States had developed a new rhetoric, if not exactly a strategy. The move toward democracy would receive a further boost with the Argentine defeat in the Falklands and the fall of its military government, for it illustrated the fragility of authoritarian regimes and the fact that U.S. support for them was not guaranteed.[51]

In Nicaragua, U.S. efforts at destabilizing the regime were rationalized as efforts to force it to live up to its democratic commitments. It was a tough sell, however, and the administration was compelled in 1983 to appoint a National Bipartisan Commission on Central America chaired by Henry Kissinger to settle on an agreed policy, and in the same year it began a "public diplomacy" campaign to influence opinion at home and abroad.[52] The result was a formal plan for "Promoting Democracy, Economic Improvement, and Peace" in the region.[53] One might well doubt the sincerity of the commitment, but it indicates accurately the context in which U.S. policy was forced to operate. The final outcome was largely shaped by the political response within the U.S. to the Iran/Contra Affair. The administration's efforts to arm and train the Contras were covert but had been well known, and there was sustained opposition, but it was the mixing up of support for the Contras with trading arms for hostages with Iran that discredited both policies utterly. The U.S. was forced to back off its support of the Contras while continuing to proclaim its support for the democratic process.[54] In practice, it acquiesced in the "Contadora Process" through which regional leaders sought to foster democracy and development. The group had come together in 1983 and issued a "Document of Objectives" that dovetailed with at least the rhetoric of American policy, calling for, among other things, "democratic, representative and pluralistic systems that will guarantee . . . fair and regular elections based on the full observation of citizens' rights . . ."[55] The process dragged on with little impact, but after Iran/Contra it became the preferred forum for negotiation. Under its auspices a ceasefire was agreed in March 1988 and elections were held in February 1990. To almost everyone's surprise, the Sandinistas lost and, equally surprising, accepted defeat. Almost by accident, the U.S. had secured a resolution that was based on democratic elections, however much prior U.S. policy had done to hinder that.[56]

The new approach was evident in American policy elsewhere, both in the developing world and in Eastern Europe. A particularly controversial variation was the strategy of "constructive engagement" toward South Africa – or, in the words of Anthony Parsons, the U.K.'s Permanent Representative to the

United Nations at the time of the Falklands War, "what is laughingly known as constructive engagement."[57] Its chief architect and exponent within the administration was Chester Crocker, Assistant Secretary of State for Africa, who proclaimed as a first premise that "As a multiracial democracy, the United States cannot endorse a system that is racist in purpose or effect." The objective was "evolutionary change toward a nonracial system" rather than a "revolutionary cataclysm." The key was to recognize that existing regimes needed reassurance, then pressure, with the pressure carefully calibrated: "The innovative feature of constructive engagement is its insistence on serious thinking about the sequencing and interrelatedness of change. Priority must be given to those areas of change that logically lead to and make possible further steps."[58] Not unreasonably, skeptics pointed out that "constructive engagement" was not a genuine path to democratization but rather the ineffective alternative to more aggressive sanctions that might actually bring about change in South Africa; indeed, by 1986 the U.S. Congress concluded that the strategy was ineffective and passed the "Comprehensive Anti-Apartheid Act" that did impose serious sanctions. Even then, the transition to majority rule and democracy was not immediate, and it would require the winding down of the Cold War for its successful completion.

Less controversial than U.S. and U.K. policies in the developing world were efforts to promote democratic transition and weaken Soviet control over Eastern Europe, though they were inspired by similar objectives. The most important case was Poland, where a strike at the Lenin Shipyards in Gdansk in August 1980 led to the creation of Solidarity, an organization that combined the features of a trade union and a much broader social movement. It grew rapidly and massively and by December it was flanked by Rural Solidarity. The authorities were unsure how to respond: local officials were dismissed, concessions were granted, and the party leadership replaced; but unrest continued and the possibility of Soviet intervention loomed. In late 1980 NATO had issued a warning to the Soviets and the Reagan administration had done the same on the day after the inauguration.[59] The Soviets would opt for a local resolution to the crisis: General Jaruzelski, appointed party leader in October 1981, proceeded in December to declare martial law and order the arrest of Solidarity's leader, Lech Walesa. In response, the United States imposed trade sanctions on Poland and on the Soviet Union. The move was ill-conceived, for its main effect was to put a halt to the construction of the gas pipeline to get Soviet supplies to Europe, a project to which the Europeans were deeply committed and in which they had invested heavily. Margaret Thatcher, America's best friend, demanded a meeting with Alexander Haig to tell him that the strategy was wrong and would be resisted by allies the U.S. administration desperately needed. Later that day, she wrote directly to Reagan.[60] Eventually, after further miscues and disputations. the impasse over the pipeline was resolved, but it rendered the initial Western response to the Polish crackdown much less effective than it might have been.[61]

Nevertheless, events in Poland had a very big impact on the thinking of the Reagan administration. Poland was truly the first serious and possibly effective challenge to Soviet domination in Eastern Europe since the USSR had imposed its will upon the region after World War II.[62] East Germany in 1953, Hungary in 1956 and the Prague Spring in 1968 were graphic demonstrations of the fact that the Soviet-backed governments in those countries lacked legitimacy, but as rebellions they were noble but quixotic efforts. In Poland, by contrast, the opposition to the regime was deeply rooted and sustained, in part because of its integral connection to the Catholic Church, while the Soviet response, ruthless as it was, demonstrated the apparent limits to what it would do to enforce the Brezhnev Doctrine. The United States took note, as did the Thatcher government in Britain. Reagan understood that Poland was a unique opportunity: "this may be the last chance in our lifetime to see a change in the Soviet Union's colonial policy re Eastern Europe."[63] The effect was to transform the defensive anticommunism that characterized the positions of the two conservative regimes when they first assumed power, and that was manifest most clearly in increased military spending, into a more aggressive and even self-confident posture. In Reagan's speech to the Houses of Parliament in London on June 8, 1982, he claimed that "Around the world today, the democratic revolution is gathering new strength" and went on to boast about the course of history:

In an ironic sense Karl Marx was right. We are witnessing today a great revolutionary crisis, a crisis where the demands of the economic order are conflicting directly with those of the political order. But the crisis is happening not in the free, non-Marxist West, but in the home of Marxism-Leninism, the Soviet Union. It is the Soviet Union that runs against the tide of history by denying human freedom and human dignity to its citizens. It also is in deep economic difficulty. The rate of growth in the national product has been steadily declining since the fifties and is less than half of what it was then.[64]

Margaret Thatcher was ecstatic: Reagan's "whole visit here has been a triumph"; and the speech "marked a new direction in the West's battle against communism. It was the manifesto of the Reagan doctrine – the very obverse of the Brezhnev doctrine . . ."[65]

The Beginning of the End

Policy would follow in the same direction as rhetoric. In Reagan's first years the emphasis had very much been on building up the nation's military capacity, both conventional and strategic, so as "to deter direct attack – particularly nuclear attack – on the United States and its Allies. Should nuclear attack nonetheless occur, the United States and its Allies must prevail." In this context:

> Deterrence can be best achieved if our defense posture makes Soviet assessments of war outcomes, under any contingency, so uncertain and dangerous as to remove any incentive for initiating attack. This requires that we be convincingly capable of responding in such a way that the Soviets or other adversary would be denied their political and military objectives. Stated otherwise, we must be prepared to wage war successfully.[66]

Inevitably, as talk of this sort leaked out beyond the narrow circle of national security experts and military men to whom it was directed, it provoked not unreasonable fears of an administration preparing to fight and win a nuclear war. But the sense of vulnerability that apparently lay behind such views began to dissipate fairly quickly and in February 1982 Reagan ordered a thorough review of National Security Strategy.[67] The new strategy was announced in May and signaled a new confidence and sense of possibility. Reagan insisted that his administration's basic posture had not altered, but now he referred specifically to "the growing but vulnerable Soviet empire."[68] The official National Security Strategy announced in May 1982 was, if anything, clearer: it was not enough to deter attack and "strengthen the influence of the U.S. throughout the world," it was also imperative "to contain and reverse the expansion of Soviet control . . ." Arms control and non-proliferation remained on the agenda, but there was now also an explicit commitment to expanding U.S. influence – "to ensure the U.S. access to foreign markets, and to ensure the U.S. and its allies and friends access to foreign energy and mineral resources" and "to promote a well-functioning international economic system . . ." This aggressiveness presupposed a Soviet Union on the defensive and less capable of thwarting U.S. ambitions. Even if the economic aims were traditional American objectives, as they no doubt were, these were now linked to the question of national security and a possible advance upon the USSR.[69]

The truly distinctive feature of the strategy was its awareness of Soviet weakness. It was assumed that "the Soviet military will continue to expand and modernize" but this would happen "despite increasing pressures on its economy and the growing vulnerabilities of its empire." These were spelled out in greater detail in a more extensive report laying out the new strategy:

the Soviets will continue to have important vulnerabilities. The economies and the social system of the Soviet Union and of most Soviet allies continue to exhibit serious structural weaknesses. The appeal of Communist ideologies appears to be decreasing throughout much of the world, including the Soviet bloc itself. The Soviet involvement in Afghanistan has revealed some of the limitations on the effectiveness of Soviet power projection capabilities. Non-Russian nationalities are growing relative to the dominant Russian population. Events in Poland have underlined, and could contribute further to, the internal weakness of most Warsaw Pact countries.

These difficulties, internal to the Soviet empire, would combine with geopolitical challenges – the hostility of China most of all – to render the Soviet leadership relatively cautious: they were unlikely to "perceive a 'window of opportunity' for the next several years" and they would instead hope "that schisms in the West and domestic inhibitions in the U.S. provide them some latitude for additional actions."[70] The Reagan administration was obviously still of two minds regarding the Soviets – fearful and yet eager to exploit weaknesses – but a consensus was forming around the belief that it was becoming increasingly possible to confront and weaken the Soviet Union and by doing so to alter Soviet behavior at its source.[71]

The confrontation would be focused at the margins, but it would have multiple targets and, it was hoped, cumulative effects. Poland represented an inviting opportunity and when Reagan met the Pope, himself of Polish origin, on June 7, 1982, they agreed on a covert plan to aid Solidarity. In the U.S., the AFL-CIO would play a major role, as would the new National Endowment for Democracy established in 1983; the Catholic Church already had its mechanisms in place.[72] In early July 1982 George Shultz had replaced Haig as Secretary of State; and Shultz would further the rethinking of policy that had already begun. In August the President ordered a review of policy toward the Soviet threat, "with emphasis on its non-military aspects" and with appropriate attention given to "the political, economic, military and ideological means at our disposal for achieving favorable changes in Soviet behavior." It was obvious by then that Brezhnev was ailing and would soon be gone and so a reckoning with the system's "strengths and weaknesses" and internal sources of change was in order.[73] Well before that review was completed, the administration decided to ratchet up the pressure on the Soviets in Eastern Europe. As of September, 1982 it was decided that "the primary long-term U.S. goal in Eastern Europe is to loosen the Soviet hold on the region and thereby facilitate its eventual reintegration into the European community of nations." The main tactic was to "differentiate" in its treatment of different regimes based on their relative independence from Moscow and thus to encourage "more liberal trends," expanded "human and civil rights" and the "pro-Western orientation" of Eastern Europeans while "lessening their . . . dependence on the USSR." The effect would be to weaken the Warsaw Pact and stimulate "more private market-oriented development." The fact that the countries of Eastern Europe were now more dependent economically on trade and credits with the West meant that such differentiation could be a more powerful tool for prying apart the Soviet bloc.[74]

Brezhnev died in November 1982 and was replaced by Yuri Andropov, who had risen to the top of the Soviet hierarchy via the KGB. Though Andropov is understood to have been far more flexible than his predecessors, the first months of his tenure brought no major initiatives and no lessening of tensions.[75] The effect, it seems, was to confirm the new and more aggressive direction of U.S. policy, which would be codified in a White House document reiterating its stance toward the Soviets while outlining the conditions for beginning, or resuming, negotiations on arms control.[76] Reagan signed NSDD–75 (National Security Decision Directive 75) on "U.S. Relations with the USSR" on January 17, 1983 and explicitly committed the U.S. to efforts to "contain and over time reverse Soviet expansionism . . . to promote, within the narrow limits available to us, the process of change within the Soviet Union toward a more pluralistic political and economic system" and, at the same time, to "engage the Soviet Union in negotiation to attempt to reach agreements which protect and enhance U.S. interests." Success would require that the U.S. "convey clearly to Moscow that unacceptable behavior" would be costly and that good behavior would be in their interests. It was important that this message be delivered and understood "during the succession period" so that it might "affect the policies of Brezhnev's successors."[77]

The plan underscored the need for the U.S. to "modernize its military forces – both nuclear and conventional – so that Soviet leaders perceive that the U.S. is determined never to accept a second place or a deteriorating military posture" and to use "economic relations with the USSR" to "serve strategic and foreign policy goals." In addition, American policy would be given an "ideological thrust which clearly affirms the superiority of U.S. and Western values of individual dignity and freedom, a free press, free trade unions, free enterprise, and political democracy over the repressive features of Soviet communism." This "major ideological/political offensive" would be pursued in "all available fora" and a special effort would be made to prevent the Soviets from "seizing the semantic high-ground in the battle of ideas through the appropriation of such terms as 'peace.'" Alliances in the West would be strengthened and the U.S. would be especially active in the Third World with "security assistance and foreign military sales"; and there should be a "readiness to use U.S. military forces where necessary." There was also a clear recognition of "important weaknesses and vulnerabilities within the Soviet Union which the U.S. should exploit" and in the Soviets' broader sphere of influence. The West should therefore seek "to loosen Moscow's hold" in Eastern Europe, "to keep maximum pressure" on the Soviets over Afghanistan and "to ensure that the Soviets' . . . costs remain high . . ." The role of Cuba would also be countered, as would Soviet efforts to ally with Third World countries. Similarly, the U.S. would continue to exploit the differences between the Soviet Union and China.

The new strategy was not premised on the likelihood of rapid success, either in transforming the Soviet Union internally or prying Eastern Europe from its grasp or in moving forward on arms control. It was conceived as a plan for the next five to ten years which, it was understood, would be a potentially volatile period during which the USSR went through "the unpredictable process of political succession to Brezhnev." It was a framework, however, built on the premise that the Soviets were now weaker, more vulnerable and stretched beyond their capacity, and on the assumption that the system would probably have to change in order to survive and that this was a moment of opportunity for the U.S. and the West. It was obviously not a plan conceived in fear and weakness by people who thought the Soviets would prevail in a prolonged contest. Nor was it a product of blind ideological fervor. There was an element of fear in it, a lingering worry about military weakness, and considerable ideological commitment, but it also reflected an intuitive grasp of the shifting balance of economic and political power and the possibilities this created for the United States and its allies. It is not impossible that an antipathy to the Soviet Union meant a greater attentiveness to its strengths and to its weaknesses. In the past such a stance had often led to an exaggerated view of Soviet communism's achievements and the threat it posed; in the early 1980s, it seems to have been a useful predisposition to have.[78]

The United States had thus evolved a new and more confident strategy toward the Soviet Union by 1983 and had gone on the offensive on that basis. In June of that year Thatcher had won a resounding victory and by the end of the year Euromissiles had begun to be deployed. Reagan's reelection was still in the future, but looked increasingly likely. The U.S. had also succeeded by 1984 in its effort to put pressure on the periphery of what it regarded as the Soviet empire – Afghanistan, Poland and Nicaragua especially – and it was in this context that the "Reagan Doctrine" had been elaborated. Most important, the rearmament of the United States was well advanced. Reagan would later recall a meeting with the Joint Chiefs of Staff in March 1984:

I had one of the most exciting hours being briefed on where we are as a result of these past three years. Our technology is so superior to what our possible adversaries have and our improvements in training and readiness are inspiring ... I wish it were possible for our people to know what has been accomplished but too much of it must remain secret.[79]

Details might remain secret, but the effect on policy was visible. Reagan was convinced that "we could now go to the summit, for the first time in years, from a position of strength" and preparations were quickly begun to make an approach to the new Soviet leader, Chernenko. Before any serious progress could be made, Chernenko took sick. He was incapacitated through most of the summer, revived briefly in the fall, but continued to decline until his death in March 1985. Only then could there be a new beginning – more accurately, the first moves toward a climax – in relations between the U.S. and the USSR and in the Cold War.

If the combination of moves made by Reagan and, to a lesser extent, by Thatcher set the terms for the climax, it was Mikhail Gorbachev whose presence actually made it happen. Gorbachev was clearly a very different person from his predecessors atop the USSR. Younger, better educated and with the self-confidence to break with convention, his personal qualities commended him to Western leaders. Thatcher made first contact. She had convened a seminar at the Prime Minister's country retreat at Chequers in September 1983 and invited outside academics to discuss the Soviet Union and its future and how Britain should respond. Her view, nurtured at the meeting, was that it was essential to focus on the next generation of Soviet leaders. In that context she first heard of Gorbachev. After Andropov's death in February 1984 several Soviet leaders were invited to Britain; and it was Gorbachev who chose to come in December 1984. He impressed everyone, but especially Thatcher. She declared on BBC TV, "I like Mr. Gorbachev. We can do business together" (December 17, 1984). She later explained the reason for her reaction:

He is totally out of the normal pattern of what we have come to regard as a typical Communist. They tend to read from a very tightly prepared paper, and when you ask them questions they never answer them. He did not have a prepared thing ... We were able to discuss for hours, which is totally refreshing, totally refreshing.[80]

Thatcher passed on her views to Reagan and urged him to talk with Gorbachev as well. Less than three months later, Chernenko died and Gorbachev was named General Secretary. Thatcher would continue to play a role as intermediary between Gorbachev and Reagan, even if it was ultimately for the two superpowers and their leaders to make peace, or not.

Reagan had already decided in 1984 it was time to reengage with the Soviet Union, but there was little to be done while Chernenko lived and Reagan campaigned for reelection. In addition, the Soviet Union had walked out of arms control talks in Geneva when Euromissiles were deployed, so that particular venue was not available for negotiations. The talks would not convene again until March 1985, but by then there was a new Soviet leader and an opportunity for more high-level bargaining. George Bush invited Gorbachev to a summit while attending Chernenko's funeral and the two sides began to prepare for the meeting that would take place in Geneva on November 19 and 20. The precise date was fixed with the help of Nancy Reagan's astrologer, as was the decision about where the President and his wife would stay. In the intervening months there were tensions but also moves to lessen tension, but the most important developments occurred on the Soviet side. In late April there was a plenary meeting of the Central Committee in Moscow at which Gorbachev made it clear that the Soviets would become more active and forthcoming on questions of arms control. He also began to sketch out a new military doctrine that was more defensive in approach and in which sufficiency in arms, not superiority, was the goal. Over the next several months the Soviets would also announce a series of proposals for a moratorium on deployment of intermediate-range nuclear forces (INF) and on nuclear testing to demonstrate their peaceful intentions and, of course, to put pressure on the U.S. The U.S. sought to counter, but mainly rejected, Soviet proposals.

The buildup to the summit, and the meeting itself, set a pattern that would be replayed in each of the summits in which Reagan and Gorbachev met – Geneva in November 1985, Reykjavik in October 1986, Washington in December 1987, Moscow in May 1988 and New York in December 1988.[81] Both sides would make seemingly bold and competing proposals that had little chance of success, but the escalating discourse of peace and disarmament nevertheless took on a life of its own; and proposals, once aired, were hard to retreat from. There was a momentum that became difficult to resist. The U.S. was most likely to resist specific commitments, presumably because it was in a stronger position but also because of the individuals involved. Reagan had surrounded himself with ideologues who shared his anticommunism but not his vision of a world without nuclear arms; and they were reluctant to bargain away any presumed advantage. Eventually, many of these people would leave or lose influence, particularly after the Iran-Contra Affair blew up in November 1986. Until then, however, they were a genuine block. Reagan's strange personal stance – in favor of confrontation and a massive increase in the quantity and quality of arms but also fascinated by the prospect of eliminating nuclear weapons – further complicated the process of reaching agreement, for it led him to propose huge steps toward disarmament while remaining utterly unwilling to compromise on the SDI program. Reagan also had this characteristically American belief that if he could sit down and talk with an opponent, they could better understand each other and perhaps even agree. It was a naive and somewhat arrogant view, but perhaps also true and useful, and it was what inspired Reagan to write long personal letters not only to Gorbachev but to his much less responsive predecessors.

Still, since the U.S. was not inclined to deal, the key to reaching agreement was the Soviets' willingness to make concessions. The question is why they ultimately chose to do so. Reagan and Thatcher and their supporters believed that the Soviets were forced to acquiesce because they could not afford to keep up with the U.S. effort to rearm and, in particular, with SDI.[82] There is undoubtedly something to this, but it is also the case that the one thing the Soviets did well was to make weapons and they continued to develop their nuclear arsenal through the 1980s and actually began to deploy two new missiles, the SS24 and the SS25, in the early 1990s.[83] At their first meeting in Geneva, in fact, Gorbachev told Reagan that the Soviet Union simply would not allow SDI to succeed: "We will not help you in your plans, we will build up in order to smash your shield." The competition in weapons was costly and it did divert attention from urgent economic problems, though not everyone in the Soviet leadership agreed on the nature or severity of the system's difficulties. Even Gorbachev did not understand the seriousness of the emerging crisis until he began to address it, and his reforms would make things worse. So a determination to shift priorities seems an inadequate explanation of Soviet decisions on defense and foreign policy. More likely and important was a change in how Soviet leaders came to understand their interests and needs on matters of security and world affairs.

Indeed, Gorbachev himself began quickly to talk about "new thinking" and about the interconnectedness of the world and the obsolescence of inherited ideas on defense. At the April Plenum of the Central Committee of the Communist Party of the Soviet Union in 1985, for example, he spoke less of confrontation and rivalry and more of "civilized relations" between states; by the Twenty-Seventh Party Congress in early 1986, he had gone much further and effectively announced that the Soviets would no longer seek to advance world revolution by direct involvement: "Today, too, we are firmly convinced that fueling revolutions from outside, and doubly so by military means, is futile and inadmissible." Gorbachev's report also made little mention of the socialist bloc, as if it did not much matter to the Soviet Union. The primary task of foreign policy was now "to provide the Soviet people the opportunity to work under conditions of a stable peace and freedom." Increased global interdependence required the "creation of a comprehensive system of international security," for "the world has become too small and too fragile for wars and for politics of force." As Eduard Shevardnadze would later explain, from that moment on "Our guidelines were precise: to stop the preparation for nuclear war; to move Soviet-American relations onto a track of normal, civilized dialog; to reject the dead, brutally rigid positions in favor of intelligent, mutually acceptable compromises" and to pursue other sensible goals such as arms reduction and getting "Soviet troops out of Afghanistan."[84]

The "new thinking" proceeding in the Soviet Union meant that its interests came to be redefined; and the new definition meant that compromises were possible on issues that had long been non-negotiable. By contrast, the Reagan administration was intent on holding firm and not compromising on what it saw as the critical issues. In the series of summits that began in Geneva the U.S. insisted that in addition to talking about arms control, the agenda should include "regional conflicts" such as Nicaragua and Afghanistan, and also human rights, thus ensuring that there would be repeated opportunities to criticize the Soviet Union on all fronts. Reagan also refused to agree to any limits on SDI, despite sustained Soviet pressure. Nevertheless, the Soviets kept negotiating. They had already decided to leave Afghanistan and to scale back support for allies and proxies, so they were able to discuss "regional conflicts" without producing stalemate. Similarly, Gorbachev for his own reasons was busy opening up Soviet society, so talk of human rights and Jewish emigration was no longer quite so threatening. It also seems that the process of negotiating did lessen fears on both sides, and talking did lead to more sophisticated understandings and even to compromises that were not openly acknowledged.

SDI is perhaps the best example. Though Reagan was deeply committed, he did talk about Soviet concerns and sought to address them by "sharing the benefits of strategic defense." The Soviets might not have believed that promise – at Geneva Gorbachev pointedly asked, "Why should I accept your sincerity on your willingness to share SDI research when you don't even share your advanced technology with your allies?" – but it became part of the record and the debate. Likewise, the Soviets pushed to restrict SDI research and development to the "laboratory" and to keep within the limits of the Anti-Ballistic Missile (ABM) Treaty of 1972. The Reagan administration wanted tests in space and to jettison the treaty, or at least reinterpret it, but instead proposed a prolonged period during which the U.S. would not withdraw from it and then another period before it would deploy any new defensive system. Disagreement would continue, but over time the U.S. commitment to SDI became effectively qualified and hedged around with promises of sharing and delaying and more talk. The Soviets were also aware that although Reagan was personally mesmerized by the prospects of strategic defense, others were not.[85] Many in Congress were opposed; funds began to be cut after 1986 and Congress insisted that the ABM Treaty be honored. America's allies were also opposed to, or at least wary of, SDI and they, too, demanded that the U.S. stick to the terms of the ABM Treaty. Even Margaret Thatcher, though formally supportive, was not a believer and it was for that reason that Gorbachev had asked her to tell Reagan not to proceed with it.[86] The Soviets also understood that Reagan would not be in power forever; and George Bush would privately tell Gorbachev that he was himself more moderate than Reagan. So Reagan claimed he would not and did not compromise, but in fact something like a compromise was what came about.

All the while the proposals for arms reduction became more sweeping, so that the prospect of nuclear conflict began to seem ever more remote. The effect was that the summits became warmer, more productive and led not only to specific agreements but to a belief, not quite justified but almost, that the Cold War was ending. In Geneva, little was agreed but the two leaders got on and they issued a communiqué stating their agreement "that a nuclear war cannot be won and must never be fought" and a joint commitment to "prevent an arms race in space and to terminate it on earth." It was also agreed that neither country was seeking military superiority and that there would be further summit meetings.

For much of the year following there were minor disputes that irritated relations and, more important, stalemate on issues central to arms control. Despite evident frustration, in September 1986 Gorbachev proposed a "quick one-on-one meeting" in which the leaders would agree on the marching orders to be given to negotiators and bureaucrats. Less than a month later Reagan and Gorbachev met in Reykjavik, where they also failed to agree because of SDI. Nevertheless, the proposals they had put on the table were genuinely radical: the Soviets proposed 50 percent reductions in nuclear weapons overall and an INF agreement that would leave out reference to British and French weapons; the U.S. responded and agreed on strict adherence to the ABM Treaty for a decade, 50 percent reductions in "strategic offensive weapons" over five years and then the elimination of all "offensive ballistic missiles" in the next five years. The Soviets were wary of the last item, because they had heavily invested in missiles while the U.S. depended more on bombers. (That was why Caspar Weinberger had favored precisely this proposal.) In the meeting, however, Reagan said that "It would be fine with me if we eliminate all nuclear weapons," to which Gorbachev responded "We can do that." Even before this stunning exchange occurred, Paul Nitze, the U.S. arms control expert, said that "This is the best Soviet proposal we have received in twenty-five years." And it was perhaps too good to be true, for Reagan continued to insist on unfettered SDI research, Gorbachev demanded it be restricted, and the two left the table without an agreement.

Disappointment was palpable, but the effects were nonetheless profound. It was very difficult to keep hold of established positions and lines of argument after these proposals were made and made public. Each side had shown the limits of its thinking and, as Gorbachev said, the talks "allowed us for the first time to look over the horizon." At one point in the meeting, Gorbachev repeated his objections to SDI and Reagan responded by saying "We are accused of wanting a first-strike capability, but we are proposing a treaty that would require the elimination of ballistic missiles before a defense can be deployed; so a first strike would be impossible."[87] Exchanges of this sort might not have led to a formal agreement, but did signal an entirely new tone, and a tone radical enough to cause great consternation among American conservatives and among U.S. allies whose security was tied to existing arrangements. On hearing what had transpired at Reykjavik, Margaret Thatcher felt "as if there had been an earthquake beneath my feet" and decided she needed to fly to Washington "to get the Americans back onto the firm ground of a credible policy of nuclear deterrence." Meeting with Reagan in mid-November, she professed herself reassured, but there was really no going back.[88]

The next summit, though less dramatic, had more substantive results. In Washington in December 1987 the INF Agreement, which removed all intermediate-range nuclear missiles, was signed and an entire class of weapons therefore eliminated.[89] Other more specific but limited deals were struck there and at later meetings. It would take much longer, until 1991, for a START treaty to be concluded, but it was also an inevitably more complicated agreement. The Moscow Summit at the end of May 1988 continued the steady progress in improving relations, but it was also a matter of display. Reagan was there asked whether the Soviet Union was still an "evil empire" and he responded, "No. I was talking about another time, another era." The very last summit was briefer still, scheduled around Gorbachev's address to the UN on December 7, 1988. Though it led to no substantive new agreement, it took place at the moment when Gorbachev made his most far-reaching statements about what "new thinking" meant for the world. He spoke eloquently at the UN of global issues and programs, of the need to take ideology out of international relations and of "the compelling necessity of the principle of freedom of choice" in governing the relations of states. The new Soviet President – he had recently created and occupied that post – also announced a bold proposal for unilateral troop cuts in Europe.[90] Gorbachev's close advisor Anatoly Chernyaev would later complain that the import of the UN speech had largely been missed in the West, and the opening it offered would certainly not be pursued by the incoming Bush administration.[91] Still, it demonstrated yet again the distance that had been traveled in U.S./Soviet relations since the antagonisms and confrontations at the peak of the Second Cold War.

When Reagan left office in January 1989, much remained to be done to finally and fully end the Cold War. That job would be left to his successors and, most important, to the peoples of Eastern Europe. What had been achieved in U.S./Soviet relations was nevertheless stunning and it had largely been achieved on Reagan's terms. The defense and foreign policy commitments that Reagan, like Thatcher, had brought into office had to a remarkable extent been fulfilled, though in ways that were unanticipated. The two conservative leaders had also largely prevailed on economic policy at home and on the governance of the world economy. Markets had been liberalized, the preference for markets made the new norm internationally, and the great opponent of markets – socialism – put very much on the defensive. Something else had happened as well. As Reagan and Thatcher did their best to restore U.S. and British influence in the world and to spread their particular vision, they had been forced to adapt their goals and aspirations to the world around them. It was a world in which human rights and democracy and self-determination were no longer the province of the lucky few in Western democracies but the expectation of people across the globe. Thatcher and Reagan were thus compelled, as the price of success and continued Anglo-American influence, to refine their own policies so as to make them acceptable in the new global context. The result was that anticommunism became not merely a defense of capital and property, but something democratic and linked to the expansion of human rights; and the promotion of markets became, by fits and starts, also the promotion of market-based democracy. These transformations were partial, often grudging and massively hypocritical, but they were real and of enormous consequence.

Of still greater importance, the U.S. and the U.K. had put in place by the end of the 1980s a new model for how the world should work, how economies should be run, how states should look and act and treat their citizens, and for the appropriate balance between state and market. The model might well be criticized on grounds of equity and fairness and even for its effectiveness, but such criticisms were at this point more caveats and qualifiers than refutations. The approach was still new and yet to be applied widely enough and for long enough to render such judgments. But because the model was in place when the Cold War ended and when the most serious alternative model of how to order the world, national economies and the state was disintegrating, it was in a position to become dominant – a new conventional wisdom whose dictates would serve to reorder the world after 1989.

CHAPTER 7

Ending the Cold War and Recreating Europe

The Emergence of "Atlantic Rules"

Ronald Reagan left office on January 20, 1989; Margaret Thatcher would be replaced as Prime Minister on November 28, 1990. The timing was classically inappropriate. Reagan, who had publicly called on Gorbachev to "tear down this wall" in Berlin in 1987 and who had made a silent and solemn visit to the wall back in 1979, was not in office to see that offensive structure isolating West Berlin literally dismantled.[1] Thatcher would see the wall fall, but she would not be in Downing Street to watch as the Soviet Union was abolished on Christmas 1991. It was instead their successors, George Bush and John Major, who got to preside over their countries' fortunes and interests as these momentous events occurred and their consequences unfolded. Bush and Major were cautious men who lacked the vision and the passion that marked Reagan and Thatcher.[2] Their pragmatism was probably an asset at a time of great uncertainty, but it was an odd twist nonetheless.

The collapse of the socialist alternative was clearly a victory for the advocates of markets and democracy and a massive defeat for the other side in the great debate of the twentieth century.[3] It was in particular a vindication of the vision that Thatcher and Reagan had articulated during the final decade of the Cold War. A success of such magnitude and with such speed would have been impossible to imagine when the two conservative leaders first took office. Thatcher and Reagan, after all, had come to power as insurgents. They and their supporters understood that they were fighting against an orthodoxy and what they regarded as a liberal and statist or "corporatist" establishment. And the initial confrontations with the old order were bruising and did not produce easy victories. Nor did it appear that the Soviet Union, or its allies and satellites in Eastern Europe, was about to give up in the competition with capitalism. These regimes appeared stable and strong, at least in terms of military power and internal security. Things began to shift by the mid–1980s, both at home and abroad. Economic growth brought at least a grudging acceptance of what Thatcher and Reagan were trying to do in terms of domestic policy. In defense and foreign policy, the process of rearmament in the United States and Britain allowed the countries' leaders to think more seriously about bargaining with the Cold War enemy. They also sensed genuine movement on the part of the Soviets and the possibility of better relations, although none dared dream of what would soon come to pass. The assumptions and techniques by which the global economy operated were also now more or less dominated by the neoliberal vision of Thatcher and Reagan and it was in 1989 that the phrase "the Washington consensus" had emerged to describe the new consensus governing international economic relations. There was in place by that time a much broader set of Washington or, better yet, Anglo-American or "Atlantic Rules" that applied not only to domestic and foreign policy but to the very consti- tution of states. The new rules were predicated on the importance of markets operating freely within countries and of expanding markets beyond national boundaries; they involved a strong preference for market-based and rights-based democracy; and they envisioned a rules-based international order.

The collapse of socialism not only created an opportunity for spreading the wisdom of economic openness and market-based democracy and extending its scope; it was also its proof and rationale. The end of "actually existing socialism" in Eastern Europe and then in the Soviet Union, and its abandonment in prac- tice farther east, had profound ideological consequences that were registered with as much force on the political left as on the right. Conservatives might gloat, but their opponents had to rethink just about everything they had come to believe. A few clung to old beliefs, but without real conviction, while most came to terms with what had happened and thought anew about what was politically possible and, still more important, what was desirable and worth fighting for. Put very simply, the failure of socialism was taken, and not without reason, to prove the superiority of markets over states in economic governance and organization. Certainly, that is how it was understood at the time, and such an understanding ruled out alternatives to free markets as viable options for the future. In Central and Eastern Europe, for example, there was much talk and some hope that Soviet-style regimes would be replaced by social- democratic governments that might find a middle path or "third way" between the command economy, with its social guarantees, and more liberal models with fewer controls over capital and less social protection and security. It did not happen. Forty years of state socialism, party dictatorship and Soviet domi- nation left citizens in these countries with no appetite for a more humane socialism. There was to be no Swedish option in Eastern Europe.

The assumption that there was no serious competitor to democratic capitalism meant that what was still to some extent new and exceptional, the sharp
turn to markets in the U.S. and the U.K., suddenly became normative. Of
course, there were considerable differences within the "varieties of capitalism"
in different parts of the capitalist world, and these would not go away.[4] It was
nevertheless the Anglo-American version that was in the ascendant, in part
because it had so successfully captured the minds and informed the policy
choices of international financial institutions.

Not only was the new dispensation of recent vintage, but the model and
its rules were not originally proclaimed from a position of strength and
confidence. They had actually been elaborated in response to a profound
sense of weakness and loss of control on the part of the U.S., the U.K. and,
to some extent, their allies as well. The relative influence of the U.S. and
the U.K. had clearly diminished since the early postwar era, and by the 1970s
the U.S. had suffered a major defeat in Vietnam and the U.K. had retreated
from exposed positions across the world. Neither government had been able to
control inflation and generate sustained growth. What Reagan and Thatcher
offered was a set of strategies – economic policies mostly, but also increases in
military spending and shifts in foreign policy – and a rhetoric that, it was
hoped, would allow both countries and their leaders to regain control and
reestablish influence. The strategies were controversial, and there might well
have been better alternatives, but there was no arguing their effectiveness by
the end of the 1980s. Success meant that what were once specific policies,
experiments even, cohered into a model – what we have called "Atlantic Rules"
but for which other terms, like neoliberalism or "market fundamentalism,"
might work as well – that could be exported to, or imposed on, places where
they were not yet the rule. This was what effectively happened in 1989 and
the years following, when the putatively socialist states across Eastern Europe
fell apart and began to put themselves, their societies and their economies
together again. The effect was to open a space for the reconstruction of a major
section of the world according to the prescriptions of these recently developed
rules. When the Soviet Union collapsed a couple of years later, the possibility
of further extending the reach of the market-oriented paradigm presented
itself. The ending of the Soviet Union and of the Cold War also meant that a
once plausible and popular, statist option for the development of poor, non-
Western nations was also no longer seen as viable; and the application of
market-based policies would now become the most likely path for developing
countries as well.

The remaking of states, economies and the global order that began in 1989
thus opened the possibility of applying the formula arrived at in the U.S. and

the U.K. – and emulated in part elsewhere and now also firmly established within the institutions that governed the world economy – on a much broader scale. The opportunity would also constitute a test of the applicability of the model to places and peoples who had had no role in its creation and who inhabited societies and polities very different to those where Atlantic Rules had been devised. Would the model prove viable in these new settings? Would the leaders of the United States and the United Kingdom, together with their allies, be capable of adapting it to new and different contexts? Was the model itself sufficiently robust to serve as a guide to countries emerging from decades of undemocratic rule and economic stagnation? Were Atlantic Rules, appropriate perhaps to the economies and political situations of Britain and the United States and the particular problems these states confronted in the early 1980s, capable of becoming "Global Rules" and of informing a new world order?

Answers to these questions would vary according to context, and a final judgment on the viability and effectiveness of "Atlantic Rules" would have to be mixed and provisional even a quarter-century on. What was clear even in the first efforts to construct a post–Cold War world were four major facts: first, the formula was arrived at in the West after a long evolution and its imposition in other contexts would inevitably produce hybrid regimes, partial successes and much backsliding; second, the leaders whose task it would be to implement the new rules were cautious realists whose instinct was to opt for continuity and who were therefore unlikely to have the imagination or enthusiasm that would be required to translate truly heroic aspirations into hard realities; third, because the commitment to markets and market-based democracy was inherently antipathetic to high levels of taxation, spending and borrowing, things would have to be done on the cheap and reform, where it occurred, would have to be locally financed; and fourth, timing mattered a great deal, for decisions made early in the process would foreclose some possibilities and make others far more likely. The fact that the extension of markets and democracy occurred first and foremost with the absorption of the former East Germany into the Federal Republic was critically important, for it established the parameters within which the rest of the East would have to develop. And because Germany's emergence as Europe's largest and most dominant state would be masked and made palatable by its further integration into Europe, the application of the neoliberal formula farther east would come largely via the European Community (soon the European Union, EU) and reflect distinctively European concerns, policies and structures.[5] It was as if the new geopolitical framework, applied to the East, would first be translated into German and French. Even so, the Anglo-American or Atlantic vision was largely ascendant at the beginning of the process and it would be dominant at its end.

The Collapse, and the Opportunity

Turning the Anglo-American experiment into the paradigm underpinning successful rights- and market-based democracies and serving as the basis for the fundamental rules of the international economy and of international relations would not have been possible at all were it not for the speed, the scale, and the definitive character of socialism's ending. Why did the regimes in Eastern Europe fall so rapidly, with so little resistance and so little bloodshed? It would seem that socialism in that part of the world had essentially no support. Nobody believed anymore, and nobody would fight to keep it going. Its leaders and theoreticians had apparently lost faith in their own rhetoric and in the system it was meant to defend. Socialism outside the Soviet Union had, of course, been an alien imposition from the beginning, though it had some local support, and over time party leaders, the military, and those few who benefited from the system developed a certain self-interested loyalty. There was also inertia and the enduring fear of repression by the state and its security forces and by the Soviet Union.

The socialist states west of the Soviet Union had been hollowed out over time and by the 1980s their inability to deliver a decent life for their citizens meant that they could not compel assent to their rule. The contrast with the prosperity of Western Europe was a continuing affront to Eastern European leaders and a rebuke to their claims and pretensions, and now these governments were increasingly in debt to, and hence dependent on, their rivals to the west. Nobody predicted the collapse of 1989, if only because repressive measures were still largely in force and, with the exception of Poland, dissident movements were mostly cowed. Still, the underpinnings of authority had eroded and when the regimes were challenged in 1989, they showed little or no resilience. These were states founded on force and maintained by fear, but in the end they lacked the will to fight for their existence. The result would be a largely peaceful series of revolutions.

Nobody could quite be sure, however, that the Soviet Union would allow this to happen. The fact that it did owed much to the decisions of Soviet leaders, Mikhail Gorbachev in particular, who not only chose not to intervene but in fact urged on the process of reform. It is not obvious just when the Soviets determined that their dependencies in Eastern Europe were a liability rather than an asset, and when that understanding led to the view that continued repression would be counterproductive. Poland was probably critical, for even when it was decided to suppress Solidarity in late 1981, it was the locals to whom the task was delegated. It was the Polish General Jaruzelski who declared the "state of war" and rounded up the leaders of the opposition on December 12–13, and for a time the repression was effective. The strong Western response to the Polish repression also mattered, for it showed that the USSR's rivals and opponents were unwilling to acquiesce to the Brezhnev Doctrine. The resilience of Solidarity, which had gone underground and managed to survive until a general amnesty was granted in September 1986, also impressed both the Soviets and the West.

Still, it would require Gorbachev and his "new thinking" in foreign policy and his talk of a "common European home" for a new strategic orientation to emerge. This was not, however, Gorbachev's original plan and in 1985–6 he still spoke of "socialist unity" and "internationalism" and sought to strengthen the unity of the Warsaw Pact. The decisive shift came, it seems, in 1987, for the signing of the INF Treaty in that year showed that the Soviets no longer regarded the border between East and West Germany as the outer perimeter of Soviet defenses. It was also a sign that the Soviet leadership had ceased to fear aggressive moves on the part of the U.S. or NATO and had become less worried about nuclear attack.[6] The clearest signal came when Gorbachev addressed the United Nations in December 1988. There he spoke about the importance of international law and "freedom of choice" as "a universal principle to which there should be no exceptions" and he coupled this new rhetoric with specific promises to reduce Soviet armed forces overall by half a million troops, including the removal of ten tank divisions from Eastern Europe.[7] The implication, grasped at the time neither in the West nor by the leaders of the Eastern European regimes, was that the Soviets would not fight to protect those regimes, and certainly not against their own peoples. On the contrary, Gorbachev and his allies wanted reform in Eastern Europe as a complement and further spur to their own efforts to promote perestroika within the Soviet Union. And they now feared that if the entrenched leaders in Eastern Europe resisted and used violence to crush their opponents, the effect would harm the increasingly warm relationship with the United States and set back the reform agenda at home.[8] Ironically, the brutality unleashed against protesters in Tiananmen Square in Beijing in June 1989 served to reinforce this sense of what a crackdown in Eastern Europe might look like and Gorbachev's determination not to allow it to happen. His allies in Berlin, by contrast, welcomed the Chinese action.

The result was that socialism disappeared from Eastern and Central Europe almost overnight. The initial breakthrough came in Poland. Faced with a deteriorating economy the government proposed a series of economic reforms that would be accompanied by measures of democratization. A referendum was held in November 1987 under the regime's auspices but, according to the rules in place, it lost. It became obvious at that point that a resolution to the deepening crisis would require compromise with Solidarity. A round of largely spontaneous strikes against price increases in the spring of 1988, and again in August, underscored the imperative of making a deal with the opposition. Jaruzelski responded by proposing "round table discussions" and Lech Walesa, Solidarity's leader, agreed. It would take until February 1989 for the discussions to start, with much jockeying for position in the run-up, and until April for an agreement to emerge, but it happened. Solidarity was legalized and a package of economic reforms was agreed: most important, a complicated political arrangement was bargained out in which there would be at least some genuinely free elections. The electoral deal seemed likely to give the ruling party continued control, but when elections were held in June 1989, Solidarity swept the openly contested seats and the Communists were crushed. After a summer of complex negotiations, to which Gorbachev contributed by telling Rakowski, the new leader of the Polish Communist Party, that the entire organization would need to be rebuilt, a coalition government dominated by Solidarity took power on August 24.[9]

The timing was propitious, for by late summer tens of thousands of Eastern Europeans, Germans especially, were on holiday elsewhere in the region. Sensing a new openness, or possibility of openness, many decided not to go home, and East Germans began asking for asylum in West German embassies in Hungary and Czechoslovakia. Hungary was following its own path to a post-Stalinist politics, though it led through reform of the party itself. It was unwilling to send people back to the east and in September allowed East Germans to cross the border into Austria en route to West Germany. Shortly after, Germans waiting desperately in Prague were also allowed to leave for the West. The East German government was furious and humiliated on the eve of its celebration of the fortieth anniversary of the founding of the DDR (or German Democratic Republic, GDR). It was a stiff and awkward celebration during which Gorbachev told Erich Honecker, the party leader, to make concessions, for "life punishes those who come too late."[10] It was in fact too late already and soon protests swelled. Within a month the Berlin Wall fell.

The transition was equally abrupt in Czechoslovakia, where the writer Václav Havel became President in December; and in Bulgaria, where reform and opposition began within the party and led to the resignation of its leader, Todor Zhivkov, on December 10. The end also came rapidly in Romania, but there it did so violently, and the dictator Nicolae Ceausescu and his wife were brutally executed on December 25. By the end of 1989 every regime but Yugoslavia's had crumbled. It was not yet clear with what they would be replaced, for a distinguishing feature of these simultaneous revolutions was that, again except for Poland, the opposition was more or less unformed. Dissidence had been suppressed with surprising effectiveness until the very late 1980s and opposition movements and organizations had mostly sprung up only recently as the regimes began to disintegrate. They were inchoate, had shallow social roots and little political experience. The weakness of the opposition would be one reason why it would take some time for the new states to develop effective political systems and to achieve relative political stability. Another, and critically important, reason was that the shape of the new order was not something that the peoples of Eastern Europe would get to decide all on their own. The interests of the superpowers were implicated; so, too, were those of the larger Western European states – Germany above all, but also France and Britain; and the European Community would come to play a big role as well. Even so, the old regimes were now gone and would not return.[11]

Reconstructing the world after 1989 would require a new geopolitical settlement as well as the creation of new political systems and the transition from command to market economies. The transformations would have to be made more or less simultaneously, for unsettled borders and unstable regimes made for bad times economically, and rebuilding the broken economies of Eastern Europe and the former Soviet Union would require a measure of stability and the confidence that political turmoil would not wreak havoc with efforts at economic restructuring. The linked transitions were made even trickier because for the first two years the Soviet Union remained a major factor and nobody wanted events in Eastern Europe to cause trouble for Gorbachev in his escalating battle with the more rigid sections of the leadership concentrated in the military and intelligence services. The attempted coup of August 1991 showed that such fears were not misplaced. The emergence, shortly after the transformations in Eastern Europe, of demands for independence in Lithuania and other Baltic countries gave Gorbachev's enemies an occasion to press their attacks on his efforts at reform.[12] The fact that the first order of geopolitical business to be settled would be about the shape of the new Germany, its alliances and its relations with neighboring countries, added to the difficulties all around, for very few people in Poland or Russia or France – or, for that matter, in Britain – could view the emergence of a new, united and more powerful Germany with equanimity.

German Unification and the New European "Architecture"

The story of German unification, and the terms on which it was agreed, is therefore essential to understand.[13] With the exception of Poland, the revolutions that toppled governments across Eastern Europe in 1989 were the products of regime collapse, not popular mobilization. They were democratic only toward the end, when the masses become active and conferred legitimacy on essentially democratic outcomes.[14] The move to unify German, however, was very different, for it was primarily a result of what the Germans themselves wanted and ultimately voted for. It should not have come as a surprise for, as the British representative in East Berlin explained to the Foreign Secretary in April 1989, to understand the situation in the east it was essential to recognize:

> the force of the attraction of the FRG [Federal Republic of Germany]. This is felt in every sphere of life and at every level in the GDR. Obsession is not too strong a word to describe both the official and unofficial attitude towards the FRG . . . at a popular level the knowledge of all aspects of life in the FRG is remarkable.[15]

With the effective disappearance of the oppressive state apparatus, this quite understandable obsession would express itself as a determination to seek reunification, and rapidly. It took just a few weeks for this sentiment to crystallize, but it was clear enough well before the end of December 1989. Planners and diplomats, who had been hedging their bets, jostling for position and thinking about interim arrangements, small steps, confederal structures and a lengthy process, now began to grasp the need to begin planning for just how and when the inevitable would happen.[16]

The Germans were not allowed to decide their fate entirely on their own, for the major powers had much at stake and demanded to be involved. That he was able largely to satisfy the demands of the Soviets, the Americans, the French and the British while eliciting and then successfully riding the wave of enthusiasm for reunification among Germans was the great achievement of Helmut Kohl, leader of the Christian Democratic Union (CDU) and Chancellor of West Germany. He was helped, of course, by the fact that outsiders held conflicting views that never cohered into a viable alternative and by his close connection to the U.S. administration. The British had begun to worry over the prospect of reunification well before the fall of the wall and Thatcher had expressed her "alarm" to Mitterrand and to Gorbachev as early as September 1989.[17] The French President sought to reassure Thatcher by invoking the likely opposition of the Soviets, and Gorbachev would later confirm to the British that they did not want reunification any more than Britain did.[18] Thatcher persisted in her efforts to slow things down, but by late January or early February 1990 even she had come round to its inevitability.

The French position was more nuanced. Mitterrand grasped the logic of German developments more quickly than Thatcher and adopted a slightly more positive stance, whatever doubts he may have privately harbored. He also understood intuitively that the Germans would be eager to win the approval and acquiescence of outside powers for any moves toward unification. Under his leadership, therefore, the French chose not to try to slow or obstruct what was soon to become unstoppable but instead to get something from agreeing to it. Because France occupied the presidency of the EC during the last half of 1989, Mitterrand was well placed to make a favorable deal. Just eleven days after the fall of the Berlin Wall he hosted a dinner at the Élysée Palace for the leaders of the twelve members of the European Community. It was his opportunity to assert the Community's interest in events in the east and its role in shaping its future; he also argued for immediate financial support for Hungary and Poland and proposed the establishment of a European Bank for Reconstruction and Development to provide more long-term aid for the transition. Kohl, for his part, reported on the situation in East Germany and, while indicating his support for "respecting the will" of the people of the GDR, did not mention reunification. Thatcher did, and made clear her opposition, but the net effect of the meeting was to reinforce French efforts to press ahead with moves toward further European integration and to make the case that the transformations occurring in the formerly socialist lands should not be allowed to defer or dilute plans to strengthen the core institutions of the EC.

The argument, and the implicit deal, were further advanced at the European Summit in Strasbourg over December 8 and 9. Diplomatic maneuvering had intensified between the two meetings. The German government was busy consulting with the United States and the Soviet Union and trying to decide how to take the initiative within Germany without upsetting either. In a bold move Kohl presented a "Ten Point Plan" to the Bundestag on November 28. The plan envisioned a series of moves – first humanitarian aid, then various cooperative ventures, followed by more substantial economic support conditioned on reforms and leading on to the creation of "confederative structures" and elections. All this was to be embedded in a broader process aimed at arms control and more involvement in the European Community: "The future architecture of Germany must fit in the future pan-European architecture," as the Plan put it. Most important, however, it would end in unification.[19]

Kohl's plan provoked an angry rebuke from the Soviets and the silence from the British side indicated a definite lack of enthusiasm in London. George Bush, by contrast, was more relaxed about it and at a dinner with Kohl on December 3 urged the Chancellor forward. The U.S. stance was not entirely straightforward, however, for earlier that same day Bush had told Gorbachev during their Malta Summit something slightly different: while "We can't be asked to disapprove of unification . . . I want you to know that we know how sensitive this is to you."[20] Secretary of State Baker would deliver a similar – that is, mixed but supportive – message when he spoke in Germany on December 12 about the "Euro-Atlantic architecture" that should frame a new German settlement. He would continue to emphasize the importance of the "Architecture of the New Atlanticism and the New Europe."[21] Though the French for their part were irritated at Kohl's decision not to consult them before proposing the Ten-Point Plan, their response was to intensify efforts to frame future choices within a European context, and they would achieve success at Strasbourg on December 8–9. Mitterrand got largely what he wanted as the Germans agreed to move forward with both monetary union and the early convening of an intergovernmental conference to work out the political and institutional changes needed to make it work. In turn, the summit ended with an accord acknowledging that "the German people will regain its unity through free self-determination." Reunification would have to be achieved "peacefully and democratically" and in accord with the Helsinki Final Act and the Conference on Security and Cooperation in Europe (CSCE) and "within the perspective of European integration." It would happen, however; and so, too, as a result of the bargaining, would the Maastricht Treaty of 1991 and all that it implied.[22]

Mitterrand's focus on a stronger and more integrated Europe was part of a more expansive and fundamentally Gaullist vision of the role of Europe in a post–Cold War world. The abiding aim was to "exit" and move beyond the divisions set at Yalta and enforced through the long years of the Cold War. Though French leaders were on good terms with those of the United States in the late 1980s and early 1990s, the assumption that America would play a diminished role continued to underpin their thinking and the easing of Cold War tensions seemed to portend a gradual decoupling. Gorbachev's rhetoric about a "common European home" was a further stimulus, as was the continued functioning of the institutional framework that had emerged from Helsinki, the CSCE.[23] The French were not eager to see the United States abandon its security guarantee to Western Europe, but they were keen to limit America's influence beyond that. It was only logical, therefore, for Mitterrand to follow up his insistence on a European path to German unification and to the integration of Eastern and Western Europe with a formal proposal on December 31, 1989 for a "European confederation in the real sense of the term, that would associate all the nation-states of our continent in a common and permanent organization of exchanges, peace, and security."[24] It was a very grand proposition, though its origins were more mundane: the French wanted to link Western Europe with the newly freed and democratic countries of the East but did not want to offer immediate and full membership in the European Community, whose institutions had to be strengthened before any such move. Holding out the prospect of this "alternative to EC membership," a key aide to Mitterrand explained, had "the immense advantage of making visible the possibility of intermediate formulas between EC membership and the current situation"; and it offered "a chance to avoid the dilution of the Community."[25]

The proposal would founder, for three reasons. It ran counter to the aims of the United States, which sought to anchor the new European settlement in an Atlantic orientation. It also failed to satisfy the leaders of the new states in Eastern Europe, who came to resent their relegation to a halfway house for not quite ready and fully civilized Europeans. And, finally, it depended for its relevance on the continued existence of the Soviet Union, for which a friendly but not close or intimate affiliation with Europe had to be found, or so it was thought in 1989. By 1991, when the French sought to put flesh on the bones of the idea and bring the new organization into existence, the future of the USSR was very much in doubt. It would disappear in December of the same year.

Like so many other schemes and options floated near the end of the Cold War, the pace of events helped to render the French plan unworkable. That it was also more or less the opposite of what the United States sought in the search for a new order did not help. It was, however, not at all clear what the U.S. wanted, for the foreign policy of the Bush administration had gotten off to a slow start. As Baker would later explain, "the new President has got to be seen to be the new leader . . . to carve out an identity for himself and a persona for himself." Reagan was a tough act to follow and Bush, as Vice-President and then as candidate for President, had been forced to be a loyal part of the team. His subsequent efforts to differentiate himself from Reagan came out in small and in large and important ways, in relations with friends and allies and with opponents. Again, Baker's comments are revealing: he notes in passing how easy it was, at least in principle, to work with the British, "because they've got the same paradigm, the same philosophy." It was not so easy for Bush to work with Margaret Thatcher: "we had the initial tensions . . . with Margaret Thatcher," Baker would later recall, "who was a wonderful friend and a terrific Prime Minister . . . But Reagan was so strong, so powerful, and so secure in his own skin he'd let her speak for the United States. Well, we couldn't do that. The United States has to be the leader of the alliance."[26] As Bush would explain, "she still wanted to speak for the special U.S.-British relationship," but "I had to speak for myself."[27] Thatcher herself grasped Bush's dilemma, but could not help but note patronizingly that the new President "had never had to think through his beliefs and fight for them when they were hopelessly unfashionable," as she and Reagan had presumably been forced to do. "This meant," she said, "that much of his time now was taken up with reaching for answers to problems which to me came quite spontaneously . . ." The Prime Minister did, nevertheless, learn to speak less and listen more.[28] Bush, in turn, was grateful at the time and more gracious afterwards.

The awkwardness with Thatcher would not matter enormously, but Bush's early insecurity had more serious consequences for policy. Gorbachev had made a series of bold statements in December 1988 that, as Condoleezza Rice would later note, were effectively a "revocation of the Brezhnev doctrine"; and he hoped for, and expected, more of a response.[29] Instead, the new administration decided on a "pause" in U.S.-Soviet relations during which they would review options and assess the worth of Reagan's dramatic moves.[30] The reviews dragged on and what emerged in late March 1989 was derided as "mush." So while the Soviets and the world awaited moves toward the reduction of nuclear weapons and the formal winding down of the Cold War, the Bush team did little. And what they did seemed oddly peripheral. Bush and Baker chose as their initial task to focus on Central America, Nicaragua in particular. The decision was to some extent a replay of Reagan's first foreign policy moves, which also centered on the Americas, but it was perhaps also an oblique effort at critiquing and distancing. Reagan's fixation on Nicaragua and Cuba had, after all, produced Iran-Contra, the major failure of his presidency. If the Bush administration could resolve the issue successfully and in bipartisan fashion, the contrast would be widely noted.

The situation on the ground in Nicaragua in 1989 was basically a stalemate. The Contras had weakened the Sandinista regime, if only by deepening the misery of the population, but the government remained firmly in control. Funding for the rebels had been cut off and their effectiveness much reduced; they had agreed to a ceasefire in March 1988 and were now mostly confined to safe havens in Honduras. Because the conflict inevitably spilled over and affected neighboring countries, the leaders of the surrounding states had already come together in the so-called Contadora process, which had proposed elections as the alternative to civil war. That effort, too, had gotten bogged down, but was revived in early 1989 and the Sandinistas agreed to hold a presidential election in February 1990. Bush and Baker agreed not to request more military aid for the Contras but instead got Congress to agree a package of aid and related measures designed to encourage the two sides to negotiate and also to pressure the Soviets (and through them, the Cubans) into ceasing aid for the government of Daniel Ortega. The deal required hard bargaining and a more sustained effort at compromise than had characterized the attitude of the Reagan administration, but it was struck by late March and the plan moved forward. Throughout 1989 there were difficult discussions with the Soviets on the matter of support for the Sandinistas, but the policy was capped with success when Ortega was defeated in the election and chose to abide by the results.[31] The negotiations with Democrats in Congress had the useful effect of ending a protracted battle that threatened to block other administration initiatives; and the ending of the conflict through elections was a model of how "regional conflicts," as they were somewhat euphemistically called, could be brought to a close when the superpowers decided that it was no longer in their interests to prolong them. It was Reagan who talked of democratic elections as the path to reconciliation, but practice had often lagged behind the rhetoric; it now began to catch up.

However successful the Bush strategy on Central America may have been, it was nevertheless something of a diversion and the administration would continue to be preoccupied with these relics of the Cold War that were classed under the rubric of "regional conflicts." As late as Christmas 1989 – with the attention of most of the world riveted on Eastern Europe – the issue at the top of the Bush foreign policy agenda was Panama and the troublesome General Noriega.[32] Eventually, Bush and his advisors would be forced to turn to the big issues concerning the Soviets, the fate of Europe and weapons. Bush moved slowly, however, and displayed a strange wariness about how to deal with Gorbachev. The U.S. was on the verge of prevailing in a forty-year conflict, but its leaders felt that they were on the defensive. Some policy-makers did not believe that the reforms occurring in the Soviet Union were serious, while others feared that reform would be reversed. Bush's advisors worried as well that Gorbachev would upstage the President by unveiling ever more attractive proposals on weapons and troops. As Bush himself explained in February, "We must take the offensive. We cannot just be seen as reacting to yet another Gorbachev move."[33] Baker, Bush and Brent Scowcroft, the head of the National Security Council, fretted also, and not unreasonably, about the impact of such gestures on U.S. allies and their willingness to remain loyal to NATO. Their views were similar to those of the French: both saw a post–Cold War world in which the United States was much less engaged with Europe, but what appealed to the French frightened the Americans. The objective of the Bush administration was thus to maintain continuity and to keep existing structures intact by making modest adaptations to what were drastically new circumstances. Such caution was deliberately uninspired and easily derided, though in the context perhaps understandable.

The most pressing and specific issue confronting the alliance was the perceived need to modernize its short-range nuclear forces by replacing the Lance missile. Pending a broader review of strategy, the Bush administration would focus on that. It was precisely the kind of decision that could elicit popular opposition and erode support for NATO and for the role of the U.S. on the European continent. The deployment of intermediate-range missiles in the early 1980s had led to large-scale demonstrations across Europe and tested the resolve of governments. The INF Agreement of 1987 would eliminate these, but would leave in place both long-range, strategic missiles and short-range missiles. The Soviets had more short-range missiles than NATO and theirs were of more recent vintage; and the USSR and the Warsaw Pact had far more troops and tanks in Europe than did NATO. To the military the logic was clear and compelling: the West needed to develop a stock of modernized short-range missiles to correct the imbalance. Many others, however, drew the opposite conclusion and believed that, having eliminated one class of weapons, the next step was to negotiate the reduction or elimination of others. With the Soviet threat no longer so apparent and the Cold War apparently winding down, there was widespread doubt about the continued need to hold on to all or any weapons of mass destruction. The summit meetings between Reagan and Gorbachev had encouraged such views, while drawing attention to strategic weapons and the possibility of major reductions. Gorbachev's UN speech in December 1988 increased pressure for further measures of disarmament, for he proposed unilateral reductions of conventional forces in Europe and negotiation on short-range missiles. No agreement on strategic or short-range nuclear weapons had been reached by the time Reagan left office, however, nor had there been much progress in talks on conventional forces, which had been dragging on since the mid–1970s.[34]

The demand for further disarmament was particularly strong in Germany and Kohl seemed eager to satisfy it. He was facing what looked to be a difficult reelection campaign and his opponents were pressing him hard. Thatcher was characteristically contemptuous of the "signs of wobble" in Bonn, and British officials worried that "German views on nuclear matters . . . are finding quite an echo with others on the continent."[35] The Bush administration recognized the growing divergence in views between the U.S. and the U.K., on the one hand, and other countries in NATO, on the other, but chose to respond more pragmatically. In March 1989 the NSC had argued: "Today, the top priority for American foreign policy in Europe should be the fate of the Federal Republic of Germany." Bush should therefore do what he could to help Kohl's reelection prospects, for his "government is now lagging in the polls behind an opposition that, as currently constituted, has too little regard either for nuclear deterrence or for conventional defense." Scowcroft was increasingly focused on Europe and the possibility of reducing troop levels and "overcoming the division of Europe through greater openness and pluralism . . ." He also raised the lingering and potentially divisive issue of the "German question" and argued that, although the Germans themselves were very cautious about the matter, the U.S. and NATO could restate their traditional support for German self-determination but "improve on this formula, make it more pointed, and send a clear signal to the Germans that we are ready to do more if the climate allows it."[36] As an aide to Baker explained, NATO had long had in place a "commitment to German unification. And there's no doubt the topic is coming back.

The real question is whether Gorbachev will grab it first. (Or else the Germans will grab it . . .) – We need to move out ahead in a way that establishes a *Western anchor* for this process."[37]

The outlines of a distinctive Bush strategy were thus beginning to take shape even as the more formal reviews of foreign policy remained incomplete. The U.S. would seek to finesse the issue of short-range missiles and shift the terms of debate about disarmament toward conventional forces in Europe. It was hoped that the move would appease German and broader European desires for more progress in reducing the military forces arrayed in and around the continent. The aim was to keep NATO solid and to tie Germany more firmly to the alliance. The Germans would be further attracted to the American proposals by the hints coming from the administration about the possibility of eventual reunification. The objective was to overcome an emerging crisis in the alliance while also getting the Soviets to cede their advantage in conventional forces upon which rested their domination of Eastern Europe. A focus on Europe, moreover, might tilt the battle for public opinion away from Gorbachev: as Bush put it: "Maybe Eastern Europe is it – get in there in his end zone. Not to stir up revolution, but we're right on human rights, democracy, and freedom."[38] Scowcroft, Bush's National Security Advisor, made a similar calculation: He wanted "to change our policy towards the Soviet Union – which had been one based on arms control directly – to a policy focused primarily on Eastern Europe . . ."[39] He advised the President to focus specifically on Berlin, for "It is clear that one point on which the Soviets are on the defensive relates to the Berlin Wall. We need throughout the coming year to bang on that theme every chance we get."[40] Of course, nobody in the administration anticipated how quickly and easily the regimes in Eastern Europe would collapse and it was almost impossible to imagine that the Berlin Wall might fall; no one predicted quick movement toward German unification; and nobody yet dared dream of the end of the Soviet Union. Still, the American strategy to cope with what was understood to be a major challenge to the Western alliance was unusually adept and even prescient, even if it grew from defensiveness and an unimaginative perspective rooted in the past.[41]

Bush proceeded cautiously even as external criticism of his apparent passivity increased and frustration built up inside the administration. Baker had visited European capitals in February 1989 and what he heard there served to push the administration toward the strategic choices that Bush was slowly groping for; and a subsequent meeting with the Soviet Foreign Affairs Minister, Eduard Shevardnadze, in Vienna in early March convinced Baker that the top leaders of the USSR regarded perestroika as genuinely revolutionary and essential.[42] In order to produce any serious initiative, however, the Bush administration seemed to require external stimuli and imposed dead-lines. White House planners in fact arranged for Bush to give a series of four major policy speeches in April and May – in Hamtramck, Michigan on April 17, at commencement ceremonies at Texas A&M University on May 12, at Boston University on May 21, and at the U.S. Coast Guard Academy on May 24.[43] The idea was to use these to come up with policies that went further than previous initiatives and that aimed to move "beyond containment." In Michigan the President announced support for reforms in Poland and a modest increase in aid, though the pronouncements generated little enthusiasm. And while Bush was struggling to articulate a new, but typically cautious, policy, allies and rivals were not so reticent. News was leaked in late April that the German government had decided to press for immediate negotiations on short-range missiles. Bush, Scowcroft and Baker were annoyed, Thatcher seriously so; and the British Prime Minister used the occasion to argue once more that the U.S. and the U.K. had to work jointly to " 'rescue' the alliance."[44]

Three weeks later, the Bush administration was again put on the defensive diplomatically when Baker traveled to the Soviet Union for meetings with Shevardnadze and Gorbachev. Shevardnadze effectively asked the U.S. to endorse perestroika and disavow skeptics; and he repeated what was now the emerging Soviet line on Eastern Europe in favor of "freedom of choice."[45] Gorbachev met Baker on May 11 and also insisted on the reality and necessity of perestroika – surely another sign that it remained precarious – but went on to discuss arms control. He made further proposals about reducing conventional weapons and troops in Europe and added that the USSR would unilater-ally withdraw 500 tactical nuclear weapons from Eastern Europe within the year and negotiate for their complete elimination within two years. When Baker demurred, Gorbachev responded pointedly that "The United States does not believe this is an urgent problem, but we in Europe feel differently." He clearly meant the remark for a Western European audience and it was fully in tune with the call for a "common European home."[46]

The United States finally came up with a meaningful response at the NATO Summit at the end of May. On May 5 Kohl spoke with Bush by phone and communicated his commitment to the alliance and, at least implicitly, a will-ingness to compromise on short-range missiles. Baker, back from the Soviet Union and still smarting from having been outmaneuvered by Gorbachev, told the President that he needed to come up with something that not only sounded bolder but that was substantial enough to respond to the domestic political needs of his allies. Over the two weeks prior to the NATO Summit a proposal for a dramatic 20 percent cut in conventional weapons was worked out, sold to doubters within the administration such as Richard Cheney and the Joint

Chiefs, and then communicated confidentially to other members of NATO countries.[47] The CFE (conventional forces) plan was to be agreed within six months and implemented not long after. The stepped-up timetable allowed the U.S. to agree in principle to negotiate on tactical nuclear weapons, but only after movement on conventional weapons. The French and Germans were pleased; Thatcher professed herself "very wary" but said in the end that "If the President wants it, of course we will do it."[48]

The meeting and the U.S. package elicited a very favorable response.[49] Bush boasted that he was proposing a "revolutionary conventional arms control agreement"; and many agreed.[50] It seemed as though Bush had at last found a vision and it was uncharacteristically bold: it was of a world "beyond containment" and beyond the Cold War, in which the Soviets would be reintegrated as a normal state. Mitterrand was especially gracious: "The President of the United States has displayed imagination – indeed, intellectual audacity of the rarest kind." (Especially rare, one must suppose, outside of Paris.) Even the Soviets, desperate for progress in whatever arena, responded positively. Perhaps equally important, Bush pressed his advantage by delivering a speech in Mainz two days later, on May 31, that praised NATO and the Germans and claimed that the new mission of the alliance was to promote European unity. "Let Europe be whole and free," he said, and in so doing he held out the alluring prospect of a Europe that was increasingly integrated, with barriers removed and reconciliation between East and West. "The Cold War began," explained Bush, "with the division of Europe. It can only end when Europe is whole. Today it is this very concept of a divided Europe that is under siege."[51] The effects of the U.S. effort at the NATO Summit were critical and long-term: the U.S. began to offer an appropriately European but also "Atlanticist" strategy for dealing with what would soon become the end of the Cold War; the strategy, still inchoate but not incoherent, would involve a revision of NATO's purpose rather than a transcending of the alliance; and with Germany, or the Federal Republic, more firmly and contentedly anchored in NATO, the Germans got de facto approval to begin thinking about reunification. It was at this stage still just a thought, a largely unexpressed wish perhaps, but events would soon put it very much on the agenda, and the position adopted by the U.S. as of mid–1989 would largely determine how that agenda would be dealt with over the next year.

The Soviets, by contrast, were fundamentally unable to put their stamp on the emerging shape of the new settlement in Europe. The failure was deeply frustrating for Gorbachev and Shevardnadze, for they had crafted their foreign policy around the idea of a "common European home" in which the Soviet Union would find its rightful place. Reducing tensions in Europe would also mean reducing arms and troops there as well, and that would allow the resources freed up from military purposes to be redeployed for domestic reconstruction. Gorbachev was also eager to find allies for his own program of reform among reformers in Eastern Europe, "to create in the Bloc little Gorbachevs."[52] More broadly, "The task of Soviet foreign policy was to shape the international environment to allow perestroika to flourish."[53] Europe was therefore at least as central to the Soviet leadership as it was to the Bush administration, for success there was effectively a precondition for Gorbachev's success at home. What Gorbachev wanted was not just an exit from the Cold War, but a "soft landing" that would guarantee the Soviet Union's status as a superpower and allow it to get on with modernizing and restructuring at home. The problem was that the Soviet empire in Eastern Europe had been constructed and held together by brute force and political repression rather than by sentiment and mutual self-interest. When authoritarian rule softened and the prospects of forceful suppression receded, nothing was left to hold the bloc together. The result was not loosening, democratization and a "soft landing" but, from the Soviet perspective, a disintegration of its empire that seemed to prefigure and encourage disintegration within its own borders.

Soviet leaders resisted the process and sought in particular to prevent or at least slow down the drive for German unification; and when it could not be prevented they tried to limit its geopolitical consequences. Gorbachev and his foreign minister were as aware as the Americans that political transformations in Eastern Europe would raise the German question once again, but until November 1989 the immediate concern was to begin the reform process in East Germany. The Soviet leadership was convinced that the determination of the leaders of the GDR to resist calls for reform would be counterproductive and lead ultimately to the regime's collapse, and Gorbachev held long-time party boss Erich Honecker in contempt. When he joined in the celebration of the Fortieth Anniversary of the GDR on October 6–7, 1989, he warned Honecker of the dangers of delay. Soon the aging leader was replaced by a reform Communist, Egon Krenz, but by then it really was too late. East Germans had already shown their preferences by choosing, in increasing numbers, to exit the system and the state that kept it and them in place.[54] Those who chose to stay also began to voice their discontent in a series of mass demonstrations led by liberal Protestant clergy. Roughly 70,000 gathered in Leipzig on the evening of October 9 and the government marshaled troops, Stasi and dogs to attack, but the protest came off peacefully.[55] The regime had lost its will and with it the capacity to repress; and as that new reality began to be understood more widely, opposition became more widespread as well. The fall of the wall on November 9 was in part accidental, but also inevitable, and it immediately raised the question of unification. Initially, the Soviets were concerned to ensure stability, whatever that meant, and both Kohl and Bush were reassuring on that score. Bush did not "dance on the wall" and Kohl sought to manage expectations, but soon the issue of Germany's future, and what it would mean for the Soviets, was engaged.

The Soviet leadership began to emit contradictory signals, indicating at one moment an openness to the idea of a united Germany and at another firm opposition. The reasons for this ambivalence were not hard to discern. Twice in the twentieth century Germany had turned east with a vengeance, bringing death and destruction and creating the conditions for the overthrow of the Tsar during World War I and unleashing, with Operation Barbarossa, a war of planned and extreme ferocity in World War II. The Soviets were determined not to allow that to happen again and the essential rationale for Soviet policy in Eastern Europe after 1945 was to make a repeat of those horrors impossible by creating a string of satellites. The onset of the Cold War made the temporary division of Germany permanent, or so it seemed for forty years, and East Germany had become the most important state within the Warsaw Pact. It was the most economically and technologically advanced, the most loyal and the most rigid of all the regimes in the region. Losing East Germany was therefore much more serious than watching Yugoslavia go its own way or contemplating the disloyalty of the Romanians or allowing a bit of leeway for the Poles. And having its most important ally absorbed wholesale into its prosperous neighbor would not only recreate a powerful German state at the center of Europe but also because the Federal Republic was a founding and still loyal member of NATO, bring the rival military alliance that much closer to the territory of the Soviet Union.

With the collapse in Eastern Europe, Soviet strategy was "overrun by events" and left "out-of-date, incoherent and shot through with potentially dangerous internal contradictions."[56] Gorbachev was forced to switch from encouraging reform to efforts to shore up the USSR's declining influence and to slow reunification. The Soviets tried several strategies. On the night after the Berlin Wall was breached Gorbachev sent urgent messages to Mitterrand, Thatcher and Bush expressing concern over "calls for reunification" and proposing that the four powers that had occupied Germany in 1945 should meet to oversee developments. Though the proposal was deflected for the moment, the Soviet leader continued to press. He also followed up with discussions designed to encourage the French, the British, the Italians and others to resist the drive to reunification; while Thatcher simultaneously pushed Gorbachev and Mitterrand in the same direction.[57] When Gorbachev met with Bush off the coast of Malta at the end of November, he invoked history, precedent and stability: "I am saying there are two states, mandated by history. Let history decide the outlook." Bush agreed that "We shall do nothing to recklessly try to speed up reunification . . .

This is no time for grandstanding or steps that look good but could prove reckless."[58] If the Soviet leader was at least partly reassured, it did not prevent him from resisting the process. Soviet leaders also spoke repeatedly about the problem of the German border with Poland: would a redrawn border respect Poland's boundaries or seek to push them back farther to the east? The issue resonated, with Poles and others. Alongside these moves, other approaches were tried out. A mid-level advisor to the Soviet Communist Party, Nikolai Portugalov, visited Horst Teltschik, Kohl's foreign policy advisor, on November 21 and delivered the "unofficial" message that "the Soviet Union was already thinking about all possible alternatives with regard to the German question, even the unthinkable." It was time, the Soviet representative suggested, to free up the two Germanies from the past and to move toward some kind of unity that would nevertheless involve Germany leaving NATO and the EC and becoming demilitarized and neutral within an "all-European order of peace."[59]

Here was the prospect that the United States and the U.K. had long feared, and it was an idea that would be echoed by what seemed, at the time, important voices in the East.[60] Honecker's successor as leader of East Germany's ruling party, the SED, was Egon Krenz, who took over on October 17, a mere ten days after the celebration of East German statehood. He had a reformist agenda, but never established his credibility and made little progress. Krenz fared better in Moscow, where he met Gorbachev and obtained his reassurance that the Soviets continued to support the existence of two separate states. It mattered little back home, where his authority continued to slip, and on November 13 another and more credible reformist, Hans Modrow, was appointed as Prime Minister. Modrow's accession promised a measure of stability and on November 17 he proposed a more ambitious program of reform that might halt the continuing disintegration of the regime. The new leader also argued for the creation of a "treaty community" linking East and West Germany. The notion was not unlike the ten-point program that Kohl would present on November 28, though it was less clear about eventual reunification. The regime's power would continue to erode, however. Krenz resigned in early December and "Round Table" talks began, bringing together what remained of the old leadership and a new generation of dissidents and members of recently revived, non-communist parties. Participants in the Round Table were not themselves eager for reunification. Those on the moderate left were sympathetic to the position outlined by a group of writers and opposition activists in late November: they spoke of "our country" and went on to explain that "Either we can insist on GDR independence" and "develop a society of solidarity, offering peace, social justice, individual liberty, free movement, and ecological conservation" or "suffer . . . a sellout of our material and moral values and have the GDR eventually taken over by the Federal Republic."[61] Accordingly, they immediately endorsed "the independence and long-term development" of their country and set about drafting a new constitution for the nation they hoped to lead.

During late 1989, therefore, ideas about federation, with actual reunification put off for the future, found considerable support within Germany, especially in the east. In critical respects these themes paralleled Mitterrand's plans for a post–Cold War order in Europe not oriented toward the Atlantic and anchored in NATO. There was also lots of talk about wider structures that would help determine Europe's fate and its borders, the CSCE most importantly. Notions of this sort were also looked upon with favor by the Soviets, who kept pushing for four-power talks that might slow down, if not entirely prevent, reunification. The plans and strategies all failed, largely because of Germany and the Germans themselves, but also because the United States was opposed. When Kohl dined with Bush on December 3, he took pains to reassure the Americans by reaffirming German's attachment to NATO and to the EC and insisting that reunification was fully compatible with its orientation to the West. Satisfied on NATO, Bush responded encouragingly. In his typical fashion, he later explained, "I probably conveyed to Kohl that I had no objection to reunification, and in a sense gave him a green light." He did more than that, for the next day the U.S. President outlined for NATO leaders his by now well-rehearsed view of "the future shape of Europe and the new Atlanticism" and the importance of crafting a new architecture for the new world.[62] The Soviets did manage to get a meeting of the four powers scheduled in Berlin on December 11, but the U.S. kept the agenda focused on Berlin and no further four-power meetings would be held.[63] Shortly after, on December 19, Kohl visited Dresden and was met with crowds clamoring "unity, unity, unity." Opinion in both halves of Germany had begun to change dramatically in December 1989 and by the end of the year the prospect of early reunification was in sight. Bargaining the details would take another six months, and the terms would matter enormously. Nevertheless, because the proposed alternatives to a united Germany lacked coherence, had little institutional backing and attracted meager public support, the viable options had begun significantly to narrow, and the outcome was no longer in any real doubt.

Four major issues still needed solving: establishing a framework for negotiating reunification that gave priority to the Germans while reassuring the Soviets and other major powers; determining what the Germans themselves wanted; deciding whether a united Germany would remain in NATO and the European Community, and on what terms; and figuring out how and when to get the nearly 400,000 Soviet troops, with an additional 200,000 dependents, out of Germany. A fifth issue had at least to be finessed and that was the question of Poland and the Oder-Neisse border with Germany.[64] The first step came in early February 1990, when the "2+4" framework was accepted by East and West Germany (the two) and the U.S., Britain, France and the Soviet Union (the four). The formula had the virtue of letting the Germans take the lead but keeping the key interested parties involved. It had been in the works for some time, although the precise description of the format was a subject of debate. The British Foreign Secretary, Douglas Hurd, may have suggested that his true preference was for "Four-plus-Zero," with the Germans left out, but the British and the French were happy with a forum that gave them a hand in the final outcome. The Germans were convinced that this was the best they could get and in late January the Soviets had proposed talks in a "group of six."[65] The eventual arrangement appealed to both Bush and Thatcher, for as a top State Department advisor explained, it was a kind of club – a "2 by 4" – that would serve "as a lever to insert a united Germany into NATO . . ."[66] After a series of intense diplomatic exchanges, the 2+4 arrangement was agreed on the margins of the Ottawa conference on "open skies" on February 13, 1990.[67] The talks would begin soon, in part because the sooner they were in process, the less opportunity there would be for other parties to demand a say and for other and more cumbersome processes, such as negotiations among the thirty-five members of the CSCE, to be set up.

The formal dealings of the six would provide an appropriate cover for the bargaining out of reunification, but the basic decisions would inevitably be taken by the Germans. The question was who would get to speak for the two German states, and with what authority. In early 1990 the answer was unclear. Informed opinion thought it likely that the Social Democrats would prevail in the East German elections scheduled for May and that, as a result, the German voice would be fractured. The Social Democratic Party (SPD) in both the east and the west was schizophrenic about unification: the revered figure of Willy Brandt supported the goal, but the party's current leadership was hesitant and found the prospect of a demilitarized and possibly neutral Germany rather attractive. Allegiances began to shift, however, as conditions in the east continued to deteriorate and the possibilities of going it alone became less and less realistic. The crisis surrounding the Stasi (Ministry for State Security) in mid-January was particularly traumatic. The repressive arm of the state had ceased its routine operations, but it was still there and the new government had decided not to abolish it outright but to replace it with a new, smaller security service. The plan was wildly unpopular and led to fears of a counterrevolution, which in turn provoked the occupation and partial destruction of Stasi headquarters on January 15, 1990.[68] The political consequence was to discredit the government, led by Modrow, and also his Round Table interlocutors. A more specific consequence was that elections were moved up to March 18. In that foreshortened time it proved impossible for the government in the east or the Round Table, several of whose members were now in the Cabinet, to put together a credible program. On February 19 the Round Table came out against continued NATO membership and insisted that a unified Germany required an immediate convention to draft a new constitution on the basis of which new elections would be held.[69] By mid-March a draft constitution was actually ready, complete with an expanded list of basic rights and a redefinition of property that did not privilege private ownership. Even after the election, various liberals, socialists and former dissidents urged their fellow citizens "to put this Constitution into force." This growing ambition was met with shrinking popularity.

The Social Democrats, with a campaign that echoed Moscow, also steadily lost public support. By contrast, the coalition that Kohl and his allies put together in early February, the Alliance for Germany, gained ground. Critical to its success was the proposal for a monetary union between east and west with very generous exchange rates for holders of East German currency. The offer, which would become reality on July 1, proved irresistible and the election resulted in an overwhelming victory for Kohl and the CDU-dominated Alliance. The Alliance won 49 percent of the vote, the SPD just under 22 percent, the former Communists (now the PDS or Party of Democratic Socialism) 16.4 percent, and others less than 14 percent. The election meant that when the representatives of East and West Germany sat down to bargain, both sides held essentially the same position. It was now merely a matter of Kohl, together with his allies and supporters, working out the details of reunification and reconciling the other powers – mainly the four former occupying powers, but also other, somewhat skeptical, members of the European Community and, of course, Poland – to what the Germans themselves decided.

The question of Germany's commitment to Europe had already been decided. In exchange for German support for moves toward further integration – monetary union and greater political coordination – the European Community would welcome Germany's expansion to the east and allow the former East Germany immediate entry into the Community. The deals were made explicit and concrete at European summits in Dublin in April and June 1990. NATO membership would, however, be especially controversial and the argument over Germany's place in the alliance far more protracted. A round of diplomacy involving the U.S., the USSR and the Federal Republic in February produced movement but also confusion. The Soviets were willing to consider a compromise by which a united Germany would remain in NATO but NATO forces would not be stationed in the former GDR. German Foreign Minister

Genscher had announced in an important speech on January 31 that "an expansion of NATO territory to the east ... would not happen" and he and James Baker reaffirmed that position in Washington two days later. Baker carried a similar message to Moscow when he visited during the following week. As Baker left, Kohl arrived and made roughly the same offer – a "united Germany tied to NATO, with assurances that NATO's jurisdiction would not shift one inch eastward ..." Gorbachev responded that "any extension of the zone of NATO would be unacceptable." The Soviet leader assumed that he had a deal to keep NATO in check, but soon the Americans and the Germans realized that they could do better. If a united Germany were genuinely and fully within NATO, it made no practical sense to restrict NATO troops and jurisdiction to the territory of the former West Germany. The best they would offer the Soviets was a temporary exclusion of the former East Germany from NATO structures, a status that would end with the withdrawal of Soviet troops.

The question of Soviet forces in Germany and that of Germany in NATO would therefore be linked and they would eventually be resolved together in a grand but amorphous and unacknowledged bargain. The ultimate basis of that was money, mostly German money. As Baker and Scowcroft have both admitted, the Bush administration was very reluctant to spend money to help end the Cold War and rebuild the states and economies of the East. Poland was a partial exception, but even the Poles would be disappointed at the total ultimately received. A division of labor evolved in which the United States would work on the geopolitical architecture and the Europeans, especially the Germans, would pay for the actual construction of a new world. The European Bank for Reconstruction and Development would help, but in limited ways. It was a French initiative that ended up headquartered in London and run first by Jacques Attali, Mitterrand's key advisor, and then by Jacques de la Rosière, former head of the IMF, and its aim was to provide development loans for the formerly socialist countries, though not the Soviet Union. Far more important in the short term were the contributions of the Germans who had, as Bush told Kohl, "deep pockets." Even before 1989 the Federal Republic was doing a great deal to support the GDR, buying goodwill and freedom for individual dissidents. In the push for unification, much more would be required, and a substantial amount would go directly to the Soviet Union. When Kohl visited Moscow in February 1990, Gorbachev made it clear that his government needed financial support. In May the Germans arranged for a loan of 5 billion DM to the Soviets. This was followed by tough bargaining over how much support the Germans would provide to assist in the removal of Soviet troops from the east and their relocation to the USSR. The Soviets demanded another 20–25 billion DM and negotiations dragged on through the summer before it was finally agreed on September 10 that the Germans would give 12 billion DM plus a line of credit worth another 3 billion DM.

The financial details of the bargain would be announced as if firmly agreed and specific, but much was left unsaid. Certainly Kohl did not tell his fellow Germans just how much it would all cost to bribe the Soviets out of East Germany and then to rebuild that neglected region. The economic side of the deal would also involve trade, between Germany and the Soviet Union, and between the Soviets and other Western countries. Again, the Germans were generous, and here the United States was also more forthcoming. Gorbachev was particularly keen on getting a trade agreement signed at the Washington Summit in June 1990 and, although it almost failed to happen, it did just get done.[70] At least as important as the economic side was the matter of security which, since it involved reducing troops and weapons and considerable savings, also had economic implications. On this the contribution of the United States would be critical. In January 1990 Bush had proposed additional measures to reduce troops and weapons, and the U.S. continued in the spring and summer to make constructive proposals and modest concessions in various arms control venues. The U.S. also did what it could to help Gorbachev get through the worsening crisis in the Baltic states, which were busy declaring themselves independent. While urging restraint on the Soviets, the U.S. did little to encourage the Lithuanians, the Estonians and the Latvians, and did not recognize Lithuania as an independent state. Instead, the Americans urged talks and compromise.

The U.S. also initiated a series of moves designed to transform NATO into something less threatening to the Soviets and to mitigate Soviet fears of a Germany unified within the alliance. At the Washington Summit meeting of May 30–June 3, 1990 leaders signed fifteen separate agreements, not every one of which was terribly important but which collectively served as a sign of a relationship that was truly going beyond containment and the Cold War. Bush was also prepared to give Gorbachev "nine assurances" about Germany and NATO. Each of these had been offered before, by the Germans themselves or the U.S., but the package was now formalized and the effect made more robust: it was agreed, for example, that Germany would not have chemical, biological or nuclear weapons, would respect its eastern borders, and would offer financial support to Soviet troops in the east; that Soviet troops would stay in East Germany during the transition and that NATO troops would stay out; that German troop levels would be reduced; that NATO would revise its strategy and move forward on reducing or eliminating short-range nuclear weapons; and that the role of the Helsinki organization, CSCE, would be enhanced.[71] The strategic implications of reunification were nearly set. At the same meeting Gorbachev acquiesced in the idea that the Helsinki Accords allowed for states and peoples to choose their alliances. He was therefore "in full agreement that the matter of alliance membership is . . . a matter for the Germans to decide."

The Bush administration followed up with a series of proposals for the NATO Summit meeting which on July 6 adopted "The London Declaration on a Transformed North Atlantic Alliance."[72] NATO declared that it would never be the first to use force and that it wanted to "reach out to the countries of the East which were our adversaries in the Cold War, and extend to them the hand of friendship." To that end it invited members of the Warsaw Pact to sign non-aggression treaties, to send observers to NATO meetings and establish regular diplomatic contact; and Gorbachev was also invited to address the organization. Additional promises were made on arms reductions. The Declaration was issued while the Twenty-Eighth Congress of the Communist Party of the Soviet Union was meeting and it gave Gorbachev an important argument to use against those who believed that in allowing the regimes in Eastern Europe to fall and in accepting German reunification he was selling out the nation's interests. Gorbachev got through the meeting with reasonable success, if not exactly wide acclaim, and met with Kohl in mid-July. He felt confident enough, about NATO and also about the negotiations with Germany over money, to formally agree to Germany's unification and its membership in NATO. The Soviet leader explained that "Whether we like it or not, the time will come when a united Germany will be in NATO, if that is its choice."[73]

With this agreement, the details were worked out quickly and efficiently. The 2+4 talks produced a formal agreement that was signed on September 12, and the two German states formally merged on October 3. All of this was ratified at the CSCE meeting in Paris on November 19–21 where leaders adopted a Charter of Paris for a New Europe and also signed the CFE Treaty.[74] And because it happened in Paris, Mitterrand was able to preside over this formal creation of a new Europe, even if the important decisions had been taken previously, elsewhere, and by others.[75] The Charter, like the London Declaration that preceded it, was a remarkable document in that it contained not only all the obligatory proclamations of good intentions and the mutual desire for peace but very specific commitments about what were in effect internal matters for states. Governments in future would be based on human rights and democracy, now defined by "its representative and pluralist character" and manifest in free elections and the rule of law, and they would also ensure "economic liberty." These were not the formulas that distinguished the original Helsinki Accord in 1975, but a package of commitments that was fundamentally Western, if not specifically Anglo-American or Atlantic. And it was these commitments that were to guide "the transition to a market economy" and to new and more democratic political systems, a recognition that there really was no longer a socialist alternative; and the Soviets themselves were happy to sign up to this genuinely revolutionary notion.

The Gulf War Intervenes

The final steps in German unification would not be taken, nor the celebrations begun, before the emerging post–Cold War order would be tested by Iraq's invasion of Kuwait on August 2, 1990. James Baker was fishing with Eduard Shevardnadze near Lake Baikal when the first word of Saddam Hussein's pending move arrived. The Soviet Foreign Minister was incredulous, but the next day's news proved him wrong. After a brief but intense set of negotiations, the two met back in Moscow on August 3 and issued a joint statement that denounced Saddam's aggression, demanded that Iraq withdraw and proposed an arms embargo. Shevardnadze announced that "this aggression is inconsistent with the principles of new political thinking and, in fact, with civilized relations between nations." He and Baker agreed that this was the moment when the Cold War actually ended. Iraq was a long-time ally of the Soviet Union and the Soviets were Saddam's major supplier of weapons. They had even trained his secret police. The Soviet leaders, Gorbachev and Shevardnadze most of all, were desperate, however, to demonstrate that the Soviet Union could be a reliable and proper member of the international community and in consequence they would choose to abandon a client.[76]

George Bush was in Washington when he learned of the invasion, but he was scheduled to meet Margaret Thatcher later in the day at the home of Henry Catto, the American Ambassador to the U.K., in Aspen, Colorado. Bush and Thatcher would meet for lunch, but even before that the U.K. and the U.S. had taken steps to freeze Iraqi and Kuwaiti assets and they had secured a near unanimous resolution of the UN Security Council condemning the invasion. The meeting to this extent made for a meeting of minds. There were stories at the time that Thatcher had to press Bush not to "go wobbly," and she did use the phrase later and in a slightly different context, but there was in fact very little hesitation on the part of Bush or Thatcher on whether to take a tough line. For Thatcher, the prospect of doing so together with the U.S. was especially appealing, for it would provide an opportunity to get past the issue of German reunification and to prove once more that Britain was still America's most important ally because only Britain was ready to stand with the U.S. when it became necessary to use force.[77]

The diplomatic isolation of Iraq was almost total and the framework for opposing the invasion was put in place very quickly. The initial UN Resolution 660, calling on Iraq to "withdraw immediately and unconditionally" had been passed by 6 a.m. on August 2; on August 5 the European Community approved an economic embargo; and it was followed very quickly by UN Resolution 661, which was adopted on August 6 and put an embargo on trade with Iraq and, now that it was under Iraqi control, Kuwait, and prohibited the transfer of funds to either country. The question of enforcement remained open, but most countries would comply voluntarily. On the same day, the Saudi king, prodded by the U.S., requested the deployment of American and British troops and planes in Saudi Arabia to prevent a possible attack by Iraq. There would be further UN resolutions, notably Resolution 678, which was approved on November 29, 1990 and gave Saddam until January 15 to comply and retreat. It was to be the basis on which the military campaign was begun on January 16, 1991.[78] Between early August 1990 and mid-January of the following year, however, there was a lot of time for things to go wrong, for agreements to unravel, for more immediate crises to distract, for the intolerable to become the normal, for doubts to take hold and for debate to obscure the clarity of initial perceptions and diminish resolve.

All this did in fact occur in the more than five months that separated the invasion of Kuwait from the start of the military campaign to reverse it. As Bush would later recall, "The fall of 1990 was spent maintaining and strengthening our international coalition while building support at home and abroad for what we were doing – and what we might yet have to do."[79] There was, to begin with, the argument over just how the crisis had come about. Saddam Hussein used two arguments to defend his actions. The first was that Kuwait essentially owed Iraq for having defended the Arab world, and the Arab oil producers in partic- ular, in the prolonged war with Iran. Now that the war was over and the Arab states secure, they should assist Iraq in rebuilding. Iraq also charged that Kuwait was exceeding OPEC's production quotas and effectively pushing down the price of oil and, in addition, drilling for oil in what was Iraq's territory. Iraq was in desperate shape economically, in part due to its decision to build up its mili- tary might. In the context, Saddam chose to regard the refusal of Kuwait, along with the United Arab Emirates and Saudi Arabia, to meet his demands as equiv- alent to an act of war: "War is fought," Saddam said, "with soldiers and much harm is done by explosions, killing and coup attempts – but it is also done by economic means. Therefore, we should ask our brothers who do not mean to wage war on Iraq: this is in fact a kind of war against Iraq."[80] After the actual invasion the Iraqi case shifted toward the historical claim that Kuwait tradition- ally had been and should again be part of Iraq. It was certainly true that there was an arbitrary quality to the line in the sand that had become the border between the two countries, but Iraq itself was an artificial and contested creation. Iraq had sought to annex Kuwait by force when the kingdom became independent in 1961, but was deterred by British intervention; and it would continue to threaten its neighbor after that. In fact, very rapidly after invading Kuwait, Iraq declared the country to be its nineteenth province. The argument from history convinced very few, however, nor did the claims for financial compensation from Kuwait serve to justify Iraq's resort to force.

The arguments were nevertheless picked up in the West and, if not many were won over, the issue did become clouded. So, too, did the debate over the past role of the United States, Britain and also France in supplying Saddam's regime with weapons and credits for a wide range of purposes. The Soviet Union may have been Iraq's closest long-term ally and largest supplier, but France was its second-largest supplier, and the U.S. and U.K. had tilted toward Iraq during the Iraq–Iran War, and both during and after the war they sold the dictator lots of weapons. The Thatcher government had been particularly interested in expanding Britain's role in the global arms trade and efforts to sell weapons were coordinated between government and private industry, with the Ministry of Defence and the intelligence services closely involved. The U.S. was equally committed to competing in the arms trade and to working constructively with Iraq. Both Britain and the U.S. became more wary in the late 1980s, as the news spread that Saddam had used chemical weapons on his own people, wiping out the Kurdish village of Halabja in March 1988, and as the scale of his ambitions became clear. The wariness led to a scaling back of economic support for the regime, but no larger policy shift.[81] As late as the summer of 1990, British and American leaders had therefore not broken with Saddam; and as the exchanges between Saddam and the American Ambassador to Iraq, April Glaspie, on July 25 made clear, the U.S. was not conspiring against Iraq or taking sides on any "inter-Arab disputes," as she put it. The Ambassador did, however, reiterate the U.S. position that it "could never excuse settlement of disputes by any but peaceful means," and Saddam in turn gave an "unconditional pledge" not to use force with Kuwait.[82]

The ambivalent attitude of the U.S. and U.K. just before the invasion of Kuwait, taken together with their prior support for Saddam, exposed both governments to charges of hypocrisy when, in August, they turned against Iraq and condemned the incursion in Kuwait. The charge was reinforced by the undeniable fact that the intensity of Western interest in the fate of Kuwait was transparently related to oil. Of course, Saddam's interest in annexing the kingdom was equally motivated by oil.

What seems actually to have worried and moved U.S. and U.K. leaders was not the possible loss of Kuwaiti oil, though that was not welcome, but the possibility that Iraq also had designs on Saudi Arabia and its oil. If Iraqi forces were solidly entrenched in Kuwait, it would be easy to move south and seize the relatively unprotected Saudi fields. This prospect was genuinely terrifying, for it would give Saddam Hussein a dominant position that would allow Iraq to dictate prices and quotas and genuinely to control the world oil market. Indeed, when the invasion took place, the first priority for the U.S. and Britain was to find ways to protect Saudi Arabia from attack. The Saudis were also worried about Iraq's plans, but they were also worried about allowing infidel forces on Saudi soil. Cheney, the U.S. Secretary of Defense, was dispatched to Saudi Arabia to discuss with the King the need for Western forces. He phoned the White House on August 4, while Thatcher was visiting, to convey the King's approval. The Saudis did not need much persuading, but they presumably did want to set down some conditions and be reassured that the U.S. would actually deliver.

The lengthy period between the invasion and the Western counterattack also allowed time for a thorough debate about the use of force. Saddam had no genuine supporters, but he had made many people afraid of him and there were widespread fears that a military confrontation would be protracted and bloody and bring with it all sorts of unforeseen consequences. Resolving the debate required that three things be proved, more or less. First, people and politicians had to be convinced that everything was done to reach a diplomatic solution. Second, and related to the first, it had to become clear that the imposition of sanctions would not by itself do the job. And third, there had to be a conviction that military action would succeed. Meeting these prerequisites required constant attention and shrewd tactics on the part of the U.S. and U.K. governments, which essentially led the effort. Bush and Baker were preoccupied throughout the fall and early winter with holding together the coalition that they had put together back in August. That meant mainly keeping the Soviets on board, not a simple task when its top leaders were under great pressure at home over both their foreign and domestic policies. Gorbachev was beginning to lose control and his enemies harped constantly on how he had lost Eastern Europe, allowed Germany to reunite while remaining in NATO and was now, in joining in the condemnation of Iraq, not only abandoning an ally but effectively giving up on the leverage that the alliance with Saddam brought with it. Gorbachev and Shevardnadze continued to support successive UN resolutions, including a resolution passed on August 25 authorizing measures to enforce the embargo on Iraq, but they exacted a price. In an effort to keep the Soviets firmly within the coalition and to get them accustomed to the idea that, in the end, force might well be necessary, the U.S. proposed a minisummit in Helsinki on September 8–9. The new partnership held, but the Soviets insisted that a thorough and permanent resolution to problems of the Middle East would also require settlement of the Arab-Israeli conflict. The Americans had for a very long time been determined not to give the USSR a formal role in Middle East negotiations, for fear of the influence that would accompany it, and therefore refused to accept this explicit "linkage." Privately, however, Bush and Gorbachev agreed that after getting Iraq out of Kuwait it would be appropriate for the U.S. and the Soviets to convene a conference on broader issues. The U.S. administration would publicly protest that there was no linkage, but the link had been established.[83] The conference would be held in Madrid at the end of October 1991, though by that time Gorbachev was not in a position to benefit from it.

Even with this concession of unacknowledged linkage, Gorbachev felt compelled for domestic reasons to continue to work for a diplomatic solution. So, too, did the French. In fact, Mitterrand used his speech to the UN on September 18 to elaborate a "logic of peace" that also linked Iraqi compliance with UN demands for a "comprehensive peace conference on the Middle East." The French were also in frequent if informal contact with Iraq over hostages. A large number of third-country nationals had been trapped in Iraq and Kuwait when hostilities had begun in August and Saddam was prepared to use them as hostages and, if it came to it, as human shields. No country was immune to this type of blackmail, and while there was yet another UN resolution on the issue and while the U.S. and U.K. made clear to Hussein that they would react very negatively to the taking and manipulation of hostages, a parade of politicians and officials from other countries met with Saddam or his surrogates – one of whom, at least on this issue, was Yasser Arafat. There were negotiations with the French as early as August and these continued into October; in October former Prime Minister Edward Heath went to Baghdad and spoke with Saddam, finding him very calm and not at all "mad," and brought home thirty-eight people; Nakasone, the Japanese Prime Minister, himself went to Iraq in early November and took home seventy-four Japanese citizens; and Willy Brandt arrived just after and came away with 180 Germans.

The most significant effort to broker a deal was made by the Soviet Union. To their credit, the Soviets were not merely concerned with hostages. Gorbachev chose to send Yevgeny Primakov, a close aide with substantial experience in the region, to negotiate with Saddam. He, too, proposed a form of linkage, with a broader peace conference promised if and when Iraq withdrew from Kuwait. The problem with this and other offers made to tempt Saddam into withdrawal was Saddam himself. He or his spokesmen, such as Tariq Aziz, would toss out suggestions that seemed to indicate flexibility and the possibility of compromise, but when they were taken up and examined, there was nothing there. The Iraqi leader basically wanted too much, certainly much more than anyone was willing to give, and so all efforts at diplomacy came to nothing. Repeated failure did not keep the Soviets from trying, right up until January 16; and even after that, Gorbachev would quickly suggest a pause in the bombing campaign to allow Saddam time to reflect and compromise. Gorbachev himself might well have hoped for a non-military solution, but it is more likely that he was playing to another, domestic audience that was growing increasingly restive with his rule.

The argument about the use of military force was conducted in a different arena and in a different register in the United States. There were actually two arguments going on simultaneously and at least indirectly influencing each other. The most interesting, surely, was the debate between the generals and the politicians. The U.S. military had not engaged in substantial and sustained warfare since Vietnam. Throughout the 1980s Reagan talked tough and increased defense spending, but did little with this enhanced military might: the invasion of tiny Grenada and the bombing of Libya barely counted. There was the disastrous deployment in Lebanon in 1983, but after the bombing of the U.S. barracks the troops were brought home. There was, it seemed, an aversion to combat that was often discussed as the "Vietnam syndrome." The phenomenon was even given a formal rationalization in what became known as the "Weinberger doctrine," after Reagan's Secretary of Defense. It held that the U.S. should not use its military unless the country was willing to commit massive forces to guarantee victory and unless political leaders could be sure of sustained popular support. The doctrine built on a relatively self-serving military reading of the history of Vietnam which held that the war could have been won if politicians had given the military the means to fight and that victory would have been possible if the folks back home had remained loyal. True or not, it led to rules of engagement that essentially precluded engagement.

When Colin Powell became head of the Joint Chiefs under Bush, what was previously the "Weinberger doctrine" now became the "Powell doctrine," and it continued to make military men cautious about when and how to use force. This wariness persisted despite the growing sophistication of American weapons and the professionalization of its all-volunteer armed forces. When the U.S. contemplated war in the Gulf, therefore, the military insisted on being able to deploy overwhelming force in order to insure victory. Constant talk on all sides about the size of Saddam's armed forces – supposedly a million strong – and their battle-hardened toughness only amplified the soldiers' worries about the nature of the coming conflict and their estimates of what it would take to prevail. The effect of this reluctance to fight unless and until backed by overwhelming force was to drag out further the time frame for acting against Saddam. The perceived need to explore all diplomatic avenues and to demonstrate that economic sanctions alone would not work also prolonged the run-up to war, but it was the fact that 500,000 troops, backed by thousands of tanks and planes and supplies, had to be transported and assembled in the desert that dictated such a protracted period of preparation. It might even be suggested that knowing how long it would take to put military forces in place to confront Saddam actually encouraged political leaders outside the U.S. in their efforts to find compromise solutions even when the likelihood of success had greatly diminished.

The military conversation about what it meant to use force provided arguments that could be used in the broader domestic debate about whether to go to war. The Bush administration was determined to win Congressional backing for the war, but received only grudging support. Opinion polls vacillated and even moderate politicians such as Sam Nunn, Daniel Moynihan and Les Aspin were skeptical of the case. When the Senate finally voted to support military action, it did so by a mere 52 to 47, with most Democrats opposing. The Democratic Party was gripped by a deep resistance to the use of force. The Bush administration did little to help itself by its shifting and not entirely convincing rhetoric and by Bush's own inarticulacy. The President might speak grandly about a "new world order" but the idea was not backed up by any credible plan for making it happen; and there was little appetite for something so vague and, to many, unrealistic. The argument from principle, though demonstrably applicable in the case of Saddam's actions, was weakened by the charge of hypocrisy and inconsistency; and the idea that it was all a "war for oil" would not go away, for it was at least partly true. Bush's occasional references to Saddam as Hitler were meant to whip up support, but they were not necessarily credible. And by the time the administration started talking about Saddam's efforts to acquire, and his evident willingness to use, weapons of mass destruction, few were moved. This was deeply ironic, for the charges were true and postwar evidence would show that Saddam had made even more progress than had been suspected.

The debate about using force also provided the occasion for what might well have been the last gasp of the antiwar movement that had grown and flourished in the late 1960s and early 1970s. The movement had gone into decline when Richard Nixon was removed from the scene in 1974, but found much to oppose during the Reagan era – the military buildup, loose talk about actually using nuclear weapons, Euromissiles, Star Wars, the Contras and more. The prospect of a real war, whatever the cause, would be an occasion to make the by now familiar arguments about the futility of force in international affairs. It was an especially apposite moment, for the ending of the Cold War suggested to many that the causes of international conflict were being reduced and the need for nuclear weapons and massive arms spending had diminished as well. It was time to end war and claim a "peace dividend," not to find new enemies to engage.[84] This more determined critique of the looming Gulf War did not lead people to take to the streets in opposition, but it served along with other criticisms and arguments to keep Americans from rallying around Bush as might have been expected given the odious character of the Iraqi regime, the blatantly illegal action that had begun the crisis, and the efforts of the Bush administration to act in a multilateral fashion.

What did work to the advantage of the U.S. and the U.K., and those who came to view war as inevitable, was Saddam Hussein's obstinacy. Numerous efforts to bargain and to give Saddam a more or less honorable exit came to naught and war came on January 16, 1991. It began with a bombing campaign that seriously degraded Iraq's war-fighting capacity and took its air force out of the contest. The Soviets made still further efforts to negotiate a settlement, but before their efforts could bear fruit, Saddam's forces began to set fire to Kuwait's oil fields. The U.S., the U.K. and their allies set a final deadline in response – Iraqi troops must begin to withdraw by February 23. They did not and the ground war began the next day; it lasted a mere one hundred hours, by which time Iraqi troops were in full retreat from Kuwait and heading back toward Baghdad. It was an ignominious defeat for Saddam Hussein and a huge victory for the coalition and its U.S. and British leaders. The decision to end the war with the liberation of Kuwait and not to move on to Baghdad did leave Saddam in power, however, and he was able to survive subsequent uprisings against his regime in the south and the north of the country. Many would later criticize this restraint on the part of the coalition, but it was largely inevitable, for the coalition had been put together for the limited purpose of getting the Iraqis out of Kuwait, not for overthrowing Saddam's regime.

If the Gulf War did not get rid of Saddam Hussein, it had important consequences nonetheless. Probably the most important was that it largely confirmed the shape of the new framework of global power. The coalition was led by the U.S. and the outcome demonstrated the reality of U.S. dominance. The United States even managed to convince its allies to pay for much of the war's cost, a sign that other states were willing for now to concede a hegemonic role to the U.S. and recognized the need to pay tribute.[85] The Gulf War also encouraged others to sign up or acquiesce to new rules and standards in terms of global security. A striking example involved the decisions, first by France and then by China, to support the Nuclear Non-Proliferation Treaty just after the conclusion of the war. The treaty had been concluded years before but with France and China not signing and with India, Pakistan and Israel pursuing their nuclear ambitions more or less openly, it was quite ineffective. France and China were members of the UN Security Council, however, so their joining up meant that the five states with veto power were all in the nuclear club and now shared an interest in restricting its membership. After 1991 the great majority of states accepted the treaty – including regional powers such as South Africa,

Argentina, and later Brazil – and the non-proliferation regime. It would be administered through the United Nations and policed by a recharged International Atomic Energy Agency through a more intrusive system of inspections. Controls were also tightened on the export of nuclear material and technology. The aim, at least in part, was to freeze the existing balance of forces at a moment when the United States and its allies were largely unchallenged and to force rising powers to commit to the new norm and to adhere to the regime as a condition of respectability. Efforts to lock in the post–Cold War security balance also led to stronger measures to enforce the Biological Weapons Convention in 1991 and to the adoption by the UN of a Chemical Weapons Convention in November 1992. These moves would mean that the prevention of the spread of "weapons of mass destruction" became a formal objective of the emerging structure of international security.[86]

By contrast the USSR, through its grudging acquiescence and almost pathetic efforts to broker a peace with Saddam, was revealed as clearly number two, perhaps no longer even a superpower except for its nuclear arsenal. More specifically, the Atlantic orientation of the new European architecture was also reinforced. As the Gulf crisis was unfolding, the French were persisting in their efforts to create a European confederation and the Germans and the French also pressed forward with proposals for a "common foreign and security policy" for Europe. The *Assises* to formalize the new confederation, held in Prague in mid-June 1991, was nonetheless a "fiasco."[87] Representatives from Eastern and Central Europe did not like the fact that the new organization might be used to delay their accession to the European Community and were unhappy at the effort to include the USSR and exclude the United States. The idea was not revived. Though there would be a rhetorical commitment to a security and foreign policy dimension to the European Union agreed at Maastricht in December 1991, that, too, would amount to very little. These initiatives failed for multiple reasons, but the lessons of the recent conflict in the Gulf were critical.

Of necessity, the Gulf War also had effects on military strategy and on the extent to which the end of the Cold War would prompt reductions in military spending. Most important, the war made it clear that even in a "New World Order" that was overall more peaceful there would be occasions that called out for the resort to force. The winding down of the Cold War would mean spending less on weapons, but military spending in the U.S. and the U.K. would not fall as far or as fast as it might have done if the Gulf War had not occurred. The war against Iraq also provided a demonstration of the future of war. The U.S. remained committed to something like the "Powell Doctrine" and its generals would continue to insist on overwhelming force, support at home and an obvious exit strategy before agreeing to deploy troops. However, the Gulf War also served to showcase the new, more technically sophisticated weapons in its arsenal. Though not everyone bought into the excessive claims about their effectiveness, they worked well enough to convince policy-makers to invest more in high-tech weapons. The ultimate effect would be a military that could fight without putting "boots on the ground," or at least that could allow for fewer troops being put at risk; and reducing the risks would mean increasing the likelihood that states, the U.S. in particular, would choose to fight. Gradually, the "Powell Doctrine" would become less compelling. It would eventually give way to a new and vastly different perspective that took as its starting point the so-called "revolution in military affairs" that was brought about by advanced technology and that led, more or less directly, to a willingness to use the new and more sophisticated weapons and to adopt military solutions for the problems of the post–Cold War world.

The Gulf War had consequences even farther afield. The "global Cold War," the contest for influence between the Soviets and the U.S., had been winding down during the late 1980s. "Proxy wars" were coming to an end as the Soviets, eager to shift resources to domestic reconstruction, began to withdraw support from clients and allies. The United States could still afford to sustain its clients, but after Iran-Contra the Reagan and then Bush administrations lacked the political support to do so. The Americans were therefore also ready to push friends and clients to settle local conflicts. The most important breakthroughs came in Africa, where the conflicts in Angola and Namibia were soon resolved. These settlements – together with international pressure and sanctions and sustained internal struggle by the African National Congress and its allies – created a framework that encouraged moves to end apartheid in South Africa. Nelson Mandela was released from prison on February 2, 1990 and began a process of negotiation that led to his election in April 1994 as President in the first genuinely democratic elections in the nation's history.[88] It was the end of the Cold War more generally, and not the Gulf War, that produced these welcome developments in the Third World. The Gulf War put a seal on the process, however, for it showed in dramatic fashion that the Soviet Union could and would abandon a long-term ally when the need arose. Soon, of course, the USSR would itself disappear, but even before its dissolution the dynamic and costly superpower rivalry for influence in Asia, Africa and Latin America had effectively ceased.

CHAPTER 8

The Shaping of the Post–Cold War World

The New Architecture and the Soviet Union

The construction of the new Europe "architecture" after the collapse of the regimes in Eastern Europe was done quickly, but great care was taken not to offend the major powers – Germany, France, Britain, the United States and, most important, the Soviet Union. Margaret Thatcher was especially worried that moving too fast on German unification would harm Gorbachev and on that she had the agreement of Bush, Mitterrand and Kohl. Soviet troops and weapons were still deployed in East Germany in 1990 even as unification was carried out, so the Germans had to be particularly careful not to provoke a reaction. These fears for the Soviet leader's future were obviously well grounded, for Gorbachev would be out of power and the Soviet Union would disappear before the end of 1991. The end of the Soviet Union did not lead to the collapse of the recently reconfigured framework of geopolitics, but it did shove it in a very particular, and very Atlantic, direction.

Gorbachev's fall and the dissolution of the state he led were the outcome of a lengthy process of decay and failed reform. The centrally planned economy never worked well. It needed mass mobilizations and terror to meet its targets and as these tools were discarded, no other mechanisms were found to replace them. Just about the only thing the Soviets did well was to build weapons, but even that came at a great cost that seemed to hold back economic development more broadly. That at least was the conclusion that Gorbachev and other Soviet leaders, and not just reformers, reached in the 1980s and it was the reason reform got as far as it did and found support even within the military. Efforts to restructure the economy, perestroika, nevertheless threatened the status and perquisites of the country's ruling elite, whose roots were in both the party and the institutions of the state. This *nomenklatura*, as they were called, would come to resist Gorbachev's plans for markets and private enterprise and so he decided that political reform, glasnost, was needed to overcome the resistance.[1] As early as 1987, Gorbachev seems to have concluded that politics was critical and he moved first to bring the Communist Party along with him but, when that proved difficult, sought to open up the party itself. When that did not work, he attempted to escape the control of the party by grounding his rule in the institutions of the state, but to do so required that the state itself be made more responsive. At the party conference in June 1988 he proposed, therefore, to create a new and elected Congress of People's Deputies as the supreme body of the Soviet state. The elections were far from open and party members continued to dominate, but they were open enough for a number of genuine reformers to gain seats and voices. Andrei Sakharov was one and an important symbol, though Boris Yeltsin was easily the most significant. The Congress opened in May 1989, the proceedings were televised, and the response was electrifying. Gorbachev was in the chair and effective in his new role, but the creation of this new political structure had provided a venue and an opening for the regime's critics as well. In particular, the effort to give life to the state beyond the party led people throughout the republics that made up the Soviet Union to use local political structures, until now largely powerless, to press their own claims against the center and the party. Openness and democracy afforded critics of Gorbachev and of reform a voice and led to an intensifying crisis of authority.

Gorbachev and his allies believed that if they were given sufficient time, reform would work and a new stable political and economic system would emerge, but time required money and there was never enough. The Soviet economy had no viable exports besides natural resources, mainly oil and gas, and there was currently a glut on the world market of these products and prices were low. With increasing desperation Gorbachev turned to the West, but he received much less than was required. The Germans were prepared to pay a steep price for reunification and they did.[2] France and Britain were willing to help, but their capacity was limited and the Soviets had to compete with other, more sympathetic, claimants in Eastern Europe – especially Poland, Hungary and Czechoslovakia. The response of the United States was therefore critical, but America was also constrained by the administration's concerns over deficits and bad debts and by domestic politics. In addition, the US administration was split in its attitude toward Gorbachev and the Soviets. Bush and Baker were relatively sympathetic, Defense Secretary Cheney and Robert Gates of the CIA were less so, and National Security Advisor Scowcroft was in the middle. In Congress the fate of Soviet Jews, of the Baltic countries and of Armenians were of overriding importance to a small number of nevertheless key lawmakers, who held the Soviets responsible and wanted assurances for their particular constituencies. Perhaps more important was the question of whether the Soviets could make effective use of the money they borrowed. The sums discussed were very large – $20 billion per year for three years of transition by one estimate, as high as $150 billion over five years in another – and the Soviet Union lacked the experience or the facilities to ensure the money was not wasted and was eventually repaid.[3]

Especially skeptical was Nicholas Brady, Secretary of the Treasury and author of the "Brady plan" for debt relief. Experienced in the ways of indebtedness, he was extremely reluctant to use U.S. funds to assist the Soviet Union when so little of the infrastructure of a modern economy and financial system was in place. Bush himself was somewhat more willing to assist Gorbachev in his plans for reform and sent Michael Boskin, chair of the Council of Economic Advisors, to Moscow to learn more about the finances of the USSR. His report was not encouraging. He met the head of the state planning agency and discussed prices. The planner knew he was supposed to reform prices, but he thought the way to do it was to sit down with Boskin and establish a new list of prices, without regard to markets and to supply and demand. The American later talked about currency convertibility with the Finance Minister, who produced a coin stamped on one side as one ruble and on the other as one dollar. Boskin would report back that it would take a decade for the Soviets to develop the institutions essential for a "functioning market economy."[4] The IMF did a major study in 1990 and reached the same conclusion: its December report was "very negative on the state of the Soviet economy" and it would "criticize reforms to date and advocate Polish-style 'shock therapy' as the antidote."[5] Clearly, nearly three-quarters of a century without the experience of markets made the transition extremely difficult, and Gorbachev himself was inconsistent in his advocacy of economic reform. Plans for selling off state assets and introducing market pricing were proclaimed and then frustrated and abandoned. Even the more moderate moves to introduce cooperatives faced resistance and sabotage. And all the while the economy deteriorated. Hence the choice to move ahead more decisively on reforming the political system. The effect, however, was to lead potential donors and investors to decide that money given to the Soviets in 1990–1 would not be well used. In the end even Soviet reformers, allies or former allies of Gorbachev, argued that loans would be misused.

Gorbachev was nevertheless desperate, and it would seem that his willingness to agree to German reunification and to various arms control agreements was due, at least in part, to his desire to get resources from the West. The Soviet leader was in fact criticized at home for trading geopolitical advantage for cash. Yuli Kvizinsky, the Soviet Ambassador to the Federal Republic, explained that it was a mistake to have Shevardnadze raise the issue of loans while negotiating the future of Germany in May 1990: "The request for a financial credit could only be the beginning of a long chain of similar pleas, which would lead to ever more humiliations and induce the West to pose ever more disagreeable political demands."[6] Gorbachev certainly understood the dilemma, but felt he had no choice. He would make repeated pleas, the most dramatic of which came when he addressed the Group of Seven (G7) meeting in London in June 1991. "The moment demanded urgent action," he wrote in his *Memoirs*, for it was a matter of "ensuring substantial economic support for the country in its most critical hour."[7] Unfortunately, the plans the Soviets presented at the meeting failed to convince. John Major, the host, led off the discussion with a series of questions about the pace and extent of market reforms and the importance of "the investment climate."[8] Scowcroft explained to Bush that "Gorbachev came to collect what he obviously felt was his due, but he never really made his case"; and Bush agreed: "The guy kind of bombed, didn't he?" Mitterrand, characteristically, was more effusive in his praise of the Soviet leader and indirectly criticized his fellow G7 leaders for lacking faith: "There is," he claimed, "a desire to evaluate an experiment before it has been completed. But the very best argument against disbelief is what President Gorbachev is doing." The French President's argument mattered little, however, and the G7 was not forthcoming. The Soviets would be granted associate membership in the IMF and the World Bank and affiliation with other institutions, but they were mainly to be given technical assistance and advice on how to proceed with economic reform.[9]

It is doubtful that even massive Western financial support could have prevented the breakup of the Soviet Union. Its problems were too deep, its elites too implicated and too threatened by reform to make a proper and peaceful transition; and the state and the party would inevitably forfeit political legitimacy as they sought to reinvent themselves. Most important in this process, which was at first gradual and then extremely rapid, was the fragmenting of what had been the Soviet empire. The Soviet Union, with its "captive nations" within its own borders and in Eastern Europe, was certainly no empire in the sense that Marxists, Lenin in particular, understood.[10] It was not an outgrowth of capitalism, let alone its highest stage, and it was not based on market mechanisms. Its subaltern parts were not systematically exploited, although certain connections were highly unequal, and it seems that for long stretches the Soviets may have run their empire at a loss and their victims may have gained. It was nonetheless an imperial creation, based on subordination to the center in Moscow, and held together by an enormous military and a ruthless party machine that spawned smaller but equally nasty party machines in Eastern Europe and wherever the Soviet model was applied. Because it was an empire, the greatest threat to its existence was that parts of the empire would secede and the entire edifice would begin to crumble.

Gorbachev was correct in believing that maintaining Soviet influence around the world, and paying for the military that underpinned that influence, was costly and a drain on resources that might be better deployed in the development of the domestic economy. He clearly failed to appreciate, however, just how the unraveling of the USSR's international position and the collapse of its allies and dependencies in Eastern Europe would lead to the coming apart of the Soviet Union itself. Others, it seemed, did, or at least claimed they did. Sergei Tarasenko, Shevardnadze's top assistant, recalled in 1993 that he and the Foreign Minister were on the beach on the Black Sea when word arrived in August 1989 of Solidarity's assumption of power in Poland. It was "an emotional moment that forced us to think about the situation." He went on:

> I remember that we stayed on the beach and started to discuss things, and we posed a question to ourselves . . .: "Do we understand what is going to happen?" The collective opinion was, "Yes, we do." That inevitably we will lose our allies – the Warsaw Pact. These countries will go their own ways. And we even acknowledged among ourselves that the Soviet Union would not manage to survive. The logic of events would force the breakup of the Soviet Union, specifically the Baltics. Because a lot of guys were from Georgia; and we were in Georgia; we were well aware even then of the problems in the Caucasus – that there was a lot of opposition there to Moscow's rule and that there could be some problems. So we did acknowledge it, even saying to ourselves, "Yes, we'll suffer. We'll lose our jobs, we'll be punished for that."[11]

Unrest on the periphery first surfaced in 1988 in Armenia, but it was the Baltic states – which shared borders and histories with Poland, where the collapse of socialism occurred first – that took the lead. In May 1989 Lithuania and Estonia declared themselves sovereign, and Latvia followed in July. The fragmentation of the Soviet state thus proceeded in parallel with the collapse of the Soviet empire in Eastern Europe and before the shape of the new Europe had been decided. The coincidence was a gift to the opponents of reform. Gorbachev's comrades on the Central Committee insisted, for example, that he go to Vilnius in January 1990 to confront those calling for independence. The move toward German reunification had scarcely begun, but its consequences were already playing themselves out within the Soviet Union; and throughout the maneuvering over Germany the Lithuanians, Latvians and Estonians pressed their claims for separation despite a distinct lack of support from the United States. It was largely this prospect of disintegration, already the reality in the Soviets' former empire in Eastern Europe and now happening within the borders of the USSR itself, that not only drove conservatives in the military, the party leadership and the KGB to oppose Gorbachev but gave them a compelling, indeed existential, argument to deploy against his reforms.

Confrontation and negotiation, then renewed confrontation, would drag on in the Baltics and restiveness would spread throughout the republics. The climactic challenge to the center, however, came ultimately from closer to home, from Russia and the Russian Federation, where Yeltsin emerged as the champion of reform and the enemy of the party and its domination. The Congress of People's Deputies of the Federation chose Yeltsin as its chair at the end of May 1990 and on June 12 the Supreme Soviet issued a declaration of sovereignty. Other republics followed suit, further undermining the authority of the USSR, whose President Gorbachev had become the previous March. The Twenty-Eighth (and, it turned out, the last) Congress of the Communist Party would meet in early July 1990. There was opposition to Gorbachev, but less than at previous meetings because by this point he had successfully got rid of many of his opponents and convinced the Central Committee to hold serious and meaningful elections to party offices and congresses. The party was nevertheless losing its central role in running the state. The same meeting of the Soviet Congress of People's Deputies that had made Gorbachev President had also eliminated the party's political monopoly. The July Party Congress would extend these efforts to loosen control internally and to separate the party from the institutions of the state. As if to mark and perhaps complete the transformation of the party's role, Yeltsin chose to resign from the Communist Party as the Congress drew to a close.

Gorbachev faced a major quandary. By the summer of 1990 the party that had brought him to power was becoming weaker and weaker, largely because of things he had done, but the Soviet state, in which his authority was now rooted, was no longer entirely sovereign even within its borders. And it would get worse: in October the Russian Federation declared that its laws were supreme and took precedence over the laws of the Soviet Union, and within days other republics made the same claim. Gorbachev was necessarily distracted from this phase of internal reform by foreign affairs, for the final stages of German unification came together with the Gulf conflict to elevate questions of the role of the Soviet Union internationally over its domestic politics. His response was to change tack in order to appease his more conservative critics and to gain further time and more room for maneuver. Though he had briefly offered support for a new and more radical plan for economic reform – the 500-Day Plan drafted by the economist and advisor Shatalin – he soon backed off and offered a watered-down compromise. Most significant, he appointed former critics to key positions in government and asked for, and was granted, emergency powers. The effect of these moves was to alienate the reformers who had once been Gorbachev's most consistent supporters and who now signed up with Yeltsin or simply quit. The most prominent defection was that of the Foreign Minister, Shevardnadze, who resigned on December 20, declaring that "The reformers have gone to seed" and warning that "Dictatorship is coming."

The mounting "paralysis of power," as Gorbachev described it on November 23, 1990, inevitably captured the attention of the United States, and the CIA issued a report that same month on "The Deepening Crisis in the USSR."[12] "The USSR," according to the report, "is in the midst of a historic transformation that threatens to tear the country apart. The old Communist order is in its death throes." What would succeed it was, however, as yet completely unclear. The CIA admitted that it had previously underestimated the threat that the growing assertiveness and independence of the republics would pose to the center and that it meant that "The Soviet Union as we have known it is finished." The political vacuum was exacerbated by the fact that the party, which constituted the sinews holding the state together, was weak and discredited and the new "governmental institutions to which Gorbachev has been attempting to shift power are ... only in their formative stages." Gorbachev himself had largely prevailed in his struggles against party conservatives, but it mattered less than it might because the party mattered so much less; and he was reluctant to move decisively on economic reform. According to the report, "Yel'tsin," who was in favor of more thorough democratization and a quicker transition to a market economy, "*appears to have the advantage over Gorbachev: he is far more popular than Gorbachev in USSR-wide opinion polls*" (emphasis in original).

What would happen next? Four scenarios seemed possible, at least in theory: deterioration short of anarchy; anarchy; military intervention (either by a coup or through the declaration of a state of emergency and the deployment of troops to maintain order); or a modest improvement – "Light at the End of the Tunnel." The analysts were careful to say that "the Intelligence Community's uncertainties about the future of the Soviet system are greater today than at any time in the 40 years we have been producing Estimates on the USSR." Still, they gave rough odds – 50/50 for deterioration short of anarchy, a bit less than 1 in 5 for either of the other three. They thought a coup unlikely, given the subordination of the military to civilian authority, but did not rule it out. It would make sense, therefore, to plan on Gorbachev and the system surviving for another year, but in a much weakened condition. For the U.S., the different scenarios had important implications, but none was a genuinely serious threat. The most unattractive was perhaps anarchy, for anything could happen; also unattractive was the possibility of military intervention and a turn to more authoritarian rule, but even so "a military-dominated regime" would "be too busy attempting to hold the USSR together to adopt a hostile military posture toward the West . . ." If Gorbachev could hang on, however, "internal *political* developments" would likely encourage him "to conclude agreements with the West as quickly as possible."

The logic of the analysis was that the West, and the U.S. in particular, should continue to work with Gorbachev while developing the relationship with Yeltsin and other emerging leaders and to use the moment of Soviet weakness to push forward on arms controls and related security issues. It was not quite so easy in practice. To shore up his political support, Gorbachev had begun to tilt toward the military and the "forces of order" who were busy making trouble in places like Lithuania, and who were reluctant to agree to further disarmament. In the spring of 1991, in fact, the Soviets began to reinterpret the treaty on conventional forces (CFE), signed in Paris the previous November, in ways that lessened their commitment to force reductions. The dispute dragged on into June 1991. Progress also slowed on strategic weapons (START) negotiations, in part because of the resistance of Brent Scowcroft, Bush's National Security Advisor, and in part because the Soviet team now routinely included representatives of the military who were there to keep tabs on the civilian negotiators. Gorbachev, Alexander Bessmertnykh (Shevardnadze's replacement as Foreign Minister) and officials working with them accepted the military's role so as to prevent them from later disowning agreements they did not like.

Two further issues caused additional awkwardness. American intelligence had figured out that the Soviets were developing two new missiles that would not be covered by the pending agreement on strategic arms. There was also troubling new information about the Soviets' continued development of biological weapons. A Soviet scientist, Vladimir Pasechnik, defected in October 1989 and told MI6 about Biopreparat, a secret organization responsible for research and production of biological weapons.[13] The British told the U.S. and in May 1990 the two countries' ambassadors made formal protests. Over the next two years the U.S. and the U.K. would continue asking for answers from the Soviets, who either denied the program's existence or denied knowledge of it, or, if it did exist, promised to end it. John Major raised the issue with Gorbachev at least twice, in March 1991 and again in September; and Bush and Gorbachev discussed it just weeks before the Moscow Summit scheduled for the end of July 1991. These more or less peripheral issues did not stop Gorbachev and Bush reaching agreement, but they did make the process harder. In the end, the U.S. decided that they had got enough from the Soviets to make the deal worthwhile. As Baker put it near the end of the negotiations, asking for more would amount to "trying to squeeze every last drop of blood out of this stone."[14] The START treaty was signed on July 31 and Bush and Gorbachev then went on their separate summer holidays.

The Soviet leader's rest would soon be violated by the attempted coup of August 18–21. The timing was far from accidental: a new Union Treaty that was to redefine relations with the republics and thus restructure the state was to be signed when Gorbachev returned from his vacation. The treaty had been in the works for more than a year and it had of necessity been Gorbachev's top priority. Without the treaty, the state he purported to run had no firm basis. The details had been bargained out as power flowed away from the center and toward the republics, Russia especially, and Gorbachev had conceded a great deal. A referendum had shown strong support for the new Union in March 1991, and on April 23 a meeting between Gorbachev, Yeltsin and the leaders of seven additional republics agreed on more or less final terms; but then, on June 12, Yeltsin was elected President of the Russian Federation. He, and others, pushed for, and obtained, more concessions; Gorbachev, for his part, convinced the Congress of People's Deputies to approve the treaty to create a "Union of Soviet Sovereign States." The date for the signing was set for August 21.

Rumors of a possible coup had circulated for nearly a year, but the prospect became much more threatening in the spring of 1991. The CIA reported on "The Soviet Cauldron" in late April and noted that "Gorbachev's credibility has sunk to near zero" and that "explosive events have become increasingly possible." The most unpleasant would be a turn to authoritarianism under "reactionary leaders." Indeed, "preparations for dictatorial rule have begun . . ." If such a move were to happen, the conservatives' "first target . . . would be Boris Yel'tsin and the Russian democrats." An attempted "putsch" might or might not succeed in the short term, and it would be ugly, but the CIA judged that it would not fare well over the long term. Still, it was now seen as much more likely than it had been only six months earlier.[15]

A further move came in June, when the Soviet Prime Minister Valentin Pavlov spoke to the Supreme Soviet and proposed that he be given emergency powers. This request, if granted, would have amounted to a "constitutional coup." Three days later the mayor of Moscow warned Jack Matlock, the U.S. Ambassador, of an ongoing plot to organize a coup.[16] The U.S. got word to both Gorbachev in Moscow and to Yeltsin, who happened to be in Washington. The Soviet leader dismissed the prospect, but did deem it necessary to appear before the Supreme Soviet in order to organize the defeat of Pavlov's proposal.

The plotters may have been discouraged but they were not deterred, for the signing of the Union treaty loomed in the very near future and they understood that it would basically ratify the demise of the Soviet Union as a major power. The coup itself was a miserable affair that fell apart quickly. Its organizers came from the military and the KGB and included ministers and officials appointed by Gorbachev himself. Their efforts were not well coordinated but, most important, the plotters could not count on the support of the armed forces or even the KGB. They were also unable to get hold of Yeltsin, who slipped away and made a genuinely heroic stand at the White House in Moscow, the seat of Russia's parliament.[17] There he was surrounded, but the elite unit of the KGB ignored orders to attack. Gorbachev also held tough, refusing to sign over his authority to a delegation sent to his dacha to secure his cooperation or, at least, his isolation. He was cut off, and he and his family feared the worst, but he did not capitulate. The plotters' inability to rally the military and security services and to fully control the cities was testimony to how far the country's transformation had proceeded. The old loyalties had frayed to the point that even the threat of force and the proclamation of a state of emergency designed to head off the end of the Soviet Union as a state evoked little popular support. The organizers of the coup soon realized the extent of their failure and gave up, and several chose to commit suicide rather than face the aftermath. On August 22, Gorbachev was brought back to Moscow and it was over.

The consequences were dramatic. The defenders of the old regime were utterly discredited. Their opponents understood immediately and so set upon dismantling what remained of it. At Yeltsin's urging the Communist Party was banned in the Russian Federation and its property seized. It chose to dissolve itself in Russia and fell apart elsewhere under similar pressures. Yeltsin and his allies simply began to take over the functions and institutions of the Soviet state, even as Gorbachev tried to make it work. Gorbachev continued his efforts to get a new Union treaty agreed, but the goal kept receding from view. When Ukraine voted for independence at the beginning of December, it was clear that nothing like the old union, or the one Gorbachev was trying to engineer, was possible, and a week later the leaders of Russia, Belarus and Ukraine met and signed an agreement to set up a "Commonwealth of Independent States." The USSR was effectively ended that day, though it was not until December 21 that the eleven republics in the CIS announced that "the USSR ceases to exist." Gorbachev, with a retirement package agreed on December 23, formally resigned on December 25. It was now primarily Yeltsin's responsibility to take over the Soviet nuclear arsenal, to manage relations with the rest of the world, to organize a stable and efficient government and to oversee the creation of a market economy. (Leaders in other republics would assume similar, but less global, responsibilities in their regions.) He would find the job rather difficult, but it was his and he did not hesitate in taking it on and shoving Gorbachev aside.

Between the coup and the formal end of the Soviet Union, Gorbachev nevertheless remained in charge of the country's relations with the world and in control of its nuclear forces. He no longer had to deal, however, with the resistance of the military in his efforts to disarm. The United States was also keen on pressing for further reductions in the aftermath of the START treaty. In August, yet another National Intelligence Estimate explained that "The decline of the Soviet Union had caused its leaders to view their national security and superpower status as hinging more than ever on strategic nuclear power." The U.S. also had in hand "evidence that five new strategic ballistic missiles are in development – two land based and three sea launched." Even if one such program were abandoned, the others would remain a serious challenge.[18] The implication was that the U.S. had a strong interest in getting the Soviets to scale back on that activity by agreeing to further measures of disarmament. The aftermath of the coup offered the possibility of doing precisely that. As the CIA noted in September, "The failed coup has created the most favorable opportunity for political democracy and a market economy in the history of the former USSR. The main institutional obstacles to fundamental changes in the system have been severely weakened" and in no sphere was that more true than in the military.[19]

Both the Bush administration and Gorbachev responded with speed and boldness.[20] Bush told the National Security Council on September 5 that he wanted a dramatic initiative, and on September 27 he announced to the country that "we now have an unparalleled opportunity to change the nuclear posture of both the United States and the Soviet Union." He proposed unilaterally to eliminate all ground- and sea-based tactical nuclear weapons, to take strategic bombers off "high-alert status" and to do the same for the 600 ballistic missiles scheduled to be deactivated as part of START, and to abandon two separate projects for nuclear modernization. The U.S. also put on the table the possibility of eliminating land-based strategic missiles with multiple warheads (MIRVs) through negotiations for a second START treaty. Bush also, though quietly, proposed "steps to permit the limited deployment of non-nuclear defenses to protect against limited ballistic missile strikes . . ."[21] The final point represented the ghost of "Star Wars," but otherwise the proposals met with an enthusiastic response and Gorbachev followed on October 5 with proposals that matched and even exceeded those made by Bush. To Bush's proposals Gorbachev added the removal of air-launched tactical nuclear weapons and the reduction of the number of warheads permitted under START from 6,000 to 5,000; and he put down a marker for new strategic negotiations by offering to cut strategic weapons by half. He also proposed a one-year moratorium on nuclear testing. Most of these decisions were unilateral, if reciprocal in spirit, and so would take effect without further negotiation. At the same time, the two sides would initiate a new round of strategic arms negotiations that would focus on "de-MIRVing" and that would lead in January 1993 to the signing of START II by Bush and Yeltsin. The arms race had gone into reverse, at least for a while.[22]

The end of the Soviet Union in December 1991 was to be the decisive climax to a period of historic geopolitical change. It effectively brought to a close the Cold War, the domination by the Soviets and their local followers of virtually the whole of Eastern Europe, the socialist experiment in the Soviet Union, and the arms race. It was transparently a triumph for the U.S. and the U.K. and their shared vision of the world, a vision shared only in part and more fitfully even by their most loyal allies in NATO and around the world. And yet the record shows little or no sign of triumphalism.[23] Instead, it shows a superpower almost obsessively concerned with proceeding cautiously, consulting allies and enlisting their support, and taking great care to replace the Cold War world order with something stable and, if possible, prosperous and democratic..

After the USSR

The European "architecture," what Gorbachev referred to as a "new structure of European security," set up with the Soviet Union and its leadership in mind, would be without its eastern pillar just over a year after it was put in place.[24] The emerging structure involved a unified and powerful Germany; a more fully integrated European Union; the continuation of NATO as the key organization for security and its continued Atlantic orientation; and a collection of new states in the east eager, for the most part, to be attached both to the European Union and to NATO. All of this would be subsumed under the United Nations, although in practice the work of the European institutions would be more important than that of the more global organization. The disappearance of the Soviet Union only made the evolving system and its architectural foundations even more "Atlanticist" as the most advanced countries in Eastern Europe queued up for membership in NATO and the EU. Having experienced the domination of their neighbor to the east, East European states and peoples opted unreservedly for a connection to the west: Poland, Hungary and the Czech Republic joined NATO as early as 1997; the Baltic countries and four others – Bulgaria, Romania, Slovakia and Slovenia – would join in 2004. The Russians were very much opposed, but were unable to stop the process.[25] EU membership would follow.

The architecture of the world economy was also skewed decisively toward an Atlantic, even Anglo-American, orientation. The "Washington Consensus" would serve to guide the transition from state-run to market economies in Eastern Europe and the former Soviet Union. The IMF played the critical, if not always an effective or enlightened, role in helping countries with macroeconomic stabilization, and its prescriptions were routinely derived from the new orthodoxy. The World Bank, which was focused on specific projects, took a similar position. Perhaps most interestingly, the new institution created to assist and supervise the transition, the European Bank for Reconstruction and Development, also adopted the Washington Consensus on what should happen in the postcommunist economies. The EBRD had been proposed by Francois Mitterrand in1989 and it was initially led by his friend and advisor Jacques Attali. The French vision for the new bank was similar to Mitterrand's plan for a European Confederation. It would be distinctly European and include the Soviet Union, and its formal ties to the United States would be more modest. The new bank was to take the lead in reconstructing postcommunist economies, effectively displacing the IMF and the World Bank, and as such it would lend to governments as well as to the private sector.[26]

Like Mitterrand's geopolitical framework, it did not work out as planned. Almost immediately, the British insisted that the U.S. be brought in more fully. The U.S. in turn objected to the inclusion of the Soviet Union and to the use of funds for loans beyond the private sector. The Americans were also determined to insist on "political conditionality of a democratic nature, built right into the mission and objectives of the Charter of the Organization."[27] On this issue there was general agreement, but a series of tense meetings in the spring of 1990 were needed to fully work out compromises on the role of the Soviet Union and the debate over public versus private sector lending. It was agreed in March that the EBRD could lend to governments, especially for infrastructure projects, but the majority of its loans (60 percent) would go to the private sector. In April the decision was made that the United States would be the largest shareholder, with a 10 percent holding, that the Soviets would take a 6 percent share but be designated not as a donor but as a "recipient" country and that its borrowings would be severely restricted. On both issues the U.S. had largely prevailed. The bank's charter was formally signed on May 29, 1990 and Attali elected as its first President. Its headquarters, however, would be in London. The very first article in the charter proclaimed the EBRD's central, and largely political, purpose: "to foster the transition towards open market-oriented economies and to promote private and entrepreneurial initiative in the Central and Eastern European countries committed to and applying the principles of multi-party democracy, pluralism, and market economies."

The EBRD would formally come into existence in 1991. Its formal structure and its ethos constituted an extremely accurate symbol of the architecture of the new Europe and the emerging post–Cold War order – headquartered in London, European in focus and personnel, with a decidedly Atlantic set of goals and rules. Its workings would reflect this orientation as well. By 1994, the bank began issuing what would become an annual Transition Report, summarizing not only its own work but assessing the transition in the formerly communist countries.[28] As part of that the bank developed a series of "transition indicators" that closely resembled and made concrete the principles of the "Washington Consensus" elaborated a few years before.

The new Europe bank did not, in fact, oversee the transition in Eastern Europe and the former Soviet Union; nobody did. Nor was there a master plan – some called for a Marshall Plan, but the will to provide that level of support was absent – or a neoliberal conspiracy. Economic reform was a complicated and often messy and uneven process whose success varied from country to country. What the story of the EBRD showed, however, was that there was no support for a transition to something other than a fully capitalist future. There was a lot of talk about various third ways or halfway houses between socialism and capitalism and between the state and the private sector, but no major state or institution was willing and able to support, or even to theorize, an alternative model. There were, of course, complaints about the social costs of too rapid transitions, of the "shock therapy" required to get it all started, but the options available to policy-makers were restricted by the "architecture" bargained out to structure the new world order and the principles on which it was based.

The decisions taken in the countries escaping Soviet domination and decades of socialist failure made it clear that the possibility of finding a third way commanded little popular support.[29] Even before the framework for the new Europe was fixed, Eastern Europeans had taken the first steps toward economic reform. Restructuring typically took place in two stages: in the first, prices were decontrolled, internal and external trade liberalized, state subsidies reduced and budgets cut to rein in inflation; the second stage involved the privatization of state-owned and controlled enterprises and the establishment of the broader set of rules and practices required for a functioning capitalist economy. In some cases, the two stages occurred together, though seldom was this a success.

In Poland the so-called Balcerowicz Plan was adopted at the end of 1989 and freed up prices at the beginning of the new year. The commission that devised it included Jeffrey Sachs, the American economist who was an early and eager advocate of "shock therapy" and who was later much criticized for his role.[30]

The short-term consequences were severe, but growth returned after two years of sharp declines. Privatization came later, and more slowly. The Hungarians had begun debating economic reform before 1989 and had taken steps to liber-alize trade and finance before the regime's demise. After the collapse prices were set free and privatization was begun quickly as well, with substantial participa-tion by foreigners. In Czechoslovakia a "Scenario for Economic Reform" was agreed in late 1989 and implementation was initiated with a "big bang" in 1990. Deregulation and macroeconomic stabilization were the top priorities and the currency was devalued in 1991. The privatization of state assets was also begun fairly soon after, with enterprises tasked with making plans for the transition and citizens given vouchers to buy into the new companies. Further east the Estonians had begun to discuss reform in 1988 and they moved quickly in 1990 to abolish price controls and free up trade. Lithuania was not far behind and undertook a speedy and widespread privatization beginning in 1992. What had been East Germany obviously followed a different path, and with a lot more help. Other states in Eastern Europe were slower to reform, and the violence in the former Yugoslavia meant that the move to markets, and to democracy, was less of a priority than physical survival. Nevertheless, economic reform was ubiquitous in Eastern Europe and it was more or less freely chosen, if some-times regretted.[31] A major motivation was to get access to the markets of Western Europe and, if possible, to secure membership in the European Union itself, with all the benefits that were presumed to flow from that.[32]

The most difficult and controversial transition occurred in Russia.[33] Economic reform was fitful at best under Gorbachev, but Yeltsin committed himself to a radical program in October 1991. In this he had strong rhetorical support from the United States, Great Britain and other G7 countries, but little substantive help. The IMF was also not inclined to push for massive aid, perhaps implicitly acknowledging the fact that it would not be forthcoming.[34] It was the Russians themselves who would undertake the task of reform, and pay for it one way or the other: Yegor Gaidar was designated to carry it out; he did and went on to suffer the political consequences. Price controls were lifted on January 2, 1992, trade was soon liberalized, and budgets were cut. Prices soared by as much as 2,500 percent during the year. A plan for massive privati-zation through a voucher system was also put in place. As Yeltsin argued, "Privatization has been going on in Russia for some time, but in a wild . . . and often criminal fashion. Today we need to seize the initiative."[35] The results were disappointing, and Yeltsin backed off plans to cut subsidies and the Russian Central Bank continued to print money, prolonging the inflation that came with the abolition of price controls. Meanwhile, managers were able to hold onto their control and as insiders they profited before and after privatization.

Political instability grew as the economy declined. Gaidar was gone within a year, and there was a major political showdown between Yeltsin and the parliament in the fall of 1993. The Russian President prevailed, but he emerged seriously weakened.[36] The process of privatization continued, but most industries ended up in the hands of former managers, officials and, often, corrupt bankers and people with backgrounds in the black market and organized crime. In 1995, as the government struggled and largely failed to collect taxes, a program of "Loans for Shares" was begun. Bankers would loan to the government in exchange for shares in privatizing industries; and huge assets were delivered into the hands of the so-called "oligarchs." By the mid–1990s the economy was recovering from its initial shocks, but the outcome was a massively unequal distribution of wealth and power and it was far from stable, as the financial crisis of 1998 would demonstrate.[37] And government itself, from 1993, would become decidedly more "presidential."

Across the former socialist lands democracy coexisted uneasily with economic reform, for reform meant a difficult transition that often tempted voters to support leaders with ties to the past, but for that very reason not burdened with the responsibility for "shock therapy" and its consequences.[38] Even when such people got back into office, however, they had few options but to continue with economic reform; and then they, too, would get blamed for its nasty side-effects.[39] Reform therefore proceeded and became irreversible; and democracy, shaky at times, became more institutionalized in the majority of formerly socialist states.

Locking In

Transitions took hold in large part because they were "locked in" by a variety of institutions and commitments and by the fact that the beneficiaries of reform developed a clear interest in defending them. An enlarged NATO and an expanded EU were two critical institutions that demanded firm commitments from new members. The integration of newly emerging states into world markets also served to lock in previous choices and block alternate paths of development. The Bush administration was particularly active in further opening world markets and in orienting and engaging the emerging economies of Eastern Europe toward the world economy. Not only did the U.S. administration sign bilateral trade agreements with Poland, Hungary, Czechoslovakia and several former Soviet republics; it also worked assiduously to negotiate the North American Free Trade Agreement (NAFTA) and to conclude the Uruguay Round of GATT talks, which led directly to the creation of the World Trade Organization (WTO). The aim was to make open markets the norm in the economic relations between states and economies and to render other possible norms, practices and approaches not merely unattractive and ineffective but illegal.[40]

In theory, regional or bilateral or even multilateral trade agreements and broader agreements to open trade on a more global basis are not entirely compatible, for a regime of partially open trading relations that effectively keeps out competitors is by definition not open.[41] The question is whether partial liberalization encourages or discourages liberalization on a larger scale. The Bush administration chose to believe that local or regional initiatives facilitated the creation of a more open world trading system. The U.S. had to some extent been forced in that direction when in 1982 it proposed a new round of GATT talks and received virtually no support. Instead, it chose to open negotiations with Canada. In early 1990, the Mexican Trade Minister proposed to Carla Hills, the U.S. Trade Representative, the creation of a free trade area encompassing the United States and Mexico. The idea soon morphed into the North American Free Trade Area including the U.S., Canada and Mexico. President Bush also announced the "Enterprise for the Americas Initiative" in June 1990, a plan to couple debt relief with investment and moves toward more open trade across Latin America. The Bush administration also worked hard to conclude the Uruguay Round and would label the process of working simultaneously on both regional and more global agreements "competitive liberalization." Striking regional or even simply bilateral bargains would, it was hoped, force others to come to terms in the bigger arena where GATT was hammered out. As Hills would argue later,

> for the U.S. to negotiate a big agreement covering North America – that is 400 million people – would bring Europe to the bargaining table because it will be concerned that we would gain a competitive edge. They will move in Uruguay Round negotiations because they will not want us to get off the reservation.[42]

Who were the others, and what did they want? As always, the array of parties to the negotiations was broad and the range of interests to be aggregated, brokered and compromised extremely complex. Early on in the Uruguay Round, the main issues seemed to be a continuation of the North–South dialogue begun in the late 1970s and adjourned in 1981. Essentially, developing countries wanted access to the markets of the more developed countries, especially for their agricultural products and for textiles. They were reluctant, however, to lower the barriers protecting their own manufacturing. The debt crisis of the 1980s led to a certain weakening of that resistance, as it became obvious that the path out of debt in the era of the "Washington Consensus" was through exports and greater openness to foreign investment.[43] The effect was to make a trade deal more likely, though it would require movement on two sectors that enjoyed substantial protection in the developed countries. Trade in textiles was managed through the Multi-Fiber Arrangement and agriculture was protected by a diverse collection of farm supports and export subsidies, the best-known of which was the Common Agricultural Policy (CAP) of the European Community. The cost of agricultural support was staggering, totaling roughly $25 billion annually in Europe and the United States. The American stance was, like Europe's, not entirely consistent. Not only did the U.S. protect agriculture and textiles, but it had also taken tough positions over Japanese imports and pressured the Japanese into a set of "voluntary import restrictions" and, with the 1988 Trade Act, it had put in place legislation that mandated the naming and shaming of countries guilty of discriminatory trade practices and, if they failed to reform, strong retaliatory measures.[44] At the same time, the U.S. in the 1980s became the loudest advocates of free trade and open markets. The stance was not entirely hypocritical, for the Reagan administration was faced with an assertive Congress determined to impose still greater restrictions on trade, and the concessions it made in response were probably inevitable; and they did serve to prevent a more decisive move to protection.[45] As Bush's top trade negotiator recalled, Reagan "talked a wonderful game of free trade, but succumbed to a lot of trade restrictions."[46] In fact, the decision to call for a new GATT round was undertaken in part to offset domestic criticism during the worst of the recession of the early 1980s.

However complex the actual trade policy of the U.S., its formal position during the Uruguay Round was a simple and orthodox assertion of the argument for free trade. The United States insisted on access to the markets of developing countries and was willing, at least on paper, to agree to opening access to the domestic market for textiles and agriculture. In July 1987, for example, the U.S. proposed a "zero option" whereby all agricultural subsidies would be eliminated by 2000.[47] The American stance was in this respect closer to that of the so-called "Cairns Group" of agricultural exporters than to the Europeans, whose commitment to the CAP precluded an alliance with this group of developing countries. The U.S. also worried that with the completion of the single market in 1992 Europe would become more closed off to American companies and imports. As U.S. Ambassador Raymond Seitz explained, "on trade issues . . . the image of Fortress Europe is never far from the American mind," and the 1992 program very much focused the mind on the prospect.[48]

On the other hand, the EU position was itself a compromise between different, and sometimes conflicting, interests and preferences. France benefited most from the CAP and so defended it most intensely. Large numbers of

German farmers also did well out of the program and so the Germans typically defended it. Britain, by contrast, did not and supported reform of the CAP and the opening up of trade both internally and externally. Further complications stemmed from the fact that trade was a community responsibility, so that individual countries were not allowed to speak for Europe. And yet the divisions within Europe were well known and in practice the U.S. and the U.K. worked together to promote a more open stance. Support for a more open and liberal position also varied by industry and by country. The French, for instance, were keen to protect their farmers, cheese-makers and *vignerons*, but with the goal of promoting their exports; and the French also felt that they, like the British, were competitive in services and so would profit from opening up trade in the service sector. The French were rather less confident that they could compete with Americans in cultural production, however, and so proclaimed "*l'exception culturelle*" and insisted on the EU's "television without frontiers" directive, whose purpose was precisely to reinforce frontiers by ensuring "that broadcasters reserve for European works a majority proportion of their transmission time . . ."[49]

The fact that the Europeans were pulled in different directions hints at the complexity and also the novelty of the Uruguay Round. Previous GATT negotiations had been taken up with efforts to lower tariffs on manufactured goods and to identify and reduce "non-tariff barriers" to trade and with finding ways to exempt agriculture and textiles.[50] The final round was to deal with those exceptions and also to extend trade rules to new areas: to services, including finance and investment and, as a corollary and support, to intellectual property.[51] The expansion of the remit of GATT (and hence the WTO) meant that trade issues moved from the borders across which exchange occurred into the domestic policies of trading nations, virtually guaranteeing greater contention and controversy but also holding out the promise of deepening the commitment to markets by embedding market values and relations in the institutions of member states. To Carla Hills, for example, "a broad trade agreement does much more than permit trade, it provides encourage[ment] to the rule of law, for an agreement sets the rules . . ."[52] These implications would make the conclusion of the round extremely difficult; and despite strenuous efforts the Bush administration would fail to achieve it before leaving office in January 1993. It would fall to the next President, Bill Clinton, to finalize the deal.

Bush did preside, however, over the signing of NAFTA in his last month in office; and his administration would preside over the breakthrough in negotiations with Europe. The original plan was to conclude the Uruguay Round by 1990, but arguments between the U.S. and Europe made that impossible. The Europeans, particularly the French but also the Germans, were determined to defend the CAP and gave their negotiators scant room for maneuver or compromise. Gradually, they came to realize the need for a deal, and within Europe itself there was dissension over the CAP.[53] Not just the British, but others were unhappy with the enormous cost of supporting mainly French and German farmers. With the conclusion of the Maastricht Treaty in December 1991 the European Commission stepped up its efforts to put in place a more sensible and defensible stance on agriculture and in May 1992 the EU came to an agreement to reform the policy. It was not a radical reform, but it did put a lid on total production, reduced support prices and took some agricultural land out of production.[54] The decision allowed negotiations between the U.S. and the EU to go forward, and by November a deal seemed within reach. But not quite: Just before the U.S. election EU Agricultural Commissioner Ray McSharry and Trade Commissioner Frans Andriessen came close to striking an agreement with the Americans on a conflict over one specific product – oilseeds – that the Europeans grew and exported in profusion. The issue was highly contentious; and the U.S. had launched a formal complaint through the GATT mechanism and prevailed and was prepared to retaliate. Resolving it was seen as key to getting a broader deal. Before the bargain could be sealed, however, the French balked and McSharry was told by Delors that he had exceeded his brief and that the deal would be rejected by member states, with France in the lead. The French had still not acquiesced to the agreement on CAP reform worked out the previous May and the government had been frightened by an outburst of dissatisfaction over CAP and the terms of the Maastricht Treaty, which was approved by a narrow margin. McSharry resigned in protest, and Delors relented. So, too, at least by implication, did the French. Shortly after, on November 18–19, the U.S. and EU reached what seemed a solid compromise at a meeting at Blair House in Washington. The Europeans would reduce by 21 percent the volume of exports subsidized and the value of subsidies by 36 percent. The oilseeds dispute was also settled on the side and it looked as though the Uruguay Round would soon be completed.

It would take another year to get a formal agreement, however, and the deal would be done by a new set of political actors. The terms of McSharry and Andriessen ran out, George Bush was not reelected and so his trade representative, Carla Hills, would be resigning. Who would replace them, and would they be as keen to reach an agreement? McSharry, who had served as Finance Minister in Ireland and had introduced a series of tough budgets, was unusually supportive of free trade as Agricultural Commissioner; Andriessen had similar views and was regarded as a genuine partner by Hills, whose perspective was even more liberal; and she reported as well that "the EC Commission staff has been pushing internally for a more open-market agricultural position."[55] Free trade was also an article of faith for George Bush and for his Secretary of State, James Baker. Their successors nevertheless proved equally eager to expand trade. The new EU Trade Commissioner was Leon Brittan, former Trade Secretary under Thatcher and former EC Commissioner for Competition. His commitment to open trade was strong, and his political skills impressive. The new Agricultural Commissioner, René Steichen of Luxembourg, was at least not French. Clinton chose to appoint a political confidante, Mickey Kantor, as U.S. Trade Representative, and Kantor and Brittan lobbied hard for the appointment of Peter Sutherland, another Irishman eager to promote freer trade, as Director-General of GATT.[56]

The key player was Bill Clinton himself. He faced a powerful set of contradictory pressures. Clinton had campaigned on the economy and insisted there should be no distinction between foreign policy and economic policy. His proposals for jobs were mostly focused on domestic measures, but there was also rhetoric about beating down the barriers to American exports. On the other hand, Clinton styled himself a "New Democrat" who would come to terms with the market-oriented political revolution that Ronald Reagan had engineered and Bush had continued, and he was personally convinced of the need for the U.S. to remain open to the opportunities created by the growth of international trade.[57] As he told an audience at American University in February 1993,

> The truth of our age is this and must be this: Open and competitive commerce will enrich us as a nation. It spurs us to innovate. It forces us to compete. It connects us with new customers. It promotes global growth without which no rich country can hope to grow wealthier. It enables our producers who are themselves consumers of services and raw materials to prosper. And so I say to you in the face of all the pressures to do the reverse, we must compete, not retreat.[58]

Clinton nevertheless had to reckon with the interests and opinions of his Democratic supporters and, as the most astute politician of his generation, he understood the need to qualify his support for open trade with promises to protect American jobs and the environment, and with specific exceptions. During the 1992 campaign, for example, he had come out in favor of NAFTA, but the endorsement was so surrounded with caveats that few could predict what he would do in office.[59] The election campaign also featured Ross Perot, whose best line in debate was about the "great sucking sound" that Americans would hear as NAFTA encouraged businesses to move jobs south, and who continued to make the argument after the election.

Clinton opted to support both NAFTA and the conclusion of the Uruguay Round and by all accounts worked hard and was effective. He had to work on two separate fronts. Internationally, the administration had to get at least token commitments from Mexico on labor and environmental issues in order to get the votes to approve NAFTA. The U.S. also faced continued hard bargaining with the Europeans. The French wanted to revisit the Blair House agreement and again criticized the EU's negotiators. The legislative elections of March 1993 saw the Socialists crushed and brought to power a center-right government in France led by Edouard Balladur who was even more committed to protecting French farmers. In May the new French government issued a paper demanding modifications to the Blair House agreement, tighter control by member states over the negotiations by the Commission and new measures that would allow the EU to retaliate more quickly and forcefully to what they saw as unfair trade practices. The argument was that the United States had similar legislation in place – famously Section 301 – and that the Europeans needed more powerful tools to fight their corner. In July the French demanded the calling of a "jumbo council" of EU ministers for agriculture, trade and foreign affairs. Though most EU members did not want to renege on Blair House and jeopardize the Uruguay Round altogether, the French position received at least partial support from Ireland, Belgium, Spain and even Germany. To appease the French, moreover, the Jumbo Council did meet in September 1993 and agreed to demand "clarification" and "amplification" of the Blair House compromise as well as greater control over the negotiating process. Later, in a final effort to mollify the French, policies designed to toughen up Europe's antidumping efforts were accepted.

The French also made an effort to talk directly to the United States, even though in theory and in law the European Commission had sole responsibility for trade. The Americans did not engage, fearing that to do so would lead to a reopening of what had already been agreed. In truth, the argument about Blair House was primarily an internal disagreement within the EU, at least until the U.S. begun the final push for a global deal in late November. What the Clinton administration did do was to set a deadline for concluding the round by December 15, 1993, at which point its "fast track" authority would expire.[60] The United States also worked closely with the British, who were themselves keen on the deal and who could push for it within the counsels of the EU. John Major was a convinced advocate of free trade and was reinforced in this preference by key officials such as Robin Renwick and Percy Craddock, who urged that the Prime Minister's top priority should be the successful conclusion of the Uruguay Round.[61] The Foreign Secretary, Douglas Hurd, was also committed to opening markets and Major and Hurd were in a position to coordinate efforts with Leon Brittan, at least informally.[62]

Meanwhile, Clinton turned his attention to securing final Congressional approval of NAFTA. It was an enormous struggle, for the President was forced to go against the strong preferences of many within the Democratic Party, especially the trade unions. The unions, after all, were among the party's biggest donors and their members were the most reliable forces on the ground working for Democrats. Democrats in Congress had also invested heavily in opposing the free trade policies of Reagan and Bush and had succeeded in imposing serious constraints on their conduct of trade policy. The still relatively new President was nonetheless eager to prove his credentials as a supporter of open trade and not unwilling to deploy his considerable political talents to that end.[63] His aides were split, with a number urging him to abandon NAFTA but with strong pressure to support it from Treasury Secretary Lloyd Bentsen. Clinton decided to push for ratification. He became deeply engaged personally, brokered a variety of deals, and he won. Along the way Al Gore challenged Ross Perot to a debate about NAFTA and, by all accounts, scored a huge victory. On November 17, the trade agreement was ratified by a vote of 234 to 200 in the House, and a majority of 61 to 38 passed it in the Senate on November 20. Only a hundred of the "yes" votes came from Democrats in Congress, but Clinton prevailed all the same.[64]

With NAFTA approved and the December 15 deadline looming, the U.S. began what would prove to be the final set of negotiations with the Europeans. Both sides were ready to compromise and on December 6 it was agreed to amend the Blair House agreement so that the cuts in subsidies were maintained, but delayed, and the base years, from which level cuts would be made, were moved up. The concessions allowed for more subsidies and more production, but the principle of reducing both was preserved. Further wrangling ensued, but the negotiations were done by mid-December: the Uruguay Round was finished, the deadline met; and a new organization to oversee international trade, the World Trade Organization, was about to come into existence.

The agreement on world trade was a major step in the creation of the institutional framework within which the post–Cold War world would develop. It put in place rules and procedures that made open markets the standard governing the economic relations between states; and it set the terms for participation in the global economy. Ironically, the initiative to create the new organization was more European than American, for the Europeans preferred a neutral arbiter of trade disputes to the U.S. practice of pressure and retaliation. The U.S. came on board quickly, however, and the outcome was of a piece with American efforts to create a new security architecture in Europe, to lock in economic reform in Eastern Europe and to encourage the enlargement of NATO and the EU. The WTO had a similar function, for joining it would be a "single undertaking": membership in the WTO meant accepting more or less the entire package of trade agreements reached under GATT and the rules and regulations to enforce them. And since the Uruguay Round itself had extended the range of trade agreements into services, agriculture, government procurement, intellectual property and patents and even investment, WTO membership involved major commitments that would have effects on domestic policy in all participating countries.[65] In signing up, countries were effectively submitting their economies and their public policies to a standard that, if not literally crafted from "Atlantic Rules" and the "Washington Consensus," was nonetheless close to and utterly compatible with those prescriptions.

Equally important, the rules of the emerging post–Cold War order had no serious rivals. Not everyone played by the new rules, of course, but they constituted a distinct set of norms. Markets, human rights and democracy had emerged in the early 1990s as a formula that dominated the rhetoric of international relations and domestic policy-making and it was assumed to have universal, or near-universal, reach. The exceptions were many and they were well known: China was no democracy and human rights were scarcely recognized there; various dictators and strongmen presided over the fate of many parts of Africa and the Middle East; and the democratic transitions in many former Soviet republics did not come close to establishing democracy. Nevertheless, the norms or at least the rhetoric of markets, rights and democracy were now pervasive in the conduct of relations between states, in international organizations and even in international law.

This discursive dominance was genuinely novel, for while democracy, markets and human rights had been on the agenda for decades, they had not always been so privileged and had typically not been understood as compatible and useful. There had been lots of talk of democracy in the 1940s and 1950s, but that tended to give way to the imperatives of the Cold War and its many unholy alliances. Rights had also been much discussed in the years after 1945, as growing knowledge of the Holocaust led to a greater understanding of what crimes against humanity and what national and individual rights looked like. Even so, the right to self-determination increasingly trumped individual and group-based rights as decolonization took hold and more and more people claimed the right to self-government and non-interference. It also turned out that the leaders of various national liberation movements were not especially committed to democracy and regarded their victories as by definition democratic and so saw no need for the trappings of democratic politics such as elections, civil rights and the rule of law.[66] The very existence of the Soviet bloc was itself an affront to any notion that democracy or human rights were potentially universal and the Soviets and their allies fought hard in the negotiations leading to the Helsinki Accords to enshrine the principle that there was no right for outsiders to question social systems internal to nation-states. They largely succeeded, but for the relatively minor concessions contained in "Basket III" of the accords.

The more fulsome commitment to human rights would come just after this, and served to expand the impact of "Basket III" in Eastern Europe and the Soviet Union. The turn toward human rights was largely a Western phenomenon, however, prompted by a desire to strike a new pose toward the Third World after the end of empire and, for the United States, after the Vietnam War.[67] The emphasis also served to isolate the worst offenders against human rights, such as Pinochet in Chile, Somoza in Nicaragua, and the Shah of Iran, and to facilitate a redrawing of the map of Cold War alliances. The U.S. in particular would disso-ciate itself from the most brutal regimes and seek to reform them or, failing that, would abandon them. Or so it was for a while under President Jimmy Carter. The Europeans had made an earlier and somewhat firmer commitment to human rights, at least internally, largely as a response to the continent's recent history of authoritarian rule. Britain hesitated to make a formal commitment, but eventually found human rights an attractive principle with which to respond to crises like that in Northern Ireland and with which to address its need for a postimperial identity. Still, the commitment to human rights remained incom-plete during the 1980s because of the stance of the two superpowers. The Reagan administration was dismayed at the outcome of Carter's policies in Iran and Nicaragua and was, at least at first, much less enthusiastic in the promotion of human rights. Over time, it found human rights a useful stick with which to beat the Soviets – over the fate of Soviet Jews especially – and it was also forced by events in Latin America, the Philippines and Haiti to abandon dictators and espouse democratic elections as the appropriate mechanism for political trans-formation. The Soviet Union, on the other hand, made no pretense of being concerned with human rights and elections until very late, and there was also little progress in Eastern Europe. All that changed between 1989 and 1991, and human rights and democracy became the norm for political life in the post-Soviet world, even if reality did not always live up to the rhetoric.

When did markets become part of the formula? To some extent the idea of private property and free markets had been on the political agenda of the advanced economies and the international organizations they founded for a long time. The Bretton Woods institutions, for example, were premised on the centrality of markets. As often as markets were praised, however, they were also regarded as flawed and needing to be contained, managed and supple-mented by the state. Such views were not literally or precisely Keynesian, but it was the broadly Keynesian consensus on economic policy that brought these ideas together and rendered them compatible. The critique of the state and of Keynes that developed in the late 1970s and early 1980s, however, shattered this relatively complacent notion; and by the late 1980s Thatcher, Reagan and their supporters had succeeded in convincing many people, not only in Britain and the U.S. but elsewhere, that markets were not merely useful tools but the key to prosperity and development. This paradigmatic revolution was firmly in place by 1989 and its assumptions became pervasive in the effort to create a post–Cold War world.

After the Cold War, therefore, democracy, markets and human rights were assumed to be consistent and self-reinforcing rather than alternatives that might be in conflict, and the evocation of these three goals not only suffused the discourse about constructing a new world but served to guide the process by which new architectures governing security and the workings of the economy, internally and externally, were set up. By the early 1990s, democracy, markets and human rights would come to be grouped together as "good governance" and the institutions that funded and supervised the restructuring of economies and societies in the former socialist bloc and in the developing world all adopted "good governance" as a prerequisite of economic support. The World Bank took the lead in adopting this normative stance, the IMF followed, and the new European development bank was in agreement as well; together, they were able to enforce a new consensus on how societies ought to be governed.[68] A 1989 report on Africa by the World Bank, for example, insisted that development meant "a systematic effort to build a pluralist institutional structure, a determination to respect the rule of law, and vigorous protection of the freedom of the press and human rights."[69] A more formal policy statement on *Governance and Development* was issued by the bank in 1992 and the emphasis on governance and rights was taken still further with the appointment of a new director, James Wolfensohn, in 1995.[70] Michael Camdessus, Director of the IMF during the late 1980s and 1990s, echoed and effectively reinforced the emphasis on governance as the complement to markets.[71] The Organization for Security and Cooperation in Europe (OSCE, formerly CSCE), with little to do on security matters, likewise chose to focus from the mid–1990s on the promotion of "Democratic Institutions and Human Rights." These formal institutions joined with semipublic agencies and with numerous non-governmental organizations (NGOs) – such as Transparency International, founded in 1993 – in what would become a virtual, and self-evidently virtuous, crusade.[72] At the same time and in a different register, Western scholars and politicians began to argue that markets and democracy brought peace. Such heady and to some extent wishful arguments had been made before, most notably before World War I, but they gained a new purchase with the apparent outbreak of peace between East and West and, shortly after, with the rallying of the coalition against Saddam Hussein in the Gulf War.[73]

It was a noble, if ultimately rather frustrating, set of beliefs to hold and to expect the international community to uphold and enforce. Two problems loomed even as the vision of the post–Cold War order was still being elaborated. The objectives were grand and the mission was global, but would the institutional framework being constructed after the Cold War deliver the resources and generate the level of commitment that the project would require? Equally important, the new principles were no longer just about peace and the resolution of disputes between states or about trade and investment flows, but also about how states were organized, how they treated their own people, how they chose to run their economies. Standards about the internal workings of states were not only hard to enforce, but it was close to impossible to come to any genuine consensus about them. What might seem obvious to outsiders, and obviously wrong and unjust, could be seen as traditional, appropriate and effective to insiders; and the very possibility of outsiders attempting to enforce such norms might well render local traditions and deviations worthy of defense. It had been a long struggle to create a world order that enshrined principles of democracy, human rights and free markets as preeminent objectives, but it would not take long to see how elusive and, in certain instances, counterproductive those goals could be.

CHAPTER 9

Order and Disorder after the Cold War

The Emerging Post–Cold War Order

The reunification of Germany in October and the signing of Charter of Paris in November 1990 began the formal construction of the post–Cold War world. A rash of agreements and understandings followed, new institutions were established and old institutions given new mandates and powers, and alliances were reconfigured around new threats and objectives. The aim was to establish a framework, an architecture, to govern international relations, security and the international economy after the collapse of communism and the disappearance of the Soviet Union. It was to be a rules-based system that was supposed to function more or less automatically, without the need for regular, heroic and potentially bloody interventions in order to make it work.[1] There was something almost utopian about the idea, and it contrasted sharply with the Cold War order it replaced, for waging the Cold War implied great vigilance, continued attention, close control over clients and allies and local conflicts, and more regular if local military engagements on both sides.

The new order was also a system that, because of the character of the rules embedded in it – with commitments to markets, democracy and human rights (or good governance) – was potentially very intrusive. Applying such rules would mean judging and seeking to alter what happened within states and in how states treated their citizens, and the effort was bound to create crises and demand the very interventions that the framework's architects hoped to avoid. Little of this would be automatic. The contradiction would push the system in unanticipated directions and toward policies – humanitarian intervention, nation-building, the "responsibility to protect," counterproliferation, antiterrorism – that eventually involved the recourse to force. It would lead, most importantly, to the ill-fated invasion of Iraq in 2003, a venture that threatened to destroy the post–Cold War system as a whole.

Well before the architecture was established, however, the new order was forced to respond to the invasion of Kuwait. Saddam Hussein's move was a flagrant violation of international law and a brutal act in itself; and his thuggish regime was virtually impossible to defend. It was thus possible to gain UN support in opposition to Iraq and to rally a broad coalition behind the effort to enforce the UN mandate. The military encounter was brief and decisive, for Iraq's forces were no match for those of the United States and its allies and the effect was to encourage grand talk of a "new world order" and a belief that, after four decades in which the United Nations and the international community were unable to cooperate to keep the peace, they would now be able to do so. In retrospect, it is clear that this was a moment unlikely to recur and that it was a mistake to regard the Gulf War, and the politics and diplomacy with which it was carried out, as a template for future action. The leaders of the Soviet Union had been distracted with what was to be that state's terminal crisis and even then it required continual negotiation to keep the tottering superpower on side. It was also no mean feat to keep the French and other Europeans from unilateral efforts for a negotiated settlement; and without firm backing from the U.S. and the U.K., the Arab opposition to Iraq might well have unraveled. Though the coalition was extremely broad, its core was the Anglo-American alliance. The experience reinforced the connection, helping to repair the damage Thatcher had done over Germany and Europe. Still, it meant the coalition was wider than it was deep. Had Saddam Hussein maneuvered with a modicum of subtlety, it could easily have fallen apart. Even the military lessons drawn from the Gulf War were unclear: the U.S. tried out a range of precision-guided weapons that were supposed to represent the new face of war, but the key to victory was the marshaling of over half a million troops in the desert.[2]

The new framework of international relations would face additional tests in Europe, in Africa and in the Caribbean.[3] In each case, the framework would be found wanting and it would be further modified in response. The disintegration of Yugoslavia, and the prolonged failure to end the civil wars and ethnic cleansing that accompanied them, was a particular challenge to the role of Europe, the European Union especially. Europe had been the focus of attention in 1989 and 1990, with questions about the future of Germany, the reconstruction of Eastern European states and the reform of their economies, the evolving role of NATO, and the meaning and effect of greater European integration and creation of the European Union dominating the agenda. These had largely been resolved in a manner that strengthened and reinforced the new framework. But Yugoslavia defied all the plans and institutions and, as Zbigniew Brzezinski put it, the fate "of Bosnia offered painful proof of Europe's continued absence" as a political force.[4] Yugoslavia, a patchwork of nationalities, ethnicities and religions first put together after the Great War, had been crafted after 1945 as a federalist state made up of six republics and two autonomous provinces. The regime had made an explicit commitment to a multiethnic identity and developed complex rules about power-sharing and regional autonomy. It had been held together largely by the personality of Josip Broz Tito, the Communist and Partisan leader who dominated the state until his death in 1980. After Tito, things came unglued and politics came increasingly to follow ethnic and nationalist divisions. The largest group was the Serbs, many of whom felt that previous arrangements had denied them the political dominance to which they were entitled. By definition the other nationalities in Yugoslavia – Croatians, Slovenes, Bosnians and the Albanians in Kosovo – would be dominated if the Serbs had their way.

As the rest of Eastern Europe turned on the party leaders who ruled over undemocratic states, the peoples of Yugoslavia turned on each other. The most prosperous republics, Croatia and Slovenia, began to envision themselves as independent states, while in Serbia the loyal communist Slobodan Milošević discovered that the appeal to nationalism was more effective than any effort to prolong or reform the system. He became leader of the Serbian party in 1987 and had soon turned it into the voice of Serbian resentment. Though the republics were organized on ethnic lines, there was lots of overlap. As tensions increased and the state moved toward breakup, Serbian leaders began to mobilize their fellow Serbs throughout Yugoslavia, in Croatia and Bosnia most notably, and effectively decided to create a greater Serbia that would include as many Serbs in as many regions as possible. To make that happen, others would have to leave and to give up their homes and lands to Serbs. "Ethnic cleansing," as the process became known, was thus central to the building of a new Serbian state. The League of Communists of Yugoslavia broke apart in early 1990 and everywhere political life came to be reorganized on a nationalist basis. By 1991 Slovenia, Croatia and Macedonia had declared their independence and civil war had broken out. Serbs in Bosnia and Croatia, allied with, and armed by, Milošević but nominally independent, committed the worst offenses, and the worst of the fighting was in Bosnia-Herzegovina. Sarajevo, the cosmopolitan capital, was under siege from April 1992 until early 1996 and suffered terrible destruction; Srebrenica, a small town further to the east, became the site of an infamous massacre in July 1995.

The crisis in Yugoslavia was highly visible to European and American leaders, but the response was slow and ineffective.[5] Trouble was visible only intermittently in Somalia, Haiti and later in Rwanda, for neither the United States nor the Europeans had vital interests in these poor and battered lands. It was no less real, however, and no less revealing about the limits of the emerging post–Cold War order. Somalia had been a Cold War battleground in the 1970s and 1980s, but was no longer; what remained were lots of weapons and a truly dysfunctional state. Civil war had erupted in 1988 and by 1992 there was no effective government and widespread famine, with approximately 300,000 deaths and many refugees. The United Nations established a peacekeeping mission with the aim of getting aid to victims. The Bush administration, facing criticism from candidate Bill Clinton over its inaction in Bosnia, agreed to U.S. participation. The limited aims of the UN mission gradually expanded, in part because UN Secretary-General Boutros Boutros-Ghali was personally invested in getting rid of General Aidid, the dominant warlord, but also because of the sheer logic of events. At the United Nations, U.S. Ambassador Madeleine Albright was busy laying out a particularly expansive vision: the aim of the intervention, she said, was to transform Somalia from a "failed state into . . . an emerging democracy."[6] As conditions in Mogadishu deteriorated, the commander on the ground requested more support, specifically a battalion of Rangers and a Delta Force unit. On October 3, 1993, it was these forces whose helicopters were shot down and who, surrounded by angry and well-armed Somalis, lost eighteen of their number, with another seventy-four injured. It was a genuine disaster, made worse by the fact that it was quickly broadcast on American television.

Just a week after the fiasco in Somalia the American warship *Harlan County* entered the harbor at Port-au-Prince in Haiti to deliver troops and advisors who were supposed to pave the way for the return of the democratically elected President, Jean-Bertrand Aristide, who had been ousted in a military coup in September 1991. On the docks was an angry crowd, organized by an ally of the military who also happened to be in the pay of the CIA, and they were shouting "Somalia! Somalia!"[7] The ship left without unloading its human cargo. It would take another year and much bargaining, with Jimmy Carter playing a not always helpful role, before Aristide would reassume the presidency.

American experiences in Somalia and Haiti were extremely embarrassing to the Clinton administration, even if much of the blame could be put on its predecessor. What mattered most, however, was the consequence, for these unhappy outcomes made the United States extremely reluctant to get involved in local conflicts in distant places whose strategic importance was unclear. The U.S. military was still deeply and appropriately scarred by the experience of Vietnam, and its leaders, both soldiers and civilians, held to what had been known first as the Weinberger and later as the Powell Doctrine, which insisted that the U.S. deploy troops only when vital U.S. interests were at stake, domestic support firm and plans for victory and for exit thorough and convincing, and even then only with overwhelming force. The Gulf War fit those conditions, nothing else in the 1990s would come close. Bosnia did not, at least in its early phases; Somalia did not; and Haiti did not. More fatefully, Rwanda did not. There the largest ethnic groups, Hutu and Tutsi, had been fighting for control of the government ever since the departure of the Belgians. The Tutsi lost and many went into exile, but in 1990 they launched an invasion that forced the ruling Hutu government to compromise and agree to share power. Hutu extremists, enamored of "Hutu power" and not eager to share anything, resisted and civil war continued. When the Hutu President's plane was shot down in April 1994, militants in the army carried out a detailed plan to massacre Tutsis. In less than four months half a million were slaughtered in the most explicit and massive genocide since World War II.[8]

Domestic Constraints

Talk of a "new world order" in international relations could not and did not survive such tragedies. In fact, it barely made it through the Gulf War. Still, the effort to craft a new order, to build its architecture and establish the institutions that would make it work, continued. The failures of the early 1990s, even if they all happened on the margins of the new order, would nevertheless rob the project of its glamor and of any triumphalism that might otherwise have accompanied it. They led as well to a public disillusionment with internationalist visions and instead encouraged a narrow focus on domestic affairs. Alliances were also strained, as divergent interests and capabilities prevented effective action to meet these crises. The details of these very public disasters would fade, as attention turned elsewhere, leaving just a bad memory and a determination not to repeat the failures. The exception, of course, was the former Yugoslavia, where Milošević remained in power and moved on from efforts to crush the Bosnians to an attempt to suppress the Kosovars. His persistence guaranteed that the question of how the new order would cope with failed or rogue states and with gross violations of human rights would remain at the top of the international agenda. The result was nearly a decade of haggling and uncertainty on the part of American, British and European leaders over when and where and whether to intervene in these troubled lands. And if the last stage of the Cold War was played out with Britain and America in close cooperation and in agreement on goals and strategy, the construction of the post–Cold War world revealed the two allies to be much less in concert and, it could be argued, less effective.

The sheer intractability of the problems was certainly one reason for disagreement and inactivity; so, too, was the fact that aside from these crises on its margins, the post–Cold War order appeared to be broadly effective and the temptation to ignore the fate of mostly non-white peoples suffering from oppression carried out by their own leaders was very strong. At least of equal importance, however, was the course of domestic politics in Britain and the United States. In both countries, voters were focused on the economy and politicians followed. In Britain, for example, the "Lawson boom" of the late 1980s produced a brief revival of inflation and was replaced by a period of slower growth; in the United States, the rapid expansion of the Reagan era was followed by a noticeable slowdown that caught the Bush administration off guard and gave Bill Clinton his opening. John Major would survive the election of April 1992, George Bush would lose his reelection bid in November.

The rhetoric with which these elections were fought differed. The Clinton campaign focused on the weak economy and succeeded, even though the data showed that recovery had already begun. In Britain the issue was whether Labour could be trusted not to ruin the economy after it had presided over the crisis of the late 1970s. The implicit charge was unfair, of course, because neither Labour nor the Conservatives had solutions to the economic woes of the 1970s, but Labour had been in office during the worst of it and was still tagged with the responsibility. The party's sharp turn to the left in the 1980s reinforced that identification, and the efforts in the late 1980s to move the party toward the center had been only partially successful. Labour presented a new program in 1992, but with Neil Kinnock as leader it was unable to regain voters' trust. And John Major, the new Tory leader, was a less controversial figure than Thatcher had been toward the end of her time in office. He was reassuring, Kinnock was not, and the tabloid press made sure to make that point.

The fundamental issue at stake in both contests, however, was whether the revolutions in public policy of the Thatcher and Reagan years would become more or less permanent or would be reversed. Despite the different issues and electoral outcomes, the effective choice in 1992 was that the market-oriented policies of the 1980s would not be reversed. Major was less ideological and far less strident than Thatcher – "In ideological terms he travelled light," as one official put it – but Tory policies remained much the same and there were few innovations during the 1992–7 government.[9] What had changed as of 1992 and would continue to evolve until 1997 was Labour: the Policy Review that Kinnock initiated after the defeat of 1987 jettisoned the party's more radical policies on the economy and foreign policy and began the process of reconciling Labour with the consequences of Thatcherism. Defeat in 1992 led Kinnock to resign as leader, with John Smith replacing him. Smith encouraged the party's shift to the center, though the process under his leadership was more plodding; when he died in 1994 and was succeeded by Tony Blair, the effort to "modernize," moderate and rebrand intensified. Blair was convinced that "the credibility of the whole New Labour project" required an acceptance of much of what Margaret Thatcher had wrought and a recognition of one "basic fact: Britain needed the industrial and economic reforms of the Thatcher period."[10] By the election of 1997, which New Labour won massively, the policy differences between the parties had become much narrower and Labour actually promised to stay within Tory budget guidelines for a full two years.

In the United States, the Democrats reconciled with the basics of the Reagan revolution even sooner, though perhaps less fully. Clinton was a so-called New Democrat, which meant specifically that he was a member and leader of the Democratic Leadership Council (DLC).[11] The DLC was founded in 1985, in the aftermath of Reagan's second election. Its leaders were typically moderate Democrats from southern states and its aim was to push Democrats toward more centrist candidates and positions. Clinton took a number of stances that did not endear him to the party's major constituencies: he was a free trader, for example, and thus broke with the unions and liberal Democrats from the northeast and midwest who had campaigned hard for protectionist legislation in the Reagan and Bush years. Clinton was personally popular with African-American voters, but he distanced himself from some of their leaders and icons, such as the rapper Sister Souljah; he also found time to fly home to Arkansas during the primary campaign to preside over the execution of Ricky Ray Rector, a black man who had been convicted of murder but was clearly mentally compromised.[12] In office he supported the Omnibus Crime Bill of 1994, which expanded the use of the death penalty. In 1996 Clinton would also support a program of welfare reform that was intended to move recipients from welfare to work, though he was also responsible for substantially extending the Earned Income Tax Credit in 1993. The Clinton administration was also fiscally conservative, eschewing big spending programs and producing a budget surplus by the end of the President's second term. He was helped in that effort by the fact that George Bush had agreed to tax increases back in 1990 – a responsible decision that did much to doom his chances of reelection. The tax increases agreed by Bush, combined with Clinton's own budgets, allowed revenues to grow steadily as the economy grew throughout the mid and late 1990s.

The elections of 1992 had the effect of embedding the shift away from government and toward the market in both Britain and the United States. Critics on the left would attack Clinton and Blair for abandoning their principles, which to some extent they clearly did, but the counter was that moving toward the political center was the only way to win and hold office. And Clinton and Blair did not simply carry out the neoliberal projects of Reagan and

Thatcher, but in fact tempered those projects with increases in spending directed at the poor and services that sustained the poor. Still, the dominant feature of domestic policy-making in both countries was continuity. This did not translate into consensus, bipartisanship or an era of compromise and good feeling. On the contrary, Clinton's moves to the center were met by further moves to the right by the Republicans, who loathed the elder Bush's willingness to compromise and who chose instead to shut down the government for nearly a month in 1995–6 over the budget. In Britain, the Tories felt little gratitude to the man who had brought them an unexpected fourth electoral victory and became increasingly obstreperous. Unrepentant Thatcherites and Eurosceptics made it increasingly difficult for Major to govern effectively and left the Conservative Party itself largely ungovernable. Add in a few sex scandals and the Conservatives were in no position to compete with Blair and New Labour in 1997.

Budgets, Strategies, Weapons

The narrowing of party differences and electoral choices and the increasing bitterness of politics itself did not dictate the stance of either the United States or Great Britain on issues such as Bosnia or Somalia or international institutions and the architecture of the post–Cold War world. There were indirect effects, however, that tended to constrain the options for political leaders charged with coping with these issues. In neither country, for example, was there much room for increased expenditures on the military or on foreign aid. The last great boost in military spending had come in the early 1980s, at the height of the Second Cold War. It had been highly controversial and elicited mass protests against nuclear weapons, and the defense buildup was largely responsible for the budget deficits that dominated the politics of Reagan's second term and compelled Bush to violate his "no new taxes" pledge. The ending of the Cold War inevitably gave rise to demands, indeed to the expectation, of a "peace dividend" that could allow taxes to be reduced or funds to be diverted to more socially useful purposes. Robert McNamara, former Secretary of Defense, in 1989 called for the defense budget to be cut in half, and in January 1992 Senator Ted Kennedy of Massachusetts called for $210 billion to be moved from defense to social purposes over seven years.[13] Similar proposals were made in the U.K. Military officials, and their political allies, would fight hard to keep defense spending high, but it was a difficult argument to win when the main geopolitical opponent simply vacated the field of battle. Defenders of the military and its budget had considerable resources at their disposal, of course, for major corporations were invested in developing and selling weapons, at home and abroad, and entire communities depended on defense spending for jobs.

The debate had begun even before the Gulf War in 1991. With the Soviet threat visibly receding, the U.S. Defense Department, under the leadership of Richard Cheney, had begun planning as early as 1989. Colin Powell, Chair of the Joint Chiefs of Staff, helped to prepare a plan that was not premised on a confrontation with the Soviet Union leading to global war. It therefore proposed a "Base Force" with roughly 25 percent fewer troops that would reduce the defense budget by 10 percent over five years. In place of a strategy designed to deter and defeat the Soviet Union and its allies, the new orientation envisioned a "regional defense strategy" that could provide the capacity for fighting regional conflicts in, for example, the Middle East or Northeast Asia. The U.S. would also retain sufficient troops and weapons to allow for the timely "reconstitution" of a major military force directed at, say, a revived and revanchist Russia or an emboldened China. But the main thrust was regional, and that meant a different configuration of military force than during the Cold War: it would require more mobile fighting units, a "forward presence" and the possibility of "force projection" in order to get them to distant battlefields. The continued development of new technologies was, of course, also a central aim.[14]

Powell, along with Paul Wolfowitz from the Defense Department, presented the new vision in May 1990 and George Bush announced its basic features in Aspen in early August. It was overshadowed, however, by Iraq's invasion of Kuwait; and the buildup to, and prosecution of, the Gulf War put discussions of long-range strategy on hold.[15] Defense Secretary Cheney nevertheless urged the process forward and was eager to lock in a strategic plan in 1992. A draft version of a new "Defense Policy Guidance" document was readied in February 1992 and immediately leaked to the *New York Times*. The *Times* broke the story on March 8 and emphasized in particular proposals that the U.S. should embrace and try to perpetuate the "unipolar moment" and seek to deter rising, and possibly rival, regional powers from challenging U.S. dominance. As the draft "Guidance" explained, its purpose was to address "the fundamentally new situation that has been created by the collapse of the Soviet Union, the disintegration of the internal as well as the external empire, and the discrediting of Communism as an ideology with global pretenses and influence." The new context had been brought into being primarily by the victory over Soviet communism but also by the recent victory over Iraq and by a "less visible one, the integration of Germany and Japan into a U.S.-led system of collective security and the creation of a democratic 'zone of peace.'" From this new reality flowed two clear objectives: the first was to "prevent the reemergence of a new rival, either on the territory of the former Soviet Union or elsewhere, that poses a threat on the order of that posed formerly by the Soviet Union." As a corollary, the U.S. would seek to "prevent any hostile power from dominating a region whose resources would, under consolidated control, be sufficient to generate global power . . ." and it would need to demonstrate "the leadership necessary to establish and protect a new order that holds the promise of convincing potential competitors that they need not aspire to a greater role or pursue a more aggressive posture to protect their legitimate interests." The second objective was to "address sources of regional conflict and instability in such a way as to promote increasing respect for international law; limit international violence; and encourage the spread of democratic forms of government and open economic systems."[16]

The *Times* story provoked a storm over the prospects of a new American empire and unilateral applications of military force by the U.S.[17] Brent Scowcroft labelled the plan "just nutty" and sought to bury it.[18] A decade later, critics would see in the plan the roots of what would later emerge as George W. Bush's National Security Strategy of 2002, with its aggressive plan to deter rivals, preempt threats and use American might to spread democracy. The neoconservatives at the Project for a New American Century, founded in 1997, made the same connection and actually embodied it.[19] Defenders of the first Bush administration's effort – including neoconservatives such as Paul Wolfowitz – have claimed that the leaked document was an early draft taken out of context and insist that in its later drafts the document reaffirmed America's commitment to allies and to multilateral action. The idea of convincing possible rivals not to contest U.S. predominance, Wolfowitz has further argued, grew out of the country's successful experience with building and maintaining alliances and was an effort to extend its reach so as "shape the future security environment" by enlarging the democratic "zone of peace."[20]

The strategy elaborated by Powell and Cheney focused mostly upon conventional weapons but assumed a relative stability in nuclear forces and hence a continued reliance on nuclear deterrence. While the implications of the new strategic posture were being argued out within the government, the defenders of the old order in the Soviet Union launched an abortive coup against Gorbachev and within a few months the Soviet state itself had disappeared. Between August and December of 1991 the U.S. and the Soviets had engaged in a process of competitive disarmament that left both sides with much reduced nuclear arsenals. The argument about defense policy would also be influenced, in somewhat contradictory ways, by the experience of the Gulf War. The mobilization against Iraq clearly put the Powell Doctrine on display and the success of the venture seemed to validate it and to make the case for the maintenance of a large army and the deployment of overwhelming force. At the same time, the apparent effectiveness of America's precision-guided weapons showed the promise of what was beginning to be called the "revolution in military affairs"

(RMA). The planning document that Cheney finally published just before leaving office in January 1993 reflected these recent but varied experiences.

Inevitably, the argument continued as the Clinton administration sought to adjust military strategy to its judgments and values. The Clinton team were clearly less eager for military engagement and initially less enamored of new weapons systems and the doctrines used to justify them, and they felt pressure from their base to reduce defense spending. In response, the new Defense Secretary, Les Aspin, promised and delivered a "Bottom-Up Review" in September 1993. The review proposed reductions in spending beyond those envisioned by Bush and Cheney, by roughly another 10 percent. Most important, it concurred with the plan that the U.S. should in future prepare itself to fight "Major Regional Conflicts" such as the Gulf War rather than a global war; and it agreed that the U.S. should be able to conduct two such conflicts simultaneously, and, if necessary, to do so with or without its customary allies.[21] Just who would be the opponents in these wars was not completely clear, but Saddam Hussein and Iraq had provided a glimpse of at least one and North Korea was routinely invoked as another.[22] Soon there was also talk in Washington of a broader variety of "rogue" and "failed" states that could fill the role, particularly if they were also seen to be interested in acquiring and using "weapons of mass destruction." Overall, the Clinton administration came to embrace a defense posture not unlike that of the previous administration: military spending would go down, but the U.S. would seek to maintain a decisive edge over potential rivals.[23] A further review in 1997 led the administration to much the same set of conclusions about the military's needs, and policy continued in the same direction.[24] Again, there was some disappointment that the Democratic administration had not undertaken a more thorough reexamination of just what forces and weapons the country would require in the new, post–Cold War era and that it had not broken more decisively with prior strategic thinking, with its commitment to nuclear weapons, and with the general aim of maintaining U.S. military predominance. The President's penchant for compromise also led him to accept the National Missile Defense Act in 1999, allowing the most controversial arms program – and the one whose value was perhaps the least obvious – to go forward. There was very little debate about this or other defense decisions, however, and no serious challenge to what was a largely bipartisan consensus.[25]

Comparable decisions to reduce existing defense capabilities while seeking to retain a capacity for major operations, presumably in league with the United States, were taken in Britain. The U.K., of course, had a bigger problem than the U.S. in determining defense expenditures. Britain had once been an empire with military forces stationed around the world, but it no longer was and it could not afford such defense commitment. Even under Thatcher the pressure to cut back was intense. The Defence Secretary John Nott had been told by the Prime Minister in 1981 to "re-establish . . . the right balance between resource constraints and our necessary defence requirements." He produced a Defence Review that called for quite serious reductions in Britain's surface fleet, proposals that looked rather misguided when Argentina invaded the Falklands a few months later. The government did not return seriously to the issue until the Cold War was coming to an end. The exercise in assessing future military needs, "Options for Change," was led by Tom King, then Defence Secretary. Planning began in 1989 and would continue for another two years, and the review would result in cuts in troop levels nearing 20 percent. Most obviously, military forces stationed in Germany – the British Army on the Rhine, which also included a garrison in Berlin – would be reduced and ultimately phased out.[26]

The process in Britain, as in the United States, would be attended by a level of controversy that disguised the fact that there was little real disagreement. Margaret Thatcher, though no longer Prime Minister, found an occasion to mock arguments for a shift to domestic spending by explaining that "the only real peace dividend is, quite simply, peace."[27] Pundits on the right echoed her sentiments; those on the left insisted on deeper cuts. The reassessment of defense needs was also complicated by external events. It had begun before German unification and before its consequences for NATO were known; and as the resolution of those issues got closer and clearer, the Gulf crisis intervened.[28] The failed coup in Moscow in August 1991 also gave policy-makers pause for thought, for there was at least a reasonable possibility that more hardline forces would prevail in the Soviet Union. As in the United States, there were voices arguing for a more radical rethinking of defense strategy and spending levels and expressing particular disappointment that neither the Conservatives nor, later in the decade, Labour chose to do so. The Strategic Defence Review of 1998, for example, continued to be premised on "the notion that Britain can maintain a seat at the 'top table' by virtue of its military prowess – the familiar idea that Britain 'punches above its weight' in matters military."[29]

Though defense spending was not reduced enough to create anything resembling a serious "peace dividend," military expenditures did decline significantly as a share of total government spending and national product.[30] Defense spending amounted to nearly 6.4% of GDP in the United States in 1985, the height of the Reagan buildup, and had fallen back to 5.5% of GDP in 1990. Just five years later, in 1994, it fell to 4.1% and dropped further the next year, to 3.8%; by 2000 it stood at 3.1%. In the U.K., defense spending was equal to 5.1% of GDP in 1985, 4% in 1990, 3% in 1995 and just 2.5% in 2000. Reductions of this magnitude did not allow for a surge in domestic spending in either country, but did permit a measure of additional social expenditure. More importantly, reduced defense spending helped repair government finances, still burdened by the expenditures and heavy debts from the 1980s, and that presumably made possible higher and more sustained rates of economic growth.[31] Fiscal recovery in Britain would also make possible a substantial increase in public spending on health, education, transport and other public services under New Labour after 2001. In the United States the great constraint on public spending – looming deficits that were the product of the Reagan-era defense buildup and a "starve the beast" approach toward government – were much lessened by the end of Clinton's second term. As of 2000 there was at least the prospect of increased domestic spending. Ironically, it was George W. Bush and the Republicans who would benefit: the solid finances left in place by Clinton allowed Bush to cut taxes, to pass an expensive prescription drug program for senior citizens, and to fight two large and costly wars.

Global Tasks and Visions

Even after modest cuts in defense spending, the U.S. and the U.K. retained resources more than sufficient for the missions that they in fact undertook in the first decade after the end of the Cold War. That was partly because the missions were of modest scope and duration, and that, in turn, was because of essentially political decisions about the deployment of force. America's military leaders persisted in their reluctance to use military force except in those rare circumstances when all the conditions were right and a quick and more or less painless victory was ensured; and British generals were no more aggressive. Political leaders were scarcely more combative, for they were acutely aware that their publics had little taste for war and the casualties and costs it might entail. It would therefore take some major rethinking, on the part of politicians and the generals, before either country, let alone their European allies, would contemplate a serious turn to force in international affairs. That would only happen in a major way with the terrorist attacks of 9/11; and even then, the preference for force and preemption would not last much beyond the failures that attended the invasion of Iraq.

The decade between the Gulf War and the military response to 9/11 would thus witness only sporadic recourse to armed force and on each occasion the choice would elicit a bout of agonizing over its usefulness and morality. As late as 1999, force was seen by leaders in the U.S. and the U.K. very much as a last resort, and as something that would happen on the margins of the international system. More central to the workings of the new order, and hence to the concerns of policy-makers, was the handling of problems stemming from the great transformations in Eastern Europe and the effort to integrate these vast areas and populations into a post–Cold War order. It was the fate of these places that animated foreign policy in the 1990s and it was in these areas that it was rather more successful.

The Clinton administration was, of course, eager to distinguish itself from the administration of George Bush, just as Bush had been keen to set a new tone after Ronald Reagan. During the election Clinton criticized Bush for his inactivity over the mounting tragedy in Yugoslavia, but there was little to argue over in other spheres. Bush's handling of the collapse of socialism in Eastern Europe was, by most indicators, a success; and while dealings with the former Soviet Union could be questioned, the alternative was not at all obvious. It was not just electoral calculations that had led the Clinton campaign to emphasize the economy, but the fact that Bush was not vulnerable on foreign policy. Equally important, as a "New Democrat" Clinton agreed with Bush on the question of free trade and was basically supportive of Bush's effort to create an "architecture" that would encompass military and security strategy, alliances, networks and global markets.[32] What was left for Clinton, then, was to supply a bit of the "vision thing" that Bush himself was unable to supply, with accompanying rhetoric, and at least the suggestion that the new administration would be more open to policies with a humanitarian objective.[33]

Though the Clinton administration did not break decisively with its predecessor, it deployed a somewhat different discourse centered on the terms "engagement" and "enlargement." Bush had spoken of engagement, of course, but with Clinton and his National Security team the word, or words, took on a more distinctive meaning. Engagement meant not only that the United States would stay engaged, but also that it would encourage allies and rivals to become more deeply engaged in international institutions and alliances and in the world economy. This type of engagement, it was argued, would encourage peace and it would also foster democracy and free markets. The effect would be to enlarge the sphere of democratic states, what Bush had labeled the "zone of democracy."[34] Enlargement would also come to take on the more specific meaning of opening membership to NATO and to the European Union, the effect of which, it was hoped, would be to further lock in the transition to democracy and free markets in the formerly socialist countries. Engagement and enlargement would therefore be linked closely to democracy promotion, a new and publicly acknowledged goal of U.S. foreign policy.

The task of crafting the Clinton foreign policy was largely delegated to Anthony Lake, head of the National Security Council, and his staff, but there was a broad consensus in support of "engagement and enlargement," democracy promotion and what was called in 1993 "assertive multilateralism." Lake offered a précis of the new approach in a speech, "From Containment to Enlargement," delivered at Johns Hopkins University on September 21, 1993. In effect, "The strategy of 'enlargement' of democracies would replace the doctrine of the containment of communism."[35] The disaster in Somalia, and troubles elsewhere, led to a reconsideration of the scope and ambition of the emerging policy. Reflecting a more cautious approach, on May 3, 1994 Clinton signed Presidential Decision Directive 25 (PDD–25), "U.S. Policy on Reforming Multilateral Peace Operations." The directive was an attempt to qualify a policy that had yet to be promulgated by laying out strict conditions that would limit the involvement of the U.S. in peacekeeping missions.[36] The new doctrine was formally set out in *A National Security Strategy of Engagement and Enlargement* in July 1994, seventeen months after the administration took office.[37] It was consistent with what Clinton had laid out in his campaign in 1992, for it insisted once again that "the line between our domestic and foreign policies is disappearing – that we must revitalize our economy if we are to sustain our military forces, foreign initiatives and global influence, and that we must engage actively abroad if we are to open foreign markets and create jobs for our people."[38]

The document proceeded to list an array of multilateral initiatives, typically involving the expansion of trade but also efforts to expand NATO and to extend and reinforce alliances in the Americas and the Asia/Pacific region. Inevitably, the statement reiterated the administration's commitment to a strong military and promised that "When our national security interests are threatened, we will, as America always has, use diplomacy when we can, but force if we must. We will act with others when we can, but alone when we must." The real thrust of the new policy, however, was to avoid the use of force and to "send American troops abroad only when our interests and our values are sufficiently at stake . . . [and] with clear objectives." Among the central objectives was the promotion of democracy and the plan was to do so through connections, interactions and institutions rather than by force:

> It is therefore in our interest that democracy be at once the foundation and the purpose of the international structures that we build . . . While democracy will not soon take hold everywhere, we know that the larger the pool of democracies, the better off we are . . . Democracies create free markets that offer economic opportunity, make for more reliable trading partners, and are far less likely to wage war on one another.

Underpinning this new orientation was a recognition that globalization was producing a more interconnected and also competitive world and that the

challenge for the United States in the new era was to further the process while
figuring out how to master it and profit from it.[39]

The U.S. had long been interested in trade and the promotion of free markets
and democracy, but the emphasis given by Clinton to opening markets, to
"commercial diplomacy," and to promoting democracy was more or less unprecedented. And it continued through the President's two terms of office, despite
setbacks in the process of democratization and a series of severe financial crises
– Mexico in 1994, the Asian crisis of 1997 and the related Russian meltdown in
August 1998 – that revealed the perils of a more open global economy. The
publication in December 1999 of *A National Security Strategy for a New Century*
represented a more or less final statement of Clinton's strategy and it repeated
the emphasis on markets and democracy. It therefore echoed the aims of the
earlier strategic plans, though it added slightly more on the forward deployment
of U.S. forces and expressed a determination that they remain technically superior to those of possible enemies and challengers; and it focused more forcefully
on the problem of "weapons of mass destruction" (WMD). All these themes had
been struck before, of course, and the overall strategic vision was largely
unchanged from 1993; and it remained fundamentally multilateral, even if it
reserved for the U.S. the right to "act alone" if necessary.[40]

The strategic vision animating British policy in the 1990s was more
restrained, but similar. With the end of the Cold War, the case for the "special
relationship" was clearly weakened and not a few commentators argued for a
turn to Europe and, more specifically, for a revitalization of the connection
with France.[41] The cooling of relations between the U.S. and U.K. during the
administrations of Clinton and Major was a further reason for thinking that a
shift might be desirable.[42] Major, and his government, had clearly favored
George Bush in the 1992 election and stories circulated that they had worked
with the Bush campaign to dig up information to discredit Clinton. For all the
lack of passion that seemed to characterize Major and Bush, their personal
connection was extremely warm. Bush had written to Major congratulating
him on his election victory in April and the Prime Minister responded with
enthusiasm and a clear promise of support: with his own reelection secured,
Major told the U.S. Ambassador that "Now the most important event of the
year is to see the President safely back – for the U.S. *and* for the rest of us . . . I
have faith he will win – he certainly deserves a thumping mandate – and if
there is any way I can help – anything at all – I will."[43] Bush particularly liked
the idea of a "thumping" victory, but the stance would not sit well with Clinton
and his advisors.

Nevertheless, the dominant feature of foreign policy under John Major and
Douglas Hurd, the Foreign Secretary, and with Bush as well as with Clinton,

was continuity – with policy toward NATO and toward Europe, and with the Anglo-American alliance. Typically, Major was the first foreign leader to visit the new President in late February 1993 and Clinton said all the right things, whatever he thought privately; far more important, the elaborate ties that linked the military and intelligence services of the U.S. and the U.K. remained close; the two countries were also, as in the past, closely aligned on trade; and they were generally on the same side in international organizations and nego-tiations. In the U.K., as in the U.S., however, there was sustained pressure for cuts in defense expenditure, a fact that might well have argued for a more fundamental reassessment but which instead led to an attitude marked by caution and realism. Hurd would insist, as was the custom, on a global role and vision: British foreign policy, he explained in July 1995, was "to make Britain more prosperous and more influential in the world, and to contribute to a safer and more decent international order."[44] Because a "stable, humane and law-abiding world" allowed British interests to flourish, Britain would use its "influence to promote standards of democracy, liberal capitalism and the rule of law . . ."[45] The rhetoric here was less heroic than that of the Clinton adminis-tration, but the substance was largely the same. Under John Major, U.K. foreign policy also followed Clinton's in its focus on economic issues: Hurd listed efforts to expand trade and investment as key aims of foreign policy; and Malcolm Rifkind, Hurd's successor, boasted in October 1995 that "we are the world's foremost champions of free trade."[46]

Until 1997, British policy would be crafted in terms markedly less visionary than that of the United States. With New Labour's victory in May 1997, Britain now had in place two spokesmen competing to articulate a grander vision for what remained of its global mission. Robin Cook, the Foreign Secretary, announced that the U.K. would now follow an "ethical foreign policy," and Tony Blair waxed eloquent on the promise and perils of the global market and the implications for foreign policy. Cook had long been critical of the arms trade and Britain's outsized role in it and revising policy on the sale of arms to repressive regimes was at the center of his efforts to render foreign policy more ethical.[47] It was a difficult task, for canceling existing contracts would be legally questionable and make the government liable for the losses incurred by the arms manufacturers; and cutting back on present and future arms sales would cost jobs and company profits. It would also, or some argued, have lessened British influence abroad. Cook's attempt to shift policy was therefore not very successful: he was forced repeatedly to compromise and was in turn denounced for hypocrisy; and little of substance changed. Cook was also more forceful on the lingering issue of Yugoslavia, but again with only modest success. And his personal stature was much diminished by the scandal surrounding his affair with Gaynor Regan, his secretary, and the subsequent breakup of his marriage.[48]

Cook's decline afforded Blair an even greater say over foreign policy – presumably a welcome relief from his recurring battles with Gordon Brown, his Chancellor of the Exchequer, over domestic policy – and his views prevailed. Like Clinton, he was a great proselytizer for globalization and the need for Britain to ready itself for a new era of competition. He used the argument to gain support for a liberalizing domestic agenda, but it seems clear he also believed it.[49] Blair and New Labour also undertook a slight pivot on Europe, replacing the hostility or at least ambivalence of many Tories with a more positive stance and a renewed emphasis on the role the U.K. could play as a "transatlantic bridge." If Britain could enhance its role in Europe, its views and interests would carry more weight with the United States.[50] Real benefits could thus accrue from the links to America and Europe and these would make it possible for Britain "to exercise a role on the international stage" And that would pay, for "a nation's chances are measured not just by its own efforts but by its place in the world. Influence is power is prosperity."[51] Blair was also much more open than Cook, and many in the party, to the use of military force. During the 1980s the Labour Party had been deeply suspicious of nuclear weapons and not especially keen on conventional forces. It had not opposed the Falklands War in 1982, but its support was lukewarm, and its 1983 program called for unilateral nuclear disarmament. The result was the party's worst election result since 1931 and a victory large enough for Margaret Thatcher to claim a popular mandate for the entire range of domestic and international policies she sought to implement. When Labour carried out its "policy review" in the late 1980s, its policies on defense and foreign policy were shifted back toward the center. With the winding down of the Cold War, however, policy on international affairs became less central to the party's image and appeal. Blair had never been on the left in terms of foreign policy and that meant that, once in power, he could take the party in new directions – toward a more explicit attachment to the United States and toward a more activist agenda globally.[52]

In fact, during the late 1990s it was Blair and the U.K. that were more ready to deploy force than the U.S. under Clinton. Eventually, the Clinton administration would agree to get involved in Bosnia and, later, to intervene more quickly and forcefully in Kosovo. Nevertheless, policy remained cautious and policy-makers averse to the ready use of force through the decade; and the U.S. devoted more time and attention to questions of trade, NATO and EU enlargement and relations with the former Soviet Union – issues more amenable to diplomacy than to military solutions. By one count, the U.S. concluded 470 trade deals during the Clinton presidency: many were small and merely bilateral, but they added up. In addition to winning approval for NAFTA and for the Uruguay Round, Clinton also secured Congressional support for granting "permanent normal trade relations" (PNTR) status to China in 2000 and he worked hard for China's subsequent admission to the WTO. The President was particularly happy to host the Asia-Pacific Economic Cooperation meeting just outside Seattle in November 1993 and continued to use that venue to push for a broadly free-trade agenda. The U.S. also moved to increase trade and trading relationships in the Americas, though with only modest success; and it passed the African Growth and Opportunity Act in 2000. As part of its emphasis on opening markets, the administration had no choice but to talk tough with Japan and won token victories, though by the end of Clinton's first term the focus shifted to matters of security, on which agreement proved easier and the benefits more obvious.[53] Even after the failed WTO meeting in 1999 – the so-called "battle of Seattle" – the administration's commitment to opening up trade and spreading democratic capitalism remained firm.

Extending the Reach of the International Order

Treaties, international institutions and the policy paradigms they established constituted the framework within which states would become integrated into the post–Cold War order. The choice to become a part of the system would necessarily be made by national political leaders, however. The policy choices in the early 1990s of three large countries outside the orbit of the developed West – India, Brazil and South Africa – would serve to make the order truly global. Faced with an enormous budget deficit, India turned in 1991 to the IMF for a huge loan. In response, it agreed to undertake a variety of measures to deregulate and open its economy. Not all were implemented, but many were. Foreign direct investment in the country went up from a very modest $132 million in 1991–2 to $5.3 billion by 1995–6. The transition to market-friendly and less statist policies in Brazil was complicated by its more or less simultaneous transition from dictatorship to democracy. A popularly elected civilian government took office in 1990, but it lacked the support to implement policies to combat inflation, which remained extremely high. In the spring of 1994, however, a new government adopted the *Plano Real* that succeeded in reducing inflation and stabilizing the economy. An IMF loan was secured in November 1998 and produced new efforts to cut regulations and subsidies and to privatize; and the country entered a period of steady and substantial growth.

South Africa confronted an even more dramatic transition in the 1990s as the African National Congress (ANC) prepared to take power with the coming of majority rule. As a revolutionary organization the ANC had been much influenced by Marxist thinking and it had received substantial material and political support from the Soviet Union and the Eastern Bloc countries. By the late 1980s the lure of Marxist economic policies had faded, however, and the level of support from the Soviet Union was less as well. Within the ANC the leading economic voice was that of Thabo Mbeki, who was a major figure in the ANC's Department of Economic Policy, and his disillusion with socialist planning was far advanced as the moment of political transition approached. He led discussions with the IMF and the World Bank in 1992 that produced a letter of intent in 1993. It promised fiscal stability and respect for private enterprise and open markets; and when Nelson Mandela assumed the presidency in May 1994 Mbeki became Deputy President responsible for carrying through on the arrangement.[54] Mandela himself was apparently brought around at Davos in 1992, convinced not by the assembled capitalists but by the advice of the Chinese and North Vietnamese.[55] Subsequently, South Africa also entered into close relations with the European Union and in 1999 signed a Trade, Development and Cooperation Act, essentially a free trade agreement with Europe. Growth was slow in post-apartheid South Africa, but it was steady, and the country became more or less locked into the international economy and post–Cold War international order.

The decision to sign up to the rigors of the global economy was also, and importantly, accompanied by commitments to human rights, good governance, transparency and democracy. The preamble to South Africa's agreement with the EU was in this regard typical in

RECOGNISING the historical achievements of the South African people in abolishing the apartheid system and building a new political order based on the rule of law, human rights and democracy . . . [and] RECALLING the firm commitment of the Parties to the principles of the United Nations Charter and to democratic principles and fundamental human rights as laid down in the Universal Declaration on Human Rights . . .[56]

There was no doubt a ritual quality to such statements, but they mattered, if only because the relationships they initiated were ongoing and consequential. These choices by emerging countries cannot be attributed primarily to the strategy of "engagement and enlargement," to the wisdom of the Clinton administration, or the dictates of the IMF and the "Washington Consensus." All these mattered, but it was ultimately a choice made by political leaders assessing the options available for generating growth and prosperity. The end of the Cold War and the apparent failure of state planning and state-led development strategies undoubtedly narrowed the range of possible futures open to all countries, but leaders in countries such as India, Brazil and South Africa could and did bargain, strike compromises, extract concessions and claim rights in their dealings with international institutions and the advanced countries that largely controlled them; and the effect was to embed their decisions more deeply.[57]

Eastern Europe, Russia, China

The consequences of the policy of engagement in Eastern Europe would serve to anchor yet another enormous region within the post–Cold War order of free market democracies, although the specific mechanisms by which this was achieved, the enlargement of NATO and the EU, were closely connected to policy toward Russia and the other states of the former Soviet Union. This was neither simple nor entirely successful. On enlargement itself the British and American positions were not identical but fundamentally congruent. The U.K.'s commitment to NATO, for example, was as intense as was that of the United States, although Major and Hurd preferred that the alliance be expanded more slowly; and Britain's enduring ambivalence over Europe meant that if there was a choice between deepening what EU membership meant and expanding and effectively diluting its meaning, enlargement was much preferred.[58] The terms of German reunification virtually guaranteed NATO enlargement and once the French realized that their plans for European defense were not going to prevail, they agreed as well.[59] The problem with enlarging NATO was the opposition, or potential opposition, of the Russians and the very real prospect that such a move by NATO would lead to a resurgence of nationalist or communist forces in Russia and set back reform. It was, of course, the very prospect of a resurgent Russia that made countries such as Poland, Hungary and Czechoslovakia (before and after it split into two separate states) so eager to join the security alliance.

The Clinton administration felt pressure from both sides. When the President visited Europe and Russia in January 1994 he chose to push for a "Partnership for Peace" as an intermediate step before joining NATO. The hope was that the plan would appease all sides, but the priority was Russia. The U.S. was especially worried about the results of the recent Russian parliamentary election, held in December 1993, in which the nationalist Vladimir Zhirinovsky's Liberal Democratic Party won nearly a third of the votes, the former Communists 12 percent and an Agrarian Party close to the Communists another 8 percent. Yeltsin's supporters had fared poorly and the outcome indicated that forces opposed to liberal reform were in the ascendant. In the context, argued ambassador-at-large Strobe Talbott and others around Clinton, it was critical to avoid "drawing a line" between Russia and the West and strengthening Yeltsin's opponents. As one Clinton official explained, they were backing Yeltsin and doing whatever was necessary to bolster his prospects: "He's our guy. We're not going to undermine him with a policy of neocontainment that boosts the hard-line empire builders. Yeltsin says that drawing a new line in Europe that shifts the Iron Curtain back to Russia's border could do just that. And we're going with his instincts."[60] When Clinton moved on from Prague to Moscow, he was eager for reassurance that the Russian leader would reaffirm his commitment to reform despite the recent electoral setback. Yeltsin obliged, and in return received an offer for Russia itself to join the Partnership for Peace. It seems that the U.S. also signaled a willingness to recognize, or at least not to contest, Russia's interest, and occasional meddling, in what it called "the near abroad," those states – like Georgia and Ukraine – that had previously been part of the Soviet Union. (The Baltic states were another matter.) The effort to strike the appropriate balance with Russia would continue to test the new administration's diplomatic abilities and the issue of NATO expansion would continue, for the Eastern Europeans were keen to join and Yeltsin's fortunes would remain uncertain. When Yeltsin won reelection in June 1996, the movement to expand NATO resumed. The NATO Summit in Paris in May 1997 ended with the signing of the NATO-Russia Founding Act in which both sides professed their peaceful intentions and willingness to cooperate.[61] It provided the background for handling expansion and in December 1997 NATO agreed that Poland, Hungary and the Czech Republic would be admitted as of 1999. Seven other Eastern European states, including the Baltics, would become members in 2004.

The decision to back Yeltsin was never in doubt, for there was no plausible alternative. With the Russian President, "what you see is what you get," Richard Nixon reportedly told Clinton, and the President himself put it more bluntly when he said in 1995 that "We can't ever forget that Yeltsin drunk is better than most of the alternatives sober."[62] The choice to back him was controversial nonetheless. At the root of the problem was the slow pace of transition in the Soviet Union and, later, in Russia. Gorbachev had been frustrated in his efforts to reform the Soviet economy, efforts that hastened, and then were overtaken by, the crisis of the regime itself. Little had been accomplished when Yeltsin assumed power at the end of 1991 and he opted for policies that amounted to a form of "shock therapy." They met with great resistance and were much compromised in execution; and the economy continued to collapse as inflation worsened. Again, economic distress produced a political crisis: opponents of Yeltsin, and of liberal economic reforms, within the Supreme Soviet seized control of the Russian "White House" on September 21, 1993 and proceeded to impeach the Russian President. After a two-week standoff support for the attempted coup weakened, the military rallied to Yeltsin and the White House was shelled and retaken on October 4. Clinton had already signaled his support for Yeltsin when the two had first met in April: "We know where we stand. We are with Russian democracy. We are with Russian reforms. We are with Russian markets. We support freedom of conscience and speech and religion . . . We actively support Russian reform and reformers and you in Russia." Warren Christopher, U.S. Secretary of State, repeated the endorsement after the defeat of the rebellious parliament.[63] The practical policies of the Clinton administration differed only marginally from those of George Bush and James Baker – the sums they promised in aid were nearly identical, if never adequate; they adopted comparable security strategies; and the attempts to balance support for NATO enlargement and for reassuring Russia were very much the same. In seeking to create a "strategic alliance with Russian reform," however, Clinton had chosen to identify much more explicitly with the reform process within Russia and hence to involve the U.S., at least indirectly, in internal issues.[64] The effect was to make the outcome of what were domestic politics in Russia a measure of the success or failure of U.S. foreign policy.

The administration therefore devoted serious time and political capital to economic and political reform in Russia. Clinton tasked Strobe Talbott to work with Larry Summers, at the Treasury Department, to find ways to provide aid to Russia, either directly or through the IMF and the G7; and a commission under Al Gore and the Russian Prime Minister, Victor Chernomyrdin, was established in order to bring American and Russian officials into closer contact and, it was hoped, to embed the commitment to reform more deeply in the bureaucracy.[65] The connection endured into 2008 and it served as a less public, and hence often more effective, mechanism for handling controversial issues. Neither of these initiatives, however, gave the U.S. any real leverage over the reform process as it played out in Russia itself; and that process was arduous and marked by repeated setbacks. Continued economic difficulties were accompanied by incessant political wrangling and instability. And then there was Chechnya, a mostly Muslim region that had declared its independence in 1991. Chechnya had long been a province of Russia, not a republic within the USSR, and its aspirations were met with hostility. A brutal war between separatists and Russian troops began in 1994 and continued until a ceasefire was agreed in 1996. Tensions persisted and in October 1999 the Russians launched a better-planned and ultimately more effective effort to crush the separatists. The United States was put in an awkward position: should it defend Yeltsin and, in effect, endorse the use of violence to keep Chechnya Russian; or condemn the repression? The choice, again, was to back the Russian President, but the conflict further tarnished Yeltsin's reputation abroad. To outsiders, it served to erode the credibility and democratic pretensions of the regime and its supposed commitment to political and economic reform; to Russians, of course, it increased support for Yeltsin and gave him leverage over his opponents.

At least as difficult for Clinton was the Russian financial crisis of 1998. It was an indirect result of the Asian crisis of the previous year, but it hit very hard in Russia due to the shaky character of its financial system and of government finances and, more fundamentally, the underlying weakness of the still largely unreformed economy. Russia announced a series of emergency measures on August 17 that involved at least a temporary default on its debts and a plan to devalue the ruble, which by the end of the year had lost 71 percent of its value. It asked as well for loans from the IMF despite the fact that it had failed to implement reforms promised as the precondition for earlier loans. The Clinton administration and the IMF were at a loss and, after some hesitation, reluctantly endorsed the request.[66] It seemed as though all the effort devoted to supporting the Russian President and the Russian economy, and seeking to assist in the transformation to a market economy and a stable polity, had been for naught. As Andrei Illarionov, a firm supporter of reform, testified in September 1998, "the largest financial assistant package in IMF history has failed in a month, international and domestic investors have borne multibillion losses, while Russia has fallen into one of the sharpest and deepest financial, economic and political crises in history."[67] The effects were disastrous: "The words 'democracy,' 'reforms,' and 'liberal' and the concepts and people associated with them have been discredited. The ideas of a market economy, liberalism and friendship with the West have been seriously undermined."[68]

Rumors swirled about Yeltsin himself being forced from power, or simply giving up, and in the United States there was a bizarre debate about "Who Lost Russia?" – as if Russia were America's to lose.[69] Clinton, now caught up in the Monica Lewinsky scandal, was scheduled to meet with Yeltsin in Moscow in early September and had to decide whether actually to go. If he canceled, it would be seen as a rebuke of Yeltsin and a virtual abandonment of administration policy; if he went, he would be accused of running away from the scandal and, if he went and Yeltsin was to fall from power or resign anyway, of poor judgment and ineffectiveness. Clinton made the trip, Yeltsin hung on and the political crisis passed. The new Prime Minister, Yevgeny Primakov, appointed in mid-September, was no reformer, but that fact probably helped him survive the crisis. In fact, the economic measures taken before or during the financial crisis began to work and a more favorable global economy, with rising oil prices and renewed growth in Asia, eased Russia's economic problems in 1999–2000.

The accession of Vladimir Putin, so problematic in so many ways, nevertheless became the occasion for instituting many of the economic and financial reforms that had proved so controversial, and had therefore been put off, during the previous decade.

Whether Clinton's policy toward Russia would be judged a success would continue to be debated, but at least it did not end in catastrophe. The verdict on the administration's policy toward China would be similarly mixed. Because so much less was expected, however, it was judged more favorably. America's relationship with China had been unprincipled since Richard Nixon's decision to recognize the Chinese communist state in order to enlist it as an ally against the Soviet Union. There was never much of a pretense that China was somehow a less nasty dictatorship than the USSR, and the opening to China predated and was in no way premised upon China's turn to markets in 1978. It was a strategic choice, and if the initial decision was taken by Nixon and Kissinger, it was Jimmy Carter, urged on by Brzezinski, who turned the tilt into something close to an alliance. Moves to allow, indeed encourage, Chinese students to attend American universities had been initiated in 1978; China was granted "most favored nation" (MFN) status in trade relations with the U.S. in 1979 – a benefit denied to the Soviets until July 1991; the Carter administration began exploring military ties and the possibility of supplying the People's Liberation Army with new military technology in late 1979 and stepped up these connections after the Soviet invasion of Afghanistan in December 1979; and in December 1980 Stansfield Turner, the CIA director, secretly visited Beijing as part of a collaboration in intelligence matters.[70]

This cozy, if slightly unsavory, relationship changed dramatically with the ending of the Cold War. As Soviet power was crumbling in Eastern Europe, the Chinese chose a bloody crackdown on dissidents in Tiananmen Square. With the Soviet Union and the United States deciding to end four decades of confrontation, the rationale for America's alliance with China disappeared almost overnight. Demands quickly surfaced to revoke China's MFN status unless and until it made progress on human rights. The Bush administration was embarrassed and publicly condemned the repression, but it refrained from serious sanctions. Clinton inherited the issue and was forced to decide whether to link human rights and trade and, most important, how hard and how far to push the Chinese on the matter. Clinton signed an executive order in May 1993 extending MFN status for a year but affirming the linkage between trade and rights and demanding that China make progress on releasing political prisoners and other measures of human rights. This did not happen and the U.S. was forced to back down. Central to the failure was the fact that China was now so much more important economically and American businessmen were now

much more involved in investing in, and exporting to, China. Business interests therefore lobbied hard against any move to deny China MFN status and
Clinton, the globalization and jobs President, felt compelled to listen. The
eagerness of America's allies, especially the Germans but also the British and
the French, to do business with China also made it clear that even if the U.S.
held back because of concerns over human rights, others would be less principled and only the U.S., and not China, would suffer.[71] The Chinese understood
this and toughened their stance, making only modest concessions. The
American military, now accustomed to dealing with the Chinese, was also
reluctant to get tough; and their instincts were reinforced by the perceived
need to get China's help in restraining North Korea's nuclear ambitions.

In response to these pressures, the Clinton team shifted and in September
1993 adopted a policy of "engagement" with China at multiple levels. It was the
same policy, in name at least, that Clinton adopted more broadly, but with
China it meant abandoning a tougher approach aimed at political reform. "Our
policy," Warren Christopher told the Senate Foreign Relations Committee on
January 13, 1993, "will be to seek to facilitate a broad, peaceful evolution in
China from communism to democracy." Just a few months later, "principled
engagement" of this sort was replaced by "economic engagement" whose positive effects – encouraging the rule of law, transparent dealing, the growth of the
middle class, personal freedoms and civil society – were understood to be indirect and very slow to work.[72] Little progress was made in a series of meetings
during late 1993 and early 1994. The Chinese Premier Li Peng told Warren
Christopher in March 1994 that "China will never accept the United States'
concept of human rights." Clinton formally conceded on May 26, 1994 that the
linking of human rights to trade had failed and announced that, despite a lack
of progress, the U.S. would extend MFN status to China yet again. He sought to
cover his retreat by claiming that the administration had developed, and would
now pursue, a "new human rights strategy" with China. Not much came of the
new plan, and what remained was whatever democratizing side-effects came
from more intense economic engagement.

The administration was clearly discomfited by its policy reversal and would
advertise its (limited) support for Taiwan as a means of expressing displeasure
with China. Its 1996 security arrangement with Japan and South Korea was also
designed in large part as an anti-China measure. Still, its basic stance remained
largely unchanged, and in 2000 the primacy of trade was yet again confirmed
when Clinton secured "permanent normal trade relations" (PNTR) for the
People's Republic from a skeptical Congress and in the face of opposition from
his supporters in the labor movement. That effort was effectively a reaffirmation of the reasoning behind the strategy of "engagement and enlargement." As

Madeleine Albright explained, in seeking WTO membership and PNTR with the U.S.,

> China committed to free itself from the "House That Mao Built," including state-run enterprises, central planning institutes, massive agricultural communes, and parasitic bureaucracies. The result should lead to more technological innovation, more use of the Internet, more frequent contact with foreigners, and more institutions and associations free from Communist Party control.

"There is no automatic connection between trade and democracy," she admitted, "but people can't help being shaped by their own experiences and observations."[73] Or so the strategy assumed, and many hoped.

Democracy Promotion

It was hard at the end of Clinton's term to point to great breakthroughs in "democracy promotion" and to assess the success of "engagement and enlargement" as a strategy guiding America's role in the world. Measurement would require a counterfactual that was impossible to specify and it was harder even to outline an alternative policy that would have been plausible, let alone effective. The transition in Russia had been slow, shaky and produced an economic order marked by corruption and cronyism and a political regime centered on a powerful president and tending toward authoritarianism. When Putin replaced Yeltsin, the new order remained formally democratic but hardly liberal and talk of partnership with the West was replaced by a more traditional emphasis on Russia's interests as a great power. Perhaps a more cautious or generous American policy toward Russia would have produced a slightly better outcome, and a more enlightened vision at the IMF could possibly have avoided some of the pain of economic reform, but was a fundamentally different approach possible, affordable and politically acceptable? It seems unlikely. Nor is there much reason to believe that, apart from the decision to expand NATO to the border of Russia, the Russians would not have opted sooner or later for a more assertive stance toward neighbors and rivals.

In China there had been no transition to democracy, but its capitalist economy was booming and its social structure evolving, slowly and unevenly, toward a more modern and mature capitalist form. Presumably, this would over time undermine the tight control of the Communist Party, but that prospect was nowhere in sight. Would greater firmness on human rights and the treatment of dissidents have forced a more liberal response from China's rulers?

The evidence does not suggest that it would have. Where transitions had been successful and locked in was in Eastern Europe where NATO membership or its prospect, or the more distant promise of EU membership, provided strong incentives to persevere in the effort to create stable democracies and market economies. Even there, more could have been done, but would voters in the United States, in Europe and in Japan have been willing to pay more? Again, it seems doubtful. And the incorporation into the post–Cold war order of India, Brazil and South Africa, major emerging countries and economies, was critical, for by expanding the reach of the new order it rendered it less American, less Eurocentric, less the preserve of the developed countries and more the property of all the states and economies that operated within it.

The lack of a credible alternative to the policy pursued by the U.S. and its allies in the 1990s was reflected in political discourse and in academic commentary. American foreign policy had few defenders among scholars in the 1970s and 1980s: respectable opinion recoiled from the policies and practices of the Nixon and Kissinger era; Carter, whose aims and rhetoric were more acceptable, inspired little respect; and Reagan was regarded as either a warmonger or a buffoon. The anticommunism that largely guided American, and also British, foreign policy was something that few serious people took seriously and the reliance on nuclear arms and on concepts such as "mutually assured destruction" (MAD) seemed mad and evil. The willingness to side with dictators in the interest of countering Soviet, or Cuban, advances elicited particularly sharp criticism and America's periodic interventions in the internal affairs of supposedly independent allies provoked outrage. The end of the Cold War stimulated a reassessment, for now it was the Soviets themselves or Soviet citizens affirming the arguments of anticommunists. It was particularly ironic that in the West the concept of "totalitarianism" had been rejected in favor of a more nuanced and "pluralistic" view of power in communist states in the late 1960s and after, but it was then resurrected by dissidents in Eastern Europe and the Soviet Union who were, after all, in a position to know.[74]

Along with the reassessment of the Cold War came a more favorable perspective on the potential of capitalism. The earlier focus on stagflation and, later, on the reasons for slow growth gave way in the 1990s to a more optimistic view that was reinforced by the return of steady growth in the U.S. and the U.K. after 1992. GDP was 36 percent higher at the end of 2000 than at the end of 1992 in Britain; GDP was more than 50 percent higher in the U.S. over the same period and more than 23 million jobs had been created in the longest boom in the nation's history. The sources of growth were several: a massive increase in investment in information technology; the integration of vast new regions into the system and investments to make it effective; as well as fiscal stability at the center, if not in Mexico, Asia and Russia. Globalization, though always controversial, came to be considered a good thing overall; and the possibilities of continued expansion seemed bright.[75]

New views on markets and capitalism and on the respective virtues of the rivals in the Cold War meant that America's post–Cold War policies were also seen in a more favorable light.[76] The fact that the U.S., and the mostly Western alliance it led, prevailed in the contest came to be seen as proof of an American dominance that was not "imperial" but rather a "liberal hegemony," which was and still is "most effective when it is indirect, inclusive, plural, heterogeneous, and consensual" and whose objective was to produce "the international dimension of liberal modernity."[77] The very idea that the United States, or Britain, or the Western alliance more broadly were genuinely interested in promoting democracy would have met with ridicule prior to 1989. Later, it was treated as a plausible description of policy, or as at least one key strand of policy – alongside such traditional concerns as security or the related goal of opening markets – that might be emphasized or not, as appropriate to time and place.[78] The same goal had also been embraced as current policy, though with perhaps less enthusiasm, by America's allies and by the European Union.[79] In fact, the effort at "democracy promotion" in the 1980s and 1990s created its own NGOs and a distinct academic discipline, if not quite a science, with journals, research centers, acknowledged experts, as well as a variety of critics and skeptics.[80] These were typically allied with the parallel efforts and organizations focused on human rights, transparency and good governance. Most could be found in Washington, but not all, and the project was genuinely international and multilateral.

The promotion of democracy and the sustained effort to open markets elicited its share of criticism, of course. Not all agreed, for example, that capitalism and democracy were fully compatible: it was obvious that undemocratic political systems could coexist with free markets for a long time without leading to democracy; and it was equally clear that democratic states could be poor and that the discontent and instability produced by poverty, inequality and economic stagnation could retard or threaten democracy. The coupling of democracy promotion and the effort to create and embed markets was therefore not always endorsed. And it was easy for skeptics to detect a degree of arrogance and naivety in the American belief that its model could be applied almost universally. Still, the alternatives were seldom defined with any precision and policy-making on matters of security and international economic policy was mostly consensual in the United States, and probably more so among America's allies.

The intensity of partisan conflict in the United States often obscured the extent of agreement on the basic questions concerning its role in the world.

American politics had been becoming more polarized for decades, but Bill Clinton's victory in the 1992 election accelerated the process. Something about the charming and canny Arkansas governor, former draft dodger and serial philanderer, drove his opponents crazy and imparted a new intensity to the partisan divide. Clinton's occasionally reckless behavior made things worse but, even before the scandal that led to the effort to impeach him, antipathy personally spilled over to critiques of his policies. The criticisms tended to be superficial and were not anchored into a compelling vision of a different policy, either domestically or abroad. Clinton was also extremely deft at deflecting attacks or, when necessary, compromising on details.

Clinton's policy on "national missile defense" was a prime example. Republicans had never given up on Reagan's "Star Wars" venture, even after the fall of the Soviet Union rendered it unnecessary and technical difficulties convinced many that the goal of missile defense was unattainable. The Clinton administration responded with scaled-back talk about "Theater Missile Defense" (TMD) that would be aimed at regional threats and rogue states and would not violate the terms of the Anti-Ballistic Missile Treaty. At the Helsinki Summit of 1997 Clinton and Yeltsin came close to a deal that would have allowed this modest plan to proceed while keeping the ABM Treaty intact and reducing strategic weapons. It fell apart when both sides went home. In Washington Republicans set up a commission led by Donald Rumsfeld that would claim the danger of "rogue states" developing missiles that could hit the United States was greater than previously assumed; and six weeks later, at the end of August 1998, North Korea made a first if abortive effort to launch its own satellite. In response, Congress insisted that the administration proceed to develop and "deploy as soon as technically possible" a more robust system of missile defense. Clinton acquiesced and signed the legislation, but also set out criteria for implementation that gave him a year to negotiate with the Russians over the ABM Treaty and to further test and assess the new technology. It proved impossible to make a deal with the Russians – Putin was elected President as talks were proceeding – but the new antimissile system failed tests in January and July 2000 and provided Clinton with a rationale for putting off a decision on deployment.[81]

The fudge over missile defense could be interpreted as another typical Clinton era compromise or, more generously, as a principled refusal to capitulate to his opponents. The return to trade politics with the grant of PNTR status to China could also be read as proof that the Clinton administration was rather more principled than critics, or even many allies, believed. These choices also meant that the legacy Clinton bequeathed to his successor was much of a piece with his administration's overall strategy of "engagement and enlargement" as it had first been articulated in 1993. The policies of the 1990s had not as yet exhausted their usefulness, although it was likely that a new administration, whether it was led by Al Gore or George Bush, would have an incentive to reassess.

New Threats, New Capabilities

The new administration would also find precedents or contradictions in Clinton's policies that could justify moves in more than one direction. Three developments stand out: the increasing frequency of terrorist attacks and the related problem of the spread of WMD; the "revolution in military affairs" that provided the U.S., and to a lesser extent Great Britain, with a decisive technological edge in war-making capacity; and the consistent difficulty of dealing with "rogue states" that seemed intent on acquiring WMD and routinely and grossly violated the rights of their own citizens. None of these, by themselves or in combination, led the Clinton administration to reorient its global strategy, but their combined effect could, in altererd circumstances, serve to justify a more aggressive set of policies.

Terrorism, to take the most potentially spectacular issue, did not become a major preoccupation during the 1990s. The bombing of the World Trade Center on February 26, 1993, came early in Clinton's first term, but it seems to have had little effect on policy-making. The "Blind Sheikh," the Egyptian cleric Omar Abdul Rahman, was arrested and convicted for his participation, but the truck filled with explosives had been driven by Ramzi Yousef, nephew of Khaled Sheik Mohammed, who would later mastermind the attack on the World Trade Center on 9/11. Yousef was arrested in 1995. Though al Qaeda was beginning to emerge as a serious force, its structure, leadership and strategy were elusive. Even its location was hard to pin down: it began as an organization to support the "Arab Afghans" who had joined the struggle against the Soviet Union, and its leader, Osama bin Laden, moved in 1992 to Sudan, then back to Afghanistan in 1996. Most important, Islamist militancy remained focused on the "near enemy," those states and rulers in Muslim countries whose ties with the West (or with atheistic communism), lack of zeal in confronting Israel, and evident corruption defined them as "un-Islamic." In this perspective the West, especially the United States but also Britain, with its long history of involvement in the Middle East, was defined as the "far away" enemy helping to sustain the local, "near" enemies of Islam.

The main battles in the early and mid–1990s were against the "near" enemies in Algeria and Egypt. The Islamist Front (FIS) in Algeria was legalized in 1989; it proceeded to win municipal elections in March 1991 and was poised in December to win national elections. The prospect led to a seizure of power by the military, cancellation of elections and the imprisonment of Islamist leaders. What followed was a brutal civil war between the forces of the state and those of the new Groupe Islamique Armé (GIA), which began a campaign of terror that spilled over into France. Soon the militants fell out with one another; and much of the public, appalled by the violence directed at civilians, turned against them as well. What had looked briefly like a major victory for radical Islam turned into a bitter defeat. Events in Egypt were equally dispiriting. Islamists were responsible for the assassination of Anwar Sadat, who had signed a peace treaty with Israel in 1981, but they paid a heavy price in the repression that followed. The Muslim Brotherhood was banned and many of its leaders imprisoned. As a result, it turned to a more moderate course of action and, for that, was attacked by militants such as Ayman al-Zawahiri, who founded the Islamic Jihad group. Its strategy focused on attacks on foreigners, tourists especially, but also government ministers. In 1993 it suffered the fate of other militants and 800 of its members were imprisoned. Zawahiri escaped to Sudan, from whence he continued to plot trouble. By 1995, he seems to have called off most active measures, but as a final gesture he helped to organize the spectacular and deadly attack at Luxor in November 1997. When it, too, failed to generate mass support and instead led to further isolation and repression, Zawahiri decided that the struggle against the "near" enemy could not succeed while the "far enemy" maintained its support.

It was time to take the fight to the United States. In this new strategy bin Laden would play a more important role: he was himself contemptuous of the U.S. and believed, reading the lessons from Vietnam and then Beirut, that it lacked the will to stand up to massive attacks on its citizens; and he also had access to the resources needed to develop the networks required to organize and carry out large-scale operations. Already in August 1996 bin Laden issued a "Declaration of War Against the Americans Occupying the Land of the Two Holy Places." Not long after teaming up with bin Laden, Zawahiri wrote a fatwa that accused the United States of "crimes and sins" that amounted to a "clear declaration of war on God, his messenger, and Muslims." In response, the fatwa insisted, "to kill the Americans and their allies – civilian and military – is an individual duty for every Muslim who can do it in any country in which it is possible . . ." The decision to focus on the United States was not uniformly embraced by militants, for it meant at least a temporary cessation of war against the "near" enemies they knew and loathed. The two leaders were nevertheless convinced, and bin Laden was reported as insisting that "our main objective is now limited to one state only, the United States, and involves waging a guerrilla war against all U.S. interests, not only in the Arab region but also throughout the world."[82]

The call to target Americans came in February 1998 and was issued by what was called the International Islamic Front for Jihad against Jews and Crusaders. Planning now began in earnest and the first move came on August 7, 1998 with simultaneous attacks on the U.S. embassies in Tanzania and Kenya. Over two hundred were killed in Nairobi. By this point, the United States had begun to understand and even to track al Qaeda and so responded with missile attacks in the Sudan and Afghanistan. The effects were counterproductive. The attack in Sudan destroyed a pharmaceutical plant and killed civilians, while bin Laden and his people avoided, though just barely, the missiles directed at Afghanistan. When al Qaeda struck again in October 2000, against the USS *Cole* off the coast of Yemen, there was no retaliation.[83]

By 1998–9 the Clinton administration was beginning to understand al Qaeda's goals, methods and potential, it had bin Laden in its sights, and the President himself claimed that "after the African slaughter I was intently focused on capturing or killing him and with destroying al Qaeda."[84] Nevertheless, little happened before Clinton left office in January 2001. The administration ratcheted up its counterterrorism efforts in 1998, but they were hampered by the inability to get different agencies to cooperate and share information and by the lack of reliable intelligence. The U.S. had few resources of its own with access to Islamist militants and was forced to rely on information passed on by notably unreliable sources in Egypt, Pakistan and Saudi Arabia. The U.S. military, concerned about its weapons and still worried over ground operations and the possibility of American casualties, was also not terribly keen on undertaking the sorts of missions that might be effective against al Qaeda.

Apparently, it would take something more dramatic than what happened in Africa to get Islamist terror to the top of the security agenda. An indication of this lack of focus was the discussion of terrorism in the description of threats in the *National Security Strategy for a New Century*, issued in December 1999. At the top of the list were "Regional or State-Centered Threats"; next were "Transnational threats" that included, on roughly equal footing, "terrorists and criminal organizations" that might engage in "terrorism" but also "drug trafficking ... illicit arms trafficking, uncontrolled refugee migration, and trafficking in human beings, particularly women and children." Cyber-attacks were also mentioned. The third most serious threat was the "Spread of dangerous technologies" to "rogue states, terrorists and international crime organizations"; the fourth was "Failed states"; the fifth was "Foreign intelligence collection"; and the last "Environmental and health threats." What was remarkable about this list was that terror and terrorism were apparently considered no more serious than criminal organizations and their enterprises and that there was no serious analysis of the way terrorists, rogue or failed states and weapons of mass destruction might be connected and the threat from each multiplied. After 9/11 the Bush administration would make these linkages the centerpiece of its aggressive policies and, in the process, exaggerate them and even imagine connections that might have been theoretically possible but did not in fact exist. The somewhat loose and incomplete reasoning of the Clinton administration was perhaps inevitable given the state of knowledge and the importance of other issues at the time. The incoming Bush administration, with its own priorities and blindnesses, proved even less effective in making the connections until reality forced itself upon its consciousness.[85]

The Clinton administration was, on the other hand, quite capable of perceiving the connection between terrorism and the Arab-Israeli conflict. The problem was what could be done about it. In September 1993 Clinton had presided over the signing of the Oslo Accords, which called for Israel to begin to withdraw from parts of the occupied territories and for the creation of a Palestinian Authority to administer the areas. A five-year time frame was also established during which the two sides would engage in "confidence-building" measures and work on a "final status" agreement. The next year Israel and Jordan signed a peace agreement and there were negotiations between Israel and Syria over the Golan Heights. Hopes were high, but were soon disappointed; and progress on the ground proved slow. The assassination of Yitzhak Rabin in 1995 was a serious blow that removed from the scene a politician with the stature to make concessions. The U.S. would sponsor another meeting at a resort on the Wye River in Maryland involving the new Israeli Prime Minister Benjamin "Bibi" Netanyahu and Yasser Arafat in October 1997. By that point it was evident that a step-by-step process was not only too slow but risked being derailed by the regular provocations of those who did not want a settlement and that what was required was a leap to a final settlement. Israeli concessions and declarations of good intentions from the Palestinians were again forthcoming, but any movement toward final status talks had to await the outcome of the Israeli election in May 1999. Netanyahu lost and was succeeded by Ehud Barak, former Chief of the General Staff of the Israeli Defense Forces and leader of the Labor Party.

The promised and much-delayed talks were held at Camp David in July 2000, but the omens were not good. Negotiations with the Syrians had already ended without agreement, and both the Israelis and the Palestinians were firming up their positions. The U.S. did manage to extract from the Israelis an offer to return roughly 90 percent of the occupied territories to the Palestinians, to allow the new state to have its capital in East Jerusalem, and to agree to a complex formula for governing Jerusalem. There would also be adjustments to the pre–1967 borders and the dismantling of a substantial number, but by no means all, of the Jewish settlements in the West Bank. What the Israelis would not do was agree to a Palestinian "right of return" to Israel, and they insisted on clear limitations on the sovereignty of a future Palestinian state. Arafat wanted considerably more, or at least believed he could hold out for more, and in any case was worried that he could not sell the deal to his followers and to the increasingly prominent insurgents in Hamas. The negotiations at Camp David failed, although the Clinton administration kept trying, with meetings in Washington, Paris, and finally in Taba in Egypt in January 2001. These, too, met with failure as the so-called "al-Aqsa intifada" swept through the territories, producing new levels of violence and convincing Israelis and Palestinians that peace was not to be had any time soon.[86]

Despite recurring tensions in the Middle East and worsening relations between Israelis and Palestinians and the increase in terrorism linked to al Qaeda, it is particularly surprising that the concern for weapons of mass destruction was not linked up in the Clinton administration's thinking with terrorists or with the actions of failed and rogue states. Instead, and not unreasonably, attention was directed at the control and possible disposal of nuclear weapons in the states of the former Soviet Union. In addition, however, the behavior of North Korea and Iran gave cause for worry. North Korea had long been interested in atomic weapons, though it had reluctantly signed on to the Nuclear Non-Proliferation Treaty in 1985. In early 1993, however, it announced its intention to withdraw, presumably to resume work on nuclear weapons. Iran's interest in new weaponry was demonstrated by its ongoing efforts to import advanced Russian technology and its missile tests in 1998. Iraq was also considered a threat; its refusal to comply with the UN inspection regime imposed after the Gulf War was regarded as proof of its ill intentions and reason enough to justify continued sanctions and bombings by U.S. and U.K. forces in 1996 and, more seriously, in "Operation Desert Fox" in late 1998. Iraq's behavior had also prompted passage of the Iraq Liberation Act, which Clinton signed at the end of October 1988.

The administration's formal policy toward Iraq and Iran was "dual containment," which meant not only limiting access to advanced weapons but also countering the two states' attempts to exert influence in the Middle East and the Persian Gulf. Policy toward Iraq had a harder edge and a more ambitious aim, however: as one Clinton aide explained, "what we're saying is that on the Iraqi side it's containment plus regime change, we're saying on the Iranian side it's containment until they are ready for engagement."[87] Rhetoric aside, actions to enforce non-proliferation had by 1998 become noticeably less effective, for in May of that year India exploded its first nuclear weapon; and a few weeks later Pakistan followed suit. It was impossible after the fact to do anything to prevent India and Pakistan from developing nuclear weapons, though it might still be possible to stop others. The contradiction between acquiescing in the possession of atomic weapons by large states, with which the United States was already allied or with which it hoped for closer relations, and denouncing, sanctioning and even bombing smaller states intent on getting their own weapons was obvious and hard to defend. The alternative was even less attractive and would be still harder to justify politically.

The danger posed by the spread of weapons of mass destruction was clear enough. Less obvious was the subtle and long-term impact of refinements in the technology used to deploy and target weapons of all sorts, nuclear and conventional alike. Throughout the Cold War there had been important asymmetries in the weapons and military forces possessed by the U.S. and the USSR. The Soviets were always superior in conventional forces, the U.S. typically ahead in nuclear weapons and delivery systems despite the achievement of rough parity by the early 1970s. The United States also maintained an edge in technology that military planners thought was essential because they feared a large-scale confrontation with the Soviets in which U.S. and Western forces would be outnumbered and outgunned by the Red Army. In the 1980s the U.S. Army devised an "Air-Land Battle Doctrine" in which success would depend on the ability to combine air and land forces and to use advanced technology and superior mobility to counter the Soviet advantage. The implication was that the U.S. should not merely maintain its existing military forces but enhance their effectiveness with new weapons and communications technology.[88]

In response, and in a tacit recognition of America's technological superiority, the Soviet General Staff became quite worried that the U.S. was on the verge of a "military-technological revolution" that would enhance its lead. This "revolution" involved "advanced technologies, especially in relation to informatics and precision-guided weaponry employed at extended ranges" that would produce a qualitative change in the character of warfare; and the prospect of developing and making use of "even more advanced technologies (e.g. lasers, particle beams, robotics, high-powered microwaves)" and even more loomed in the not too distant future.[89] When linked together, these innovations would be the basis of a new and more deadly "reconnaissance-strike complex." American military planners lagged behind in theorizing the "revolution in military affairs," as they would call it, but intuitively grasped its potential and during the Reagan administration made efforts to push it forward. The Strategic Defense Initiative, proposed in 1983, owed its origins to the President's fervid imagination rather than to such considerations, but the military understood that even if it did not literally work, it would make available additional funds for developing these new military technologies. By the early 1990s, the administration and the U.S. military leadership had became convinced of the idea and estimated that they were in the early stages of a transformation that could "run another one or two decades." In order to make the most of this revolution, the U.S. needed to continue to spend on new technologies and on the hardware and software required to link them up, to restructure procurement priorities in order to ensure an adequate supply of the latest weapons and support systems, to invest in training so that soldiers and officers could operate the latest equipment and, most important, to reframe military strategy and organization.

Reshaping the military and its war-fighting doctrines would mean major shifts in what the armed forces would look like and in how and when they were expected to fight; and there was resistance to changing both. Though the Gulf War provided "a glimpse" of this new world of high-tech war, it also showed the attachment of the military to the lessons learned from Vietnam.[90] The generals insisted on deploying overwhelming force, on the ultimate need to combine air and ground forces, on having a clearly defined and delimited mission with an exit strategy, and on being able to count on sustained support at home. These principles, whether labeled the "Weinberger Doctrine" or the "Powell Doctrine", retained their grip on the military imagination and Powell saw it as his role to ask hard questions about the use of force and to keep the enthusiasms of his civilian bosses in check. In a famous exchange with Madeleine Albright over the possible use of U.S. troops in the Bosnian conflict, the Ambassador had asked, "What are you saving this superb military for, Colin, if we can't use it?"[91] Powell was extremely put out and insisted that "American GIs were not toy soldiers to be moved around on some sort of global game board."[92]

The "revolution in military affairs" would not resolve the debate over the use of American forces during the 1990s, and the argument would be rehearsed more than once. Still, the U.S. did deploy air power twice in the Balkans and it seems reasonable to assume that the possibility of using advanced technology and "network-centric warfare" to obtain the desired results, without putting troops at risk, made it easier to make the choice for war. It also seems likely that the increasing sophistication of American weapons, surveillance, targeting and delivery systems had an impact on the question of national missile defense. What had seemed mere fantasy in 1983 was becoming a more realistic prospect in the late 1990s and thus harder to resist. Equally important, the quest for a missile defense system together with the broader effort to develop more advanced technologies was extremely expensive and it is also likely therefore that it was a factor leading the Clinton administration in 1999 to propose an increase in defense spending of $112 billion over five years.

The availability of more sophisticated weaponry had two further effects. It meant that for the U.S., and perhaps for some of its allies, the future of warfare led away from nuclear weapons and toward the use of more powerful and precise conventional weapons. If so, it would become even more important to stop the spread of nuclear weapons to states that did not yet have them. Not that the United States, or Britain, or France – or Israel – would be giving up their nuclear weapons, but in the context of weapons that did not need to be nuclear to be lethally effective, it seemed especially urgent to deprive "rogue states" of the ability to bluster and blackmail using nuclear weapons. The military-technical revolution also meant that the United States and its closest allies would need to rethink what was involved in linking their military efforts. Among America's allies, Germany and Japan presumably had the capacity to match the sophistication of U.S. weapons, but not the will to do so; the French would probably make an effort but fall short. Only the U.K., which for decades had made "interoperability" with the U.S. military a guiding principle in training and procurement, could effectively fight alongside the Americans.[93] The effect of this emerging reality was to reinforce the Anglo-American connection in intelligence and military cooperation while, somewhat ironically, making the U.S. slightly more open to unilateral action.

The question of when to work with allies and when to avoid the entanglement was also raised pointedly by the recurring conflicts in the former Yugoslavia. The Bush administration had been deeply involved in crafting the post–Cold War security and geopolitical architecture of Europe, but its aim was to put in place the framework and let the details and the local decisions be more or less automatic, or, when the issue was European, the responsibility of the Europeans themselves. The Clinton team largely shared this objective, even if they had attacked Bush for inaction over Bosnia during the campaign. The Europeans were divided, however: the Germans had been early supporters of the Croatians and Slovenians in their quest for independence and the French and British saw this as encouraging the breakup of Yugoslavia. Fighting in Yugoslavia erupted first over Slovenian independence, but died down quickly. Much more serious conflict occurred during the Croatian War of Independence. In response, the UN set up a United Nations Protection Force (UNPROFOR) in late February 1992. UN forces, mostly from Britain and France, were therefore already on the ground and in the way when Bosnia – technically Bosnia and Herzegovina – declared its independence and a new round of fighting broke out. In March 1991 Milošević and the Croatian leader, Franjo Tudjman, had met and agreed to divide up Bosnia. The declaration of independence a year later provided the opportunity. Croatian forces attacked the unprepared and outgunned Bosnians and the Bosnian Serbs (roughly a third of the population), backed by Serbia, joined in and did by far the greatest damage and carried out the most brutal atrocities. Soon the Croatian and Serbian forces had carved

out large swathes of the country for themselves and the Bosnians were pushed
back. The region contained some areas that were populated largely by Bosnians,
typically Muslim, and other localities where Serbians or Croats dominated, but
there were also many areas of mixed settlement. The effect was that as Croatian
and Serbian forces expanded their reach, Bosnians were often trapped in
enclaves surrounded by hostile forces. It was a recipe for disaster and a standing
temptation to turn the battle into an effort not merely to secure greater territory but ethnically cleanse recently won territory.

With Europeans split, it was difficult to craft a strategy to end the fighting in
a manner that did not reward the aggressors – the Croatians and especially the
Serbs. Indeed, an arms embargo was declared which had the effect of keeping
the Bosnians weak while the Bosnian Serbs were amply supplied and resupplied
by Serbia. The presence of UN troops, commanded by the British General Sir
Michael Rose, was itself to prove an impediment to further action, for it gave
force to the argument that air strikes against the Serbs would endanger the
humanitarian mission and perhaps even provoke further outrages. The most
important factor preventing an effective response, however, was the stance of the
British government. Britain was America's closest ally and uniquely willing to
deploy its military in joint ventures such as the Gulf War. The readiness to do
this declined markedly, however, under John Major, who effectively delegated
foreign and defense policy to Douglas Hurd, the Foreign Secretary, and to
Malcolm Rifkind, the Secretary of Defense. They were all "realists" marked by a
"conservative pessimism," as a top Foreign Office official put it, and also keenly
aware of Britain's limited resources and determined not to squander them in
unrealistic pursuits.[94] Hurd was also skeptical about the vision of a new post–
Cold War security architecture as envisioned by Bush and embraced by Clinton.
As he explained in July 1993, "Britain has every interest in and commitment to
regional and global security . . . This is a matter of building, brick by brick, not
pretending that a great structure of a new world order already exists." Hurd,
Rifkind and Rose – along with Lord Carrington, who was delegated to mediate
the conflict early on – were not only wary of interventions to enforce order on
the borders of Europe but predisposed to regard the parties as equally at fault.
Carrington thought the protagonists were "all impossible people . . . all as bad as
each other" and Rose referred to the Bosnians as "savages." British policy-makers
were also in the grip of paralyzing historical analogies: they remembered
Sarajevo as the strange place with fanatical people who brought the world to war
in 1914. They were also desperate not to repeat the experience of Northern
Ireland, where what they saw as an unrewarding and seemingly endless effort to
separate warring ethnicities left Britain and its soldiers exposed and responsible
and where, as Hurd explained in September 1991, "we have experience of

fighting from village to village and from street to street." It was obviously an experience not to be repeated on behalf of the unfortunate Bosnians.[95]

The U.S. was also ambivalent and not eager to get involved militarily, but the Clinton administration felt compelled to do something. Typically in such a situation, it would proceed by developing a strategy and then selling it to its European allies. It would ordinarily consult with Britain, France, Germany, in that order, and then others in NATO. There was no really good policy at hand, however, and the administration settled upon an awkward plan to "lift and strike." The idea was to lift the embargo on supplying weapons to the Bosnians and to carry out air strikes on the Bosnian Serbs. It was not an ideal solution, but it had the twin virtues of promising to break the Serb dominance on the ground and allowing the Bosnians the opportunity to arm themselves and begin to fight back; and it did not commit additional Western troops.[96] It was the job of the Secretary of State, Warren Christopher, to take the proposal to Europe and the most important stop would be Britain. Relations between the new U.S. administration and the Major government were not warm to start with and they would be set back further by the brusque dismissal of the plan at a meeting in early May 1993 held at Chevening, the Foreign Secretary's grand retreat.[97] Hurd equated the proposed lifting of the arms embargo with a policy of trying to bring about, not peace, but "a level killing field."[98] Christopher himself, it appears, was less enthusiastic about the plan than others back in Washington such as Anthony Lake, Madeleine Albright and Al Gore, and it seems the President also had doubts. Still, the unwillingness of the U.K. to play its customary role was not welcomed in Washington. It should therefore not have come as a surprise to British leaders when, the following year, the U.S. decided to granted a visa to Gerry Adams, the leader of Sinn Fein.[99]

The crisis in Bosnia went on as successive peace plans were offered and then rejected, ceasefires agreed and then violated, and atrocities committed with what seemed to be impunity. Sarajevo remained under siege for nearly four years and was shelled repeatedly, most notably in February 1994, and massacres of Muslims were reported from places where Serb forces had the ability to carry them out. The most famous instance was in Srebrenica in July 1995. Eventually the Clinton administration, prodded by critics in the press and in Congress, stiffened its resolve and in 1994 began, more or less unilaterally, to implement a variation of "lift and strike." The Europeans, including the British, were also finally convinced to abandon their even-handed stance in favor of putting pressure on the Bosnian Serbs and their Serb backers. France played a critical role, for the new President, Jacques Chirac, decided to reverse French policy and turned decisively against the Serbs. In June 1995 he proposed to deploy a NATO "Rapid Reaction Force" to augment and stiffen UN forces.[100]

An alliance between Croatia and Bosnia had meanwhile been cobbled together and left the Serbs more isolated. The Croatians began to push the Bosnian Serbs back and the revelation of what had transpired in Srebrenica swayed international opinion decisively. So, too, did the Serbian decision to seize UN peacekeepers and use them as hostages. In the end, it was the combination of NATO air strikes and the arming of the Bosnians that made the crucial difference. A Bosnian offensive was launched in August 1995 and recaptured much of the territory seized by the Serbs. Diplomatic activity was ratcheted up at the same time and the Russians brought on board. A ceasefire was agreed in October and the parties moved on to serious negotiations in Dayton, Ohio, led by the American diplomat Richard Holbrooke. The Dayton Accords were signed on November 21, 1995.[101] Bosnia was independent, and the war brought to a close. The deal was by no means perfect, but it was far better than had seemed possible while the fighting went on. The difficulty of agreeing on a coordinated policy among the U.S. and its allies, and then of taking joint action to make it happen, was sobering to all involved; and led to a determination not to allow it to recur. The memories of inaction in Bosnia would combine with memories of doing nothing while genocide unfolded in Rwanda and become a potent argument for humanitarian intervention in the future.[102]

The resolve to prevent future crises from festering until disaster struck and to ensure that the U.S. and its allies and "the international community" responded more effectively was not easily translated into a set of policies, procedures and doctrines to make it real. NATO did emerge from the Bosnian crisis with increased credibility; so, too, did the Clinton administration. Clinton's reelection in 1996 also made him bolder, at least until he was caught up in the Lewinsky scandal and the impeachment proceedings. The U.S. military also became marginally less averse to the use of force, at least in the air. Nevertheless, in the U.S., the U.K. and other NATO countries there was still no great appetite for involvement. Nor was there much confidence in the mechanisms that might be used to organize and legitimize the use of force. The United Nations had passed resolutions, imposed sanctions and sent in peacekeepers, but had been bypassed at critical moments. Increasingly, it seemed, interventions would have to be done ad hoc, by groups such as NATO or by what came to be called "coalitions of the willing," and these would depend upon the political leaders in the most powerful states. Would they do so? Should they? And just how would their actions be justified? By what principles, if any, would they be guided?

These questions were posed sharply during the mid and late 1990s and debated widely. Many on the left insisted on the need for humanitarian intervention, while others denounced "the imperialism of human rights." Commentators on the right were also split: "neoconservatives" supported muscular efforts to police the world, while more traditional conservatives warned of the dangers and difficulties of "nation-building."[103] An answer of sorts, though it was much contested, would be offered by Tony Blair during the next crisis in the Balkans, this one over Kosovo, and the collaboration between Blair and Clinton in that conflict would provide a template, again not uniformly agreed, for the practice of intervention. The coming to power of New Labour would in fact inaugurate a new era of Anglo-American cooperation. Blair and Clinton were much more compatible than Major and Clinton, in matters of personal style as well as in politics. The political affinity was most important: Clinton campaigned and governed as a "new Democrat"; Blair and his allies literally invented "New Labour" and sought to find a "third way" between Conservatism and what was understood as "old Labour." Perhaps by coincidence, center-left leaders also found themselves in office at about the same time in Germany, France and Italy. Blair and Gerhard Shröder, the German Chancellor, even co-authored a manifesto on the "Third Way" and Blair and Clinton would create an international forum devoted to bringing together "progressive" leaders from around the world.[104] A sense of shared mission came to characterize the relation between the two leaders and served to reestablish the closeness of the relationship between the two countries after the frostiness of the mid–1990s.

The first product of the collaboration was the Good Friday Agreement between the parties to the conflict in Northern Ireland. The Clinton administration had effectively decided in 1993 that progress toward peace might be possible in the troubled province. The moderate nationalist leader John Hume told the Americans that the leadership of Sinn Fein, especially Gerry Adams, might be interested in an end to violent struggle and a negotiated solution. It was suggested that his hand would be strengthened if he were able to visit the United States and claim American support for peace. That would mean "engaging a terrorist," but the prospective payoff was considerable. Also, the U.K. and Irish governments had agreed in December 1993 on a "Joint Declaration" of principles in which the Irish would renounce their formal claim on the North and the British would agree to accept the wishes of the citizens living there. After much debate, and in the face of considerable British pressure, Clinton had decided at the end of January 1994 to grant Adams a visa to come to New York. The U.S. pressed hard for a sign of goodwill from Sinn Fein and the IRA announced a cease-fire in August of that year.[105] What made the time "ripe" for a resolution, at least in part, was the promise of substantial financial support from both the United States and the European Union. Contacts continued in 1995, but talks were put on hold when the cease-fire was broken in early 1996, and resumed after New Labour took office. The government of John Major had been wary of U.S. involvement and Britain's position had long been that the conflict was an internal affair. Blair, by contrast, saw the possibility of a deal and he and Clinton began a carefully coordinated effort that led to a plan for power-sharing agreed on Good Friday, April 10, 1998.[106]

Belfast was not much like Kosovo, but the pattern of cooperation that was established, or restored, over Northern Ireland would be put to further use in the second major crisis caused by the collapse of Yugoslavia. Kosovo was populated largely by ethnic Albanians who were mostly Muslim and were becoming increasingly restive in the last days of Yugoslavia and actually declared independence in 1990. Milošević took a hard line that actually helped him to consolidate his leadership inside Serbia and the struggle turned violent with the creation of the Kosovo Liberation Army (KLA) in 1991. The situation continued to deteriorate and by 1998 the KLA was becoming bolder in its attacks and the Serbians more brutal in their repression. The U.S., Britain, France and other NATO countries demanded that Serbia back off and threatened air strikes to add pressure, but there was reason to believe that threats might serve only to convince the Serbs to step up their efforts. A conference was held at Rambouillet, near Paris, in February 1999 in order to work out a deal that would be accepted by the Serbs and the KLA. It failed, and the Serbian government chose to intensify its attacks, creating a flood of refugees and provoking further demands that they cease. In late March NATO began a bombing campaign that would grow wider and continue into early May, but Serbia was defiant. With the accidental bombing of the Chinese Embassy in Belgrade on May 7 there were fears that international support for air strikes would begin to ebb and it appeared increasingly likely that ground troops might be required to secure NATO's aims.

Britain and the U.S., along with NATO allies, had already begun to talk about possible ground deployments, but the talk was accompanied by intense debate over whether actually to do it. The American General Wesley Clark was eager and by late May 50,000 troops stood on the border, ready to invade. Clinton held back, however, and it was in this context of uncertainty that Tony Blair emerged as an advocate of greater force and, if necessary, ground troops. Blair had visited Brussels in early April and talked extensively with Clark, who reinforced his more aggressive instincts. He was also scheduled to attend a NATO Summit in late April in Washington. At a dinner with Clinton and his advisors, Blair struck an agreement in which the British would talk less about ground troops while the Americans would begin planning for their actual use. It was assumed that the Serbs would get the message. The next day, April 22, Blair gave a speech to the Economic Club of Chicago in which he outlined what he called a new "Doctrine of International Community." The speech made the case for humanitarian intervention and listed six conditions, all very subjective if otherwise unobjectionable, that needed to be met before deciding on action. At the heart of the speech was the argument that an increasingly interdependent world made it impossible not to act: "Twenty years ago," he explained, "we would not have been fighting in Kosovo. We would have turned our backs on it. The fact that we are engaged is the result of a wide range of changes – the end of the Cold War, changing technology, the spread of democracy. But it is bigger than that. I believe that the world has changed in a more fundamental way. Globalization has transformed economies and our working practices. But globalization is not just economic, it is a political and security phenomenon."[107]

The link between intervention and globalization was instructive: Clinton had based his entire geopolitical and international economic strategy on the advance of globalization; and Blair had done much the same. By 1999, the implications for foreign and security policy were finally realized and articulated. Or so Blair would argue, even if Clinton was rather more cautious. And, of course, not everyone agreed with Blair, but his vision was consistent with the policy frameworks within which Clinton and Blair had been working, and he made a uniquely coherent case for them.[108] The argument was also compelling in practical terms, since it recognized that although the post–Cold War order may have been designed to function automatically, it would not always do so. There would be periodic crises requiring more active measures, and these would have to be taken with a decisiveness and a speed of which existing international institutions, the United Nations above all, were simply not capable. Interestingly and appropriately, Blair's speech also insisted on the need to reform the UN. And the United Nations itself seemed to agree. The intervention in Kosovo had been led by NATO, but the UN retroactively gave its blessing and assistance.[109] An independent commission also decided that although the intervention was technically "illegal," it was also "legitimate."[110] The decision had inevitably aroused controversy but the UN Secretary-General, Kofi Annan, countered forcefully: "if humanitarian intervention is, indeed, an unacceptable assault on sovereignty, how should we respond to a Rwanda, to a Srebrenica – to gross and systematic violations of human rights that affect every precept of our common humanity?" "If the collective conscience of humanity . . . cannot find in the United Nations its greatest tribune," he had explained even earlier, "there is a grave danger that it will look elsewhere for peace and for justice."[111] In response to this obvious and growing dilemma an International Commission on Intervention and State Sovereignty was established under the auspices of the Canadian government, and in December 2001 it issued a report proposing a new doctrine, embodied in its title, *The Responsibility to Protect*. If the rulers of a state would not or could not protect their citizens or, worse, if they turned against their own people, then they forfeited the right to sovereignty and it was the right and duty of the international community to intervene.[112] The policy was approved by the UN General Assembly in 2005.[113]

The war in Kosovo ended without the use of ground troops. The United States convinced the Russians to abandon their wayward ally in exchange for a role in the peacekeeping and Milošević caved in on June 3, 1999.[114] Blair's new doctrine and the articulation of a new "responsibility to protect" remained untested, to be used and abused soon after. The outcome was a sign that, for all the moves toward the use of force and despite the mounting evidence of threats that might make it necessary, the strategic framework worked out in response to the end of the Cold War remained largely intact. The first Bush administration had spoken of it in terms of a new architecture; Clinton had talked about "engagement and enlargement," and his policies, if not always brilliantly conceived and executed, largely followed that prescription. Though the words were not used, the order that the U.S. sought to build after the Cold War was a fundamentally Anglo-American inspiration and the principles on which it would be constructed were in effect "Atlantic Rules." The work of creating that order, bargaining out its details and managing its crises, fell in the 1990s primarily to the United States, in part because it truly was the dominant global power and, in some part also, because the U.S./U.K. alliance was not terribly close between the Gulf War and the coming to power of Tony Blair. When the relationship was repaired after 1997, and a more active collaboration reestablished, it became easier to see that the post–Cold War order was indeed a product of that partnership and to understand why it was Blair and Clinton who were most determined to make it work.[115] The challenges of the new millennium would test the ability of the U.S. and the UK, as well as that of their allies, to do so or, failing that, to find a more agreeable alternative. Clearly, if it were to function and endure, it would have to become the common property of more than just America and its closest ally and, to that extent, escape the limits of its origins. The supreme test of the new post–Cold War order, then, would be whether Atlantic Rules could became Global Rules.

Epilogue: Global Rules in Question

The effort to put together the post–Cold War order was a project for leaders in politics and business and for policy-making elites. Ordinary citizens had little say and often little knowledge of what their leaders were up to. They were seldom asked to vote for or against specific policies or strategic decisions, and the edifice as a whole was not theirs to understand, debate or vote upon. In democratic systems they could judge their masters and change them, though the choices were ordinarily determined by questions of domestic policy. Shaping the new world did involve lots of arguments, of course, and it required tough and complicated bargaining, but it was largely a matter for leaders unconstrained by popular opinion. Pundits and academics debated as usual, but few outside a narrow circle were really paying attention when the key choices were made.

The attacks on the World Trade Center and the Pentagon would change that overnight. Americans asked plaintively, and naively, "Why do they hate us?" and received a lot of answers that raised profound questions about America's role in the world order that the United States and its allies had worked to build. The aftermath of 9/11 ensured that the questions and answers would keep coming and they would be less about why the U.S. had been on the receiving end of terror and more about its response: the invasions of Afghanistan in late 2001 and Iraq in March 2003. As those ventures went wrong, and local resistance grew, further questions were posed not only about the wisdom of the decisions but also about the capacity of the United States to continue to play the dominant role in the post–Cold War order. And if the U.S., even with support from its traditional allies – most prominently the U.K. – and ad hoc "coalitions of the willing," was incapable of anchoring the world order it had done so much to shape, what would this do to that order itself? Would it remain as it had been at the turn of the millennium, would it disintegrate, or would it be radically transformed or even replaced? These questions were still being debated when the "great recession" of 2008 demonstrated the precarious character of the global economy that was so central to the post–Cold War order. Just about everything that seemed secure, stable and promising in 2000 was in doubt by the time Barack Obama became President and therefore subject to debate.

The events prompting such doubts were indeed dramatic and more or less unprecedented. The collapse of the twin towers seemed to come from the realm of fantasy and nightmare rather than from the world of organizations, alliances, negotiations, threats, and on occasion wars, that typically define international relations. The notion of religious fundamentalists somehow managing to turn the latest technology against the nation that largely invented it was particularly stunning. The decision to go after bin Laden by invading Afghanistan and overthrowing the regime there was equally bold, a major departure from the practice of military intervention since end of the Vietnam War. Invading Iraq was bolder still, for by then the claim of pursuing bin Laden could no longer be invoked. It was, rather, a considered decision that required an entirely new set of arguments. (Making the arguments, in turn, required data that proved wrong.) Equally unpredictable, at least to most, was the incompetence that followed once these odious regimes were overthrown. In both Afghanistan and Iraq, in consequence, the occupying powers confronted insurgencies that they had largely provoked but had not planned for. Failure was on a scale that far exceeded the worst-case scenarios of almost all of the critics of the decisions to go to war and that produced a rapid disillusion at home, both in the United States and in Great Britain.

As leaders began to recognize the folly of these nation-building efforts and to scale back their ambitions, they would be confronted with a financial crisis more severe than anything since the Great Depression. It was a crisis that also defied previous understandings, for its roots lay in the collapse in the value of products and investments that political leaders and their advisors from business and the academy did not understand. Derivatives, collateralized debt obligations and credit default swaps were all new devices made possible by the financial deregulation that attended and encouraged the globalization of finance over the previous quarter-century. The crisis, therefore, required rapid and massive interventions made largely on faith, or on the authority of people who now commanded little trust. Both the crisis and the supposed solutions served to cast doubt on an entire era of economic policy and its guiding philosophy.

Doubt, debate and uncertainty were thus very much the order of the day. Predictably, the arguments were not always helpful. The urgency of the moment allowed little time for reflection or for research that might make sense of what was an extraordinary series of events rapidly following one another. The typical response was to give voice to established opinions and find ways to link them to recent events. Long-time critics of American foreign policy, for example, explained the origins of 9/11 in the lengthy record of America's imperial pretensions and adventures. The overthrow of the Mossadegh government in Iran in 1953, a joint U.K./U.S. project, would be repeatedly invoked. Among scholars of international relations, realists or neorealists echoed what they had said repeatedly about "national interest" narrowly calculated as the sole basis for action and so argued against an aggressive American response. Liberal internationalists, by contrast, fretted over the abandonment of multilateralism by the Bush administration and urged a return. Defenders of the administration tended to downplay the novelty of its policies and insisted that it was following policies similar to those of its predecessors but responding to new threats and circumstances. Overall, the tendency was to repeat old nostrums and propose familiar formulas with which to endorse or critique current policy.

The weakness of contemporary commentary is understandable, and some contributions were quite insightful. More than a decade after 9/11 and the invasions of Afghanistan and Iraq it ought, however, to be possible to comment on the events themselves and the intense debates they provoked with a bit more perspective.[1] Truly definitive accounts will take time to emerge, but it is presumably not too soon to try to place these tumultuous years in the context of the broader post–Cold war era of which they are so prominently a part. Doing so should at least make it easier to avoid the two common and equally mistaken arguments: that "9/11 changed everything" and so whatever we thought we knew before that is outdated; or, conversely, that recent events are just the latest manifestations of phenomena we have long known about and already understood. More specifically, it should be possible to assess whether the policies of the Bush administration represented a continuation of policies already in place, with perhaps minor variations, or something very different; and to suggest whether, if the Bush policies were new and different, they were temporary aberrations or considered alternatives likely to last. The added perspective gained since 9/11 and its immediate aftermath also ought to allow a tentative judgment on whether the events of the century's first decade witnessed the birth of a new American imperium or the beginning of the eclipse of American power. As the recovery from the "great recession" is far from complete, it will be harder to decide what consequences it will ultimately have for the world economy and for economic policy-making. Even so, it should be possible to describe the range of potential outcomes and to see which options are more or less likely to be adopted.

The Bush Dispensation

George W. Bush was not Clinton, and his administration, like every new administration seeking to define itself against what went before, adopted a slightly different rhetoric on foreign policy and made a number of different decisions. The shifts were marginal, however, and even in the heat of the election campaign of 2000 Bush had not veered far from the path Clinton had trod. Debates between Bush and Gore focused very little on security and foreign policy and revealed few differences. Bush was decidedly more cautious on the question of "nation-building." He hinted at a greater toughness with potential adversaries, and he seemed more inclined toward unilateral action. These were differences merely in degree, however, and few expected much difference in practice. Especially telling was the fact that when supporters of Al Gore watched with horror as the Supreme Court handed victory to Bush, they did not argue that the election would mean a fundamentally different and threatening foreign policy. They worried over the consequences for domestic policy, but Bush had not given them sufficient reason in the campaign to elicit serious concern over matters of national security. In office the Bush administration would adopt a more aggressive and unilateralist stance on the new International Criminal Court, on the Kyoto Protocol and on the Anti-Ballistic Missile Treaty. None of these decisions were unexpected, however, and it is not obvious that a Democratic administration would have decided differently or, if they had, that they would have been capable of convincing Congress to go along with their plans. Clinton, after all, had already begun negotiating with the Russians to revise the ABM Treaty and he had chosen merely to delay the deployment of a missile defense system.

Nor was there any indication of a new course when Bush met with Tony Blair in late February 2001. Their joint statement reaffirmed the alliance between the two countries in world affairs and the continued importance of NATO. They pledged their commitment to sustained efforts to bring peace to the Balkans and to shape it into "a region, fully embedded in Europe, where commerce supplants conflict, where borders are venues for cooperation and not reasons for conflagration, and where the rule of law prevails and war criminals are brought to justice." The language on weapons of mass destruction was slightly more forceful, though nothing that had not been said before.[2] Iraq was often mentioned by Bush and those who worked for him, but not as a dire or looming threat. When the President addressed the graduating class at the Naval Academy on May 25, 2001, for example, he spoke of the importance of forward deployment to deter aggression and noted the presence of U.S. ships and troops in the Persian Gulf "deterring any mischief Saddam might contemplate." "Mischief," however annoying, is clearly not an existential threat. Bush went on to tell the newly minted officers that "Today, you inherit a world that is safer and more peaceful" than the world that the class of '51 had entered fifty years before and that the greatest challenge for their generation was to master new technologies and reshape the military accordingly: "we must build forces that draw upon the revolutionary advances in the technology of war that will allow us to keep the peace by redefining war on our terms."[3] Restructuring the military to be leaner, meaner and more tech-savvy was also, it would appear, the priority of Bush's Secretary of Defense, Donald Rumsfeld, who for that reason was constantly at odds with his generals.[4]

George W. Bush, like Blair, came to power without experience in foreign relations and was often derided for that. His response was that the depth of experience of his defense and foreign policy team made up for his own lack of knowledge. Critics have seen the President as therefore uniquely dependent on the people around him and vulnerable in particular to the supposed "neocon-servative" views of the Vice President, Dick Cheney, and Rumsfeld and his Deputy Secretary of Defense, Paul Wolfowitz.[5] Cheney and Rumsfeld are perhaps better understood as conservative foreign policy "realists" or "assertive nationalists" than as "neoconservatives," though they had been supporters of the neoconservative Project for a New American Century and its hawkish agenda.[6] The leader of Bush's team of foreign policy advisors, the self-styled "Vulcans," was Condoleezza Rice, also more of a realist than a neoconservative in that, like Cheney and Rumsfeld, she was skeptical about America's ability to spread democracy and undertake "nation-building" in places that lacked the history, culture and social structure necessary to sustain it.[7] The most promi-nent member of the Bush team, of course, was Secretary of State Colin Powell and he was also extremely cautious about when and for what ends to deploy military force. Neither the personnel who made up the Bush administration nor Bush himself provided reason to believe that a major transformation in foreign affairs and security policy was in the offing prior to 9/11.

After 9/11, the United States would undertake two major military actions that would add up to a genuine transformation and the administration would articulate a national security strategy markedly different in tone and moder-ately distinct in substance not merely from that of the Clinton administration but also from those of the Bush and Reagan administrations before it. Taken together, the effect was a definite break from at least the recent past. The deci-sion to invade Afghanistan was not terribly controversial, for there was little doubt that the Afghan regime was deeply implicated in bin Laden's enterprise and little expectation that it would offer him up to the United States for a proper trial. The U.S. had also received support from the UN. Even so, the intervention was swift and brutal and effectively unilateral and it led directly to "nation-building," something Bush and his advisors had long opposed. The plan, which was not well thought out, was to do it lightly, encouraging local political forces to come up with a new leadership and to begin putting together a new state. The results were not encouraging.

Well before it was clear whether the invasion and occupation of Afghanistan would succeed in generating a stable government, the United States moved on to a confrontation with Iraq. The idea was contentious from the beginning and although the UN Security Council approved a resolution in November 2002 declaring Iraq to be in material breach of previous resolutions and giving it "a final opportunity to comply with its disarmament obligations," very few believed that the UN intended to support the invasion that followed in March 2003. While U.S. allies had mostly supported, and made modest contributions to, the war in Afghanistan, the "coalition of the willing" that supported the war in Iraq was embarrassingly narrow. The critical ally was Great Britain, and the British decision proved the undoing of Tony Blair, whose reputation never fully recovered. The argument over Iraq was bitter, though often misdirected. The case for the invasion rested on the claim that Iraq possessed and was hiding "weapons of mass destruction," or at least making efforts to develop them in violation of various UN resolutions. The claim was not controversial, for at the time both proponents and opponents of the war believed it to be true. In fact, it was precisely because it seemed self-evidently true that the U.S. used WMD as the excuse for war. The French President, Jacques Chirac, accepted that Iraq had such weapons, but opposed the use of force to disarm him. And why else, U.S. leaders asked then and later, would Saddam Hussein have refused to allow inspections if there was not something to hide? The alternative – that he was doing so as a bluff – seemed hardly credible. Assuming WMD existed, the temptation to massage the data and exaggerate its importance was hard to resist and the Bush and Blair governments made claims that would prove to have been embarrassingly inaccurate and that they came to regret. Prior to the war, however, the WMD argument was not seriously debated.

The debate centered instead on whether and when to use force to obtain Iraq's compliance, and that turned largely on the question of how long and how bloody the conflict would be. Critics claimed that Iraq's powerful and battle-tested military, the Revolutionary Guard in particular, would be a formidable foe and that victory would take time and be very costly in terms of military losses and the collateral damage that would be inflicted on Iraqi civilians and on the nation's infrastructure. It was even argued that Saddam Hussein might in desperation make use of the WMD he was thought to have at his disposal. Opponents of the war also saw the overthrow of Saddam Hussein as a possible precedent that they did not want to see set. A U.S.-led coalition had already invaded Afghanistan and ousted the Taliban; if it could do this again in Iraq, why not do it elsewhere? The fear was that Iraq was but a step in a broader, bolder effort to assert an American hegemony throughout the world.

The Bush administration insisted that it was not interested in empire but that it sought to promote a "freedom agenda."[8] Whatever the objective, the U.S. was clearly prepared to use force – in new ways and with fewer restrictions – in order to achieve it. After Afghanistan and before Iraq, in fact, the U.S. had explicitly proclaimed a new "national security strategy" that was far more belli-cose than previous strategic doctrines.[9] The doctrine reflected, it appeared, the triumph within the administration of "neoconservative" thinking. The first articulation of the strategy came in Bush's address to graduates of West Point in early June 2002, where he claimed the right to take preemptive action and proclaimed that "We must take the battle to the enemy, disrupt his plans and confront the worst threats before they emerge." America "fights . . . for a just peace," Bush explained, and added that "we will extend the peace by encour-aging free and open societies on every continent."[10] Three weeks later, the President announced a key decision on the Middle East. The Second Intifada showed no signs of ebbing and hopes for a negotiated settlement were fading and Bush, rather than calling for a new round of talks, insisted instead that the Palestinians replace Yasser Arafat: "I call on the Palestinian people to elect new leaders, leaders not compromised by terror."[11]

In September the administration issued a new *National Security Strategy* that went still further. It again claimed the right and duty to take preemptive and unilateral action against terrorists: "While the United States will constantly strive to enlist the support of the international community, we will not hesitate to act alone, if necessary, to exercise our right of self-defense by acting preemp-tively against such terrorists . . ." The document reiterated America's attach-ment to allies and alliances, but it was clear where the leadership of these shifting coalitions would come from. The administration announced, for example, that the U.S. intended to remain the dominant military power in the world and promised that "Our forces will be strong enough to dissuade poten-tial adversaries from pursuing a military build-up in hopes of surpassing, or equaling, the power of the United States." The document also committed the United States to "a distinctly American internationalism" and to the global spread of democracy, insisting on "a single, sustainable model for national success: freedom, democracy, and free enterprise" and to doing what it could to expand trade and foster capitalist development. Rather more ominously, it thoroughly rehearsed the case for dealing roughly with "rogue states" willing to use "weapons of mass destruction."[12]

The Bush administration could claim credit for three controversial innovations in strategy thinking. The first was the deployment of the phrase "War on Terror," used by Bush on September 20, 2001, or, later, the "Global War on Terror." It had the virtue of not being something much worse – a declaration of war on Islam or Islamic fundamentalism or Islamist terror – but little else to recommend it. As critics pointed out, one makes war on an enemy, not a tactic, and without an enemy to defeat the battle can last forever. The second innovation was the so-called "one percent doctrine," a corollary invented by Vice-President Cheney. He apparently used it in a planning meeting in November 2001: "If there's a one percent chance that Pakistani scientists are helping al-Qaeda build or develop a nuclear weapon, we have to treat it as a certainty in terms of our response. It's not about our analysis . . . It's about our response."[13] It was a particularly clear example of the thinking that led to a policy of preemption. The third new coinage was "axis of evil," which Bush used in his State of the Union Speech in 2002.[14] It was made up of three states, Iraq, Iran and North Korea, all loathsome regimes but hardly an axis. The use of the phrase was a fairly clumsy and transparent attempt to begin the campaign to gather support for the invasion of Iraq, but it was extremely unhelpful as a guide to foreign policy.[15] Evil, like terror, is easy enough to be opposed to, but the label serves only to reduce flexibility and narrow the range of possible strategies.

These components of the "Bush Doctrine" served well enough to convince the Bush administration, as well as Congress and many Americans, of the wisdom of an aggressive military posture, especially toward Iraq. Bush presumably did believe that the choice to invade Iraq was an example of a "distinctly American internationalism," although to others it seemed part of a plan for world domination. The reaction to the new American policy and posture was intense and bitter, even within the United States, but especially among America's allies. Americans, and the Bush administration more than most, were in turn uncomprehending and angry. They should not have been so surprised. The expressions of solidarity that had followed 9/11 – such as Le Monde's famous headline "Nous sommes tous Américains" – were characteristically fleeting and soon replaced by more familiar sentiments that mixed sympathy with critique and suspicion about American motives.[16] More typical, at least of intellectuals if not of ordinary people, was the post–9/11 issue of the London Review of Books, in which a number of well-known authors fretted more about "retribution" and retaliation than about the attack itself and what it might portend. Mary Beard, the Cambridge classicist, perhaps spoke only for herself but she was clearly pleased to report that, after the initial shock, a "more hard-headed reaction set in. This wasn't just the feeling that, however tactfully you dress it up, the United States had it coming. That is, of course, what many people openly or privately think. World bullies, even if their heart is in the right place, will in the end pay the price." "But," she continued, "there is also the feeling that all the 'civilised world' (a phrase which Western leaders seem able to use without a trace of irony) is paying the price for its glib definitions of 'terrorism' and its refusal to listen to what the 'terrorists' have to say." In his contribution the veteran campaigner and journalist Paul Foot implied at least a rough equivalence between the United States and those who had attacked it: he was writing, he said, in the "ominous lull between the talk of vengeance and vengeance itself" and "without much optimism." Throughout the essays, the theme was of symmetry, of comparable guilt on both sides, even if it was necessary to go back a long way or to distant places to find the equivalent outrage committed by the United States, and of fear of what the United States would do in response.[17] Writing in the same vein in the *New Yorker*, Susan Sontag also came down hard on the United States and its "robotic President" while insisting that the terrorists "were not cowards." "And if the word 'cowardly' is to be used," she maintained, "it might be more aptly applied to those who kill from beyond the range of retaliation, high in the sky, than to those willing to die themselves in order to kill others."[18]

Criticism of America was not new. In France, it was an established genre that had as much to do with defining what it meant to be French – namely, not American – than it did with a serious engagement with the study of the United States.[19] In Britain, despite the "special relationship," there was always an undercurrent of contempt for the upstart colonists whose power and influence had displaced Britain's own. The sentiment was found on the right but also, in a different register, on the left. There was also a broader worry, noticeable across Europe, that American culture and its products were eroding local distinctions, traditions and producers. McDonald's, Coca-Cola and American films were widely consumed but just as widely denounced.[20] And there was certainly ample precedent for opposing American foreign policy. European leaders often recoiled from the American embrace, resented its power and were grudging in their support for decisions and policies with which they did not really disagree and from which they largely benefited. The British more often stood publicly with the United States, but were often quietly critical as well. U.S. policy since the end of the Cold War had produced a unique period of ambivalence. The first President Bush did not gloat over victory in the Cold War; and the focus on building the architecture of world order seemed harmless and, to some, helpful and important. Clinton's effort at "engagement and enlargement" was also not a very threatening prospect, coupled as it was with a marked reluctance to deploy force except in rare circumstances. The decade following the

collapse of socialism was nevertheless clearly a time of American global dominance, of the U.S. as "*hyperpuissance*," as the French Foreign Minister Hubert
Védrine labeled it, or as "the indispensable nation," as Madeleine Albright
rather tactlessly claimed. Resentment was ubiquitous, although it lurked
beneath the outward calm of alliances and the ritual invocations of friendship
and consensus. It found an outlet after 9/11, especially when the United States
responded with two wars and a doctrine that seemed to threaten still more.

The critique of U.S. policy that began to emerge shortly after 9/11 would
intensify with the invasion of Afghanistan and with the move toward the invasion of Iraq. Though it was not unprecedented and had deep roots, it reached a
particular intensity, and generated a special bitterness, in the unique circumstances brought about by 9/11. For most Americans, for example, the attacks
were uniquely undeserved and allowed of no ambiguity in terms of cause and
in how to respond. Claims that U.S. policies of the past were ultimately responsible did not resonate with a public whose memories seldom stretched further
back than the Gulf War in 1991, when the U.S. intervened to restore the sovereignty of a Muslim country attacked by Saddam Hussein and stationed troops
in Saudi Arabia at the request, or with the acquiescence, of its leaders. Since
then, the United States had used force to protect Muslims in Bosnia and
Kosovo. America's long-term relations with Iran were scarcely remembered by
most people in the U.S., even if the second oil shock, the impotence of Jimmy
Carter, and the fate of the hostages were firmly lodged in the nation's folk
memory. Americans did know rather more about the conflict between Israelis
and the Palestinians, though the U.S. role seemed uncontroversial: it was
defending an ally whose very existence was a reminder of what its people had
suffered and it was working, off and on at least, to broker peace. Things obviously looked different to many in the Islamic and Arab worlds, but regular
reports of suicide bombings and terror did not elicit any great sympathy from
Americans. In reacting to 9/11, therefore, Americans were not inclined to look
inward and question their own role in bringing on the tragedy.

It was not that Americans were prone to accept what its leaders told them or
that they were cowed by the atmosphere of repression supposedly generated by
the Bush administration. Ever since Vietnam, voters in the U.S. had been reluctant to go to war and were highly suspicious of whatever foreign ventures and
entanglements their leaders proposed. The first President Bush learned to his
dismay that even a successful war brings little electoral benefit, and Clinton's
slow and cautious moves toward intervention in the Balkans were carefully
calibrated so as not to get too far ahead of public opinion and not to provide
openings to Republican opponents, who might well advocate tough measures
against foreign powers but who were ready to turn against the President if they

backfired. Such caution was shared and indeed codified into military doctrine. The sources of the more aggressive posture adopted by Americans after 9/11 are thus better sought in the nature of the event itself and in the response of particular leaders than in the country's deeper history and character.[21] Again, the unprecedent character of 9/11 and the break it produced in U.S. defense policy and security strategy, even if it was short-lived, were closely linked.

A second, and fairly obvious, reason why Americans were not likely to respond with self-criticism and a turning of the cheek after 9/11 was that Islamic fundamentalism was extremely hard to defend. Throughout the Cold War there were people in the U.S. and allied countries who were in sympathy at least with the aims and aspirations of Soviet communism, if not with the USSR's policies. Likewise, there was considerable support for national liberation movements and their resistance to the former colonial powers. *Tiermondiste* sentiments were much weaker in the U.S. than in Europe, especially France, but not entirely absent; and groups such as the Sandinistas in Nicaragua evoked considerable sympathy and support. There would and could be nothing comparable when the U.S. was attacked by Islamist movements, whose ideology was so antithetical and unattractive and whose practice seemed to embody a medieval brutality. Even if Americans had bothered to read the pronouncements of al Qaeda or the thinkers who inspired them, they were unlikely to be convinced of the portrait painted of the U.S., or Western, enemy or of its vision of the just society, with its religious conformity, oppression of women and unusually harsh justice.

For U.S. allies in Europe, the attitude toward Muslims and Islamic fundamentalism was rather more complex. Britain, France and Germany all had large Muslim communities, many of them recent immigrants, and huge problems integrating them into society. Policies differed greatly, but nowhere were they reckoned an overwhelming success.[22] In consequence, there were large pockets of impoverished, isolated and alienated young men (and women, but mostly men) in the cities of all three countries and resentment among native-born and mostly white populations that occasionally burst forth in nasty, anti-immigrant politics. Governments and mainstream parties were unsure what attitude to strike; and after 9/11 they were fearful of possible domestic reactions to what they worried would be an intemperate American response. In the United States, with a much smaller Muslim population, there was far less antipathy and discrimination directed at Muslim communities. There was an increase in anti-Islamic sentiment right after 9/11, but it subsided quickly.[23] Instances of intolerance and suspicion have continued, stoked occasionally by local controversies over the location of mosques and by opportunistic politicians and ministers, but not on the scale feared just after 9/11. For its part the Bush administration, so cavalier about many things, was careful to discourage such action and eager to assert that Islam was a fundamentally peaceful religion whose teachings were distorted and hijacked by al Qaeda.[24] For America's European allies, however, such rhetorical gestures were insufficient and not unreasonably they worried over the reactions that U.S. actions would have both in the Arab and Islamic world and among their own Muslim populations.

For a variety of reasons, therefore, Europeans were at least as concerned over America's response to 9/11 as they were with what the attacks of 9/11 might mean for the United States and for other Western countries that were also considered enemies of Islam. As a result, the French and the Germans simply refused to go along with American policy and formally opposed the invasion of Iraq. The French President promised to veto any UN resolution authorizing further action. The only major ally to join the "coalition of the willing" in that venture was Britain, and even there opposition was widespread. Demonstrations were held across the country on February 15, 2003 and over a million gathered in London. Blair managed to win a vote for the war on March 18, 2003 and the invasion began the very next day. Though the vote was not close, the arguments were angry and intense and Blair's support for the U.S.-led action would dog him for the remainder of his time in office, and in fact beyond. The joint action by the U.S. and the U.K. might well have represented something of a last gasp of the "special relationship," at least in the sense that after Iraq any such cooperation would be more highly scrutinized and debated than before.[25] The intimacy and frequency of contact would, of course, continue: Condoleezza Rice reported that, as Secretary of State "I talked to the Brits every day."[26] Nevertheless, as the U.S. and the U.K. began eventually to reckon with the disastrous consequences of the invasion of Iraq, it become much less likely that the two nations would undertake similar controversial ventures in the future. Apart from a mission that simultaneously united them and separated them from other countries, it would become less important to stand together in the world.

The Anglo-American connection would be central to the run-up to Iraq, however, and it was Blair who had made the strongest case for humanitarian intervention in his speech on "international community" in 1999. His ideas formed an essential background to the argument made by the Bush administration for the invasion. Had Blair not previously laid out the rationale, the Bush administration would certainly have done so on its own. Still, it was useful to have the backing and useful as well to be able to refer to recent UN discussions about the "responsibility to protect." And this more intellectual discourse had the additional effect of recruiting some unlikely allies to the cause. A distinctive feature of the angry debates over 9/11 and the invasion of Iraq – Afghanistan was less controversial – was that they often divided people normally allied. The bellicose and unilateralist plans of the Bush administration were cheered by neoconservatives but regarded with horror by many traditional conservatives who preferred a more realist and cautious posture. On the left a surprising number of commentators came to believe that American power was finally being deployed for good ends rather than to prop up friendly dictators and, as secular liberals, they identified fanatical religion as the main enemy. They also, and regrettably, somehow forgot the lessons of the national liberation struggles and counterinsurgencies, Vietnam most notably, that had marked the end of empire and that taught the foolishness of efforts to impose democracy at the point of a gun. Bush administration policy, and its new strategic doctrine, managed simultaneously to spark a culture war among liberals and to engender a pattern of bitter recrimination among conservatives.[27]

Ironically, the controversies that attended the decision to invade Iraq would be quickly replaced by an entirely new set of questions once the war began. Nothing went as planned and the hopes and fears of all sides were displaced by different concerns. To begin with, the feared bloodbath never materialized: Saddam's forces put up very little resistance and the regime was dispatched in a matter of weeks; Baghdad was in the hands of U.S. and allied forces by April 9. Instead of welcoming the occupying, or "liberating," forces, however, many Iraqis turned to looting as the old order melted away. Fears of a protracted battle soon gave way to worries about maintaining order and to the question of whether the leaders of the "coalition of the willing" had any serious plans for how to occupy and reconstruct Iraq. The fears that the invasion might trigger the use of chemical or biological weapons were also soon eclipsed by the realization that there might not be any weapons of mass destruction in the country. The failure to find evidence of WMD puzzled both supporters and opponents of the war and it led to a renewed focus on what had always been the underlying rationale for the invasion: regime change. The case for war, which before its outbreak relied on the argument about Saddam's weapons programs, now rested on the success or failure of the occupation and its ability to create a stable, democratic (or at least not grossly undemocratic) regime. On that standard it largely failed, for the toppling of Saddam Hussein did not lead to a rapid flowering of democracy but to a brutal insurgency that elicited intemperate and at times ferocious responses by the military forces of the occupying powers, to sustained sectarian violence aimed mainly at redressing the grievances of Iraq's Shiite population, and finally to a government that was sectarian, illiberal and corrupt.[28] It also produced many casualties.

Occupation policies contributed mightily to these unhappy outcomes, not only by way of specific decisions but also because of their overall inadequacy. Two specific decisions, both made by Paul Bremer but approved at higher levels, were to disband the Iraqi army and to pursue a strict policy of "de-Baathification" designed to root out the lingering influence of Saddam Hussein's Baath Party and its leader on the military and bureaucracy. The effect was to put tens of thousands of armed, trained and now angry soldiers out of work and to make the state even less effective. In the context it was inevitable that more and more responsibility would fall to the occupying powers, or what came to be called the Coalition Provisional Authority, and that it would be blamed when it failed in those responsibilities. But failure was in its genetic make-up, for the people who made war did remarkably little to prepare for postwar. In fact, while the U.S. State Department sought to develop a plan – and America's closest ally, Britain, pushed in the same direction – the effort was met with contempt by people closest to President Bush – Cheney and Rumsfeld in particular.[29]

It seems clear in retrospect that the strongest proponents of war, though hard-headed realists in their own imaginations, had an almost mystical belief that overthrowing a dictator would more or less automatically unleash the democratic sympathies and energies of oppressed peoples. Scholars of democratic transition might insist on the need for a vibrant civil society, for a long period in which to engender social trust, and for an extended experience with democratic institutions and procedures. To the Bush administration, however, none of this seemed to matter and so its postwar strategy was ad hoc and incoherent. Its perspective was classically laissez-faire, assuming that competing interests would result in order; and its preferred style was to distrust formal administration in favor of subcontracting and privatizing, on the assumption that markets and competition were more effective than bureaucratic routine and that formal administrative structures were self-serving and inefficient; and when government itself did need to act, it was best to rely on people you knew and could trust rather than on people with merit and experience. These were the neoliberal principles that Thatcher and Reagan championed and on which a generation of conservatives made their careers, flavored under Bush with a shot of "good ole boy" cronyism.

The disastrous nature of the occupation effectively ended the debate on whether to invade Iraq. It had clearly been a mistake. The failed occupation, however, provoked an insurgency that would bedevil efforts by the U.S., the U.K. and their diminishing cast of allies to end the fighting and leave Iraq. Between 2003 and 2006 a series of steps were taken to draft a constitution, hold elections and set up a government run by Iraqis, but there was little prospect that the Iraqi government would actually work. More important, by late 2005 and early 2006 it was clear that the insurgency was holding its own against the forces of the occupation and the fledgling government. Perhaps even more important, it was evident to people inside and outside the country that the battle against insurgents had brutalized the occupiers and led them to adopt thuggish and counterproductive tactics. Shaken and confused by the resistance they met, American forces had begun to detain and interrogate suspected insurgents in the fall of 2003. The abuses at Abu Ghraib prison (and elsewhere) and the use of "enhanced interrogation" techniques – effectively torture – were the result. When these became public in early 2004, the credibility of the occupation forces and of the entire effort was permanently undermined and the insurgency flourished.[30] Support for the war and occupation dissipated rapidly among America's old and new allies and began to ebb in the United States as well. It was nevertheless not until the midterm elections of 2006 that voters were able to register their disapproval with the Bush administration. In response, Bush got rid of Donald Rumsfeld as Defense Secretary and began to talk more of leaving Iraq. Before doing so, however, the administration turned in desperation to what it labeled a "surge" in Iraq. Closely associated with General David Petraeus and his doctrine of "counterinsurgency," the plan was to send additional troops to Iraq with the primary goal of protecting civilians and weaning them away from the insurgents.[31] In fact, Iraqis were already turning against the more violent jihadists themselves in what came to be called the "Sunni Awakening." The turn was welcomed by the American military, which decided to pay local Sunni leaders to oppose the insurgents. The combined effects of the "Awakening" and the surge were a decline in violence and a period of relative stability that allowed the U.S. to claim victory and begin the process of disengagement.

The Anglo-American intervention in Iraq therefore came to be understood as a failure very quickly, even if it dragged on well past the end of George Bush's presidency.[32] Failure had serious consequences. The very first casualty, it would seem, was the "Bush Doctrine" that was articulated with such force in 2002. The debate over the strategy document's embrace of preemption and its acceptance of the need for unilateral action began immediately and was at least partially responsible for the administration's decision to work through the United Nations prior to going to war and to seek a UN mandate for the governance of Iraq after the war. The United States also worked hard to get allies to share in the reconstruction of Iraq, even if such efforts stopped short of ceding any meaningful control of the process. When Condoleezza Rice replaced Colin Powell as Secretary of State in January 2005, she launched a project of "transformational diplomacy" which, though consistent with Bush's almost messianic "freedom agenda," was more nuanced and multilateral and worked hard to overcome the tensions with allies caused by Iraq.[33] These were signs that the neoconservative moment in foreign policy was over and they were confirmed when prominent neoconservatives came to dissociate themselves with the course of policy in Iraq.[34] Indeed, policy had begun to change, to revert back toward a more cooperative and multilateral pattern, and away from the more unilateralist and militaristic turn that the Bush administration had adopted after 9/11, even as Bush continued to make his case for the policy.[35]

The rapid rise and fall of the Bush strategic doctrine does not mean that its authors had never believed in it. What it does suggest, however, is that it was an unstable and incoherent mix of beliefs that came together briefly in response to the attacks of 9/11. Bush and his closest allies were surely convinced of America's unique virtues and they had few doubts about the ability of the United States to project power. They were firm believers in the "revolution in military affairs" and understood that it gave the United States a capacity to act quickly, unilaterally and effectively.[36] At the same time the Bush team were very skeptical about the possibilities for "nation-building" and "democracy promo-tion" and they had criticized Bill Clinton because he was less so and more open, though not by much, to committing the United States to such projects. Even after 9/11 and the decision to invade first Afghanistan and then Iraq, the antip-athy to nation-building persisted. In place of a strategy for building a new and democratic nation in Iraq was a naive faith that democracy would somehow happen once the evil regime was overthrown. It was a strategy of hope, of possibility, influenced perhaps by the vague memory of what happened, or what was thought to have happened, after the end of the Cold War. Russia and Eastern Europe had not descended into chaos and in most countries some-thing resembling democracy had taken root by the end of the first decade of transition. These were countries in which an oppressive state had done its best to stifle opposition and abort the development of the institutions of civil society. If they could be democratized, why not Iraq and other countries in the region? The answer, in large part, was that the nations of Eastern Europe and the former Soviet Union had not been invaded and democracy, such as it was, was not imposed by an alien military force. The distinction was lost in the frenzied atmosphere that followed 9/11. The aggressive and militaristic aims of the administration never really overcame the more cautious and skeptical understanding with which it took office, however, and the result was a policy that combined maximum force with minimal planning for reconstruction and for building a democratic society and polity. It was a policy doomed to fail and therefore destined not to last.

Aftermath: Back to the Millenium?

Of course, the policy lasted long enough to do great damage – to Iraq, to the United States, and to the relationships between the United States, linked closely to Great Britain, and their allies – but not long enough to constitute a funda-mental change of policy.[37] As early as 2006, well before George W. Bush was succeeded by a Democratic President, America's foreign and security policy had begun to display more continuities with the era before 9/11 than would have seemed possible in the two or three years just after that catastrophic event.[38] Neither Bush nor his Secretary of State would talk as Clinton did in terms of "engagement and enlargement" – to them the words would have seemed to indicate weakness and passivity – but in practice the administration acted much the same as had the previous administration. The question, obvi-ously, was whether the misadventure in Iraq had made it impossible to resume the more multilateral and less militaristic policies of the early post–Cold War era. America's reputation had undoubtedly been blackened, as it was now asso-ciated with aggression and torture as much as with democracy and rights; its relations with allies had suffered, even if efforts to repair them were under-taken during Bush's second term; and, perhaps equally important, the United States and its allies had apparently failed to work their will in Iraq and Afghanistan. The United States might still be the world's dominant power, but that dominance was now seen as less overwhelming and less compelling than before. After Iraq there seemed less need to acquiesce to "Atlantic Rules" and the vision of world order that the United States and its closest allies had crafted, and less likelihood that defying them would incur any meaningful penalty.

It was also far less likely, after the multiple failures in Iraq, that voters in the United States or in the U.K. would support sending troops to enforce compli-ance with the wishes of their governments. Bush may have won reelection in 2004, but he would have failed a year later. Blair did lead the Labour Party to a third victory in 2005, but the margin of victory was diminished and his oppo-nents within the party emboldened. He would leave office in 2007, and Bush would leave at the end of his second term. Though the British role in Iraq was secondary, Blair became a despised figure for many and his actions were subjected to repeated investigations: the first led by Lord Hutton, which reported its findings early in 2004; the second, focused on the flawed intelli-gence in the run-up to the war and chaired by Lord Butler, which reported in July 2004; and the third led by Lord Chilcot, which began deliberations in 2009 and whose report was scheduled for 2014. What some have called "Blair rage" became the common currency of center-left discourse. Blair's perfidy was depicted on stage and in mock trials and he was even the subject of a novel and subsequent film that could explain his actions only by reference to manipula-tions by the CIA.[39] In the U.S., resentment against George Bush – some of his supporters called it "Bush derangement syndrome" – was tempered mainly by the addition of sarcasm. Bush was notoriously inarticulate and it was not hard to draw a line connecting his inability to speak with a more basic incompetence as President. The effect, nevertheless, was to damage the President's credibility and to erode support for his foreign policy. By 2006, if not earlier, public support for the war in Iraq had ebbed in both Britain and the United States and public opinion was extremely wary of further foreign adventures. Something like an "Iraq syndrome" had come to replace, or perhaps to reinforce, the earlier "Vietnam syndrome."[40]

This shift of public opinion was mirrored among political leaders and public intellectuals and it looked as though it might become permanent, a settled preference for leaders and led alike. The brief consensus behind the decisions to invade Afghanistan and Iraq had been produced by a unique and spectacular event which for a short time overcame the tendency of voters, already evident in the 1990s, to look inward. When that resolve evaporated, it was unlikely ever to be reconstituted. The rejection of the specific policies pursued in Iraq was in this sense both a commentary on the particular choices of American and British leaders, but also a reflection of a broader transformation in the relationship between governments and citizens. A top British official explained that actions such as the invasion of Iraq were simply no longer possible in a democracy.[41] The implication, it seemed, was that military adventures of this sort, and occupations maintained against the will of determined adversaries, were ugly and vicious and that the transparency of democratic government, aided by a free press and enhanced by unprecedented access to information over the internet, now rendered these impossible. Without popular backing, they could not be sustained; and if they could not be sustained, they would of necessity fail; and potential opponents would understand that as well as U.S. leaders and America's allies.

Bush's successor, Barack Obama, shared in this emerging consensus of caution and restraint and he worked hard to make it the foundation of U.S. foreign and security policy. It was not a simple undertaking. Obama inherited two ongoing wars of occupation and resistance in Iraq and Afghanistan and Osama bin Laden remained at large, a symbol of both the limits of U.S. power and the unlimited nature of the "war on terror." In the 2008 campaign the future President had argued for leaving Iraq as soon as possible, but the price he was forced to pay for that pledge was a plan to focus more attention on Afghanistan. In consequence, the rundown of military forces in Iraq would be accompanied by a new, if brief, "surge" in Afghanistan. In order to deflect criticisms that he was weak on terror, Obama also stepped up drone attacks on al Qaeda and the Taliban in Pakistan and al Qaeda affiliates in Africa, and pressed the hunt for bin Laden until he was killed on May 2, 2011.[42] Obama's careful moves in matters of policy were linked to a series of equally deliberate shifts in rhetoric and doctrine.[43] His first major speech on combating terrorism came in May 2009, when he began seriously to distance himself from the excesses of the Bush administration.[44] The following year the administration issued its own National Security Strategy, a document that echoed those of the Clinton administration with its embrace of "globalization," "engagement" and alliances. It went further, however, in its mostly implicit critique of the Bush administration by warning of the dangers that follow "when we overuse military might," by redefining the war on terror as a "broad, multinational effort," by assuming that the Bush administration's policies had left America weaker and by insisting that in response "we must pursue a strategy of national renewal and global leadership ... that rebuilds the foundation of American strength and influence."[45]

The final step in laying out a new approach toward defense and toward terror was Obama's quite bold speech to the National Defense University on May 23, 2013. The President claimed that with al Qaeda's leadership largely destroyed, it was possible to envision an end to the war on terror. The continuing threat to the U.S., Obama argued, was akin to what it had been before 9/11 and it could and should be met by tactics different from those employed after that date. It would remain U.S. policy to discover, disrupt and dismantle violent networks such as al Qaeda, but it would do this legally and locally, with allies and through diplomacy, and it would cease to act as if it were engaged in an all-out war of global reach. Obama also reiterated his pledge to close the prison at Guantanamo Bay. The administration would also rein in the use of drones, with greater restrictions in place and with responsibility for drone attacks eventually transferred to the military and taken away from the CIA, which would be restructured to refocus once more on intelligence; and it would seek a revision of the "Authorization to Use Military Force" that Congress granted George Bush right after 9/11.[46] Obama was criticized by the right for what he proposed and by the left for what he did not propose, but the criticism was muted, for what he articulated was what most Americans and most of America's allies wanted to hear.[47] If proof of this were lacking, it would come soon enough when rebel forces in Syria were attacked by chemical weapons in August 2013. All indicators pointed to the government and its supporters and the United States felt compelled to threaten military action. But American allies baulked, and it soon became clear that Congress and voters were hesitant as well. Obama retreated and accepted a Russian compromise in September 2013. Later that month the President spoke to the United Nations about U.S. interests in the Middle East and chose not to list efforts "to promote democracy and human rights and open markets" as "core interests."[48] These would remain high on the list of values and preferences, of course, and part of the rhetoric of international relations. It was now accepted, however, that the United States lacked the means or the will or the international support to achieve them in anything but the very long term.

Obama's move back toward the foreign and defense policies that had been developed and followed during the 1990s was obviously based on his belief that the position of the United States in the world had been weakened both by its misguided adventures in Afghanistan and Iraq and by the "Great Recession" of 2008. Up until 2008 it was reasonable to believe a shift in foreign policy by itself might suffice to repair the damage done by the policies of George W. Bush. A very strong argument could still be made for regarding the United States, the global order and the rules on which it was constructed with respect and even support. That argument was based largely on the sustained association between America, its global vision, and prosperity. So long as this connection held, America's role in the world was relatively secure, its position unlikely to be contested, and the world order it had labored to create appeared stable and functional. However, the "great recession" would break that link and make it possible to conceive of a world not ordered on principles based on Anglo-American traditions.

Remarkably, the link had been maintained after 9/11 and through most of the Bush presidency. The attack on the World Trade Center was intended in part as an attack on capitalism and it was assumed that it would seriously disrupt the American, and possibly the world, economy. Robert Zoellick, U.S. Trade Representative, claimed just after 9/11 that "the terrorists deliberately chose the World Trade towers as their target. While their blow toppled the towers, it cannot and will not shake the foundation of world trade and freedom."[49] His boast proved prescient, for the shock to the U.S. economy did not last and very quickly the center of global capitalism was again thriving. So, too, was the economy of Great Britain. In both the U.S. and the U.K., economic policy continued on paths charted in the 1980s and 1990s and growth continued. In the United States, the Bush administration's top priority was to cut taxes and its first major cuts were signed into law in June 2001. Its provisions were to be phased in gradually, but a second Act was passed in May 2003 to make them effective more quickly. The cuts were made possible by the frugality of the Clinton administration, which had left office with a balanced budget; and they were obviously consistent with the thrust of Republican economic policy since Reagan. The Bush administration also won passage of a plan to provide prescription drug coverage to senior citizens in December 2003. These moves would wipe out most of the budget gains made under Clinton. This, too, was consistent with Reagan, for he and his administration had been relatively complacent about deficits. There was yet a further parallel:

the Reagan recovery was boosted by a policy of militarized Keynesianism in which his budget-cutting was largely offset by the economic stimulus provided by Reagan's military buildup; Bush, twenty years later, chose to fight two wars and to build an elaborate security apparatus without raising taxes, providing a stimulus to the economy while incurring additional debt.

How much of this was a conscious imitation and how much the product of a more fundamental ideological stance toward markets is unclear and may not matter. What is clear is that the Bush administration was worried about a possible slowdown after 9/11 and did whatever was necessary to prevent it. It was abetted by the actions of Alan Greenspan, Chair of the Federal Reserve, who was not only unfazed by the growth of government debt but who also encouraged the accumulation of personal debt through the "housing bubble." He declared that rising house prices did not constitute a bubble and in so doing likely exacerbated it.[50] Ideology surely played a role as well. Just as a light footprint and a predisposition toward cronyism in the occupation of Iraq was a uniquely accurate reflection of the beliefs that motivated the Bush administration, so, too, were its failures in domestic policy. An unwillingness to raise or even maintain taxes and a lax approach to regulating and running the economy were very much of a piece with the administration's two most visible failures prior the collapse of 2008: the unsuccessful campaign to replace Social Security and its response to Hurricane Katrina. Bush famously declared that he intended to spend the "political capital" he had won in the 2004 election and chose to use it to sell a plan designed ultimately to privatize the nation's most popular social program. Throughout 2005 the President campaigned strenuously, but he got nowhere. And while that effort was going on, a massive hurricane struck New Orleans and the surrounding coastline on August 29. It caused over 1,800 deaths and over $80 billion in property damage. The administration's response was delayed and anemic, and the public was outraged at what seemed complacency on the part of the White House. Bush's famous statement praising the work of Michael Brown, the head of the enfeebled Federal Emergency Management Agency – "Brownie, you're doing a heckuva job" – was taken reasonably enough as a sign that Bush himself was out of touch and, more importantly, that his administration was incompetent. It was undoubtedly a manifestation of its general disdain for government and its preference for markets and private initiative or, if necessary, action by state and local governments.

The policy choices of the Bush administration were not unique, of course, and in Britain a government of a very different complexion implemented a set of economic policies that was not terribly different. Where New Labour differed with the Bush administration was on tax cuts. Blair and Brown made few changes to the budgets they inherited until after they won reelection in 2001. In that contest they promised a small increase in national insurance contributions (the equivalent of social security taxes in the United States) and by combining these new taxes with the additional revenue produced by steady growth they had available sufficient funds to undertake a significant increase in social spending. Spending on health care, education and transport was greatly increased, partly on the grounds that a succession of Tory governments had bequeathed a legacy of run-down services and partly on the promise of reducing child poverty and getting people back to work.[51] Policy continued to be generous after the election of 2005 and the government could boast of real gains in welfare.

In both Britain and the United States the effect was to prolong the 1990s boom through 2007. Job growth was maintained and living standards continued to increase, if more slowly and unevenly. In both countries, however, growth after 2000 was centered on the two sectors – financial services and housing – most affected by deregulation and, in the last years, most prone to speculation. Thatcher and Reagan had begun the process of deregulating finance, and it had been pushed forward by Clinton and Blair and then by Bush. The housing market was likewise sustained by the ease of borrowing, itself partly a function of looser regulation and of the new-found ability of investors and bankers to repackage and sell mortgage-backed securities. The fates of housing and finance came to be closely intertwined; and their success and profitability created the underpinnings of a period of growth led not by investment and innovation but by consumption, debt and the proceeds of financial transactions. When these sectors faltered, as began to happen in 2007 and as happened catastrophically in 2008, the engine of growth for the economy as a whole came to a screeching halt. The ensuing recession would turn into the worst economic crisis since the 1930s.[52]

The "Great Recession" threatened the prevailing global economic order in two major ways. It marked the end of the widespread faith in neoliberalism, in the fundamental wisdom of markets, and opened up the possibility that the countries that had invented and imposed the "Washington Consensus" might themselves abandon it. Martin Wolf, the respected *Financial Times* writer and a defender of globalization and neoliberalism, proclaimed in 2009 that "The assumptions that ruled policy and politics over three decades suddenly look as outdated as revolutionary socialism."[53] And there seemed a very real prospect that governments in the United States and the United Kingdom, and perhaps other European governments, might turn away from the market-oriented policies associated with Thatcher and Reagan and once again decide to adopt the more interventionist and state-oriented policies associated with John Maynard Keynes and an earlier era of economic policy-making. The other, and perhaps more ominous, possibility was that countries whose commitment to open markets and trade was more recent and less deeply rooted would defect from the global market and seek their prosperity on their own or through regional groupings. Regional trade groupings already existed, after all, and there were periodic rumblings of discontent about the fact that most of the world's trade and finance was conducted in dollars.[54] The countries most affected by the 1997 Asian financial crisis had already taken measures to insulate themselves from the volatility of global financial markets and, in effect, opted not to work with the IMF; and in 2001 Argentina had decided to default on its debts.[55] In addition, the so-called BRIC countries (Brazil, Russia, India and China), joined by South Africa, would soon begin meeting and talking about setting up sources of finance outside the orbit of the IMF and the World Bank.[56] The Chinese were also the main sponsors of the Shanghai Cooperation Organization, which included Russia and several states from the former Soviet Union, though its remit was not extensive. Finding an alternative to the existing system, global in character and centered on the dollar, seemed even more attractive and potentially viable when the world economy was pushed into recession because of financial problems at the center. As Wolf fretted, "the combination of a financial collapse with a huge recession, if not something worse, will surely change the world. The legitimacy of the market will weaken. The credibility of the U.S. will be damaged. The authority of China will rise. Globalisation itself may founder."

The twin crises – economic and geopolitical – that confronted the United States in 2008 were reminiscent of those it had faced in the late 1970s. A growth model had failed and the nation's global power was checked and seemingly ebbing away. Americans shared that fate with Britain in the 1970s and again in 2008. The accumulating difficulties of the 1970s would lead to the elections of Thatcher and Reagan and the adoption of a new approach to the economy and to government and a new aggressiveness in foreign and security policy. A philosophy of government friendly to the market and antipathetic to the state had replaced an "embedded liberalism" in which markets were constrained by public policy and government took responsibility for generating growth and employment and made use of interventions guided by Keynesian economic theory; and a stance overtly hostile to communism, at least as it manifested itself in the Soviet Union, had replaced a policy of containment and détente. The shift in the 1970s and 1980s was dramatic and lasting.

Nothing quite like it occurred after 2008. Keynes came briefly back into fashion and in 2008–9 governments in the U.S., the U.K. and Europe adopted policies designed to counter the downturn with a measure of stimulus. The sums involved in the "bailout" of the banking and insurance industries in the United States and in the stimulus package were substantial and it was argued that the more modest spending plans in Europe, augmented as they were by "automatic stabilizers" built into the systems of social provision, had a comparable effect. At the time Keynesians argued that it was too little. The main problem was that it did not last. Very soon, and certainly by 2010, calls for austerity overwhelmed the advocates of stimulus and the Keynesian lessons of the 1930s were, if not quite forgotten, no longer considered compelling. In the United States, the midterm elections of 2010 gave Republicans control of the House of Representatives and made further efforts to stimulate the economy impossible. Instead, the Federal Reserve worked to increase demand by keeping interest rates low and by increasing liquidity through what became known as "quantitative easing" (QE). In Britain, the election of May 2010 ended thirteen years of Labour government and brought to power a coalition that could agree on little else but the need to reduce government debt and expenditure. In Europe, the mounting financial crisis affecting its southern tier – Greece, Spain and Italy – and also Ireland, caused policy-makers to turn away from even a modest policy of expansion toward a brutal austerity that plunged southern Europe and Ireland into a deep recession. Austerity became the norm whether or not it was effective.[57]

Rather than displacing the prevailing free-market orthodoxy, the "Great Recession" left it in place.[58] Nor was there a major shift in the structure of the international economy or the institutions overseeing it. Progress had long ago slowed on the Doha Round of trade negotiations, launched in 2001, though efforts to open trade further produced a modest WTO agreement on "trade facilitation" in Bali at the end of 2013.[59] Bilateral agreements were also hard to achieve, but negotiations on both a Trans-Pacific Partnership and a Transatlantic Trade and Investment Partnership would continue.[60] Despite serious unemployment in the United States and Europe and brief declines in exports from emerging economies, there was no major retreat from international markets and more or less free trade. The system for overseeing the international economy that was in place when the crisis broke proved durable, though its governance was broadened and it became more tolerant of diversity in how nations responded to the crisis. The system had already been modified in response to the Asian financial crisis of 1997, which had led to the establishment in 1999 of the G20, which brought together finance ministers from a broader range of countries for informal meetings, and the Financial Stability Forum. These innovations may not have done much to prevent the next major financial crisis, but they did bring the leaders of the major emerging economies – China, Brazil, Russia and India – into the governance of the regime. Giving rising powers a stake in the system was an explicit aim of the United States during the Bush administration. As Robert Zoellick, by now Deputy Secretary of State, explained in September 2005, "It is time to take our policy beyond opening doors to China's membership in the international system . . . We need to urge China to become a responsible stakeholder in that system."[61] The regime would become that much stronger, because more legitimate, if China, Russia, India, Brazil and South Africa were brought within it and transformed from potential challengers to "status quo" powers.[62]

In November 2008 the G20 became more formal, as heads of state met in the United States to coordinate the response to the crisis. Less than a year later it was agreed that the G20 would take over from the G8 as the main body responsible for coordinating international economic policy.[63] The Financial Stability Board was also established as a more formal successor to the Financial Stability Forum in 2009. The G20 would remain less formal than the IMF, but it began giving instructions to the IMF, which was expected carry out assessments and to adopt and implement G20 recommendations.[64] These reforms were a further step in granting more input in the governance of the global economy to emerging powers, especially China, India and Brazil. They also gave them a greater stake in the system and enhanced their commitment to it. There were still occasional demands for a "de-Americanized" economic order, but they were not accompanied by serious moves in that direction.[65] Instead, the existing order was modified. One effect, it would seem, was a shift in the stance of the IMF, which became less of a scourge upon debtors, more concerned about growth and the provision of adequate social services, and at least mildly critical of austerity.

On balance, the economic crisis did not bring about fundamental change in economic policy, either domestically or internationally. If the shock of 2008 did not do more to alter the post–Cold War global economic order, it was even less likely that the challenges confronting the U.S. and its allies would produce a major realignment in international relations. And they did not, in large part because the policies of the Bush administration did not last. After 2006, it was highly unlikely that the United States would choose to invade another Middle Eastern or Muslim country and it was even less likely that, should it for some reason choose to do so, it would have any allies in the adventure. Its cautious response to the Arab Spring and its efforts to deal with Iran primarily through sanctions, while restraining the Israelis from taking military action, testified to the chastened outlook of U.S. leaders, both military and civilian. So, too, did the consistent efforts of the Obama administration to undo Bush's national security policy and to replace it with a more modest set of objectives and with methods that aroused far less opposition. In this respect it appears that the war in Iraq will cast as large and as long-lasting a shadow over defense policy in the United States and in Britain as did the experience of Vietnam. When the U.S. suffered defeat in Vietnam, however, there was a rival superpower to take advantage of its weakness and isolation and the USSR did so. Failure in Iraq had no such consequences, for no other power was ready, eager or able to displace the United States from its dominant, if now a bit less dominant, role. Russia, whatever Putin's fantasies was simply not in a position to challenge the United States and preferred to join other major powers in governing the world rather than to attempt to refashion the system. China, the truly rising power, might well look forward to replacing the United States as the world's most powerful nation over the course of the twenty-first century, but it had not yet decided to challenge the existing global order. China and Russia were clearly interested in extending their influence locally – in the East and South China Seas, in Georgia and Ukraine – but these were not global ambitions, however threatening they could be to regional stability.[66]

The Resilience of "Global Rules" of Atlantic origin

Just why the world failed to turn in 2008 or after and why the order put in place after the end of the Cold War endured and continued to operate on largely "Atlantic Rules" will remain something of a mystery until events and forces ultimately combine to transform this world order. There are reasons to doubt an imminent and dramatic transformation, however, for three distinct features of the post–Cold War order make it more likely that it will evolve rather than be rejected and replaced outright. The first test of whether the Anglo-American vision of how to order the world and run the global economy could prove viable in the long term was whether it could transcend its origins and be embraced, if not openly then in a de facto manner, by other powerful countries. The United States – with the support of the UK and other allies – constructed and bargained out the architecture, the framework, with which power would be wielded internationally and by which the world economy would function, and most of the world has accepted it and joined the institutions that make it up. They did so, it would seem, because order itself is a public good and the post–Cold War order offered benefits to those who signed up to it. As the creator and anchor of the system, the United States has perhaps the greatest interest in its successful functioning, but that means it has borne much of the cost. The U.S. has been and remains party to a variety of security agreements that tend, more often than not, to keep the peace; and when it has been necessary to restore the peace or prevent humanitarian disasters, the U.S. has typically been in the lead in whatever the international community has done.

The U.S. is also central to the world economy, not only because of its trade, its investments, and its financial contributions and the pivotal role it plays in its governing institutions, but also as a massive consumer of other people's products. The U.S. derives benefits from taking on these roles, but incurs substantial costs as well. It frequently provokes anger and irritation, but these reactions would seem almost inevitable and do not of themselves prove that U.S. is failing in, or profiting disproportionately from, its dominant position.[67]

Of comparable importance, and part of the same calculus of advantage and disadvantage, are the forces and interests that have come to be arrayed around and on behalf of the existing world order. Over time more and more states and their peoples have come to depend on the international economy and the global order that makes it possible.[68] Not only have interests become more aligned, they have actually been recreated by participation in the world economy. As trade has become more open, industries oriented to importing and exporting have grown and become an interest committed to open trade. When financial flows liberalized, the financial sector grew bigger, generated more profits, employed more people and found itself in a position to put its increasing influence behind policies aimed at maintaining or increasing the unimpeded flow of capital. The difficulty in reforming the banking and financial sector even after 2008 is eloquent testimony to the entrenched power of this relatively new interest.

What this means is that over three decades market-oriented policies have created their own constituencies. People and firms that did not exist prior to the era of neoliberalism have grown, waxed powerful, and become its firm supporters; and their massive contribution to the health of national economies has meant that governments must listen. The multinationals whose reach was remarked upon and feared a generation ago, if not earlier, have now been joined by tens of thousands of enterprises and millions of their workers who share vital interests in making the global market function.[69] In addition, entire networks of professionals and institutions linked to the international economy and the emerging global polity have grown up and constitute a weighty inertial force on behalf of an open, market-oriented world order.[70] Inevitably, the globalization of the world economy has produced losers as well as winners, prospective opponents as well as cheerleaders, but declining industries and their owners and workers by definition have declining influence. There are exceptions, of course, as even a brief glance at agricultural policy will confirm, but such exceptions underscore the rule that new industries whose fate is tied to the global marketplace will on balance favor the economic order and the economic policies that have nurtured and sustained them. Economy and society have been restructured by the market-friendly policies first implemented by Reagan and Thatcher and, truly a world away, Deng Xiaoping, and the result is that there are now millions of Thatcher's and Reagan's and Deng's children employed around the world and they are unlikely to repudiate the conditions that made their working lives possible.

The other defining feature of the post–Cold War order, and one that makes it likely that the global rules guiding it will be adapted and modified rather than discarded, is that the system is flexible and open. Economic openness is at its heart. Its political requirements are minimalist and mostly negative: it seeks to avoid war and human rights abuses, and on principle favors the rule of law and peaceful political transitions. Democracy is preferred but, as China's role demonstrates, optional. Its governance, moreover, is not forever fixed, centralized and resistant to change, for it is fundamentally a thing of rules and institutions and not mere domination; and it is not an empire in any meaningful sense of the term. The United States has been for a long time eager to get the Europeans involved in what it sees as the burdens of global governance, and it has recently become desperate to get the governments of emerging nations involved. Reforming peak institutions such as the United Nations, and its Security Council, has been and will remain difficult, but that is itself a sign that the organization long ago transcended its origins and now serves different purposes and different interests than it did in 1945 – a useful, and on the whole beneficial, evolution.[71]

The changing distribution of economic might, by contrast, means that the direction of the global economy must and will be shared in a new and different manner in order to be effective. The United States and its European allies understand that, however, and so the institutions governing the international economy have already begun to adapt. There can be no doubt that the post–Cold War order will look different in the future, that new powers and peoples will speak more loudly, even if they do so in English, that the specifically British contribution to its workings will become ever more residual, and that the United States will have to content itself with bargains rather than victories, with influence rather than domination. The possibilities for the post–Cold War order would therefore seem not yet exhausted, even if the optimism with which its birth was announced has faded and even if the claim that the spread of global capitalism would bring with it greater concern for human rights and the spread of democracy no longer carries much conviction. And it seems likely that for some time it will continue to be recognized as a work of Anglo-American provenance, the product of the unusually successful efforts of the United States and Great Britain, for many years the closest of allies with leaders who crafted a shared vision of the world and had the opportunity and the resources to ensure that it came to prevail over the principles and practices on offer from their Cold War rival.

Notes

1 Remaking the World, Again

1. It is surely significant that Eric Hobsbawm, who had no sympathy with bold claims about the "end of history," should nonetheless end his *Age of Extremes* (1995) with the end of the Soviet Union in 1991, when something did end and something very different clearly began. For a forceful exposition of the position that Hobsbawm and many other historians would dispute, see Francis Fukuyama, *The End of History* (1992).
2. See Andrew Williams, *Failed Imagination?* (2007); G. John Ikenberry, *After Victory* (2001); Charles Maier, "Empires or Nations?" (2002); and also Samuel F. Wells and Paula Bailey Smith, eds., *New European Orders* (1996).
3. The idea is that world orders, and the dominant powers that tend to preside over them, generate "public goods" whose systemic benefits make lesser powers willing to participate or at least acquiesce. For an effort to specify the notion of public goods in the aftermath of 9/11, see Joseph Nye, "The American National Interest and Global Public Goods" (2002); also Elizabeth Cobbs Hoffman, *American Umpire* (2013); and Wesley Wooley, *Alternatives to Anarchy* (1988). Order itself can be counted a public good, but it does not typically look like that to states and leaders that feel order comes at their expense and benefits primarily the hegemonic power or powers.
4. Ideas about world order have a much longer history, of course, but the crises and conflicts of the twentieth century created a new intensity to the interest. See Mark Mazower, *Governing the World* (2012).
5. On the link between Wilsonianism and the British liberal tradition, see David Reynolds, "Rethinking Anglo-American Relations" (1988–9), p. 102, who argues reasonably that "for all the diverse sources of Wilson's thought, Wilsonianism can legitimately be seen as British Liberalism transformed by America's crusading sense of mission and energized by American power."
6. The British government enlisted J. M. Keynes to develop a critique of the German model for a new Europe, and Arnold Toynbee, who had relocated with the rest of Chatham House to Balliol College, Oxford, wrote early memos on what an Anglo-American world order would look like. See Robert Skidelsky, *Keynes*, vol. 3 (2000); and William H. McNeill, *Arnold J. Toynbee* (1989), pp. 179–85, 189. Keynes himself insisted that any response by Britain should not suggest that they are "the champions of the pre-war economic *status quo* ..." See Keynes to Harold Nicolson, Nov. 20, 1940, TNA, INF 1/871.
7. See the memo by the Foreign Research and Publication Service, "British-American World Order," July 1941, TNA, CAB 117/98; and also the interesting preliminary report by the same group on "The Non-White Races in a British-American World Order," June 24, 1941, TNA, AVIA 38/1129. On the diplomacy that helped bring the U.S. and the U.K. together around these aims, see B. J. C. McKercher, *Transition of Power* (1999); David Reynolds, "Roosevelt, Churchill, and the Wartime Anglo-American Alliance, 1939–1945" (1986); John Charmley,

Churchill's Grand Alliance (1995); John Kent, *British Imperial Strategy* (1993); and Patrick Hearden, *Architects of Globalism* (2002).

8. On Soviet uses of "antifascism," see Tony Judt, *Postwar* (2005), pp. 215–17.

9. See Fraser Harbutt, *The Iron Curtain* (1986); Ritchie Ovendale, *The English-Speaking Alliance* (1985); Terry Anderson, *The United States, Great Britain, and the Cold War* (1981); David Reynolds, "The Origins of the Cold War" (1985); and John Harper, *American Visions of Europe* (1994).

10. James Cronin, *The World the Cold War Made* (1996); Judt, *Postwar*; Odd Arne Westad, *The Global Cold War* (2005); and, more recently, Melvyn Leffler and Odd Arne Westad, eds., *The Cambridge History of the Cold War* (2010); and Joel Isaac and Duncan Bell, *Uncertain Empire* (2012).

11. The transition from Cold War to post–Cold War has not received the attention it deserves from either historians or scholars of international relations. Three exceptions are G. John Ikenberry, *Liberal Leviathan* (2012); Michael Hunt, *The American Ascendancy* (2007); and Tony Smith, *America's Mission* (2012).

12. See Walter Russell Mead, *God and Gold* (2007). Air power and nuclear weapons would radically change such calculations, however, as H. W. Brands argues in "The Age of Vulnerability" (1989).

13. Lately there have been a number of comparisons of Britain and America – and occasionally others – in terms of empire. See Charles Maier, *Among Empires* (2006); Bernard Porter, *Empire and Superempire* (2006); Patrick O'Brien, "The Myth of Anglophone Succession" (2003); and Niall Ferguson, *Colossus* (2004). For a much earlier statement, see D. Cameron Watt, *Succeeding John Bull* (1984); and, for a more popular treatment, Norman Moss, *Picking up the Reins* (2008).

14. See Kathleen Burk, *Old World, New World* (2007) and "Old World, New World" (2009); Burk's book and essay constitute a useful introduction to what is a vast literature on the "special relationship." Among the more helpful and analytical contributions are Wm. Roger Louis and Hedley Bull, eds., *The Special Relationship*; David Reynolds, *Britannia Overruled* (2000); D. Cameron Watt, *Succeeding John Bull*; John Dumbrell, *A Special Relationship* (2001); John Baylis, *Anglo-American Defence Relations* (1984); Ritchie Ovendale, *Anglo-American Relations* (1998); C. J. Bartlett, *'The Special Relationship'* (1992); Alex Danchev, *On Specialness* (1998); John Dickie, *'Special' No More* (1994); Alan Dobson, *Anglo-American Relations* (1995); Alan Dobson and Steve March, eds., *Anglo-American Relations: Contemporary Perspectives* (2013); and, of course, Christopher Hitchens, *Blood, Class and Empire* (2004); as well as Peter Hennessy and Caroline Anstey, *Moneybags and Brains* (1990. Baylis's document collection, *Anglo-American Relations since 1939* (1997), is especially helpful. For a recent celebratory account, see Andrew Roberts, *A History of the English-Speaking Peoples since 1900* (2007).

15. The label can easily be debated, but the idea has much to commend it. The most forceful argument is James Belich, *Replenishing the Earth* (2009), but see also John Darwin, *The Empire Project* (2009). A similar notion underpins David Edgerton's claims about British war-making capacity in his *Britain's War Machine* (2011). For an assessment, see James Cronin, "Britain in the World" (2012).

16. The argument here is that the international context critically affects the decisions of even dominant actors, both internally and externally. For discussions of the role of international factors, see the extensive literature on the "new international history" as well as the related work of scholars of international relations on the interactions of foreign and domestic policy. Useful starting points are Niall Ferguson, Charles Maier, Erez Manela and Daniel Sargent, eds., *The Shock of the Global* (2010); Ira Katznelson and Martin Shefter, eds., *Shaped by War and Trade* (2002); and William Mulligan and Brendan Simms, ed., *The Primacy of Foreign Policy in British History* (2010).

17. Debate continues on just who got the better of the bargaining at the end of the war. See, for example, Benn Steil, *The Battle of Bretton Woods* (2013), and the reviews by Jamie Martin in the *London Review of Books*, Nov. 21, 2013, pp. 16–18, and by Robert Kuttner in *American Prospect* 24.6 (Nov.–Dec. 2013): 76–9.

18. The meaning of "containment" has been much debated, at the time and since. See, among many others, Thomas McCormick, *America's Half-Century* (1995); Anders Stephanson, *Kennan and the Art of Foreign Policy* (1989); and John Lewis Gaddis, *George F. Kennan* (2011). The text of NSC-68 can be found in *FRUS, 1950*, vol. 1, pp. 235–92; for an analysis, see Ernest May, ed., *American Cold War Strategy* (1993).

19. On the UN, see Robert Hildebrand, *Dumbarton Oaks* (1990); and David Bosco, *Five to Rule Them All* (2009).

20. Acheson, as reported in Memorandum of Conversation on "Tripartite Atomic Energy Negotiations," July 6, 1949, in *FRUS, 1949*, vol. 1: *National Security Affairs, Foreign Economic Policy*, p. 472.

21. See Alan Milward, *The United Kingdom and the European Community*, vol. 1 (2002), pp. 1–9, 415–20; and Stephen Wall, *The Official History of Britain and the European Community*, vol. 2 (2013).

22. "Evidence of U.K.-French-Israeli Collusion and Deception in Connection with Attacks on Egypt," report by W. Park Armstrong, Special Assistant for Intelligence, U.S. State Department, Dec. 5, 1956, in *FRUS, 1955–1957*, vol. 16: *Suez Crisis July 26–December 31, 1956*. See also Wm. Roger Louis and Roger Owen, eds., *Suez 1956* (1989); and Louise Richardson, *When Allies Differ* (1996).

23. Memorandum of Conversation, Ambassador Dillon's Residence, Paris, Dec. 10, 1956, in *FRUS, 1955–1957*, vol. 16: *Suez Crisis*. See, more generally, Stephen Kinzer, *The Brothers* (2013).

24. "Outline of Future Policy," reprinted in the *New York Times*, Aug. 5, 1957.

25. Memorandum by the Counselor of the Department of State (G. Frederick Reinhardt), Sept. 11, 1958, in *FRUS, 1958–1960*, vol. 7, part 2: *Western Europe*.

26. See S. J. Ball, "Military Nuclear Relations between the United States and Great Britain" (1995). After this it became impossible to talk credibly about Britain's independent nuclear deterrent. See Dan Plesch, "The Future of Britain's WMD" (2006).

27. McGeorge Bundy, Memorandum for the Record, Dec. 7, 1964, in *FRUS,1964–1968*, vol. 13: *Western Europe Region*, p. 139. On Ormsby-Gore's involvement in the deliberations over the Cuban missile crisis, see the interview with Sir John Oliver Wright in BDOHP.

28. See the *New York Times* of Dec. 6, 1962, the day following the speech.

29. On Kennedy and the "special relationship," see Nigel Ashton, *Kennedy, Macmillan and the Cold War* (2002); David Nunnerly, *President Kennedy and Britain* (1972); Alistair Horne, "Kennedy and Macmillan" (1999); and Michael Hopkins, "David Ormsby Gore, Lord Harlech, 1961–65" (2009).

30. John Baylis, *Anglo-American Defence Relations*, p. 154; Harold Wilson, *The Labour Government* (1974), p. 341; McGeorge Bundy to President Johnson, Sept. 10, 1965, in *FRUS, 1964–1968*, vol. 12: *Western Europe*, p. 506.

31. Ball's report of Sept. 9, 1965 on his meeting with Wilson is included as an attachment to Bundy's memo, above.

32. See Jonathan Colman, *A 'Special Relationship'?* (2004); James Ellison, *The United States, Britain and the Transatlantic Crisis* (2007); John Young, "Britain and Vietnam" (2002) and "Ambassador David Bruce and LBJ's War" (2011); and Alan Dobson, *The Politics of the Anglo-American Economic Special Relationship* (1988), pp. 236–7.

33. Saki Dockrill, *Britain's Retreat from East of Suez* (2002).

34. Johnson to Wilson, Jan. 11 and Jan. 15, 1968; State Department paper, undated but presumably issued c. June 1, 1968 and formally discussed by the National Security Council at its meeting of June 5, 1968, in *FRUS, 1964–1968*, vol. 12: *Western Europe*, pp. 555–7, 609–11, 618–27. For analysis, see Jeffrey Pickering, *British Withdrawal from East of Suez* (1998); and Helen Parr, "Britain, America, East of Suez and the EEC" (2006).

35. George Ball to President Johnson, July 22, 1966, in *FRUS, 1964–1968*, vol. 12: *Western Europe*, pp. 546ff.

36. On U.S. policy toward Europe, see Geir Lundestad, *'Empire' by Integration* (1998).

37. "Underlying Elements in Anglo-U.S. Relations," paper prepared by the British Embassy and the FCO Planning Staff, Jan. 17, 1969, TNA, FCO55/744, also in FCO32/376.

38. Henry Kissinger, *White House Years* (1979), pp. 86–96, esp. p. 91.

39. Henry Kissinger, *Years of Renewal* (1999), pp. 606–10.

40. See Melvyn Leffler, *A Preponderance of Power* (1993).

41. See Jeremy Suri, *Power and Protest* (2003) for an argument linking détente to the activism of the 1960s.

42. Howard Malchow, *Special Relations* (2011), pp. 57–63.

43. Michel Crozier, Samuel P. Huntington and Joji Watanuki, *The Crisis of Democracy* (1975).

44. On the formation and functioning of alliances, see Stephen Walt, "Alliance Theory and the Balance of World Power" (1985). Walt distinguishes between strategies of "balance" and

"bandwagoning" and identifies the at times obsessive concern of U.S. leaders with maintaining credibility and keeping allies from defecting as an example of bandwagoning. In theory, such a strategy can be counterproductive, but the U.S. largely avoided this because it worked so often through multilateral institutions, exercised "strategic restraint" and delivered significant "public goods." On these, see G. John Ikenberry, *After Victory* and *Liberal Leviathan*; and, more recently, Josef Joffe, *The Myth of America's Decline* (2014).

45. On the 1970s as a major turning point, see Niall Ferguson et al., *The Shock of the Global*; Thomas Borstelmann, *The 1970s* (2012); and Christian Caryl, *Strange Rebels* (2013).

2 Vietnam to Helsinki: A Seventies Trip

1. Among many accounts, see Frank Snepp, *Decent Interval* (1977); and Henry Kissinger, *Years of Renewal* (1999), pp. 543-4. Many have detected a profound cynicism in the actions of Nixon and Kissinger who, it is argued, knew well the fate that would befall their South Vietnamese allies but wanted merely a decent interval to elapse between the peace agreement and American withdrawal, with the inevitable collapse and North Vietnamese victory. It is difficult to know precisely what Nixon and Kissinger thought, but Edward Heath reported on a meeting with Nixon in February 1973 at which Nixon said that he believed the North Vietnamese wanted ultimately to control a "united Vietnam" but that various constraints would "enable the settlement to hold for perhaps two years." Heath to Trudeau, Feb. 15, 1973, TNA, PREM15/2082.

2. On the earlier history, see Stephen Kinzer, *All the Shah's Men* (2003).

3. Heath was always clear about his intentions. See Edward Heath, *Old World, New Horizons* (1970); and Heath, *The Course of My Life* (1998).

4. The party had also adopted a radical program in 1973, but the party's leaders were by no means committed. See James Cronin, *New Labour's Pasts* (2004), chs. 4-5.

5. The episode was never entirely forgotten, particularly by Kissinger, who devoted the better part of two chapters to the venture in his memoir *Years of Upheaval* (1982). A still more comprehensive record has recently been made available by the Foreign and Commonwealth Office in Keith Hamilton and Patrick Salmon, eds., *The Year of Europe* (2006). See also Keith Hamilton, "Britain, France and America's Year of Europe, 1973" (2006); as well as the essays by Daniel Mochli, Alastair Noble and Fabian Hilfrich in Matthias Schulz and Thomas Schwartz, eds., *The Strained Alliance* (2010). See also Catherine Hynes, "'A Year of Bickering'" (2009) and *The Year That Never Was* (2009); Thomas Robb, "Henry Kissinger, Great Britain, and the 'Year of Europe'" (2010); Silvia Pietrantonio. "The Year That Never Was" (2010); Alistair Horne, *Kissinger: 1973* (2009); Alex Spelling, "Edward Heath and Anglo-American Relations 1970-74" (2009); and more broadly, Andrew Scott, *Allies Apart* (2011). The controversy is also discussed in Robin Renwick, *Fighting with Allies* (1996), pp. 298-305; and Denis Greenhill, *More by Accident* (1992); and Kissinger's initiative is referred to as having "established a new gravity record for lead balloons" by Raymond Seitz in his memoir, *Over Here* (1998), p. 333.

6. For a review of the issues, see James Ellison, "Britain and Europe" (2005).

7. Philip Ziegler, *Edward Heath* (2010), pp. 392-3; John Campbell, *Edward Heath* (1993), pp. 340-1.

8. See Christopher Hill and Christopher Lord, "The Foreign Policy of the Heath Government" (1996), pp. 285-6.

9. "Underlying Elements in Anglo-U.S. Relations," a paper prepared by the British Embassy and the FCO Planning Staff, Jan. 17, 1969, TNA, FCO55/744, also in FCO32/376.

10. Hill and Lord, "The Foreign Policy of the Heath Government," pp. 308-9.

11. Cited in Stephen Wall, *A Stranger in Europe* (2008), p. 3.

12. Heath to Nixon, Oct. 30, 1972, in Hamilton and Salmon, *The Year of Europe*, no. 1. Heath would later describe the communiqué as "the finest of . . . modern times." See John Young, "The Heath Government and British Entry into the European Community" (1996), p. 279.

13. Kissinger, *Years of Upheaval*, p. 142.

14. Pierre Asselin, *A Bitter Peace* (2001).

15. The literature on the Vietnam War and its consequences is voluminous. An insightful guide is John Dumbrell, *Rethinking the Vietnam War* (2012).

16. Margaret MacMillan, *Nixon and Mao* (2007); for the context, see William Kirby, Robert Ross and Gong Li, eds., *Normalization of U.S.-China Relations* (2005).

17. Henry Kissinger, *White House Years* (1979), p. 763.
18. See Robert Litwak, *Détente and the Nixon Doctrine* (1984), esp. pp. 139–43; and William Bundy, *Tangled Web* (1998).
19. Charles Maier, *Among Empires* (2006), p. 236.
20. Rick Perlstein, *Nixonland* (2008), pp. 368–71. See also Robert Dallek, *Nixon and Kissinger* (2007), pp. 473–6, on how the relationship played out on the issue of the "Year of Europe."
21. Kissinger, *Years of Upheaval*, p. 142.
22. A minimalist document was agreed and announced as the "Ottawa Declaration" at the NATO Summit of June 1974. See the "Declaration on Atlantic Relations issued by the North Atlantic Council," June 19, 1974, NATO On-line Library, also reproduced in *Selected Documents relating to Problems of Security and Cooperation in Europe, 1954–1977*, Cmnd. 6932 (1977), pp. 184–6. The U.S. had originally wanted a joint declaration with the European Community and with NATO, not simply with NATO.
23. Kissinger, *Years of Upheaval*, p. 193.
24. The most thorough account is Kissinger's, which is obviously not the entire story. On the limitations of Kissinger's account, see Scott, *Allies Apart*, pp. 144–5, 204.
25. Stanley Hoffman, *Dead Ends* (1983), pp. 58–9.
26. The official was Crispin Tickell, then head of the Western Organisations Department. See Tickell to Wiggin (and others), May 4, 1973, in Hamilton and Salmon, *The Year of Europe*, no. 85. Tickell would later play a critical role in the negotiations leading to the Helsinki Accords and he would become an early advocate of efforts to address climate change.
27. "Record of a Meeting at the British Embassy, June 4, 1973," in Hamilton and Salmon, *The Year of Europe*, no. 108.
28. The phrases concerning "symbolic satisfaction" and "form for substance" come from a Foreign Office paper of August 1973 on "The Identity of the Nine vis-à-vis the United States," in Hamilton and Salmon, *The Year of Europe*, no. 193; "the form of words" quote is from Tickell's note of May 4.
29. "The Identity of the Nine," Aug. 1973.
30. On the broader issue, see Giuliano Garavini, *After Empires* (2012).
31. "Record of Conversation between the Foreign and Commonwealth Secretary and the American Secretary of State, Sept. 24, 1973," in Hamilton and Salmon, *The Year of Europe*, no. 232.
32. Kissinger had been mad enough to discontinue U.S./U.K. intelligence cooperation during the summer. It would happen again in the autumn during the fallout over the Middle East. See Richard Aldrich, *GCHQ* (2010), pp. 277–98.
33. Cited in Ziegler, *Edward Heath*, p. 378.
34. Cromer to Dennis Greenhill (Permanent Undersecretary, FCO), Oct. 3, 1973, TNA, FCO82/306.
35. Cited in Ziegler, *Edward Heath*, p. 386.
36. See Timothy Garton Ash, *In Europe's Name* (1993); and Mary Sarotte, *Dealing with the Devil* (2001).
37. "Report of the Joint Intelligence Committee on the Soviet Attitude to MBFR," July 12, 1973, in Gillian Bennett and Keith Hamilton, eds., *Détente in Europe, 1972–1976* (2001), p. 50.
38. "How the Soviets View the Strategic Balance," National Security Study Memorandum no. 24, May 1969, DNSA.
39. Robert Osgood, "The U.S. in the International Environment," May 21, 1969, memo to NSC staff, DNSA.
40. For a summary, see Richard Crockatt, *The Fifty Years War* (1995), pp. 224–34. A fuller account is available in Raymond Garthoff, *Détente and Confrontation* (1994).
41. Kissinger, *Years of Upheaval*, p. 280.
42. "Record of a Discussion at Camp David, 2 February 1973," between Heath, Nixon, Kissinger and Trend, in Hamilton and Salmon, *The Year of Europe*, no. 22.
43. Cromer to Brimelow, Mar. 7, 1973, in Hamilton and Salmon, *The Year of Europe*, no. 44.
44. Kissinger, *Years of Upheaval*, p. 167. By this Pompidou apparently meant the electoral progress of Communist parties, a prospect made more real soon after by the attractions of Eurocommunism.
45. McCracken to Nixon, June 2, 1971, in *FRUS, 1969–1976: Nixon-Ford Administrations*, vol. 3, Document no. 157.

46. No formal papers were prepared for the meeting and no official record exists, though H. R. Haldeman and William Safire have written accounts. See *FRUS, 1969–1976: Nixon-Ford Administrations*, vol. 3, Document no. 168.

47. See Allen Matusow, "Richard Nixon and the Failed War against the Trading World" (2003); and Francis Gavin, *Gold, Dollars, and Power* (2006).

48. See Diane Kunz, *Butter and Guns* (1997), ch. 10, on Nixon's focus on domestic politics and hence the domestic economy.

49. Heath to Douglas-Home, Sept. 8, 1970; Douglas-Home to Heath, Sept. 18, 1970, TNA, CAB164/988. The incident is also recounted in Andrew Roberts, *A History of the English-Speaking Peoples since 1900* (2007), pp. 486–7.

50. Author interviews with Sir Michael Palliser, June 13, 2007, and with Lord (David) Owen, June 26, 2007.

51. Account by R. T. Armstrong (Private Secretary to Heath) to Antony Acland (Principal Private Secretary to Foreign Secretary), June 19, 1973, in Hamilton and Salmon, *The Year of Europe*, no. 133. The dinner was on June 13.

52. See, for example, the report by Michael Palliser, "1973: Year One in the European Communities," prepared for the Foreign Secretary, Jan. 25, 1974, in Hamilton and Salmon, *The Year of Europe*, no. 517, on the assumptions with which Britain approached the first year of EC membership and the attendant disappointments. Palliser was U.K. Permanent Representative in Brussels and would eventually become Permanent Under-Secretary at the FCO. See also Stephen Wall, *The Official History of Britain and the European Community*, vol. 2 (2013), ch. 9.

53. While the U.S. did not support the development of nuclear weapons by the French during the 1960s, it shifted its stance during the following decade. In fact, it was at the contentious meeting in San Clemente with Jobert on June 29–30, 1973 that Kissinger conveyed a U.S. offer of technical assistance to the French. Pompidou accepted, though he apparently never told Jobert, and the collaboration was extremely secretive. See Michael Sutton, *France and the Construction of Europe* (2007), pp. 193–4.

54. The framework is elaborated in Henry Kissinger, *The Troubled Partnership* (1965). See also Jeremi Suri, *Henry Kissinger and the American Century* (2007), pp. 170–7.

55. Kissinger, *Years of Upheaval*, p. 541.

56. On European rates, see Tony Judt, *Postwar* (2005), pp. 455–6.

57. Douglas-Home message to Washington, Nov. 11, 1973, TNA, FCO46/962.

58. "Permanent Under-Secretary's Monthly Meetings on Coordinating U.S./U.K. Relations," TNA, FCO82/306. The British emissary to the Saudis was Lord Aldington, Chairman of Grindlays Bank and former Deputy Chairman of the Conservative Party.

59. Heath and Jobert are both cited in Kissinger, *Years of Upheaval*, pp. 720, 710.

60. Lord Cromer to J. O. (Oliver) Wright, Nov. 2, 1973, in Hamilton and Salmon, *The Year of Europe*, no. 361.

61. "The European Identity," English translation of a French-language draft agreed by officials, Nov. 1973, in Hamilton and Salmon, *The Year of Europe*, no. 392.

62. Notes on a discussion between Schlesinger and Lord Carrington, U.K. Defence Secretary, held at The Hague, Nov. 7, 1973, in Hamilton and Salmon, *The Year of Europe*, no. 379.

63. Schlesinger in discussion with Carrington, Nov. 7, 1973.

64. Scott, *Allies Apart*, p. 193.

65. Even Willy Brandt, who would take a leading role in arguing for a Euro-Arab Dialogue and later become a tribune for the "global South" on the issue of commodity prices, felt defensive about the Europeans' role in the Middle East conflict and about the conference in Copenhagen in December. See Brandt, *People and Politics* (1976), pp. 275 and 462 (on the EEC's performance in general), p. 276 (on the December meeting), and pp. 472–6 (on the Arab world and commodity prices more generally). See also David Allen and Andrin Hauri, "The Euro-Arab Dialogue, the Venice Declaration, and Beyond" (2011).

66. Quoted in Kissinger, *Years of Upheaval*, p. 900. The discussion apparently occurred in early February 1974.

67. Walter Isaacson, *Kissinger* (1992), pp. 538–45.

68. Douglas-Home telegram, Oct. 15, 1973, in Hamilton and Salmon, *The Year of Europe*, no. 292.

69. Cromer to Douglas-Home, Nov. 24, 1973, in Hamilton and Salmon, *The Year of Europe*, no. 412.

70. See the interesting record of the discussion of the "Cabinet European Unit" on Jan. 23, 1974, in Hamilton and Salmon, *The Year of Europe*, no. 515, which refers to "disappointment in the rest of the Community at what were taken to be selfish policies pursued bilaterally by the United Kingdom and France, notably to conclude bilateral deals with oil producing countries. Declarations that we regarded North Sea oil as available for our own benefit alone . . . further encouraged suspicion within the community."

71. Thomas Brimelow to Cromer, Jan. 10, 1974, in Hamilton and Salmon, *The Year of Europe*, no. 498, reports on the December 12 meeting and appends a new set of policies about communications between the U.S., U.K. and other European countries. The note suggests continued irritation at Kissinger and the U.S., but represents a shift in policy nonetheless.

72. In the words of Michael Palliser, "Those of us who took part in . . . the meeting . . . in Copenhagen on 14–15 December last would be forgiven for saying 'Never Again'. The meeting . . . was a shambles . . ." See Palliser, "1973," in Hamilton and Salmon, *The Year of Europe*, no. 517.

73. Brimelow, for example, remained antipathetic to the U.S., but people in Washington such as Cromer and Richard Sykes were more positive. The pro-Europeanists within the Foreign Office such as Palliser became less optimistic about its value in a crisis. See Palliser, "1973"; Brimelow to Sykes, Jan. 18, 1974, and Sykes to Brimelow, Jan. 25, 1974, in Hamilton and Salmon, *The Year of Europe*, nos. 513 and 518. See also Lord Kennet to Callaghan, Mar. 18, 1974, Callaghan Papers, Box 221, Bodleian Library, Oxford. Kennet had dined with Kissinger's advisor Hal Sonnenfeldt who, like his boss, was appalled at the decision to begin a Euro-Arab Dialogue.

74. Jagdish Bhagwati, "Rethinking Global Negotiations" (1984), pp. 23–6; Kissinger, *Years of Renewal*, pp. 674ff.

75. Gerald Ford, speech to the World Energy Conference, Sept. 23, 1974, PPPUS.

76. D. G. Holland to Sir Donald Maitland, Dec. 13, 1974, TNA, FCO96/16. Maitland was U.K. Permanent Representative to the UN, 1973–4.

77. George Shultz would represent the U.S., Eric Roll the U.K., Wilfried Guth of Deutsche Bank would speak for Germany, Raymond Barre for France, and Hide Suzuki for Japan. See Robert Putnam and Nicholas Bayne, *Hanging Together* (1984), pp. 15–16.

78. James Reston, "A Chat with Giscard," *International Herald Tribune*, June 16, 1975, quoted in Putnam and Bayne, *Hanging Together*, p. 15.

79. The quotes from the Rambouillet meeting can be found in Kissinger's *Years of Renewal*, pp. 694 and 678.

80. Preparations and negotiations for the Conference and the eventual accord are thoroughly documented in Gillian Bennett and Keith Hamilton, eds., *The Conference on Security and Cooperation in Europe, 1972–75* (1997). Further documentation is available in Bennett and Hamilton, *Détente in Europe*, and focused primarily on the roughly simultaneous and occasionally linked talks on Mutual and Balanced Force Reductions, the "diplomatic sibling" of the talks leading to Helsinki. Unlike the Helsinki process, the MBFR talks never reached an agreement and dragged on until 1989. A final report to Sir Geoffrey Howe made what seemed the obvious point that without greater imagination and will, "we can spend another fifteen years without result" (R. J. O'Neill to Howe, Feb. 17, 1989, in Bennett and Hamilton, *Détente in Europe*, Appendix 3.). Spoken just a bit too soon.

81. "Note by the Defence Policy Staff on 'Mutual and Balanced Force Reductions: The Situation in NATO,'" Apr. 21, 1972, in Bennett and Hamilton, *Détente in Europe*, no. 1; Kissinger, *White House Years*, pp. 938–49.

82. Crispin Tickell to C. D. Wiggin, July 3, 1974, and Callaghan memo to various embassies on the NATO meeting of June 19, 1974, TNA, PREM16/391.

83. Quoted in the Callaghan memo.

84. Sara Snyder, *Human Rights Activism and the End of the Cold War* (2011).

85. Crispin Tickell memo of Mar. 26, 1974, TNA, PREM16/391.

86. Kissinger, *Years of Renewal*, p. 609.

87. See David Butler and Uwe Kitzinger, *The 1975 Referendum* (1996).

88. Heath himself acknowledged the failure of the European option, writing in his memoir that "After the oil crisis of 1973–4 the Community lost its momentum and, worse, lost sight of the philosophy of Jean Monnet: that the Community exists to find common solutions to common problems. Each member state drifted back to seeking its own, unilateral solution to unemployment and inflation." See Heath, *Course of My Life*, p. 395.

89. Meeting of Permanent Secretaries, Feb. 28, 1974, TNA, FO49/503.
90. "British Foreign Policy: The Scope for Change," transmitted with a cover letter from J. E. Cable, Head of the Foreign Office Planning Staff, Feb. 12, 1974, TNA, FO49/503.
91. Brimelow to Hunt, Feb. 27, 1974, with the paper, "A Policy for the Lean Years," attached, TNA, FO49/503.
92. To this extent it was not unreasonable to conclude, as did David Watt, that "since the 1970s Anglo-American relations, considered entirely by themselves, have ceased to be very important or very interesting." See David Watt, "Introduction" (1986), p. 13. Whether such a conclusion remained apt in the mid–1980s and beyond is another matter.

3 Détente, Human Rights and Economic Crisis

1. Odd Arne Westad, ed., *The Fall of Détente* (1997).
2. On the transition in Europe, see Barry Eichengreen, *The European Economy since 1945* (2006). The U.S. experienced a broadly similar trajectory.
3. The meaning of Keynesianism varied from one country to another. See Peter Hall, ed., *The Political Power of Economic Ideas* (1989).
4. Judith Stein, *Pivotal Decade* (2010), pp. 159–61.
5. Data here has come from Susan B. Carter et al., eds., *Historical Statistics of the United States* (2006), online edn.; and Lawrence Mishel, Jared Bernstein and Heidi Shierholz, *The State of Working America* (2009), as well as data made available online from the Bureau of Labor Statistics.
6. On Carter's turn, see David Calleo, *The Imperious Economy* (1982), pp. 125–7, 145–53.
7. Robert Collins, *More* (2000), pp. 179–82.
8. Peter Hall, "Policy Paradigms, Social Learning and the State" (1993). At least one American, Milton Friedman, played a very active role in the U.K. debate. See Edward Nelson, "Milton Friedman and U.K. Economic Policy" (2009).
9. The Carter administration tried something similar in the wake of the second oil shock, but it was much too little and far too late. See Stein, *Pivotal Decade*, pp. 221–4.
10. See the discussions recorded in TNA, PREM16/1708 and T366/217. There was talk, for example, of denying strikers social security payments, of imposing taxes so as to discourage or at least postpone car purchases from Ford's U.K. and foreign rivals, and of government departments and agencies punishing Ford by refusing to purchase its vehicles. Officials tended to discourage these options, but Cabinet members continued to express interest.
11. See James Cronin, *New Labour's Pasts* (2004), pp. 178–85; Kathleen Burk and Alec Cairncross, *Goodbye, Great Britain* (1992); and Ben Clift and Jim Tomlinson, "Negotiating Credibility" (2008).
12. Labour Party, *Report of the Seventy-Fifth Annual Conference of the Labour Party* (1976).
13. Transcript of a press conference held at Millbank Tower, Mar. 21, 1978, TNA, PREM16/1805 "North Sea Oil White Paper 1978."
14. As Sir John Hunt explained to Kenneth Stowe in advance of the Bonn Summit, "The 'locomotive theory' may be largely discredited but what we are seeking is a concerted action package." See Hunt to Stowe, June 25, 1978, TNA, PREM16/1916.
15. The apparent success of the Bonn Summit served as the key illustration of "the logic of two-level games" that Robert Putnam described in "Diplomacy and Domestic Politics" (1988). See also G. John Ikenberry, "Market Solutions to State Problems" (1988); and Kenneth Morgan, *Callaghan* (1997), pp. 606–7.
16. Henry Kissinger, *Years of Renewal* (1999), pp. 606–10.
17. Reported in Michael Palliser to David Owen, Feb. 17, 1977, TNA, FCO82/687.
18. Kissinger, *Years of Renewal*, p. 926.
19. On the history of human rights politics, see Erez Manela, *The Wilsonian Moment* (2007); Elizabeth Borgwardt, *A New Deal for the World* (2005); Mark Mazower, "The Strange Triumph of Human Rights, 1933–1950" (2004); A. W. Brian Simpson, *Human Rights and the End of Empire* (2001); Mary Ann Glendon, *A World Made New* (2001); Johannes Morsink, *The Universal Declaration of Human Rights* (1999); John Humphrey, *Human Rights Law and the United Nations* (1984); Andrew Moravcsik, "The Origins of Human Rights Regimes" (2000); Kenneth Cmiel, "The Recent History of Human Rights" (2004); Samuel Moyn, *The Last Utopia* (2010); Nicolas Guilhot, *The Democracy Makers* (2005); Stephen Hopgood, *The*

Endtimes of Human Rights (2013); and Akira Iriye, Petra Goedde and William I. Hitchcock, eds., *The Human Rights Revolution* (2012).

20. Michael Ignatieff, ed., *American Exceptionalism and Human Rights* (2005); Kenneth Cmiel, "The Emergence of Human Rights Politics" (1999).

21. See Roland Burke, *Decolonization and the Evolution of International Human Rights* (2010), chs. 4 and 5; and also Ryan Irwin, *Gordian Knot* (2012).

22. See John Dumbrell, *A Special Relationship* (2001), p. 80, for a summary; and the documents in Gillian Bennett and Keith Hamilton, eds., *The Conference on Security and Cooperation in Europe, 1972-75* (1997) for the details.

23. The most recent assessment is Jonathan Haslam, *The Nixon Administration and the Death of Allende's Chile* (2005).

24. John Dinges, *The Condor Years* (2004).

25. Kissinger conversation with Cesar Guzzetti, June 10, 1976, cited in Jeremi Suri, *Henry Kissinger and the American Century* (2007), p. 240.

26. Kissinger, *Years of Renewal*, p. 757.

27. See Robert Kaufman, *Henry Jackson* (2000), ch. 14; and Julian Zelizer, "Defence and Domestic Politics" (2009).

28. Henry Kissinger, *Diplomacy* (1994), p. 753.

29. The coalition behind Jackson-Vanik, which included antiwar liberals and people and newspapers ordinarily favorable to détente, provoked particular anger from Kissinger. See Henry Kissinger, *Years of Upheaval* (1982), pp. 251-2.

30. Jackson speech to the U.S. Senate, Mar. 29, 1973, cited in Kaufman, *Henry Jackson*, pp. 267-8.

31. Ann Marie Clark, *Diplomacy of Conscience* (2001).

32. Nicholas Henderson, *Mandarin* (1994), p. 280.

33. While Britain regarded itself as an exemplar of human rights, the issue had never been a top priority in foreign policy. The Foreign Office had had a human rights officer since at least 1964, but as John Coles, who held the job, remembered, "I cannot say that much attention was paid to my work." At roughly the same time the Foreign Secretary in the Labour government was deciding not the ratify the UN Convention on the Elimination of Racial Discrimination. See John Coles, *Making Foreign Policy* (2000), pp. 118-19.

34. "First Report of the Working Group on Human Rights," Jan. 27, 1976, TNA, HO274/36.

35. See Edmund Dell to James Callaghan, Jan. 7, 1977, in which he reports that his fellow Cabinet members worry that the European Convention "would impede radical action by Labour governments"; also Benn to Callaghan, Dec. 21, 1976, arguing that "the special circumstances of Northern Ireland should not be allowed to influence constitutional decisions elsewhere"; and Merlyn Rees to Callaghan, Nov. 26, 1976, saying that a resolution of the Irish conflict might require a bill of rights there and, by extension, elsewhere; TNA, PREM16/1294.

36. Luard described the process in a meeting at the State Department with Patricia Derian, whom Carter put in charge of U.S. human rights policy, on June 20, 1977, TNA, FCO82/806.

37. Shakespeare to Hugh Carless, Latin American Department, FCO, Sept. 30, 1976, TNA, FCO7/3021.

38. For an assessment of Carter's foreign policy, see Gaddis Smith, *Morality, Reason and Power* (1986); and also John Dumbrell, *The Carter Presidency* (1993), esp. chs. 5-7. On the rivalry between Zbigniew Brzezinski, the National Security Advisor, and Cyrus Vance, the Secretary of State until April 1980, see their and the President's memoirs: Zbigniew Brzezinski, *Power and Principle* (1983); Jimmy Carter, *Keeping Faith* (1982); and Cyrus Vance, *Hard Choices* (1983).

39. Brzezinski, cited in Dumbrell, *The Carter Presidency*, p. 113.

40. Jimmy Carter, Address at the University of Notre Dame, May 22, 1977, PPPUS.

41. "Human Rights," Presidential Directive/NSC-30, Feb. 17, 1978, DNSA.

42. See Peter Jay's Sept. 24, 1977 memo to Callaghan on a meeting with Brzezinski during which the National Security Advisor gave "a more hawkish account of the American approach to Belgrade" – the site of the upcoming meeting on Helsinki – than Jay, the Ambassador, had expected; TNA, FCO88/806.

43. Record of meeting between Derian and Luard, Dec. 9, 1977, TNA, FCO82/806.

44. G. N. Smith to Michael Simpson-Orlebar, Feb. 17, 1977, TNA, FCO82/687; David Owen, *Time to Declare* (1991), p. 319. See also Callaghan's discussion with officials and foreign leaders after the funeral service for Tony Crosland on what attitude to take toward Carter and his human rights initiatives, Mar. 7, 1977, TNA, PREM16/1262.

45. David Owen, *Personally Speaking* (1987), p. 135.
46. Smith to Simpson-Orlebar, Feb. 17, 1977.
47. See Odd Arne Westad, *The Global Cold War* (2005), pp. 194–206. Brezhnev spoke of the new "correlation of forces" in his report to the Central Committee of the Communist Party in February 1976.
48. Report to the National Executive of the Labour Party by Callaghan and Tom McNally on their visit to the Soviet Union, Aug. 7–13, 1972, in Callaghan Papers, Box 148, Bodleian Library, Oxford.
49. Stanley Hoffmann, *Dead Ends* (1983), p. 125. Hoffman's essay had first appeared in the *New York Review of Books* on April 16 and 30, 1981.
50. Fred Halliday, *The Making of the Second Cold War* (1983).
51. See Keith Hamilton and Patrick Salmon, eds., *The Southern Flank in Crisis, 1973–1976* (2006).
52. Kissinger, *Years of Renewal*, pp. 626–9.
53. See Tony Judt, *Postwar* (2005), pp. 495–6; and, more generally, Rudolf Tökés, ed., *Eurocommunism and Détente* (1978). The 1978 kidnapping and murder of Aldo Moro by the Red Brigades also helped to derail the Eurocommunist initiative.
54. N. Trench to Wiggin (Ambassador to Spain), June 5, 1974, in Hamilton and Salmon, *The Southern Flank in Crisis*, no. 109.
55. Walter Isaacson, *Kissinger* (1992), pp. 673–4.
56. Notes on a meeting in Lisbon involving Callaghan, Tom McNally, Soares and others, Feb. 6, 1975, Callaghan Papers, Box 221. Soares feared that the Portuguese Communists were busy plotting a coup.
57. Kissinger, *Years of Renewal*, p. 631.
58. Report of Meeting of Socialist Party Leaders and Heads of Government," Stockholm, Aug. 2, 1975, Callaghan Papers, Box 148. The phrase "which should be discussed in a smaller group" was added in pen to the typed report. At the meeting Olaf Palme, the host, and Brune Kreisky of Austria largely supported Callaghan and Wilson, while Bettino Craxi was vague and Willy Brandt for some reason thought that a better approach to the problem would involve Yugoslavia, Romania and Algeria. Soares comes across as slightly hysterical, though perhaps he had reason to be.
59. I. J. M. Sutherland to Callaghan, July 18, 1975, in Hamilton and Salmon, *The Southern Flank in Crisis*, no. 134.
60. Record of meeting between Wilson and Costa Gomes, Helsinki, Aug. 1, 1975, in Hamilton and Salmon, *The Southern Flank in Crisis*, no. 136.
61. Minute by Sir J. Killick (British Ambassador to Moscow, 1971–3, Deputy Under-Secretary at the Foreign Office, 1973–5), Sept. 1, 1975, reporting on a meeting with Soviet Chargé d'Affaires (Brussels), Y. A. Semenov, in Hamilton and Salmon, *The Southern Flank in Crisis*, no. 140.
62. This was the view of Soviet theoretician Karen Brutents, interviewed by Westad and cited in *The Global Cold War*, p. 241.
63. Kissinger testimony to the Senate Foreign Relations Subcommittee on African Affairs, Jan. 29, 1976, cited in Isaacson, *Kissinger*, p. 684.
64. Raymond Garthoff, *Détente and Confrontation* (1994), p. 592. See also Peter Ramsbottom (U.K. Ambassador to Washington) to Callaghan, "'Peace through Strength' – U.S.-Soviet Relations in 1976," Mar. 31, 1976, in Gillian Bennett and Keith Hamilton, eds., *Détente in Europe, 1972–76* (2001), no. 89, pp. 442–9, on the multiple factors causing the U.S. administration to stop using the term "détente."
65. The Soviet Ambassador to Ethiopia, Anatoly Ratanov, felt that in getting rid of his enemies Mengistu was proving himself a "resolute and uncompromising leader." See Westad, *The Global Cold War*, p. 270.
66. Brzezinski, *Power and Principle*, p. 184.
67. Brzezinski, *Power and Principle*, p. 189. The Secretary of State, Cyrus Vance, took a very different view. See Vance, *Hard Choices*, pp. 72–5, 84–8.
68. "Study in Response to National Security Study Memorandum 39: Southern Africa," Dec. 9, 1969, DNSA, SA00379. (The original memo was issued by Kissinger on April 10.) The study merely outlined the options, but it was "Option 2," the so-called "Tar Baby" option, that prevailed. See Isaacson, *Kissinger*, pp. 686–7; Anthony Lake, *The Tar Baby Option* (1976).
69. Kissinger, *Years of Renewal*, chs. 30–2; Isaacson, *Kissinger*, pp. 685–92.

70. Margaret Thatcher, *The Downing Street Years* (1993), pp. 72–8.
71. Owen, *Time to Declare*, p. 296 and more generally, pp. 291–318.
72. Vance, *Hard Choices*, p. 267. Brzezinski did not think much of the Anglo-American collaboration and told Carter that Britain was "leading us by the nose." Brzezinski, *Power and Principle*, p. 141.
73. Brzezinski, *Power and Principle*, p. 142, reports that in December 1979 Carter informed him that Callaghan had called, and said "He wants to move on his own – with some U.S. involvement."
74. See the interviews with Robin Renwick (Lord Renwick of Clifton), no. 33, and with Anthony Parsons, no. 10, BDOHP.
75. In an effort to appease critics on the right, however, Andrew Young was ordered to abstain on a United Nations resolution denouncing the internal settlement. See Sean Wilentz, *The Age of Reagan* (2008), p. 104.
76. See David Reynolds, *America, Empire of Liberty* (2009); and Julian Zelizer, "Conservatives, Carter, and the Politics of National Security" (2008), pp. 273–5; on how the issue played into the hands of Carter's opponents.
77. Morgan, *Callaghan*, pp. 607–9.
78. Paul Nitze, "Assuring Strategic Stability in an Era of Détente" (1976). Nitze and like-minded conservatives would soon be appointed by Ford and CIA Director George Bush as "Team B," charged with providing an alternative and less benign assessment of Soviet intentions and capabilities. Their report was released shortly before Jimmy Carter took office. The detailed arguments are reviewed in Garthoff, *Détente and Confrontation*, pp. 865–77; and Richard Crockatt, *The Fifty Years War* (1995), pp. 260–7.
79. Memo by the North America Department to David Owen, Sept. 20, 1977, TNA, FCO82/760.
80. See Timothy Garton Ash, *In Europe's Name* (1993); and Mary Sarotte, *Dealing with the Devil* (2001).
81. Brzezinski, *Power and Principle*, p. 164.
82. Schmidt, "The 1977 Alastair Buchan Memorial Lecture" (1978). The lecture had been delivered on Oct. 28, 1977.
83. See David Yost and Thomas Glad, "West German Party Politics and Theater Nuclear Modernization" (1982); and Jeffrey Herf, *War by Other Means* (1991).
84. See the accounts in Brzezinski, *Power and Principle*; Garthoff, *Détente and Confrontation*; and Ezra Vogel, *Deng Xiaoping* (2011).
85. Owen, *Time to Declare*, p. 405.
86. The British had already been moving in the same direction and reassessing détente. See, for example, "Planning Paper on Détente and the Future Management of East/West Relations by the Foreign and Commonwealth Office," Nov. 23, 1976, no. 93, pp. 461–5, and "Record of a Meeting held in the Foreign and Commonwealth Office on December 7, 1976," no. 94, pp. 466–71, in Bennett and Hamilton, *Détente in Europe*.
87. Dumbrell, *The Carter Presidency*, pp. 200–1.
88. The new accord permitted the development of one new type of intercontinental ballistic missile while prohibiting more than that and provided for new verification and notification procedures. The two sides also agreed on certain limits on long-range cruise missiles and the Soviets acquiesced to American pressure to restrict the development of the Backfire bomber. For further detail, see Crockatt, *The Fifty Years War*, pp. 266–7.
89. The phrase is Owen's, *Time to Declare*, p. 386.
90. See David Farber, *Taken Hostage* (2005).
91. Anthony Parsons interview, BDOHP, no. 10.
92. Toasts of the President and the Shah at a State Dinner, Tehran, Iran, Dec. 31, 1977, PPPUS.
93. Owen, *Time to Declare*, p. 395. It was not only politicians and diplomats who failed to understand the forces at work in Iran. An example was Michel Foucault, who was moved by the "political spirituality" of the Islamist movement and much impressed by Khomeini. See Janet Afary and Kevin Anderson, *Foucault and the Iranian Revolution* (2005).
94. Sir Anthony Parsons, "Internal Difficulties in Iran," Jan. 31, 1978, TNA, FCO8/3183.
95. P. (Peter) J. Westmacott to Miss A. M. (Marriot) Sanderson, Mar. 1, 1978, TNA, FCO8/3183.
96. M. S. Weir to Parsons, Feb. 24, 1978, TNA, FCO8/3183. *Savak* was the Shah's secret police.
97. As a default option there was always the invocation of principle. As a top Foreign Office official put it on November 14, 1978, "On damage limitation . . . politically there is no obvious successor regime with which we could re-insure: we should concentrate on stressing our

support for liberalisation and fair and free elections rather than for any particular group." See EY (Economic Strategy) Committee meeting, Tuesday, Nov. 14, 1978, TNA, FCO8/3195 Anglo-Iranian Relations – Contingency Planning 1978.

98. The Carter administration was prepared to give a lot to get the hostages back. Secretary of State Cyrus Vance met with Thatcher and Carrington on February 21, 1980 in London and told them a deal was imminent. Among other concessions to Iran, an international commission would be established to "investigate the Shah's period in office" and go to Tehran to take evidence, meet with hostages and with the Revolutionary Council. It would prepare a document for the United Nations but insist the hostages be transferred to the government. The document would go to the UN and shortly after that the hostages would be released. See report on Vance's visit in TNA, PREM 19/383.

99. Lawrence Freedman, *A Choice of Enemies* (2008), pp. 62–83.

100. See Brzezinski, *Power and Principle*, pp. 505–9; and Carter, *Keeping Faith*, p. 594, who admits that toward the end "The release of the American hostages had almost become an obsession with me."

101. Henderson, *Mandarin*, p. 325.

102. President Jimmy Carter, "State of the Union Address," Jan. 23, 1980, PPPUS.

103. Dumbrell, *The Carter Presidency*, pp. 200–3; Brzezinski, *Power and Principle*, pp. 454–9; "Nuclear Weapons Employment Policy," Presidential Directive 59 (PD-59), 25 July 1980, NSA "Nuclear Vault."

104. On the campaign, see Wilentz, *The Age of Reagan*, pp. 120–5.

105. The index would have been 14.6%, not much above what it had been in 1976.

106. John Gillingham, *European Integration* (2003), pp. 307–8; Robert Putnam and Nicholas Bayne, *Hanging Together* (1984).

107. I. M. Destler, *Making Foreign Economic Policy* (1980), pp. 190–202.

108. It is worth noting that these negotiations were characterized by much better communication and coordination between the U.S. and the U.K. than might have been the case earlier in the decade. Even though the U.K. stance over trade was officially coordinated through Europe, the U.S. and the U.K. talked regularly about the process. Thus Callaghan could tell Carter on July 13, 1978, just days before the critical Bonn Economic Summit, "I thought . . . that you would wish to have an indication of the line we will be taking in the Community's deliberations on the main outstanding issues"; Callaghan to Carter, TNA, PREM16/1896.

109. See Diane Kunz, *Butter and Guns* (1997), pp. 245–7; and Daniel Yergin, *The Prize* (2008), pp. 656–80.

110. The phrase was much in use in the 1970s. See Donella Meadows et al., *The Limits to Growth* (1972).

111. "The Energy Problem: Address to the Nation," Apr. 18, 1977, PPPUS.

112. "National Energy Plan: Message of the President," Apr. 29, 1977, PPPUS.

113. Quoted by Carter in *Keeping Faith*, p. 112.

114. The text of the summit declaration, together with material on the bargaining that led up to it, can be found in TNA, PREM19/27, "Tokyo Economic Summit." This would be Margaret Thatcher's first summit and the decision to stand firm against inflation, if nothing else, pleased the new Prime Minister. The harsh tone toward OPEC was undoubtedly a reaction to the proceedings of the OPEC meeting that ended the day before and announced further oil price increases. See the OPEC Press Release of June 28, 1979, in PREM19/27.

115. "Address to the Nation on Energy and National Goals," July 15, 1979, PPPUS.

116. Carter followed up his "malaise" speech with the replacement of several Cabinet members and it was accompanied by a set of legislative proposals. Some were enacted in highly modified form, but neither legislation nor new personnel could offset the political consequences of the administration's failure to offer genuine leadership during the most sustained political and economic crisis of the postwar era. See, among others, Wilentz, *The Age of Reagan*; Dumbrell, *The Carter Presidency*; and Haynes Johnson, *In the Absence of Power* (1980).

4 Thatcher, Reagan and the Market

1. See Keith Joseph to Margaret Thatcher, May 9, 1979, TNA, PREM19/93.

2. Richard Allen, "Ronald Reagan: A Man with a Plan" (2010).

3. Martin Anderson, Reagan domestic policy advisor, recalls that the administration assumed they had only a year to put their stamp on things. See Anderson's interview of Dec. 11–12, 2001, POHP.

4. *President Ronald Reagan's Initial Actions Project*, introduction by Arthur Laffer (2009), pp. 5–6. The report itself was drafted by Richard Wirthlin and David Gergen.

5. Peter Jay to David Owen, "How the Americans See Us," Feb. 13, 1979; Report of Callaghan's meeting with Jay, Mar. 5, 1979; TNA, PREM16/2290.

6. Carter had met Thatcher previously in 1977 and recorded in his diary that "She's obviously an overbearing, not unattractive woman." See Jimmy Carter, *White House Diary* (2010), entry for Sept. 13, 1977, p. 97.

7. Excerpted in Jimmy Carter, *Keeping Faith* (1982), p. 113.

8. Nicholas Henderson to Lord Carrington, Jan. 20, 1981, TNA, FCO 82/1088. The key sections come from an earlier report by David Thomas and Stephen Wall that was attached to Henderson's memo.

9. Margaret Thatcher, *The Downing Street Years* (1993), pp. 68–9. See also Nicholas Henderson, *Mandarin* (1994), pp. 490–3.

10. Text of Thatcher's speech to the Pilgrims Society, Jan. 29, 1981, and cable from Reagan to Thatcher, Feb. 2, 1981, CAC, Papers of Baroness Thatcher, NSC Files, THCR AS 10/2/CD-ROM 1.

11. Thatcher to Reagan, Mar. 5, 1981; Thatcher to Reagan, Mar. 30, 1981; Richard Allen to Reagan, "Letter to Prime Minister Thatcher," n.d. but presumably mid-April 1981; K. L. Kachigian to Dennis Blair, Mar. 16, 1981; CAC, THCR AS 10/2/CD-ROM 2.

12. Lou Cannon, *President Reagan* (1991), p. 466; Reagan to Thatcher, Aug. 4, 1981, CAC, THCR AS 10/2/CD-ROM 4A.

13. See Geoffrey Smith, *Reagan and Thatcher* (1991); Nicholas Wapshott, *Ronald Reagan and Margaret Thatcher* (2007); and Richard Aldous, *Reagan and Thatcher* (2012); and also G. R. Urban, *Diplomacy and Illusion at the Court of Margaret Thatcher* (1996).

14. James Rentschler to Richard Allen, Apr. 28, 1981; Allen to Rentschler, July 31, 1981, "John Louis on a Drifting UK"; Allen to Reagan, "Britain Drifts," n.d. but presumably just after; Allen to Louis, Aug. 17, 1981; CAC, THCR AS 10/2/CD-ROM 4A.

15. Robert McFarlane to Reagan, July 27, 1984; Reagan to Charles Price, July 31, 1984; CAC, THCR AS 10/2/CD-ROM 4A. Reagan and Thatcher would remain protective of one another even after leaving office. See, for example, Ronald Reagan, "Margaret Thatcher and the Revival of the West" (1989); and their respective memoirs.

16. Official quoted anonymously in Robert Putnam and Nicholas Bayne, *Hanging Together* (1987), p. 184. See also Smith, *Reagan and Thatcher*, pp. 106–11.

17. Reagan to Thatcher, June 15, 1983, CAC, THCR AS 10/2/CD-ROM 4A; Thatcher to Reagan, n.d. but clearly Nov. 1984 and, in response, Reagan to Thatcher, Nov. 13, 1984, CAC, THCR AS 10/2/CD-ROM 2.

18. Whether the specific economic reforms put in place by Thatcher and Reagan were effective remains a matter of debate. For one moderately supportive assessment of the Thatcher policies, see David Card, Richard Blundell and Richard B. Freeman, eds., *Seeking a Premier Economy* (2004).

19. Peter Hall, "Policy Paradigms, Social Learning and the State" (1993), pp. 275–96, offers an account focused on the British case alone. For a broader perspective that treats Britain in comparison with Chile, Mexico and France, see Marion Fourcade-Gourinchas and Sarah Babb, "The Rebirth of the Liberal Creed" (2002). Including the U.S. would seem critical, however, for it would also magnify the importance of the shift by emphasizing its effective reach. On the United States, see Ted McAllister, "The Transformation of American Conservatism" (2003); and, for an economists' perspective, James Tobin and Murray Weidenbaum, eds., *Two Revolutions in Economic Policy* (1988). Just why the United States and Great Britain were more susceptible to the appeal of the market is not entirely obvious, but see Monica Prasad, *The Politics of Free Markets* (2006).

20. Eric Hobsbawm, for example, quite likes the phrase. See, for example, his *Globalization, Democracy and Terrorism*, 2007.

21. Friedrich Hayek, *The Road to Serfdom*, 50th anniversary edn. (1994).

22. Andrew Gamble, *Hayek* (1996), p. 76. Gamble's book is a very useful summary of Hayek's life and thought. In his preface to the 1956 paperback edition, Hayek suggests that because the book was published in 1944, with the war on, and with Britain and the United States allied for the moment with the Soviet Union, the critique was unbalanced. As he explained: "in order to get a hearing I had somewhat to restrain myself in my comments on the regime of

our wartime ally and to choose my illustrations mainly from developments in Germany." See *Road to Serfdom*, p. xxvii.

23. See Richard Cockett, *Thinking the Unthinkable* (1994); Angus Burgin, *The Great Persuasion* (2012); Daniel Stedman Jones, *Masters of the Universe* (2012); and also Philip Mirowski and Dieter Plehwe, eds., *The Road from Mont Pèlerin* (2009).

24. Hayek, "'Free' Enterprise and Competitive Order," paper given at the Mont Pelerin Society, Apr. 1, 1947, cited in Cockett, *Thinking the Unthinkable*, p. 113.

25. Milton Friedman, "Preface, 1982," in *Capitalism and Freedom*, 40th anniversary edn (2002), pp. xiii-xiv. This rather uncontroversial comment serves as the starting for Naomi Klein in *The Shock Doctrine* (2007), p. 7.

26. Hayek letter to fellow economic liberals, Dec. 28, 1946, cited in Cockett, *Thinking the Unthinkable*, p. 103.

27. Keith Joseph, interviewed and cited by Cockett, *Thinking the Unthinkable*, p. 237; Andrew Denham and Mark Garnett, *Keith Joseph* (2001), pp. 238-44.

28. See Charles Heatherly, ed., *Mandate for Leadership* (1981); and also Garrett Graff, *The First Campaign* (2007), pp. 27-8, who claims that by the end of the second Reagan administration something like two-thirds of the book's 2,000 recommendations had been implemented.

29. Kevin Phillips, *The Emerging Republican Majority* (1969) was the playbook.

30. Rick Perlstein, *Nixonland* (2008).

31. Irving Kristol, *Reflections of a Neoconservative* (1983). See also John Ehrman, *The Rise of Neoconservatism* (1995); Jacob Heilbrunn, *They Knew They Were Right* (2008); and Justin Vaisse, *Neoconservatism* (2010).

32. Robert Kuttner, *Revolt of the Haves* (1980).

33. Thatcher speech to the Conservative Party conference, Oct. 8, 1975, cited in John Campbell, *Margaret Thatcher*, vol. 1 (2000), p. 391.

34. Cockett, *Thinking the Unthinkable*, pp. 272-4.

35. See John Hunt to Thatcher, May 5, 1979 on the budget and T. P. Lankester's response, addressed to Vile, May 8, 1979, TNA, PREM19/29.

36. Lankester, Report of meeting between Prime Minister and Treasury ministers and officials, May 16, 1979, TNA, PREM19/29. The meeting constituted a dramatic dressing down of the Chancellor of the Exchequer, Geoffrey Howe, in front of his officials and occurred less than two weeks after coming to power. Howe makes no mention of the meeting in his memoir. See Geoffrey Howe, *Conflict of Loyalty* (1994), pp. 126-32.

37. John Campbell, *Margaret Thatcher*, vol. 2 (2004), pp. 51-2. The phrase "dogmatically inegalitarian" came from the *Observer*, June 17, 1979.

38. Cannon, *President Reagan*, pp. 118, 235; Sean Wilentz, *The Age of Reagan* (2008), pp. 140-1.

39. Murray Weidenbaum, Memorandum for the President, "Audit of the U.S. Economy as of January 20, 1981," Feb. 6, 1981, RPL, Weidenbaum Files, OA11007.

40. Martin Anderson insists that the administration was not a captive to supply-side myopia. See Anderson interview, POHP.

41. Alongside the theory went some very fanciful numbers as well, mainly the creation of Reagan's budget director, David Stockman. See William Greider, *The Education of David Stockman and Other Americans* (1982).

42. See M. Adeney and John Lloyd, *The Miners' Strike* (1986).

43. Howe, *Conflict of Loyalty*.

44. The quotes are directly from Kinnock; the estimate of 57% is inferred from Kinnock's statements in response to Scargill as recorded in the transcript of a "Telephone Conversation between Neil Kinnock and Arthur Scargill," Apr. 9, 1994, CAC, Papers of Neil Kinnock, Papers on the Miners' Strike, KNNK 3/23. On April 19, 1984 the NUM formally altered the rule that 55% of workers had to vote yes in order for a strike to be called and substituted 50%, but the executive still did not hold a ballot. See Martin Westlake, *Kinnock* (2001), pp. 288, 298.

45. Reagan to Thatcher, undated but July 18, 1984; and Thatcher to Reagan, July 23, 1984, CAC, NSC Head of State File, THCR.

46. Sir Antony Acland, Interview, BDOHP.

47. Wilentz, *The Age of Reagan*, p. 143; Ronald Reagan, *An American Life* (1990), p. 283.

48. Nicholas Henderson was especially perceptive on the shared sensibilities of Reagan and Thatcher, explaining that the American President "is like Thatcher in having no sentiment or guilty feelings about underdogs." Henderson, *Mandarin*, pp. 485-6.

49. See, for example, David Vogel, *National Styles of Regulation* (1986).
50. Lawson in the House of Commons, Nov. 5, 1981, cited in Campbell, *Margaret Thatcher*, vol. 2, p. 97.
51. Campbell, *Margaret Thatcher*, vol. 2, pp. 94–6, 236–43; Simon Jenkins, *Thatcher and Sons* (2006), p. 92.
52. The total was 368, according to Wilentz, *The Age of Reagan*, p. 187.
53. Data from the International Labour Organization, Labour Statistics Online Database.
54. Data on unemployment has come from the OECD and the U.S. Bureau of Labor Statistics.
55. Wilentz, *The Age of Reagan*, pp. 171–5.
56. Wapshott, *Reagan and Thatcher*, p. 260.
57. Thatcher, speaking to the Conservative Central Council, Mar. 15, 1986, cited in Campbell, *Margaret Thatcher*, vol.. 2, p. 499.
58. Richard Vinen, *Thatcher's Britain* (2010), p. 260.
59. Thatcher, *The Downing Street Years*, p. 661.
60. Cannon, *President Reagan*, pp. 539–45.
61. See Greta Krippner, *Capitalizing on Crisis* (2011), pp. 92–105.
62. Reagan, *An American Life*, p. 335.
63. See Jeffrey Birnbaum and Alan Murray, *Showdown at Gucci Gulch* (1987); Wilentz, *The Age of Reagan*, pp. 205–6; Cannon, *President Reagan*, pp. 565–6; and Cathie Jo Martin, *Shifting the Burden* (1991). The rate on capital gains was, however, increased from 20% to 38%.
64. The original Act was ruled unconstitutional, requiring the passage of the revised version in 1987. This was in turn replaced by the Budget Enforcement Act of 1990, which was the context in which George Bush violated his "no new taxes" pledge and permanently alienated the antitax enthusiasts in the Republican Party.
65. Jonathan Rauch, "Gramm-Rudman" (2005).
66. James Baker to Howard Baker, "Draft memo to the Boss . . . on budget," Sept. 16, 1987, BP, Box 98, Folder 4.
67. Reagan, *An American Life*, pp. 335–6.

5 Market Rules and the International Economy

1. Eric Helleiner, *States and the Reemergence of Global Finance* (1994); Kathleen McNamara, *The Currency of Ideas* (1998), ch. 4.
2. By summer 1981 the Reagan administration had put together a four-point program on trade that Alexander Haig referred to as "Free trade tinged with patriotism." "The programme," according to John Fretwell (Chargé d'Affaires, Washington), "is regarded within the Administration as the most dedicated commitment to free trade by any US Government for many years." Fretwell to Lord Carrington, June 29, 1981, TNA, FCO 82/1128.
3. Greta Krippner, *Capitalizing on Crisis* (2011).
4. Judith Stein, *Pivotal Decade* (2010), pp. 154–75.
5. Ronald Reagan, *The Reagan Diaries* (2007), entry for July 20–21, 1981, pp. 31–2.
6. See Robert Putnam and Nicholas Bayne, *Hanging Together* (1987), pp. 127–8, which also quotes from Reagan's Sept. 29, 1981 speech to the Annual Meeting of the World Bank and the IMF.
7. McNamara, *Currency of Ideas*, pp. 136–9; Rawi Abdelal, *Capital Rules* (2007), pp. 58–64. See also Ben Clift, *French Socialism in a Global Era* (2003); and George Ross, "The Limits of Political Economy" (1996).
8. Trichet and Naouri were interviewed by Abdelal and quoted in *Capital Rules*, p. 62.
9. Baker swapped jobs with Donald Regan. See Lou Cannon, *President Reagan* (1991), pp. 555–9.
10. Regan, speaking at the IMF, cited in Harold James, *International Monetary Cooperation since Bretton Woods* (1996), p. 431.
11. James Baker with Steve Fiffer, *"Work Hard, Study . . . and Keep Out of Politics!"* (2006), pp. 427–33.
12. On the new arrangement within the administration, see the White House announcement, Apr. 11, 1985, BP, Box 96, Folder 9; and also Peter Kilborn, "How the Big Six Steer the Economy" (1985).

13. The move had the support of centrist Democrats such as Bill Bradley who regarded devaluation as a mechanism to hold back more protectionist efforts in Congress. See memos in RPL, Beryl Sprinkel Papers, OA17741.

14. James, *International Monetary Cooperation since Bretton Woods*, pp. 435–7.

15. Alasdair Roberts, *The Logic of Discipline* (2010), pp. 58–62.

16. David Butler and Uwe Kitzinger, *The 1975 Referendum* (1976); Stephen Wall, *The Official History of Britain and the European Community*, vol. 2 (2013), ch. 10.

17. Margaret Thatcher, *The Downing Street Years* (1993), p. 64.

18. P. Lever to M. Alexander, Nov. 30, 1979, TNA, PREM19/55 and also the correspondence in PREM19/133.

19. John Campbell, *Margaret Thatcher*, vol. 2 (2004), pp. 59–69, 305–7; Geoffrey Howe, *Conflict of Loyalty* (1994), pp. 401–3; Stephen Wall, *A Stranger in Europe* (2008), pp. 18–40.

20. Andrew Glyn, *Capitalism Unleashed* (2006), pp. 37–49.

21. Jeffry Frieden, *Global Capitalism* (2006), pp. 392–412.

22. See George Ross, *Jacques Delors and European Integration* (1995), pp. 1–15, 26–9.

23. Thatcher, *The Downing Street Years*, p. 314.

24. "Europe – The Future," June 1984, TNA, PREM19/1229. For the background, see Wall, *A Stranger in Europe*, pp. 41–2, 47–9; and Duccio Basosi, "The European Community and International Reaganomics" (2013).

25. Ross, *Jacques Delors and European Integration*, pp. 30–3, sees the successful negotiation of the Single European Act largely as a victory for Delors and the Commission itself. That its mandating of the single market project should also have been a signal British, indeed Thatcherite, achievement was ironic, but in certain ways appropriate.

26. Abdelal, in *Capital Rules*, ch. 4, somewhat mischievously attributes the move toward more open markets to an emerging "Paris Consensus," and he is echoed by Mark Mazower, *Governing the World* (2012), pp. 409–10.

27. See High Level Group on the Functioning of the Internal Market, *The Internal Market after 1992* (1992). Sutherland would go on to serve as the final Director of the GATT and the first Director of the World Trade Organization (WTO) and would then join Goldman Sachs.

28. Abdelal, *Capital Rules*, pp. 65–71. The quote from Delors is on p. 66.

29. OECD, *Forty Years' Experience* (2002), pp. 27–8.

30. Abdelal, *Capital Rules*, pp. 86–106.

31. Margaret Thatcher, speaking to the Franco-British Council in November 1984, quoted in Wall, *A Stranger in Europe*, pp. 46–7.

32. Ross, *Jacques Delors and European Integration*, pp. 40–5. Especially provocative was Delors's decision to speak at the British Trades Union Congress in 1988. It was clear to Thatcher that by 1988 Delors "had altogether slipped his leash as a *fonctionnaire* and become a fully-fledged spokesman for federalism." See Thatcher, *The Downing Street Years*, p. 742; and also Campbell, *Margaret Thatcher*, vol. 2, p. 603.

33. Michael Clarke, *British External Policy-Making in the 1990s* (1992), p. 47.

34. Leon Brittan, 1996, quoted in Sophie Meunier, *Trading Voices* (2005).

35. "Fast-track" authority allows the President and the Trade Representative to negotiate a package and have it voted up or down by Congress as a whole, making it harder to pick agreements apart. The first such grant was made in 1974 as part of the Trade Reform Act.

36. See John Gillingham, *European Integration* (2003), pp. 105–20, for a useful discussion of "The New Protectionism" and "Neomercantilism" in Europe during the 1970s.

37. See I. M. Destler, *American Trade Politics* (1995).

38. Steve Dryden, *Trade Warriors* (1995), pp. 275–7. William Brock, America's top trade negotiator, came up with a White Paper on trade in 1981 and presented its contents to Congress in July, but encountered considerable opposition.

39. William Niskanen, *Reaganomics* (1988), p. 138.

40. See James Shoch, *Trading Blows* (2001), chs. 3–5; Dryden, *Trade Warriors*, chs. 13–16; and Niskanen, *Reaganomics*.

41. Claude Cheysson, France's Foreign Minister, had responded to the announcement of the U.S. pipeline decision in June 1982 by claiming: "This day could well go down as the beginning of the end of the Atlantic Alliance." Cited in Dryden, *Trade Warriors*, pp. 282–3.

42. William Drake and Kalypso Nicolaïdis, "Ideas, Interests and Institutionalization" (1992).

43. Unemployment rose to 7.4% in the summer of 1985 and hovered just over 7% for the next year or more. Data from the OECD and the U.S. Bureau of Labor Statistics.

44. The "Multi-Fiber Agreement," one of the most significant deviations from free trade principles, had been negotiated in the mid–1970s but was about to expire in 1986. The Reagan administration secured a five-year extension.
45. Cited in Shoch, *Trading Blows*, p. 113.
46. Hugo Paemen and Alexandra Bensch, *From the GATT to the WTO* (1995), pp. 43–60, 269–80.
47. De Clercq, cited in Drake and Nicolaïdis, "Ideas, Interests and Institutionalization," p. 57, see also p. 77.
48. See BP, Box 98, Folder 4 on the "Trade Bill 1988."
49. See I. M. Destler, "U.S. Trade Policy-Making in the Eighties" (1991); Shoch, *Trading Blows*; and Jagdish Bhagwati and H. T. Patrick, eds., *Aggressive Unilateralism* (1990).
50. See David Kynaston, *The City of London*, vol. 4 (2001); and Richard Melcher, "The City of London Wanted Competition – But Not This Much" (1987).
51. Gillingham, *European Integration*, p. 271.
52. Helleiner, *States and Global Finance*.
53. Daniel Rodgers, *The Age of Fracture* (2011), p. 74.
54. Kathryn Lavelle, *Legislating International Organization* (2011), ch. 5.
55. Ngaire Woods, *The Globalizers* (2006), pp. 28–33; and also Sarah Babb, *Behind the Development Banks* (2009).
56. See John Toye and Richard Toye, *The UN and Global Political Economy* (2004).
57. See Jagdish Bhagwati and John G. Ruggie, eds., *Power, Passions and Purpose* (1984).
58. "The Mexico Summit," Report by the Official Committee on Relations with Developing Countries, July 8, 1981, TNA, PREM 19/445. See also the correspondence and reports on the Brandt Commission in PREM 19/435, which includes an intervention by Edward Heath sharply critical of the U.K. government's stance.
59. Thatcher, *The Downing Street Years*, pp. 168–70.
60. Reagan's remarks reported in TNA, FCO 82/1104.
61. James Broughton, *The Silent Revolution* (2001), p. 2.
62. These have since been joined by the European Bank for Reconstruction and Development, set up in 1991.
63. U.S. Treasury Department, *United States Participation in the Multilateral Development Banks in the 1980s* (1982), cited in Babb, *Behind the Development Banks*, pp. 88, 99.
64. See Helleiner, *States and Global Finance*, pp. 176–83; Joseph Kraft, *The Mexican Rescue* (1984).
65. See Babb, *Managing Mexico* (2004).
66. Kraft, *The Mexican Rescue*, p. 39; *New York Times*, Sept. 2 and Oct. 1, 1982.
67. Nigel Lawson, *The View from Number 11* (1992), p. 520, cited in Toye and Toye, *The UN and Global Political Economy*, p. 260.
68. The details on these various packages come mainly from James, *International Monetary Cooperation since Bretton Woods*, ch. 12.
69. For an example of the administration's change of tune, see RPL, Beryl Sprinkel Papers, OA 17757, which mentions a White House Dinner on Third World Debt on Sept. 10, 1986 and includes among the notes for discussion "LDC Growth Benefits the United States Directly" and "LDC's Need to Become Outward Rather than Inward Looking."
70. The OECD would also publicly commit to the new orthodoxy. OECD, *OECD Jobs Study* (1994).
71. See Babb, "The Washington Consensus as Policy Paradigm" (2103).
72. See John Williamson, "What Washington Means by Policy Reform" (1990), pp. 7–20. The paper came from a conference held in November 1989.
73. John Williamson, "Did the Washington Consensus Fail?" (2002).
74. Anne Krueger, "Trade Policy and Economic Development" (1997).

6 Cold War Ironies: Reagan and Thatcher at Large

1. There is a rather large literature about how the making of foreign policy differs fundamentally from the making and execution of domestic policy. For a classic statement, see Aaron Wildavsky's 1966 essay on "The Two Presidencies," which suggests that U.S. Presidents have an easier time abroad than at home.
2. The comment was made and first reported in the *Wall Street Journal*, June 3, 1980, and cited again by Anthony Lewis in the *New York* Times, Oct. 20, 1980.

3. Margaret Thatcher, "Speech to the Zurich Economic Society" (1987), p. 25; and *The Sinews of Foreign Policy* (1978), in Margaret Thatcher, *In Defence of Freedom* (1987), p. 50.
4. Ronald Reagan, *The Reagan Diaries* (2007), entry for Feb. 26, 1981, p. 5.
5. See the tense correspondence in TNA, PREM19/1048.
6. A major contribution of Odd Arne Westad's *The Global Cold War* (2005) has been to document and explain Soviet assertiveness in the age of détente, esp. pp. 202–6.
7. Morris Blachman and Kenneth Sharpe, "De-democratising American Foreign Policy" (1986).
8. "Excerpts from Haig's Remarks at First News Conference as Secretary of State," *New York Times*, Jan. 29, 1981; Elliott Abrams, "The Main Threat to Human Rights Is the Soviet Union," *U.S. News and World Report*, Sept. 10, 1984, cited in Raymond Garthoff, *The Great Transition* (1994), pp. 24, 26; and Jeane Kirkpatrick, "Dictatorships and Double Standards" (1979).
9. The move was sudden and some observers regarded it as merely an effort to update Western strategies for maintaining global hegemony. See Nicolas Guilhot, *The Democracy Makers* (2005); and also William Robinson, *Promoting Polyarchy* (1986).
10. James Mann, *The Rebellion of Ronald Reagan* (2009).
11. See James Cronin, *The World the Cold War Made* (1996) on the background.
12. On at least one issue, the grain embargo, Reagan was less aggressive than Carter, for he believed it "had probably hurt our American farmers more than it hurt the Russians." Ronald Reagan, *An American Life* (1990), p. 238.
13. Haig, Sept. 13, 1981; and Reagan, Mar. 1982, cited in Garthoff, *Great Transition*, pp. 40–1; entry for Feb. 18, 1981, *Reagan Diaries*, p. 70; excerpt from Reagan's letter to Brezhnev, in Reagan, *An American Life*, p. 271.
14. Thatcher, in the House of Commons, June 5, 1980, quoted in John Campbell, *Margaret Thatcher*, vol. 2 (2003), p. 188. See also Margaret Thatcher, *The Downing Street Years* (1993), pp. 239–44.
15. Tami Davis Biddle, "Shield and Sword" (2007), p. 175. See also Sean Wilentz, *The Age of Reagan* (2008), p. 154.
16. Reagan, "Remarks and a Question-and-Answer Session at a Working Luncheon with Out-of-Town Editors," Oct. 16, 1981, PPPUS.
17. The plan is outlined in National Security Decision Directive 6-83, "Study on Eliminating the Threat Posed by Ballistic Missiles," Apr. 18, 1983, DNSA. The British were always skeptical, but Thatcher was formally supportive. See TNA, PREM 19/1188.
18. See, among others, Jeffrey Herf, *War by Other Means* (1991).
19. Reagan, "Remarks at the Annual Convention of the National Association of Evangelicals," Mar. 8, 1983, PPPUS.
20. The Reagan administration moved quickly to exploit the incident to discredit the Soviets at what was a critically important moment – just before the deployment of Euromissiles. See National Security Decision Directive 102, "U.S. Response to Soviet Destruction of KAL Airliner," Sept. 5, 1983, DNSA. As the Directive put it, "Soviet brutality in this incident presents an opportunity to reverse the false moral and political 'peacemaker' perception that their regime has been cultivating."
21. The Soviets were genuinely worried about U.S. rearmament and its possible aggressive intent. They became especially agitated during the NATO military exercise known as "Able Archer 83" in November 1983. See Garthoff, *Great Transition*, pp. 138–40.
22. Thatcher, *The Downing Street Years*, pp. 242–3.
23. David Gergen, quoted in Jeffrey Knopf, *Domestic Society and International Cooperation* (1998), p. 224.
24. *New York Times*, July 28, 1982.
25. See Reagan's "Address to the Nation on Defense and National Security," Mar. 23, 1983, PPPUS.
26. Reagan, *An American Life*, p. 566.
27. Thatcher, *The Downing Street Years*, p. 267.
28. Interview with Lord Hurd, Mar. 9, 2011.
29. Paul Lettow, *Ronald Reagan and His Quest to Abolish Nuclear Weapons* (2005); and Beth Fischer, *The Reagan Reversal* (1997).
30. James Carroll, *House of War* (2006), pp. 385–95.
31. See Chris Saunders and Sue Onslow, "The Cold War and Southern Africa" (2010).
32. Thatcher, *The Downing Street Years*, p. 73.

33. Campbell, *Margaret Thatcher*, vol. 2, p. 71.
34. Interview with Anthony Parsons, British Ambassador to the UN, BDOHP. There was tremendous suspicion of Britain at the UN, Parsons recalls, and he concludes that "if it hadn't been for the existence of the Commonwealth I don't think we would have got through this . . ."
35. For a striking example, see the chapter on "Human Rights and Wrongs" in Margaret Thatcher's *Statecraft* (2002), pp. 248–81, in which she concludes that "Conservatives everywhere must go on the counter-offensive against the New Left human rights brigade . . ."
36. Garthoff, *Great Transition*, pp. 712–13, 725–30.
37. See John Dinges, *The Condor Years* (2004); John Coatsworth, "The Cold War in Central America" (2010); and Thomas Borstelmann, *The 1970s* (2012), pp. 219–20.
38. In his memoir *Caveat* (1984), Alexander Haig claims that it was the Falklands that cost him his job.
39. "U.S. Actions in the South Atlantic Crisis," National Security Council Decision Directive 34, May 14, 1982, DNSA, PD01627; Caspar Weinberger, Background Interview, Aug. 1997, for *CW*, LHCMA. More broadly, see Lawrence Freedman, *Official History of the Falklands Campaign* (2005) and also Robin Renwick, *A Journey with Margaret Thatcher* (2013), chs. 4–5.
40. Memcon [memorandum of conversation] Reagan to Thatcher, May 31, 1982, RPL, U.K., 1/20/81–8/31/81, Box 20. A transcription of the same phone call can be found in TNA, PREM 19/633; and it is summarized in Freedman, *The Official History of the Falklands Campaign*, vol. 2, p. 516.
41. See "U.S. Policy toward the Americas as a result of the Falklands Crisis," June 23, 1982, National Security Study Directive 10–82, DNSA, PD01514, which ordered a review of strategy after the end of the war and the resignation of Galtieri, leader of the Argentine junta.
42. Thatcher, *The Downing Street Years*, pp. 326–35. Geoffrey Howe believes that the U.K. backed the U.S. over the Libyan air strikes in part because of Ireland. The U.S. and U.K. were at the time nearing a deal with the U.S. Senate to ratify the U.S./U.K. Supplementary Extradition Treaty, which the Senate approved in July 1986. Author interview with Lord Howe, Mar. 9, 2011.
43. George Shultz, *Turmoil and Triumph* (1993), p. 621.
44. See Thomas Carothers, *In the Name of Democracy* (1991); Hal Brands, *Latin America's Cold War* (2010); and Peter Smith, *Talons of the Eagle* (2012). On democratic transitions more broadly, see Larry Diamond and Marc Plattner, eds., *The Global Resurgence of Democracy* (1996); Juan Linz and Alfred Stepan, *Problems of Democratic Transition* (1996); and Larry Diamond, *The Spirit of Democracy* (2008). The most remarkable turnaround in U.S. policy occurred in Chile, where the U.S. began to qualify its support as early as 1983. By the time of the plebiscite on the continuation of Pinochet's rule in October 1988, the U.S. had become actively involved in ensuring that the vote was fair and its result was respected by Pinochet. Recent documents suggest that Pinochet was prepared to ignore the vote against him, but that the U.S. played a crucial role in preventing that. See National Security Archive Electronic Briefing Book No. 413, Feb. 22, 2013, ed. Peter Kornbluh, NSA website; and also Stern, *Battling for Hearts and Minds* (2006).
45. "Assessing America's Options in the Philippines," Feb. 3, 1986, transcript of meeting held by the House Committee on Foreign Relations, Subcommittee on Asian and Pacific Affairs, DNSA.
46. Shultz, *Turmoil and Triumph*, p. 625.
47. On the process, see Robert Jackson, "The Weight of Ideas in Decolonization" (1993); and Gerry Simpson, "The Diffusion of Sovereignty" (2000).
48. See Tony Smith, *America's Mission* (1994), ch. 2. Those closest to the scene attributed Marcos's fall, and the peaceful transition that accompanied it, largely to the Catholic Church and its local leader, Cardinal Sin. For a more general argument about the role of the Catholic Church in the process of democratization in this period, see Samuel Huntington, *The Third Wave* (1993). See also Jeremi Suri, *Liberty's Surest Guardian* (2012), ch. 3.
49. Shultz, *Turmoil and Triumph*, pp. 623–4.
50. "U. S. National Security Strategy," Apr. 1982, DNSA, PR01452. There is no single articulation of the Reagan Doctrine, though Reagan's own speeches are clear enough in their meaning and Shultz sought to give it more weight and coherence in a series of pronouncements. The State Department, on its website, points to two particular statements – National Security

Decision Directive 75 on "U.S. Relations with the USSR," Jan. 17, 1983, DNSA, PR01485; and Reagan's 1985 Inaugural Address.

51. See Carothers, *In the Name of Democracy*, esp. ch. 1 and also pp. 130–1.
52. Efforts to influence public and Congressional opinion of course predated this. See "National Security Decision Directive on Cuba and Central America," DNSA, NSDD 37, May 28, 1982.
53. "Central America: Promoting Democracy, Economic Improvement, and Peace," DNSA, NSDD 124, Feb. 7, 1984.
54. Post-Iran/Contra strategy is laid out in the National Security Decision Directive on "Central America," Oct. 22, 1986, DNSA (NSDD no. obscured on copy).
55. Shultz, *Turmoil and Triumph*, pp. 401–4.
56. Westad, *The Global Cold War*, pp. 394–5. In the elections themselves, the indirect role of the U.S. was quite significant. U.S. meddling had severely disrupted the economy and led many Nicaraguans to believe that getting rid of the Sandinistas would bring material benefits.
57. Interview with Sir Anthony Parsons, BDOHP.
58. Chester Crocker, "South Africa: Strategy for Change" (1980–1) and also "Southern Africa: Eight Years Later" (1989).
59. Haig, *Caveat*, p. 242.
60. Thatcher met with Haig on Jan. 29, 1982. See Thatcher, *The Downing Street Years*, pp. 254–6.
61. The resolution did not come until November 1982, when Shultz negotiated a deal whereby the U.S. would remove the embargo and in exchange other Western countries would limit future gas purchases and in general tighten Soviet access to credit and technology. See "East-West Economic Relations and Poland-Related Sanctions," National Security Decision Directive 66, Nov. 16, 1982, DNSA 01477.
62. On that earlier process, see Anne Appelbaum, *The Iron Curtain* (2012).
63. Reagan, *The Reagan Diaries*, entry for Dec. 21, 1981, p. 57.
64. Ronald Reagan, "Address to Members of the British Parliament," June 8, 1982, PPPUS.
65. Record of Meeting between Ronald Reagan and Margaret Thatcher, June 9, 1982, TNA, PREM 19/942. See also Thatcher, *The Downing Street Years*, p. 258. The invitation to Reagan was controversial and the President's advisors considered cancelling. The idea for the speech was apparently William Whitelaw's, but Thatcher was especially eager that it happen. See the telegram from the American Embassy, London, to the Secretary of State, Mar. 22, 1982, RPL, U.K., Box 20, which explains that "The Prime Minister considers it very important that the President address Parliament and believes it would be a serious error to be seen to bow to opposition pressure and not make a speech."
66. "Nuclear Weapons Employment Policy," National Security Decision Directive 13, Oct. 19, 1981, DNSA 01443.
67. "U.S. National Security Strategy," National Security Study Directive 1–82, Feb. 5, 1982, DNSA 01646.
68. "Proposed Statement by the President," May 13, 1982, DNSA 01453.
69. "U.S. National Security Strategy," National Security Decision Directive 32, May 20, 1982, DNSA 01451.
70. "U.S. National Security Strategy," Apr. 1982.
71. This was the argument made by Richard Pipes, who was at the time working within the National Security Council. See Pipes, *Vixi* (2003), pp. 188–202.
72. Garthoff, *The Great Transition*, p. 31. The Mossad also lent a hand.
73. "U.S. Policy toward the Soviet Union," National Security Study Directive 11–82, Aug. 21, 1982, DNSA 01654.
74. "United States Policy toward Eastern Europe," National Security Decision Directive 54, Sept. 2, 1982, DNSA 01475.
75. Shultz, *Turmoil and Triumph*, pp. 126–7.
76. See Jack Matlock, *Reagan and Gorbachev* (2004), pp. 52–4, and Garthoff, *Great Transition*, p. 33, for slightly different interpretations of the document's significance.
77. "U.S. Relations with the USSR," National Security Decision Directive 75, Jan. 17, 1983, DNSA 01485.
78. The Team B exercise in 1976 was a classic example. Team B was appointed by then CIA Director George Bush to review and, by implication, to second-guess internal CIA assessments of Soviet capabilities and intentions. Pipes was involved in this earlier exercise as well as in the drafting of the new U.S. strategy toward the Soviets. See Pipes, *Vixi*, pp. 132–43.

79. Reagan, *An American Life*, p. 594. The excerpt comes from Reagan's diaries but is not included in the published version of the *Diaries*.

80. Thatcher used virtually the same words during a meeting with Reagan a few days later. See TNA, PREM 19/1394. For her recollection a couple of years later, see Thatcher, interview in the *New Yorker*, Feb. 10, 1986. In her memoir Thatcher used the phrase "wooden ventriloquism" to describe the behavior of the typical Soviet leader. See *The Downing Street Years*, pp. 450–3, 459–63.

81. The summits have been well chronicled. The memoirs of Reagan, Thatcher, Shultz and Howe give quite thorough accounts as do the biographies of Reagan and Thatcher by Cannon and Campbell. Garthoff's account in *The Great Transition* is even more detailed, but see also Don Oberdorfer, *From the Cold War to a New Era* (1998); Matlock, *Reagan and Gorbachev*; and David Reynolds, *Summits* (2007), ch. 7.

82. Peter Schweizer, *Reagan's War* (2002).

83. Biddle, "Shield and Sword," pp. 177–8.

84. This paragraph relies on summaries of Soviet thinking in Garthoff, *Great Transition*, pp. 214–15, 253–65. The Shevardnadze quote is from his book, *The Future Belongs to Freedom* (1991).

85. See Sidney Drell, Philip Farley and David Holloway, *The Reagan SDI* (1985).

86. On UK attitudes and discussions with the US over "Star Wars", see TNA PREM 19/1188, "Military Uses of Laser Technology in Space: The US Strategic Defense Initiative."

87. Reagan and Nitze are both quoted in Shultz, *Turmoil and Triumph*, p. 760.

88. Thatcher, *The Downing Street Years*, pp. 470–3.

89. Gorbachev recognized the importance of the breakthrough and told the Politburo that it represented the "normalization of the international situation in general." See Gorbachev's Report to the Politburo Session of Dec. 17, 1987, CWIHP, Document Reader on "The Euromissiles Crisis and the End of the Cold War: 1977–1987," part 4, section B.

90. Garthoff, *Great Transition*, pp. 365–8.

91. Philip Zelikow and Condoleezza Rice, *Germany Unified and Europe Transformed* (1995), p. 16.

7 Ending the Cold War and Recreating Europe

1. Ronald Reagan, "Remarks on East-West Relations at the Brandenburg Gate in West Berlin," June 12, 1987, PPPUS; and Fred Taylor, *The Berlin Wall* (2006).

2. George Bush and Brent Scowcroft, *A World Transformed* (1998), pp. 148–51. (Bush and Scowcroft's book is written in three separate voices. There are sections in Bush's words, sections in Scowcroft's words, and a third voice, a "narrative 'we' that represents the two of us and, more broadly, the Administration." This third voice was most likely that of James McCall, who seems to have overseen the research and much of the writing.) See also Margaret Thatcher, *The Downing Street Years* (1993), pp. 793–4; and John Major, *The Autobiography* (1999), p. 277.

3. This was, of course, the import of Francis Fukuyama's essay on "The End of History" (1989), and his subsequent book, *The End of History and the Last Man* (1992). He was not foolish enough to think that history was at an end, although he did fool some academics into thinking that was his point. For a judicious assessment, see David Runciman, *Confidence Trap* (2013), pp. 225–41. Fukuyama was working at the State Department when his essay was written and published, and presumably it was aimed at furthering the strategic aims of the Bush administration. In fact, Fukuyama was quite directly involved in the framing of U.S. policy on Europe and German unification. See James Baker with Thomas DeFrank, *The Politics of Diplomacy* (1995), p. 168; and Philip Zelikow and Condoleezza Rice, *Germany Unified and Europe Transformed* (1995), pp. 113, 132.

4. The scholarly interest in different styles of capitalism was itself a product of the fact that after 1989 non-capitalist paths were no longer seen as viable options for development. See Peter Hall and David Soskice, eds., *Varieties of Capitalism* (2001).

5. In *1989* (2009), Mary Elise Sarotte argues convincingly that what prevailed in a united Germany was a "prefab" model crafted in West Germany. More globally, however, it was a more Anglo-American, or neoliberal, model that was predominant, albeit with many local variations. See also Wade Jacoby, *The Enlargement of the European Union and NATO* (2004).

6. Melvyn Leffler, *For the Soul of Mankind* (2007), pp. 417–21.

7. Raymond Garthoff, *The Great Transition* (1994), pp. 365–7.

8. Mark Kramer, "The Demise of the Soviet Bloc" (2011).

9. Gale Stokes, *The Walls Came Tumbling Down* (1993), pp. 121–30, for a compelling narrative. See, for a more recent assessment, Stephen Kotkin with Jan Gross, *Uncivil Society* (2009). On Germany in particular, see Charles Maier, *Dissolution* (1997).

10. Gorbachev, cited in Garthoff, *The Great Transition*, p. 602. More generally, see Hannes Adomeit, *Imperial Overstretch* (1998); Jonathan Haslam, *Russia's Cold War* (2011); and Vladislav Zubok, *Failed Empire* (2007).

11. On the options opened up and the outcome, see Sarotte, *1989*.

12. Michael Beschloss and Strobe Talbott, *At the Highest Levels* (1993), pp. 171–5.

13. There is now a substantial literature on German unification and the end of the Cold War and the documentary record is unusually full and open. When Bush, Baker and Scowcroft wrote their firsthand accounts, of course, they had direct access to all the documents. Beschloss and Talbott were clearly also given relatively free access for *At the Highest Level* and Zelikow and Rice also had the key documents at hand when writing *Germany Unified and Europe Transformed*, and Raymond Garthoff seems to have seen everything and talked with nearly everyone. So, too, Dan Oberdorfer. There are several major works based on apparently different levels of access: Konrad Jarausch's study, *The Rush to German Unity* (1994), for example, does not seem to be based on privileged access, but is full nonetheless. He and others – e.g., Frank Costigliola, "An 'Arm around the Shoulder'" (1994) – were apparently able to piece things together by making use of the extensive documentation made available even as the events proceeded. The largest early selection was collected in Lawrence Freedman, ed., *Europe Transformed* (1990). More recent studies, such as Sarotte's and Frédéric Bozo's important *Mitterrand, the End of the Cold War, and German Unification* (2009) make new and interesting arguments and they have tracked down many of the original sources on which earlier studies were based. They have not, by and large, revised or refuted those accounts. For a recent addition to the documentary record, see the important collection of British government documents: Patrick Salmon, Keith Hamilton and Stephen Twigge, eds., *German Unification, 1989–1990* (2010). Also added since the early 1990s are various oral history interviews. A number were recorded in 1997 as part of a British documentary (*CW*, LHCMA); many more were done under the auspices of the Miller Center at the University of Virginia.

14. Eric Hobsbawm puts the issue clearly enough, taking the late Tony Judt and others to task for "creating the fairy tale of the Velvet and multicoloured revolutions of 1989 and after. There were no such revolutions, only different reactions to the Soviet decision to pull out." See Eric Hobsbawm, "After the Cold War" (2012), p. 14.

15. Nigel Broomfield to Geoffrey Howe, Apr. 20, 1989, in Salmon, Hamilton and Twigge, *German Unification*, p. 11.

16. Zelikow and Rice, *Germany Unified and Europe Transformed*, p. 148.

17. Thatcher was not alone among British politicians in her concerns over Germany. James Callaghan, the former Prime Minister, wrote to George Bush that though German unification was inevitable, "it must be channeled into a wide European settlement that will render harmless that Teutonic tendency to give way to angst at regular intervals." Callaghan to George Bush, June 3, 1989, BPL, WHORM Subject Files, FO006-01, "NATO Summit in Belgium, 5/29–30/89.

18. Sir Patrick Wright to Stephen Wall, Oct. 30, 1989, in Salmon, Hamilton and Twigge, *German Unification*, pp. 78–80. Wright was Permanent Under-Secretary at the Foreign and Commonwealth Office and Wall was private secretary to the Foreign Secretary, Geoffrey Howe.

19. Sarotte, *1989*, pp. 72–5.

20. On the Malta Summit of Dec. 3, 1989, see BP, notes in Box 176, Folder 9.

21. Andrew Carpendale to Thomas DeFrank, "Top Ten Meetings, Moments, Mistakes, Controversies," May 24, 1993, BP, Box 176, Folder 33; and "Notes for Post-Malta Discussions with European Leaders," BP, Box 108, Folder 12 (Dec. 1989).

22. Bozo, *Mitterrand*, ch. 3.

23. Gorbachev had begun talking of "Europe" as "our home. Home, and not a 'theatre of military operations'" as early as December 1984, when he spoke to the British Parliament. See Garthoff, *The Great Transition*, 587. The contrast with Vladimir Putin, who chooses to regard Europe as a decadent force to be resisted, makes it clear how remarkable a figure Gorbachev was.

24. Mitterrand's New Year's Eve message is quoted in Bozo, *Mitterrand*, p. 147.

25. Elisabeth Guigou to Mitterrand, early January 1990, cited in Bozo, *Mitterrand*, p. 347.
26. Interview with James Baker III, Mar. 17, 2011, POHP.
27. Bush, in Bush and Scowcroft, *A World Transformed*, pp. 67, 69–70.
28. Thatcher, *The Downing Street Years*, pp. 782–3. Thatcher regarded Baker even less favorably, as a mere "fixer."
29. Condoleezza Rice, interviewed Dec. 17, 1997 for the Cold War series, CW, LHCMA.
30. See Baker's note from the new administration's first Cabinet meeting, Jan. 23, 1989, BP, Box 108, Folder 1.
31. Baker, *The Politics of Diplomacy*, ch. 4.
32. Noriega had taken refuge in the Papal Nunciature in Panama City and Baker was trying to contact the Vatican on Christmas Day. See BP, note in Box 108, Folder 12.
33. The remark was made in a discussion with the Canadian Prime Minister, Brian Mulroney, and is quoted in Baker, *The Politics of Diplomacy*, p. 86.
34. These were the Mutual and Balanced Force Reduction talks and were originally part of the negotiations that produced Helsinki.
35. The phrase actually came from Charles Powell, Thatcher's top advisor. See Powell's Feb. 9, 1997 interview, CW, LHCMA. See also Sir John Fretwell, FCO, to Sir Christopher Mallaby, May 18, 1989, in Salmon, Hamilton and Twigge, *German Unification*, p. 16.
36. NSC Memo and Scowcroft note to Bush, "The NATO Summit," Mar. 20, 1998, cited in Zelikow and Rice, *Germany Unified and Europe Transformed*, p. 28.
37. "May 15th Draft NATO Policy," by RBZ (Robert Zoellick), BP, Box 115, Folder 6.
38. Bush's remarks had been made in a discussion with Brian Mulroney on February 10, 1989 and are cited in Baker, *The Politics of Diplomacy*, p. 86.
39. Interview with Brent Scowcroft, Nov. 12–13, 1999, POHP.
40. Scowcroft to Bush, May 25, 1989, in BPL, WHORM Files FO006–1. Earlier, in 1986, the Reagan administration had proposed a plan for a "Berlin without Barriers" initiative, to be timed for the twenty-fifth anniversary of the building of the wall. It was meant to embarrass the Soviets and East Germans but also to influence German opinion: "The time is also right for a broad initiative to counter the spreading German view that the Allied role in Berlin is outdated." See Steve Sestanovich to Admiral Poindexter, July 24, 1986, RPL, files of the NSC, European and Soviet Affairs Directorate, Box 1.
41. As Charles Maier has argued insightfully, "The crisis of the Soviet empire precluded a crisis of American hegemony in Europe." See Charles Maier, *Among Empires* (2006), p. 247.
42. See Baker's notes on his March 8 meeting with Shevardnadze, BP, Box 108, Folder 6.
43. "Remarks to Citizens in Hamtramck," Apr. 17, 1989; "Remarks at the Texas A&M University Commencement Ceremony," May 12, 1989; "Remarks at the Boston University Commencement Ceremony," May 21, 1989; "Remarks at the U.S. Coast Guard Academy Commencement Ceremony," May 24, 1989, all available at PPPUS.
44. Bush, in Bush and Scowcroft, *A World Transformed*, p. 68.
45. On April 29 Richard Cheney, the Secretary of Defense, had expressed doubts about Gorbachev's ability to reform the USSR successfully. The statement contradicted Washington's general line and he was rebuked. The Soviets remembered and wanted a more public affirmation of the administration's support, presumably for internal reasons.
46. Baker, *The Politics of Diplomacy*, pp. 75–6, 80–2.
47. The figure of 20% was reached by focusing only on combat troops, not other forces; and the proposed reductions would lower Soviet forces by 325,000 while U.S. forces would shrink by only 30,000.
48. Bush and Scowcroft, *A World Transformed*, p. 80.
49. See Dan Oberdorfer, *From the Cold War to a New Era* (1998), pp. 345–52; and Beschloss and Talbott, *At the Highest Levels*, pp. 79–83.
50. "Remarks Announcing a Conventional Arms Control Initiative," May 29, 1989, PPPUS; more generally, see the notes on the NATO Ministerial Meeting in BP, Box 176, Folder 7.
51. "Remarks to the Citizens of Mainz, Germany," May 31, 1989, PPPUS.
52. Scowcroft Interview, POHP.
53. Leffler, *For the Soul of Mankind*, p. 416.
54. See A. O. Hirschman's essay "Exit, Voice, and the Fate of the German Democratic Republic" (1993), which takes as its starting point his earlier book *Exit, Voice, and Loyalty* (1970).
55. Jarausch, *The Rush to German Unity*, pp. 33–4.

56. Sir Rodric Braithwaite (U.K. Ambassador to Moscow) to Douglas Hurd, Nov. 11, 1989, in Salmon, Hamilton and Twigge, *German Unification*, pp. 106–8.
57. As summarized in a letter from Charles Powell to Stephen Wall, Nov. 10, 1989, in Salmon, Hamilton and Twigge, *German Unification*, pp. 103–4.
58. Gorbachev and Bush, in Bush and Scowcroft, *A World Transformed*, p. 167.
59. For a more detailed discussion, see Sarotte, *1989*, pp. 70–2. The possibility of a united and neutral Germany, and its implications for NATO and U.K./U.S. strategy, had been discussed in the Foreign Office in September 1987, though it was not regarded as something that would happen any time soon. See Rodric Braithwaite, *Across the Moscow River* (2002), pp. 126–7.
60. At a dinner with the President and his top advisors on November 13, Henry Kissinger had explained just why the Soviets would respond to the crisis in Eastern Europe with plans either to extract the two Germanies from the Warsaw Pact and NATO or to "get both alliances disbanded." These options would have allowed the Soviet Union a strategic gain despite the collapse of their erstwhile empire. See Bush in Bush and Scowcroft, *A World Transformed*, p. 191. For more detail, see Richard Nixon to George Bush, Nov. 16, 1989, BP, Box 115, Folder 10.
61. Cited in Jarausch, *The Rush to German Unity*, p. 67.
62. Bush, in Bush and Scowcroft, *A World Transformed*, pp. 199–200. The French reaction was predictably allergic. Thatcher ought to have been happier, given the echoes of her Bruges speech in the concept of a "new Atlanticism," but she was not. On the French, see Bozo, *Mitterrand*, pp. 143–5; on the Atlanticism of the Bruges speech of September 1988, see Richard Aldous, *Reagan and Thatcher* (2012), pp. 273–4.
63. Shevardnadze to Baker, Dec. 8, 1989, BP, Box 108, Folder 12. The Germans were offended at this reenactment of the moment of occupation and Baker felt compelled to apologize. The effect was to reaffirm the support offered by Bush in early December and to rule out future meetings of this sort.
64. Large sections of the current Polish state had been carved out of the eastern portions of Germany and both sides fretted over lingering revanchist sentiments among the Germans displaced from the east. Polish fears and claims were magnified because they received a sympathetic hearing abroad – in France, Britain and the United States.
65. Zelikow and Rice, *Germany Unified and Europe Transformed*, pp. 162–3; Beschloss and Talbott, *At the Highest Levels*, p. 185.
66. Harvey Sicherman to S/P – Dennis Ross, Mar. 12, 1990, BP, Box 176, Folder 14.
67. The text can be found in BP, Box 176, Folder 11.
68. Jarausch, *The Rush to German Unity*, pp. 95–7.
69. On whether a constitutional convention was legally required, see Sarotte, *1989*, pp. 129–32.
70. Two issues stood in the way of a deal: the Soviet treatment of the Baltic states, and, more importantly, the emigration of Soviet Jews. See Beschloss and Talbott, *At the Highest Levels*, pp. 216–18, 222–4.
71. Garthoff, *The Great Transition*, p. 427.
72. "The London Declaration on a Transformed North Atlantic Alliance," July 6, 1990, NATO Online; see also Stanley Sloan, *Permanent Alliance* (2010), 94–5.
73. Beschloss and Talbott, *At the Highest Levels*, p. 238.
74. The Charter was a modest document, but its implications were enormous. See Philip Bobbitt, *The Shield of Achilles* (2003), pp. 636–9.
75. Bozo, *Mitterrand*, p. 300.
76. Baker, *The Politics of Diplomacy*, pp. 1–16.
77. According to George Bush, it was in a late August discussion about enforcing the embargo on Iraq that Thatcher used the phrase. See Bush, in Bush and Scowcroft, *A World Transformed*, p. 352. The memoir and recollections of Henry Catto, at whose ranch the two leaders met, are in this respect unhelpful. See Henry Catto, *Ambassadors at Sea* (1998); and the interview with Catto, Apr. 20, 2000, POHP. See also Campbell, *Margaret Thatcher*, vol. 2 (2004), pp. 662–71; and Thatcher, *The Downing Street Years*, pp. 816–28.
78. The most thorough account is Lawrence Freedman and Efraim Karsh, *The Gulf Conflict, 1990–1991* (1993); but see also Freedman's subsequent, more abbreviated account in *A Choice of Enemies* (2008), chs. 11 and 12.
79. Bush, in Bush and Scowcroft, *A World Transformed*, p. 357.
80. Saddam Hussein, cited in Friedman, *A Choice of Enemies*, p. 216.
81. Senator Robert Dole was tasked with expressing the Bush administration's displeasure in April 1990. See White House Meeting Agenda, Apr. 11, 1990, BP, Box 115, Folder 7.

82. As recounted in Freedman and Karsh, *The Gulf Conflict*, pp. 52–5.

83. Beschloss and Talbott, *At the Highest Levels*, pp. 260–7.

84. The case made for and against the war can be assessed though two collections: Micah Sifry and Christopher Cerf, eds., *The Gulf War Reader* (1991); and Phyllis Bennis and Michel Moushabeck, eds., *Beyond the Storm* (1991).

85. The Americans even convinced the Saudis to give $4 billion to the Soviets to keep their loyalty. The war cost $61 billion and the U.S. received offsetting contributions of $54 billion. See U.S. Department of Defense, *Conduct of the Persian Gulf War, Final Report to the U.S. Congress*, Apr. 1992; and Freedman and Karsh, *The Gulf Conflict*, pp. 358–61, whose figures differ slightly but make the same overall point.

86. See Norman Dombey, "The Nuclear Non-Proliferation Treaty" (2008) and Peter Gowan, "Twilight of the NPT?" (2008); Susan Watkins, "The Nuclear Non-Protestation Treaty" (2008); and, more generally, Richard Rhodes, *The Twilight of the Bombs* (2010).

87. Bozo, *Mitterrand*, p. 357.

88. Odd Arne Westad, *The Global Cold War* (2005), pp. 364–95.

8 The Shaping of the Post–Cold War World

1. Anatoly Chernyaev, Gorbachev's foreign policy advisor, dates the moment when Gorbachev and his allies began to realize that their reforms could mean the undoing of the state itself to mid-1988: "It is starting in the fall of 1988 that the conscious resistance to Gorbachev's policies among the Party *nomenklatura*" began in earnest, he recalled. See William C. Wohlforth, ed., *Witnesses to the End of the Cold War* (1996), p. 112. For a useful overview, see Stephen Kotkin, *Armageddon Averted* (2008).

2. Hannes Adomeit, *Imperial Overstretch* (1998), pp. 539–56.

3. The higher estimate came from Jeffrey Sachs, the Harvard economist who made the calculation as part of an effort, led by the Kennedy School's Graham Allison, to strike a "grand bargain" over reform. The lower estimate came from Yevgeni Primakov during the Camp David meeting in 1990. See Michael Beschloss and Strobe Talbott, *At the Highest Levels* (1993), pp. 237, 381–90.

4. Michael Boskin interview, July 30–31, 2001, POHP.

5. White House Meeting agendas, Dec. 1990, BP, Box 115, Folder 7.

6. The comment is from Kvizinsky's 1993 memoirs and is cited in Adomeit, *Imperial Overstretch*, p. 543.

7. Mikhail Gorbachev, *Memoirs* (1995), p. 611.

8. In retrospect, Major was even more critical: "Gorbachev had changed the face of Russia, yet he was unable to grasp even the basic essentials of the free market into which he had released his country." See John Major, *The Autobiography* (1999), p. 500.

9. Scowcroft's and Bush's remarks are cited in Beschloss and Talbott, *At the Highest Levels*, p. 407; Mitterrand's is reproduced in Gorbachev's *Memoirs*, p. 614.

10. Adomeit, *Imperial Overstretch*, pp. 25–48, provides a useful review of debates about the Soviet Union as an empire.

11. Tarasenko, in Wohlforth, *Witnesses to the End of the Cold War*, pp. 112–13.

12. Gorbachev is quoted in Raymond Garthoff, *The Great Transition* (1994), p. 441. For the CIA report see Director of Central Intelligence, "The Deepening Crisis in the USSR: Prospects for the Next Year," National Intelligence Estimate, Nov. 1990, in CWIHP, *The End of the Cold War* (2006).

13. David Hoffman, *The Dead Hand* (2009), chs. 15–16; Gorbachev, *Memoirs*, p. 666.

14. Beschloss and Talbott, *At the Highest Levels*, p. 405.

15. Central Intelligence Agency, Office of Soviet Analysis, "The Soviet Cauldron," Apr. 25, 1991, in CWIHP, *The End of the Cold War*. The date for the next National Intelligence Estimate for the Soviet Union was appropriately pushed up to June and the report, "Implications of Alternative Soviet Futures," laid out four scenarios, but since "No one can know what the duration or the ultimate outcome of the revolution will be," it did not give odds on which would prevail.

16. Jack Matlock, *Autopsy on an Empire* (1995), pp. 537–9; Rodric Braithwaite, *Across the Moscow River* (2002), p. 244.

17. Timothy Colton, *Yeltsin* (2008), pp. 196–203.

18. Director of Central Intelligence, "Soviet Forces and Capabilities for Strategic Nuclear Conflict through the Year 2000," Aug. 8, 1991, in CWIHP, *The End of the Cold War*.

19. Director of Central Intelligence, "The Republics of the Former USSR: The Outlook for the Next Year," Special National Intelligence Estimate, Sept. 1991, in CWIHP, *The End of the Cold War.*

20. Yeltsin had proposed comparable reductions much earlier, but was not in a position actually to deliver on them. See the transcript of the phone call from James Baker to President Bush, Jan. 29, 1990 describing his "extraordinary discussion with President Yeltsin," BP, Box 108, Folder 12.

21. George Bush and Brent Scowcroft, *A World Transformed* (1998), pp. 545–7; George Bush, "Address to the Nation on Reducing United States and Soviet Nuclear Weapons," Sept. 27, 1991, PPPUS; Garthoff, *The Great* Transition, pp. 490–1.

22. For an assessment of Gorbachev's proposals, see Director of Central Intelligence, "Soviet Tactical Nuclear Forces and Gorbachev's Nuclear Pledges: Impact, Motivations, and Next Steps," Interagency Intelligence Memorandum, Nov. 1991, in CWIHP, *The End of the Cold War.*

23. Others see it differently. See the essays in Ellen Schrecker, ed., *Cold War Triumphalism* (2004).

24. Gorbachev, *Memoirs*, p. 548.

25. Bill Clinton did agree to put off enlargement to 1997 in order not to cause Yeltsin further difficulties in his 1996 reelection bid. See Colton, *Yeltsin*, p. 363.

26. See P. A. Menkveld, *Origin and Role of the European Bank for Reconstruction and Development* (1991); Lilian Barria and Steven Roper, "Economic Transition in Latin America and Post-Communist Countries" (2004); and Steven Weber, "Origins of the European Bank for Reconstruction and Development" (1994).

27. Richard McCormack, Under Secretary for Economic Affairs, to Stapleton Roy, "Meeting at Treasury on European Bank," Jan. 9, 1990, BP, Box 115, Folder 7.

28. EBRD, *Transition Report 1994* (1994).

29. See United States Institute of Peace, *Prospects for Conflict or Peace in Central and Eastern Europe* (1990).

30. Sachs has strongly defended his role ever since. See, for example, his essay "What I Did in Russia" (2012).

31. The literature on transition is now enormous, but see, among others, Sachs, "The Transition at Mid-Decade" (1996); Jan Svejnar, "Transition Economies" (2002); EBRD, *Transition Report 1999* (1999); and Mitchell Orenstein, "What Happened in East European (Political) Economies?" (2009).

32. Milada Anna Vachudova, *Europe Undivided* (2005).

33. See, among others, Harold James, *International Monetary Cooperation since Bretton Woods* (1996), ch. 16. For a critique of the process as carried out in the former Soviet Union, see Stephen Cohen, *Soviet Fates and Lost Alternatives* (2009).

34. Sachs is particularly scathing about the recommendations proffered by John Olding-Smee, the IMF official most responsible. See Sachs, "What I Did in Russia;" and, by way of response, John Olding-Smee, "The IMF and Russia in the 1990s" (2004).

35. Colton, *Yeltsin*, pp. 226–30.

36. Despite Yeltsin's many difficulties, the Bush administration backed him strongly. "Yeltsin is in trouble," the U.S. Ambassador reported on June 4, 1992, but the "current Russian leadership, genuinely committed to political and economic reform (even if they are determined to do it their own way) is the best we are going to get here . . . Any successor . . . will be worse . . ." See report in BPL, National Security Council Files, CF00273–006. Clinton would reach the same conclusion.

37. See Strobe Talbott, *The Russia Hand* (2002); and James Goldgeier and Michael McFaul, *Power and Purpose* (2003).

38. For a recent and comprehensive effort to assess the impact of economic reforms in Eastern Europe, Russia and the states of the former Soviet Union, see Michael Mann, *The Sources of Social Power*, vol. 4 (2013), ch. 7. His conclusion is appropriately mixed.

39. On the fate of former Communists and other people in center-left parties after 1989, see Jean-Michel De Waele and Sorina Soare, "The Central and Eastern European Left" (2011).

40. See John Ruggie. "At Home Abroad, Abroad at Home" (1995).

41. For the argument that the two are incompatible, see Jagdish Bhagwati and Anne Krueger, *The Dangerous Drift to Preferential Trade Agreements* (1995).

42. Interview with Carla Hills, Jan. 6, 2004, POHP. See also Hills's comments on the essay by Christopher Meyerson, "Trade Policy Making in the Bush Administration" (2002), in the same volume.

43. Jeffrey Schott, *The Uruguay Round* (1994), pp. 4–7.

44. On the 1988 Act and the "Super 301" provision, see James Shoch, *Trading Blows* (2001), ch. 5.

45. Just after the Plaza Agreement of September 1985, James Baker noted that he and other finance ministers were "All agreed – protectionism main threat to economic growth and all must resist." Protectionist pressures did not notably lessen over the next three years. See Baker's notes on the memo on "Supplementary Press Guidance," Sept. 22, 1985, BP, Box 96, Folder 13.

46. Interview with Carla Hills.

47. See Steven Dryden, *Trade Warriors* (1995), pp. 348–9; and Sophie Meunier, *Trading Voices* (2005), p. 102.

48. Raymond Seitz, *Over Here* (1998), pp. 333–4.

49. Youri Devuyst, "The European Community and the Conclusion of the Uruguay Round" (1995), p. 457.

50. The approach to dealing with non-tariff barriers was to estimate their negative effects and to determine what level of tariff would have achieved the same effect, then to impose that level of tariff and, it was hoped, begin to reduce it.

51. See John Barton, Judith Goldstein, Timothy Josling and Richard Steinberg, *The Evolution of the Trade Regime* (2006), chs. 4 and 5; and also David Deese, *World Trade Politics* (2007).

52. Interview with Carla Hills.

53. Carla Hills was largely responsible for administration policy. See her memo "Uruguay Round Strategy," June 17, 1991, in BPL, Chief of Staff (John Sununu) Files OA/ID, Box 89, 003.

54. Meunier, *Trading Voices*, p. 108; George Ross, *Jacques Delors and European Integration* (1995), pp. 109–14, 211–12.

55. "US/EC Declaration," Oct. 31, 1990, BP, Box 115, Folder 7.

56. A profile in the *Financial Times*, July 28, 2006, called him "the charming enforcer."

57. Shoch, *Trading Blows*, pp. 7–8.

58. William J. Clinton, "Remarks at the American University Centennial Celebration," Feb. 26, 1993, PPPUS.

59. Dryden, *Trade Warriors*, p. 383.

60. Officially, the date was agreed by others, but the internal U.S. deadline was essential.

61. Craddock was a key advisor to Major and claims that in 1992 he "saw the first task, in time and probably importance, as the conclusion of the current round of negotiations in GATT." Percy Craddock, *In Pursuit of British Interests* (1997), p. 191. Renwick recalled that "When I was Ambassador we did work together very closely with the Americans in achieving a successful outcome to the Uruguay Round of trade negotiations leading to the setting up of the WTO . . . and I worked very closely with Mickey Kantor as did Sarah Hogg from John Major's office and, of course, above all, Leon Brittan . . ." Renwick interview in BDOHP.

62. Major, *The Autobiography*, pp. 499, 513–14; author interview with Douglas Hurd, May 2010; Interview with Robin (now Lord) Renwick, U.K. Ambassador to Washington, 1991–5, BDOHP.

63. See John Dumbrell, *Clinton's Foreign Policy* (2009), ch. 3.

64. John Harris, *The Survivor* (2005), pp. 95, 101; Shoch, *Trading Blows*, pp. 177–85.

65. Schott, *The Uruguay Round*, pp. 14–16.

66. See Roland Burke, *Decolonization and the Evolution of International Human Rights* (2010).

67. See Samuel Moyn, *The Last Utopia* (2010), esp. ch. 4.

68. See Nicolas Guilhot, *The Democracy Makers* (2005), ch. 6; and Ngaire Woods, "The Challenge of Good Governance" (2000).

69. World Bank, *Sub-Saharan Africa* (1989).

70. World Bank, *Governance and Development* (1992). More generally, and critically, see Galit Sarfaty, *Human Rights and the Culture of the World Bank* (2012).

71. See Michael Camdessus, "The IMF and Good Governance" (1998), for a review of the policy.

72. See Elizabeth Cobbs Hoffman, *American Umpire* (2013), p. 9.

73. On the debate on the "democratic peace," see Miles Kahler, "Introduction: Liberalization and Foreign Policy" (1997).

9 Order and Disorder after the Cold War

1. Robert Zoellick, a key participant, believed that the framework "tried to reconcile Friedrich von Hayek's 'spontaneous order' of markets with international governmental cooperation." See Zoellick, "An Architecture of U.S. Strategy after the Cold War" (2011), p. 28.
2. Lawrence Freedman and Efraim Karsh, *The Gulf Conflict, 1990-1991* (1993).
3. See Tony Smith, *America's Mission* (2012), ch. 11.
4. Zbigniew Brzezinski, *The Grand Chessboard* (1997), p. 59.
5. Given its continuing role in the Cold War, Yugoslavia was much watched and top American diplomats were typically posted there. See David Halberstam, *War in a Time of Peace* (2001), p. 42; and Warren Zimmermann, *Origins of a Catastrophe* (1996). For an indictment focusing on British policy, see Brendan Simms, *Unfinest Hour* (2001); and for a still broader indictment, see David Rieff, *Slaughterhouse* (1995).
6. Madeleine Albright, "Yes, There Is a Reason to Be in Somalia" (1993). On Albright as a spokesperson, see Andrew Bacevich, *Washington Rules* (2010), pp. 139-45.
7. Halberstam, *War in a Time of* Peace, p. 271.
8. Philip Gourevitch, *We Wish to Inform You* (1998); Samantha Power, *"A Problem from Hell"* (2002), ch. 10.
9. Percy Craddock, *In Pursuit of British Interests* (1997), p. 34.
10. Tony Blair, *A Journey* (2010), p. 101.
11. John Harris, *The Survivor* (2005), pp. xv-xvi.
12. On Sister Souljah, see Bill Clinton, *My Life* (2004), pp. 411-12.
13. Robert McNamara, *Out of the Cold* (1989); *Toronto Star*, January 8, 1992; and *Financial Times*, January 14, 1992. The specific number comes from the *Toronto Star*, but there's a broader discussion in the *FT*.
14. Paul Wolfowitz, "Shaping the Future" (2011), pp. 49-54.
15. Carroll, *House of War* (2006), p. 434.
16. Dale A. Vesser to Secretaries of the Military Departments, Chairman of the Joint Chiefs of Staff, Under Secretary of Defense for Acquisition, Assistant Secretary of Defense for Program Analysis and Evaluation, and Comptroller of the Department of Defense, "FY 94-98 Defense Planning Guidance Sections for Comment," Feb. 18, 1992, Secret, Excised Copy, Document 3 in the online collection "The Nuclear Vault: The Making of the Cheney Regional Defense Strategy, 1991-92," NSA.
17. The *Times* article was written by Patrick Tyler. On the furor and subsequent debate, see James Mann, *Rise of the Vulcans* (2004), pp. 208-15; Eric Edelman, "The Strange Career of the 1992 Defense Policy Guidance" (2011); Justin Vaisse, *Neoconservatism* (2010), ch. 7; Nicholas Guyatt, *Another American Century?* (2003), pp. 119-20; and, more generally, Carroll, *House of War*, ch. 8.
18. Richard Rhodes, *The Twilight of the Bombs* (2010), p. 271.
19. The Project's organizers explicitly linked their efforts to Cheney's in Thomas Donnelly et al., *Rebuilding America's Defenses* (2000), p. ii.
20. Wolfowitz, "Shaping the Future," pp. 58-62. Wolfowitz has an obvious interest in getting out his side of the story. For the final document from the Secretary of Defense, see Richard Cheney, *Defence Strategy for the 1990s* (1993).
21. Daniel Wirls, *Irrational Security* (2010), pp. 41-5.
22. See Bruce Cumings, "The Assumptions Did It" (2011), which discusses America's continued fixation on North Korea.
23. Andrew Krepinevich, *The Bottom-Up Review* (1994); Michael Klare, *Rogue States and Nuclear Outlaws* (1995).
24. U.S. Department of Defense, "Report of the Quadrennial Defense Review" (1997).
25. Stephen Walt, "Two Cheers for Clinton's Foreign Policy" (2000). Criticism was often confined to minor variations in language. See, for example, Richard Haass, *The Reluctant Sheriff* (1997); and also Charles Kupchan and Peter Trubowitz "Dead Center" (2007).
26. Robert Self, *British Foreign and Defense Policy since 1945* (2010), pp. 168-73.
27. Speech by Margaret Thatcher, Mar. 8, 1991, BPL, WHORM Subject Files, CO167, United Kingdom, Box 1, -221973.
28. *Guardian*, Jan. 22, 1991.
29. David Edgerton, "Tony Blair's Warfare State" (1998), p. 127.
30. Data from the Stockholm International Peace Research Institute. They are available in SIPRI, *SIPRI Yearbook 1995* (1995) and SIPRI, *SIPRI Yearbook 2002* (2002).

31. The "peace dividend," in short, was used to cope with long-term deficits. See Wirls, *Irrational Security*, pp. 40, 46–7.

32. Zoellick, "An Architecture of U.S. Strategy," pp. 26–33, notes the interconnectedness of the framework.

33. The final statement of the Bush administration policy can be found in The White House, *National Security Strategy of the United States* (1993), with a statement by President Bush, Jan. 19, 1993, PPPUS.

34. For a more disenchanted view, see Max Singer and Aaron Wildavsky, *The Real World Order* (1993).

35. See Anthony Lake, "From Containment to Enlargement" (1993); and William Hyland, *Clinton's World* (1999), p. 6. For a critique, see Andrew Bacevich, *American Empire* (2002). For a review of the making of the new doctrine, see Michael Cox, "Wilsonianism Resurgent?" (2000).

36. Power, *"A Problem from Hell"*, p. 342.

37. The White House, *A National Security Strategy of Engagement and Enlargement* (1994), with a statement by President Clinton, July 21, 1994, PPPUS.

38. This and subsequent quotations come from the revised version: The White House, *A National Security Strategy of Engagement and Enlargement* (1995), with a statement by President Clinton, Feb. 28, 1995, PPPUS.

39. John Dumbrell, *Clinton's Foreign Policy* (2009), pp. 45–50; and more generally, Derek Chollet and James Goldgeier, *America between the Wars* (2008). By the end of the Clinton presidency the focus on "globalization" had largely replaced the terms "engagement" and "enlargement." See, for example, Samuel Berger, "A Foreign Policy for a Global Age" (2000). Berger had served as Lake's assistant and became Clinton's National Security Advisor in 1997.

40. The White House, *A National Security Strategy for a New Century* (1999). For a discussion, see Arnold Offner, "Liberation or Dominance?" (2007), p. 36.

41. See, for example, Christopher Coker, "Britain and the New World Order" (1992); William Wallace, "British Foreign Policy after the Cold War" (1992); and Lawrence Freedman, *The Politics of British Defence* (1999), p. 42.

42. See John Dickie, *'Special' No More* (1994).

43. John Major to Ray Seitz, Apr. 18, and Ray Seitz to George Bush, Apr. 23, 1992, BPL, WHORM Subject Files, CO167, United Kingdom, Box 1, –324829.

44. Hurd, cited in Michael Howard, "Introduction," in *DBFSP* (1998), p. xiii. Hurd made many of the same points in an interview with the author on Mar. 10, 2011.

45. *Statement on the Defence Estimates 1995*, in *DBFSP*, p. 3.

46. See "Speech by the Foreign Secretary . . . to the 'Britain and the World' conference, 29 March 1995," in *DBFSP*, pp. 41–5; and Rifkind, cited in Howard, "Introduction," p. xxi.

47. Richard Little and Mark Wickham-Jones, eds., *New Labour's Foreign Policy* (2000); and Oliver Daddown and Jamie Gaskarth, eds., *British Foreign Policy* (2011).

48. John Kampfner, *Robin Cook* (1998).

49. Colin Hay and others have emphasized Blair's use of the discourse on globalization to further New Labour's more or less neoliberal agenda, but in doing so tend to underestimate the real importance of the process itself. See, for example, Colin Hay and Matthew Watson, "The Discourse of Globalisation and the Logic of No Alternative" (2003).

50. The U.S. State Department and the British Foreign Office had come to a similar conclusion in the late 1960s. See above, Chapter 1. On the recurring dilemmas over Britain's role in Europe, particularly as they were manifest in the Labour Party, see Andrew Gamble, *Between Europe and America* (2003); and Patrick Diamond, *Shifting Alliances* (2008).

51. Blair, speech to the Labour Party Annual Conference, 2002. More generally, see Steve Kettel, *New Labour and the New World Order* (2011), pp. 10–14.

52. Denis Healey, former Labour Cabinet minister, recalled that the Labour Party had not resolved its divisions over foreign policy in the 1980s. The issues had been "kicked into the long grass" and therefore there was no real policy on offer in 1997. Author interview with Healey, Apr. 23, 2007.

53. Dumbrell, *Clinton's Foreign Policy*, pp. 50, 54–61; Clinton, *My Life*, pp. 560–1; "United States and Japan Joint Declaration on Security," Apr. 17, 1996.

54. Mark Gevisser, *A Legacy of Liberation* (2009), esp. ch. 30.

55. Andrew Ross Sorkin, "How Mandela Shifted Views on Freedom of Markets" (2013).

56. "Agreement on Trade, Development and Cooperation" (1999).

57. See Harold James, *The End of Globalization* (2001), p. 208.
58. Margaret Thatcher, *Statecraft* (2002).
59. The effort to craft a common European Security and Defense Policy would continue throughout the 1990s and beyond. Its most significant achievements were the "Joint Declaration on European Defense" signed at the Franco-British Summit at St. Malo on Dec. 4, 1998 and the "European Security Strategy," approved by the European Council on Dec. 12, 2003. Little came of either, but they did keep the idea alive. See Jolyon Howorth, *Security and Defence Policy in the European Union* (2007).
60. As quoted in Michael Kramer, "The Case for a Bigger NATO" (1994). More generally, see Hyland, *Clinton's World*, pp. 94–106.
61. "Founding Act on Mutual Relations, Cooperation and Security between NATO and the Russian Federation signed in Paris, France," May 27, 1997, NATO website.
62. Strobe Talbott, *The Russia Hand* (2003), p. 185. See also Hyland, *Clinton's World*, p. 85.
63. See Warren Christopher, "A New Generation of Russian Democrats," speech to the Academy of the National Economy, Moscow, Oct. 23, 1993, cited in Hyland, *Clinton's World*, p. 89.
64. The phrase was the title of a March 1993 memo by Christopher and endorsed, maybe even originated, by Talbott. See Dumbrell, *Clinton's Foreign Policy*, p. 106.
65. James Goldgeier and Michael McFaul, *Power and Purpose* (2003), pp. 106, 164–6.
66. The Asian and Russian financial crises served to stimulate the most thorough critique of globalization and the role of institutions suh as the IMF as yet conducted. See, for example, Paul Bluestein, *The Chastening* (2002); and Joseph Stiglitz, *Globalization and Its Discontents* (2003).
67. The testimony, on September 10, is cited in Nigel Gould-Davies and Ngaire Woods, "Russia and the IMF" (1999), p. 1.
68. Illarionov, "The Roots of the Economic Crisis" (1999), cited in Goldgeier and McFaul, *Power and Purpose*, p. 233.
69. For a sampling, see Jonathan Broder, "Who Lost Russia?" (1998); John Lloyd, "Who Lost Russia? The Devolution of Russia" (1999); George Soros, "Who Lost Russia?" (2000); Stephen Cohen, *Failed Crusade* (2001) and *Soviet Fates and Lost Alternatives* (2009); and Dimitri Simes, *After the Collapse* (1999).
70. See James Mann, *About Face* (1999), ch. 5; and Juliette Bourdin, "The US Debate on China Policy, 1992–2007" (2009).
71. On Britain, see Self, *British Foreign and Defence Policy*, pp. 222–5.
72. The useful distinction between "principled engagement" and "economic engagement" comes from Dumbrell, *Clinton's Foreign Policy*, pp. 111–12, who also discusses "military engagement."
73. Madeleine Albright, *Madam Secretary* (2003), p. 552.
74. On the theory and its uses, see Abbott Gleason, *Totalitarianism* (1995); and, for its revival and later use by Soviet dissidents, see Martin Malia, *The Soviet Tragedy* (1994), pp. 13–14.
75. The debate on globalization reflects this. See Stiglitz, *Globalization and Its Discontents*.
76. There was not, however, much of a debate about the origins and diplomacy of the Cold War itself. The revisionist critics of American foreign policy complained about the "triumphalism" of their opponents; and one "postrevisionist" scholar wrote a book claiming to have been right all along, more or less – John Lewis Gaddis, *We Now Know* (1997). Despite the opening up of Soviet archives, there has been less revision than one might have anticipated. For the current state of the debate, see Melvyn Leffler, *For the Soul of Mankind* (2007); and Melvyn Leffler and Odd Arne Westad, *The Cambridge History of the Cold War* (2010).
77. Bruce Cumings, "Still the American Century" (2000). See also *Millennium*, "The Globalisation of Liberalism" (1995).
78. A book such as Tony Smith's *America's Mission*, for example, is unlikely to have appeared or been taken seriously prior to when it was first published in 1994. After the arguments he had made were refashioned by others into a justification for the invasion of Iraq, of course, he was appalled and restated his position. See Tony Smith, *A Pact with the Devil* (2007); and the expanded and updated version of *America's Mission*, published in 2012.
79. Richard Youngs, *The European Union and the Promotion of Democracy* (2001).
80. See, for example, the work of Thomas Carothers, Director of the Democracy and the Rule of Law Project at the Carnegie Endowment – *Aiding Democracy Abroad* (1999) and *Critical Mission* (2004). For an assessment, see Michael Cox, G. John Ikenberry and Takashi Inoguchi, eds., *American Democracy Promotion* (2000); and, for still more long-term assessments, see Larry Diamond, *The Spirit of Democracy* (2008); and Kathryn Stoner and Michael McFaul,

eds., *Transitions to Democracy* (2013). For a specific effort to update the concept and the practice after Iraq, see McFaul, *Advancing Democracy Abroad* (2010).

81. Talbott, *The Russia Hand*, pp. 372–399; Dumbrell, *Clinton's Foreign Policy*, pp. 142–3.

82. The recollection comes from an assistant to Zawahiri and is repeated in Lawrence Wright, *The Looming Tower* (2006), p. 261.

83. See, among others, Lawrence Freedman, *A Choice of Enemies* (2008), ch. 16; and Gilles Kepel, *Jihad* (2002).

84. Clinton, *My Life*, p. 798.

85. See Mark Danner, "Donald Rumsfeld Revealed" (2014).

86. See Dumbrell, *Clinton's Foreign Policy*, ch. 8; and Freedman, *A Choice of Enemies*, ch. 15.

87. Martin Indyk, cited in Freedman, *A Choice of Enemies*, p. 308.

88. See James Kurth, "Variations on the American Way of War" (2007), pp. 53–98; and Andrew Bacevich, "Elusive Bargain" (2007).

89. Andrew Krepinevich, "The Military-Technical Revolution" (2002). The report was initially prepared in 1992 and reissued a decade later. See also Michael Vickers and Robert Martinage, "The Revolution in War" (2004).

90. Eliot Cohen, *Supreme Command* (2002), p. 199.

91. Albright, *Madam Secretary*, p. 230.

92. Colin Powell with Joseph Persico, *My American Journey* (2003), p. 561. Neither Albright nor Powell gives the date of the exchange, but it was presumably in 1993. The precise words quoted differ marginally, but the meaning and tone come through clearly in each account. Powell's comment comes from his memoir. What he said at the time is not reported.

93. Christopher Coker, in "The Anglo-American Defense Partnership" (2001), has suggested that Britain is also falling behind the U.S. technologically, though less so than other European countries. The commitment to "interoperability" has a long history and a continuing relevance. Geoffrey Hoon, the former Defence Minister under Blair, is reported to have said that "the first principle of British defense planning was to be interoperable with the U.S. forces." See Jeffrey McCausland, "When You Come to a Fork in the Road, Take It" (2007).

94. Author interview with Patrick Wright, Permanent Under-Secretary at the Foreign Office, on June 11, 2007.

95. Hurd's comments on the new world order come from the *Guardian*, July 1, 1993 and his reference to Ireland was reported in several sources in September 1991; Carrington made his comments in an interview on Feb. 20, 2001; and Rose's recollection comes from his memoir, Michael Rose, *Fighting for Peace* (1998), p. 72. The citations are reproduced in Simms, *Unfinest Hour*, pp. 7, 10, 17 and 176.

96. John Major understood this and was very unhappy about it. As he later argued, "Gallingly, this approach avoided committing American troops, yet maintained a high moral tone and a strident appearance of engagement with the crisis. The neatness of the 'lift and strike' formula belied the fatal damage it would do to humanitarian operations . . ." John Major, *The Autobiography* (1999), p. 540.

97. See Halberstam, *War in a Time of* Peace, pp. 224–30; and Simms, *Unfinest Hour*, pp. 87–9.

98. Douglas Hurd, *Memoirs* (2003), p. 460.

99. The move was denounced as a "reward for terrorism" by Christopher Meyer, then John Major's press secretary, in his memoir, *DC Confidential* (2005), p. 108.

100. Halberstam, *War in a Time of Peace*, p. 304.

101. Albright, *Madam Secretary*, pp. 236–43.

102. Ivo Daalder, *Getting to Dayton* (2000).

103. On the need for a set of principles to guide interventions to protect human rights, see Bernard Kouchner, "Humanitarian Intervention" (1999). The idea that humanitarianism represents an "imperialism of human rights" and hence a kind of neo-imperialism has long been argued by Third World leaders, many of them clearly guilty of human rights abuses. See, for different sides of the argument, Eric Hobsbawm, "After the Winning of the War" (2003) and "World Distempers" (2010); Slavoj Žižek, "Against Human Rights" (2005); and Michael Ignatieff, "The Attack on Human Rights" (2001). For the long history behind this, see Anthony Pagden, "Human Rights, Natural Rights and Europe's Imperial Legacy" (2003).

104. Tony Blair and Gerhard Schröder, *Europe* (1999). See also Gerhard Schröder, ed., *Progressive Governance for the XXI Century* (2002). The Progressive Governance Conference would become the Progressive Governance Network.

105. See Nancy Soderberg, *The Superpower Myth* (2005), pp. 68–75. Soderberg had worked for Senator Edward Kennedy before joining the Clinton administration and in consequence had extensive contacts with Irish and Irish-American politicians.

106. See Blair, *A Journey*, ch. 6; and Clinton, *My Life*, passim. On the need for an understanding of the conflict in Northern Ireland as something beyond a local struggle, see Megan Myers, "An International History of the Northern Ireland Conflict, 1969–1998" (2011).

107. Blair, "Doctrine of International Community" (1999). See Robert Jackson, *The Global Covenant* (2000), pp. 355–60 for an assessment of the doctrine. The speech owed much to the academic Lawrence Freedman, who was nevertheless surprised to see his words appear in the speech. The penultimate draft was done by John Kerr, Permanent Under-Secretary at the Foreign Office at the time. Author interviews with Freedman, July 6, 2006 and with Lord Kerr, July 8, 2013.

108. See James Cronin, *New Labour's Pasts* (2004), pp. 450–1; John Kampfner, *Blair's Wars* (2004), pp. 50–2; and David Coates and Joel Krieger, *Blair's War* (2004), pp. 19–21, 107–10.

109. David Bosco, *Five to Rule Them All* (2009), pp. 209–13.

110. Independent International Commission on Kosovo, *The Kosovo Report* (2000).

111. Kofi Annan, "We the Peoples: The role of the United Nations in the 21st Century," Mar. 27, 2000, and "Annual Report to General Assembly," Sept. 20, 1999, cited in Anne Orford, *International Authority and the Responsibility to Protect* (2011), p. 33.

112. This qualification of sovereignty meant a weakening of the theoretical underpinnings of the so-called Westphalia system. See G. John Ikenberry, *Liberal Leviathan* (2012), pp. 239–54; and Beth Simmons, *Mobilizing for Human Rights* (2009).

113. ICISS, *The Responsibility to Protect* (2001); Orford, *Responsibility to Protect*, p. 2; Kampfner, *Blair's Wars*, p. 51; Coates and Krieger, *Blair's War*, p. 139.

114. There would be some final dickering over the precise role the Russians would play. See Albright, *Madam Secretary*, pp. 533–41; and Talbott, *The Russia Hand*, pp. 342–9. More generally, see Ivo Daalder and Michael O'Hanlon, *Winning Ugly* (2001); Andrew Bacevich and Eliot Cohen, eds., *War over Kosovo* (2002); and Lawrence Freedman, "The Age of Liberal Wars" (2005).

115. According to Robert Skidelsky, "Flaws in the New World Order" (1999), "The New Doctrine [of international community] unashamedly identifies the good of the world with Anglo-American values." That was in many ways its strength, its anchor, but may have also defined its limits.

Epilogue: Global Rules in Question

1. A helpful starting point is Melvyn Leffler, "September 11 in Retrospect" (2011).

2. George W. Bush, "Joint Statement with Prime Minister Tony Blair of the United Kingdom," Feb. 23, 2001, PPPUS.

3. George Bush, "Commencement Address at the United States Naval Academy in Annapolis, Maryland," May 25, 2001, PPPUS. It is actually traditional for new Presidents to use addresses of this sort and at this stage in their tenure to outline the basic vision underlying their foreign policy, but no "Bush Doctrine" emerged until well after 9/11.

4. Donald Rumsfeld, "Transforming the Military" (2002).

5. Though Peter Baker, *Days of Fire* (2013), gives Bush a more prominent role.

6. Ivo Daalder and James Lindsay, *America Unbound* (2005), p. 55. Unsurprisingly, the Project for a New American Century was wrapped up in 2006.

7. See James Mann, *The Rise of the Vulcans* (2004), on the background; and also Stefan Halper and Jonathan Clarke, *America Alone* (2004); and Justin Vaisse, *Neoconservatism* (2010). The connection between neoconservatism and support for Israel has often been noted. For an informed but controversial discussion of the issue, see John Mearsheimer and Stephen Walt, *The Israel Lobby and U.S. Foreign Policy* (2007).

8. The actions of the Bush administration prompted a new round of arguments on whether the United States should be regarded as an empire. The point of view adopted here is that while the term captures many aspects of the American past, it also obscures the very real difference between that experience and what empire looked like elsewhere. For background, see Wolfgang Mommsen and Jürgen Osterhammel, eds., *Imperialism and After* (1986), especially the essays by Klaus Schwabel on the United States and Ronald Robinson on the "excentric

idea of imperialism"; Tony Smith, *The Pattern of Imperialism* (1981); Michael Cox, "Empire by Denial" (2005); various contributions to the "Forum on the American Empire" in the *Review of International Studies* (2004), including Cox, "Empire, Imperialism and the Bush Doctrine"; G. John Ikenberry, "Liberalism and Empire"; and Michael Mann, "The First Failed Empire of the 21st Century," and *Incoherent Empire* (2005). See also, for contrasting views, Niall Ferguson, *Colossus* (2004); Michael Ignatieff, *Empire Lite* (2003); John Lewis Gaddis, *Surprise, Security and the American Experience* (2004); Andrew Bacevich, *American Empire* (2002); and Richard Falk, *The Decline of World Order* (2004). On the comparison with the British empire, see Eric Hobsbawm, "Why America's Hegemony Differs from Britain's Empire," in his *Globalization, Democracy and Terrorism* (2007), pp. 49–73; Bernard Porter, *Empire and Super-Empire* (2006); Patrick O'Brien, "The Myth of Anglophone Succession" (2003); and, for a broader comparative perspective, Charles Maier, *Among Empires* (2006). For a specific application to the Middle East, see Rashid Khalidi, *Resurrecting Empire* (2005); and for a useful collection of views on empire and the American experience, see Andrew Bacevich, ed., *The Imperial Tense* (2003).

9. For analyses and critiques, see Mann, *Rise of the Vulcans*, ch. 20; Daalder and Lindsay, *America Unbound*, ch. 8; Halper and Clarke, *America Alone*; Robert Zervis, "Understanding the Bush Doctrine" (2003); Ian Shapiro, *Containment* (2007); Timothy Lynch and Robert Singh, *After Bush* (2008); and James Cronin, "The United States In, or Against, the World" (2010).

10. George Bush, "Commencement Address at the United States Military Academy at West Point, New York," June 1, 2002, PPPUS.

11. George Bush, "Remarks on the Middle East," June 24, 2002, PPPUS.

12. The White House, *The National Security Strategy of the United States of America* (2002). The "Bush Doctrine" had at least a faint echo in Britain with the publication in 2003 of the FCO White Paper on *UK International Priorities*, Cm 6052, and the Ministry of Defence's White Paper, *Delivering Security in a Changing World*, Cm 6041. See Hew Strachan, "The Lost Meaning of Strategy" (2005).

13. Ron Suskind, *The One Percent Doctrine* (2006).

14. George Bush, "State of the Union," Jan. 29, 2002, PPPUS.

15. More generally, see Nick Ritchie and Paul Rogers, *The Political Road to War in Iraq* (2007).

16. The essay itself mixed sympathy with critique. See Jean-Marie Colombani, "Nous sommes tous Américains" (2001).

17. "11 September," *London Review of Books*, Oct. 4, 2001, pp. 20–5. The effort to find equivalence or appropriate comparisons was in fact the dominant theme of much of the contemporary commentary from "critical intellectuals." The American historian Eric Foner, for example, confessed to not knowing "which is more frightening: the horror that engulfed New York City or the apocalyptic rhetoric emanating daily from the White House." He was relieved to have learned, however, that people in London and elsewhere were immune to the views supposedly common in the United States: "Americans reluctant to embark on an armed 'crusade' to rid the world of evil," he explained, "are now relying on our allies to impose some restraint on the White House." Others went further afield: Fredric Jameson chose to invoke the massacre of Indonesian and Iraqi communists by way of indirect explanation; Terry Eagleton reached back to Cambodia; many mentioned the Palestinians. The penchant for highlighting supposed symmetries was widespread. Tariq Ali's book *The Clash of Fundamentalisms* (2003) does so in its very title, but the equation betrays an utter ignorance of twenty-first century America. In a slightly similar, if less straightforward, way Jean Baudrillard, the French theorist of "the spectacle" and "hyper-reality," likewise tried to suggest an equivalence, or appropriateness, between the "unbearable power" of the United States and the violence so spectacularly directed against it: "Moral condemnation and the sacred union against terrorism are equal to the prodigious jubilation engendered by witnessing this global superpower being destroyed; better, by seeing it more or less self-destroying, even suiciding spectacularly. Though it is (this superpower) that has, through its unbearable power, engendered all that violence brewing around the world, and therefore this terrorist imagination which – *unknowingly* – inhabits us all." See Jean Baudrillard, "L'esprit du terrorisme" (2001). Mike Davis, "The Flames of New York" (2001), was similarly struck by the sense of 9/11 as a spectacle that was somehow appropriate to New York as the spectacular symbol of global capitalism.

18. See Sontag's contribution to the set of reflections on 9/11 published in the "Talk of the Town" section in the *New Yorker*, Sept. 24, 2001.

19. See Philippe Roger, *The American Enemy* (2005); Jean-François Revel, *L'obsession anti-américaine* (2000); Richard Kuisel, "What Do the French Think of Us?" (2004); Sophie Meunier, "Anti-Americanisms in France" (2005); and Peter Katzenstein and Robert Keohane, eds., *Anti-Americanisms in World Politics* (2007), who note the ubiquity of anti-Americanism but also its modest effects.

20. Victoria de Grazia, *Irresistible Empire* (2005); Mary Nolan, *The Transatlantic Century* (2012), esp. ch. 8.

21. There is a recurring tendency among historians of American foreign policy to attribute the country's foreign policy decisions to deep-seated traditions and character traits – to the nation's relentless pursuit of markets, to its sense of superiority and exceptional virtue and to its utopian, and arrogant, desire to share the benefits of democracy and capitalism with less fortunate peoples, or to its implicit and occasionally explicit racism. The problem is that American foreign policy changes and periodically breaks with previous patterns. Some commentators have responded to this variety by identifying different and competing traditions in the history of U.S. foreign relations. Two impressive variations are Walter McDougall, *Promised Land, Crusader State* (1997), and Walter Russell Mead, *Special Providence* (2001). The approach adopted here takes various legacies seriously but is more attentive to the distinctions between successive moments in America's relations with the world.

22. See Jonathan Laurence, *The Emancipation of Europe's Muslims* (2012); and Robert Leiken, *Europe's Angry Muslims* (2012).

23. After a sharp increase in late 2001, incidents declined by two-thirds in 2002 and remained at a relatively low level through 2010. In March 2002, moreover, a Pew survey asked if Islam was more prone to violence than other religions and by 2 to 1 Americans who had an opinion rejected the idea (51% said no, 25% yes, the rest did not know or did not respond). Getting reliable data on such matters is extremely difficult, for all the obvious reasons.

24. To argue, for example, that anti-Arab and anti-Muslim violence was rampant after 9/11 and could be understood as "the good ole boy equivalent of Kristallnacht" is hardly credible, however much it might satisfy a certain caricature of U.S. culture. See Davis, "The Flames of New York."

25. Alex Danchev, "Tony Blair's Vietnam" (2007); Con Coughlin, *American Ally* (2006).

26. Condoleezza Rice, *No Higher Honor* (2011), p. 425.

27. See, for example, Stefan Halper and Jonathan Clarke, *The Silence of the Rational Center* (2007); Tony Judt, "Bush's Useful Idiots" (2006); Perry Anderson, "Arms and Rights" (2005); and Andrew Bacevich, *Breach of Trust* (2013), pp. 138–53.

28. There is a substantial and highly informative literature on the invasion and occupation of Iraq. In addition to works previously cited, see George Packer, *The Assassins' Gate* (2005); Thomas Ricks, *Fiasco* (2006) and *The Gamble* (2009); and for a critical insider account, Ali A. Allawi, *The Occupation of Iraq* (2007).

29. The British also pushed hard for a plan for postwar planning, but were unable to force the Bush administration to take the issue seriously. According to Michael Jay, Permanent Under-Secretary at the Foreign Office, Colin Powell at the U.S. State Department tried to induce Jack Straw and the British government to get messages about the importance of postwar planning to Condoleezza Rice. His own access was blocked by Cheney and Rumsfeld. Interview with Michael Jay, Nov. 11, 2009. See also Jack Straw, *Last Man Standing* (2012), pp. 393–413.

30. See Mark Danner, *Torture and Truth* (2004); and Ricks, *Fiasco*, ch. 12.

31. The idea that a strategy of "counterinsurgency" was invented in 2006–7 is wildly ahistorical, for it had been the strategy used by the British in Malaysia and other parts of the empire and by the U.S. in Vietnam. It was, of course, discredited and therefore needed not rediscovery but rehabilitation for use in Iraq. For a critique of the new strategy, see Andrew Bacevich, *Washington Rules* (2010), ch. 5.

32. The sense of failure was as intense on the right as on the left. See, for example, James Dobbins, "Who Lost Iraq?" (2007), and, more generally, David Hendrickson and Robert Tucker, "Revisions in Need of Revising" (2005). The rush by former supporters of the Bush administration to dissociate themselves from its failures left the principals on their own to defend it. See George W. Bush, *Decision Points* (2010); Dick Cheney with Liz Cheney, *In My Time* (2011); and Donald Rumsfeld, *Known and Unknown* (2011).

33. The most forceful statement of the "Bush Doctrine" was probably Bush's second "Inaugural Address," Jan. 20, 2005, though by this time the doctrine and the practice were already being superseded. On "Transformational Diplomacy," see Rice, *No Higher Honor*, ch. 30; and on her efforts with allies, ch. 22.

34. See, for a prominent example, Francis Fukuyama, "After Neoconservatism" (2006) and *After the Neocons* (2006).

35. The reversion began even before some of the more forceful critiques and counterproposals had been published. Among the most forceful critiques, see Fred Kaplan, *Daydream Believer* (2008); Andrew Bacevich, *The New American Militarism* (2005); Robert Merry, *Sounds of Empire* (2005); and John Mearsheimer, "Imperial by Design" (2011). Critique and counterproposal were typically combined. Among many, see especially Stephen Walt, *Taming American Power* (2005); Richard Haass, *The Opportunity* (2005); Anatol Lieven and John Hulsman, *Ethical Realism* (2007); G. John Ikenberry and Anne-Marie Slaughter, *Forging a World of Liberty under Law* (2006); G. John Ikenberry, Thomas Knock, Anne-Marie Slaughter and Tony Smith, *The Crisis of American Foreign Policy* (2008); and David Calleo, *Follies of Power* (2009).

36. See Halper and Clarke, *The Silence of the Rational Center*, pp. 146–50, on the work of Alfred Wohlstetter and others at the "Office of Force Transformation," established in 2001.

37. Charles Maier, "Privileged Partners" (2008), labels the period an "imperial interlude," p. 30. See also Geir Lundestad's "Introduction" and "Conclusion" to the same volume, Geir Lundestad, ed., *Just Another Major Crisis?* (2008).

38. The *National Security Strategy* of 2006 was notably more focused on alliances and multilateral efforts than its predecessors.

39. Robert Harris wrote the novel, *The Ghost* (2007), and Roman Polanski directed the movie, *The Ghost Writer*, in 2010. In the end it was not the Blair character, Adam Lang, who worked for the CIA, but his wife.

40. As Ronald Steel argued in 2006, "I think there's an Iraq syndrome. I think it will be a very long time before there will ever be public support for this kind of adventure." See Steel's comments at the online forum on "The Iraq War's Impact on the Future of U.S. Foreign and Defense Policy" sponsored by the Council of Foreign Relations, New York, Oct. 6, 2006.

41. Author interview with Michael Jay.

42. See Mark Mazzetti, *The Way of the Knife* (2013) on the use of drones; and, more generally, David Sanger, *Confront and Conceal* (2012).

43. See James Mann, *The Obamians* (2012).

44. Barack Obama, "Remarks at the National Archives and Record Administration," May 21, 2009, PPPUS.

45. The White House, *National Security Strategy* (2010). The emphasis on the home front was echoed by Richard Haass, *Foreign Policy Begins at Home* (2013).

46. See the transcript of the speech "As Delivered: Obama's Speech on Terrorism," *Wall Street Journal*, May 23, 2013. The U.S. had not previously acknowledged the use of drones, but Obama's speech was remarkably candid about what he called "lethal, targeted action" and its victims. The new limits and procedures governing drone attacks were detailed in a "Presidential Policy Guidance" document signed on May 22. Further information about drone attacks was simultaneously provided to Congress.

47. Congressional Republicans reacted as one might expect, but their criticisms did not seem to resonate. More liberal critics, who long decried Obama's failure to close Guantanamo and the use of drones, seemed finally to acknowledge Obama's desire to break with the policies of the Bush administration. See, for example, David Cole, "Obama's Long Road to Peace" (2013). See also Vali Nasr, *The Dispensable Nation* (2013), for a criticism that sees caution and restraint as retreat; also Walter Russell Mead, "The End of History Ends" (2013); and Stephen Sestanovich, Maximalist (2014).

48. "Remarks by President Obama in Address to the United Nations General Assembly," Sept. 24, 2013, White House press release. Secretary of State John Kerry and Defense Secretary Chuck Hagel further elaborated on, and defended, Obama's stance at the Munich Security Conference in February 2014. See *New York Times*, Feb. 1, 2014.

49. Robert Zoellick, "Countering Terror with Trade" (2001).

50. See Alan Greenspan, "The Mortgage Market and Consumer Debt," speech at America's Community Bankers Annual Convention, Washington, DC, Oct. 19, 2004, Federal Reserve Board website.

51. Polly Toynbee and David Walker, *Better or Worse?* (2005).
52. Most of the discussion of the causes of the "Great Recession" has reasonably enough centered on housing, finance and the lack of regulation in both sectors. There have also been efforts to situate it a longer historical frame. See, for example, Peter Temin and David Vines, *The Leaderless Economy* (2013); Menzie Chinn and Jeffry Frieden, *Lost Decades* (2012); and Thomas Palley, *From Financial Crisis to Stagnation* (2013).
53. Martin Wolf, "Seeds of Its Own Destruction" (2009).
54. For a skeptical view of how much this matters, see Barry Eichengreen, *Exorbitant Privilege* (2011).
55. Robert Kuttner, *Debtors' Prison* (2013), pp. 258–64.
56. The discussions culminated in March 2013 in a proposal to create a new development bank. See Lydia Polgreen, "Group of Emerging Nations Plans Development Bank" (2013).
57. On the broad politics of austerity, see Kuttner, *Debtors' Prison*; Mark Blythe, *Austerity* (2013); Nancy Bermeo and Jonas Pontusson, eds., *Coping with Crisis* (2012); and Miles Kahler and David Lake, eds., *Politics in the New Hard Times* (2013).
58. There is not a necessary relation between neoliberalism and austerity, but rather a recurring historical one. See Martin Wolf, "How Austerity Has Failed" (2013); and Paul Krugman, "How the Case for Austerity Has Crumbled" (2013).
59. Interestingly, it was a Brazilian Director-General, Roberto Azevêdo, who was critical to securing the deal. *Financial Times*, Dec. 7, 2013.
60. The appointment of Mike Froman as U.S. Trade Representative in June 2013 signaled the administration's determination to focus on trade and market opening. *Financial Times*, Dec. 23, 2013.
61. Cited in Daniel Drezner, "The New New World Order" (2007), p. 41
62. See Alastair Iain Johnston, "Is China a Status Quo Power?" (2003) and *Social States* (2008).
63. Ngaire Woods, "The G20 and Global Governance" (2013).
64. See Temin and Vines, *Leaderless Economy*, pp. 249–51.
65. The government shutdown and fiscal crisis in the U.S. in October 2013, for example, prompted the Chinese to call for a "de-Americanized world." *New York Times*, Oct. 15, 2013.
66. There is now a very large literature about the decline of the United States and the rise of rival centers of power. For thoughtful reviews from diverse perspectives, see Fareed Zakaria, *The Post-American World* (2011); Perry Anderson, "Imperium" (2013); Charles Kupchan, *No One's World* (2012); and Robert Kagan, "A Changing World Order?" (2013). At the center of the discussion is the rise of China and the other BRICS countries (Brazil, Russia, India, China and South Africa) and its possible impact. The case of China has elicited the sharpest disagreements. See, for example, Martin Jacques, *When China Rules the World* (2012); and Ben Chu, *Chinese Whispers* (2013); as well as Pranab Bardhan, *Awakening Giants, Feet of Clay* (2010); and Richard Rosecrance, *The Resurgence of the West* (2013).
67. See Michael Mandelbaum, *The Case for Goliath* (2005); Drezner, "The New New World Order"; and G. John Ikenberry, *Liberal Leviathan* (2012).
68. Noah Feldman, *Cool War* (2013), makes this point about relations between the United States and China and labels it "positive-sum interdependence."
69. Not all commentators see economic interconnectedness as precluding political tensions and conflicts. See, for example, Jens van Scherpenberg, "Trade Is No Superglue" (2008) and Kathleen McNamara, "The Ties That Bind," (2008). These essays, both in Jeffrey Anderson, G. John Ikenberry and Thomas Risse, eds., *The End of the West?* (2008), are based on the state of economic relations between Europe and the United States.
70. See Anne-Marie Slaughter, *A New World Order* (2004); and Rosemary Foot, S. Neil MacFarlane and Michael Mastanduno, eds., *US Hegemony and International Institutions* (2003). There is also a substantial literature on global governance, non-governmental organizations and civil society. See, among others, David Held, *Cosmopolitanism* (2010); and Mary Kaldor, Henrietta Moore and Sabine Selchow, eds., *Global Civil Society 2012* (2012).
71. On the UN and its evolution, see Paul Kennedy, *The Parliament of Man* (2006); Mark Mazower, *No Enchanted Palace* (2009) and *Governing the World* (2012).

Bibliography

Documentary Sources (including online)

Abbreviations

BDOHP	British Diplomatic Oral History Programme
BP	James Baker Papers
BPL	George Bush Presidential Library
CAC	Churchill Archives Centre
CW, LHCMA	*The Cold War*, television documentary archive, Liddell Hart Centre for Military Archives
CWIHP	Cold War International History Project
DBFSP	*Documents on British Foreign and Security Policy*, vol. 1: *1995–1997*
DBPO	*Documents on British Policy Overseas*
DNSA	Digital National Security Archive
FCO	Foreign and Commonwealth Office
FRUS	*Foreign Relations of the United States*
NARA	National Archives and Records Administration
NSA	National Security Archive
NSC	National Security Council
POHP	Presidential Oral History Project
PPPUS	Public Papers of the Presidents of the United States
RPL	Ronald Reagan Presidential Library
TNA	The National Archives (U.K.)
WCDA	Wilson Center Digital Archive

U.S. Sources

Cold War International History Project. Woodrow Wilson Center, Washington, DC. The project has been central to the effort to open up documents from the Cold War era and make them available to scholars. Its documents are integrated with several other collections in the Wilson Center Digital Archive (WCDA). Works closely with the National Security Archive.

Digital National Security Archive. Maintained by the National Security Archive, George Washington University, available online. Additional material available on the NSA website.

Foreign Relations of the United States. State Department, Washington, DC.

George Bush Presidential Library. Texas A&M University, College Station, Texas, administered by the National Archives and Record Administration.

James Baker Papers. Mudd Library, Princeton University.

Presidential Oral History Project. Organized and maintained by the Miller Center, University of Virginia. Archive available online.

Public Papers of the Presidents of the United States. American Presidency Project, University of California-Santa Barbara. Available online.

Ronald Reagan Presidential Library. Simi Valley, California, administered by the National Archives and Records Administration.

U.S. Department of Defense, *Conduct of the Persian Gulfwar, Final Report to the U.S. Congress,* April 1992.

U.S. Department of Defense, "Report of the Quadrennial Defense Review," May 1977.

U.K. Sources

British Diplomatic Oral History Programme. Maintained at Churchill Archives Centre and available in hard copy and online.

Churchill Archives Centre, Churchill College, Cambridge.

The Cold War, television documentary archive, Liddell Hart Centre for Military Archives, King's College, London. A collection of interviews made as part of a television documentary on the Cold War.

Documents on British Foreign and Security Policy, vol. 1: *1995–1997,* ed. Marcus Walker and Richard Coleman. London: Stationery Office, 1998.

Documents on British Policy Overseas. Foreign and Commonwealth Office, London, with various publishers and dates.

Foreign and Commonwealth Office. *UK International Priorities. A Strategy for the FCO,* Cm. 62052. London: Stationery Office, 2003.

The National Archives, Kew.

Selected Documents Relating to Problems of Security and Cooperation in Europe, 1954–1977, Cmnd. 6932. London: HMSO, 1977.

Articles and Books

Abdelal, Rawi. *Capital Rules: The Construction of Global Finance.* Cambridge, MA: Harvard University Press, 2007.

Addison, Paul and Harriet Jones, eds. *A Companion to Contemporary Britain 1939–2000.* Oxford: Blackwell for the Historical Association, 2005.

Adeney, M. and John Lloyd. *The Miners' Strike, 1984–85: Loss without Limit.* London: Routledge, 1986.

Adomeit, Hannes. *Imperial Overstretch: Germany in Soviet Policy from Stalin to Gorbachev.* Baden-Baden: Nomos, 1998.

Afary, Janet and Kevin Anderson. *Foucault and the Iranian Revolution: Gender and the Seductions of Islam.* Chicago: University of Chicago Press, 2005.

"Agreement on Trade, Development and Cooperation." *Official Journal of the European Communities,* L 311, vol. 42, Dec. 4, 1999.

Albright, Madeleine. "Yes, There Is a Reason to Be in Somalia," *New York Times,* Aug. 10, 1993.

Albright, Madeleine. *Madam Secretary.* Paperback edn. New York: Miramax Hyperion, 2003.

Aldous, Richard. *Reagan and Thatcher: The Difficult Relationship.* London: Hutchinson, 2012.

Aldrich, Richard. *GCHQ: The Uncensored Story of Britain's Most Secret Intelligence Agency.* London: HarperCollins, 2010.

Ali, Tariq. *The Clash of Fundamentalisms.* London: Verso, 2003.

Allawi, Ali., A. *The Occupation of Iraq: Winning the War, Losing the Peace.* New Haven: Yale University Press, 2007.

Allen, David and Andrin Hauri, "The Euro-Arab Dialogue, the Venice Declaration, and Beyond," in Daniel Möckli and Victor Mauer, eds., *European-American Relations and the Middle East* (ch. 6). London: Routledge 2010.

Allen, Richard. "Ronald Reagan: A Man with a Plan," *New York Times,* Jan. 31, 2010.

Anderson, Jeffrey, G. John Ikenberry and Thomas Risse, eds. *The End of the West? Crisis and Change in the Atlantic Order.* Ithaca, NY: Cornell University Press, 2008.

Anderson, Perry. "Arms and Rights: Rawls, Habermas and Bobbio," *New Left Review,* no. 31 (Jan.–Feb. 2005): 5–40.

Anderson, Perry. "Imperium," *New Left Review,* no. 83 (Sept.–Oct. 2013): 5–111.

Anderson, Terry. *The United States, Great Britain, and the Cold War, 1944–1947.* Columbia: University of Missouri Press, 1981.

Appelbaum, Anne. *The Iron Curtain: The Crushing of Eastern Europe, 1944–1956.* New York: Doubleday, 2012.

Ashton, Nigel. *Kennedy, Macmillan and the Cold War: The Irony of Interdependence.* London: Palgrave, 2002.

Asselin, Pierre. *A Bitter Peace: Washington, Hanoi, and the Making of the Paris Agreement.* Chapel Hill: University of North Carolina Press, 2001.

Babb, Sarah. *Managing Mexico: Economists from Nationalism to Neoliberalism.* Princeton: Princeton University Press, 2004.

Babb, Sarah. *Behind the Development Banks: Washington Politics, World Poverty, and the Wealth of Nations.* Chicago: University of Chicago Press, 2009.

Babb, Sarah. "The Washington Consensus as Policy Paradigm: Its Origins, Trajectory, and Likely Replacement," *Review of International Political Economy* 20.2 (2013): 268–97.

Bacevich, Andrew. *American Empire: The Realities and Consequences of U.S. Diplomacy.* Cambridge, MA: Harvard University Press, 2002.

Bacevich, Andrew. *The New American Militarism: How Americans Are Seduced by War.* New York: Oxford University Press, 2005.

Bacevich, Andrew. *Washington Rules: America's Path to Permanent War.* New York: Metropolitan Books, 2010.

Bacevich, Andrew. *Breach of Trust: How Americans Failed their Soldiers and their Country.* New York: Metropolitan Books, 2013.

Bacevich, Andrew, ed. *The Imperial Tense: Prospects and Problems of American Empire.* Chicago: Ivan Dee, 2003.

Bacevich, Andrew. "Elusive Bargain: The Pattern of U.S. Civil-Military Relations since World War II," in Andrew Bacevich, ed. *The Long War: A New History of U.S. National Security Policy since World War II* (207–64). New York: Columbia University Press, 2007.

Bacevich, Andrew and Eliot Cohen, eds. *War over Kosovo.* New York: Columbia University Press, 2002.

Baker, James with Thomas DeFrank, *The Politics of Diplomacy: Revolution, War and Peace, 1989–1992.* New York: Putnam's, 1995.

Baker, James with Steve Fiffer. *"Work Hard, Study . . . and Keep Out of Politics!" Adventures and Lessons from an Unexpected Public Life.* New York: Putman's, 2006.

Baker, Peter. *Days of Fire: Bush and Cheney in the White House.* New York: Doubleday, 2013.

Ball, S. J. "Military Nuclear Relations between the United States and Great Britain under the Terms of the McMahon Act, 1946–1958," *Historical Journal* 38.2 (1995).

Bardhan, Pranab. *Awakening Giants, Feet of Clay: Assessing the Economic Rise of China and India.* Princeton: Princeton University Press, 2010.

Barria, Lilian and Steven Roper. "Economic Transition in Latin America and Post-Communist Countries: A Comparison of Multilateral Development Banks," *International Journal of Politics, Culture, and Society* 17.4 (Summer 2004): 619–38.

Bartlett, C.J. *'The Special Relationship': A Political History of Anglo-American Relations since 1945.* London: Longman, 1992.

Barton, John, Judith Goldstein, Timothy Josling and Richard Steinberg. *The Evolution of the Trade Regime: Politics, Law, and Economics of the GATT and the WTO.* Princeton: Princeton University Press, 2006.

Basosi, Duccio. "The European Community and International Reaganomics, 1981–1985," in Kiran Patel and Kenneth Weisbrode, eds., *European Integration and the Atlantic Community in the 1980s* (133–53). Cambridge: Cambridge University Press, 2013.

Baudrillard, Jean. "L'esprit du terrorisme," *Le Monde*, Nov. 3, 2001.

Baylis, John. *Anglo-American Defence Relations: The Special Relationship.* London: Macmillan, 1984.

Baylis, John, ed. *Anglo-American Relations since 1939.* Manchester: Manchester University Press, 1997.

Belich, James. *Replenishing the Earth: The Settler Revolution and the Rise of the Anglo-World, 1783–1939.* Oxford: Oxford University Press, 2009.

Bennett, Gillian and Keith Hamilton, eds. *The Conference on Security and Cooperation in Europe, 1972–1975.* DBPO, series 3, vol. 2. London: Stationery Office, 1997.

Bennett, Gillian and Keith Hamilton, eds. *Détente in Europe, 1972–1976.* DBPO, series 3, vol. 3. London: Frank Cass, 2001.

Bennis, Phyllis and Michel Moushabeck, eds. *Beyond the Storm: A Gulf Crisis Reader.* New York: Olive Branch Press, 1991.

Berger, Samuel. "A Foreign Policy for a Global Age," *Foreign Affairs* 79.6 (Nov.–Dec. 2000): 22–38.

Bermeo, Nancy and Jonas Pontusson, eds. *Coping with Crisis: Government Reactions to the Great Recession.* Cambridge: Cambridge University Press, 2012.

Beschloss, Michael and Strobe Talbott. *At the Highest Levels: The Inside Story of the End of the Cold War.* Boston: Little, Brown, 1993.

Bhagwati, Jagdish. "Rethinking Global Negotiations," in Jagdish Bhagwati and John G. Ruggie, eds., *Power, Passions and Purpose: Prospects for North–South Negotiations.* Cambridge, MA: MIT Press, 1984.

Bhagwati, Jagdish and Anne Krueger. *The Dangerous Drift to Preferential Trade Agreements.* Washington, DC: American Enterprise Institute, 1995.

Bhagwati, Jagdish and H. T. Patrick, eds. *Aggressive Unilateralism: America's 301 Trade Policy and the World Trading System.* Ann Arbor: University of Michigan Press, 1990.

Bhagwati, Jagdish and John G. Ruggie, eds. *Power, Passions and Purpose: Prospects for North–South Negotiations.* Cambridge, MA: MIT Press, 1984.

Biddle, Tami Davis. "Shield and Sword: U.S. Strategic Forces and Doctrine since 1945," in Andrew Bacevich, ed., *The Long War: A New History of U.S. National Security Policy since World War II.* New York: Columbia University Press, 2007.

Birnbaum, Jeffrey and Alan Murray. *Showdown at Gucci Gulch: Lawmakers, Lobbyists and the Unlikely Triumph of Tax Reform.* New York: Random House, 1987.

Blachman, Morris and Kenneth Sharpe. "De-democratising American Foreign Policy: Dismantling the Post-Vietnam Formula," *Third World Quarterly* 8.4 (Oct. 1986).

Blair, Tony. "Doctrine of International Community," Speech to Economic Club of Chicago, Apr. 22, 1999.

Blair, Tony. *A Journey: My Political Life.* New York: Knopf, 2010.

Blair, Tony and Gerhard Schröder. *Europe: The Third Way/Die Neue Mitte.* London: Labour Party and Social Democratic Party, 1999.

Bluestein, Paul. *The Chastening: Inside the Crisis That Rocked the Global Financial System and Rocked the IMF.* New York: Public Affairs, 2002.

Blythe, Mark. *Austerity: The History of a Dangerous Idea.* Oxford: Oxford University Press, 2013.

Bobbitt, Philip. *The Shield of Achilles: War, Peace and the Course of History.* New York: Knopf, 2003.

Borgwardt, Elizabeth. *A New Deal for the World: America's Vision for Human Rights.* Cambridge, MA: Harvard University Press, 2005.

Borstelmann, Thomas. *The 1970s: A New Global History from Civil Rights to Economic Inequality.* Princeton: Princeton University Press, 2012.

Bosco, David. *Five to Rule Them All: The UN Security Council and the Making of the Modern World.* Oxford: Oxford University Press, 2009.

Bourdin, Juliette. "The US Debate on China Policy, 1992–2007," in Lori Maguire, ed., *The Foreign Policy Discourse in the United Kingdom and the United States in the "New World Order"* (162–89). Newcastle: Cambridge Scholars, 2009.

Bozo, Frédéric. *Mitterrand, the End of the Cold War, and German Unification,* trans. Susan Emanuel. New York: Berghahn, 2009.

Braithwaite, Rodric. *Across the Moscow River: The World Turned Upside Down.* New Haven: Yale University Press, 2002.

Brands, Hal. *Latin America's Cold War.* Cambridge, MA: Harvard University Press, 2010.

Brands, H. W. "The Age of Vulnerability: Eisenhower and the National Insecurity State," *American Historical Review* 94.4 (1989): 963–89.

Brandt, Willy. *People and Politics: The Years 1960–1975,* trans. J. Maxwell Brownjohn. Boston: Little, Brown, 1976.

Broder Jonathan. "Who Lost Russia?" Salon.com, Sept. 1, 1998.

Broughton, James. *The Silent Revolution: The International Monetary Fund, 1979–1989.* Washington, DC: International Monetary Fund, 2001.

Brownlee, W. Elliot and Hugh Graham, eds. *The Reagan Presidency: Pragmatic Conservatism and Its Legacies.* Lawrence: University of Kansas Press, 2003.

Brzezinski, Zbigniew. *Power and Principle: Memoirs of the National Security Adviser.* New York: Farrar, Straus, & Giroux, 1983.

Brzezinski, Zbigniew. *The Grand Chessboard: American Primacy and its Geostrategic Implications.* New York: Basic, 1997.

Bundy, William. *Tangled Web: The Making of Foreign Policy in the Nixon Presidency.* New York: Hill & Wang, 1998.

Burgin, Angus. *The Great Persuasion: Reinventing Free Markets since the Depression*. Cambridge, MA: Harvard University Press, 2012.

Burk, Kathleen. *Old World, New World: The Story of Britain and America*. London: Little, Brown, 2007.

Burk, Kathleen. "Old World, New World: Great Britain and America from the Beginning," in John Dumbrell and Axel Schäfer, eds., *America's 'Special Relationships': Foreign and Domestic Aspects of the Politics of Alliance* (24–44). London: Routledge, 2009.

Burk, Kathleen and Alec Cairncross. *Goodbye, Great Britain: The 1976 IMF Crisis*. New Haven: Yale University Press, 1992.

Burke, Roland. *Decolonization and the Evolution of International Human Rights*. Philadelphia: University of Pennsylvania Press, 2010.

Bush, George H. W. and Brent Scowcroft. *A World Transformed*. New York: Knopf, 1998.

Bush, George W. *Decision Points*. New York: Crown, 2010.

Butler, David and Uwe Kitzinger. *The 1975 Referendum*, 2nd edn. Basingstoke: Macmillan, 1996.

Calleo, David. *The Imperious Economy*. Cambridge, MA: Harvard University Press, 1982.

Calleo, David. *Follies of Power: America's Unipolar Fantasies*. Cambridge: Cambridge University Press, 2009.

Camdessus, Michael. "The IMF and Good Governance," Speech to Transparency International, Paris, Jan. 21, 1998. Available on the IMF website.

Campbell, John. *Edward Heath: A Biography*. London: Jonathan Cape, 1993.

Campbell, John. *Margaret Thatcher*, vol. 1: *The Grocer's Daughter*. London: Jonathan Cape, 2000.

Campbell, John. *Margaret Thatcher*, vol. 2: *The Iron Lady*. London: Pimlico, 2004.

Cannon, Lou. *President Reagan: The Role of a Lifetime*. New York: Touchstone, 1991.

Card, David, Richard Blundell and Richard B. Freeman, eds. *Seeking a Premier Economy: The Economic Effects of British Economic Reforms, 1980–2000*. Chicago: University of Chicago Press, 2004.

Carothers, Thomas. *In the Name of Democracy: U.S. Policy toward Latin America in the Reagan Years*. Berkeley: University of California Press, 1991.

Carothers, Thomas. *Aiding Democracy Abroad: The Learning Curve*. Washington, DC: Carnegie Endowment for International Peace, 1999.

Carothers, Thomas. *Critical Mission: Essays on Democracy Promotion*. Washington, DC: Carnegie Endowment for International Peace, 2004.

Carroll, James. *House of War: The Pentagon and the Disastrous Rise of American Power*. Boston: Houghton Mifflin, 2006.

Carter, Jimmy. *Keeping Faith: Memoirs of a President*. New York: Bantam, 1982.

Carter, Jimmy. *White House Diary*. New York: Farrar, Straus, & Giroux, 2010.

Carter, Susan B. et al., eds. *Historical Statistics of the United States: Millennial Edition*. 5 vols. Cambridge: Cambridge University Press, 2006.

Caryl, Christian. *Strange Rebels: 1979 and the Birth of the 21st Century*. New York: Basic, 2013.

Catto, Henry. *Ambassadors at Sea: The High and Low Adventures of a Diplomat*. Austin: University of Texas Press, 1998.

Charmley, John. *Churchill's Grand Alliance: The Anglo-American Special Relationship, 1940–1957*. London: Hodder & Stoughton, 1995.

Cheney, Dick. *Defence Strategy for the 1990s: The Regional Defense Strategy*. Washington DC: Department of Defense, Jan. 1993.

Cheney, Dick with Liz Cheney. *In My Time: A Personal and Political Memoir*. New York: Simon & Schuster, 2011.

Chinn, Menzie and Jeffry Frieden. *Lost Decades: The Making of America's Debt Crisis and the Long Recovery*. New York: Norton, 2012.

Chollet, Derek and James Goldgeier. *America between the Wars: From 11/9 to 9/11: The Misunderstood Years between the Fall of the Berlin Wall and the Start of the War on Terror*. New York: Public Affairs, 2008.

Chu, Ben. *Chinese Whispers: Why Everything You've Heard about China Is Wrong*. London: Weidenfeld & Nicolson, 2013.

Clark, Ann Marie. *Diplomacy of Conscience: Amnesty International and Changing Human Rights Norms*. Princeton: Princeton University Press, 2001.

Clarke, Michael. *British External Policy-Making in the 1990s*. London: Macmillan and Royal Institute for International Affairs, 1992.

Clift, Ben. *French Socialism in a Global Era: The Political Economy of the New Social Democracy in France.* New York: Continuum, 2003.

Clift, Ben and Jim Tomlinson. "Negotiating Credibility: Britain and the International Monetary Fund, 1956–1976," *Contemporary European History* 17.4 (2008): 545–66.

Clinton, Bill. *My Life.* New York: Knopf, 2004.

Cmiel, Kenneth. "The Emergence of Human Rights Politics in the United States," *Journal of American History* 86.3 (Dec. 1999): 1231–50.

Cmiel, Kenneth. "The Recent History of Human Rights," *American Historical Review* 109.1 (Feb. 2004): 117–35.

Coates, David and Joel Krieger. *Blair's War.* Cambridge: Polity, 2004.

Coatsworth, John. "The Cold War in Central America, 1975–1991," in Melvyn Leffler and Odd Arne Westad, eds., *The Cambridge History of the Cold War*, vol. 3: *Endings* (201–221). Cambridge: Cambridge University Press, 2010.

Cobbs Hoffman, Elizabeth. *American Umpire.* Cambridge, MA: Harvard University Press, 2013.

Cockett, Richard. *Thinking the Unthinkable: Think-Tanks and the Economic Counter-Revolution, 1931–1983.* London: HarperCollins, 1994.

Cohen, Eliot. *Supreme Command: Soldiers, Statesmen and Leadership in Wartime.* New York: Free Press, 2002.

Cohen, Stephen. *Failed Crusade: America and the Tragedy of Post-Communist Russia.* New York: Norton, 2001.

Cohen, Stephen. *Soviet Fates and Lost Alternatives: From Stalinism to the New Cold War.* New York: Columbia University Press, 2009.

Coker, Christopher. "Britain and the New World Order: The Special Relationship in the 1990s," *International Affairs* 68.3 (July 1992): 407–21.

Coker, Christopher. "The Anglo-American Defense Partnership," in Barry Rubin and Thomas Keaney, eds., *US Allies in a Changing World* (75–92). London: Frank Cass, 2001.

Cole, David. "Obama's Long Road to Peace," *New York Review of Books* blog, May 24, 2013. Online.

Coles, John. *Making Foreign Policy: A Certain Idea of Britain.* London: John Murray, 2000.

Collins, Robert. *More: The Politics of Economic Growth in Postwar America.* Oxford: Oxford University Press, 2000.

Colman, Jonathan. *A 'Special Relationship'? Harold Wilson, Lyndon B. Johnson and Anglo-American Relations 'at the Summit', 1964–1968.* Manchester: Manchester University Press, 2004.

Colombani, Jean-Marie. "Nous sommes tous Américains," *Le Monde*, Sept. 13, 2001.

Colton, Timothy. *Yeltsin: A Life.* New York: Basic, 2008.

Costigliola, Frank. "An 'Arm around the Shoulder': The United, States, NATO, and German Reunification, 1989–90," *Central European History* 3.1 (1994): 87–110.

Coughlin, Con. *American Ally: Tony Blair and the War on Terror.* London: Politico's, 2006.

Cox, Michael. "Wilsonianism Resurgent? The Clinton Administration and the Promotion of Democracy," in Michael Cox, G. John Ikenberry and Takashi Inoguchi, eds., *American Democracy Promotion: Impulses, Strategies and Impacts.* Oxford: Oxford University Press, 2000.

Cox, Michael. "Empire, Imperialism and the Bush Doctrine," *Review of International Studies* 30.4 (2004): 585–608.

Cox, Michael. "Empire by Denial: The Strange Case of the United States," *International Affairs* 81.1 (Jan. 2005): 15–30.

Cox, Michael, G. John Ikenberry and Takashi Inoguchi, eds. *American Democracy Promotion: Impulses, Strategies and Impacts.* Oxford: Oxford University Press, 2000.

Craddock, Percy. *In Pursuit of British Interests: Reflections on Foreign Policy under Margaret Thatcher and John Major.* London: John Murray, 1997.

Crockatt, Richard. *The Fifty Years War: The United States and the Soviet Union in World Politics, 1941–1991.* London: Routledge, 1995.

Crocker, Chester. "South Africa: Strategy for Change," *Foreign Affairs* 59.2 (Winter 1980–1).

Crocker, Chester. "Southern Africa: Eight Years Later," *Foreign Affairs* (Fall 1989).

Cronin, James. *The World the Cold War Made.* London: Routledge, 1996.

Cronin, James. *New Labour's Pasts: The Labour Party and Its Discontents.* London: Longman, 2004.

Cronin, James. "The United States In, or Against, the World," *Government and Opposition* 45.1 (Jan. 2010): 114–41.

Cronin, James, George Ross and James Shoch, eds. *What's Left of the Left*. Durham, NC: Duke University Press, 2011.

Cronin, James. "Britain in the World: Implications for the Study of British Politics," *British Politics* 7.1 (2012): 55–68.

Crozier, Michel, Samuel P. Huntington and Joji Watanuki. *The Crisis of Democracy: Report on the Governability of Democracies to the Trilateral Commission*. New York: New York University Press, 1975.

Cumings, Bruce. "Still the American Century," *Review of International Studies* 25.5 (Winter 1999): 271–299. Also published in Michael Cox, Ken Booth and Tim Dunne, eds., *The Interregnum: Controversies in World Politics, 1989–1999*. Cambridge: Cambridge University Press, 2000.

Cumings, Bruce. "The Assumptions Did It," in Melvin Leffler and Jeffrey Legro, eds., *In Uncertain Times: American Foreign Policy after the Berlin Wall and 9/11* (131–49). Ithaca, NY: Cornell University Press, 2011.

CWIHP. *The End of the Cold War*. Document Reader compiled for conference June 15–17, 2006. Online.

Daalder, Ivo. *Getting to Dayton: The Making of America's Bosnia Policy*. Washington, DC: Brookings Institution, 2000.

Daalder, Ivo and James Lindsay. *America Unbound: The Bush Revolution in Foreign Policy*. Washington, DC: Brookings Institution, 2005.

Daalder, Ivo and Michael O'Hanlon. *Winning Ugly: NATO's War to Save Kosovo*. Washington, DC: Brookings Institution, 2001.

Daddown, Oliver and Jamie Gaskarth, eds. *British Foreign Policy: The New Labour Years*. New York: Palgrave Macmillan, 2011.

Dallek, Robert. *Nixon and Kissinger: Partners in Power*. New York: HarperCollins, 2007.

Danchev, Alex. *On Specialness: Essays in Anglo-American Relations*. New York: St. Martin's, 1998.

Danchev, Alex. "Tony Blair's Vietnam: The Iraq War and the 'Special Relationship' in Historical Perspective," *Review of International Studies* 33 (2007).

Danner, Mark. *Torture and Truth: America, Abu Ghraib and the War on Terror*. New York: New York Review of Books, 2004.

Danner, Mark. "Donald Rumsfeld Revealed," *New York Review of Books*, Jan. 9, 2014, pp. 65–9.

Darwin, John. *The Empire Project: The Rise and Fall of the British World System, 1830–1970*. Cambridge: Cambridge University Press, 2009.

Davis, Mike. "The Flames of New York," *New Left Review*, no. 12 (Nov.–Dec. 2001).

Deese, David, *World Trade Politics*. London: Routledge, 2007.

de Grazia, Victoria. *Irresistible Empire: America's Advance through Twentieth-Century Europe*. Cambridge, MA: Harvard University Press, 2005.

Denham, Andrew and Mark Garnett. *Keith Joseph*. Chesham: Acumen, 2001.

Destler, I. M. *Making Foreign Economic Policy*. Washington, DC: Brookings Institution, 1980.

Destler, I. M. "U.S. Trade Policy-Making in the Eighties," in Alberto Alesina and Geoffrey Carliner, eds., *Politics and Economics in the Eighties* (251–81). Chicago: University of Chicago Press, 1991.

Destler, I. M. *American Trade Politics*, 3rd edn. Washington, DC: Institute for International Economics, 1995.

Devuyst, Youri. "The European Community and the Conclusion of the Uruguay Round," in Carolyn Rhodes and Sonia Mazey, eds., *The State of the European Union*, vol. 3: *Building a European Polity?* Boulder, CO: Lynne Rienner, 1995.

De Waele. Jean-Michel and Sorina Soare. "The Central and Eastern European Left: A Political Family under Construction," in James Cronin, George Ross, and James Shoch, eds., *What's Left of the Left* (290–318). Durham, NC: Duke University Press, 2011.

Diamond, Larry. *The Spirit of Democracy: The Struggle to Build Free Societies throughout the World*. New York: Times Books, 2008.

Diamond, Larry and Marc Plattner, eds. *The Global Resurgence of Democracy*, 2nd edn. Baltimore: Johns Hopkins University Press, 1996.

Diamond, Patrick. *Shifting Alliances: Europe, America and Britain's Shifting Global Strategy*. London: Politico's, 2008.

Dickie, John. *'Special' No More: Anglo-American Relations: Rhetoric and Reality*. London: Weidenfeld & Nicolson, 1994.

Dinges, John. *The Condor Years: How Pinochet and His Allies Brought Terrorism to Three Continents*. New York: New Press, 2004.

Dobbins, James. "Who Lost Iraq? Lessons from the Debacle," *Foreign Affairs* 86.5 (Sept.–Oct. 2007): 61–74.

Dobson, Alan. *The Politics of the Anglo-American Economic Special Relationship.* Brighton: Wheatsheaf, 1988.

Dobson, Alan. *Anglo-American Relations in the Twentieth Century.* London: Routledge, 1995.

Dobson, Alan and Steve March, eds. *Anglo-American Relations: Contemporary Perspectives.* London: Routledge, 2013.

Dockrill, Saki. *Britain's Retreat from East of Suez: The Choice between Europe and the World?* London: Palgrave Macmillan, 2002.

Dombey, Norman. "The Nuclear Non-Proliferation Treaty: Aims, Limitations and Achievements," *New Left Review*, no. 52 (July–Aug. 2008).

Donnelly, Thomas et al. *Rebuilding America's Defenses: Strategy, Forces and Resources for a New Century.* Washington, DC: Project for a New American Century, Sept. 2000.

Drake, William and Kalypso Nicolaïdis. "Ideas, Interests and Institutionalization: 'Trade in Services' and the Uruguay Round," *International Organization* 46.1 (Dec. 1992): 37–100.

Drell, Sidney, Philip Farley and David Holloway. *The Reagan SDI: Technological, Political and Arms Control Assessment.* Cambridge, MA: Ballinger, 1985.

Drezner, Daniel. "The New New World Order," *Foreign Affairs* 86:2 (2007).

Dryden, Steve. *Trade Warriors: USTR and the American Crusade for Free Trade.* New York: Oxford University Press, 1995.

Dumbrell, John. *The Carter Presidency: A Re-evaluation.* Manchester: Manchester University Press, 1993.

Dumbrell, John. *A Special Relationship: Anglo-American Relations in the Cold War and After.* New York: St. Martin's, 2001.

Dumbrell, John. *Clinton's Foreign Policy: Between the Bushes, 1992–2000.* London: Routledge, 2009.

Dumbrell, John. *Rethinking the Vietnam War.* New York: Palgrave, 2012.

Dumbrell, John and Axel Schäfer, eds. *America's 'Special Relationships': Foreign and Domestic Aspects of the Politics of Alliance.* London: Routledge, 2009.

EBRD (European Bank for Reconstruction and Development). *Transition Report 1994.* London: EBRD, 1994.

EBRD (European Bank for Reconstruction and Development). *Transition Report 1999: Ten Years of Transition.* London: EBRD, 1999.

Edelman, Eric. "The Strange Career of the 1992 Defense Policy Guidance," in Melvin Leffler and Jeffrey Legro, eds., *In Uncertain Times: American Foreign Policy after the Berlin Wall and 9/11* (63–77). Ithaca, NY: Cornell University Press, 2011.

Edgerton, David. "Tony Blair's Warfare State," *New Left Review*, no. 230 (July–Aug. 1998).

Edgerton, David. *Britain's War Machine: Weapons, Resources and Experts in the Second World War.* London: Allen Lane, 2011.

Ehrman, John. *The Rise of Neoconservatism: Intellectuals and Foreign affairs.* New Haven: Yale University Press, 1995.

Eichengreen, Barry. *The European Economy since 1945: Coordinated Capitalism and Beyond.* Princeton: Princeton University Press, 2006.

Eichengreen, Barry. *Exorbitant Privilege: The Rise and Fall of the Dollar and the Future of the International Monetary System.* Oxford: Oxford University Press, 2011.

Ellison, James. "Britain and Europe," in Paul Addison and Harriet Jones, eds., *A Companion to Contemporary Britain, 1939–2000* (517–38). Oxford: Blackwell for the Historical Association, 2005.

Ellison, James. *The United States, Britain and the Transatlantic Crisis: Rising to the Gaullist Challenge, 1963–68.* Basingstoke: Palgrave Macmillan, 2007.

Falk, Richard. *The Decline of World Order: America's Imperial Geopolitics.* London: Routledge, 2004.

Farber, David. *Taken Hostage: The Iran Hostage Crisis and America's First Encounter with Radical Islam.* Princeton: Princeton University Press, 2005.

FCO (Foreign and Commonwealth Office). *UK International Priorities: A Strategy for the FCO,* Cm 6052. London: Stationery Office, 2003.

Feldman, Noah. *Cool War: The Future of Global Competition.* New York: Random House, 2013.

Ferguson, Niall. *Colossus: The Price of America's Empire.* New York: Penguin, 2004.

Ferguson, Niall, Charles Maier, Erez Manela and Daniel Sargent, eds. *The Shock of the Global: The 1970s in Perspective*. Cambridge, MA: Harvard University Press, 2010.

Fischer, Beth. *The Reagan Reversal: Foreign Policy and the End of the Cold War*. Columbia: University of Missouri Press, 1997.

Foot, Rosemary, S. Neil MacFarlane and Michael Mastanduno, eds. *US Hegemony and International Institutions: The United States and Multilateral Institutions*. Oxford: Oxford University Press, 2003.

"Founding Act on Mutual Relations, Cooperation and Security between NATO and the Russian Federation signed in Paris, France," May 27, 1997. NATO website.

Fourcade-Gourinchas, Marion and Sarah Babb. "The Rebirth of the Liberal Creed: Paths to Neoliberalism in Four Countries," *American Journal of Sociology* 108.3 (2002): 533–79.

Freedman, Lawrence. *The Politics of British Defence, 1979–1998*. New York: St. Martin's, 1999.

Freedman, Lawrence. "The Age of Liberal Wars," *Review of International Studies* 31 (2005): 93–107.

Freedman, Lawrence. *The Official History of the Falklands Campaign*. 2 vols. London: Routledge, 2005.

Freedman, Lawrence. *A Choice of Enemies: America Confronts the Middle East*. New York: Public Affairs, 2008.

Freedman, Lawrence, ed. *Europe Transformed: Documents on the End of the Cold War*. New York: St. Martin's, 1990.

Freedman, Lawrence and Efraim Karsh. *The Gulf Conflict, 1990–1991: Diplomacy and War in the New World Order*. Princeton: Princeton University Press, 1993.

Frieden, Jeffry. *Global Capitalism: Its Fall and Rise in the Twentieth Century*. New York: Norton, 2006.

Friedman, Milton. *Capitalism and Freedom*, 40th anniversary edn. Chicago: University of Chicago Press, 2002.

Fukuyama, Francis. "The End of History," *National Interest* (Summer 1989).

Fukuyama, Francis. *The End of History and the Last Man*. New York: Free Press, 1992.

Fukuyama, Francis. *After the Neocons: America at the Crossroads*. London: Profile, 2006.

Fukuyama, Francis. "After Neoconservatism," *New York Times Magazine*, Feb. 19, 2006.

Gaddis, John Lewis. *We Now Know: Rethinking Cold War History*. Oxford: Oxford University Press, 1997.

Gaddis, John Lewis. *Surprise, Security and the American Experience*. Cambridge, MA: Harvard University Press, 2004.

Gaddis, John Lewis. *George F. Kennan: An American Life*. New York: Penguin, 2011.

Gamble, Andrew. *Hayek: The Iron Cage of Liberty*. Boulder, CO: Westview, 1996.

Gamble, Andrew. *Between Europe and America: The Future of British Politics*. London: Palgrave, 2003.

Garavini, Giuliano. *After Empires: European Integration, Decolonization and the Challenge from the Global South, 1957–1985*. Oxford: Oxford University Press, 2012.

Garthoff, Raymond. *Détente and Confrontation: American-Soviet Relations, Nixon to Reagan*, rev. edn. Washington, DC: Brookings Institution, 1994.

Garthoff, Raymond. *The Great Transition: American-Soviet Relations and the End of the Cold* War. Washington, DC: Brookings Institution, 1994.

Garton Ash, Timothy. *In Europe's Name: Germany and the Divided Continent*. New York: Random House, 1993.

Gavin, Francis. *Gold, Dollars, and Power: The Politics of International Monetary Relations, 1958–1971*. Chapel Hill: University of North Carolina Press, 2006.

Gevisser, Mark. *A Legacy of Liberation: Thabo Mbeki and the Future of the South African Dream*. New York: Palgrave, 2009.

Gillingham, John. *European Integration, 1950–2003: Superstate or New Market Economy?* Cambridge: Cambridge University Press, 2003.

Gleason, Abbott. *Totalitarianism: The Inner History of the Cold War*. New York: Oxford University Press, 1995.

Glendon, Mary Ann. *A World Made New: Eleanor Roosevelt and the Universal Declaration of Human Rights*. New York: Random House, 2001.

Glyn, Andrew. *Capitalism Unleashed: Finance, Globalization and Welfare*. Oxford: Oxford University Press, 2006.

Goldgeier, James and Michael McFaul. *Power and Purpose: U.S. Policy toward Russia after the Cold War*. Washington, DC: Brooking Institution, 2003.

Gorbachev, Mikhail. *Memoirs.* New York: Doubleday, 1995.

Gould-Davies, Nigel and Ngaire Woods. "Russia and the IMF," *International Affairs* 75.1 (Jan. 1999).

Gourevitch, Philip. *We Wish to Inform You That Tomorrow We Will Be Killed with Our Families.* New York: Farrar, Straus, & Giroux, 1998.

Gowan, Peter. "Twilight of the NPT?" *New Left Review,* no. 52 (July–Aug. 2008).

Graff, Garrett. *The First Campaign: Globalization, the Web and the Race for the White House.* New York: Farrar, Straus, & Giroux, 2007.

Greenhill, Denis. *More by Accident.* York: Wilton, 1992.

Greider, William. *The Education of David Stockman and Other Americans.* New York: Dutton, 1982.

Guilhot, Nicolas. *The Democracy Makers: Human Rights and International Order.* New York: Columbia University Press, 2005.

Guyatt, Nicholas. *Another American Century? The United States and the World since 9/11.* New York: Zed Books, 2003.

Haass, Richard. *The Reluctant Sheriff: The United States after the Cold War.* New York: Council of Foreign Relations, 1997.

Haass, Richard. *The Opportunity: America's Moment to Alter History's Course.* New York: Public Affairs, 2005.

Haass, Richard. *Foreign Policy Begins at Home: The Case for Putting America's House in Order.* New York: Basic, 2013.

Haig, Alexander. *Caveat: Realism, Reagan, and Foreign Policy.* New York: Macmillan, 1984.

Halberstam, David. *War in a Time of Peace: Bush, Clinton and the Generals.* New York: Scribner, 2001.

Hall, Peter. "Policy Paradigms, Social Learning and the State: The Case of Economic Policy-making in Britain," *Comparative Politics* 25.3 (Apr. 1993): 275–96.

Hall, Peter, ed. *The Political Power of Economic Ideas: Keynesianism across Nations.* Princeton: Princeton University Press, 1989.

Hall, Peter and David Soskice, eds. *Varieties of Capitalism: The Institutional Foundations of Comparative advantage.* Oxford: Oxford University Press, 2001.

Halliday, Fred. *The Making of the Second Cold War.* London: Verso, 1983.

Halper, Stefan and Jonathan Clarke. *America Alone: The Neo-Conservatives and the Global Order.* Cambridge: Cambridge University Press, 2004.

Halper, Stefan and Jonathan Clarke. *The Silence of the Rational Center: Why American Foreign Policy Is Failing.* New York: Basic, 2007.

Hamilton, Keith. "Britain, France and America's Year of Europe, 1973," *Diplomacy and Statecraft* 17 (2006): 871–95.

Hamilton, Keith and Patrick Salmon, eds. *The Year of Europe: America, Europe and the Energy Crisis, 1972–1974. DBPO,* series 3, vol. 4. London: Routledge, 2006.

Hamilton, Keith and Patrick Salmon, eds. *The Southern Flank in Crisis, 1973–1976. DBPO,* series 3, vol. 5. London: Routledge, 2006.

Harbutt, Fraser. *The Iron Curtain: Churchill, America and the Origins of the Cold War.* New York: Oxford University Press, 1986.

Harper, John. *American Visions of Europe.* Cambridge: Cambridge University Press, 1994.

Harris, John. *The Survivor: Bill Clinton in the White House.* New York: Random House, 2005.

Harris, Robert. *The Ghost.* New York: Simon & Schuster, 2007.

Haslam, Jonathan. *The Nixon Administration and the Death of Allende's Chile: A Case of Assisted Suicide.* London: Verso, 2005.

Haslam, Jonathan. *Russia's Cold War: From the October Revolution to the Fall of the Wall.* New Haven: Yale University Press, 2011.

Hay, Colin and Matthew Watson. "The Discourse of Globalisation and the Logic of No Alternative: Rendering the Contingent Necessary in the Political Economy of New Labour," *Policy and Politics* (Mar. 2003).

Hayek, Friedrich. *The Road to Serfdom,* 50th anniversary edn. Chicago: University of Chicago Press, 1994.

Hearden, Patrick. *Architects of Globalism: Building a New World Order during World War II.* Lafayettville: University of Arkansas Press, 2002.

Heath, Edward. *Old World, New Horizons: Britain, Europe and the Atlantic Alliance.* Cambridge, MA: Harvard University Press, 1970.

Heath, Edward. *The Course of My life: My Autobiography.* London: Hodder & Stoughton, 1998.

Heatherly, Charles, ed. *Mandate for Leadership: Policy Management in a Conservative Administration.* Washington, DC: Heritage Foundation, 1981.

Heilbrunn, Jacob. *They Knew They Were Right: The Rise of the Neocons.* New York: Doubleday, 2008.

Held, David. *Cosmopolitanism: Ideas, Politics and Deficits.* Cambridge: Polity, 2010.

Helleiner, Eric. *States and the Reemergence of Global Finance: From Bretton Woods to the 1990s.* Ithaca, NY: Cornell University Press, 1994.

Henderson, Nicholas. *Mandarin: The Diaries of an Ambassador, 1969–1982.* London: Weidenfeld & Nicolson, 1994.

Hendrickson, David and Robert Tucker. "Revisions in Need of Revising: What Went Wrong with the Iraq War," *Survival* 47.2 (Summer 2005): 7–32.

Hennessy, Peter and Caroline Anstey. *Moneybags and Brains: The Anglo-American "Special Relationship" since 1945.* Glasgow: Department of Government, University of Strathclyde, 1990.

Herf, Jeffrey. *War by Other Means: Soviet Power, West German Resistance, and the Battle of the Euromissiles.* New York: Free Press, 1991.

High Level Group on the Functioning of the Internal Market. *The Internal Market after 1992: Meeting the Challenge.* Report presented to the Commission, Oct. 28, 1992. In the online Archives of European Integration.

Hildebrand, Robert. *Dumbarton Oaks: The Origins of the United Nations and the Search for Postwar Security.* Chapel Hill: University of North Carolina Press, 1990.

Hill, Christopher and Christopher Lord. "The Foreign Policy of the Heath Government," in Stuart Ball and Anthony Seldon, eds., *The Heath Government, 1970–1974: A Reappraisal* (285–314). London: Longman, 1996.

Hirschman, A. O. *Exit, Voice, and Loyalty: Responses to Decline in Firms, Organizations, and States.* Cambridge, MA: Harvard University Press, 1970.

Hirschman, A. O. "Exit, Voice, and the Fate of the German Democratic Republic: An Essay in Conceptual History," *World Politics* 45.2 (Jan. 1993): 173–202.

Hitchens, Christopher. *Blood, Class and Empire: The Enduring Anglo-American Relationship.* New York: Nation Books, 2004.

Hobsbawm, Eric. *The Age of Extremes: A History of the World, 1914–1991.* New York: Pantheon, 1995.

Hobsbawm, Eric. "After the Winning of the War – United States: Wider Still and Wider," *Le Monde Diplomatique* (June 2003).

Hobsbawm, Eric. *Globalization, Democracy and Terrorism.* London: Little, Brown, 2007.

Hobsbawm, Eric. "World Distempers," *New Left Review,* no. 61 (Jan.–Feb. 2010).

Hobsbawm, Eric. "After the Cold War," *London Review of Books,* Apr. 26, 2012, p. 14.

Hoffman, David. *The Dead Hand: Reagan, Gorbachev and the Untold Story of the Cold War Arms Race.* New York: Doubleday, 2009.

Hoffman, Stanley. *Dead Ends: American Foreign Policy in the New Cold War.* Cambridge, MA: Ballinger, 1983.

Hopgood, Stephen. *The Endtimes of Human Rights.* Ithaca, NY: Cornell University Press, 2013.

Hopkins, Michael. "David Ormsby Gore, Lord Harlech, 1961–65," in Michael Hopkins, Saul Kelly and John Young, eds., *The Washington Embassy: British Ambassadors to the United States, 1939–77* (130–49). London: Palgrave, 2009.

Horne, Alistair. "Kennedy and Macmillan," in Douglas Brinkley and Richard Griffiths, eds., *John F. Kennedy and Europe* (3–15). Baton Rouge: Louisiana State University Press, 1999.

Horne, Alistair. *Kissinger: 1973, the Crucial Year.* New York: Simon & Schuster, 2010.

Howard, Michael. "Introduction," in Marcus Walker and Richard Coleman, eds., *Documents on British Foreign and Security Policy,* vol. 1: *1995–1997* [*DBFSP*]. London: Stationery Office, 1998.

Howe, Geoffrey. *Conflict of Loyalty.* New York: St. Martin's, 1994.

Howorth, Jolyon. *Security and Defence Policy in the European Union.* London: Palgrave, 2007.

Humphrey, John. *Human Rights Law and the United Nations.* Dobbs Ferry: Transnational, 1984.

Hunt, Michael. *The American Ascendancy: How the United States Gained and Wielded Global Dominance.* Chapel Hill: University of North Carolina Press, 2007.

Huntington, Samuel. *The Third Wave: Democratization in the Late Twentieth Century.* Norman: University of Oklahoma Press, 1993.

Hurd, Douglas. *Memoirs.* London: Little, Brown, 2003.

Hyland, William. *Clinton's World: Remaking American Foreign Policy* Westport, CT: Praeger, 1999.

Hynes, Catherine. "'A Year of Bickering': The European Response to Kissinger's Atlantic Initiative," in Catherine Hynes and Sandra Scanlon, eds., *Reform and Renewal: Transatlantic Relations during the 1960s and 1970s* (129–50). Newcastle: Cambridge Scholars, 2009.

Hynes, Catherine. *The Year That Never Was.* Dublin: University College Dublin Press, 2009.

ICISS (International Commission on Intervention and State Sovereignty). *The Responsibility to Protect.* Report. Ottawa: International Development Research Centre, Dec. 2001.

Ignatieff, Michael. "The Attack on Human Rights," *Foreign Affairs* 80.6 (Nov.–Dec. 2001): 102–16.

Ignatieff, Michael. *Empire Lite.* London: Vintage, 2003.

Ignatieff, Michael, ed. *American Exceptionalism and Human Rights.* Princeton: Princeton University Press, 2005.

Ikenberry, G. John. "Market Solutions to State Problems: The International Politics of American Oil Decontrol," *International Organization* 57.1 (Winter 1988): 151–77.

Ikenberry, G. John. *After Victory: Institutions, Strategic Restraint, and the Rebuilding of Order after Major Wars.* Princeton: Princeton: Princeton University Press, 2001.

Ikenberry, G. John. "Liberalism and Empire: Logics of Order in the American Unipolar Age," *Review of International Studies* 30.4 (2004): 609–30.

Ikenberry, G. John. *Liberal Leviathan: The Origins, Crisis and Transformation of the American World Order.* Princeton: Princeton University Press, 2012.

Ikenberry, G. John and Anne-Marie Slaughter. *Forging a World of Liberty under Law: The Princeton Project on National Security.* Princeton: Princeton University Press, 2006.

Ikenberry, G. John, Thomas Knock, Anne-Marie Slaughter and Tony Smith. *The Crisis of American Foreign Policy: Wilsonianism in the Twenty-First Century.* Princeton: Princeton University Press, 2008.

Illarionov, Andrey. "The Roots of the Economic Crisis," *Journal of Democracy* 10 (Spring 1999).

Independent International Commission on Kosovo. *The Kosovo Report: Conflict, International Response, Lessons Learned.* Oxford: Oxford University Press, 2000.

Iriye, Akira, Petra Goedde and William I. Hitchcock, eds., *The Human Rights Revolution: An International History.* Oxford: Oxford University Press, 2012.

Irwin, Ryan. *Gordian Knot: Apartheid and the Unmaking of the Liberal World Order.* Oxford: Oxford University Press, 2012.

Isaac, Joel and Duncan Bell eds. *Uncertain Empire: American History and the Idea of the Cold War.* New York: Oxford University Press, 2012.

Isaacson, Walter. *Kissinger: A Biography.* New York: Simon & Schuster, 1992.

Jackson, Robert. "The Weight of Ideas in Decolonization," in Judith Goldstein and Robert O. Keohane, eds., *Ideas and Foreign Policy* (111–38). Ithaca, NY: Cornell University Press, 1993.

Jackson, Robert. *The Global Covenant: Human Conduct in a World of States.* Oxford: Oxford University Press, 2000.

Jacoby, Wade. *The Enlargement of the European Union and NATO: Ordering from the Menu in Central Europe.* Cambridge: Cambridge University Press, 2004.

Jacques, Martin. *When China Rules the World: The End of the Western World and the Birth of a New Global Order.* London: Penguin, 2012.

James, Harold. *International Monetary Cooperation since Bretton Woods.* Washington, DC: IMF; New York: Oxford University Press, 1996.

James, Harold. *The End of Globalization.* Cambridge, MA: Harvard University Press, 2001.

Jarausch, Konrad. *The Rush to German Unity.* Oxford: Oxford University Press, 1994.

Jenkins, Simon. *Thatcher and Sons: A Revolution in Three Acts.* London: Allen Lane, 2006.

Joffe, Josef. *The Myth of America's Decline: Politics, Economics and a Half Century of False Prophecies.* New York: Liveright, 2014.

Johnson, Haynes. *In the Absence of Power: Governing America.* New York: Viking, 1980.

Johnston, Alastair Ian. "Is China a Status Quo Power?" *International Security* 27.4 (Spring 2003).

Johnston, Alastair Ian. *Social States: China in International Institutions, 1980–2000.* Princeton: Princeton University Press, 2008.

Judt, Tony. *Postwar: A History of Europe since 1945.* New York: Penguin, 2005.

Judt, Tony. "Bush's Useful Idiots," *London Review of Books*, Sept. 21, 2006.

Kagan, Robert. "A Changing World Order?" *Washington Post*, Nov. 15, 2013.

Kahler, Miles. "Introduction: Liberalization and Foreign Policy," in Miles Kahler, ed., *Liberalism and Foreign Policy* (1–23). New York: Columbia University Press, 1997.

Kahler, Miles and David Lake, eds. *Politics in the New Hard Times: The Great Recession in Comparative Perspective*. Ithaca, NY: Cornell University Press, 2013.

Kaldor, Mary, Henrietta Moore and Sabine Selchow, eds. *Global Civil Society 2012: Ten Years of Critical Reflection*. London: Palgrave Macmillan, 2012.

Kampfner, John. *Robin Cook*. London: Victor Gollancz, 1998.

Kampfner, John. *Blair's Wars*. London: Free Press, 2004.

Kaplan, Fred. *Daydream Believer: How a Few Grand Ideas Wrecked American Power*. Hoboken, NJ: Wiley, 2008.

Katzenstein, Peter and Robert Keohane, eds. *Anti-Americanisms in World Politics*. Ithaca, NY: Cornell University Press, 2007.

Katznelson, Ira and Martin Shefter, eds. *Shaped by War and Trade: International Influences on American Political development*. Princeton: Princeton University Press, 2002.

Kaufman, Robert. *Henry Jackson: A Life in Politics*. Seattle: University of Washington Press, 2000.

Kennedy, Paul. *The Parliament of Man: The United Nations and the Quest for World Government*. London: Allen Lane, 2006.

Kent, John. *British Imperial Strategy and the Origins of the Cold War, 1944–49*. Leicester: Leicester University Press, 1993.

Kepel, Gilles. *Jihad: The Trail of Political Islam*. Cambridge, MA: Harvard University Press, 2002.

Kettel, Steve. *New Labour and the New World Order: Britain's Role in the War on Terror*. Manchester: Manchester University Press, 2011.

Khalidi, Rashid. *Resurrecting Empire: Western Footprints and America's Perilous Path in the Middle East*. Boston: Beacon, 2005.

Kilborn, Peter. "How the Big Six Steer the Economy," *New York Times*, Nov. 17, 1985.

Kinzer, Stephen. *All the Shah's Men: An American Coup and the Roots of Middle East Terror*. Hoboken, NJ: Wiley, 2003.

Kinzer, Stephen. *The Brothers: John Foster Dulles, Allen Dulles, and Their Secret World War*. New York: Times Books, 2013.

Kirby, William, Robert Ross and Gong Li, eds. *Normalization of U.S.–China Relations: An International History*. Cambridge, MA: Harvard University Asia Center, 2005.

Kirkpatrick, Jeane. "Dictatorships and Double Standards," *Commentary* (Nov. 1979).

Kissinger, Henry. *The Troubled Partnership: A Re-appraisal of the Atlantic Alliance*. New York: Council of Foreign Relations, 1965.

Kissinger, Henry. *White House Years*. Boston: Little, Brown, 1979.

Kissinger, Henry. *Years of Upheaval*. Boston: Little Brown, 1982.

Kissinger, Henry. *Diplomacy*. New York: Simon & Schuster, 1994.

Kissinger, Henry. *Years of Renewal*. New York: Simon & Schuster, 1999.

Klare, Michael. *Rogue States and Nuclear Outlaws*. New York: Hill & Wang, 1995.

Klein, Naomi. *The Shock Doctrine: The Rise of Disaster Capitalism*. New York: Picador, 2007.

Knopf, Jeffrey. *Domestic Society and International Cooperation: The Impact of Protest on US Arms Control Policy*. Cambridge: Cambridge University Press, 1998.

Kotkin, Stephen. *Armageddon Averted: The Soviet Collapse, 1970–2000.*. New York: Oxford University Press, 2008.

Kotkin, Stephen with Jan Gross. *Uncivil Society: 1989 and the Implosion of the Communist Establishment*. New York: Modern Library, 2009.

Kouchner, Bernard. "Humanitarian Intervention: New Global Code Must Emerge," *Toronto Star*, Oct. 20, 1999.

Kraft, Joseph. *The Mexican Rescue.*. New York: Group of Thirty, 1984.

Kramer, Mark. "The Demise of the Soviet Bloc," *Journal of Modern History* 83.4 (Dec. 2011): 788–854.

Kramer, Michael. "The Case for a Bigger NATO," *Time*, Jan. 10, 1994.

Krepinevich, Andrew. *The Bottom-Up Review: An Assessment*. Washington, DC: Defense Budget Project, 1994.

Krepinevich, Andrew. "The Military-Technical Revolution: A Preliminary Assessment," Center for Strategic and Budgetary Assessments, Washington, DC, 2002.

Krippner, Greta. *Capitalizing on Crisis: The Political Origins of the Rise of Finance*. Cambridge, MA: Harvard University Press, 2011.

Kristol, Irving. *Reflections of a Neoconservative*. New York: Basic, 1983.

Krueger, Anne. "Trade Policy and Economic Development: How We Learn," *American Economic Review* 87.1 (Mar. 1997): 1–22.

Krugman, Paul. "How the Case for Austerity Has Crumbled," *New York Review of Books*, June 6, 2013, pp. 67–73.

Kuisel, Richard. "What Do the French Think of Us? The Deteriorating Image of the United States 2000–2004," *French Politics, Culture and Society* 2 (2004): 91–119.

Kunz, Diane. *Butter and Guns: America's Cold War Economic Diplomacy*. New York: Free Press, 1997.

Kupchan, Charles. *No One's World: The West, the Rising Rest and the Coming Global Turn*. New York: Oxford University Press, 2012.

Kupchan, Charles and Peter Trubowitz. "Dead Center: The Demise of Liberal Internationalism in the United States," *International Security* 32.2 (Fall 2007): 7–44.

Kurth, James. "Variations on the American Way of War," in Andrew Bacevich, ed., *The Long War: A New History of U.S. National Security Policy since World War II* (53–98). New York: Columbia University Press, 2007.

Kuttner, Robert. *Revolt of the Haves: Tax Rebellions and Hard Times*. New York: Simon & Schuster, 1980.

Kuttner, Robert. *Debtors' Prison: The Politics of Austerity versus Possibility*. New York: Knopf, 2013.

Kynaston, David. *The City of London*, vol. 4: *A Club No More*. London: Chatto & Windus, 2001.

Labour Party. *Report of the Seventy-Fifth Annual Conference of the Labour Party*. London: Labour Party, 1976.

Lake, Anthony. *The Tar Baby Option*. New York: Columbia University Press, 1976.

Lake, Anthony. "From Containment to Enlargement," Speech at School of Advanced International Studies, Johns Hopkins University, Washington, DC, Sept. 21, 1993.

Laurence, Jonathan. *The Emancipation of Europe's Muslims: The State's Role in Minority Integration*. Princeton: Princeton University Press, 2012.

Lavelle, Kathryn. *Legislating International Organization: The US Congress, the IMF and the World Bank*. Oxford: Oxford University Press, 2011.

Lawson, Nigel. *The View from Number 11: Memoirs of a Tory Radical*. London: Bantam, 1992.

Leffler, Melvyn. *A Preponderance of Power: National Security, the Truman Administration, and the Cold War*. Stanford: Stanford University Press, 1993.

Leffler, Melvyn. *For the Soul of Mankind: The United States, the Soviet Union, and the Cold War*. New York: Hill & Wang, 2007.

Leffler, Melvyn. "September 11 in Retrospect," *Foreign Affairs* (Sept.–Oct. 2011).

Leffler, Melvyn and Odd Arne Westad, eds. *The Cambridge History of the Cold War*. 3 vols. Cambridge: Cambridge University Press, 2010.

Leiken, Robert. *Europe's Angry Muslims: The Revolt of the Second Generation*. Oxford: Oxford University Press, 2012.

Lettow, Paul. *Ronald Reagan and His Quest to Abolish Nuclear Weapons*. New York: Random House, 2005.

Lieven, Anatol and John Hulsman. *Ethical Realism: A Vision for America's Role in the World*. New York: Vintage, 2007.

Linz, Juan and Alfred Stepan. *Problems of Democratic Transition and Consolidation: Southern Europe, South America and Post-Communist Europe*. Baltimore: Johns Hopkins University Press, 1996.

Little, Richard and Mark Wickham-Jones, eds. *New Labour's Foreign Policy: A New Moral Crusade?* Manchester: Manchester University Press, 2000.

Litwak, Robert. *Détente and the Nixon Doctrine: American Foreign Policy and the Pursuit of Stability, 1969–1976*. Cambridge: Cambridge University Press, 1984.

Lloyd, John. "Who Lost Russia? The Devolution of Russia," *New York Times Magazine*, Aug. 15, 1999.

Louis, Wm. Roger and Hedley Bull, eds. *The Special Relationship: Anglo-American Relations since 1945*. Oxford: Clarendon, 1986.

Louis, Wm. Roger and Roger Owen, eds. *Suez 1956: The Crisis and Its Consequences*. Oxford: Oxford University Press, 1989.

Lundestad, Geir. *'Empire' by Integration: The United States and European Integration, 1945–1997*. Oxford: Oxford University Press, 1998.

Lundestad, Geir, ed. *Just Another Major Crisis? The United States and Europe since 2000*. Oxford: Oxford University Press, 2008.

Lynch, Timothy and Robert Singh. *After Bush: The Case for Continuity in American Foreign Policy*. Cambridge: Cambridge University Press, 2008.

MacMillan, Margaret. *Nixon and Mao: The Week That Changed the World*. New York: Random House, 2007.

Maier, Charles. *Dissolution: The Crisis of Communism and the End of East Germany*. Princeton: Princeton University Press, 1997.

Maier, Charles. "Empires or Nations? 1918–1945–1989," in Carl Levy and Mark Roseman, eds., *Three Postwar Eras in Comparison: Western Europe 1918–1945–1989* (41–6). London: Palgrave, 2002.

Maier, Charles. *Among Empires: American Ascendancy and Its Predecessors*. Cambridge, MA: Harvard University Press, 2006.

Maier, Charles. "Privileged Partners: The Atlantic Relationship at the End of the Bush Regime," in Geir Lundestad, ed., *Just Another Major Crisis? The United States and Europe since 2000*. Oxford: Oxford University Press, 2008.

Major, John. *The Autobiography*. New York: HarperCollins, 1999.

Malchow, Howard. *Special Relations: The Americanization of Britain?* Stanford: Stanford University Press, 2011.

Malia, Martin. *The Soviet Tragedy*. New York: Free Press, 1994.

Mandelbaum, Michael. *The Case for Goliath: How America Acts as the World's Government in the Twenty-first Century*. New York: Public Affairs, 2005.

Manela, Erez. *The Wilsonian Moment: Self-Determination and the International Origins of Anticolonial Nationalism*. New York: Oxford University Press, 2007.

Mann, James. *About Face: A History of America's Curious Relationship with China, from Nixon to Clinton*. New York: Knopf, 1999.

Mann, James. *Rise of the Vulcans: The History of Bush's War Cabinet*. New York: Viking, 2004.

Mann, James. *The Rebellion of Ronald Reagan: A History of the End of the Cold War*. New York: Viking, 2009.

Mann, James. *The Obamians: The Struggle Inside the White House to Redefine American Power*. New York: Penguin, 2012.

Mann, Michael. "The First Failed Empire of the 21st Century," *Review of International Studies* 30.4 (2004): 631–53.

Mann, Michael. *Incoherent Empire*. London: Verso, 2005.

Mann, Michael. *The Sources of Social Power*, vol. 4: *Globalizations, 1945–2011*. Cambridge: Cambridge University Press, 2013.

Martin, Cathie Jo. *Shifting the Burden: The Struggle over Growth and Corporate Taxation*. Chicago: University of Chicago Press, 1991.

Matlock, Jack. *Autopsy on an Empire: The American Ambassador's Account of the Collapse of the Soviet Empire*. New York: Random Houses, 1995.

Matlock, Jack. *Reagan and Gorbachev: How the Cold War Ended*. New York: Random House, 2004.

Matusow, Allen. "Richard Nixon and the Failed War against the Trading World," *Diplomatic History* 27.5 (2003): 767–72.

May, Ernest, ed. *American Cold War Strategy: Interpreting NSC 68*. New York: Palgrave Macmillan, 1993.

Mazower, Mark. "The Strange Triumph of Human Rights, 1933–1950," *Historical Journal* 47.2 (2004): 379–98.

Mazower, Mark. *No Enchanted Palace: The End of Empire and the Ideological Origins of the United Nations*. Princeton: Princeton University Press, 2009.

Mazower, Mark. *Governing the World: The History of an Idea*. New York: Penguin, 2012.

Mazzetti, Mark. *The Way of the Knife: The CIA, a Secret Army, and a War at the Ends of the Earth*. New York: Penguin, 2013.

McAllister, Ted. "The Transformation of American Conservatism," in W. Elliot Brownlee and Hugh Graham, eds., *The Reagan Presidency: Pragmatic Conservatism and Its Legacies* (40–60). Lawrence: University of Kansas Press, 2003.

McCausland, Jeffrey. "When You Come to a Fork in the Road, Take It . . . Defence Policy and the Special Relationship," Paper presented to the American Political Science Association, Chicago, Aug. 2007.

McCormick, Thomas. *America's Half-Century*. Baltimore: Johns Hopkins University Press, 1995.

McDougall, Walter. *Promised Land, Crusader State: The American Encounter with the World since 1776*. Boston: Houghton Mifflin, 1997.

McFaul, Michael. *Advancing Democracy Abroad*. Stanford: Hoover Institution; New York: Rowman & Littlefield, 2010.

McKercher, B. J. C. *Transition of Power: Britain's Loss of Global Pre-eminence to the United States, 1930–1945*. Cambridge: Cambridge University Press, 1999.

McNamara, Kathleen. *The Currency of Ideas: Monetary Politics in the European Union*. Ithaca, NY: Cornell University Press, 1998.

McNamara, Kathleen. "The Ties That Bind: US/EU Economic Relations and the Institutionalization of the Atlantic Alliance," in Jeffrey Anderson, G. John Ikenberry and Thomas Risse, eds., *The End of the West? Crisis and Change in the Atlantic Order* (157–85). Ithaca, NY: Cornell University Press, 2008.

McNamara, Robert. *Out of the Cold*. New York: Pantheon, 1989.

McNeill, William. *Arnold J. Toynbee: A Life*. Oxford: Oxford University Press, 1989.

Mead, Walter Russell. *Special Providence: American Foreign Policy and How It Changed the World*. New York: Knopf, 2001.

Mead, Walter Russell. *God and Gold: Britain, America and the Making of the Modern World*. New York: Knopf, 2007.

Mead, Walter Russell. "The End of History Ends," *American Interest* (Dec. 2013), online.

Meadows, Donella et al. *The Limits to Growth: A Report for the Club of Rome's Project on the Predicament of Mankind*. New York: Universe, 1972.

Mearsheimer, John. "Imperial by Design," *National Interest*, no. 111 (Jan.–Feb. 2011): 16–34.

Mearsheimer, John and Stephen Walt. *The Israel Lobby and U.S. Foreign Policy*. New York: Farrar, Straus, & Giroux, 2007.

Melcher, Richard. "The City of London Wanted Competition – But Not This Much," *Business Week*, Aug. 10, 1987.

Menkveld, P. A. *Origin and Role of the European Bank for Reconstruction and Development*. London: Graham & Troutman, 1991.

Merry, Robert. *Sounds of Empire: Missionary Zeal, American Foreign Policy and the Hazards of Global Ambition*. New York: Simon & Schuster, 2005.

Meunier, Sophie. "Anti-Americanisms in France," *European Studies Newsletter* 34.3–4 (Jan. 2005).

Meunier, Sophie. *Trading Voices: The European Union in International Commercial Negotiations*. Princeton: Princeton University Press, 2005.

Meyer, Christopher. *DC Confidential*. London: Weidenfeld & Nicolson, 2005.

Meyerson, Christopher. "Trade Policy Making in the Bush Administration," in Meena Bose and Rosanna Perotti, eds., *From Cold War to New World Order: The Foreign Policy of George H. W. Bush* (43–62). Westport, CT: Greenwood Press, 2002.

Millennium. "The Globalisation of Liberalism." Special issue, 26.3 (1995).

Milward, Alan. *The UK and the European Community*, vol. 1: *The Rise and Fall of a National Strategy, 1945–1963*. London: Whitehall History with Frank Cass, 2002.

Ministry of Defence. *Delivering Security in a Changing World*, Cm 6041. London: Stationery Office, 2003.

Mirowski, Philip and Dieter Plehwe, eds. *The Road from Mont Pèlerin: The Making of the Neoliberal Thought Collective*. Cambridge, MA: Harvard University Press, 2009.

Mishel, Lawrence, Jared Bernstein and Heidi Shierholz. *The State of Working America, 2008/2009*. Economic Policy Institute. Ithaca, NY: ILR Press, 2009.

Mommsen, Wolfgang and Jürgen Osterhammel, eds. *Imperialism and After: Continuities and Discontinuities*. London: Allen & Unwin for the German Historical Institute, 1986.

Moravcsik, Andrew. "The Origins of Human Rights Regimes: Democratic Delegation in Postwar Europe," *International Organization* 54.2 (Spring 2000): 217–52.

Morgan, Kenneth. *Callaghan: A Life*. Oxford: Oxford University Press, 1997.

Morsink, Johannes. *The Universal Declaration of Human Rights: Origins, Drafting, Intent*. Philadelphia: University of Pennsylvania Press, 1999.

Moss, Norman. *Picking up the Reins*. New York: Overlook Press, 2008.

Moyn, Samuel. *The Last Utopia: Human Rights in History*. Cambridge, MA: Harvard University Press, 2010.

Mulligan, William and Brendan Simms, eds. *The Primacy of Foreign Policy in British History, 1660–2000*. London: Palgrave Macmillan, 2010.

Myers, Megan. "An International History of the Northern Ireland Conflict, 1969–1998," PhD Thesis, Boston College, 2011.

Nasr, Vali. *The Dispensable Nation: Foreign Policy in Retreat*. New York: Doubleday, 2013.

Nelson, Edward. "Milton Friedman and U.K. Economic Policy, 1938–1979," *Federal Reserve Bank of St. Louis Review* (Sept.–Oct. 2009), part 2: 465–506.

Niskanen, William. *Reaganomics: An Insider's View of the Policies and the People.* New York: Oxford University Press, 1988.

Nitze, Paul. "Assuring Strategic Stability in an Era of Détente," *Foreign Affairs,* 54.2 (Jan. 1976): 207–32.

Nolan, Mary. *The Transatlantic Century: Europe and America, 1890–2010.* Cambridge: Cambridge University Press, 2012.

Nunnerly, David. *President Kennedy and Britain.* New York: St. Martin's, 1972.

Nye, Joseph. "The American National Interest and Global Public Goods," *International Affairs* 78.2 (2002): 233–44.

Oberdorfer, Don. *From the Cold War to a New Era: The United States and the Soviet Union, 1983–1991.* Baltimore: Johns Hopkins University Press, 1998.

O'Brien, Patrick. "The Myth of Anglophone Succession," *New Left Review,* no. 24 (Nov.–Dec. 2003): 113–34.

OECD (Organization for Economic Co-operation and Development). *Forty Years' Experience with the OECD Code of Liberalisation of Capital Movements.* Paris: OECD, 2002.

OECD (Organization for Economic Co-operation and Development). *OECD Jobs Study: Evidence and Explanations.* Paris: OECD, 1994.

Offner, Arnold. "Liberation or Dominance? The Ideology of U.S. National Security Policy," in Andrew Bacevich, ed., *The Long War: A New History of U.S. National Security Policy since World War II* (1–52). New York: Columbia University Press, 2007.

Olding-Smee, John. "The IMF and Russia in the 1990s," IMF Working Paper, WP/04/155, 2004.

Orenstein, Mitchell. "What Happened in East European (Political) Economies? A Balance Sheet for Neoliberal Reform," *East European Politics and Societies* 23 (Nov. 2009): 479–90.

Orford, Anne. *International Authority and the Responsibility to Protect.* Cambridge: Cambridge University Press, 2011.

Ovendale, Ritchie. *The English-Speaking Alliance: Britain, the United States, the Dominions and the Cold War, 1945–51.* London: Allen & Unwin, 1985.

Ovendale, Ritchie. *Anglo-American Relations in the Twentieth Century.* New York: St. Martin's, 1998.

Owen, David. *David Owen: Personally Speaking to Kenneth Harris.* London: Weidenfeld & Nicolson, 1987.

Owen, David. *Time to Declare.* London: Michael Joseph, 1991.

Packer, George. *The Assassins' Gate.* New York: Farrar, Straus, & Giroux, 2005.

Paemen, Hugo and Alexandra Bensch. *From the GATT to the WTO: The European Community in the Uruguay Round.* Leuven: Leuven University Press, 1995.

Pagden, Anthony. "Human Rights, Natural Rights and Europe's Imperial Legacy," *Political Theory* 31.2 (Apr. 2003): 171–99.

Palley, Thomas. *From Financial Crisis to Stagnation: The Destruction of Shared Prosperity and the Role of Economics.* Cambridge: Cambridge University Press, 2013.

Parr, Helen. "Britain, America, East of Suez and the EEC: Finding a Role in British Foreign Policy," *Contemporary British History* 20.3 (Sept. 2006): 403–21.

Perlstein, Rick. *Nixonland: The Rise of a President and the Fracturing of America.* New York: Scribner, 2008.

Phillips, Kevin. *The Emerging Republican Majority.* New Rochelle, NY: Arlington House, 1969.

Pickering, Jeffrey. *British Withdrawal from East of Suez: The Politics of Retrenchment.* London: Macmillan, 1998.

Pietrantonio, Silvia. "The Year That Never Was: 1973 and the Crisis between the United States and the European Community," *Journal of Transatlantic Studies* 8.2 (2010): 158–77.

Pipes, Richard. *Vixi: Memoirs of a Non-Belonger.* New Haven: Yale University Press, 2003.

Plesch, Dan. *The Future of Britain's WMD.* London: Foreign Policy Centre, 2006.

Polgreen, Lydia. "Group of Emerging Nations Plans Development Bank," *New York Times,* Mar. 26, 2013.

Porter, Bernard. *Empire and Superempire: Britain, America and the World.* New Haven: Yale University Press, 2006.

Powell, Colin with Joseph Persico. *My American Journey.* New York: Ballantine, 2003.

Power, Samantha. *"A Problem from Hell": America and the Age of Genocide.* New York: Basic, 2002.

Prasad, Monica. *The Politics of Free Markets: The Rise of Neoliberal Policies in Britain, France, Germany and the United States*. Chicago: University of Chicago Press, 2006.

President Ronald Reagan's Initial Actions Project, edited with an introduction by Arthur Laffer. New York: Threshold, 2009.

Putnam, Robert. "Diplomacy and Domestic Politics: The Logic of Two-Level Games," *International Organization* 57.3 (Summer 1988): 427–60.

Putnam, Robert and Nicholas Bayne. *Hanging Together: The Seven-Power Summits*. Cambridge, MA: Harvard University Press, 1984.

Rauch, Jonathan. "Gramm-Rudman – A Bad Idea Whose Time Has Come Again," *Atlantic*, Feb. 15, 2005. Online.

Reagan, Ronald. "Margaret Thatcher and the Revival of the West," *National Review*, May 19, 1989.

Reagan, Ronald. *An American Life*. New York: Simon & Schuster, 1990.

Reagan, Ronald. *The Reagan Diaries*, ed. Douglas Brinkley. New York: HarperCollins, 2007.

Renwick, Robin. *Fighting with Allies: America and Britain in Peace and War*. London: Macmillan, 1996.

Renwick, Robin. *A Journey with Margaret Thatcher: Foreign Policy under the Iron Lady*. London: Biteback, 2013.

Revel, Jean-François *L'obsession anti-américaine*. Paris: Plon, 2000.

Reynolds, David. "The Origins of the Cold War: The European dimension, 1944–1951," *Historical Journal* 28.2 (Mar. 1985): 497–515.

Reynolds, David. "Roosevelt, Churchill, and the Wartime Anglo-American Alliance, 1939–1945," in Wm. Roger Louis and Hedley Bull, eds., *The Special Relationship: Anglo-American Relations since 1945* (17–41). Oxford: Clarendon, 1986.

Reynolds, David. "Rethinking Anglo-American Relations," *International Affairs* 65.1 (Winter 1988–9): 89–111.

Reynolds, David. *Britannia Overruled: British Policy and World Power in the 20th Century*. London: Longman, 2000.

Reynolds, David. *Summits: Six Meetings That Shaped the Twentieth Century*. New York: Basic, 2007.

Reynolds, David. *America, Empire of Liberty*. New York: Basic, 2009.

Rhodes, Richard. *The Twilight of the Bombs*. New York: Knopf, 2010.

Rice, Condoleezza. *No Higher Honor: A Memoir of My Years in Washington*. New York: Crown, 2011.

Richardson, Louise. *When Allies Differ: Anglo-American Relations during the Suez and Falklands Crises*. New York: St. Martin's, 1996.

Ricks, Thomas. *Fiasco: The American Military Adventure in Iraq*. New York: Penguin, 2006.

Ricks, Thomas. *The Gamble: General David Petraeus and the Military Adventure in Iraq, 2006–2008*. New York: Penguin, 2009.

Rieff, David. *Slaughterhouse: Bosnia and the Failure of the West*. New York: Simon & Schuster, 1995.

Ritchie, Nick and Paul Rogers. *The Political Road to War in Iraq*. London: Routledge, 2007.

Robb, Thomas. "Henry Kissinger, Great Britain, and the 'Year of Europe': The 'Tangled Skein,'" *Contemporary British History* 24.3 (Sept. 2010): 297–318.

Roberts, Alasdair. *The Logic of Discipline: Global Capitalism and the Architecture of Government*. Oxford: Oxford University Press, 2010.

Roberts, Andrew. *A History of the English-Speaking Peoples since 1900*. New York: HarperCollins, 2007.

Robinson, William. *Promoting Polyarchy: Globalization, US Intervention, and Hegemony*. Cambridge: Cambridge University Press, 1986.

Rodgers, Daniel. *The Age of Fracture*. Cambridge, MA: Harvard University Press, 2011.

Roger, Philippe. *The American Enemy: The History of French Anti-Americanism*, trans. Sharon Bowman. Chicago: University of Chicago Press, 2005.

Rose, Michael. *Fighting for Peace: Bosnia 1994*. London: Harvill, 1998.

Rosecrance, Richard. *The Resurgence of the West: How a Transatlantic Union Can Prevent War and Restore the United States and Europe*. New Haven: Yale University Press, 2013.

Ross, George. *Jacques Delors and European Integration*. New York: Oxford University Press, 1995.

Ross, George. "The Limits of Political Economy: Mitterrand and the Crisis of the French Left," in Anthony Daley, ed., *The Mitterrand Era: Policy Alternatives and Political Mobilization in France*. New York: New York University Press, 1996.

Ruggie, John. "At Home Abroad, Abroad at Home: International Liberalisation and Domestic Stability in the New World Economy," *Millennium* 24.3 (1995): 507–26.

Rumsfeld, Donald. "Transforming the Military," *Foreign Affairs* 81 (May–June, 2002): 20–32.

Rumsfeld, Donald. *Known and Unknown: A Memoir*. New York: Sentinel, 2011.

Runciman, David. *The Confidence Trap: A History of Democracy in Crisis from World War I to the Present*. Princeton: Princeton University Press, 2013.

Sachs, Jeffrey. "The Transition at Mid-Decade," *American Economic Review* 86.2 (May 1996): 128–33.

Sachs, Jeffrey. "What I Did in Russia," Mar. 14, 2012. Available at jeffsachs.org.

Salmon, Patrick, Keith Hamilton and Stephen Twigge, eds. *German Unification, 1989–1990. DBPO*, series 3, vol. 7. Abingdon: Routledge, 2010.

Sanger, David. *Confront and Conceal: Obama's Secret Wars and the Surprising Use of American Power*. New York: Crown, 2012.

Sarfaty, Galit. *Values in Transition: Human Rights and the Culture of the World Bank*. Stanford: Stanford University Press, 2012.

Sarotte, Mary. *Dealing with the Devil: East Germany, Détente, and Ostpolitik, 1969–1973*. Chapel Hill: University of North Carolina Press, 2001.

Sarotte, Mary. *1989: The Struggle to Create Post–Cold War Europe*. Princeton: Princeton University Press, 2009.

Saunders, Chris and Sue Onslow. "The Cold War and Southern Africa, 1976–1990," in Melvyn Leffler and Odd Arne Westad, eds., *The Cambridge History of the Cold War*, vol. 3: *Endings* (222–43). Cambridge: Cambridge University Press, 2010.

Schmidt, Helmut. "The 1977 Alastair Buchan Memorial Lecture," *Survival* (Jan.–Feb. 1978).

Schott, Jeffrey. *The Uruguay Round: An Assessment*. Washington, DC: Institute for International Economics, 1994.

Schrecker, Ellen, ed. *Cold War Triumphalism: The Misuse of History after the Fall of Communism*. New York: New Press, 2004.

Schröder, Gerhard, ed. *Progressive Governance for the XXI Century*. The Hague: Kluwer Law International, 2002.

Schulman, Bruce and J. Zelizer, eds. *Rightward Bound: Making America Conservative in the 1970s*. Cambridge, MA: Harvard University Press, 2008.

Schulz, Matthias and Thomas Schwartz, eds. *The Strained Alliance: U.S.-European Relations from Nixon to Carter*. Cambridge: Cambridge University Press for the German Historical Institute, 2010.

Schweizer, Peter. *Reagan's War: The Epic Story of His Forty-Year Struggle and His Final Triumph over Communism*. New York: Anchor, 2002.

Scott, Andrew. *Allies Apart: Heath, Nixon and the Anglo-American Relationship*. London: Palgrave, 2011.

Seitz, Raymond. *Over Here*. London: Weidenfeld & Nicolson, 1998.

Self, Robert. *British Foreign and Defense Policy since 1945*. London: Palgrave Macmillan, 2010.

Sestanovich, Stephen. *Maximalist: America in the World from Truman to Obama*. New York: Knopf, 2014.

Shapiro, Ian. *Containment: Rebuilding a Strategy against Global Terror*. Princeton: Princeton University Press, 2007.

Shevardnadze, Edvard. *The Future Belongs to Freedom*. New York: Free Press, 1991.

Shoch, James. *Trading Blows: Party Competition and U.S. Trade Policy in a Globalizing Era*. Chapel Hill: University of North Carolina Press, 2001.

Shultz, George. *Turmoil and Triumph: My Years as Secretary of State*. New York: Scribner's, 1993.

Sifry, Micah and Christopher Cerf, eds. *The Gulf War Reader*. New York: Random House, 1991.

Simes, Dimitri. *After the Collapse: Russia Seeks Its Place as a Great Power*. New York: Simon & Schuster, 1999.

Simmons, Beth. *Mobilizing for Human Rights: International Law in Domestic Politics*. New York: Cambridge University Press, 2009.

Simms, Brendan. *Unfinest Hour: Britain and the Destruction of Bosnia*. London: Penguin, 2001.

Simpson, A. W. Brian. *Human Rights and the End of Empire*. Oxford: Oxford University Press, 2001.

Simpson, Gerry. "The Diffusion of Sovereignty: Self-Determination in the Post-Colonial Age," in R. McCorquodale, ed., *Self-Determination in International Law*. Aldershot: Ashgate, 2000.

Singer, Max and Aaron Wildavsky. *The Real World Order: Zones of Peace/Zones of Turmoil.* London: Chatham House, 1993.

SIPRI (Stockholm International Peace Research Institute). *SIPRI Yearbook 1995.* New York: Oxford University Press, 1995.

SIPRI (Stockholm International Peace Research Institute). *SIPRI Yearbook 2002.* New York: Oxford University Press, 2002.

Skidelsky, Robert. "Flaws in the New World Order," *Independent,* June 22, 1999.

Skidelsky, Robert. *Keynes,* vol. 3: *Fighting for Freedom.* New York: Viking, 2000.

Slaughter, Anne-Marie. *A New World Order.* Princeton: Princeton University Press, 2004.

Sloan, Stanley. *Permanent Alliance: NATO and the Transatlantic Bargain from Truman to Obama.* London: Bloomsbury, 2010.

Smith, Gaddis. *Morality, Reason and Power: American Diplomacy in the Carter Years.* New York: Hill & Wang, 1986.

Smith, Geoffrey. *Reagan and Thatcher.* New York: Norton, 1991.

Smith, Peter. *Talons of the Eagle: Dynamics of U.S.-Latin American Relations.* New York: Oxford University Press, 2012.

Smith, Tony. *The Pattern of Imperialism: The United States, Great Britain, and the Late-Industrializing World since 1815.* Cambridge: Cambridge University Press, 1981.

Smith, Tony. *A Pact with the Devil: Washington's Bid for World Supremacy and the Betrayal of the American Promise.* London: Routledge, 2007.

Smith, Tony. *America's Mission: The United States and the Worldwide Struggle for Democracy.* Princeton: Princeton University Press, 1994; revised edition 2012.

Snepp, Frank. *Decent Interval.* New York: Random House, 1977.

Snyder, Sara. *Human Rights Activism and the End of the Cold War: A Transnational History of the Helsinki Network.* Cambridge: Cambridge University Press, 2011.

Soderberg, Nancy. *The Superpower Myth: The Use and Misuse of American Might.* Hoboken, NJ: Wiley, 2005.

Sorkin, Andrew Ross. "How Mandela Shifted Views on Freedom of Markets," *New York Times,* Dec. 10, 2013.

Soros, George. "Who Lost Russia?" *New York Review of Books,* Apr. 3, 2000.

Spelling, Alex. "Edward Heath and Anglo-American Relations 1970–74: A Reappraisal," *Diplomacy and Statecraft* 20.4 (2009): 638–58.

Stedman Jones, Daniel. *Masters of the Universe: Hayek, Friedman and the Birth of Neoliberal Politics.* Princeton: Princeton University Press, 2012.

Steil, Benn. *The Battle of Bretton Woods: John Maynard Keynes, Harry Dexter White and the Making of a New World Order.* Princeton: Princeton University Press, 2013.

Stein, Judith. *Pivotal Decade: How the United States Traded Factories for Finance in the Seventies.* New Haven: Yale University Press, 2010.

Stephanson, Anders. *Kennan and the Art of Foreign Policy.* Cambridge, MA: Harvard University Press, 1989.

Stern, Steven. *Battling for Hearts and Minds: Memory Struggles in Pinochet's Chile, 1973–1988.* Durham, NC: Duke University Press, 2006.

Stiglitz, Joseph. *Globalization and Its Discontents.* New York: Norton, 2003.

Stokes, Gales. *The Walls Came Tumbling Down.* New York: Oxford University Press, 1993.

Stoner, Kathryn and Michael McFaul, eds. *Transitions to Democracy: A Comparative Perspective.* Baltimore: Johns Hopkins University Press, 2013.

Strachan, Hew. "The Lost Meaning of Strategy," *Survival* 47.3 (Autumn 2005): 33–54.

Straw, Jack. *Last Man Standing: Memoirs of a Political Survivor.* London: Macmillan, 2012.

Suri, Jeremi. *Power and Protest: Global Revolution and the Rise of Détente.* Cambridge, MA: Harvard University Press, 2003.

Suri, Jeremi. *Henry Kissinger and the American Century.* Cambridge, MA: Harvard University Press, 2007.

Suri, Jeremi. *Liberty's Surest Guardian.* New York: Free Press, 2012.

Suskind, Ron. *The One Percent Doctrine.* New York: Simon & Schuster, 2006.

Sutton, Michael. *France and the Construction of Europe, 1944–2007.* New York: Berghahn, 2007.

Svejnar, Jan. "Transition Economies: Performance and Challenges," *Journal of Economic Perspectives* 16.1 (Winter 2002): 3–28.

Talbott, Strobe. *The Russia Hand: A Memoir of Presidential Diplomacy.* New York: Random House, 2002.

Taylor, Fred. *The Berlin Wall: August 1961–9 November 1989*. London: Bloomsbury, 2006.

Temin, Peter and David Vines. *The Leaderless Economy: Why the World Economic System Fell Apart and How to Fix It*. Princeton: Princeton University Press, 2013.

Thatcher, Margaret. *The Sinews of Foreign Policy*. Brussels: Les Grandes Conférences Catholiques, 1978. Repr. in *In Defence of Freedom*, 1987.

Thatcher, Margaret. *In Defence of Freedom: Speeches on Britain's Relations with the World, 1976–1986*, introd. Ronald Butt. Buffalo, NY: Prometheus Books, 1987.

Thatcher, Margaret. "Speech to the Zurich Economic Society," in Margaret Thatcher, *In Defence of Freedom: Speeches on Britain's Relations with the World, 1976–1986*, introd. Ronald Butt. Buffalo, NY: Prometheus Books, 1987.

Thatcher, Margaret. *The Downing Street Years*. London: HarperCollins, 1993.

Thatcher, Margaret. *Statecraft: Strategies for a Changing World*. New York: HarperCollins, 2002.

Tobin, James and Murray Weidenbaum, eds. *Two Revolutions in Economic Policy: The First Economic Reports of Presidents Kennedy and Reagan*. Cambridge, MA: MIT Press, 1988.

Tökés, Rudolf, ed. *Eurocommunism and Détente*. New York: New York University Press, 1978.

Toye, John and Richard Toye. *The UN and Global Political Economy: Trade, Finance and Development*. Bloomington: Indiana University Press, 2004.

Toynbee, Polly and David Walker. *Better or Worse? Has Labour Delivered?* London: Bloomsbury, 2005.

United States Institute of Peace. *Prospects for Conflict or Peace in Central and Eastern Europe: A Report of a Study Group*. Washington, DC: U.S. Institute of Peace, May 1990.

Urban, G. R. *Diplomacy and Illusion at the Court of Margaret Thatcher*. London: I. B. Tauris, 1996.

U.S. Department of Defense, "Report of the Quadrennial Defense Review," May 1997.

U.S. Department of Defense, *Conduct of the Persian Gulf War, Final Report to the U.S. Congress*, April 1992.

Vachudova, Milada Anna. *Europe Undivided: Democracy, Leverage, and Integration after Communism*. Oxford: Oxford University Press, 2005.

Vaïsse, Justin. *Neoconservatism: The Biography of a Movement*, trans. Arthur Goldhammer. Cambridge, MA: Belknap, 2010.

Vance, Cyrus. *Hard Choices: Critical Years in American Foreign Policy*. New York: Simon & Schuster, 1983.

van Scherpenberg, Jens. "Trade Is No Superglue: The Changing Political Economy of Transatlantic Relations," in Jeffrey Anderson, G. John Ikenberry, and Thomas Risse, eds., *The End of the West? Crisis and Change in the Atlantic Order* (127–56). Ithaca, NY: Cornell University Press, 2008.

Vickers, Michael and Robert Martinage. "The Revolution in War," Center for Strategic and Budgetary Assessments, Washington, DC, 2004.

Vinen, Richard. *Thatcher's Britain: The Politics and Social Upheaval of the 1980s*. London: Pocket Books, 2010.

Vogel, David. *National Styles of Regulation: Environmental Policy in Great Britain and the United States*. Ithaca, NY: Cornell University Press, 1986.

Vogel, Ezra. *Deng Xiaoping and the Transformation of China*. Cambridge, MA: Harvard University Press, 2011.

Wall, Stephen. *A Stranger in Europe: Britain and the EU from Thatcher to Blair*. Oxford University Press, 2008.

Wall, Stephen. *The Official History of Britain and the European Community*, vol. 2: *From Rejection to Referendum, 1963–1975*. London: Routledge, 2013.

Wallace, William. "British Foreign Policy after the Cold War," *International Affairs* 68.3 (July 1992): 423–444.

Walt, Stephen. "Alliance Theory and the Balance of World Power, *International Security*, 9, 4 (Spring, 1985), 3–43.

Walt, Stephen. "Two Cheers for Clinton's Foreign Policy," *Foreign Affairs* 79.2 (Mar.–Apr. 2000).

Walt, Stephen. *Taming American Power: The Global Response to U.S. Primacy*. New York: Norton, 2005.

Wapshott, Nicholas. *Ronald Reagan and Margaret Thatcher: A Political Marriage*. New York: Sentinel, 2007.

Watkins, Susan. "The Nuclear Non-Protestation Treaty," *New Left Review*, no. 54 (Nov.–Dec. 2008): 5–26.

Watt, D. Cameron. *Succeeding John Bull: America in Britain's Place, 1900–1975*. Cambridge: Cambridge University Press, 1984.

Watt, David. "Introduction: The Anglo-American Relationship," in Wm. Roger Louis and Hedley Bull, eds., *The Special Relationship: Anglo-American Relations since 1945*. Oxford: Clarendon, 1986.

Weber, Steven. "Origins of the European Bank for Reconstruction and Development," *International Organization* 48.1 (Winter 1994): 1–38.

Wells, Samuel F. and Paula Bailey Smith, eds. *New European Orders, 1919 and 1991*. Washington, DC: Woodrow Wilson Center, 1996.

Westad, Odd Arne, ed. *The Fall of Détente*. Oslo: Scandinavian University Press, 1997.

Westad, Odd Arne. *The Global Cold War*. Cambridge: Cambridge University Press, 2005.

Westlake, Martin. *Kinnock*. London: Little, Brown, 2001.

The White House. *National Security Strategy of the United States*. Washington, DC: The White House, Jan. 1993.

The White House. *A National Security Strategy of Engagement and Enlargement*. Washington, DC: The White House, July 1994.

The White House. *A National Security Strategy of Engagement and Enlargement*. Washington, DC: Brassey's, 1995.

The White House. *A National Security Strategy for a New Century*. Washington, DC: The White House, Dec. 1999.

The White House, *The National Security Strategy of the United States of America*. Washington, DC: The White House, Sept. 2002.

The White House, *National Security Strategy*. Washington, DC: The White House, May 2010.

Wildavsky, Aaron. "The Two Presidencies," *Trans-Action* 4 (Dec. 1966).

Wilentz, Sean. *The Age of Reagan*. New York: HarperCollins, 2008.

Williams, Andrew. *Failed Imagination? The Anglo-American New World Order from Wilson to Bush*, 2nd edn. Manchester: Manchester University Press, 2007.

Williamson, John. "What Washington Means by Policy Reform," in John Williamson, ed., *Latin American Adjustment: How Much Has Happened?* (7–38). Washington, DC: Institute for International Economics, 1990.

Williamson, John. "Did the Washington Consensus Fail?" Outline of speech at the Center for Strategic and International Studies, Washington, DC, Nov. 6, 2002.

Wilson, Harold. *The Labour Government, 1964–70*. Harmondsworth: Penguin, 1974.

Wirls, Daniel. *Irrational Security: The Politics of Defense from Reagan to Obama*. Baltimore: Johns Hopkins University Press, 2010.

Wohlforth, William C., ed. *Witnesses to the End of the Cold War*. Baltimore: Johns Hopkins University Press, 1996.

Wolf, Martin. "Seeds of Its Own Destruction." *Financial Times*, Mar. 8, 2009.

Wolf, Martin. "How Austerity Has Failed," *New York Review of Books*, July 11, 2013, pp. 20–1.

Wolfowitz, Paul. "Shaping the Future: Planning at the Pentagon, 1989–93," in Melvin Leffler and Jeffrey Legro, eds., *In Uncertain Times: American Foreign Policy after the Berlin Wall and 9/11* (44–62). Ithaca, NY: Cornell University Press, 2011.

Woods, Ngaire. "The Challenge of Good Governance for the IMF and the World Bank Themselves," *World Development* 28.5 (2000): 823–41.

Woods, Ngaire. *The Globalizers: The IMF, the World Bank, and Their Borrowers*. Ithaca, NY: Cornell University Press, 2006.

Woods, Ngaire. "The G20 and Global Governance," in Joseph Stiglitz and Mary Kaldor, eds., *The Quest for Security: Protection without Protectionism and the Challenge of Global Governance* (343–54). New York: Columbia University Press, 2013.

Wooley, Wesley. *Alternatives to Anarchy: American Supranationalism since World War II*. Bloomington: Indiana University Press, 1988.

World Bank, *Sub-Saharan Africa: From Crisis to Sustainable Growth*. Washington, DC: World Bank, 1989.

World Bank, *Governance and Development*. Washington, DC: World Bank, 1992.

Wright, Lawrence. *The Looming Tower: Al-Qaeda and the Road to 9/11*. New York: Knopf, 2006.

Yergin, Daniel. *The Prize: The Epic Quest for Oil, Money and Power*. New York: Free Press, 1992. Repr. with new epilogue, 2008.

Yost, David and Thomas Glad. "West German Party Politics and Theater Nuclear Modernization since 1977," *Armed Forces and Society* 8.4 (Summer 1982): 525–60.

Young, John. "The Heath Government and British Entry into the European Community," in Stuart Ball and Anthony Seldon, eds., *The Heath Government, 1970–1974: A Reappraisal* (259–84). London: Longman, 1996.

Young, John. "Britain and Vietnam," *Cold War History* 2.3 (Apr. 2002): 63–92.

Young, John. "Ambassador David Bruce and LBJ's War: Vietnam Viewed from London," *Diplomacy and Statecraft* 22.1 (2011): 81–100.

Youngs, Richard. *The European Union and the Promotion of Democracy.* Oxford: Oxford University Press, 2001.

Zakaria, Fareed. *The Post-American World: Release 2.0.* New York: Norton, 2011.

Zelikow, Philip and Condoleezza Rice, *Germany Unified and Europe Transformed: A Study in Statecraft.* Cambridge, MA.: Harvard University Press, 1995.

Zelizer, Julian. "Conservatives, Carter, and the Politics of National Security," in Bruce Schulman and J. Zelizer, eds., *Rightward Bound: Making America Conservative in the 1970s* (265–87). Cambridge, MA: Harvard University Press, 2008.

Zelizer, Julian. "Defence and Domestic Politics," *Diplomatic History* 33.4 (2009): 653–70.

Zervis, Robert. "Understanding the Bush Doctrine," *Political Science Quarterly*, 118 (Fall 2003): 365–388.

Ziegler, Philip. *Edward Heath.* London: Harper, 2010.

Zimmermann, Warren. *Origins of a Catastrophe: Yugoslavia and Its Destroyers – the Last Ambassador Tells What Happened and Why.* New York: Times Books, 1996.

Žižek, Slavoj. "Against Human Rights," *New Left Review*, no. 34 (July–Aug. 2005): 115–31.

Zoellick, Robert. "Countering Terror with Trade," *Washington Post*, Sept. 20, 2001.

Zoellick, Robert. "An Architecture of U.S. Strategy after the Cold War," in Melvin Leffler and Jeffrey Legro, eds., *In Uncertain Times: American Foreign Policy after the Berlin Wall and 9/11.* Ithaca, NY: Cornell University Press, 2011.

Zubok, Vladislav. *Failed Empire: The Soviet Union in the Cold War from Stalin to Gorbachev.* Chapel Hill: University of North Carolina Press, 2007.

Acknowledgments

Historians often write as if they are merely giving voice to the documents, to the records that they find and decipher. In truth, we do more than report, translate and let the material speak for itself. We debate, interpret and reinterpret, and we routinely engage with other scholars whose work and arguments frame our own. We are in consequence very much in their debt. Writing history feels like a lonely pursuit, but it is in fact a collective effort. A book that covers the actions of two major countries over forty years, in matters of foreign and domestic policy and their implications for the international order and the international economy, is more collective than most and could not be done without incurring massive debts. The most obvious debts, to scholars and to archives, are acknowledged in the notes and references, but here I would like to note some that might not be so obvious.

Just to get started on this project, and oriented toward the right questions and sources, I sought advice from a number of scholars of foreign policy and international relations in Britain and the United States. These included John Baylis, Kathleen Burk, Alex Danchev, John Dumbrell, Sir Lawrence Freedman, Stefan Halper, Michael Hunt, Michael Kandiah, David Reynolds, Tony Smith, Odd Arne Westad, Andrew Williams and John Young. Along the way I got advice from scholars with a still wider range of interests, among them Sarah Babb, Andrew Gamble, Erik Goldstein, Eric Hobsbawm, Peter (now Lord) Hennessy, Ira Katznelson, Charles Maier, and Mark Wickham-Jones. I am especially grateful to colleagues who arranged for me to speak at seminars they organized. Pat Thane and Tim Lynch did this in London, Mark Wickham-Jones at Bristol, Larry Wolff at New York University and Andrew Bacevich at Boston University. Their efforts created opportunities to discuss the project with many others – among them Judith Allen, Peter Bailey, David Edgerton, Sonya Rose, Donald Sassoon, Rodney Lowe, Molly Nolan and Robert Taylor. I also profited greatly from comments by Peter Hall and Seth Jacobs on a working paper published by the Minda de Gunzburg Center for European Studies at Harvard University.

The breadth of this project required research in several distinct fields: U.S. and U.K. foreign policy, economic history and the history of economic policy-making; domestic policy and politics in both America and Britain; and the history of international institutions and relations. The documentation for each of these fields varies, and it varies considerably between the U.S. and the U.K. Americans have more experience in using the Freedom of Information Act, for example, whereas in Britain the involvement of professional diplomats and civil servants has been greater than in the U.S. and policy-makers at this level tend to be more accessible than their counterparts in the United States. What is available in the two countries is somewhat different, therefore, but each has produced a rich historical record.

For the U.S. side, I want to thank the various colleagues who guided me to the sources. I am especially grateful to Mary Sarotte, who helped me access and navigate collections at the Ronald Reagan Presidential Library in Simi Valley, California, the George Bush Presidential Library at College Station, Texas, and who directed me to the James Baker Papers at the Mudd Library at Princeton. I want also to thank the archivists at these institutions and James Baker, formerly Secretary of the Treasury and Secretary of State, for granting permission to examine his papers. In some ways the most impressive U.S. sources are the online collections created and maintained by the National Security Archive at George Washington University, the Miller Center at the University of Virginia and the Cold War International History Project at the Wilson Center. These institutions have done a great service to scholars working on the recent history of the United States.

Having worked in British archives for many years, I needed a bit less help in locating sources, but I nevertheless benefited greatly from meetings with Patrick Salmon and the FCO Historians and with Lawrence Freedman. I am also particularly grateful to the Churchill College Archives Centre, who not only sponsored and housed the British Diplomatic Oral History Project but also hold the Thatcher Archives. The Thatcher Archives is closely linked to the Thatcher Foundation, which has taken it upon itself the job of collecting and making available not only the papers of Margaret Thatcher but also relevant papers from the United States, recently declassified material from the Ronald Reagan Presidential Library in particular. The Centre was kind enough to allow me to purchase a collection of CDs produced by the Thatcher Foundation documenting Reagan's and Thatcher's interactions. I also found very useful material at the Liddell Hart Centre for Military Archives at King's College

London and at the Bodleian Library at Oxford. Of course, the main repository for materials on recent British history is The National Archives at Kew.

A number of politicians and officials in Britain were willing to speak with me about both process and substance. Much of the discussion served as background, but some of it was on the record. These include Sir Arthur John Coles; Lord Healey (Denis Healey); Patrick Holdich; Lord Howe of Aberavon (Geoffrey Howe); Lord Hurd of Westwell (Douglas Hurd); Lord Jay of Ewelme (Michael Jay); Sir Gerald Kaufman, MP; Lord Kerr of Kinlochard (John Kerr); Lord Owen (David Owen); Sir Michael Palliser; and Lord Wright of Richmond (Patrick Wright). Healey held numerous positions in government, as Defence Secretary and as Chancellor of the Exchequer and he was also Deputy Leader of the Labour Party; Howe, Hurd, and Owen had been Foreign Secretary; Coles, Jay, Palliser and Wright had served as Permanent Under-Secretary at the Foreign and Commonwealth Office; Kaufman was Shadow Foreign Secretary from 1987 to 1992; and Holdich was Head of the Americas Research Group in the FCO from 1998 to 2006. Their insights have been invaluable.

A number of institutions made serious contributions to this project. The most sustained support came from Boston College, especially Dean David Quigley, but also from colleagues in the History Department. The department has become a hive of scholarly activity in recent years and a stimulating place to work. I have also been aided by a great collection of students at Boston College. Three research assistants — Michael Franczak, Kevin Walton and Paul Wooten – did important work. Equally important, I have had the privilege of teaching a very talented group of graduate students who have taught me much and forced me to think harder and to read more widely. They are Megan Meyers, Jon Kuiken, Anna Haas Kolchinsky, Peter Moloney, Amy Limoncelli, Jesse Tumblin, Shannon Monaghan, Michael Franczak, Jamie Clifton and Erica Foss. The Minda de Gunzburg Center for European Studies also played a critical role, providing space and colleagues whose expertise was central to the issues around which this book had been structured. I was privileged to share an office there with two distinguished visitors, Alexander Geppert and Jörn Leonard, who provided important encouragement. The Marion and Jasper Whiting Foundation provided critical support for research in Britain in 2007 and the Earhart Foundation supported a semester of research and writing in 2008. The Centre for Contemporary British History and the Institute for the Study of the Americas, both parts of the University of London, appointed me as visiting fellow in 2007 and made me feel very welcome.

Finally, I want to thank those special friends who constituted the more intimate community in which this book took shape. Old friends, such as Paul Breines, Richard Price and Jon Schneer, continued to give advice and encouragement. Lou Ferleger, George Ross and Jim Shoch again served as sources of information, criticism and support. In 2011 George, Jim and I managed, with Lou's connivance, to publish a collection, *What's Left of the Left*, which compared the experience of the center-left in the United States and Europe over the past thirty years. Work on that project may have delayed the completion of this book, but I learned a great deal that proved useful in this effort and I very much want to thank my co-editors and our contributors, especially Art Goldhammer, Jonas Pontusson and Ruy Teixeira. My education in things American was further advanced by the experience of organizing a conference in October 2012 on "The Election of 2012 in Comparative and Historical Perspective" at Boston College. Again, I want to thank all those who participated and, in particular, Vlad Perju of the Clough Center, which funded and provided logistical support for the event. These recent efforts, typically undertaken with help from old friends, substantially enlarged the circle of friends and colleagues on whose knowledge and understandings I drew for this project.

Five people deserve thanks beyond what is normal. Heather McCallum, editor at Yale, took an interest in the book from the beginning and saw the entire process through to the end. Her suggestions were always helpful. Three close friends – Jim Obelkevich, George Ross and Larry Wolff – read the entire manuscript in its semifinal form and their criticisms made it much better. Larry's writing is itself a source of inspiration; and he was and remains a model colleague. Most important, my wife, Laura Frader, was there at the beginning, in the middle and at the end of the project. She was always encouraging, endlessly patient, and she made everything better.

Index